Laurier

Laurier

THE FIRST CANADIAN

BY JOSEPH SCHULL

MACMILLAN OF CANADA
A DIVISION OF CANADA PUBLISHING CORPORATION
TORONTO, ONTARIO, CANADA

Canadian Cataloguing in Publication Data

Schull, Joseph, 1910-1980.
Laurier, the first Canadian

Bibliography: p.
Includes index.
ISBN 0-7715-9567-0

1. Laurier, Wilfrid, Sir, 1841-1919. 2. Prime ministers - Canada - Biography. 3. Canada - Politics and government - 1896-1911.* I. Title.

FC551.L38S28 1965 971.05'6'0924 C66-245
F1033.L38S28 1965

Originally published in hardcover 1965 by The Macmillan Company of Canada Limited

Reprinted 1966

First published in softcover 1987

Cover design and illustration by David Montle

Printed in Canada

To Hélène, my wife

Contents

List of drawings ix

Preface x

1. 'A valedictory address was read in French' to 1864 1
2. A *Rouge* in Montreal 1864-1866 25
3. The Bois-Francs 1866-1868 51
4. 'Those days of Arthabaska' 1868-1874 71
5. Back-bencher 1874-1876 96
6. 'I have unfurled the Liberal standard' 1877 112
7. A Fixed Fact 1878-1881 132
8. 'Things must be taken as they are' 1881-1884 147
9. Riel 1885-1886 166
10. 'A high and honourable ambition' 1886-1887 184
11. 'I am convinced of my deficiencies' 1887-1889 201
12. 'This man would be a giant' 1889-1891 229
13. The Ripening West 1892-1894 261

14. 'I ask this parliament not to proceed any further with this bill' 290
1894-1896
15. 'Is it not a considerable triumph?' 321
1896
16. 'Let the bugle sound, let the fires be lit on the hills' 336
1897
17. 'The times of Saint-François de Sales' 361
1897-1899
18. 'Sir Wilfrid Laurier is too English for me' 376
1899-1900
19. Foreshadowings and Departures 398
1901-1902
20. 'We cannot wait because time does not wait' 413
1902-1903
21. New Provinces 429
1903-1905
22. A Time To Go 455
1906-1908
23. Ships and Men 480
1909-1910
24. 'Governments are born to grow and die' 499
1910-1911
25. 'I will stay with the boys for a while' 534
1911-1914
26. 'There is in Canada but one mind and one heart' 556
1914-1916
27. 'The only tactics of the Tories will be "French Quebec"' 574
1916-1917
28. 'I have no fault to find with life' 602
1918-1919

A note on sources 623
Books and publications used 624
Notes 628
The Laurier Ministry 646
Index 649

Drawings

Cartoon from *L'Opinion Publique,* January 3, 1878 129

Sir Richard Cartwright, drawn by Henri Julien 138

Sir Charles Tupper, drawn by Henri Julien 139

'The Great British North America "Act" '. Cartoon by J. W. Bengough in *Grip,* April 16, 1887 189

'Home, sweet home'. Cartoon by J. W. Bengough, September 1, 1897 358

Cartoonist's comment on Boer War policy 389

'Sir Charles has a shocking disagreement with the most eminent statesman of his acquaintance!' Cartoon by J. W. Bengough in the Toronto *Globe,* October 17, 1900 396

1904 election. Cartoon by Fergus Kyle 440

Sir Wilfrid Laurier. Pen-and-ink sketch by Henri Julien 449

1908 election. Cartoon by Fergus Kyle 474

Sketch of Sorel meeting by George E. McElroy in the Montreal *Star,* September 7, 1908 475

'Let Laurier finish his work?' Cartoon by N. McConnell in the Toronto *News,* October 10, 1908 477

'For Canada and the Empire': the navy plan. Cartoon by Fergus Kyle 495

Post-election comeback. Cartoon by Fergus Kyle in the *Globe* 543

'Is this to be the fate of the last free parliament in the world?' Cartoon by Fergus Kyle in the *Globe* 549

'Hi: let Laurier in!' Cartoon by N. McConnell in the Toronto *News,* December 13, 1917 598

Preface

THE STUDY of Laurier's life was begun some seven years ago on commission from the Canadian Broadcasting Corporation. After the radio work was done Mr. John Gray of Macmillan proposed that research be expanded and deepened to produce a short biography. During the course of the work I received a Canada Council Fellowship and *Weekend* Magazine expressed its interest. Out of all this encouragement the present book has resulted.

It is longer than first intended because it seemed impossible to treat adequately of Laurier and his times in less detail. Since the man was inseparable from politics through all his adult life, and dominant in politics through much of it, his story becomes of necessity a part of the story of the political development of the nation. For an understanding of his attitudes it seemed as important to portray him in his early years as in the years when he was Prime Minister. All this came to be attempted, whether rashly or not I do not know. I can only say that I have been given generous scope and assistance by my publishers, that I have found the work rewarding, and that I hope it will prove to be of some value.

I have to thank Professor Frank H. Underhill of Ottawa for much assistance and encouragement on many occasions, and for a most valuable reading of the first draft of the manuscript. The same thanks are due to Professor H. Blair Neatby, whose thesis 'Laurier and a Liberal Quebec' was one of the valued references for the work. Mrs. H. Blair Neatby, the former Jacqueline Côté of the Government Archives, also was kind enough to read the manuscript in draft and to provide some insights and criticisms that could ill have been spared. None of these authorities, it should be said, reviewed the manuscript in its final form or should be held responsible for any part of it.

Mr. A. Kirk Cameron of Montreal, a long-time friend of Laurier, has been for me a mine of anecdote and assistance. I have, like every researcher in Canadian history, to give thanks to Dr. W. Kaye Lamb and his staff of the National Archives for unstinting help. I should like in particular to acknowledge the kindness of Mr. Pierre Brunet, Assistant Government Archivist, whose office I never left without some nugget of information or the suggestion of some new and useful line of inquiry.

I am indebted to Mme L.-H. Gariépy, the former Jacqueline Migneau and a niece of Yvonne Coutu, for information about the Laurier household and about the couple's life in Ottawa. Professor Julian Gwyn of Ottawa University directed me to several important sources of information. Professor Marc La Terreur, formerly of Ottawa University and now of the University of Alberta, gave generously of his time, advice, and material; and Mr. D. C. McArthur of Ottawa was another unfailing source. I should like to acknowledge the help of Miss Norah Story, formerly of Ottawa and now of Toronto, of M. Alcide Fleury of Arthabaska, of Miss Marie Baboyant of the Montreal Public Library, and of Mrs. Charlotte Kyle of Montreal, who made me a gift of several of the political cartoons of her late husband, Fergus Kyle. The staff of the Ontario Provincial Archives and Mr. Bernard Weilbrenner and M. Antoine Roy of the Quebec Provincial Archives were generous in response to any call for material. I should like to acknowledge the early support of the CBC and the help of my friends J. Frank Willis, Robert Weaver, Frank Lalor, and Robert Allen.

To John Gray of Macmillan, always at hand in difficult times, my thanks are due in connection with this work and much else. I am a grateful beneficiary of the Canada Council; and have also to thank Hugh Shaw of *Weekend* Magazine for his own encouragement and that of his publication.

To my sister, Helen, I am deeply indebted for many hours spent in the typing of the manuscript; and finally to my wife, Hélène, I owe the fact, good or not, that it ever came to completion.

JOSEPH SCHULL

'These people do not understand Laurier; he has a governing mind; he wants to do things; he has plans. He will walk the great way of life with anyone of good intention who will join him.'

J. ISRAEL TARTE *to* JOHN DAFOE,
July 1896.

'A VALEDICTORY ADDRESS WAS READ IN FRENCH'

to 1864

THE FIRST DAY of Convocation for McGill University's class of 1864 was much dampened by rain, but the second broke clear and sunny. It was Wednesday, May 4. Standing alone on a swampy strip of farmland hardly divided yet from surrounding fields, the Arts Building looked down to the sketchy beginnings of Sherbrooke Street. Behind it to the north and west the slopes of Mount Royal climbed away, ragged and rich, with wild-flowers flaring in dank undergrowth and elms and maples just breaking into leaf. Below it, across Sherbrooke and a mile or so to the south and east, the grey stone huddle of Montreal, spiked with spires, dominated by the square-cut towers of Notre Dame, began its course along the river.

Sherbrooke Street had once been a country road, patched with the shade of old elms and curving gracefully along a slope of rising meadows. Now, where it passed below the mountain, it was lined with a fence and widened out and graded, for it served as a link joining the estates of a few prosperous merchants. They had moved up from Notre Dame or St. James Street as the spicy smells of the river's commerce began to be dominated by the pervading aroma of sewage, and their search for fresh air and rural surroundings had been combined with a shrewd assessment of property values which time was already vindicating. In the haphazard green belt between the fence and the city there were now a few houses, a spire or two, and the occasional stone business establishment, squat and ugly as a jail. Sprouting streets were fingering out from the east, and along St. Catherine, the most venturesome of them, the clip-clop of the horse-cars sounded once an hour. For all the promise of things to come, however, the area was still a gap-toothed outskirts and a domain of country squires. The fashionable and wealthy might bowl along Sherbrooke in their carriages, but the ordinary dweller in the city climbed to McGill by raw new cart-roads or cut through fields and woods along the ancient foot-paths of the Indian and the voyageur.

Few students and fewer still of their elders were accustomed to make the trip. Of McGill's half-dozen faculties, most were housed uncomfortably in the city below. It was not much of a university as yet and James McGill, the old fur-trader, slept in the tomb that would one day come to grace the forecourt of the Arts Building, with little more than the ghosts of his hopes about him.

Fifty-five years before this Convocation Day, musing in his old age on the state of the divided, ignorant, and Frenchified colony that had made him rich, he had bent an ear to the persuasive vehemence of the young John Strachan, Rector of York. Ten years out from Scotland, still far from a bishop but already on his way in Upper Canada, Strachan had time for the concerns of the lower province too. He had no time to heed the lessons of its past. Ignorance and Frenchness must depart, rooted out by education. McGill had money and McGill had Burnside, forty-six acres of rich land rolling down from the mountain's foot. What better gift, what better monument could a loyal, prosperous, God-fearing Briton leave behind him than the means to found a college bearing his name? The bounty of a grateful state would surely be added. The halls and towers and sunny walks of a great university would rise, securely Anglified. The sons of the priest-ridden habitant, side by side with their English betters, would 'by Degrees be induced to embrace the Protestant Religion'.

It was the long-deferred and unrelinquished hope, conveyed by the English conquerors to their first governor in Quebec. McGill, with fifty years' experience of this benighted land, may have felt a doubt or two. The vanquished had defeated the pious hopes of many Strachans. Seventy thousand leaderless, exhausted peasants at the time of the conquest, cut away from their homeland, alone in North America – nothing had seemed more certain than that they would be quickly and painlessly absorbed by the two million stout British Protestants to whom the continent and the future belonged. Instead, obdurately French, immovably Catholic, they had clung on in the farms and villages of the St. Lawrence basin, listening to their priests, breeding innumerable children, doggedly defying progress. Neither the American Revolution nor the flooding-back of Loyalists nor the division of Canada into an upper and a lower province had changed them at all. Constitutional government, with its elected House of Assembly, had changed them only for the worse. The English returning from the lost American colonies had gone west to the upper province beyond the Ottawa River. The French had remained where they were. When elections came, fourteen-fifteenths of the population of Lower Canada had been French, and Frenchmen had elected Frenchmen. In the first session of the new House James McGill had found himself one of an outraged British minority contending vainly against a notary by the name of Papineau for the use of the King's English as the sole official language. Proceedings thereafter, as the frustrating years went by, had come to be almost completely dominated by French representatives speaking their own tongue. Only the other blessings of the British constitution – the appointed governor, the appointed upper house, and a loyal swarm of officials who throve on English bounty – prevented the conquered from making and changing laws.

The Roman Catholic Church, which had cast its lot with England in the War of the Revolution, waxed and grew strong. Authority *in excelsis,* it was comfortable with all authority. Suavely, eternally watchful, it was undisputed custodian of the hearts and minds of its people. If it disliked an English king, it abhorred American democracy. If it feared English Protestantism, the grim divines of Boston were its fiercest, oldest enemies. To the hopes of raucous rebels it had opposed a chill loyalty; it had been and it remained a bulwark of British rule in Lower Canada, exacting its own price. The Church tolerated was now the Church entrenched. Religion, language, Frenchness, watered by churchmen and endured by London, all persisted and grew. To an old man mindful of the victory on the Plains of Abraham the province was a strange and maddening anomaly, moving at a crab-like walk through Papist darkness. In Upper Canada all was British, Protestant, progressive. Lower Canada remained forever the same or changed for the worse. The clamorous, jabbering Assembly was reaching out for the strings of power, always with more skill and impudence. The notary Papineau was rearing up a more obnoxious son.

Nevertheless the long hope remained and many voices spoke with the voice of Strachan. In 1811 James McGill made his bequest and in 1813 he moved to his tomb. His beloved Burnside, now the property of McGill College, became at once another of many battlegrounds on which the obstinate vanquished still turned back the victors. The Roman Catholic Church turned a basilisk-eye on Protestant-directed schooling. French-Canadian legislators throttled the state's purse. The battle for the purse became a battle for control of the state as the star of Louis-Joseph, son of the first Papineau, climbed in a darkening sky. Rebellion came and was crushed. Reunion of the provinces followed, clamping the mutinous antipathies of Upper and Lower Canada into one rasping frame. Still the French, outnumbered now and destined to be swamped in Britishness, would vote no funds for the work. In forty years two buildings rose on McGill's land out of the increment of McGill's fund. They remained half-completed, housing a few shivering students and complaining teachers and subsiding little by little into penury and decay. Leanly-paid professors of the arts gave room and board to their scholars among the rafters of building number two. At night in the ghostly garret of building number one the professor of medicine carved up next day's cadaver by wind-blown candlelight with the blizzards of the winter wilderness howling round him and battalions of rats scurrying down the walls as the snow blew in.

William Dawson, fourth in the line of principals, had arrived from Nova Scotia in 1855 to find 'two blocks of unfinished and partly ruined buildings and a wilderness of excavators' and masons' rubbish overgrown with weeds, pastured at will by herds of cattle cropping the grass, browsing in the shrubs . . . with the only access from town by a circuitous and ungraded cart track almost impassable at night'. After nine years of hard work he had managed to complete the two unfinished buildings and supplement them by a third which bore the name of its donor, William Molson the brewer. The three had been joined together by corridors, again with Molson's money, and the whole now stood in more or less symmetry as the Arts Building.

Parts of the 'campus' had been drained and ditched. Spindly saplings, grown by the principal himself and laid out under his knowledgeable eye, ran down the drive from the Arts portico to a wooden gate at Sherbrooke Street. The nutters 'from the eastern parts of the city' who had come since time immemorial to strip the butternut trees at the mountain's foot had been discouraged. Rowdy sportsmen from the town who had played their games on McGill's field and the purveyors of strong drink who had set up booths to serve them now found the law on hand to spoil their fun.

It was not much, and for the moment it was about all that could be hoped for in this land of the uncompleted conquest, this country paved with the wreck of good British intentions. There was still no help from the state; the partners of the shotgun marriage that had made united Canada were as flinty-eyed as ever. Yet out of the arid rock one fountain bubbled. The 'stream of private liberality' begun with James McGill had resumed with William Molson. In a few years it would be swelled by William Macdonald, the non-smoker whose 'cut plug' was just beginning to harvest its millions from the smokers and chewers of the continent. For the English college, if not for the English cause, a beneficent age of beer had succeeded the age of furs and the age of tobacco lay not far in the future.

Where money talked the other race would listen. Learning was learning and McGill dispensed it, deferring other hopes. The son of the habitant came to the classrooms now, to depart as French as ever. The English shared their bounty as the French partook of it, grudgingly and warily. But the times had grown politer, the graduation of a year's crop of students was now a thing to be noticed, and the Convocation of 1864 was a fashionable affair. By mid-afternoon of this sunny second day, according to the Montreal *Gazette*, 'a numerous and brilliant attendance completely filled the William Molson Hall'.

2

THE AUDIENCE found itself listening to the valedictorian for the eleven graduates of the faculty of law. His teachers, sitting on the platform behind him, had been drawn from the upper echelons of the Montreal bar and most of them gave their services as lecturers on a part-time basis. French and English, usually deep in politics, they were more often than not violently at odds outside these walls. Of the graduates, six were English and five French. The man at the lectern had not been, technically, the most brilliant of the class. One man, never to be heard of again, had outranked him in several subjects and a second had equalled him in one or two. He had gained his present place on the strength of a general record that had been considered impressive and a graduation thesis devoted mainly to constitutional law.

He was just over six feet tall and he looked almost bulky in a long, square-cut coat that hung to his knee-joints, and trousers of some wrinkled homespun stuff that had never known an iron. The effect was an illusion created by a country tailor. The body tapering up to the wide shoulders was in reality frail, with a grace that would be set off by elegance in dress long before he was able to afford it. One of the sharpest pangs of three hard student years in Montreal had been the lack of suitable clothes for many functions he would have liked to attend.

The head was striking, with the broad front swept by a mass of chestnut hair, thick and inclined to curl. The nose was aquiline and strong. The mouth was a curious, almost conflicting compound of masculine strength and feminine beauty. It had not yet settled into the repose of maturity, the romantic was still at war with the realist, but already the long, dominant upper lip was imposing its control on the gentle sensuousness of the lower. About the eyes, concentrated though they were at the moment on the effort to deliver carefully prepared phrases, there was a hint of something melancholy and detached. They were the eyes of an observer as well as an actor, of a man who would play out the game of life never quite obsessed with its prizes because they would never be bathed for him in the glow of exuberant health. He coughed once or twice as he turned the pages before him, and stopped occasionally to sip at a glass of water. The breaks were something more than oratorical pauses. The voice was liquid with an attractive, slurring emphasis, pleasantly modulated for so young a man, but it came quite evidently from a weak chest.

He was speaking of the mission of the lawyer in the modern world. 'Messieurs,' he had begun, recalling old battles to his hearers with the first word, 'de toutes les missions qu'il a été donné d'exercer à l'homme vivant en société, je n'en sache pas de plus grande que celle de l'homme de loi.' Knowing no greater mission than that of the man of law, he had gone on in his mother tongue to discuss the work of the lawyer in the maintenance of liberty and the place of the lawyer in a free society.

Not unnaturally, he considered this place to be of the highest. The lawyer preserved the circle of rights traced out by the people's will, the lawyer repulsed the bold and upheld the weak. The lawyer, of all men in this country, had pushed to its furthest extent the union of French and English.

The transition to politics and the Canadian scene was so skilful as to seem almost instinctive and was also made on high ground. Two races today shared the soil of Canada. It could be said in this place, since such times were now past, that the two races had not always been friends. He hastened to add, however, 'and I say it to our glory, that the struggles of race are ended on Canadian soil. There is here now no other family than the human family, whatever the language they speak or the altars at which they kneel. There is glory in this fraternal union of which Canadians can never be sufficiently proud; mighty nations, indeed, might well come to us to seek a lesson in justice and humanity. . . . The mission of the man of law in Canada embraces first justice, the most noble of all human perfections; secondly patriotism, the most noble of all the social virtues; and finally union between the peoples, the secret of the future. Here, gentlemen, we see our goal; it is for us to ensure that our efforts be worthy of it.'

He concluded with a graceful *adieu* to his teachers, an *au revoir* to fellow graduates 'whom we shall meet again on the way of our profession', and a line of Virgil. The audience before him had long since divided almost as visibly as Montreal was divided, into French and English sections. Even among those who understood him, however, there was a touch of quizzical restlessness not quite accounted for by the youthful soporifics. The young man's diction had an undeniable touch of elegance but it was at the same time oddly and unsettlingly coloured by a tincture of Scotch. 'A valedictory address was read in French by one of the members of the graduating class,' noted the *Gazette* reporter for his newspaper, and Wilfrid Laurier, twenty-two years old and now a Bachelor of Civil Law, resumed his seat on the platform.

3

HE WAS NOT very far from his home and nearer still to the place of first beginnings for his line in Canada. Below, along the river, lay Place Royale, crowded in now among cobbled streets and granite quays. It had been a forest clearing pocked with stumps, overgrown with rank grass, and starred with wild-flowers when Augustin Hébert had landed there on May 18, 1642. A burly Jack of all trades from Caen in Normandy, he had come with the forty men and five women brought by Maison-neuve and Jeanne Mance to 'plant the banner of Christ in an abode of desolation and a haunt of demons'. He had been long dead from an Iroquois tomahawk when, thirty-four years later, his granddaughter Jeanne had walked to the notary's with the soldier François Cottineau, called Champlaurier from some family field of laurels in his native Guyenne. In the house of the Sieur Forestier, the dowry of the milch cow and the hundred livres of Tours had been agreed to, the contract had been signed and witnessed, and the line of the Champlauriers had begun.

As children and grandchildren multiplied and the prefix dropped from the name, Lauriers had crossed from the Island of Montreal to the Island of Jesus. They had crossed again to the woods of Lachenaye, glooming along the north shore. Still later, as the narrow ribbons of cleared land and the steep-roofed, whitewashed houses began to crowd each other along the St. Lawrence, other Lauriers had turned to the north-west along the River Achigan. It looped out in a wide arc, feeding to the greater river from the foothills of the Laurentians, and the soil was rich along its course. Year by year and generation by generation the woods had come down and new farms had been cleared. The face of the great Laurentian plain had begun to emerge, lined with forked-rail fences or fences of piled stones.

The eighth generation of Lauriers had come to rest at St-Lin on the Achigan, twenty-five miles from the landing-place of Augustin Hébert. Here, on November 20, 1841, Henri Charles Wilfrid, the first son of Carolus Laurier, was born. About his cradle, inescapable now, were the memories of a race. He was a part of the Norman artisan who had stood with Maisonneuve to hear the first Mass on the Island of Montreal. Somewhere in his blood the memory of the first night lingered on: the men silent by the bivouac fires, the white circle of the Host exposed on the altar of boughs in the midst of the great forest, the fire-flies glimmering round it strung on threads by the women. He was a part of François Cottineau the soldier, of the men mangled by the Iroquois, of the men who had hacked down the forest, and of the women who had borne their children. He was a part of nameless and forgotten Lauriers who had left the half-cleared fields for the long canoes and followed the gleam of water to the mid continent and the Gulf of Mexico. He was a part, too, of the great-great-grandfather who had heard that Quebec was taken and Montcalm dead, and had watched from the woods of Lachenaye as the boats of the redcoats came to Montreal. In all of it he was no more nor less than two-thirds of the children who were to grow up with him in his village, yet like them he came of Normans who had made and lost a conquest twenty times as great as that of William of Bayeux.

He had been born in the year that the two provinces of Canada were reunited, following rebellion, sealing a second conquest. It had been a pitiful enough thing, that rebellion, but he had grown up with the myths and memories of it, scarred with its scars, divided by the new divisions it had made. Papineau – Louis-Joseph Papineau – was the name inseparably linked with it, and in that name were the seeds of all division.

The son of the first disputant with James McGill had always been a man apart. He had been a seigneur but not of the old seigneurs: his lands along the Ottawa had been purchased by his father from the earnings of a notary who had prospered with the country. Louis-Joseph had grown up a lawyer of some means, one of the small group of educated men whom education placed at the head and set apart from the mass of an illiterate people. The habitant or the artisan worked for his daily bread, accommodated himself to ever-advancing Englishness. Papineau had time to brood on the glories of the past, to magnify them, to feel and resent the pressure of the dismal English oligarchy that aped and improved on the worst snobberies of the homeland and managed all government behind the mask of the constitution. The priests had taught Papineau but he moved apart from the priests, resenting their acquiescence to English authority. Absorbing the ideas let loose on the world by the American and French revolutions, fired and obsessed by them, he was still and forever the *parvenu* seigneur. The nostalgia in him for the days and dreams of New France was a fiercer thing than it was in the few sons and grandsons of authentic old aristocrats who lingered on in Canada. Many of these seemed to adjust to the English with cynical pliability. He detested them while he envied them. He envied the English everything. Handsome, magnetic, vain, a born leader who had been born French, he found the prospect of this life in another England an affront not to be endured. Accommodation itself was an affront. The facts of the conquest were unbearable facts.

He had emerged as the leader of the French party in the Assembly at about the time James McGill went to his last rest. For twenty-five years after that he had fought the Tory rulers in the name of responsible government. The times had been ripe for him; the same struggle went on in Upper Canada. But beyond the Ottawa, brother wrestled with brother for control of an English state; here Papineau led the French in a war of survival he had made and shaped. It was to be a survival of total identity, total and conscious as it had never been before. To the smug English certainty of final absorption he opposed the myth he had rescued from the past, the wholly united people, wholly resolved to continue as itself. There could be no concession to the milder souls, making their peace with the times, making their way in them. Detesting Englishness, he detested the industrial age. Always provided with his daily bread, he had only scorn for the thrusting English progress that might bring an English plenty.

There was no repose for him as there was for the Church in the mere preservation of faith and tongue. The Church held to them, but it held to them blindly and blandly, trusting in everything he did not trust. Ignorance and isolation and the faith of treaties, they were the Church's bulwarks. Untaught by the English, unseduced by the English, the habitant might find his way to heaven; he would never advance on earth. Nor would he find his grandson speaking French. If the old hopes of the conquerors seemed asleep in England they did not sleep here. They spoke every day through the mouths of squires and parsons to whom the first condition of the life they wished for was the disappearance of all Frenchness. Papineau had beaten back many a squire and parson in his twenty-five years; he had gained much, but always the realities of power had been withheld. British authority, a bayonet-bristling rock in the midst of a French sea, would not haul down its flag.

He had come to require no less as he reached middle age. Estranged from the Church, he had moved beyond his party and most of his people. He no longer spoke of reform. Savage and embittered, always demanding the loaf where crumbs were given, he was lost now in the dream of a French republic. Perhaps it would link itself with the United States, living still French behind some shadowy safeguards. Perhaps and best of all it might exist shut in on itself in the St. Lawrence valley, a land of peasants and devoted seigneurs reviving a golden age. In either case he would be first seigneur, free of the English at last.

Cloudy and hopeless as his vanities and angers, the dream was not to die. Generation by generation, always changing in form, always returning to its source, it would haunt the years ahead. At each rasping moment in the country's history young men would search and yearn for those wide horizons clear of the Union Jack. French-Canadian 'nationalism', that dream of a people apart, denying the whole essence of the age-long English hope, would rise to confront the English. Another divisive current would run athwart it, reversing the priorities of the Church, setting the claims of race above religion. Both were to be Papineau's legacy, and neither had saved Papineau.

He had given to a whole people a troubling awareness of itself. He had shaped forces that would never rest again, and he had no more to give. The priest, stirred and torn though he was by newly-awaked Frenchness, drew back from the unbeliever. The bishop, French as his priests, still saw in the hopes of this baleful prophet the certainty of absorption by the United States, bringing with it the twin anathemas of Protestantism and democracy. The politician, looking at English might, was appalled by the spectre of conflict. The mass of the people sat mute, shaken in old loyalties, never again so wholly one with their priests, yet reluctantly abandoning Papineau. The man of words, as he came to the brink of deeds, had found himself almost isolated. He had tried to draw back but there had been men who would not. He and his few young dreamers had drifted into the strange camps of the annexationists and the revolutionaries and the fishers in troubled waters. The power of his words had sharpened blunt steel and loaded old muskets in a few stormy counties. Egged on by Tories hoping for the worst, left now with an Englishman, an Irishman, and a sodden Swiss freebooter as his principal lieutenants, he had stumbled into rebellion. He had watched its onset, dazed, and had run from the results.

He had been a squalid enough figure, riding away through a November dawn while a huddle of trapped peasants awaited the advancing redcoats. Yet the scars of the redcoats' work would live longer than that memory. St-Lin itself, on a black December night four years before the birth of Wilfrid Laurier, had seen the last and heaviest of the blows of the mailed fist. The guns and muskets of two thousand British regulars had sounded from St-Eustache, twenty miles away. The flames of the village had climbed above the woods, the handful of *patriotes* had died in the roofless church, unblessed and unforgiven by their priests. Sobbing men had come by the rutted roads, throwing away their hay-forks and their rusty swords and firelocks. Women with frozen

number of invisible spirits subordinated to the will of God. Such are the good angels, our tutelaries, our guardians. Such also are the bad angels who seek our destruction. The winds, for example, are spirits invisible and heavenly and in great numbers.'

Midway between the heavens of Copernicus and the earth of the survey lines stood politics, the work of man. This also Charles Laurier viewed in the light of 'nature, morality, and reason'. The faint echo of Rousseau, strange in the shadow of the village steeple, was not so foreign as it seemed. From America and from France the cries of the revolutions had whispered over the farmlands. They had grown to a shout with Papineau. They were muffled now, but not quelled. The old surveyor was a dutiful son in church but he thought for himself outside.

Carolus followed his father in his own leisurely way. Neither man was a politician and neither missed a political meeting. Sundays they went to Mass, week-days they tramped about the country, *Rouge* in their opinions, genial in defence of them. The priest at the altar must be heard in silence, but he could be argued with in the village street. The English, taken as a whole, were a problem and a menace; the Englishmen they knew, scattered about on neighbouring farms, were men to be lived with. The Lauriers were popular in St-Lin. Seven miles away in the village of New Glasgow, where Irish immigrants and Scots from disbanded regiments had taken land, they were equally popular. So was the boy who sometimes came along with them.

Wilfrid was ten years old and he had been crossing the road to the parish schoolhouse of St-Lin for three years when he was told that he was to go to New Glasgow to learn English. Adeline had doubts and so had the curé, but Charles and Carolus had made up their minds. A man was not a vegetable and he was not all patriot. If he must make his way in a country of two peoples it was necessary to be a little of each and not hobble on one crutch. The plan, through a long summer of excited preparations, was that he should live with the Kirks, who were Irish Catholics. At the last moment, however, Mrs. Kirk fell ill and John Murray came forward, a sound Scotch Presbyterian. The calèche, when it rolled into New Glasgow on a cool September evening, deposited the boy at his door.

It was not much of a risk and not much of an uprooting. John Murray had been a friend of the Lauriers for years. His store, an hour's drive from home along the Achigan, had been a haunt of sweets and treasure for the boy as long as he could remember. To an eleven-year-old who mastered the basics of communication in his stride, contemporary New Glasgow was not much different from contemporary St-Lin. 'I remember how I fought with the Scotch boys and made school-boy love to the Scotch girls, with more success in the latter than in the former.'

Yet there were differences, and deep ones. The boy came home each week a little changed. At the Murrays in the evenings, as the head of the house prepared to intone the Scriptures during family prayers, he offered to excuse Wilfrid. The boy demurred. The deep voice and the rich phrasings stirred him; they would stir him all his life. All his life he would read the Bible, and memorize much of it, in the King James version. All his life he would carry on his tongue, whether he spoke in English or in French, the memory of John Murray. He clerked in the Murray store in his spare time and was one of the family. Even when Mrs. Kirk recovered and he moved there he was back to the Murrays in the afternoons to help out behind the counter and in the evenings to listen to the psalms and canticles and the wild music of Isaiah. Yet he made his mark with the Kirks too. Forty years later the father of Nancy Kirk, 'now over a hundred and beginning to wander in his mind . . . does not see us at all, but talks of Wilfrid and Ireland'.

School in New Glasgow complemented the atmosphere of the home. Sandy Maclean sat at the master's desk, rich and overflowing with his store of English poetry, a glass of whisky at his left hand, the straps of the tawse dangling from the desk at his right. Milton, Shakespeare, and Burns sank deep in the young mind, always flavoured with the burr, always mingling in the long memories of the days beside the Achigan the scent of heather with the scent of pine.

He came back from New Glasgow a boy of twelve, different from the boys of St-Lin, already divided a little from the half-brothers who had been born to Carolus and Adeline. He had travelled and lived apart. He spoke English and knew a little of English ways. Now he was to embark on a longer journey and on the real business of education. In September 1854, two months before his thirteenth birthday, his bag was packed again and the calèche rolled away to the east on the twenty-mile trip to L'Assomption.

The college of L'Assomption in 1854 was everything that McGill was not. Founded in 1832, it was the fifth of the French ecclesiastical schools of secondary education. It gave a good deal to the few where there was little or nothing for the many. It was the fruit of unity and purpose, and the purpose, older than Papineau, was still survival. *Parare Domino Plebem Perfectam* was the inscription carved above its door – to prepare a people perfect to the Lord – and for seven years the young Wilfrid was to be shaped to the priest's conception of this mould.

There was no tawse here, no Sandy Maclean and no glass of Scotch. There was instead an almost monastic discipline. The students rose at five-twenty-five in the morning. There was a half-hour for recreation at noon and another forty-five minutes in the late afternoon. Eight in the evening was bedtime and ten minutes later the lights were out. Latin and the Latin classics filled a great part of each day. Literature was the French literature of the days before the revolution, supplemented by a little Greek and some of the English classics, which were treated with cool respect as the fruits of a foreign tongue. There was a little mathematics and more of philosophy and history, all taught by priests and heavily shaded by the Church's view. L'Assomption was seminary as well as college, and each boy thought of the priesthood as a possibility either for himself or the boy at the next desk. It was, after all, one of the four choices open to him in a country where commerce, industry, and capital were all in English hands. The cloth would never be strange to him, even though he did not wear it. Doctor or lawyer, notary or priest of the future, each knew the other here as a boy and would understand him later, for better or worse, as a man.

The blue sash of the college was worn day in and day out. Each weekday began with morning Mass in the chapel. Each Sunday the whole school, in blue and black coat and collegian's cap, trooped to the church in town. Yet Sunday afternoons, under the benevolent eyes of the masters, there were games and horseplay on the campus and the shouts of youngsters from whom the imp had not been removed. Thursday was the day of days. On the campus each Wednesday evening young faces turned imploringly to heaven and young voices rose from the heart in the refrain of the canticle, 'Grant us a good day.' And next morning, if the sun shone, the flag rose to the top of the maypole and the whole school took to the woods on the long holiday.

Life was strenuous at L'Assomption, but the world beyond the walls was hard and treacherous. The masters' work, according to their view, equipped the boy to meet it. They were not always sure of the young Laurier. He had listened by many a hot stove to Charles and Carolus. He had stood hand in hand with them under many a political platform. He had been to New Glasgow and he had read whatever he could lay his hands on. The business of law and courts fascinated him and he was frequently missing from his classes when the Assizes came to L'Assomption. He could not be kept away from the clamour of elections and the great *assemblées contradictoires* held at the church door. He raised his own small storm on one occasion and was squelched midway in a debate resolving 'that in the interests of Canada the French kings should have permitted the Huguenots to settle here'. Nevertheless, if the priests could discipline they could also discern, and they were well aware that they had a potential leader on their hands.

'The very appearance of Wilfrid Laurier indicated his future,' wrote Arthur Dansereau, one of the fellow students who was to be a problem of that future. 'He exercised a veritable domination within the walls. He was the most popular pupil, the pupil with the greatest following and the most influence.' The comment was made in long retrospect but the political flavour might have been prophetic. There were other lads wearing the blue sash at that time who were later to be of importance to Laurier for good and ill. In his last year at L'Assomption the diminutive, sharp-eyed, stuttering Israel Tarte entered the college and was quickly a friend. He was to be an enemy later and a friend again and again an enemy, but through all of it the years at L'Assomption would colour their careers and lives.

Here, on his own ground, Laurier became a man. The associations were to be lifelong, the memories graven deep. He would come, old and sick, a few months before his death, to look at the grey stone walls and touch them for the last time. Through all the years ahead he would crave the approval of this Alma Mater and dread its censure. Whenever his thoughts would stray to L'Assomption a light of humour and tenderness would grow in his eyes and some story of the days there would spring to mind. He was nineteen when the days ended. He had spent a third of his life with the teacher-priests; he was French again. But he was not yet prepared for life in this Canada of the two peoples.

5

HE WAS PREPARED now, as the rites of Convocation came to an end in Molson Hall. The three years at McGill had followed the years at L'Assomption because McGill, with all its shortcomings, had scraped together the only faculty of law in the province. Only at McGill could a young man of the minority learn to thread his way through the tangle of French and English jurisprudence that governed the land and put himself on an equal footing with the English lawyer. Without that there could only have been a French practice, perhaps in a country village. It would not have been enough for the grandson of Charles Laurier.

As he passed down the muddy drive toward Sherbrooke Street the pages of the valedictory crackled in his breast pocket, to be carefully preserved. He had meant what he said, but in the orator's way, surveying remote peaks. Now, while the numerous and brilliant attendance dispersed about him, the squalid verities of life came crowding back.

It is not likely that he was greatly troubled with nostalgic campus memories or gave much thought to the fact that he was passing through the wooden gateway for the last time. The faculty of law was housed in an upper room of Burnside Hall, a quarter of a mile below. He had journeyed that far 'from the eastern parts of the city' to take his five weekly lectures from four to six in the afternoons. He had seldom gone farther, and the grounds of McGill were almost as strange to him as to the visitors. McGill itself, with its old purposes blunted on hard facts and its private convictions unchanged, had the feel of foreign territory. One was accepted here because one stubbornly existed; one came here, *faute de mieux*, to fit oneself for competition with the English. That done, one left without a backward glance.

2

A *ROUGE* IN MONTREAL

1864-1866

LAURIER, Archambault & Desaulniers – Avocats'. The domicile was Montreal and the letterheads were printed in October of 1864. The three partners in the bare little office on Ste-Thérèse street, five minutes' walk from the clamour of Merchants' Pier, were all of an age. Oscar Archambault had been a classmate of Laurier at L'Assomption. Henri Lesieur Desaulniers had been one of his closest competitors in the law classes at McGill.

There was plenty of time at first for the barristers to reminisce about school days and reconsider the position of the lawyer in the modern world. They were three additions to the annual surplus of *avocats* and notaries turned out by the French colleges, and the men who climbed the narrow steps to their door were mostly of their own age and profession, briefless as themselves. Their single second-floor window looked across to the Canada Hotel, one of the cheaper houses in the area of the quays. As the bustle of the sailing season rose to its autumn peak there was liveliness and colour to make up for the lack of clients. Sailors, porters, and ship's passengers crowded into the raucous bar of the Canada or stumbled out of it. To the left and right, down St-Gabriel and St-Vincent streets, a daily stream of carters' wagons pounded along the cobbles bound for St-Paul street and the docks. Then as October waned a bite crept into the air. Ice filmed the river in the early mornings and the last ships cleared. The Canada Hotel fell into its winter doze, the streets about it emptied of horses and wagons, and the first wet snowflakes came. The Montreal of the waterfront settled to grey-brown silence, waiting the real cold.

Ste-Thérèse joined St-Gabriel and St-Vincent streets. It was a narrow little ribbon of dankness along which decaying old houses were being converted into cheap office space. Low rents and proximity had made it a warren of notaries, lawyers, and journalists. A block above it ran Notre Dame, the great avenue of the island, lined with its busy shops. Just across Notre Dame were the Court House and the City Hall where the business of the law centred, and behind the Court House on the wide drill-ground of the Champ de Mars the public meetings gathered, the speakers of the day held forth, and politics reared its enthralling head.

It was all familiar ground to Wilfrid Laurier. The lectures at Burnside, during his three years at McGill, had taken up only about two hours of each working day. The rest of his time had been spent as an articled clerk in the office of Rodolphe Laflamme, who was not only one of the busiest lawyers in Montreal but one of the liveliest of the lecturers at McGill. A brisk, handsome, hard-living bachelor with the tastes of an aristocrat if not the purse, Laflamme had taken at once to his clerk and student. He had given him every chance not only to familiarize himself with the routine of courts and the law but also to become acquainted with the practitioners. Laurier now knew and was known by most of the prominent French barristers in Montreal, and since they were all politicians of greater or less degree it was as natural as breathing to find himself involved in politics.

It was also inevitable that he should find himself a *Rouge*. The twig had been first bent in that direction and his new mentor was not long in freeing him from the deep-blue atmosphere of L'Assomption. Laflamme was only fourteen years older than Laurier, but he had been one of the youngsters who had clustered round the returning Papineau to found the *Rouge* party. He was still one of its liveliest if not of its steadiest lights. Enjoying his carriage, his good horses, his good clubs, and the sparkle of convivial society, he treated the law as a game. If a case bored him he became a bore. If it stirred his interest he could galvanize a courtroom. A fighter to his finger-tips, with no unnecessary respect for authority civil or religious, he had spent much of his life at vigorous odds with the Church.

The word 'ultramontanism' was soon to make its entry into Canadian politics and the force was already felt. At bay in Europe, with its lands and temporal power shorn away, the Roman Catholic Church had hardened round one of the first principles of its conservatives. Ultramontanism was older than the Reformation; it had, indeed, never accepted the Reformation. Kings and states and individual men might rebel, sects secede, society change; the ultramontanist still looked beyond the mountains to the chair of Peter for authority over all. It was authority absolute and undivided; there could be no rent in the seamless robe of Christendom. It acknowledged no bounds. Religion entered everywhere into the lives of men and states; therefore the power of the papacy was above men, their rulers, and their laws.

Always implicit in the central teachings of the Church, always defying liberalizing Popes, the doctrine had emerged in armour to confront the turmoil of the mid nineteenth century. Shaken by political and industrial revolution, undermined by social unrest, attacked by new ideologies, the Church would yield nowhere. To yield on any point was to yield everything. A few bitter experiences had taught reforming Popes that atheist republicanism advanced under the name of liberal thought. It reached inside the fold, still in the name of reform, to create the new heresy of Catholic Liberalism. Liberalism, whatever the cloak it wore, was the central enemy to be stamped out. In place of compromise there would be new assertions of authority. In the face of growing doubt there would be new projections of dogma. Physically powerless now, the Church would rise with a stronger, sterner voice to command the minds of men.

If ultramontanism had not been much heard of in French Canada it was largely because the doctrine had been taken for granted. In few countries of the world was the Church more authoritarian, and in few countries had the authority been better deserved. The bishops of New France, in the days of the old régime, had been almost co-equal rulers. The Church had been the one mainstay, the one source of leadership when the conquest came and the beaten generals, prosperous seigneurs, and thieving officials departed. Its place in the habitant's heart was wholly secure. Yet it no longer embraced the whole life of a whole people. The leaders of the future still came out of the ecclesiastical colleges. They still came out as Catholics, sons of the world-wide Church. A sizeable number of them, in a year or so, were to be recruited with much colour and ceremony for service as Papal Zouaves in the last struggle against republican Italy. Yet another sizeable number, steadily growing, were embarked on a contrary course. Authority, in question everywhere, was coming to be questioned here. Some of the props of religion were being questioned. Men, young and rash and loud, speaking with Papineau's voice, were examining the relation of the Church to the state.

L'Institut Canadien, a province-wide cluster of study groups with its headquarters in Montreal, was one of the principal manifestations of the new mood. Laflamme had been one of its founders and he had soon introduced Laurier to its fascinations and its perils. Described innocently enough as a club for reading, study, and debate on the questions of the day, the Institut was in addition and inevitably a hotbed of *Rouge*-ism. Taking all knowledge for its province, it had stacked its shelves with many books that figured prominently in the Index. It had accepted Protestant members as well as Catholic. It had been stirred to enthusiasm rather than abhorrence by the success of revolution and the growth of liberal thought in Europe. It had approved with youthful sanctimony the decline of the Church as a temporal power and it had turned a hard eye on the claims of the Church at home. Liberalism, socialism, communism, the still half-defined words and half-born forces of Europe, had been accepted as tidings of a new Great Awakening and had found a place in the Institut's political programs.

The Church had watched for a while, hoping that years would cool the hot young heads. By the time Laurier came on the scene, however, its stony disapproval had turned to active hostility.

Bishop Bourget of Montreal, who had assumed the episcopal chair in the year Laurier was born, had once looked with some sympathy on the cause of Papineau and the *patriotes*. All that was changed now. The *Rouges* were beginning to speak of themselves as Liberals. The bishop equated liberalism with socialism and communism, as some of the *Rouges* themselves were inclined to do, but he went a step beyond them. He equated all three with the deadly heresy that assailed the Church in Europe. Bishop Bourget was an ultramontane, and ultramontanism, transposed to Canada in his hands, was to be the great defender. Over the faithful, as he firmly believed, his authority was absolute. In the case of the Institut Canadien he had already put forth his claim to regulate all proceedings and to censor all books in the club's library.

The claim was resisted with varying degrees of heat. As the issue sharpened it had troubled the devout of the club and thinned the membership, and there had been a good many attempts at compromise. Laurier, in his second year at McGill, had been one of a deputation that called on the bishop to 'consider means of settling the difficulties which have arisen between His Grace the Bishop of Montreal and the Institute'. The proposal had been that a catalogue of the club's library be left with His Grace and that all books of which he disapproved be placed under lock and key. They were to remain in the custody of the Institut, however, for release by the president to such members as he should consider qualified to absorb them. The ingenious device for transferring authority he considered his own to one of the beardless intellectuals of the club had not met with the approval of the bishop. The deputation had been heard with fatherly courtesy and ushered out. All prohibitions remained and the club lay under the ban. Now, a year and a half later, Laurier had become one of its vice-presidents. He went about with the chip of liberalism on his shoulder, the threat of excommunication over his head, and some inkling of what life as a *Rouge* might be.

2

LIFE WAS exciting enough in any case. This was the autumn of 1864, the autumn of the Charlottetown Conference and the Quebec Conference from which had emerged the Confederation Scheme. Laurier and his partners were hardly established in the new office when Ste-Thérèse street began to hum with the angry industry of journalists, pamphleteers, and lesser politicians organizing the fight against it. A few doors down the street Laurent-Olivier David, devout and quiet-spoken but still a *Rouge* of *Rouges,* decanted his vitriol to fill the columns of *L'Union Nationale.* Médéric Lanctôt, owner of the paper and young man of many affairs, stormed in and out, much too busy with the plans of battle to pay any attention to his law practice. It was the same with Laflamme a block or two away in his more elegant quarters; and oftener and oftener now one was likely to find Laflamme in conference with the Dorions, the great lights of the party. Wherever Laurier moved in these haunts of the law and politics he could feel the rising tension. Wherever he looked he was apt to catch a glimpse of a man who might be making history. The Canada he had always known was in for a time of change.

The union that was just the same age as himself was already decrepit and paralysed. He had no regrets over that. He had learned to know it as a work of English revenge, the last stroke intended to complete the conquest. The joint parliament with its equal representation for the two sections, which were now known as West and East rather than Upper and Lower, had been a parliament shamelessly rigged against the realities of popular government and popular representation. Now conditions had changed; minorities had become majorities. Thirteen hundred thousand English west of the Ottawa and two hundred thousand to the east of it had grown keenly alive to the justice of representation by population. A million French faced them, grotesquely equal in power, behind the bulwark of the old rigged plan. Canada East and Canada West, as much divided as ever for political purposes into citadels of French and English, wrestled each other to a standstill.

Party politics cut across racial lines, for business had to be done. The country was booming and prosperous, with the Civil War to the south creating a mighty demand for its products and the Reciprocity Treaty opening the border. The Grand Trunk Railway was building, showering largesse impartially and demanding favours in return. Montreal, dominated by English money, was thriving as the centre of commerce for the rich St. Lawrence basin. An envious, rising Toronto, seeking a counterpoise, was eyeing the western wilderness beyond the Great Lakes. There was talk of another railway that would run the length of the river to connect the maritime colonies with the colony of the centre, and perhaps run on in time linking new colonies all the way to the Pacific. Businessmen dreamed big dreams and politicians shared them, sometimes sought to realize them. John A. Macdonald of Kingston jockeyed his Tories into shifting alliances with George Etienne Cartier's *Bleus*. George Brown's Upper Canadian Liberals were the uneasy bedfellows of Antoine-Aimé Dorion's *Rouges*. Yet everywhere, ultimately, the rock of race thrust up, splitting alliances and defeating progress. When it came to the fundamentals, the sharing of power, the education of the young, to anything that affected the future of divided peoples, the two faces glared and the two voices spoke with all the old fear and suspicion. Real government, whichever of the parties claimed it, was a two-headed monstrosity in which each section of the province wielded equal power and held the other at bay.

If there was wry irony in the working out of Durham's plan there was little reassurance. The parties had come to complete deadlock and government was no longer possible within the framework of the union. Yet there had to be government and would be, and that mighty majority of the English pressed ever more formidably against its paper barriers. On both sides the work of the past had failed and the men of the past and present stood up in a harsh new light.

Lafontaine had just died, a baronet and Chief Justice of Canada East. Thirteen years out of politics and dead at fifty-seven, the stocky, solid judge with the features of Napoleon had accomplished much and had pointed the way to more. Even the

Rouges who had destroyed him admitted that now. He had found the source of survival in the wells of English liberalism. But he had lost it again as Papineau returned, and not only because of Papineau. The source itself was changing; the wells beyond the Ottawa were brackish now. Liberalism today was still the unresting enemy of entrenched privilege and reactionary authority, but it was also the enemy of the dearest safeguards of the French. It was the liberalism of George Brown of Toronto, harshly English, grimly Protestant, only to be embraced at peril.

Papineau would never embrace it, and all the chords of a young *Rouge* still vibrated at that name. Yet Laurier had met Papineau by now and been vaguely disappointed. The old man lived in baronial seclusion on his estate along the Ottawa, and it was a retirement as welcome to the party as to himself. In his second coming he had been potent enough to catalyse the dreams and resentments of young men, to disrupt French Canada, and to send a disgusted Lafontaine into retirement. But there had been nothing more. Hatred of the English and hostility to the Church had not been enough; the dream of a pastoral democracy had been passed by in an age that was blackening the sky with train-smoke and the smoke of new factories. The *Rouges* had followed Papineau along a road that had led only to the dead end of his retirement in 1854. They still gathered round him for the occasional *vins d'honneur* which marked his rare appearances in Montreal, and Laurier had been among them. He had listened to the loyal eulogies and the old man's words in reply, impressed and moved. There was something real and tragic here, never to be forgotten or abandoned, but the magnificent white head, seething with ancient wrongs, was fixed immovably on the past.

Lafontaine dead, Papineau silent and impotent: that chapter was closed. There was nothing to be hoped for from Cartier, the conservative realist, the railway lawyer, the dreamer of practical dreams. That rebel of 1837 had taken over the wrecked party of Lafontaine. He had dedicated it to the proposition that business must be done with the English. No one could deny the power of the man nor his achievements. There were Catholic denominational schools in Ontario now, outraging every instinct of George Brown, because Cartier had forced them through. The English complained, and not without a show of reason, that Cartier dominated the country; certainly he was the strongest figure in parliament. Yet the party of Cartier was also the party of the Church, of big business, of commercial Montreal. The gulf between *Rouge* and *Bleu* had never been deeper. To the men who had walked with Papineau and the younger men who followed, Cartier was the nearest, dearest enemy. Whatever they conceded to Lafontaine they denied to him. All that they had once hoped to find in the old leader they now seemed to find in the Dorions.

Laurier had met both brothers through Laflamme. Each in a different way they stirred and excited and convinced him. There was fire enough in them for any *Rouge* but there was also a strain of hard practicality. The one could dream but he could also act. The other could resent the past and present without being blinded to the shape of the future.

Eric Dorion, thirty-nine years old and still '*l'enfant terrible*' to the party elders, had had a great part in shaping the program that had set the course for the *Rouges.* He clung as he always would to the dream of independence, but he had worked for much else along the way. He had founded his first newspaper at nineteen and closed it at twenty. By the time he was twenty-two his second newspaper, *L'Avenir*, was bristling with *Rouge* manifestoes. When *L'Avenir* had been brought down after a few exciting years by the combined hostility of the *Bleus* and the Church he had promptly embarked on a new venture.

The Eastern Townships, lying between the south shore of the St. Lawrence and the borders of New England, had been in the early days of the colony a wilderness carefully maintained for defence against the Americans. Later they had become a preserve of English settlement into which the French rarely ventured. Dorion had plunged into the heart of the English county bearing Durham's name and had founded there the village of L'Avenir. Colonization had been one of his great themes as an editor and now he intended to put his words to work. This town of 'the future' was to be a place of model farms, a living symbol of the enterprise he preached and an example of the new life he dreamed of for French Canadians. Hard as he had fought the

Church, his first act in the new town had been to build a chapel with his own hands to show that opposition to priests in politics did not mean enmity to religion.

L'Avenir, in the dozen years since its founding, had not fulfilled his hopes. The era of the Grand Trunk had intervened, drawing all growth like a magnet toward its lines, and the line had gone to Victoriaville, twenty-five miles away. Yet Dorion had fired the progress of the whole region and he had won the respect not only of the French settling about him on a widening circle of cleared farms but of the English who had been there before them.

In his third newspaper, *Le Défricheur* – 'The Pioneer' – he still thundered forth his *Rouge* doctrines, mellowing only a little toward the Church, as French-Canadian politicians were accustomed to do with advancing years. He preached also, however, the gospel of every frontier: the need for harmony and mutual help, the need for thrift and industry, the need for better farming and better education. He had been twice elected to the provincial parliament for the constituency of Drummond-Arthabaska, which embraced his village, and English, Scotch, and Irish farmers had combined with the French to send him there. He was a member of the House now, often in Montreal in this autumn which was to be the last of his life. He chafed as always in the bonds of an English state. He still fought for the goals he would never reach, but he had made a little of the land bloom along his way. Frail, passionate, intense, and still youthful-looking, he was the perfect example of the untamed, unregenerate *Rouge*, a man to inspire young men.

Antoine-Aimé Dorion was the elder brother, now forty-seven. The coolest and oldest head among Papineau's cluster of young, he had become the leader of the party on Papineau's retirement ten years before. He had been constantly in the provincial House, constantly in touch with the realities of government and of the French position in Canada. He had seen the issue of survival become the lesser quarrel of French or English 'domination', and he had seen the quarrel submerged for a time under the bustle and boom of progress. He had seen the businessmen take over on both sides of the racial line and the Grand Trunk become a power in the land. He had moved into wary alliance with George Brown as Conservatives and *Bleus* linked hands. Then, as the population of Upper Canada moved steadily ahead, the issue of race had emerged again, more threatening than before. The voice of George Brown had become the loudest voice in the country crying for representation by population.

Dorion had known that it must come, with all its dangers for the French. That certainty he shared with Cartier. He still leaned toward the ways of American democracy, as Cartier did not, but he no longer saw an escape in independence or annexation. He had abandoned whatever hopes he had had of joining the United States as he saw that union torn apart by civil war. He had found his solution in a new division of Canada. Durham's 'legislative union', which had given all power to a central government and tried to make the two peoples one in everything, had been a failure. Dorion's goal was a 'federal union' in which French and English Canada, like two of the American states, would be united under the Crown but each supreme in its separate sphere. He had been urging the plan for years now, in parliament and out, and his *Rouges* had come to accept it as the one pale hope. It would be a refuge at least from the dangers of 'Rep. by Pop.', a half-way house for the French on the long, forked road to independence or the United States.

Instead, out of obscure stirrings in the Maritime Provinces there had come the Charlottetown Conference in September of 1864, with Canadians there as half-invited guests. The junketings of delegates about the country had followed, and then from behind the locked doors of that other conference room in Quebec had come a plan of the English and of Cartier, breath-taking in its insolence. To the million and a half English of the Canadas were to be added the three hundred and thirty thousand English of Nova Scotia, the two hundred and fifty thousand English of New Brunswick, and the hundred thousand English of Prince Edward Island and Newfoundland. In one enormous and grotesque conglomeration, defying all the facts of economics and geography, the English of North America were to be brought together to swamp the million French. Nor were the people of any province, English or French, to be allowed to pronounce on the matter. It was all to be done 'at a bound'. The resolutions of the Quebec Scheme were to be forced through provincial legislatures under the thumbs of their leaders. They were then to be hurried to England for incorporation into an Act of the Imperial Parliament and the confederation of British North America would be a fact.

Neither the elder *Rouges* nor the raw recruits who listened to them could yet take the outrageous plot quite seriously. It was too obviously the work of desperate politicians: of Macdonald, helpless before George Brown's Liberals; of Cartier, moneygrubber and man of the Grand Trunk, with his consuming thirst for bigness. Yet the very thought of it heightened all fears and sharpened all perceptions. One was alive for the first time to the hugeness of this continent on which one lived, cut off from the tap-root of the old French homeland. One had hardly thought of those seaside colonies seven hundred miles away across the wilderness, still less of that vaster wilderness reaching to the west beyond the Canadas. It all had to be thought of now – George Brown thought of that west as the home of future millions, English millions – and there was still more than that.

The streets of Montreal were bright, as they had been for three years now, with red jackets and gold lace. Six chartered steamers had filled Montreal with troops as the Civil War began and England embroiled herself with Washington. The old resentments came with the sight of those troops, but a new fear as well. Unwelcome as they were, they would be hopelessly few for their purpose when the war ended, as it was now certain to do, in favour of the North. Canada, lying defenceless along the St. Lawrence and the Great Lakes, all the sprawling half-emptiness of this British North America, would be faced by the mighty armies of a restored and hostile union.

England – America – the sense of relentless pressures and the power of great contenders was suddenly oppressive about one. The anxious, angry conferences of the Dorions and Laflammes and Lanctôts could not dispel it. The maledictions of young lawyers, the clacking of hand-presses, and the stream of broadsheets and pamphlets seemed curiously unreal. The days were drawing in, darkening earlier now, deepening the mood. The idle barrister of Ste-Thérèse street felt small and lost, angry and impotent, as he turned home each evening with the first of the cold snows blowing in his face and the winter cough coming on.

3

THERE WAS a good deal more than politics to depress him these days. The drab little upstairs office contrasted painfully with the surroundings in which he had spent three years as Laflamme's privileged clerk. The new dignity of the B.C.L. hardly made up for the lack of a monthly stipend. Above all he was still adjusting rather painfully, after more than a year of it, to a change in his domestic life.

He had been a young man on his own during his first two terms at McGill. With the beginning of the third term, however, Carolus and the family had moved in from St-Lin to make a home for him, and he was now living at 23 St-André street, just below Dorchester on the northern fringes of the city's built-up area. It was a very good move in Carolus's view, since it kept the family together and saved Wilfrid the expense of boarding out. Grandfather Charles, who had died a year or so before, was no longer on hand to point out that both the farm and the business of the surveyor might suffer from the change. Adeline accepted it with a shrug and made the best of it. It was good to have Wilfrid near at hand, and impossible to change Carolus. To him the life and excitement of Montreal made up for all inconveniences. He was not, however, able to provide a great deal with his diminished income, and St-André was not a very good neighbourhood. One woke in the morning to the sound of carpenters, cobblers, and mechanics starting off for their benches followed by the yells of their wives and the squalls of their children. One came home to the same in the evenings and endured it with good-humoured loyalty; but it made the two previous years on St-Louis street, just off the Champ de Mars, all the sweeter in retrospect.

The house on St-Louis street was the home of Dr. Séraphin Gauthier. It was spacious and comfortable and full of children and it was loud in the evenings with good music and good talk, which was the way the doctor liked it. He was interested in everything and had his own opinions on everything, some of them violently at odds with those of his colleagues. He had been a druggist before he became a doctor and he now practised both professions successfully and with great relish. Genial, gregarious, and unconventional, with little respect for the orthodox view in any field, he was admirably matched with his wife, Phoebe.

Phoebe Gauthier was enjoying life with her second husband of the same name. She had been born Phoebe Lyons, daughter of a Jewish merchant of Manchester in the wholesale jewellery trade. Her father had come to the United States in the 1840s to set up some outlets for his prosperous business and she had come along with him, a girl of seventeen. She had spent some time with him in Montreal and had there made the acquaintance of a young Dr. Séraphin Gauthier who was practising in the village of St-Lin. The two were in love before the appalling prospect of a mixed marriage had even dawned on their parents and they did not wait for the explosion. Instead they made off by calèche for Lacolle, thirty miles to the south of Montreal, and were there married. Since it had been an overnight journey and the parents knew their children, nothing remained but to fetch them back and marry them over again.

Phoebe had embraced the Catholic faith with her Catholic husband but Lewis Lyons, after the first shock, bore it well. He lingered on in the United States and Canada and was a frequent visitor at St-Lin where two daughters, Emma and Hannah, were born to the young couple. Two years after the marriage he was called on to provide a home in Montreal for Phoebe and the children when Séraphin Gauthier died of consumption and left her a widow of twenty-one. Perhaps he cherished hopes of her return to Manchester and the faith of her fathers, but if so they were disappointed. The second Séraphin Gauthier, a cousin of the first, appeared on the scene, and it was not long before another marriage was in train. It was destined to be a long and successful one, as Lewis Lyons was soon reassured. There was no doubt of the affection and competence of the second Séraphin, nor of his abounding health and vitality. As the children of the later marriage began to come along, Lewis Lyons yielded at last to the calls of home. 'I am leaving you,' he wrote his daughter, 'and perhaps we may never meet again. Be good and virtuous and honour your parents and all your friends who love you.'

The dark-eyed Phoebe heeded her father's injunction and the house on St-Louis street was a pleasant rendezvous for many friends. The strangely-assorted turned up there surprisingly and found themselves at ease, and it was seldom that either the doctor or his wife spent an evening quite alone. The friends of the children crowded in when there were no guests for the elders; sometimes there was a mingling of both groups, and often there were some who did not quite fit into either.

Of these, a Mme Zoë Lafontaine, married to Napoléon-Godefroi Lafontaine, a bailiff, became one. Napoléon-Godefroi was not a good provider, and was so frequently absent from home that many of Mme Lafontaine's neighbours thought her a widow in narrow straits. The latter part of the supposition, at least, was true. She had become a teacher of music in order to support herself and her daughter, Zoë, and one of the homes at which she called was that of the Gauthiers. When her health began to fail the daughter took the mother's place at the piano and music lessons went forward with new enthusiasm. Mlle Lafontaine was soon a favourite of all the Gauthier children and the bosom companion of the elder daughters, Emma and Hannah.

Napoléon-Godefroi's absences from home became more prolonged and Mme Lafontaine's health worse. Her slender resources dwindled until they consisted of her piano and a certificate for sixteen shares in a building society valued at eight hundred dollars, both reserved for her daughter's dowry. In such circumstances, on the urgent invitation of the Gauthiers, she and Zoë came to join the household.

About a year later the nineteen-year-old Wilfrid Laurier appeared at the door, a student just enrolled at McGill. He was not unexpected. During Phoebe's two years at St-Lin she had been a friend of Marcelle Martineau Laurier. Her first Séraphin had been for a while the Lauriers' family doctor. She had given a promise, in the last weeks of Marcelle Martineau's life, that she would do what she could to help in the education of young Wilfrid and she had been mindful of her promise ever since.

The connection with St-Lin had been maintained; she was aware of the boy's abilities and of the family's plans. Wilfrid found a room prepared for him and was at once a member of the family circle.

He was something of an enigma for a while, a very handsome, rather frail, and bookish young man, troubled by a cough. He was inclined at first to keep to his room a good deal in the evenings, or to pass down the stairs with an absent-minded nod on his way out. The last Friday of each month was taken up by the evening meetings of the Institut des Lois, where McGill students joined in free-swinging debate on the questions of the day. Here the young man who had deplored the policy of the French kings toward the Huguenots found much support and many more intriguing avenues of discussion opened up. Then came the much more serious business of the Institut Canadien, and he was soon a regular attendant at all political meetings. Meanwhile there were still the notes from his lectures to be conned in the evenings at home.

He was nevertheless not a man to be ignored by the Gauthiers, nor to wish to be ignored. There was too much life below stairs, there was too much good talk and there was too much music. Oftener and oftener as the months went by he became a member of the groups that gathered about the piano while Mlle Lafontaine played. He was very often preoccupied and sometimes looked pale and ill but he was soon conscious, not at all unpleasantly, of the eyes of three young women glinting and glancing away.

Emma Gauthier, already a widow, was more or less out of the running. She had contracted a marriage briefer than that of her parents, ended by the death of her husband in this town of damp and reek where *les poumons* seemed to be a topic of incessant and subdued conversation. Hannah was only fourteen, and in any case soon saw the lay of the land. From the beginning it was Zoë Lafontaine for Wilfrid Laurier.

She was slight and small-boned, with hands grown graceful over the piano keys and roughened a little from the many tasks of nursing an ailing mother. Her dark hair was parted in the middle and brushed back severely to either side. Both the limitations of her wardrobe and her duties in the household enforced plainness in dress; she was seldom garnished by the waves of embroidery and the mutton-chop sleeves of the day. Among the flamboyant Gauthiers she seemed at first retiring and demure, but that impression soon passed. The wide, hazel eyes held their own in any company and the mouth with its lovely, delicate moulding, still midway between that of the child and the woman, matched them. Mlle Lafontaine looked at the world from a position that was scarcely an advantageous one at the moment, but she looked at it unafraid, with shrewd appraisal and with gentleness and humour.

The beginnings of the courtship were apparent to the bystanders long before the participants were quite sure what they were about. The symptoms, indeed, were well enough disguised from any but the sharp-eyed and the uninvolved, for they emerged first in the hot political discussions of the drawing-room. There had always been talk before, but it became better talk as Laurier grew intimate with the family and began to bring home some of his associates. David and Lanctôt, as young familiars, were frequently on hand. Laflamme made an appearance, liked what he found, and was soon returning often. Eric Dorion and even Antoine-Aimé began to drop in. Since the family circle by no means excluded priests and *Bleus*, it all made for exhilarating evenings and the ladies were inclined to linger. Dr. Gauthier himself was a wildly exuberant *Rouge*. The young student of L'Assomption, now released from L'Assomption, glowed bright red. Zoë, generally silent in the background, nevertheless began to wear the flags in her cheeks.

The household divided about the pair into camps of observant conspirators: the doctor for, his wife against, and the elder daughters siding with their father. Wilfrid, the absorbed student, became Wilfrid the troubled lover, often growing silent and abstracted in the midst of the liveliest discussion. Zoë, alone with the women and children during the day, conducted her music lessons and went about her other work with composure, but she was subject to alternating fits of brightness and depression in the late afternoons as the time neared for the homecoming of the men. Everything was noted by the alert family, and much provided for. Uninhibited comings and goings were rearranged to provide opportunities for tête-à-têtes of the two; the evening musicales developed a habit of breaking up early and absent-mindedly, leaving the same two alone at the piano. Ten-year-old Louis Gauthier, creeping down from his room upstairs to listen at the door, heard Zoë's music and Wilfrid's voice rising with it, clear and a little off key:

> How may it be, you ask, that I adore you?
> Do you not know your lips and brow and eyes,
> Your voice that lingers when the song is stilled?
> Do not love me, but only let me love.

Once more, however, as so often in his life, Wilfrid Laurier was living in a house where death hovered in an upstairs room. Mme Lafontaine was dying; there could be no thought of marriage for Zoë at the moment. There could be no thought of it in any case for an impecunious law student, and this in its own bleak way was for the best. The eternal cough held on through the winter's cold and the slush and rains of the long springs. Dr. Gauthier violently maintained that Laurier was not consumptive, but he could not convince his wife. Laurier was not convinced. Two summers had seemed to free him for a while of the sick lethargy, but everything returned with the autumn winds, a little worse. He could not forget his mother or Malvina or the weak chests of his half-brothers.

He would come out of McGill with little money and less in the way of prospects. If he was a man whose time was short he must make his way alone. The break came with Carolus's decision to move to Montreal. It meant the end of the pleasant life at the Gauthiers', and it was almost a relief. Perhaps it was a relief for Phoebe Gauthier too, friend though she was. The one-time lass of Manchester was a curious link for Laurier with the old days of New Glasgow, brightening the half-blurred memories. She tempered the fires of his Frenchness sometimes with a flash of sharp Midlands humour, and he liked her for it. He had come to her once with a fistful of scarf-pins brought from a shopkeeper on approval, and she had pointed instantly to the horseshoe pin – 'for luck'; he wore it now. He had taken her advice on many things, but on this she would not advise him. There was no need: he knew her mind. She remembered the last days of Marcelle Martineau, of her own first husband, and of Emma's husband, and she loved Zoë Lafontaine.

He had moved his things to 23 St-André street as he began his last term at McGill. Now, as the autumn of 1864 passed into the winter of 1865, the break was lengthening into a second year. It was far from a complete separation; he was still often at the Gauthiers'. But he came as a visitor now, and already his place seemed to be filled. Mme Lafontaine was gone. François-Xavier Coutu was on hand as a new suitor for Emma, and sometimes Pierre Valois, a handsome young doctor from Pointe-Claire, was present with his eyes on Zoë.

It made the surroundings of 23 St-André street more drab; it made the long journey to the office each morning more tiring. With his coat collar bundled about his ears, the barrister would come along by the big houses on Dorchester Street to take the horse-car at St-Dénis. He would get off at Gosford and walk by the Champ de Mars and the City Hall to Notre Dame and on down to Ste-Thérèse. Very often, with the thought of that briefless desk ahead, he would stop midway along Gosford and look up St-Louis toward the well-known house. Sometimes she would come to meet him for a word, often she could not, but always she was there.

4

ON FRIDAY FEBRUARY 3, 1865, in the third session of the eighth provincial parliament of Canada assembled at Quebec, the Honourable Sir Etienne-Pascal Taché rose to move:

> That an humble address be presented to Her Majesty praying that she may be graciously pleased to cause a measure to be submitted to the Imperial Parliament for the purpose of uniting the Colonies of Canada, Nova Scotia, New Brunswick, Newfoundland and Prince Edward Island in one Government with provisions based on the following Resolutions, which were adopted at a Conference of Delegates from the said Colonies, held at the city of Quebec on the 10th of October, 1864.

Having read the seventy-two resolutions, he commenced a speech in French which was immediately interrupted by the Honourable John Ross, a life member of the Legislative Council, with the request that he speak in English. Sir Etienne agreed, since 'as there were English members who did not understand French at all, while the French members all understood English, it would be best for him to speak in the latter language'.

If there was a barb in the statement it was unpoisoned and well concealed. The polite and accommodating Taché, now seventy years old and within a few months of his death, was author of the celebrated promise that 'the last cannon shot fired in defence of English power in America will be fired by a French Canadian'. He was a man of the era of Lafontaine and Baldwin, he had seen the rights of his language entrenched in the country's statutes. He could not make the English listen to it, but he had come to accept that as one of the enduring facts of life in this Canada, and it did not greatly matter on the present occasion. Taché, though premier of the province, was merely a reluctant figurehead. Behind him moved the great alliance headed by Macdonald, Cartier, and Brown, and the real debate was opened by Macdonald on February 6.

For the *Rouges* of Montreal the incredible was now all too real; the black six weeks had begun. George Etienne Cartier, the French Canadian who no longer even spelt his name in the French way, was the prop and underpinning of the whole scheme. For him Canadian bigness, British or not, was the only answer to American bigness. The Church was with him, always in dread of Protestant America, always seeing in the British connection at least 'a plank of safety'. As the days of the debate dragged by, the savage protests of the younger Dorion and the cold sarcasm of the elder went alike for nothing, even though they were supported by the reasoned arguments of a few English members. 'Why are we engaged in discussing Confederation?' Eric cried out, and answered his own question. The government had collapsed; it had been defeated on a question of maladministration. It had advanced $100,000 to the always-hungry Grand Trunk without authority of parliament. Discredited and bankrupt Tories had allied themselves with their ancient enemy George

Brown and with those unknown men from the Maritimes to produce a scheme that would save their hides and make them greater than before.

Cartier promised safety for the French in this new union; of what value was the word of Cartier in the face of an English parliament? George Brown, that great hater of Frenchness and above all of separate schools, now conceded the right of separate schools. How long would that concession last? George Brown wanted representation by population, English dominance, and that was what he would get.

Confederation was spoken of as a union of autonomous provinces, a federal union. All the world knew that John A. Macdonald stood for the legislative union in which a central government would be supreme. Cartier could never openly agree to that, but it would come. Even in the present scheme the central government had the power of veto; it could disallow and override provincial laws. The powers of the provincial legislatures were strictly defined and limited; the power at the centre embraced all else and was open to every expansion in an unknown future. To call this federalism, said Eric Dorion, was 'nonsense and repugnant to truth. All is strength and power in the federal government, all is weakness, insignificance, annihilation in the local government. The autonomy of Lower Canada is menaced and placed at the mercy of a parliament of one hundred and ninety-four members of whom forty-seven or at most forty-eight would represent the views of the majority of its peoples.' It was 'a legislative union in disguise'. His brother icily agreed. 'It is evident', said Antoine-Aimé, 'that it is intended eventually to form a legislative union of all the provinces.'

This scheme, said Eric, was advanced in the name of defence against the United States, and what it would achieve was an indefensible frontier sixteen hundred miles long, a country 'without its like under the sun. In geographical form it resembles an eel. Its length would be everything, its breadth nothing.' There was a promise in the scheme to build the long-promised intercolonial railway joining Quebec to Halifax, but there was no word as to the route or the cost. There was the still wilder prospect of an inter-oceanic railway across three thousand miles of unknown wilderness to reach the territories of British Columbia. Everything about the scheme could be dismissed as the work of fools or rogues or both. 'These gentlemen', said Antoine-Aimé Dorion, 'only found that Confederation was a panacea for all evils when their seats as ministers were in danger. I see in it nothing but another railway scheme for the benefit of the few.'

There were signs, even as the debate went on, that the plan was falling apart. Prince Edward Island began to draw away from it. The government of New Brunswick was forced to the people on the issue, and went down. In Nova Scotia the determined Tupper, one of the principal framers of the plan, was being backed to the wall by an adamant opposition. 'Will the honourable gentlemen go to England and press on the scheme under such circumstances?' asked Antoine-Aimé Dorion on March 6. 'I say that this scheme is killed. I repeat that it is killed.'

One week later, on Monday March 13, the resolutions of the Confederation Scheme were approved and the Address to the Throne was agreed to by a vote of ninety-one to thirty-three, with twenty-one of the dissenting votes French-Canadian. On the following day the Speaker informed the House that His Excellency the Governor General would 'have much pleasure in transmitting it to the Secretary of State for the Colonies, in order that it may be presented to the Queen'.

5

IN MONTREAL about a month later, and with rather less attention from the public, the firm of Laurier, Archambault & Desaulniers was dissolved. There had been few clients, there was now no money, and, at least in Laurier's case, there had always been too much politics. The Institut Canadien had whetted his appetite. He was close to the centre of things and he had been noticed. He was convinced, personable, and ambitious; the attention of leaders was flattering and there was always work for young men. While the debate in the House went on he had taken to the snowy roads and addressed some meetings for the Dorions. They had not been particularly successful, but one meeting had led to another; and they had all led back at last to the briefless desk and the mound of unpaid bills. The way on from there led straight to Médéric Lanctôt.

Laurier had been sought by the new partner long before he left the old ones. Now such doubts as he may have had were brushed aside. It was a matter not only of the means to live but of his own mood. Lanctôt was twenty-seven, just three years older than himself. He had a good practice which he neglected almost completely, and therefore he required a partner. Above all he was a fierce opponent of Confederation who regarded the closing of the debate as merely the beginning of the fight.

There had never been a time, in either of their memories, when the fear of some such measure had not been in the wind. Lanctôt had been born in 1838, the son of a condemned rebel. His mother had carried him to the docks, an infant in arms, to see his handcuffed father walk up the deck of a convict ship bound for exile in Australia. He had grown up within the union, hating it, watching it move toward collapse, always expecting worse. He blazed with the resentments of the past and chafed at the frustrations of the present, and for a few angry months in this spring and summer of 1865 he seemed to strike a deeper chord in Laurier than any other man.

They were both young, and wherever they looked the future seemed closed. The English had always had the money; the English built the canals and railways, the English owned the shops and factories, the big houses growing in the mountain's shadow were all English. The Confederation Scheme might fail but there would always be other schemes. Sooner or later the realities of power must be reflected in the final reality of political power, in increased representation in the House, in the domination of the province by an English majority. What would remain then for the man who thought in French even though he spoke in English, for the man who clung to his roots and hoped to grow from them in a land of his own making?

It seemed sometimes that one could find the answer in Lanctôt himself. He had a brilliant, dogmatic mind. He was a genial companion and a generous partner. He had fire and humour and discernment and a gift for admiration. 'Let me present you to Laurier, my partner.' The introductions punctuated their walks wherever they went. 'There is a head for you! Mark my words, he is a coming man. He is a poet, an orator, a philosopher, a jurist – my God, I can't name all his talents, but he will be heard of. Don't forget that face.' Time after time the words followed the junior partner down the corridors of the Court House as the senior broke away to attend to his many concerns. It was pleasing and it was stimulating. It made one resigned to doing all the work, but it began to be troubling too.

Lanctôt, like Laurier, was the child of the long memories. They were darker for him, and held him in a fiercer grip. Instinctive rebellion was the way of his life. He was ambitious and the English stifled his ambition; therefore he fought them. The Church was authority incarnate; therefore he fought the Church. He resented English prosperity; therefore he sought prosperity for himself in the wildest commercial schemes. He had no time for the easy success he might have had in the courts; there were always his business promotions, there was always *L'Union Nationale*, and now there was the Club Saint-Jean Baptiste, a secret anti-Confederation society even more to his taste. He delighted in this battle, but it was not a battle for the future. It was a battle with himself, with the old angers, with the old, gnawing sense of inferiority, with the unaccepted conquest. Was this the fate of the *Rouge*, then, of the intellectual, of the French Canadian risen above the horde – always to be blindly struggling for he never quite knew what, always to be beaten by the self-made enemies of the present and encompassed by the shadows of the past?

6

THE QUESTION grew more insistent as the hopes of 1865 began to die away with the spring of 1866. Anti-Confederation petitions still poured in on the government. Great meetings filled the Champ de Mars and crowded in on the church doors of the country towns as the Dorions took to the road. Newfoundland was drawing away from the scheme as well as Prince Edward Island. In Nova Scotia Joseph Howe was tearing the plan to shreds. Yet nothing seemed to avail. The handful of provincial premiers and party politicians who had always wavered before held on unwaveringly now. The address passed by the parliament at Quebec lay before the Queen; Canada had declared herself. On April 17, 1866, Tupper forced his resolution through the Nova Scotia legislature. On June 12, Tilley of New Brunswick came back to power, pledged to Confederation.

Antoine-Aimé Dorion was a beaten man; Eric was dying. Lanctôt was still of the irreconcilables, rushing from meeting to meeting and plot to plot. In the tumbledown office on Ste-Thérèse street he and David and their handful of hot-eyed youths still scrawled out the jeremiads of *L'Union Nationale* or gathered for the meetings of the Club Saint-Jean Baptiste. Laurier was sometimes with them, but it was only in the evenings now. He seemed to have nothing to contribute and he was usually tired out from a long day at his desk or in the courts. The business, after all, had to go on; it was earning less and less each month but there was no money from any other source. David, the best of his friends as his feelings toward Lanctôt cooled, often looked up at him. 'I seem to see Laurier as he was then, ill and sad, grave and indifferent to all the turmoil raised around him. He passed through the midst of it like a shadow and seemed to say to us, "Brother, we must all die." '

He was looking at the stragglers of a lost battle and he knew it as the summer wore away. The familiar chill crept into his bones with autumn, and the cough shook him. Eric Dorion was gone, dead of a heart attack. Laurier was a sick man with a living to earn. He dragged himself through the routine of courts and offices, a little contemptuous in his heart now of Lanctôt and the rest. They craved excitement and they were achieving excitement; nothing else.

In the evenings he sometimes tried to read in the house on St-André street, but gave it up irritably, disgusted with the clamour of the street outside. He went to the Gauthiers' a good deal, but even from there he returned more dejected. The conversations of the *Rouges* were subdued and gloomy. The groups about the piano included not only Emma's François-Xavier Coutu but Pierre Valois, now the open and ardent suitor of Zoë.

She had given Valois little encouragement through the summer and that thought had brightened the hot dry days for Laurier, when he felt better in any case. On some of the evenings he had taken Zoë's arm and they had walked down to look at the stores on Notre Dame Street or gone along St. James, still bright with the uniforms of soldiers. There had been the drills with fife and drum on the Champ de Mars, and they had often strolled to Dalhousie Square to hear the regimental bands and look in at the mysteries of the officers' mess. A man had felt hope at times like those, turning homeward at the sound of the sunset gun, with that hand on his arm.

But the summer was gone now, and the health and hopes with it. Lanctôt was bitter and despondent and drinking as well, a hopeless partner. Laurier could hardly force himself to what little work there was. The cough was worse than it had ever been, and at last on a grey afternoon in October he collapsed across his desk with blood spouting from his lips and staining the paper before him. He was conscious of hurrying feet and of the faces of Lanctôt and David as they bent over him. Then there was a black bag on the desk and the voice of a doctor came from far off: 'The poor lad – he will have to take good care of himself to live ten years.'

Later there was Zoë at the bedside and his hand in hers. He drew it away. Antoine-Aimé Dorion came, grey in defeat and still dulled by his grief for Eric. But there was something for Laurier in that very grief. There was no lawyer at L'Avenir, and there was now no editor for *Le Défricheur*. It was a place of opportunity for a young man and it was high country where the air was clean. It would require a little money but when he was well again, or well enough to go on, the money would be found.

By the beginning of November it was all arranged. On the night before he was to leave Lanctôt arrived, brisk, sober, and well groomed, to drag him off to the Hotel Saint-Louis, where he found a sizeable banquet arranged in his honour. It was a bright and lively gathering with most of the *Rouge* leaders there and Laflamme and Lanctôt setting the pace. Since Laurier drank very little he was able to judge the speeches with a clear head and they had a sincerity and warmth that genuinely surprised him. He had done nothing he particularly cared to remember, but this was a consolation prize for the man who might have been.

3

THE BOIS-FRANCS

1866-1868

IT WAS mid November when he arrived at L'Avenir. On the twenty-eighth of the month the first edition of *Le Défricheur* appeared with 'Wilfrid Laurier – Rédacteur' replacing the name of Eric Dorion at the masthead. Two weeks later *Le Pays* of Montreal noted with approval that '*Le Défricheur* has resumed its regular publication. Mr. Laurier . . . is an energetic and distinguished writer . . . one of the most solid and at the same time most brilliant young men we know. He is in a position to render important services to the Eastern Townships and to the Liberal party while preparing himself for a glorious career.'

It was a pat on the back from his *Rouge* friends, continuing the mood of the banquet. His own mood, however, was better reflected by the condition of the paper when it arrived, damp and bedraggled like all his mail from a rough trip over snow-drifted lumber-trails. Limp, dejected, and far from familiar surroundings, he was already convinced that the first step in the glorious career had been a false one.

L'Avenir, the town of Dorion's dream, lay in the heart of what had come to be known as the Bois-Francs country. Around it high hills and magnificent forests seamed by a dozen rivers rolled away to the borders of Maine, New Hampshire, and Vermont. For thirty years a new generation of French Canadians, urged to possess their soil, had come to this 'land of the free woods'. A man had only to hack down the forest, the cry went, and he had a wealth of logs for burning down to potash. He had soil rich from a thousand years of mould on which a crop could be harvested the first season. It was to be the answer to the bustling English, 'the California of Quebec', the home of a people happy, contented, and above all French. And so it was for a few. But from the window of Dorion's cluttered office, with the hand-press clacking away in the back room, one looked out at the log houses of farmers and woodsmen straggling along a single village street. The future had been swept off to the north, twenty-five miles away, where English power and money had brought the Grand Trunk to Victoriaville. L'Avenir was a hopeless backwater. The choice was the old choice: follow the English or remain a pastoral relic.

About the middle of December he bundled himself into a sleigh and made the trip to Victoriaville. Ten days of plodding about the booming railway town dispelled whatever hopes he had had of it. It stood up half-built, hideous, and clanging on a patch of frozen table-land which became swamp each spring as the high hills around it fed their waters down. It was acrid with train-smoke and swarming with contractors, promoters, and money-makers in hip-boots. It was all Grand Trunk, it was all English, it was all *Bleu*. It was 'the Froggery' to the disdainful citizens of St-Christophe d'Arthabaskaville, three miles away across the little Gosselin River.

He hired another sleigh and set off on the road for the Gosselin. It wound away from Victoriaville station over a dismal, snowy plain where the reeds of summer swamps poked up through drifts and rail fences wound crazily away toward a few farm-houses scattered in the distance. Then it dipped down to an old wooden bridge across the river and began to climb on the other side. The driver pointed to Mont Christo and Mont St-Michel as the steep slope undulated ahead and the woods closed in around them; they were now, he said, on the main street of St-Christophe.

To the jaundiced eye of a city man the houses were a long time in coming and sparse and scattered when they came, but they were surprisingly good. Some of them stood up tall and gauche, with all the fantastic elaboration of a country builder; others were clustered together like top-heavy gossips under their sloping, oversized roofs. They all had good grounds, however, and crisp-cut paths through the snow-drifts led to welcoming doorways. There was a sense of ease and comfort. The court-house stood long and severe in yellow brick, surrounded by a field-stone wall. The post-office was equally imposing, and beyond the post-office were a half-dozen prosperous-looking stores, each with a patch of clean-swept wooden sidewalk in front of it. Laurier observed the polished name-plates of doctors, lawyers, and notaries, and was impressed by the bustle of comings and goings between them. He was even more impressed as the road wound out of the business district and divided in two forks. On the left it bent down under a stark lattice of maple branches that would be an arch of shade in summer, and to the right it climbed under tall elms up the slope of Mont Christo. The sleigh took the right fork past a group of mansions of ascending elegance, each in its own wide grounds, and Laurier could see that there were similar houses on the road below. He was far from the glories of Montreal here, but he was equally far from the primitive isolation of L'Avenir.

The white-painted wooden church stood long and low on the brow of the little mountain. It was much cursed for its location, the driver said as he paused to breathe the horse, because every cartload of wood or other freight had to be broken up into two half-loads before making the climb. Beyond the church the street sloped away again down the other side of the hill, passing the cemetery and running along by the bank of the River Nicolet. The frozen thread of the river disappeared under a long, covered bridge, emerged again by a grist-mill, and wound out into a valley dazzling white with snow and shadowed by blue hills. Laurier got out of the sleigh and drew a long breath, so deep it made him cough. He was eight hundred feet above Montreal here and the air was sharp and dry. Whether to live in or, as he suspected, to die in, he had found his place.

2

HE WOUND UP his few affairs in L'Avenir over a Christmas and New Year's that he always remembered as the most wretched of his life. By the first week of January 1867 he had crossed the Gosselin again and was installed as a paying guest in the home of Dr. Edouard Modeste Poisson. A few days later his press and printshop equipment arrived, accompanied by Dorion's printer, whose occupation was gone in L'Avenir. The search for business quarters led to a small frame building standing empty on 'the street of the church'. It was cut up into four square rooms heated by a single stove let into a sheet metal alcove at the rear, and only one of its five windows looked onto the street. It provided space, however, for printer, press, master, and office equipment, and the rent was reasonable. He signed a year's lease and came home that night feeling for the first time in months that his fate was in his own hands.

It was not quite true. He had been bound here, whether he knew it or not, from the first moment he stepped into Eric Dorion's shoes. St-Christophe d'Arthabaskaville, whose name was soon to be shortened down to Arthabaska, was one of the earliest and most successful of the Bois-Francs settlements. It had grown quickly to a certain affluence and a certain elegance as prosperous farmers settled down to enjoy their holdings. More importantly in this land of litigation, it had become the judicial seat of the county. As a place of courts and lawyers, it was also a place of politicians, most of whom had blossomed in the Dorion era and wore the Dorion hue. It was often visited by the barristers and judges of Quebec and Montreal. Close enough to the large centres to feel the pulse of the times, it was also important enough in its own region to exert considerable influence. Eric Dorion, as a figure already prominent in the province and a man to whom men came, had been able to live apart from it. Wilfrid Laurier, so long as he cherished any hopes of a career, was not.

He did not arrive as a complete unknown. The first half-dozen issues of the new *Défricheur* had been read with interest here. He had been provided in Montreal with letters of introduction.

The early fruits were the genial companionship and the comfortable house of the middle-aged widower, Dr. Poisson. It was quite certain, however, that the newspaper, the letters, and his own brief record would be known of in other quarters. Along with waiting friends, he could look for watchful enemies.

He was a *Rouge* of Montreal and a member of L'Institut Canadien. He could therefore be sure that his first appearance in the white church on the hill would bring a hard stare from the pulpit. When it came it was not overly alarming. Father Philippe-Hippolyte Suzor was the first curé of Arthabaska and had come with the creation of the parish in 1851. He was an indefatigable builder and an equally indefatigable politician. His activities through a long and lively incumbency were to become the stuff of legend. Priests of the future, faced with the inheritance of his dusty battles, were to come to Arthabaska with sighs of dread and depart with hosannahs of relief. At the moment Father Suzor was in his early forties, a tall, rather slender man who walked with dignity and carried his head well. Out of an otherwise acceptable face, however, protruded an aquiline nose that had the habit of reddening when he was disturbed, and in the same moments his large mouth opened eccentrically, giving the effect of an irritated fish. He was not blessed with a sense of humour and his copious pulpit oratory was accompanied by a series of wildly unrelated gestures which not only his sheep but some of his fellow shepherds found irresistibly comic. Without humour he was also without luck; unsought comedy followed him everywhere. 'Anecdotes?' said an old acquaintance of the cloth, replying to a question years later. 'How could I select an anecdote about him? – his whole life is an anecdote!'

Invisible behind the occupant of this pulpit, however, was a very different figure. Louis-François Laflèche, Grand Vicar of the diocese of Three Rivers, which embraced Arthabaska, was soon to become a bishop and had always been an ultramontane. He stood already at the right hand and perhaps a little in advance of Bishop Bourget of Montreal. A man in his middle age now, he had behind him twelve years of service with the missions of the Church in the Northwest. He had been passionately devoted to the dark-skinned Métis people who lived, free as Indians, in the lands of the Red River. They were the descendants of French-Canadian voyageurs, trappers, and buffalo hunters who had come west and married among the tribes of the plains. Laflèche had seen in them, as others had seen before him, the nucleus of a daughter people, French and Catholic, bringing Quebec to the west. He had come back, embittered, as the first comings of English immigration threatened the dream. In the homelands of the St. Lawrence, he was determined, the Church should hold its place; and his conception of that place had all the clear-cut, authoritarian vigour of the bishops of New France.

'Each nation', he had written a year before, 'has received from Providence a mission to fulfil. The mission of the French-Canadian people is to constitute a centre of Catholicism in the New World.' He answered the pretensions of the *Rouges* in flat words: 'The best form of government is a moderate monarchy: the most imperfect is democracy. Authority derives from God. Liberalism commits the fundamental error of seeking to build society on other than religious principles. Electors not only exercise a right; they fulfil a duty for which they are responsible before God. The priest thus has the right to guide them. It is an error condemned by reason, by history, and by revelation to say that politics is a field in which religion has no right to enter and in which the Church has no concern.'

The newly-arrived editor went back from church to his office with this shadow over him and other troubles waiting. Somehow, in spite of all his comings and goings, he had managed to bring out the weekly editions of the paper more or less on schedule. He had launched his first issue with an elaborate statement of program and principles which he had composed in Montreal before he left. It had been much admired by *Le Pays* on publication. For all the remote encomiums, however, he had not yet found his feet. He was only beginning to discover how treacherous the footing was. He was editing Dorion's paper, but he was not Dorion. He found himself self-committed to 'retaining in *Le Défricheur* its spirit and turn of thought', while occupying himself, 'as did Dorion, with political economy, agriculture, and industrial education'. Since all three subjects were Greek to him, he was somewhat at a loss for material. The old Dorion motto,

'Work Ennobles', flew at the left of his masthead and the old Dorion injunction, 'Read, People of the Fields!' at the right, but when he tried to fill the columns beneath them he was ill at ease and ill-informed; he floundered and copied.

It was not so when he turned to politics, but in some ways it was rather worse. Dorion's great last cause had been the battle against Confederation. It was a lost cause now and little remained but a spiteful rearguard action. Yet it had to be fought by the man in Dorion's shoes, writing for Dorion's subscribers, the young man with a name to make for himself. On Laurier's desk at L'Avenir the *Bleu* newspapers had piled up, smug and complacent over the approaching victory. Most irritating among them, if not most prominent, had been the *Journal des Trois Rivières,* which spoke with the voice of Bishop Laflèche, and *L'Union des Cantons de l'Est,* which was published in Arthabaska and of which Father Suzor was the life and soul. Laurier had answered both in his first issues with all the flamboyant bitterness of Dorion himself.

'We politicians of the Papineau school' found the *Bleus*' support of Confederation 'a miserable pretext; the real reason is hatred of the Liberal party and of Liberal ideas. . . . You have succeeded, gentlemen; you have obtained a temporary triumph; but you have killed nationality.' Against the American union this new Canadian union would be 'armed with an egg-shell to stop a bullet; you will have placed a wisp of straw in the way of a giant'. Confederation would be 'the tomb of the French race and the ruin of Lower Canada'.

He had enlarged on the bleak prophecy in the last editorial written from L'Avenir, and the words would be dredged up against him long after. 'When the Ministers undertook their Confederation,' he had written, 'the basis of all their calculations, of all their hopes, of all their projects, was always the *English Colonies.* We do not care a fig for the English Colonies – we think only of Lower Canada and the French race. In this strange union every contrary element will meet face to face; the Catholic element and the Protestant element, the English element and the French element. From this moment there will be strife, division, war, anarchy; the weakest element, that is to say the French and

Catholic element, will be dragged along and swallowed up by the strongest.'

He was no longer quite in the mood of those drab December days. As he tried to resume the strain from the desk in Arthabaska there was only a sense of futility. It was bad enough to be a voice crying in a wilderness; it was worse to be no longer sure that he believed what he said. This pleasant, busy, bickering town was preparing to live under Confederation. The lawyers and doctors and comfortable landed men to whom he had come with his letters of introduction were all certainly *Rouge* but they were just as certainly resigned. There was going to be strife and division, but when had there not been? War and anarchy there would not be; never another 1837. The meeting of contrary elements, the swallowing of the French by the English, were more than political processes and they would go on with or without Confederation.

Where was a workable alternative? The young *Rouges* still talked of a future union with the United States. Laurier was a young *Rouge*. Yet more and more as he thought of the arms of that giant enclosing him he was content to delay the embrace. The plan of the elder Dorion, thought through to the end, offered only a return to the past and more years of hopeless stalemate. Against it stood Macdonald, ingratiating as always, and confident and earnest as never before in his life. Against it stood George Brown, trumpeting and self-complacent in the victory, yet somehow impressive and reassuring because he had sacrificed so much of his Englishness and Protestantism to gain it. Against it, above all, stood Cartier and the spark of eloquence struck from that uneloquent man: 'Shall we be content to maintain a mere provincial existence when by combining together we could become a great nation?'

It was certain by the end of the winter that the British North America Act would be passed. With acceptance of that, for Laurier, came an apathy that was almost relief. There would no longer be any need to search and divide himself, to feel guilt at the tug of new thoughts drawing him away from old loyalties. Right or wrong, the Dorions and their cause had been beaten. Eric was at rest and Antoine-Aimé with his usual cool-headedness was preparing to adapt himself to new conditions. A lone journalist, twenty-five years old, in the woods of the Eastern Townships, might be forgiven for doing the same.

It was not going to matter much in any case. He was now under the cold eye of Father Suzor and observed by Bishop Laflèche. He sparred weekly and bitterly with both *Le Journal des Trois Rivières* and *L'Union des Cantons de l'Est*. His views on the larger political question might have been forgiven him; Confederation, for the bishop, was the least of many evils but hardly a cause dear to his heart. It was a different matter, however, when *Le Défricheur*'s proprietor began to take a dutiful interest in local affairs and emerge as a friend and champion of the Pacauds.

They were a large and lively family whose seven branches had seeded and intertwined themselves through the Bois-Francs country over a long time. To the devout and obedient of the diocese they were known interchangeably as the seven deadly sins or the seven plagues of Egypt. Most of them still remained firmly within the fold, but the clergy, in their view, were more accustomed to lead sheep than lions. The man who could tame the Pacauds had not yet appeared. Laurier had soon become acquainted with the white-haired and magnificent Edouard Pacaud who was the dean of the Arthabaska bar. He had seen and heard him in church, occupying pew number four on the Epistle side, chanting the Mass off key, to the obvious discomfiture of Father Suzor. It was Charles Pacaud of nearby Stanfold, however, who had provided a *casus belli*.

'L'Oncle Charles', one of the family's stormiest petrels, was a prominent man in Stanfold. A little before Laurier's arrival he had become involved, not for the first time, in litigation with his curé. The dispute turned on some obscure and intricate matter of principle and involved about twenty dollars in tithes, but when it came before the court Pacaud was ordered to pay the tithe or declare himself no longer a Catholic. With all the constancy of a Pacaud he chose the latter course and brought down on himself a storm of condemnation. The new editor, without much looking before him, leaped to the defence. 'We do not know the facts of the case,' he admitted, and probably the decision was right. 'That, however, is no reason for insulting Mr. Pacaud, the condemned party. Every party . . . before a court exercises a legitimate right, and to make it a reproach to him that the court did not see it as he did is foolishness if not bad faith.' The righteous words brought considerable applause from many new-made friends. They also served, however, to deepen clerical frowns, to slow subscriptions to a trickle, and to increase the editor's dependence on one friend he could have spared.

Louis-Adélard Sénécal of Pierreville, forty miles to the west on the St. Francis River, had been Eric Dorion's political and financial backer and was now the chief creditor of *Le Défricheur*. He was a rarity in French Canada, a self-made baron of business who had fought his way to prominence with all the single-minded ruthlessness of an American tycoon. He had had a half-dozen years of education in a parish school and two or three years of apprenticeship in a general store. Out of this he had emerged in 1853 with the means to purchase a decrepit old steamer that was lying at Ogdensburg, New York. He had brought her down to Montreal the following April through a mass of floating ice, and the not inconsiderable feat had earned him the title of 'Captain' Sénécal, which he wore with unashamed pleasure. In a few more years he had half a dozen ships running freight on Canadian rivers and plying to American ports. The Civil War and the Reciprocity Treaty, of which he took full advantage, built up his fleet and made his fortune. He traded in lumber and grain, he took over defunct businesses and put them on their feet, and he ran the going concerns of competitors into the ground for the purpose of buying them up cheap. He had turned Dorion's colonizing enthusiasm neatly to his own account by buying up large blocks of land and putting settlers to work clearing them. By the time Laurier came on the scene Sénécal owned nearly the whole of near-by Upton township and could boast that he turned over an annual three million dollars of business without ever leaving Pierreville. 'One of the most striking traits of his character', as he caused to be written of himself, 'was that he never allowed himself to be legally or financially cornered and he always gained his object.'

It was not a character that could have had much appeal for

Laurier in the best of circumstances, and the circumstances were not good. Dorion, in spite of the money he owed, had remained his own master and Sénécal's master, much too tall in the country to be pulled down by debt. Laurier was in no such position. He was soon aware that, with Dorion gone, Sénécal had political ambitions of his own. They did not square with those of the young man who was being pointed out on the streets of Arthabaska and invited to some of the big houses. Times were changing, there was much talk of railways mixed with the talk of Confederation, and railway building and politics would be a profitable combination. Louis-Adélard Sénécal, it was clear, felt that he could do very nicely without Wilfrid Laurier and *Le Défricheur*.

Bishop Laflèche and Father Suzor, for quite other reasons, were of the same opinion. The editor began to be met on Sundays by messages of condemnation from the pulpit and on Mondays by demands for money he could not raise. Subscribers were already on the wing, advertisers had been frightened off, and even the problem of finding his printer's wages became a weekly nightmare. Along with it all came the blizzards of late March, the flush and chills of the fever, and finally the haemorrhages. On March 28, 1867, the first polite notice of himself appeared in the columns of *L'Union des Cantons de l'Est* as a paid advertisement. 'Mr. Laurier,' it read, 'suffering for a long time from a malady of the lungs which has suddenly come to assume alarming proportions, finds it necessary to interrupt for some time the publication of *Le Défricheur*.'

3

Sweet butterfly, my solitary light
Scarce glows in the still night
Before you come, drawn to the fatal gleam,
And sink, a fluttering dream . . .

What cruel pleasure moves thy golden wings
To seek these sufferings? . . .

Like thee, drawn by the flame of hope,
I sought a treacherous slope,
And now, my best blood spent in search of fame,
Wait here, a victim of ambition's flame.

He gave it the title 'To a Butterfly' and filed it away among his papers. It had been the only effort of a listless May, and he could not quite bring himself to tear it up. Perhaps some day he would show it, or at least send it, to Zoë.

He had had six weeks in bed, tossing under heavy blankets with all the windows sealed. So far as he could tell he had only grown weaker for the treatment, and he had certainly grown restless and irritable. But the haemorrhages had not returned, the cough had become less insistent, and finally Dr. Poisson had allowed him to sit up. After that he had thrown discipline to the winds when he was alone and opened his windows to the dangerous night air. It seemed to have done him no harm, and it had at least brought in the butterfly and inspiration.

By the end of the month he was taking little walks; the doctor who shut him up in an airless room while he was sick was a great man for fresh air and sunshine during convalescence. There seemed to be something contradictory in these two phases of the treatment, but Laurier was too indifferent and too sceptical to raise the question, and it was pleasant to be abroad in Arthabaska in early June. It was not so pleasant to look in on the dusty office, with press and printer already gone, and tot up the unpaid bills, invoices, and promissory notes. But it had to be done, and if he was going to live for a while this load of debt would somehow have to be shouldered.

He had forgotten his first profession since he came; he had been all journalist. Now he would have to be all lawyer, and as little of the politician as was humanly possible. In any case, while Sénécal pulled the strings politics would have few attractions. The invalid began to resume some idle conversations he had held with young Eugène Crépeau, a lawyer who had been in Arthabaska about a year longer than himself. Crépeau was a *Bleu* if he was anything, but he was first of all a business-getter. He was enthusiastic about the prospects in Arthabaska, he wanted Laurier as a partner, and the former printshop could be made an office for both. By the end of June it was all arranged, and Crépeau and Laurier were in business.

Prospects were fair enough. The paper had made him known, and it had made him more friends than enemies. A man in the law did not have to worry too much about the hostility of priests and bishops: there was usually an anti-clerical client on one side of any case. Debt hung over him but he felt goodwill about him. He knew he could find his feet if he could gather his scattered wits and make the effort.

He had lost all control of his thoughts during the long weeks of his convalescence. They had returned incessantly to Montreal; they had haunted St-Louis street. That book was closed, he told himself now; it must remain closed. It was already plain from Zoë's letters, with the slight touch of formal reticence creeping into them, that she was near to an understanding with Pierre Valois. He wished her well, more than well, and it was all he could do. His business was to be a good partner to Crépeau, to get to know the district, to conduct himself as if he really were what the town seemed willing to consider him, a rising young barrister.

His letters began to come more regularly to the house on St-Louis street. They told of improving health; his cough had hardly bothered him since June, he was making new friends in Arthabaska and even getting some briefs. He was taking longer walks, and they seemed to be doing him good.

There was no talk, however, of returning even for a visit. The departed Wilfrid was writing more and more as a polite friend and few of the letters came to Zoë. They were passed round by Hannah, his 'dear Annette', for he was still *Rouge* enough to cling to the French form of her name. With Hannah he had always been at ease, usually playful, and often more inclined to confide in her than in any of the others. The confidences were lacking now, though the old tone remained. Hannah was becoming his intermediary with the family, and what he seemed to be negotiating through her was a gentle severance of the old relations. It became doubly difficult for Zoë to write him; Pierre Valois was always on hand and always more urgent, while Laurier seemed tacitly giving the other man his blessing. There was nothing she could say, or at least nothing that mattered. Phoebe Gauthier pursed her lips and evaded discussion when Zoë attempted to broach the subject, and the doctor boomed about the house apparently noticing nothing.

As July 1, 1867, approached, Montreal prepared for Confederation with resounding apathy. Around the middle of June a first committee reported that public indifference made any attempt at a celebration impossible. The mayor, who had presided reluctantly at the meeting, announced with considerable relief that the matter was closed. On the twenty-eighth of the month another meeting called in the Mechanics' Hall managed to squeeze a thousand dollars from the city and another thousand from the banks. A Mr. James Lyman was sent to Boston for a supply of fireworks and set pieces. By the next day, however, the mayor was being difficult again. Even though a celebration might be desirable, he said, the city's insurance agents were opposed to dangerous illuminations and since the gas-works were under repair sufficient gas could not be supplied for outdoor lighting.

The squabbles continued right up to the return of Mr. Lyman with his fireworks. In the end the city obtained on the night of July 1 a state of 'partial illumination' chiefly confined to the English business section. About nine o'clock shells and rockets began to go up against the background of the mountain and Mr. Lyman's set pieces broke out with various loyal and congratulatory mottoes. It was all very limp, and soothing to the heart of the *Rouge* who read of it in Arthabaska. There could be no escape from the thought, however, that Zoë had probably watched it with her hand on the arm of Pierre Valois.

By the middle of July Arthabaska, like all the rest of the Dominion, was in the throes of the first general election campaign. Laurier did not participate. The constituency of Drummond-Arthabaska was in Sénécal's pocket now, and it was Sénécal who was elected to the Dominion House in the place of Eric Dorion. For good measure he was also elected to the seat of Yamaska in the provincial legislature. The lawyer who had forsaken journalism watched with prim distaste as the liquor flowed in the taverns, the brawls broke out on the streets, and the bribed or scared electors climbed to the open platforms to announce their votes. He was no political lily; he had seen his share of elections in Montreal and in St-Lin and in L'Assomption. But it occurred to him for the first time, as he watched the campaign of this man who always gained his object, that there was some point in the carpings of the ecclesiastical autocrat of Three Rivers. Democracy, at work in its lower regions, could be a very ugly sight.

4

THE TIDE of matrimony was now running very strongly in the house on St-Louis street, and was carrying Zoë with it. By early autumn Emma had become engaged to François-Xavier Coutu. The marriage was arranged for the spring, and the eyes of the bride-to-be were often on Zoë. There had been talk of double weddings in the days of Laurier, silly perhaps, but not so silly now. Zoë was fond of Pierre Valois, Emma pointed out, and she must face facts.

There were always the friends on hand with their advice too. A girl had not forever to make up her mind; she must think of the future. One was sad about Wilfrid, but he was a sick man who in any case had removed himself from the running. Pierre Valois would not wait forever; he was attractive and he had health and prospects. One did not live a romantic novel; the business of a woman after all was to find a husband and make a home. Hannah stood apart from it all, irreconcilably for Laurier, but she stood alone and she was only seventeen. Neither of the elder Gauthiers said anything. Zoë held out until the new year, but early in January she gave way. She would marry Pierre Valois. Emma would have her double wedding in May.

The news was not long in coming down to Arthabaska, and Laurier absorbed it as the winter passed. By spring he had come to accept it, almost to welcome it. It seemed to remove the one uncertain factor in his life. His first summer in the Bois-Francs country had been rather a good one. He had travelled around a little and come to know the district. He had found some clients, he had shaken off the depression of the spring, and there had been few lonely evenings when he watched the butterflies circling his lamp. He had almost felt himself a well man. But the fall and the winter had brought the fevers and the cough, returning with pendulum-like inevitability. They always would return, each year a little worse. He was an invalid nibbling away at a hopeless load of debt for the sake of his self-respect. He was a lawyer practising his profession because he could not sit with folded hands. There was nothing in this he could ask a woman to share, and it would be easier with the last temptation removed. When one was sick and alone, it seemed, one was able to face facts.

He lived comfortably and companionably with Dr. Poisson, always with the thought that there was care at hand when he needed it. In April, as he began to feel better in any case, the household was enlivened by the addition of young Edouard Richard, a nephew of Poisson. Richard was a thoroughgoing invalid who had suffered at times from cerebral congestion, gastric trouble, and liver trouble and was now threatened with consumption. In spite of it all he was lively, volatile, intense, and well-educated, a reader of history who was also going to write it.

His turn of mind was wholly congenial to Laurier and equally so to Crépeau. By the end of April he had become the third member of the firm. He was hardly in condition to work but Crépeau supplied energy enough for all three and Laurier was, he flattered himself, bringing in his share of business. Life was a pattern of greys with that one pang of violent separation ahead at the end of May but beyond that the view seemed quietly endurable.

His court pleadings were mainly those concerned with the small affairs of a litigious countryside. He had a better case in hand, however, for May 14. On the afternoon of the twelfth he was preparing for it with some zest when a rig jounced over from Victoriaville with a telegram for him. It was from Montreal and it was signed Séraphin Gauthier. 'Come at once,' it said. 'A matter of urgent importance.'

It was like the doctor's own vigorous hand clapping him on the shoulder, tumbling down the precarious framework of his tranquillity. 'Come at once' – into that household where two weddings were preparing, where he would have to see Zoë again and pull his face into a smile or walk through all the excitement like a mummy at the feast. 'A matter of urgent importance' – it was not sickness or a death, Gauthier would not have worded it that way. It could not concern Carolus or Adeline or any of the

Lauriers; they had all been back at St-Lin for nearly two years. It was something else, one of those brisk decisions the doctor was given to, generally followed by cataclysmic upheaval. Laurier had a dim suspicion of what it was, and wanted no part in it. His life lay neat and clear before him and he would not change it now. He had a case in court the day after tomorrow. He would not even reply; he would simply not go.

He had changed his mind by train-time; and at eight o'clock next morning the doctor met him at the station in Montreal. Gauthier was irritable and uncommunicative and seemed to be suffering from lack of sleep. Laurier had been prepared to meet outlandish proposals with a stiff and dignified refusal, but since none was forthcoming the conversation in the carriage on the way to St-Louis street was a little forced. It turned on the matter of his health, but the doctor was not listening to the replies to his questions. Quite as a matter of course he shoved Laurier into the surgery when they arrived, ordered him to strip, and was soon thumping, tapping, and listening in his accustomed fashion. Even in this, however, his manner was absent and preoccupied; he was quite evidently neither finding nor expecting to find anything new. It was all both annoying and disconcerting; shivering and stripped in the early-morning surgery, the proper attitude seemed hard to find. The only sign of the presence of the rest of the family had been a glimpse of Hannah, peering cautiously from a window as they arrived.

When the examination was concluded the doctor waved the patient to his clothes. Laurier put them on in stiff silence and came out of the little dressing-room. Gauthier was standing by his desk in no mood either for dignity or protest. He waved both aside, flatly and abruptly. 'You are not consumptive and you never have been; is that clear? You have bronchitis, chronic bronchitis, and you will have to live with it. But you can live with it, if you are careful, to a ripe old age. And you will certainly live longer than Zoë Lafontaine if things go on like this.'

The doctor, it became apparent, had had enough. The double wedding was now ten days off, but for two months a red-eyed Zoë had been coming down to breakfast after tearful, sleepless nights. She had been upsetting Emma, spoiling everything. At last, yesterday, Gauthier had taken her in hand and she had confessed all. She did not wish to marry Pierre Valois; it was Wilfrid Laurier for her or no one. 'And then', Gauthier concluded ominously, 'I sent the telegram.'

Laurier found himself protesting inanely that he had a case in court tomorrow. The doctor glared at the picayune objection and waved it off. If the case was so desperately important there was plenty of time to get back. The business in hand did not concern tomorrow, it concerned today. Or rather it concerned the whole of Laurier's life and whether he wanted to live it like a man. It concerned Zoë Lafontaine. It concerned the peace of the Gauthier household. By the end the breakfastless listener in the cold surgery was aglow with unreasoning anger. So far as his health was concerned he was no more convinced than before. Gauthier was a good doctor but he could be wrong: he was not inclined to review evidence or revise a first conviction. He was not entitled to make himself Zoë's spokesman in an affair like this. And, whatever else might come of the matter, the quiet pattern of life in Arthabaska, so laboriously built up, was now shattered beyond redemption.

He had been a fool to come, Laurier told himself, and now he could not go back without at least explaining to Zoë. The house was still strangely silent when he met her in the library and he had a feeling of hushed conspirators about them, huddling in other rooms. He was angrier than ever and most of all with himself; he had half guessed what was in the wind. A wave of shamed despair came over him at the sight of Zoë's startled face. For her, at least, all this was a complete surprise.

It did not take her long to sense the situation as his fumbling words began to fit in with the atmosphere of the house. A flush rose in her cheeks and there was a dangerous glint in her eyes. Gauthier, thought Laurier, might be in for some memorable words if he were here now. He could never remember, afterward, the point at which his explanations broke down and the tears came out of her anger, and then for both of them the warm wave of certainty and release. It was Hannah, inevitably, who first looked in to find them in each other's arms and after that the house exploded about them.

Phoebe Gauthier, laughing and crying by turns, ordered the servants on a dozen errands at once. François-Xavier Coutu arrived at Emma's urgent summons to learn that his wedding was to take place ten days earlier than expected. Messengers were dispatched to the essential relatives, and a special emissary went off to locate Napoléon-Godefroi Lafontaine. By noon the dispensations for the double wedding had been obtained from the bishop's palace. The afternoon was a blur of legal phrases, totally uninteresting, for once, to the barrister of Arthabaska, as Notary L. N. Dumouchel, in the presence of Zoë, Laurier, Phoebe, and the doctor, with Emma and Coutu squirming beside them, droned through the terms of the marriage contract. To the union the future husband brought only his office furniture, personal effects, and books, undertaking also to provide an annuity of three hundred dollars for his future spouse, payable quarterly from the first quarter after his decease. The goods of the bride, of which she was to retain full control, consisted of her sixteen shares in the building society, her piano, clothing, and household effects. It was nearly five when the papers were handed across the desk, signed and sealed, with the customary injunction that they were legal documents which 'conveyed no privileges'.

The party returned to plunge back once more into the pandemonium of the house. There was a hasty meal, a flurry of dressing and making ready in crowded rooms and borrowed clothes. At seven-thirty the carriages arrived. Ten minutes later the quiet of the little brick chapel on Dorchester Street descended on them mercifully, and at eight the double wedding took place.

The first sight that greeted Laurier as he came back to the house with Zoë on his arm was the face of Pierre Valois. Zoë gasped and ran forward contritely. It was unforgivable – she had sent no message – her head had been in a whirl all day. The forgotten suitor took her hand and then the hand of the bridegroom, forcing a smile that pained a happy man to see. There must always be winners, there must always be losers, said Valois; he had never quite believed in his luck. He raised his glass with the others when the toasts came.

In an hour the toasts were ended and the Lauriers, on the

station platform, were preparing for a first parting. Zoë required a day or two before leaving Montreal to gather her wits and possessions. For the barrister of Arthabaska there was the case in court tomorrow. Surely he could forget that, Gauthier had said, but Zoë had studied her husband's face for an instant and made the decision. He would not forget it, it was important to him; she would join him by the end of the week. As the train came in her lips closed on his. Then he was in the carriage and looking from the window, watching her smile and wave beside the beaming Gauthier. The cars groaned and jerked, there was the familiar belch of wood-smoke, and the face of his wife fell behind him among the other faces on the platform. He was on his way; he was on his way indeed.

4

'THOSE DAYS OF ARTHABASKA'

1868-1874

THOSE DAYS of Arthabaska, so faint, so remote that they seem almost a dream. We were young then, and youth paints only *en couleur de rose*. Those days of Arthabaska! How gladly would I return to them.' The words were to be written fifty years later, in the last year of his life. He was entering now upon the unforgettable prime.

Dr. Poisson was dumbstruck and incredulous as the bachelor of the early morning returned that night a benedick. He was more than a little disgusted to find the married man proceeding with spurious calm to try his case in court next day. When Zoë arrived, however, he took an instant fancy to her and Edouard Richard became her devoted slave. The three largest, sunniest rooms of the house were set aside for the new couple. Zoë's piano soon arrived from Montreal, and there was music in this former refuge of congenial invalids. The town's best, vastly titillated by the breath-taking speed of the romance, scarcely allowed a decent interval to pass before they were calling to inspect the bride. Zoë charmed them all, played for them all, and was soon presiding over evening musicales as gay as any the Gauthiers had known.

Very often there were Gauthiers on hand to assist, for they came down from Montreal in ones and twos to beam over the results of their work. There were visits from David and Lanctôt and Laflamme, and from the family at St-Lin who had missed the excitement of the wedding and had to make up for it now. Eugène Crépeau added his contribution to the mood of the summer by providing a second bride, Zélia Larivière of near-by St-Norbert, as companion for the first.

Zoë, the product of Montreal's grey stone and cobbled streets, revealed an atavistic hunger for the earth and an amazingly green thumb. The stumpy wilderness behind the house became parcelled off under her hand into little squares of rich black loam. The country girl in the kitchen was an admiring helper, recruiting labour for the heavy digging. There was always a neighbour or a passing farmer to answer questions and contribute a word of advice. Green vegetables began to come to the table and vases of late-blooming flowers appeared about the rooms as the summer passed. Next year, said Zoë, there would have to be an earlier start. There would have to be tools and trellising and shrubs and manure.

She was happy, there was no doubt about it. The change in his own world still left Laurier a little breathless. He had the promise of life, a long life, perhaps; and there was Zoë to share it. He was no longer a celibate invalid waiting for release; he was a man, a husband. He was still a bankrupt journalist but he was also a lawyer on his feet, in demand. The debt that had seemed such an impossible burden was now merely an obstacle to be cleared away. There seemed to be nothing he wanted that he did not have or could not get.

There was never enough time alone with her, living as they did among a growing circle of lively friends. Arthabaska's summer was a time of gathering families, of leisurely incessant entertaining. There were few week-days and no week-ends when visitors from Montreal, many of them prominent, were not enjoying the cool of well-groomed lawns and imparting the latest gossip. It was often important, it was always witty and informed; it swept away the barrier of rural isolation and made one part of the larger world. He did not want Zoë to miss it, he did not want to miss it himself; and more and more for such gatherings the Lauriers were in demand.

Yet there were still afternoons when they could slip off together with a picnic basket to explore the windings of the Nicolet or climb the slopes of Mont Christo. They soon succumbed to the charm of Pont Bernard, the favourite rendezvous of the town's youth. The old wooden bridge, sagging and warped, was the one Laurier had taken across the Gosselin on the first day he came to Arthabaska. It had been built by the earliest pioneers of the district in the middle of a grove of ash trees standing tall and long-branched on either side of the river. The pale, silky bark of the tree-trunks rose glinting in sunlight and the shaded paths were carpeted by generations of rust-coloured leaves. The ancient cedar of the bridge rails, with the bark long since peeled away, was scarred everywhere by the pen-knives of lovers. Some of the initials and twined hearts and secret symbols were as fresh-cut as the new spring, others had been carved by those who were grandparents now. It was a place that Father Suzor viewed with not unjustified suspicion, but it was also a place where the young came to decide their destinies and the old to be sweetly sad. One walked home from it with the sense of life like the sound of the river in one's ears, always passing, always on the flow.

On such afternoons bride and bridegroom drew together as man and wife. In this Zoë Lafontaine of St-Louis street Wilfrid Laurier had acquired his secure anchor, his unfailing prop. Witty and shrewd in all her assessments of men, warm and deep in her understanding of him, she would grow as he grew. She would complement all his growth, supply each new need, yet never relinquish herself. There would still be something lacking, in him no less than in her; for he was what he was. To the lawyer of Arthabaska, as new vistas opened about him, a kind of emptiness was revealed in the foreground. Beyond Zoë and life and health, beyond an interesting practice and congenial friends, he did not know what he wanted. Nor could she help him there. She wanted Wilfrid Laurier as he was and as he wished to be; she had no thought of probing and changing, no seed of her own to plant, no wish to thrust him on. Sometimes, perhaps, he missed it; it might have been the final gift. He walked beside her always happy, always a little alone, feeling in the hour of high, unblemished serenity a hint of the troubling vacancy that lay at its heart.

It was only in the late fall, as the stripped branches of the maples began to toss under grey skies and the leaves blew along the streets soggy with rain, that his mood changed. The cough came back as usual, bringing the old depression. Gauthier's words were only words after all. Poisson did not believe them. Zoë did not believe them. He had never really believed them himself. It occurred to him that much as Zoë delighted in children she never spoke of children of their own. She did not expect them, then; she did not want children who must carry in their veins and tissues the doom of Marcelle Martineau. Her happiness would be in him and would end with him; it must have been her thought from the beginning. It must have been his own thought, and by some strange and intricate process never to be fathomed he justified the selfishness. Perhaps it was a part, an essential part, of the marked man. The old spur came back, sharpened now, with the cough and the blood-flecked handkerchiefs. If life was to be short, then it must be lived to the full. If one was to die without sons then it would be good to leave a name, for himself and for her.

2

HE WAS twenty-seven now and it was to go on for three years, this easy rhythm of life and growth. The stirrings of ambition were always there but they were softened by contentment and diffused by recurrent illness. He was no longer the young man of *Le Défricheur,* tilting at windmills for the sake of proving himself. He grew sure of his own abilities and it made him patient. He could never be sure of his physical strength and it made him careful. He watched, waited, studied, and let friendships grow about him, easily and enduringly. Most of them would be lifelong, for Zoë as for himself. They had the gift for friendship, both of them, and here in this pleasant ground their roots sank deep.

With it all, and inevitably, they wore the tinge of *Rouge*. The close-knit, lively community embraced all shades of opinion, and always beneath politeness faction lurked. Laurier could not have divorced himself from his beginnings if he had wished to, and this was a society largely of professional people. There could be no evening without shop talk, the law was inseparable from politics, and politics grew always a little more acrid and more intertwined with religion. It made for some awkward pauses, some little coolnesses, and some uncomfortable moments in church, but Zoë accepted them as facts of life. She had, after all, been a *Rouge* in Montreal.

By the spring of 1870 Eugène Crépeau, true *Bleu* and already overshadowed by his partner, felt that it was time to go. Richard remained, a good friend and an enlivening companion but a restless junior more interested in writing and politics than in the law. Laurier did the work and it was soon as heavy as he cared to make it. He was beginning to be known in the surrounding towns, and an endless series of disputes over wills, land-parcels, fences, and road allowances found their way to his desk. A good deal of his time was spent in keeping would-be clients out of court, but he still found himself with a full calendar when the sessions came to Arthabaska and enough to keep him busy on the circuit. He was known as a lawyer not too hungry for a fee, and he was beginning to sense the advantages of his antecedents in this region where English, Irish, Scotch, and French had grown to a casual intermingling under the shadow of Eric Dorion.

His income began to rise toward the comfortable figure of two thousand dollars a year, and there were other satisfactions. It was good to feel himself in demand, to sense the little stir about him in a courtroom as he rose. It was good to know that he commanded the respect of judges and that opposing counsel were wary of him, as they had good reason to be. He had an almost passionate respect for the law and therefore he made certain that he knew the law. He prepared his cases carefully and he had mellowed since his days as a student debater. He soon learned to keep his temper, to watch and wait for an opening, and to thrust quickly and cleanly when it came.

He was often tired and half-sick, often impatient and oppressed by the insignificance of the matter he was pleading, and for that very reason he seldom became completely involved. It made a certain reserve and detachment natural to him, it made it easier for him to be courteous, and as he saw the advantages of these attitudes they settled on him like a cloak. He acquired and cultivated an easygoing daytime air of indolence which was often belied by painful industry at night. There was more than a bit of the actor in him, and more than one occasion on which Zoë caught him out. If she was amused, however, she was tactful, and she had always known her man.

By the end of 1870 they were still living *en pension* with Dr. Poisson and Richard, quite comfortable yet not quite anchored to domesticity. He had been in the mood for some house-hunting in the early summer but it had come to nothing. The cottage of William Duval, a fellow lawyer, had been on the market and they had gone so far as to inspect it and inquire the terms. Zoë had decided that the price was too high, Laurier that the place was a little drab, and the search had ended there.

He suspected that with Zoë the matter of money was outweighed by the matter of his health. It was her great preoccupation and she was not inclined to share it even with the care of a house. Here, moreover, she had Dr. Poisson always at hand to assist in the watch on her husband's diet, to see that he got his ration of fresh air, and to harp without much success on his habit of sitting up late. In this last he was confirmed now, almost beyond the possibility of redemption.

One of their three rooms had been set aside as his inviolable study. With each mail Zoë laid a pile of newspapers on his desk and each evening he devoured them. He could afford more books now and they were coming in new profusion, crowding the older ones along the shelves, becoming dog-eared and overscrawled by pencilled notes as the oil went down in the lamp and Zoë watched the ribbon of light stream in under the closed bedroom door.

He followed the daily disasters of the Franco-Prussian War and went to their roots in books, feeling the same shocked sense of loss and isolation that troubled the country round him. Whenever he moved out on the circuit he saw people in the little towns clustered about store windows or newspaper offices reading the latest bulletins, stunned by the unbelievable collapse of France. For them, as for him in this year of 1870, the atheist republic from which they had been severed for generations was suddenly a mother again.

Religion was an insistent contrapuntal theme. He found himself following with absorbed interest the stormy debate that was rocking the Church in Europe. Shorn of her temporal power, encircled by hostile republics, her spiritual office undermined by heretics outside and liberals within the fold, the Holy Mother was girding herself for a gesture of magnificent authority. It came on July 18, 1870, when the Vatican Council, the twentieth General Council of the Church, proclaimed and made dogma the old cloudy theory of papal infallibility. From that day forth Pius IX, speaking from the chair of Peter on matters of faith and morals, became the voice of unanswerable truth. He was an old man, a liberal who had been betrayed by liberals and had turned against them. Half the world heard in that Council not the whisper of the Holy Ghost but the voice of bitter reaction. It would be ridiculed and resented by enemies, while all too many believers would set no limits whatever to that ground of faith and morals. Everywhere the new and the old, the liberal and the ultramontane, were coming to fiercer grips. It must all be reflected here among this people whose roots were deep in France and Rome.

Much was reflected already. Two years before, under the urgings of Bishop Bourget and Bishop Laflèche, the contingent of Papal Zouaves had marched off from Montreal to the defence of the Vatican lands. In the solemn ceremonies and genuine fervour that surrounded the departure of the one hundred and thirty-five young men there had seemed to be a complete triumph for the spirit of ultramontanism, for the old ideal of the authoritarian Church. The impression was only deepened by the fact that it was Napoléon Bourassa, son-in-law of Papineau, who had designed the banner that flew at the head of the contingent, with its silver band and its beaver and maple leaves on a field of blue. Yet, whatever might happen to his relatives, the spirit of the old unbeliever still flowed through the land and gathered strength. When the Church turned with its new authority against the Institut Canadien, child of the *Rouges*, results were different. The printer Joseph Guibord, with the enthusiastic co-operation of Rodolphe Laflamme, was now making news that disturbed and intrigued the country.

The man had been a printer in Montreal and had succeeded Laurier as one of the vice-presidents of the Institut. He had died in office and he had died a steadfast free-thinker, even under threat of excommunication. The priest of his parish of Notre Dame, with the approval of Bishop Bourget, had refused him the last rites and Christian burial. Laflamme and some of the leaders of the Institut had arranged a procession with his body to the gates of the Catholic cemetery and been turned away. They had then gone to Guibord's widow and urged recourse to the law. The wider issues had been somewhat beyond the lady as she could neither read nor write, but she had wished her husband to lie in consecrated ground and had agreed to bring suit.

It was the kind of case that set Laflamme alight, and he had won a brilliant victory before a judge of the lower court. Notre Dame's priest had been condemned to grant full Christian burial to the rebel. The priest had appealed on the instructions of his bishop, and the verdict had been reversed by the appeal court. Now a counter-appeal was before the Court of Queen's Bench while the newspapers of English Canada as well as of Quebec argued it out in their columns. Laflamme was becoming famous and amid the distractions of the greater case had found time to sue a priest who had called him an atheist and win a retraction with costs. He was more than ever determined that the law should unlock the treasury of the sacraments. Bishop Bourget was equally resolved that no Catholic should be allowed to think for himself. The antagonisms of the *Bleu* and the *Rouge* were newly hardening into the antipathies of believer and unbeliever. Joseph Guibord still lay with his resting-place unsettled, and amidst the rancorous uproar French Canada was becoming a spectacle of medieval archaism and fatuous division to the whole country.

Nor was there much reassurance to be found in the state of the Dominion itself. It was building its Intercolonial Railway. It was even talking of the inter-oceanic railway to the Pacific. But Confederation's brief moment of reconciliation and reassurance had passed into history. In the east New Brunswick was preparing to abolish Catholic separate schools, repudiating the very essence of the pact between French and English and opening up a quarrel of which no man could see the end. The first westward step, the taking over of the Red River country, had led to another half-war. Louis Riel was now a name and a cause.

The blundering thrust of the new Canada into the old lands of the Hudson's Bay Company had meant for the Church the end of its dream of colonization and conversion. For the Métis people it had meant the replacement of a wild, free life by English civilization in its crudest, most truculent form. Riel had risen as the champion in revolt and Riel's 'provisional government', in its short life before the army came, had executed one of the principal rowdies opposed to it. Thomas Scott, the stupid, blustering Orangeman, was in his grave now and his half-breed executioner had disappeared, bribed to get out of the country by a federal government whose conduct admitted everything its words denied. Nor would the politicians leave bad enough alone. Burly British Protestantism had acquired a shabby martyr while newly-resentful Frenchness cheered for a dingy hero. Manitoba, the newest province, was the worst of the mounting problems.

The confusion made one fretful in the evening quiet of the study, and yet glad to be there. There was little a *Rouge* could do in any case, for federally and provincially the Conservatives who had made Confederation still rode high. Luxuriously half-concerned, the young barrister might toss down the newspapers and turn for solace to his nightly quarter-hour with the Bible, absorbing the mighty rhythms and the great words that dwarfed division and dogma. It was always the English Bible, always the King James version, and more and more he found his other reading veering away toward the English. It was with the English, after all, that the key to this confusion lay, if it lay anywhere. He re-read Shakespeare and Milton and Burns. He sought out the riddle of English history in Burke and Bright and Fox and Macaulay. Lincoln, so much nearer, just beginning to tower out of the recent past, became a consuming interest with him. He collected everything he could find that had yet been written about the man. He studied the speeches, tried to imagine the many motives behind them, reached for the inner core as though he were groping for something in himself. Perhaps he was. Here was a master politician who had almost solved the riddle of a divided nation. Here had been a man, lonely, obscure, and long-preparing, suddenly called to a great task for which he was ready.

3

HIS OWN CALL, when it came, was something less than that. The Quebec provincial parliament, the first since Confederation, was due to dissolve in the spring of 1871. It was two-thirds *Bleu* and the next was certain to be the same, but the riding of Drummond-Arthabaska was a patch of Dorion country where a *Rouge* had an even chance. There was much discussion of prospects at the home of Edouard Pacaud, and it soon became flatteringly apparent that the thoughts of prominent men were centring on Laurier.

He had his doubts, and reasons enough to support them. But he had also acquired a new friend who was never to be troubled with doubt. Ernest Pacaud was Edouard's nephew, still in his early twenties and just out of college. Bristling, diminutive, and eager for a career in journalism, he had arrived in Arthabaska several months before and had conceived an admiration for Laurier that would remain just this side idolatry as long as he lived. It would shorten his life and it would cost him dear, but no man would ever hear him express a word of regret for it. At this moment he had found the first of his causes, and he was almost irresistible. Ernest Pacaud would neither rest himself nor let anyone else rest until Wilfrid Laurier sat in the provincial House.

For the kind of campaign that lay ahead it might have seemed to the potential candidate that he was saddled with Pacauds enough. The case of Uncle Charles, which had helped *Le Défricheur* on the way to its end, was still unforgotten. There was the newer friendship with Georges-Jérémie Pacaud who had departed the Church with wife and family on the promulgation of the dogma of infallibility, thereby becoming to the devout not only a name of execration but the possessor of a house haunted by demons. Edouard Pacaud himself, persistent churchgoer though he was, seemed to persist mainly as the thorn in Father Suzor's flesh. His greatest acts of merit had a certain salty venom about them, and he was not given much credit in clerical quarters even for the dozen souls he had recently saved from the near-by parish of St-Paul de Chester. The townsmen had come to him furiously aggrieved because their church was to be removed to another village, and determined to respond by having themselves legally declared Protestants. Pacaud had listened to their representations, solemnly prepared the necessary forms, and submitted them to each client with a bill for one hundred dollars. Then, as the astounding fee brought murmurs of consternation, he had proposed an alternative. 'Remain in the faith of your fathers, my friends, and I won't charge you a penny for my work.' Quarrels with priests and bishops, he had gone on to explain, had nothing to do with religion. He himself had fought the autocrats of the cloth through most of his life, yet he still remained a good Catholic.

It was not a view with which priests and bishops concurred and they were going to be heard from, louder than ever before, in this election. Bishop Bourget was not too occupied with the case of Joseph Guibord to be vigilant in other matters. Both he and Bishop Laflèche had returned from the Vatican Council with all their purposes mightily reinforced. To Bishop Laflèche the dogma of infallibility was 'the great remedy which God in his mercy has prepared to cure the frightful social evils of our times'. He had little doubt that the Holy Ghost spoke from Three Rivers as surely as from the chair of Peter and no doubt at all that liberalism was the great enemy. He was now engaged, with Bishop Bourget and the highest of the high ultramontane politicians, on a formidable project. The result of the consultations, when it appeared in the newspapers on April 20, 1871, appalled not only the *Rouges* but a good many hard-headed Conservatives and some of the bishops as well.

There was to be in effect a new Catholic party within the Conservative party, and a new 'Catholic Program' to be enforced on the electors with all the authority of the Church. With regard to elections the program decreed: 'If the contest is between two Conservatives it goes without saying that we shall support the one who accepts the program which we set forth. If . . . it is between a Conservative of any shade whatever and an adept of the Liberal school, our active sympathies will be given to the former. If the only candidates who come forward in a constituency are both Liberals or oppositionists, we must choose the one who will accept our conditions.' Finally, in the event of an election in which neither candidate was satisfactorily committed to the program, 'we would advise Catholic electors to refrain from voting'.

By the beginning of May the issue was ablaze in all the newspapers and was being fought out behind the scenes in the chancelleries of the Church itself. Archbishop Taschereau of Quebec, whose younger brother was a Liberal member of parliament and who himself represented that strain of liberalism always at war with ultramontanism within the Church, thoroughly disliked the program. He was supported in varying degrees by other bishops. George Etienne Cartier, as the federal Conservative leader who had taken Quebec into Confederation, was aghast at the new prospect. Bishop Bourget and Bishop Laflèche, however, were adamant and aflame. They had lighted the torch of battle and all the rains of reason were not to be allowed to put it out. Bishop Bourget was already at odds with Cartier and had no objection to splitting the ranks of the *Bleus*. Bishop Laflèche saw only the Church marching triumphant to the control of a Catholic state. Neither bishop was concerned by the certainty of an aroused Protestantism in the wider field of the Dominion. The Church's eternal war against evil and error went on. The greater enemy would be dealt with when the *Rouges* were crushed.

The couple at Dr. Poisson's were living now in the last days of their tranquillity. The columns of *L'Union des Cantons de l'Est* began to fill up with long expositions of the Catholic Program and savage denunciations of the *Rouges*. Father Suzor took up the attack each Sunday, in longer and longer sermons ever more wildly athletic in their gestures. The man Zoë had married was changing under her eyes. He was not recovering as usual from the early spring cough. He came home in the evenings tense and fretful, going moodily to the study after dinner or starting out irritably for long evening meetings. He returned from each a little more tired and evasive, withdrawn into a half-world of doubt and indecision where she could not enter. She could understand the fears and share some of the doubts, she could ache for the lost content of the quiet country lawyer. Beyond that she could only wait out the days and nights.

By the last Sunday of May she knew that her prayers had been refused. The church on the hill was unusually crowded for High Mass. Father Suzor's sermon was more prolonged and more desperately emphatic than ever. Just at the close of Mass, a little too late to be a sin, a little too early to be polite, and exactly at the moment to command maximum attention, there was a stir in pew number four on the Epistle side. Edouard Pacaud rose deliberately to his imposing height, stepped out of the pew, genuflected, and, with his hat in his hand and his missal under his arm, walked up the aisle toward the door.

The Lauriers did not join in the first hasty outrush, but waited until Father Suzor had left the altar and the general exodus began. When they came out Pacaud was standing on the topmost of the stone steps basking in the sunshine. Below him the congregation was forming rank on rank in a wide semicircle. The town's sprinkling of Protestants and the shamefaced Mass-missers who would not miss this were hurrying up the hill from below. Around the fringes of the crowd marched a sweating crier beating his drum, announcing the purpose of the meeting, and clearing dogs, chickens, cows, and children from his path.

As Zoë slipped down the steps to take her place at the rear with the womenfolk, the drum-beating and the clamour of livestock ceased. Pacaud laid his hat at his feet, put on his steel spectacles, and began his address, tapping his missal for emphasis. Point by point, with all the suave virulence of a good lawyer and without ever referring to the sermon just delivered, he tore it to shreds. He went back over past sermons and lifted out titbits for further mangling. He deplored the work of those unnamed who would soil the robes of the Church by dragging it into the grimy political arena. He could not resist a reference to newly enlightened Europe where the Church had been taught its place. He brought cheers and jeers when he dwelt on the incapacity of Hemming, the stodgy lawyer of Drummondville, who would be the *Bleu* contender. He drew a roar of laughter when he raised his arms in an elaborate gesture never seen anywhere on earth except in the pulpit inside. The near-by presbytery window was open and the curtains fluttered as he spoke. They came down with a decisive swirl as he turned to Wilfrid Laurier and the chosen of the party stepped forth to declare himself a candidate for the provincial riding of Drummond-Arthabaska.

The first *assemblée contradictoire* took place, after much acrimonious dispute between party organizers, on the neutral courtyard of the Hotel Dorais. It was immediately apparent that Hemming of Drummondville was woefully outclassed by his opponent. The politely indolent lawyer was no more and the wary politician had not yet arrived. This was a young man who had flung his hat and was following it into the ring with everything he had. The voice that had piped and faltered in the days of *Le Défricheur* was now clear and sharp. The *Rouge* candidate was not content with defying the Catholic Program, he was critical of the Vatican itself. He had all the young man's scorn for decrepit elder *Bleus,* he was unrepentant of his old leanings toward annexation, and he was as scathingly critical as Eric Dorion had ever been of the state of education in the province.

'This novice in politics,' cried Father Suzor's *L'Union des Cantons de l'Est,* 'does he not presume to judge the acts of venerable men who have passed their lives in working for the country? What would happen if Liberals of the Laurier stripe came to power? It would be down with the oldest institutions of the country – up with the laws most hurtful to religion!'

Laurier here was far from Joseph Guibord, but Guibord came after him. The first law this *Rouge* would work for, prophesied *L'Union des Cantons de l'Est,* 'would be to oblige the bishop or the curé to bury an excommunicated person . . . what he loves above all, this M. Laurier, is that beautiful goddess of the Liberals which authorizes all freedom to think and act without any control.'

It was in the name of this freedom that the *Rouge* candidate dared to attack Quebec's system of education. He spoke of it, said the newspaper, as a shame on the province, and 'what this really means is "shame on you electors of Arthabaska who are so ignorant, and shame on the clergy who have education under their control" '. This 'ignorant, beardless youth', this 'ridiculous dancing-jack of politics', had criticized the Pope as arbitrary and intolerant because he did not permit Protestant worship in the papal states. He was a Liberal annexationist, a professor of anti-Catholic doctrines condemned by the Church – 'let readers be on their guard!'

Bleus saw to it that the past of the *Rouge* followed him up and down the country roads, and some of his friends were equally helpful. The brilliant Arthur Buies came from Quebec, a journalist so red that even the deliveries of his newspaper were made in a red wagon. In addition to his other qualities Buies was a determined Bohemian not unknown in Arthabaska. *L'Union* welcomed him with a detailed account of his visit the year before, on which he had marched stark naked through the corridors of the Hotel Dorais. 'And this', it concluded, 'is the man whom people will hear in public assemblies. This is the man who is here to support M. Laurier!'

It was nevertheless apparent by the first week in July that Laurier was running ahead. Father Suzor, on the last Sunday before polling, rose to a desperate effort. Acting, as he said, in obedience to a letter from his bishop, he recalled his parishioners to their duties in the struggle against Catholic Liberalism. If they failed in them, he concluded, rising to a climax of his own, he would forthwith resign his curacy and leave the parish. That evening he received a call from two hundred repentant parishioners who had cheered Edouard Pacaud's reference to Pilate and Herod as patrons of the Conservative party. Yet, if the pastor was comforted, comfort was soon dispelled.

The results of the polling for the constituency of Drummond-Arthabaska came in on July 9. The candidate of the *Rouges* had been elected by a resounding majority of seven hundred and two votes. He received the returns at home, an exhausted wreck. The letters of congratulation poured in and among them was one from his old classmate and partner, Oscar Archambault. He answered it with a warmth that had in it more than a trace of hysteria. 'When I saw your writing and read the postmark our whole life in college – a whole world – passed before my eyes like a flash. With what joy I would throw to the winds my deputy's seat if I could find myself back in that blessed time!' Nor would the discerning among his constituents have been greatly impressed by his program for the future. 'I am entering public life', he wrote, 'without any preconceived ideas, without seeking any personal advantage, I might say without desire, or if I have any it is that of making my ideas triumph.'

'There was a time', concluded the twenty-nine-year-old deputy, 'when I felt tremendously ambitious, but age has dissipated those wraiths of adolescence; I am turning into a positivist.'

4

POSITIVIST or not, he was aware as he always would be of the virtues of fence-mending. Politics was one thing, a priest another, and the threat of Father Suzor's departure hung like a blight over the whole parish. Even amid the celebrations of victory it was a worrisome thought, and the rites were hardly ended when Laurier, Pacaud, and some of the leading *Rouges* were in conference with their late enemies.

Wholly reluctant to leave but still a man of his word, the shepherd of the flock had somehow to be delivered from the snare of his promise. The plan evolved at last took the shape of a parish picnic from which all hint of politics would be banished. As the guest of honour, Father Suzor would be presented with an illuminated address. It would gratefully remind him of his long years of service and tactfully insist that those services be long continued. He would receive the address seated in a chair of honour under a triumphal arch and there was hardly a possibility that he could refuse such pleadings. The scars of battle would be healed and the parish would be whole again under its old head.

Everyone entered into the spirit of the occasion with great goodwill. The weather on the day was magnificent and all went for a while with dignity and grace. The only thing that had not been provided for among all the careful arrangements was the luck of Father Suzor.

He arrived as he was supposed to arrive, apparently unaware of the purpose of the celebration. He moved among his people benevolently accepting their homage, and a generous picnic meal moved on to its conclusion. Then he was ushered, politely protesting, to the chair of state over which an elaborate floral crown had been suspended from the arch, bearing the inscription 'He Has Well Deserved It'.

He took his place, the address was duly read and replied to, and there was no doubt that Father Suzor would remain. The ceremony, however, had had a curiously unsatisfactory quality, punctuated as it was throughout by continual pointings and ripples of laughter. An hour or so before, while their elders sat at the long tables, some of the mischievous youth of the village had been at the floral crown. By the time Father Suzor took his place in the chair of honour the flowers had disappeared and only the loop of rope that had held them in place remained. It hung down now above his head, dangling and sinister, still with the legend 'He Has Well Deserved It'.

5

THE QUEBEC HOUSE met on November 7, 1871, and on November 10, the new member for Drummond-Arthabaska rose among the back benches to move the address in reply to the Speech from the Throne. By the end of the afternoon he knew he had made his mark. The morning papers confirmed it. Even the correspondents of the *Bleus* conceded him an 'elegance and purity of style', a 'sympathetic and sonorous voice'. The few journals of the *Rouges* were elated by his attack on the lethargic complacency of the government and by the manner in which he had 'thrown thorns among the roses'.

It was an easy enough success. He had had a fatuous self-congratulatory Speech from the Throne to attack, larded with nothing but the usual praises of Quebec's prosperity and happiness. Where did that happiness lie, he had asked, when thousands of Canadians moved each year to the United States in search of the crust of bread they could not find here? The province, according to the government, was rich, rich in mines, forests, resources of every sort. Tantalus had been rich too, but Tantalus had starved eternally in the sight of plenty. Educational reforms promised for years had not yet come. French Canadians congratulated themselves on what they were and what they had been, while the English moved ahead of them in every branch of the country's development. 'We know only how to flatter our prejudices and our self-love. That is not a true patriotism, and it is not mine. My patriotism will consist rather in telling my country the hard truths which will waken it from its lethargy and make it enter at last into the true way of progress and prosperity.'

He was not specific as to the way, and his hard truths bounced back from the rock of a solid *Bleu* majority. This was a House dominated by the old hands who had made Confederation. Since the system of 'double mandates' allowed a member to hold a federal seat and a provincial seat at the same time, Cartier sat here as well as in Ottawa. Sir George Etienne Cartier now, he dominated all proceedings and pulled all strings. Sir Hector Langevin sat beside him, Minister of Public Works in Ottawa and also a member here. Another of the Confederation Fathers, knighted with his chief, Langevin waited a little uneasily for the time when he would be called on to fill Cartier's shoes. Meanwhile, however, with the patronage of the Department of Public Works at his disposal, he was a power in himself.

The shopworn Joseph Cauchon, of dingy reputation and dubious loyalties, was hardly in the same class. A *Bleu* now, he was a former Liberal who had deserted Dorion at the time of Confederation and had always kept himself as comfortably as possible under the wing of the Church. Dangerous, shifty, and the friend of bishops, few men were more disliked and distrusted by the *Rouges*.

Behind Cauchon, however, looming among the younger members, rose the spectacular black mane of Joseph-Adolphe Chapleau. He was a mechanic's son, a year older than Laurier, who had been taken in hand by one of the substantial Conservative families of Quebec and educated for the law. With a mighty physique which he was already devastating by work and dissipation, he combined the power and magnetism and a good many of the ideals of Eric Dorion. Yet he had gone Cartier's way at the time of Confederation and he drove on, a man of the Cartier mould, thrusting, dominant, not to be set aside. He would be heard from and deserve to be heard; Laurier granted him that. The two men would be at each other's throats through much of their lives but there would never be dislike between them.

For the moment Chapleau sat among the seats of the mighty though a little apart, and the *Rouge* sat among the helpless. There was little to be gained by attack but bruising failure. Laurier's only other speech during the session was delivered against the double mandate that allowed such men as Cartier and Langevin to be here. It made Quebec, he said, 'an appendage of Ottawa'. Then with the end of the session he went home, his duty done.

Ernest Pacaud, the ever-hopeful journalist, was now ready with another proposal. By March of 1872 it had taken flesh. *Le Journal d'Arthabaska* appeared with Pacaud as proprietor and Laurier as contributing editor who would also be called on frequently to contribute money. When the time came for the second session of the Quebec House the member for Drummond-Arthabaska departed with his neglected law practice and the demands of journalism tugging at his thoughts. Neither left him much time to give to his public duties, though what he did give was well enough delivered. 'Mr. Laurier', commented his old friend *Le Pays* at the end of the session, 'has definitely carried off the sceptre of eloquence. I cannot, however, help reproaching him for not taking part often enough in the debates.'

His difficulty was not so much that he was busy but that he was bored, and bored not with politics but with provincialism. Provincial politics at the moment were certainly a sorry spectacle. The Catholic Program was beginning to bear down with full force and even the liberal churchmen who opposed it could make no headway. Quietly warring bishops trooped back and forth to Rome but Rome remained silent, and in default of her voice the loudest voices in Quebec were those of Bishop Bourget and Bishop Laflèche. Their proclaimed ideal was now 'the submission of the State to the Church, and the State dependent upon the Church . . . submissive to God'.

This meant in practical terms that the greasiest *Bleu* time-servers were being driven to align themselves with genuinely devout ultramontanes to the disgust of both, while the *Rouges* were dividing into two hapless wings, neither of which offered any hope for the future. On the one hand a hard core of unregenerates answered the invectives of the clergy with savage defiance and abuse of all things Catholic. On the other, a hopeful group of compromisers banded themselves into a *Parti National* which tried to cling to a remnant of principle while licking the hand that chastised it. Its official newspaper protested 'our entire devotion and our filial obedience to the Church'. The party would be, it said, 'a national party because, before all, we are attached to our nation . . . but as the special organ of the Catholic population . . . when occasion arises we shall concur with Catholic opinion, and we repudiate in advance anything which may inadvertently be overlooked in the hasty editing of a daily paper'. The weasel talk spoke eloquently of the state of *Rouge* fortunes and it was quite clear that all the divisions of the *Bleus* would not be enough to improve them.

On the other hand the federal scene became steadily more intriguing. Sénécal was a *Bleu* now and had relinquished his federal ambitions for the sake of railway contracts in Quebec. If it was the worse for Quebec, it at least cleared the way for a new man in Drummond-Arthabaska. The second general election in August 1872 gave clear evidence of the decline of the Conservative party. Most spectacular of all was Cartier's shattering defeat in Montreal East. He had quarrelled with Bishop Bourget and he had opposed the Catholic Program, and though neither of these causes gave the *Rouges* a stick to beat him with, Riel was another matter. Cartier, as a member of the government, could be held responsible for its treatment of Riel, and Riel emerged forthwith as a *Rouge* cause.

Still better was to come the following spring, while Cartier lay dying in England. On April 2, 1873, the scandal surrounding the project of the Pacific Railway broke in parliament. Cartier, Macdonald, and the whole Conservative party were tarred with the brush of electoral bribery and corruption. All through the summer the storm rumbled over the heads of the Tory government, and on October 27 debate reached the floor of the House. On November 5, 1873, Macdonald resigned; Alexander Mackenzie and his Liberals crossed the aisle to become the government and a new general election was in the wind. It was the time, if there was ever to be a time, for a *Rouge* to make the leap.

Edouard Richard went first. Late in 1873 he was offered the nomination for neighbouring Mégantic county and left to take up residence there. It was hard to see him go after a pleasant five years together, and it was an ominous sign for Zoë. She was only partially reassured when Joseph Lavergne arrived from Princeville, a few miles away up the line of the Grand Trunk, to become the new partner. The twenty-seven-year-old Joseph was a good friend and a likely man; his arrival might mean that her fretful husband was settling down to consider the future of his law practice. On the other hand it might mean that he was providing himself with a *locum tenens* and that his purposes were straying after his thoughts.

Early in December, as the town began to seethe with election excitement and talk of nominations filled the air, Laurier's decision seemed to have been made for him. A cold grew to a fever and then the first of the haemorrhages came. He was in his bed, sweating and on the edge of delirium, as the committee of nomination gathered in Arthabaska. There was a bitter fight ahead as every *Rouge* knew, and it would be no fight for a sick man.

Two days later a deputation from the meeting presented itself at Dr. Poisson's house. Its members were tired from long wrangling, reticently polite to Zoë, and quite determined, if it were possible without danger to his health, to see Mr. Laurier. There was every danger, Zoë insisted; surely another time would do? It would not; they shook their heads without moving. It was now or never, and as their intentions became clear the voice of the invalid was heard from the bedroom asking that the gentlemen come in.

He was sitting propped on pillows with books and newspapers strewn beside the bed, for once careless both of his appearance and of the fitness of things. Every window of the room was closed tight; it was steamy and stale with the smell of old medicine. He had drawn a blanket about his shoulders and the feverish flush was rising in his cheeks. He would not meet Zoë's eyes as she ushered the men in and he was still looking carefully away when she went out, closing the door.

She had no need to ask what his decision had been after the deputation left. He was already looking better, the flush in his cheeks was excitement now, and he was peeling off his blankets. If he had to die, he said, he was going to die in harness; and she could only nod at the heroics.

Four weeks later, on January 22, 1874, he came home elected to the federal seat of Drummond-Arthabaska by a majority of 238. He was utterly, cheerfully exhausted but the cough was gone. He had driven through blizzards on every road in the two counties, he had spoken by hot stoves and open windows, on the platforms of draughty halls, and in wind-swept courtyards. He had averaged four hours' sleep a night. But he had escaped from boredom and indecision, he had escaped from the stifling room, and the winter air of the Arthabaska highlands had wrought its miracle.

6

HE WAS NOW a member of the third parliament of the Dominion of Canada and a supporter of the first Liberal Prime Minister, Alexander Mackenzie. He knew Mackenzie only as a Scot from Sarnia, a Presbyterian, and a friend and disciple of George Brown. Among Mackenzie's lieutenants he knew of Edward Blake. That man of towering abilities already stood higher in the country than Alexander Mackenzie and it was common gossip that he could have had Mackenzie's position for the asking. If it had been offered he had rejected it, and he had only recently stepped out of the cabinet completely, pleading pressure of other work. His personality seemed as enigmatic as his reported speeches seemed formidable and tortuous, and two years before, when he had been premier of Ontario, he had offered $5,000 reward for the arrest of Louis Riel. There was not much promise here for a *Rouge* who had made Riel one of his election cries.

Richard Cartwright of Kingston was another vaguely inimical figure. Acidly English, mightily bewhiskered, he was a former Conservative who had quarrelled bitterly with John A. Macdonald and crossed the aisle. Commercial Montreal, predominantly English and always Tory, detested him as a free-trader, but beyond his vendetta with Macdonald there was little to recommend him to the French. There would be Antoine-Aimé Dorion, who now stood close to Mackenzie as Minister of Justice; yet even this friend and mentor was likely to be lost soon. Dorion was growing deaf and wanted to retire.

Of the country outside his province Laurier knew nothing but what he had read or what he had been told. He was a citizen of a Dominion whose making he had opposed, and he was not even yet quite comfortable or secure in it or convinced of its permanence. As a French member in an English parliament he was nothing without Quebec and he had no need to be reminded, fresh as he was from his battles with curés and *Bleus,* that Quebec was quicksand under his feet.

He felt very young and ill at ease as he arrived at the Russell Hotel in Ottawa. Greater men bustled round him in the cold March twilight. His room was both expensive and lonely. He missed Zoë and was depressed at the realization that the pleasant wholeness of life in Arthabaska had come to an end. So long as he was a member of parliament Ottawa would claim a great deal of his time, and it was a bleak prospect. The parliament buildings rose on the hill incongruously beautiful by contrast to the squalid streets below them. Pipes for the city's water supply were being laid and there were ditches to be gone round, with piles of excavated earth at every crossing, all slimy with spring mud. There was worried talk of a typhoid fever epidemic. The country lawyer, fresh from Arthabaska, wandered through the Ottawa market and was disgusted at the sight of housewives, clerks, servants, and mackinawed lumberjacks jostling each other around rank-smelling tubs of butter, scooping up samples on penny-pieces, old tobacco-knives, or thumb nails. His card arrived for the Governor General's drawing-room, but he was shy and unsure of himself and stayed away.

He stood up for the first time in the Dominion House on March 30, 1874, well back among the junior members. Once again he was to reply to a Speech from the Throne, speaking in French, while the English reply was made by another new-comer. He had not been the first choice for the honour, such as it was. The party elders had selected Louis Fréchette, poet and journalist, who was a distant connection of Marcelle Martineau and sat beside Laurier in the House. Fréchette, however, had gracefully retired in favour of his desk-mate.

James Young of Galt, member for Waterloo, sat near by watching Laurier as he rose. 'At first glance', he recorded, 'he looked like an unsophisticated country boy. His long, chestnut-tinged hair naturally inclined to be thrown back on both sides and his clean-shaven face deepened the impression. Many supposed him much younger than he really was.'

The impression soon changed, however. Laurier, once on his feet, felt the mood of the last few days slipping away. The benches were pretty well filled; there was always a benevolent curiosity about new members. There was less decorum here than at Quebec: more top hats tilted on bald heads or pulled down over closed eyes, more feet on desks or in the aisles. The heavy air was stirred by waftings of tobacco and alcohol as late-comers pushed in from the smoking-rooms or the bar, and some of the honourable gentlemen showed the effects of their lingering. None of them seemed very formidable or very concerned; there was a kind of ease, even an untidy homeliness about the place in these first days of the session. He began to speak, as Young watched him, 'with all the self-possession of the practised orator, a charm of manner, a touch of dignity, an air of candour, a natural eloquence'.

It was perhaps not difficult for him to exert his charm. The manner of the speech in this case was more important than the matter. He disclaimed for the Liberals of Quebec any taint of the radical liberalism of France. He sounded the glories of the British constitution which had been framed and handed down as a perfect instrument after the wisdom of centuries had gone to its making. 'Mr. Laurier spoke in French,' the Toronto *Globe* was to report next day, 'a circumstance that deprived many members of the pleasure of fully understanding . . . but . . . he addressed the House with the quiet but earnest manner of the practised debater.'

As he sat down Mackenzie rose to congratulate him. Then from across the aisle the other Scot was on his feet, standing with an easy, jocular grace that belied his status as a fallen man. The honourable member for Drummond-Arthabaska, declared John A. Macdonald without unduly committing himself, had fully justified the reputation he had brought with him.

BACK-BENCHER

1874-1876

ON THE MORNING of March 31, one day after the delivery of his maiden effort, Laurier was summoned urgently to a party caucus. The day before, at just about the time he was speaking, the country's most ticklish problem had materialized briefly under the same roof. Louis Riel had come east from Manitoba, crossed the river at Hull, and presented himself before an astonished clerk to sign the roll as a member of the House of Commons. Then, after thriftily trying to collect his expenses for the trip, he had walked out of the building and disappeared.

The word of the visit had taken some hours to spread, but it was now everywhere. As the doors closed on the Liberal caucus other doors were closing on anxious Tories. The uproar was resounding through the city and speeding out on the telegraph wires to arouse the constituencies. Under the baleful power of that name Riel, party allegiances were dissolving. Liberals and Conservatives alike were dividing and re-forming as English and French. To Quebec, Riel was the duly elected member for the constituency of Provencher in Manitoba. To Ontario he was a rebel and indicted murderer with a warrant out for his arrest. Around that single shabby figure all the resentful frustrations, all the hopes and fears of the seven-year-old Dominion lay ready to meet and clash.

The man was now twenty-nine years old. He had been born at St-Boniface on the Red River, in the heartland of the Métis. His father's mother was a woman of the Montagnais tribe, his own mother was the daughter of the first white woman to settle in the west, and his paternal ancestry ran back through four generations of French Canadians to a Reilly in Ireland and beyond that to a Reilson in Scandinavia. At fourteen, a brilliant boy with a precocious interest in religion, he had been sent to the College of Montreal to study for the priesthood. At twenty he had come home, no priest, and already with an ominous background. He had been too much for his teachers. He had left the college after three years and drifted as far as the western states, always embarked on some obscure crusade and always in search of money to support it. He was a half-educated mystic devoured by a sense of religious calling. He was a natural leader and a powerful, magnetic speaker. He was a Métis of the Métis and a restless son of the Church, quickened and torn by the old dream of another Quebec on the prairies. In the lands of the Red River he was not long in finding his mission.

He had been twenty-five in 1869 when the English survey parties arrived in the west with word that the Red River country had been taken over from the Hudson's Bay Company. He had watched these agents of the Dominion of Canada running their neat block lines across the wavering strips of river frontage held by the Métis. He had seen their officers cannily taking title to the best of the vacant lands. He had listened to French troublemakers and English troublemakers and to American annexationists who came up from St. Paul with word that the rights of the Métis were to be extinguished. Half-informed, misinformed, and blandly lied to like the rest of his people, he had been the exposed nerve in the west, throbbing at each new blunder of Macdonald's cabinet. He had been the inevitable leader when the Métis rose, the inevitable head of the cluster of ignorant men who called themselves a provisional government and sought to make terms with the Dominion. Still inevitably, when revolt had culminated in the single execution, he had become the symbol of the races. Murdering outlaw to the English, he was the champion of a people to the French. Against the onward-lunging Protestantism of George Brown stood the lost and aching hope of a Catholic west.

As he sat uneasily among the junior members in caucus, Laurier was aware of the authentic depths of the problem. He was also aware of muddy swirls above them. Both he and his leaders had ridden to their present places partly at least on Riel's coat-tails. The four years since Scott's death had been years of shoddy manoeuvre by each of the parties. Macdonald had played both sides with less skill than usual and with few scruples. He had sent a military expedition to the Red River and been cheered by Ontario. Yet when the provisional government evaporated without a shot being fired he had turned at once to the work of appeasing Quebec. The manageable Riel had received promises or half-promises of amnesty. He had been bribed, with money supplied by Macdonald, to leave the country. When he drifted back without leave his help had been gratefully accepted as an organizer of Métis resistance to Fenian raiders from the United States. He had been allowed to stand as candidate for the federal constituency of Provencher and had only stepped aside when George Etienne Cartier came west looking for a seat after the débâcle in Montreal East. The man whom Ontario saw as traitor and murderer had helped to elect Cartier. Hailed by Quebec as a hero, he had still been sought officially under a warrant for high treason. It had been too much for either province to stomach and Riel had played his part, along with the Pacific scandal, in dragging Macdonald down.

Now Mackenzie was in the high seat, riding the two horses. In 1870 he had lined up squarely with Ontario, demanding 'five, ten, twenty thousand men if necessary' to restore order in the Red River country. Yet as Prime Minister he had made no move when a new election became necessary for the seat of Provencher, vacated by Cartier's death. The author of all disorder, still unpunished and a free man, had run and had been elected.

Blake was not here in caucus this morning, nor even in the government, but every Liberal wanted him back and most wanted him as leader in Mackenzie's place. Yet Blake, who had offered a reward for Riel's head, would be in no better position. He could have Riel if he wanted him, but it would be at the cost of nearly every French-Canadian member of the party. It would be at the cost of Laurier for one, reflected the junior member. Riel had been too well used on the stumps of Arthabaska to be abandoned now. The game had to be played out as it had begun.

That afternoon Mackenzie Bowell of Belleville, Ontario, rock-ribbed Conservative and Grand Master of the Orange Order, rose in the House to move that Riel be ordered to attend in his place next day. There was no probability that he would, and nothing to be less desired. The Liberal answer was the appointment of a commission of inquiry to decide whether Riel had or had not been promised amnesty. There was a two weeks' wait during which no culprit appeared, and then the Conservative party split neatly into its two wings. Bowell, the English Conservative, moved for Riel's immediate expulsion. Mousseau, a French *Bleu,* moved that he be granted unconditional amnesty. Between them the Liberals sat on their prickly hedge, moving for delay until the commission of inquiry reported.

On April 15, after the debate had been under way for a day or so, the member for Drummond-Arthabaska rose. The atmosphere of the House was no longer as genial as it had been for his first speech and there was a flinty gleam in some of the eyes that watched him, but this time he was speaking in the other tongue. 'Mr. Speaker,' he said, 'I must apologize to the House for using a language with which I am imperfectly acquainted. Really I should claim a complete amnesty, because I know only too well that in the course of the few remarks I wish to make I shall frequently murder the Queen's English.'

It got him his little laugh, and he was launched on his first parliamentary speech in English. He was not quite at home in the language as yet and it would be a good many years before the accent and the slight inversions of construction would disappear. 'To do' and 'to make' would trip him up in absent-minded moments to the end of his life. But he was not nervous and he had all the powers of his voice at his control. The little tinge of Scotch was an advantage now and he had neither hope nor fear of accomplishing anything by his words. He was speaking from the fence and on the law – a lawyer's speech.

He stood for the Liberal amendment: no judgment on Riel without the report of the Commission. How could the House judge him when the evidence was not in, when the late Macdonald government would neither admit nor deny that an amnesty had been granted? Ontario was impatient with such objections; it called them technicalities, legal subtleties. Yet these technical expressions, these legal subtleties, were the guarantees of British liberty. The execution of Scott was a crime; granted; but it was the political act of a provisional government. It was a political execution. And, taken all in all, if the events at Red River had not been stained with the blood of Thomas Scott, he would have regarded them as a glorious page in Canadian history. Until the question of amnesty had been cleared up he would never declare Riel a fugitive from his country's justice.

It was, said the Montreal *Herald* next day, 'the best speech of the whole debate – calm, logical and thoughtful. He has made his mark and placed himself at once in the front rank of our debaters.' He had not done much for Riel. The leader of the Métis was expelled from the House by a vote of 123 to 68, returned five months later by the voters of Provencher to a seat he dared not take, and remained in his status of elected outlaw. The member for Drummond-Arthabaska did move up in the party, however, partly by his performance and rather more by erosion. At the end of the session in May Antoine-Aimé Dorion retired to become a judge, leaving a notable gap in the row of heads along the treasury benches. Of all men in Ottawa Laurier could least spare him, and he was more worried than cheered by the improvement in his own prospects. 'We have no man in Quebec that can lead the party,' he wrote to James Young a few weeks later from the quiet of Arthabaska.

The two men had become good friends in Ottawa, and Young showed a flattering respect for Laurier's opinions. Under the warmth of it the young *Rouge*, back among the troubles of home, expanded jauntily. 'I am now busy with courts and judges,' he wrote on July 18. 'You have a good crop, you tell me. We have a very poor one. Some religious papers tell us that God is punishing us for the sins of the last election. This, if true, is rather perplexing, for it would be evidence that the Ontario heretics are better in the eyes of heaven than the orthodox believers of Quebec. This cannot be admitted.'

'Do you see,' he wrote a week or so later, 'when I let loose the bridle to my imperfect English, I cannot control it but it controls; it is for me a sort of wild horse which drives me into all sorts of mistakes and blunders.' He was clear enough and candid enough, however, when he wrote Young in September on the matter of Riel. English and French, each and equally, had played politics with the man. Each had inflamed the issue out of all proportion. 'There is but one solution. Either we must yield to you, or you must yield to us. Either we must bring the accused to trial or grant an amnesty. You might say that we should yield because you are the strongest. I do not believe so; you must adopt our policy because it is the more liberal policy in the matter and because it must some day be finally adopted; its adoption is only a question of time. Since, therefore, we must come to it some day, better to make up our minds at once and act accordingly.'

2

HE WAS to have two more years to enjoy his status as a promising junior pundit without undue responsibility. His advice on Riel was not taken when the new session opened in February of 1875, but neither was it wholly ignored. The solution was another of the familiar straddles: Riel was to be banished for five years but amnesty was to apply at the end of that term. Laurier supported it in a little speech, quite as well aware as his leaders that Riel had not left the country and showed no haste to do so.

He had particular grounds for his own knowledge, since he had met Riel during the summer as a guest of one of the curés in the Bois-Francs country. It had been a surprise encounter of which he had not been forewarned and of which he would not have expected much, but he had found this half-breed outlaw who wandered aimlessly from hiding-place to hiding-place a memorable and disturbing man. Riel had shown a surprising grasp of Canadian, American, and European politics. He had been powerful, fluent, and well informed, rising to passionate eloquence when he spoke of his own people. It was only when religion was touched that clarity became a flame-shot nebula and the talk of missions and money grew hopelessly jumbled in a wild harangue. Here was unquestionably a madman but a force too, thrown up by mightier forces which were not yet quelled. It was difficult to believe, as the tired acrimonies of debate drew to an end, that that wild spirit and unsettled mind had finally been disposed of.

It was becoming, in fact, a little difficult to believe that this parliament and this government would ever dispose of anything. John A. Macdonald, official Father of Confederation, was now a scandal-haunted, bibulous party leader. One saw him at the end of the grey winter afternoons tottering down Parliament Hill in the old Red River sash and coat and the mink-skin cap that he had made famous in better days. Very often he walked quite alone, with others even of his own party making a wide sweep to avoid him. He was unquestionably in low water and there was even talk of his replacement, but it did not mean that the fortunes of his enemies were on the rise.

For Mackenzie Laurier felt a liking and respect that never quite grew to warmth. He could admire the downright debater, the 'grand man on his legs', always sure of his facts and merciless with an opponent. He could respond to the rare glints of pawky humour in the stonemason who had bid unsuccessfully on the contract for the parliament buildings and now considered their dim corridors more suitable for monks than legislators. He could take pride in the dour, uncompromising honesty of the administration. But he could not fail to see that the grim old leader, spending interminable days and nights at his desk on work that would have been better left to auditors, was losing his grip on the party and the country.

Times were bad and threatening to become worse, and the government's only remedy seemed to be to pare expenses. Its bits of railway building in the west compared dismally to the grand project of a transcontinental line which had collapsed with the Pacific scandal. In place of Macdonald's flamboyant vision Mackenzie offered a procession of short lines and linking waterways that would jog on toward the foothills of the Rockies and climb over them by means of a wagon road, if even the wagon road should prove feasible. The heart of settlement for a generation to come would be Manitoba, from which colonization lines would radiate out as population and revenue justified them. It was a prudent policy for sketchily-linked communities groping together across a wilderness, but it was not the policy that had made Confederation. There seemed to be no vision in it of the nation spanning the continent; rather there was the old prospect of divided regions pulling away to the south. British Columbia, which had entered the Dominion on the promise of the railway, was threatening to leave again and Mackenzie seemed willing to let her go.

With the Red River quarrel unhealed, the railway at a standstill, and depression on the way, the country was crawling doggedly and unimaginatively toward the threat of dissolution. It did not make for a happy session and the member for Drummond-Arthabaska sat it out almost in silence. He was not even much cheered by the return of Edward Blake, who accepted Dorion's portfolio as Minister of Justice. Blake did not replace Dorion, so far as Laurier was concerned, and the new strength he brought was coupled with a new sense of uncertainty and division. One felt at first only a commanding presence that could dominate but not attract. The bulky, tweedy figure seemed to move in a cold aura, forbiddingly remote to a junior member. Here was a great lawyer who could be Prime Minister if he would say the word. Everyone knew that Mackenzie would step aside unhesitatingly, and the knowledge changed all attitudes. It changed, above all, the attitude of the brilliant, jealous Cartwright who had been Mackenzie's right-hand man. The second was now third, the first was uneasily aware that he held his position by default, and the stress and strain in the cabinet vibrated down through every level of the party.

All this on returning to Arthabaska began to seem shadowy and remote. By midsummer Laurier was following with absorbed interest a by-election in Charlevoix county where Langevin was seeking to re-enter politics after his downfall in the Pacific scandal. The election was important in itself because Langevin's return would give Macdonald the lieutenant he needed for Quebec. It had the new feature of secret balloting, which had been introduced by the Mackenzie government. Above all it was overshadowed by the 'undue influence' clause that had been written into the electoral act as an almost direct answer to the Catholic Program. Adopted from a British statute designed to prevent bribery, the definition of undue influence could be made to apply equally to the threats of confessional or pulpit.

The election, fought out by tough and experienced professionals who were not impressed by change, proved to be a memorable one. 'Whackers' and party paymasters and imported intimidators performed as of old on both sides. Langevin's *Bleus* used all the weapons of the Church. His brother was bishop of the diocese in which the county lay, and clerical vehemence rose to such heights that it called forth not only protests from the liberal-minded diocese of the Archbishop of Quebec but counter-claims of hellfire from Protestant pulpits. Langevin squeaked through to victory, but his election was promptly challenged under the 'undue influence' clause and two priests of the Church found themselves on charge in a civil court. A new phase had opened in the war of *Rouge* and *Bleu* just as an old battle moved to its final stages.

Rodolphe Laflamme had carried the case of Joseph Guibord from the Quebec Court of Appeals to the Privy Council in London. He was now back with a verdict. Guibord was to have full Christian burial, with costs. Not only was the parish of Notre Dame to perform the rites, it was also to pay the six thousand dollars in lawyers' fees piled up by the various cases.

On September 2 the body of the printer was exhumed from the Protestant cemetery where it had lain for over four years and taken to the Catholic cemetery. The gates were shut on it in the face of a great crowd. It returned to the Protestant cemetery to lie for another two and a half months under the protection of an armed guard. Then on November 16, while Bishop Bourget urged the people of Montreal to remain calm, it moved through the streets again with an escort of twelve hundred troops. The gates of the Catholic cemetery stood open, the body of the infidel was laid in earth, and two hours later a stroke of the bishop's pen wiped out the result of all parades and litigation by declaring the ground no longer consecrated.

Steaming at his desk in Ottawa while cool breezes fanned the woods of Arthabaska, Mackenzie pondered the troubles of his headless party in Quebec. The man on his horizon seemed to be Joseph Cauchon, the old *Bleu* Cauchon of the Quebec legislature, who was now again *Rouge*. Muddied with scandal and twice a political turncoat, Cauchon seemed nevertheless to retain his influence with the Church. What little help the *Rouges* had received in Charlevoix had come through his efforts. He was now busy explaining away the undue-influence charges that had been brought by *Rouges* against priests. It began to seem to Mackenzie that with all Cauchon's flaws he was the one hope in the province.

Still hesitating as autumn came on, the Prime Minister consulted his old oracle, George Brown. On November 15 Brown wrote him, bringing up for the first time an alternative prospect. 'Should you be led to the conviction', he said, 'that Cauchon could not safely or wisely be ventured upon then you have no doubt to choose between the old, respectable gentleman in question and the young, vigorous, popular and eloquent man of the day – Laurier, I think, is his name.'

Laurier did not know about this but he knew Cauchon. His antipathy for the man was as old as his loyalty to the Dorions. He knew more than Mackenzie about the methods of the fight in Charlevoix and he was not impressed by the pronouncements of a few of the milder clergy, which Cauchon was supposed to have inspired. He had no hope that the bringing of priests into court would be forgiven. Neither could it be disavowed. This burnt-out politician and demi-*Rouge* was employing the same weaseling tactics that had launched the *Parti National*, and they would fail. He would not win the bishops, and the attempt to placate them would merely arouse Protestants. The Liberal party had not much longer to live with one face turned to the country and another to Quebec. Either the hard core of ultramontanism would be met head-on or the war with the Church would grow to a war with the English.

On December 7 Cauchon was sworn to office as President of the Privy Council. Mackenzie had plumped for a policy of appeasement. Two weeks later a Protestant Defence Association was formed in Montreal. On December 30 Lucius Seth Huntington, Mackenzie's Postmaster-General and the most prominent English Liberal in Quebec, spoke his mind. The time had come, he said, for Liberals to ally themselves with English Protestants. The common enemy was the Quebec *Bleu* who went to parliament as the apostle of ultramontanism, condemned to declare 'that the English-speaking people of this province are no longer British; that tolerance and fair play have no charms for them and that their highest pleasure is to make the state the mere machinery for registering the decrees of the Church'.

Bishop Bourget had already neatly staked out the ground of the ultramontanes. 'Hear Jesus Christ in hearing the Church,' he wrote in a pastoral letter. 'Each of you can and should say to himself in the depths of his soul: "I hear my curé, my curé hears the Bishop, the Bishop hears the Pope, the Pope hears our blessed Saviour Jesus Christ. With this rule I am sure not to stray and I am certain to walk in the way of justice and truth." '

With the English aroused, the Church more truculent than ever, and Cauchon generally despised, the search for new leadership among the *Rouges* of Quebec was desperate. There was little pleasure at the moment in the thought that it was centring on Arthabaska. 'As to myself,' Laurier wrote Young, 'I have the bones and sinew of the Liberal party. They push me ahead and would have me take a more active part in politics than I have done hitherto. I, however, feel very reluctant to do it. I am at present quiet and happy. The moment I accept office I will go into it actively and earnestly, and from that moment my quiet and happiness will be gone. It will be a war with the clergy, a war of every day, of every moment . . . Political strifes are bitter enough in your province, but you have no idea of what it is with us . . . I will be denounced as Anti-Christ. You may laugh at that, but it is no laughing matter to us.'

3

HIS THIRD session of parliament opened in February 1876 and closed in April. It provided two months of dismal weather and undistinguished debate which he did little to brighten. Huntington's outburst of the previous December had reverberated through the country and it was quite to be expected that the ultramontanes of his province would fall on him in a body. To the delight of every Conservative, however, Luther Holton, Huntington's English colleague from Quebec, joined in attacking him and was followed by Joseph Cauchon. Holton was jealous of Huntington and his motives for the break were otherwise mixed, but Cauchon's were painfully clear. He was in hot water with the clergy and he had to lower the temperature, even at the expense of his standing in Ottawa. The creakings and groanings of the Liberal party were now public property, and the dismayed Mackenzie was learning how much he could expect from his new minister.

Laurier sat through the debate in masterful silence and spoke only three times in the entire session. On March 10 he made his first essay on the question of the tariff, speaking partly as the child of commercial Montreal and more as a hopeful philosopher: 'I do not deny that I have been a Protectionist, which I am still. It is asserted by many that Free Trade is a Liberal principle and Protection a Conservative principle – I see nothing political about it – it is purely a matter of social economy.'

The tariff did not interest him and his task in the other two speeches was positively distasteful. Two Liberal members had been forced to resign for accepting government contracts, and there had to be an eye for an eye. The counterbalancing victim was discovered in the elderly Currier, Conservative member for Ottawa, whose lumber firm had had some official dealings without his knowledge. The choice of hatchet-man fell on Laurier, and though he was graceful and sympathetic in performing his work Currier went out. The member for Drummond-Arthabaska, as he neared the treasury benches, was being hardened for political war.

By the middle of April he was back in Arthabaska. Affairs in

Ottawa were little more than a distraction; it was in Quebec that the heads rolled and the time of decision drew near. The political map was speckled with by-elections and the drumfire of clerical invective and *Rouge* counter-invective rose with each. Ernest Pacaud's *Journal d'Arthabaska* was savagely at war with Father Suzor's *Union des Cantons de l'Est*, and the toning-down of Pacaud's worst excesses was a constant preoccupation. On the other hand there was no safety in the moderation of Laurent-Olivier David, with whose lingering affection for the Church and tendency for hopeful compromise Laurier had often been impatient. 'No Catholic is allowed to proclaim himself a moderate Liberal,' said Bishop Bourget, and in Montreal in May David's *Bien Public* came out with its final issue. 'Certain facts which I need not mention', said the closing editorial, 'have finally convinced me that the profession of politics has become intolerable in this province to anyone who has more independence of character than of purse. It would appear that there is now but one crime in the world, but one mortal sin, that of voting for a Liberal candidate.'

In spite of the new election law, *Rouge* was 'the colour of hell-fire' in country pulpits. Liberals were 'ravening wolves come to raise a disturbance in the flock', 'serpent Catholic Liberals', 'false prophets who wish to bring dissension between you and your legitimate pastors'. Bonaventure had now been added to Charlevoix as a constituency where priests were on trial for using undue influence in an election. Quebec judges inclined toward the Church, but it would be the Supreme Court of Canada that would pronounce the final verdict. Throughout the country now the position of the Church was in question. Lawyers were at odds with bishops, bishops with other bishops, and religion and politics were almost indistinguishable in the newspapers. The Catholic family quarrel was becoming a national quarrel.

Everything that was done in Ottawa seemed to worsen the position in Quebec. Cauchon squirmed and Mackenzie drifted, grasping always at the wrong straws. At the end of the long summer, after a fierce election battle in a Montreal constituency, Laflamme went to Ottawa and the cabinet. One could be loyal to Laflamme, one could admire many of his qualities, but one could not see his presence, after the years of the Guibord case, as adding anything but fuel to the flames. 'The plain, unvarnished truth', Laurier confided to Young in one of his autumn letters, 'is that our party is going to the dogs in Quebec. I am fully convinced that the next election will make a terrible sweep in our ranks. I would tremble for my own fate', he added, 'were it not for the fact that my constituency numbers about three hundred heretics like yourself who will vote me and all liberty and reform and who will make the contest an easy one. Notwithstanding what the Church may say, I do say that there is something good in heresy.'

Yet even in the wider realms of the heretics he foresaw trouble. The Mackenzie government was not only failing in Quebec; it was disappointing the country. 'I certainly admire the great qualities of Mackenzie,' he wrote, 'but he has no zest to carry a party on.' Cauchon was the great bone in his craw; he could not and would not stomach the man. 'As to Cauchon, he never will think of going out as long as he will not have brought the government into some dirty and disgraceful scrape.'

In spite of it all his unpredictable health had seldom been better. He was too busy now, too much sought out, to brood on his pains and aches. Mackenzie made it clear to him that the appointment of Cauchon had been a mistake and that he was only waiting for an opportunity to ease him gracefully out. There would then be a cabinet seat for Laurier, and dubious though the attractions were, it was an assurance that he was not stagnating. He could retire to the study concerned but not responsible for the woes of his leader. He could still enjoy a leisure that was his own choice. He read Trevelyan's life of Macaulay that summer, and Trevelyan sent him back to Macaulay's history. 'I am now concluding the fourth volume,' he wrote Young in October. 'The history of England has for a foreigner like myself a charm which I am sure it has not for one accustomed from his infancy to English ideas and traditions. As you follow in Macaulay's pages that constant struggle between liberty and despotism and the slow and steady progress and at last complete triumph of liberty the student of French history is struck with amazement. This is the reason why I admire you so much, you Anglo-Saxons.'

It had been, all in all and in spite of politics, a good summer. He was in debt once more but this time it was a pleasanter burden and one he had shouldered of his own choice. He had bought seven acres of ground at the foot of Mont Christo and was now going ahead with plans for a house that Zoë considered to be of rather frightening proportions. But he was a coming man, a man with a good practice and many prospects. There were often important visitors to be entertained, and it was a little deflating to receive them in rooms at Dr. Poisson's. One was entitled, it seemed, to live according to his station and even, perhaps, a little in the future.

They were familiars of all the large houses in Arthabaska now, not least the haunted house of Georges-Jérémie Pacaud, where many *Rouge* festivities went on to the horror of the devout. At one of the summer parties had appeared Emilie Barthe, a niece of one of the Pacauds. She was an elegant young lady recently returned with her family from several years in Paris and a year in London, and her entrance had created a stir. Above all, it had stirred Joseph Lavergne, and the wedding that followed was the event of the season.

The Lavergnes were settled as neighbours now, and Mme Lavergne was undoubtedly brightening and improving the social life of Arthabaska. She was perhaps a little beyond the staid Joseph, who seemed at times to be rather dazed by his luck. Her Paris gowns and her taste for English ways combined the best of two worlds, both European, and both likely to prove something of a strain on the income of an Arthabaska lawyer. Yet she was proving a delightful hostess, always with some new and tasteful surprise in her arrangements and always with a fund of conversation that was at least as interesting to the men as to the women.

She seemed taller than she was because of the grace with which she carried herself. She was not quite beautiful nor even pretty; her chin was a little strong and her teeth were not quite regular. There was sometimes a tinge of yellow in the whites of her eyes because she was a woman who read late and preferred candlelight to sunlight. Yet they were beautiful eyes, sparkling in a mobile face, and the flow of her talk ranged easily and impressively over politics, literature, and history. She was brilliant, she was well read, she was usually witty and light, and she was capable of a deft flick of sarcasm. Members of the local society were sometimes made to feel a little gauche in her company and even Laurier, Zoë noticed, did not quite escape. The wives of the two partners saw a good deal of each other, but Mme Lavergne was not to be found in an old hat gossiping among flower-beds with gloves over sunburned hands. A woman, said Zoë, who would always prefer the drawing-room to the garden. Yes, Laurier agreed thoughtfully, a woman for the soirée and the salon.

6

'I HAVE UNFURLED THE LIBERAL STANDARD'

1877

THE OTTAWA of February 1877 was subtly changed for him from the capital he had known for three years. He came back a prospective cabinet minister and a marked man. The days of responsibility were overshadowing him; he would not be able much longer to think of himself as a lawyer playing at politics. Nor would his official enemies. He figured now in the calculations of Tories, and responded as one who knew it.

He found himself more vocal than in the three earlier sessions. He twitted John A. Macdonald on the new phrase in the air. The 'National Policy', said Laurier, like the resolution in which it had been introduced, was loose and vague. It was framed not to embarrass Macdonald when the Conservatives came back to power, as they must in the natural order of things. It was designed 'to catch the wind, no matter from what point of the compass it came'. He was derisive of the Quebec protectionists who supported it, veering a little himself from his earlier position on the tariff. They 'would stop short of nothing to obtain position. They would tax the people's bread, they would attack the Bench, and the ferocity of a she-bear deprived of her cubs was nothing compared with that of the Tory party when deprived of the spoils of office.'

It was all in the politician's vein and all in the mood of a parliament that had passed its peak and was coasting down the slope toward a general election. A sign of the growing stature of Wilfrid Laurier was the fact that some of his old words were now being dug up and thrown back at him. *Bleu* archivists went back to his speeches in the Quebec House and on the stumps of Arthabaska. The honourable gentleman, they recalled, had paid French Canadians the distinguished compliment of considering them inferior to other races so far as commerce and manufacturing were concerned. He had also derided their system of education. The honourable gentleman fended off the attacks with ease. He yielded nothing to any man in his pride of race, but so far as commerce and manufacturing were concerned he had stated facts. He had certainly attacked the educational system of Quebec, and if he were still a member of the provincial House he would do it again.

'I am more than anxious to reach the end of the session,' he wrote to Ernest Pacaud on March 31, 'as I am lonesome for my friends and each day more impatient to return to them.' He had other reasons for impatience, and release when it came on April 28 brought only a plunge into the real problems of the year. The court decisions in the undue-influence cases had now been handed down. In the case of Charlevoix the Supreme Court of Canada had reversed a Quebec court by voiding the election and condemning the priests for their political activities. In the case of Bonaventure the decision had been the same and it had been rendered by a Quebec court. The fire of the ultramontanes was now turned not only on the *Rouge* party but on the courts and judges of the land. It did not spare the liberal-minded among the clergy who seemed disposed to tolerate the banishment of priests from politics. Church, province, and nation were thoroughly ablaze and divided, while Quebec so blessed with bishops was about to receive another.

Early in May Bishop Conroy of the famous see of Ardagh in Ireland arrived in Canada as apostolic delegate. Rome was at last aroused. Bishop Bourget, Bishop Laflèche, and other ultramontane prelates had crossed the ocean half a dozen times to present their case. So had their adversaries among both the clergy and the laity. Amid the confusion of comings and goings one thing was clear: the quarrels of Canadian bishops were becoming a public scandal. The apostolic delegate was to bring peace to embattled sees and he was to define the attitude of the Church to politics and political parties.

It would be a momentous visit. A verdict for the ultramontanes would mean the silencing of liberal opinion in the Church and would be all but a death-blow to the Liberal party in Quebec. It would be a good deal more than that, for no Protestant and few English Catholics would accept the judgment. Bishop Bourget and Bishop Laflèche would have their Catholic party in good truth, but it would be faced by a Protestant party and it would be cut adrift from the rest of Catholic Canada.

By the latter part of June Bishop Conroy had visited Quebec, Montreal, and Ottawa. In each city he had heard the bishops and the politicians and a host of other advisers. He had then returned to Quebec, rather pointedly avoiding the palace of the liberal Archbishop, and established himself on the neutral ground of a house in the suburbs. Floods of mail and streams of distinguished callers poured in on him each day and only silence came forth. The elderly cleric walked and read and listened in his pleasant garden at Ste-Foy while *Rouges* and bishops and *Bleus* lay on their arms waiting.

For Laurier, meanwhile, the problem of Cauchon and the cabinet had been settled. Cauchon was to go, and he was to go before Laurier assumed a portfolio. At the moment, through the usual dismal irony of the Liberal position, he had to be kept on because he had played a considerable part in bringing Bishop Conroy to Canada and he was now the party's intermediary with the legate. Cauchon prepared the memoranda, Cauchon answered the Bishop's inquiries, Cauchon was the front that liberalism presented to the Church. But he had been informed that he was to become Lieutenant-Governor of Manitoba at a moment of Mackenzie's choosing and at that moment Laurier would replace him. The prospective junior minister had been about as stiff-necked and righteous as it was possible to be. If he were to enter the cabinet while Cauchon was still a member, he had said, he could not possibly approve even the new appointment that Cauchon was receiving.

By the end of May he seemed to have assured his political future on his own terms. He was settled into the fine new house at the foot of Mont Christo. He had a good and growing practice and it would soon be supplemented by a cabinet minister's salary. So far as life in Arthabaska was concerned only the death of Dr. Poisson, who had been ailing for months, had darkened a pleasant spring. It was not a moment when one welcomed Fate with a momentous choice, but the lady was now at hand.

The letter from the Young Men's Liberal Association of Quebec had arrived late in May. It conveyed an invitation to address a public meeting in the Salle de Musique of Quebec City on June 26. It was not unexpected and it differed from many similar invitations only in the fact that the audience was to be particularly large and distinguished. The Young Liberals, the men like Pacaud and David who were the very core of Laurier's strength in the party, had decided to set the scene for his entrance as acknowledged leader.

Laurier had accepted and had begun the writing of his speech about the time that Bishop Conroy secluded himself in Ste-Foy. Very soon, as the June days and nights went by, he had felt the tug of depths and whirlpools he would have liked to avoid. He detested Cauchon because Cauchon had neither principles nor convictions; now he had to find his own. He had to express them, if he dared. Standing as he now stood in all but formal ratification as the head of a beleaguered band of Quebec Liberals, he had to define their aims as politicians and as French Canadians. He had to define the French Canadian in relation to the English state in which he lived and in relation to that Church, so outrageous in its claims, that still held a larger place in his life than any state. The easy angers of a *Rouge* seemed to evaporate as he scrawled down his sentences and crossed them out and started again. One was looking beyond elections to the whole sprawling process of democracy, so untidy, so disorderly and formless, often so dirty. Laurier the liberal was not dealing here with a few old, intolerant, and reactionary clerics: he was searching for a philosophy. The whole position of man as a social being seemed to stand in question, and no answer was easy. He had not found many answers as the late days of June came, but he had written a dangerous speech and he was a different man.

He sent a précis of what he intended to say to Mackenzie and on June 21 Mackenzie replied. 'I have been discussing your proposed lecture with Laflamme, Pelletier and also with Mr. Blake,' he wrote, 'and the opinion seems to prevail that if you could postpone the lecture until the Legate has finished his mission it would be the safer course.'

It was the voice of the old Liberal policy and the worried Mackenzie had good and tempting reasons. 'I had a long discussion with the Legate,' he went on, 'and it was quite plain that he had been imbued by some of the clerical party with the belief that we are an extreme revolutionary party closely related to the Red Republican Communists of France and Italy. For myself I have no faith in clerical dignitaries being favourable to liberal opinion in itself, and if Doctor Conroy decides to report against the Bishops it will be because he considers their policy is calculated to injure the Church in the other Provinces. On the other hand the impression is general that he is now favourable both on principle and policy and that we had better avoid challenging controversy for a time.'

The letter arrived in Arthabaska on June 22, and was read by a man as worried as the writer. It was almost a command to silence. The heads of the party, even the reckless Laflamme, were advising caution, and the man who went against them took his future in his hands. He took the future of the party in Quebec in his hands. One looked across the street at the fine new house and thought of the load of debt overhanging it. It would be a heavy burden on a man suddenly without prospects. The cabinet post, for all the doubts he had of it and all the difficulties he had made, grew in attractiveness as he saw it threatened. The peaceful life in Arthabaska was all very well while one clung to it as a matter of choice. It would be a different affair to be relegated to obscurity after an act of political suicide.

'This is a subject', he wrote Mackenzie in unheroic English all too eloquent of the state of his mind, 'which gives me a great deal of uneasiness and I feel at times sorry of having accepted to go into it. However, I am studying to make it as prudent as possible. There is but one subject on which I might be open to objection; it is the *undue influence*. I cannot but speak upon it. An effort is to be made during next session of the local parliament to have this law amended, and the Liberal party would make a fool of itself if it were to assent to this amendment, and unless we do something to shape the opinion of our friends here they will bolt. . . . It seems to me that if we cannot speak . . . plain common-sense language, which we must have to speak some day, the fate of our party is in a desperate condition.

'Upon the whole, however,' he added, 'I am disposed to abide by your judgment, and if you do not approve the views I now express, I would wish you to telegraph me, on Monday at the St. Louis Hotel, Quebec.'

He mailed the letter on the night of Thursday June 22. On Sunday evening he took the train to Quebec. Monday morning he insured himself so far as he could by showing the manuscript of his speech to the Abbé Benjamin Paquet, the right hand of Archbishop Taschereau and the leading theologian of Laval University. There was no objection expressed, but that did not mean much, for these liberal churchmen had never been the men to fear. He returned to the St. Louis Hotel and from his window watched the sun slope down golden along the proud old streets. There was no telegram from Mackenzie. At eight in the evening, flanked by his official party, he entered the Salle de Musique to find it crowded to the doors with two thousand of the social, intellectual, and political élite of the province.

2

THE PRELIMINARIES of the evening were soon over and it was time for the main address. 'He rose deathly pale,' recorded an observer afterwards, 'and his friends thought him ill.' There was a moment of absolute stillness while the speaker and his audience looked at each other. His voice trembled a little as he began to speak, though his opening sentences were calm and deliberate, 'but his eyes were scanning the bearing and his judgment deliberately searching the temper of the audience. Then, the kindling . . .'

There was no trace here of the halting uncertainty of the letter to Mackenzie. That was behind him; and he was speaking in his own tongue. For a little over an hour, as the rustle of the hall deepened into an intense silence hardly broken by a spatter of applause, he offered himself to his people as he had offered himself to Mackenzie, on his own terms.

'I do not deceive myself with regard to the position of the Liberal party in the Province of Quebec. . . . I know that in the eyes of a portion of our people . . . liberalism is a new form of evil, a heresy carrying with it its own condemnation. I know all this and it is because I know it that I have accepted the invitation to come here. To my mind . . . the only way to defend our ideas and our principles is to make them known.'

He made the old distinction so often hammered home: political liberalism had nothing to do with the doctrines of the Church. Liberalism and conservatism were inherent in the system of responsible government so hardly won by French and English Canadians alike. They represented the opposed and balanced forces by which the state was held together. 'On the one hand you have those who govern, and on the other those who watch. On the one hand you have those who are in power and have an interest in remaining there, and on the other those who have an interest in getting there.'

What was the sentiment, what was the principle that made some men conservatives in politics and some men liberals? 'You will see together those who are attracted by the charm of novelty and you will see together those who are attracted by the charm of habit. You will see together those who are attached to all that is ancient, and you will see together those who are always disposed to reform.

'Is the one radically good and the other radically bad? Is it not evident that both are what are termed in moral philosophy *indifferents,* that is to say that both are susceptible of being appreciated, pondered, and chosen? Would it not be as unfair as it would be absurd to condemn or approve either the one or the other as absolutely bad or good?

'For my part,' he went on, 'I am a liberal. I am one of those who think that always and everywhere in human things there are abuses to be reformed, new horizons to be opened up, and new forces to be developed. The principle of liberalism is inherent in the very essence of our nature, in that desire of happiness with which we are born into the world, which pursues us throughout life, and which is never completely gratified on this side of the grave. Our souls are immortal but our means are limited. We constantly gravitate towards an ideal which we never attain. We dream of good but we never realize the best. We only reach the goal we have proposed to ourselves to discover new horizons opening up, which we had not before even suspected. . . . This condition of our nature is precisely what makes the greatness of man, for it condemns him irrevocably to movement, to progress. Our means are limited but our nature is perfectible and we have the infinite for our arena. Thus there is always room for improvement of our condition, for the perfecting of our nature, and for the attainment by a larger number of an easier life.'

He moved on to compare the parliamentary tradition of England and the work of constitutional reform with the spectacle of absolutism in Europe and the fate that had overtaken it. 'Wherever there is compression there will be explosion, violence, and ruin. I do not say this to excuse revolutions. But I am less inclined to cast the responsibility on those who make them than on those who provoke them by their blind obstinacy.'

He admitted the wildness and excesses of the early *Rouge* program. 'If, by the wave of some magic wand, the twenty-one articles of that program had been realized in a single night, the country in the morning would have been no longer recognizable, and the person who should have left it the evening before and returned the next day would not have known where he was. The only excuse for these Liberals', he added dryly, creating the sole ripple of smiles throughout his speech, 'was their youth. The oldest of them was not more than twenty-two years of age.'

He admitted the harm that had been done by attacks on the Church. But who had invited them if not the politicians who had built their platforms under the shelter of the Church? His voice hardened and his head rose from the lectern as he came to the heart of his speech.

'I have too much respect for the opinion of my adversaries ever to insult them, but I reproach them with understanding neither their time nor their country. I accuse them of laboriously

. . . working to degrade religion to the simple proportions of a political party.

'In our adversaries' party it is the habit to accuse us, Liberals, of irreligion. I am not here to parade my religious sentiments, but I declare that I have too much respect for the faith in which I was born ever to use it as the basis of a political organization.

'You wish to organize a Catholic party' – his voice rose again – 'but have you not considered that if you have the misfortune to succeed you will draw down upon your country calamities of which it is impossible to foresee the consequences?

'You wish to organize all the Catholics into one party, without other bond, without other basis than a common religion; but have you not reflected that by that very fact you will organize the Protestant population as a single party and that then . . . you throw open the door to war, a religious war, the most terrible of all wars?'

He turned to the charge that the Liberal party wished to 'hinder the clergy from meddling in politics and to relegate them to the sacristy. In the name of the Liberal party and of Liberal principles I repel this assertion. I maintain that there is not one Canadian Liberal who wants to prevent the clergy from taking part in political affairs if they wish to do so. In the name of what principle should the friends of liberty seek to deny to the priest the right to take part in political affairs? Why should the priest not have the right to say that if I am elected religion will inevitably be destroyed, when I have the right to say that if my adversary is elected the state will go into bankruptcy? No, let the priest speak and preach as he thinks best; such is his right and no Canadian Liberal will dispute that right.'

Then he went on more deliberately. 'That right, however, is not unlimited. We have no absolute rights amongst us. The rights of each man end precisely at the point where they encroach upon the rights of others. The right of interference in politics finishes at the spot where it encroaches on the elector's independence. It is . . . perfectly legitimate to alter the elector's opinion by argument and by all other means of persuasion, but never by intimidation. When by terror you force him to vote, the opinion you cause him to express is your opinion. If such a state of things continues and is repeated, if after each election the will expressed is not the real will of the country, you do violence to the constitution, responsible government is no longer anything but an empty name, and sooner or later, here as elsewhere, the pressure will culminate in explosion, violence, and ruin.'

There was another pause, another long, steady look over the unreadable audience. He resumed more quietly. 'I am not one of those who parade themselves as friends and champions of the clergy. However, I say this: like most of my young fellow countrymen I have been reared among priests and among young men who have become priests. I flatter myself that I have among them some sincere friends and to them, at least, I can and do say: see if there is under the sun a country where the Catholic Church is freer or more privileged than it is here. Why then should you, by claiming rights incompatible with our state of society, expose the country to agitations of which it is impossible to foresee the consequences?

'But I address myself to all my fellow countrymen without distinction and I say to them: We are a free and happy people, and we are so owing to the liberal institutions by which we are governed, institutions which we owe to the exertions of our forefathers and the wisdom of the mother country. The policy of the Liberal party is to protect those institutions, to defend them and spread them, and under the sway of those institutions to develop the country's latent resources. That is the policy of the Liberal party and it has no other.'

With his peroration he carried the audience out on a wide sweep over the Plains of Abraham. Could their ancestors, he asked, dying defeated in the mud of that September day, have dreamed of a nation in which the conquered would rise again to the place of the French in Canada? Then it was over. The core of it all had lain in two sentences: 'People are not wanting who say that the clergy have a right to dictate to the people what are its duties. I simply answer that we are here under the government of the Queen of England.' For the most implacable of his enemies the rest was empty eloquence and meaningless sophistry. He had broken no new ground, he had not even posed the riddle of man in God and man in the State; he never would. But he had opened a wide doorway; the cathedral gloom of the Middle Ages was invaded by the light of day, and as he turned from the lectern a great gust of applause swept through the hall.

3

OVERNIGHT he had become a national figure quoted with zest in every English paper. The midsummer doldrums slipped by in Arthabaska enlivened by much correspondence and many important visitors. Mackenzie was already consulting him as the leader of the party in Quebec. By early September he had to ask that the Prime Minister write rather than telegraph him as the *Bleu* operator in the railway office at Victoriaville was giving away secrets.

On October 7 Cauchon resigned from the cabinet and on the eighth Laurier went to Ottawa to be sworn in. On the ninth he returned to Arthabaska to find a triumphal arch and a procession of two hundred carriages waiting for him, and to be driven to his home through streets overhung with flags and bunting. Two days later came a note of final triumph, sounded this time by unlikely and unwilling lips. On the sunny Sunday of October 11 Father Suzor read from the pulpit by command a general pastoral letter to the clergy of Quebec declaring that the strictures of the Holy See against Catholic Liberalism were not to be applied to any political party.

Priests were privately forbidden in an accompanying circular 'to teach from the pulpit or anywhere else that it is a sin to vote for any particular candidate or party. You are never to give your personal opinion from the pulpit.' Both letters had been inspired by Bishop Conroy and neither had any visible connection with Laurier or his speech. The timing, however, could scarcely have been more opportune. Bishop Laflèche's *Journal des Trois Rivières* mourned the coming of 'the epoch of concessions to liberalism and of cowardice, the epoch of the triumph of Catholic Liberalism'. The *Rouges* hailed the work of the new man, whose rise had only to be confirmed now by the formality of a by-election.

There were hopes for a while that even the by-election could be dispensed with. The bothersome necessity of presenting oneself for the approval of one's constituents after accepting a cabinet portfolio was often avoided by a graceful acclamation. It was soon apparent, however, that there was to be no grace in Arthabaska. Laurier was now marked down for destruction by revengeful ultramontanes. To Langevin, safely seated at Macdonald's side by another election in Charlevoix, he represented the new threat in Quebec. He was the long-time enemy of the *Bleus* in the provincial House, and to the Conservatives of English Canada he was a still-unmortared keystone that might be pried loose to topple the whole Mackenzie structure. For all these reasons the incumbent minister was soon declaring somewhat waspishly through the columns of *Le Journal d'Arthabaska,* 'I know it is the custom in England to allow those whom Her Majesty calls to her cabinet to be elected by acclamation. That is how they act in the ancient home of liberty and fair play, but a similar favour is not to be expected from the Conservatives of this country. The struggle waits me; I am ready.'

Both in the dignified sanctuary of the office on Church Street and in the clamorous committee room of *Le Journal d'Arthabaska* there seemed every reason for an almost contemptuous confidence. Désiré-Olivier Bourbeau, who emerged as the opposing statesman, was a merchant of Victoriaville. He was tall, bearded, and heavy, principally distinguished for a cane that rattled the wooden sidewalks and a voice that shook the windows of the church when he sang. His platform, so far as it was discernible, was built on the conviction that merchants should be sent to parliament because there were enough doctors and lawyers there already. According to Ernest Pacaud 'the big Burgundian' discussed the tariff 'like a blind man speaking of colours; talked of hay, oats, and buckwheat and was stopped by his friends at the moment he was going to pass the potatoes'.

He was nevertheless a man suddenly in possession of a host of distinguished admirers who poured into the constituency from Montreal and Quebec and even from the remote fastnesses beyond the Ottawa. They were supported by the voice of the old schoolfellow Arthur Dansereau, now editing Quebec's ultramontane *La Minerve,* and they were under the expert personal direction of another editor and comrade of L'Assomption, J. Israel Tarte.

The little man's chin, which had been fresh and downy fourteen years ago, now wore a trim Vandyke. The stutter was still with him and the quick black eyes were humorous as ever, sharpened by ten years in seamy provincial politics. He was here to do the work of Langevin and the rising Chapleau, with a thought for his own concerns in the long future. The *Rouge* of Arthabaska stood in the way of them all. 'I am met with a contestation the bitterness of which I did not expect,' Laurier reported to Mackenzie on October 22, 'but everything is going well. The only thing I fear is bribery. If there is no bribery the majority cannot be less than 300.'

By that time, as the twenty-day campaign rose to its climax, there had been almost everything else. The silence imposed on the pulpits was too new to have much effect; the opinions of priests were still well known and well conveyed to their flocks. The old stridency of Father Suzor, moreover, would have been almost welcome compared to the new ways of the imported laity. Brawls and broken heads were a feature of every meeting and at one of the loudest of them a *Rouge* supporter was kicked to death. His memory was glorified each day in the columns of *Le Journal d'Arthabaska*, but the capacities of the martyr as a vote-getter remained doubtful. The counter-clamour of the *Bleus* was too sustained and their methods too efficient. 'Elections are not won by prayers,' Tarte was to say at some point in his career, and whether or not he had yet said it he had mobilized a corps that fully shared the conviction.

Loudest of all the loud and agile band was one Charles Thibeault, a lawyer of Montreal, seemingly equipped with seven-league boots, certainly with a thunderous voice, and possessed of a portable grandmother who had been born within a mile of every stump he spoke from. The pious Charles was here to rescue Quebec from the atheist Laurier. He came as the familiar of bishops and the instructor of priests, as a builder of convents, hospitals, and seminaries. He spoke to the electors of Drummond-Arthabaska as the confidant of the Pope, and he usually held in his hand a telegram of support received that day from the Vatican.

Panting *Rouge* speakers, alarmed at last in the late days of the campaign, followed him from village to village. They found it necessary to deny that Laurier was going to Ottawa 'to become a Protestant Minister'. They were called upon to point out that Laurier 'not one of whose children has been baptized' was not blessed with children. They were still battling a Thibeault who was always a town ahead of them when it was discovered that the *Bleu* secretary of the municipality had 'forgotten' to post the electoral lists of Arthabaska at the registry bureau, thus depriving many *Rouges* of their votes. The final blow fell on the evening of October 26, the night before the election, when Louis-Adélard Sénécal arrived at Victoriaville station with two prosperous friends.

'I telegraphed you this morning', Laurier wrote to Mackenzie three days later, 'that I had been beaten by 24 votes. This has been the most violent election that has taken place in the province for many a year . . . all the vilest passions have been let loose . . . and what I mostly dreaded has at last come out, bribery. The three largest parishes in the county of Drummond, St. Guillaume, St. Germaine, St. Bonaventure, have been bribed over. I had calculated upon 150 votes majority in these three places and the day previous to the election it was perfectly sure, but my former friend Mr. Sénécal along with two other railway contractors of the provincial government came there on the night of Friday to Saturday and went on buying votes as in the good old times. My majority there was reduced to two votes. I have an offer to run for Quebec Centre. I feel extremely averse to stand another election at once – my health is very much broken down. But of course I will have to do it. Let me hear from you as soon as possible.'

The defeat was perfectly incredible, said the stunned Ernest Pacaud. He had had to go through the figures twenty times to believe it. Yet it was true, and on the final count the hostile majority stood at five votes more than Laurier had told Mackenzie. 'I was with him that evening,' wrote the poet Louis Fréchette, his old desk-mate in the House. 'We felt overwhelmed. Yet his good humour never varied by a hair's breadth from his habitual calm and his hand did not shake with the slightest quiver as he raised his glass in a toast to better days.'

4

THE BRAVE MASK covered the face of a shaken and angry man. Mackenzie, equally shaken, came down to Montreal on October 30, and Laurier met him there. By that time the prospect of running for Quebec Centre was gone. The sitting member, who had old ties with Cauchon, had decided not to resign. There were other offers but none of them had hardened yet, and the question was what to do. In Ottawa, Conservative papers were trumpeting the party's intention to pursue Laurier from constituency to constituency. They had high hopes now, by defeating him wherever he went, of forcing the government to resign. His own stature in any case was already sharply reduced. 'Mr. Laurier', said the Ottawa *Free Press,* 'is being degraded by his professed friends who are hawking him about the various divisions to be bid for by the electors. An upset price has been put on his head and unless the amount is sufficient he will be withdrawn.'

The young oracle of Quebec, the man who had come home a cabinet minister less than a month before, was painfully conscious that he now stood in a different light. 'I suspect he suffered a little from over-confidence,' was to be George Brown's comment, and it was clear from Mackenzie's uneasy bearing that he already shared the suspicion. He might even be feeling that he had over-estimated the services and the value of this new lieutenant. There was no point in protesting that the election had been flagrantly corrupt and that it would almost certainly be annulled in the courts. The process would take months and Laurier would still limp back to Ottawa with the smell of defeat about him. If he was to go on in politics at all, and never before had he so much wanted to go on, there had to be a fight now. It had to be a winning fight and Mackenzie had to be steeled to it.

Returning to Arthabaska with nothing decided, Laurier spent the next two days in prodding Ernest Pacaud. That wounded and exasperated beaver was scurrying about among the *Rouges* of Quebec City, firing back telegrams and letters. By the evening of November 1 there was news to report to Mackenzie. The members for Quebec East, Mégantic, Montmagny, and Iberville had offered to give up their seats and Quebec East was the likeliest choice. Laurier was recovering, he said, from the strains of the past campaign. 'Rest is all that I require and in a few days more I will be ready for another conflict.'

He wished to leave no doubt in the mind of the Prime Minister either as to his own value or as to what would be required to secure him. 'I am the last card of the party in this province,' he wrote. 'If I am sent down the party is well nigh gone down completely – at least our adversaries act under this assumption. They spent $5,000 before and will again. I cannot undertake a new fight unless we are determined to carry it.'

By November 6 the die had been cast in Ottawa. The whole prestige of the party would go to support Laurier in Quebec East. On November 7 a deputation from Quebec arrived in Arthabaska, formally tendering him the nomination. Next day he set off, a candidate, surrounded by beaming supporters. As the train pulled into Lévis, across the river from Quebec which as yet had no railway, Laurier was met by Isidore Thibodeau, the retiring member, and a large crowd. The campaign began at that moment and from then to polling day Quebec East was the political centre of the country. 'Every nerve is being strained', commented John Willison, the rising young journalist of the Toronto *Globe*, 'to defeat Mr. Laurier and thus, if possible, disgust him with public life.'

Tarte and his band of *Bleus* began with the same tactics that had succeeded in Drummond-Arthabaska. Money flowed even more freely than before. This time, however, the assault was met by as tough a band of *Rouges*. They were not impoverished, they were no longer so easily confident, and they had learned much. The party workers of the *Bleus* who went from house to house found that the *Rouges* had been there before them. Familiar claims brought new and startling answers. Liberalism would end, warned a *Bleu*, by making the people march knee-deep in the blood of priests. 'Oh well,' said a stubborn old *Rouge* shoemaker, well prepared for the visit, 'we'll put on high boots.'

Twenty *Rouge* shadowers were assigned to a watch on the railway station at Lévis and the ferry dock at Quebec. Each new arrival was promptly followed. The ineffable Thibeault was one of the first, and began his confident march in the light of a new vision. The *Rouges*, he had discovered, were descended in a direct line from Cain, the first Liberal of the world. This time, however, he was met at every platform, talked down by a well-briefed speaker, and heckled by ready foes. Sweating and flustered under the new treatment he came out at last with the great and hoped-for gaffe. 'Laurier', he shouted, 'is disliked by the country, he is disliked by his home counties – and he is disliked by his wife!'

The howl from the crowd around him was echoed next day in every *Rouge* paper and even by some of the *Bleus*. The tactics of Drummond-Arthabaska had begun to recoil; shame-faced Conservatives, unable to stomach Thibeault any longer, found the dragging in of Zoë's name the last straw. Thibeault's final appearances were devoted to explanations: he had been misquoted, he had meant to say not that Mme Laurier disliked her husband but that she disliked his involvement with politics, which everyone knew. His audiences, however, had heard what they had heard. By November 23 the correspondent of the Ottawa *Free Press*, stationed in Quebec, was able to report, 'Thibeault left in disgust last night. Sénécal, Tarte, and Langevin have no show.'

November 28 was polling day. Early in the morning a battery of artillery and several squads of police were drawn up in Jacques-Cartier Square. Gangs of election 'whackers' moved restlessly about, but under the mouths of the guns and the eyes of the constabulary not a club was lifted. Polls opened at nine with the strong-arm men of the parties standing by at the ready and again there were only glares. All day, under a drumming rain that turned the outlying roads to swamps, an undisturbed stream of voters moved to the polls. By noon the trend to Laurier was unmistakable. It wavered a little in the afternoon and the predicted majority of 500 came down to 150. By the time the polls closed there had been another turn and hopes had risen to the neighbourhood of 300. Then with darkness came the final

FROM *L'Opinion Publique*, JANUARY 3, 1878

ecstatic pronouncement: a *Rouge* plurality of 316. The mile-long procession formed in Jacques-Cartier Square, and the man rejected by Drummond-Arthabaska stood in the light of a thousand torches. 'I have unfurled the Liberal standard above the ancient citadel of Quebec,' he cried in a voice for once hoarse and unmusical, 'and there I will keep it waving.'

In Ottawa the news clicked over the wires to crowds waiting in front of the telegraph office, the *Free Press* office, and the Russell Hotel. Dour Tories turned homeward and Liberals adjourned to make a night of it. There were speeches at Matthewman's Block on the corner of Wellington and Elgin streets, but these were for the commonalty. The more important assembled in a mightily festive gathering at Bourget's restaurant. By dawn, amid a welter of empty bottles and cigar butts, a committee had been formed to arrange for the victor's reception.

November 30 was to be the day of departure from Quebec. In chilly morning sunlight flags blew and bunting streamed from the roofs and cornices of every building that boasted a *Rouge* proprietor. A special train waited in Lévis station with steam up, ready for the start to Ottawa. Then all arrangements collapsed when it was discovered that there was a muddle over official returns. The lost day gave Laurier time for a breathless reply to a breathless note of congratulation from Marie-Louise Pacaud, wife of Ernest. 'I know that there is no one to whom the victory has caused more pleasure than to Ernest, for I have no friend more devoted. I cannot tell you all I owe your dear husband. The enthusiasm, energy, and efficiency he displayed throughout this election cannot be repaid, nor can I express in words my affection for him.'

By Saturday December 1 the two candidates and their lawyers had resolved the imbroglio of the ballots. The special train waiting across the river was once more under steam. Two brass bands and a crowd of six thousand people escorted the new member for Quebec East to the ferry dock. Cheers billowed round him, the flags and bunting snapped, and his carriage was filled with flowers. He was shoved onto the ferry's deck at the centre of a flying wedge that carved its way among a thousand yelling supporters. The ramps came up, the engines shuddered below, and then there was a brief parting in the sea of heads and shoulders as an aisle was cleared to the rail for him. A new wave of cheering billowed out from shore, and he raised his hand in salute to the constituents he would represent for the rest of his life.

The special train went on by Stanfold to Arthabaska and a day of rest. On Tuesday December 4 Laurier reached Montreal. 'I have gone to the very door of the Quebec government,' he confided to a huge crowd from the balcony of St. Lawrence Hall, 'and there defied and defeated the Conservative.' On Wednesday December 5, his Ottawa reception committee, with all plans completed, met him *en route* at Prescott. By 4:40 in the afternoon, bound for the capital, the train was lumbering through a sleety dusk lighted on both sides of the track by fireworks and calcium flares.

It was pouring with rain in Ottawa, but the Liberal triumph went grimly on as planned. In an open carriage, drawn by four white horses which were soon black, Laurier passed by Sussex Street and St. Patrick Street, by Friel and Clarence and Cumberland, and by Rideau, Sparks, and Wellington on the way to Mackenzie's house.

A great bonfire burning on the outskirts at Taylorville cast its glow into the wet sky. At the head of the procession moved an illuminated carriage with the word 'Laurier' blazing on each side and the magic figure 316, his majority in Quebec East, glowing above. Fireworks and calcium flares spouted up from the dashboard and sprayed down on the soaked bystanders. Three bands followed, then the Grand Marshal, then the carriages of the managing committee, and then the four-in-hand containing Laurier. The carriages of the less-important followed in a long string interspersed by three more bands, while a stubborn crowd on foot plodded behind. Drenched and shivering, with the blare of bands in his ears and the sputter of flares overhead, the conqueror came at last to Mackenzie's house. The Prime Minister stood on his veranda waiting and the Prime Minister's words were an echo of the words of Quebec. Mackenzie was confident, he said, that 'we shall be able to carry the banner of victory which has floated over the ancient capital of Quebec in triumph over every province of the Dominion'.

7

A FIXED FACT

1878-1881

FOR THE next week he moved through official Ottawa in a kind of exhausted trance, playing out the triumph. He dined with the Dufferins at Government House, no longer as 'one of the French members' but as Mr. Laurier, the Minister of Inland Revenue. He accepted the congratulations of his cabinet colleagues, aware now of a new glint of speculative appraisal in their eyes. He met with his deputy minister and with senior officers of his department, and he was still a source of good copy to the reporters who dogged his steps.

His remarks, in the aftermath of Drummond-Arthabaska, were hardly the usual gracious platitudes. It had been an election to redden the ears of the toughest party hack; it was quite certain to be annulled by the courts, and some of the Conservative leaders came to him with tentative apologies. There were even hints that he might have the seat by acclamation if he chose to run again. They did not soften him; he was still in the fighting mood of Quebec East. He had been beaten, he told reporters, for the simple reason that 3,800 votes had been cast in a constituency with 3,200 registered voters. Next time, he added grimly, the six hundred imported strangers would find plenty to do at home.

It was good to escape from the grisly weather of Ottawa in mid December and live out the inevitable relapse in Arthabaska.

He came home, already sick, impatient of another welcome, hardly able to sit through an interminable series of addresses. Every man on the platform, he told himself ill-humouredly, had done him favours and would expect favours in return. As he settled into the spacious comfort of the new bedroom the cough and the fevers came on. All the accumulated fatigues of the two campaigns descended on him in one enormous lassitude. Even Zoë, resigned to her fate now and well on the way to becoming a knowledgeable politician, could not stir him out of it. The angry, elated conqueror of two weeks ago seemed a ridiculous stranger to himself. What had he really gained but the tedium of administering a dull department in a doomed government? He sat here now, shivering and sick, one of the supposed masters of a country he hardly knew, with the tides already gathering to sweep him away.

He roused himself with difficulty to enjoy the visits of the family and the first Christmas in the new house. By the beginning of January he was sufficiently restored to pay his respects to late enemies who were going on as before. Tarte and other ultramontane politicians, still unsilenced by decrees that had silenced bishops, were now dubious of the wisdom of the Vatican itself. 'The Church, that good mother,' commented the angry *Rouge* in the columns of *Le Journal d'Arthabaska*, 'allowed these wretched *enfants terribles* to have their way, but as impunity gave them courage our high and mighty ultramontanes set themselves to smashing the whole shop. Now Rome has spoken. But what of our high and mighty ultramontanes? Are these submissive children of the Church? Pouah! What Tartuffes!'

He left for Ottawa with this parting shot and the work of the new session began on February 7. It came to an end in the small hours of May 10 amid a savage brawl in which John A. Macdonald and Tupper sought to prevent their fellow Conservative, Donald A. Smith, from raking over the embers of the Pacific scandal. Black Rod's knock on the chamber door synchronized with Macdonald's last shout, 'That fellow Smith is the biggest liar I ever met!' Often drunk and truculent on other nights of the session, Macdonald had been throughout a sorry sight.

Watching him, it was easy to pardon Mackenzie for the confidence with which he faced the coming election. It was not so easy to share it.

The body of Torydom might be torn with quarrels and tainted by corruption but it was raucously alive. Liberalism, with the stern erectness of Mackenzie and the chill dignity of Blake, had all the appeal and colour of a granite tomb. Macdonald's drinking had not prevented him from knitting the party together behind the National Policy. Catch-phrase it may have been, catch-phrase it was still so far as Mackenzie was concerned; but the tariff, in despite of all pious hopes, would henceforth and forever be a political issue. Some protection against American competition was certainly necessary for the half-born industry of a half-built country. Hungry manufacturers and thousands of unemployed workmen were already clamouring for help. The National Policy offered it on a grand scale. The Liberals had nothing to counter with but a little less of the same. The Liberals had not built the railway to the Pacific; the Tories would, or the Tories said they would. The Liberals had not brought prosperity; they had come to power in the doldrums and their sails still hung flat. They had provided honest, upright, economical government, and the more they spoke of it the more they bored and irritated a country that was finding a dollar hard to make. Canada as a whole was not interested in the austerities of sound administration: it wanted a government of imagination and flair and it wanted good times. It had just about given up hope that the Liberals could provide them.

The mood of Quebec was the same, with the old differences. Laurier had heard his speech on political liberalism much quoted in the House during the three months of the session, but it had been quoted mainly by the English and admired only by the converted. The *Bleus* who sat with Macdonald shifted and evaded uneasily as the ringing phrases were thrown up to them in the nation's parliament. On their own ground they were unchanged. The Church would be circumspect but the Church was hostile. In provincial politics Louis-Adélard Sénécal, deep *Bleu* now and prospering as never before, sat at the centre of all things, spinning his webs. Drummond-Arthabaska, unrepentant over the duly-annulled election, had once more gone to the *Bleus* in a new campaign. The omens were so bad that even Ernest Pacaud had taken to shelter. The beloved *Journal* was no more; the little man fidgeted uneasily now as Prothonotary of Three Rivers.

Laurier remained at his desk in Ottawa till the end of May, clearing up the work of his department and doling out the last bits of patronage. Arthabaska in June had never seemed so attractive, but he was allowed barely a glimpse of it. The summer was a dusty blur of country roads, hot hotels, and noisy platforms as he moved out to cover almost every constituency in Quebec. He came home with no doubt that disaster lay ahead.

He moved over to the Ontario constituencies, spoke a few times under the wing of Cartwright, and returned more than ever deflated. He had mastered the parliamentary style in English as well as in French but he had not mastered the ways of the Ontario stumps. He could feel his words falling flat. He could almost see the bristles rising along sunburned necks at the accent that still plagued him. Yet he was not greatly concerned at his own failure; he had not expected much. The real sign of the times was the new Macdonald, sparkling, sober, and confident, cutting a wide swath through every Liberal constituency. Behind him plodded Mackenzie, still hopeful and a little pathetic because of it, upright, dour, and dull.

To the last day of the campaign the stonemason retained his confidence. He had been clean-handed and hard-working, he had given the country honest government; he could not believe that it would return itself to the men of the Pacific scandal. Doggedly, in meeting after meeting, he ticked off the sure constituencies, totted up his certain majority. On September 17 the results came. Ontario had gone for Macdonald by fifty-nine seats to twenty-nine, Quebec by forty-five to twenty, and the country as a whole by one seat less than two to one.

Laurier was safe in Quebec East, a private member now. On October 9, 1878, with the rest of Mackenzie's government, he handed in his portfolio. He had held his cabinet office for a year and a day.

2

IT WAS the time for a man to retire, if there was to be a time of his own choosing. The mortgage weighed more heavily on the new house now, the neglected practice could no longer be left entirely to Joseph Lavergne, and the political view from the desk in Arthabaska was almost completely black. Yet it was also the time when a man felt more strongly than ever the tug of friendships and allegiances, of expediencies and necessities, which made up party loyalty. He had had seven years in politics and they had hardened and sobered him. He knew the country a little or he was beginning to know it, and he had had a taste of the real work that went to its making. The taste bred the appetite for more but beyond that was a new thing, a sense of responsible involvement. The work of the seven years could not be dropped at convenience if it had meant anything in the first place. He had spoken in parliament and shouted on a thousand platforms of things that could and should be done. They were still to do. He could not go yet.

It was apparent from the first bleak days of February, when the new session opened, that the Liberal party had suffered more than an electoral defeat. It was almost completely demoralized, and the first casualty was Mackenzie himself. He was stunned and disillusioned and his health was failing. He had lost confidence in the country and in himself and he had lost the confidence of the party. Still in his place as leader, he knew that the men who sat with him on the wrong side of the aisle waited impatiently for the hour of his going. Laurier knew it, and shared the feeling. Something must be done, and soon, for the new Macdonald was better than the old had ever been and so was the Conservative party. It had come back to power on the strength of flamboyant promises and a dubious slogan, but it was electric with the vitality and confidence of twelve years before. The Fathers of Confederation were in the saddle again.

Tilley of New Brunswick brought down the new tariff on March 12, fulfilling and more than fulfilling election promises. 'Tell us what you want and we will give you what you need,' Macdonald had said to the manufacturers and industrialists. He had been told and had complied. The country was embarked on the National Policy. It was embarked, too, with overwhelming approval and in high spirits. That was all too apparent as the debate on the budget ran its course and the newspaper editorials and the letters from the constituencies poured in. There was no mistaking the sense of elation and purpose, the new release of vigour. The whole nation seemed quickened by the thought of that towering wall of customs duties to be erected against the United States, and the new factories, industries, jobs, and wealth that would spring up behind it. Cartwright could not withstand the flood of opinion with all his bitter eloquence. Laurier was half-hearted even in the attempt. He had no convictions on the tariff. He did not need Cartwright to tell him that the natural channels of continental trade ran north and south, that tariffs were artificial barriers delaying a certain future, that reciprocity and probably union with the United States were the obvious national destiny. All that had been a part of his own thinking since the days of the Dorions. But Confederation itself was an artificial thing, built in defiance of geography and economics, dependent on sentiments and times and men. Macdonald, if he had not quite made Confederation, was determined to preserve it. He was the master of government, the man for this country, alive to its needs and mood. Once more he had caught a new tide at the full and the tide was irresistible.

On May 10 Tupper brought down the first proposal for the building of the transcontinental railway, and once more Liberal policy was dwarfed to insignificance. The country was to build the railway in co-operation with the Imperial government. One hundred million acres of land were to be appropriated. All the ungranted lands within twenty miles of the line of the road were to be set apart as a railway reserve. The plan in its reckless scope was only a proposal as yet. It was obvious that the government were muddled in their minds as to how to go about the work. Yet it was equally clear that they were determined, and even clearer that they had caught the imagination of the country.

Blake, the deadliest enemy of the railway, was not in the House. A sick man, recovering in England when the general election came on, he had been defeated *in absentia*. Without him

SIR RICHARD CARTWRIGHT, DRAWN BY HENRI JULIEN

the Liberals sat planless, disorganized, and irritable, attacking rainbow hopes. They could point out that the government was chasing a mirage in its search for English money. There were no completed surveys, there was no idea of how the line was to run. The government was mortgaging the lands of future generations in pursuit of a wild dream.

There was truth in every argument and few of the thrusts could be answered. Yet the formless plan had a stubborn life of its own. The session came to an end with everything hanging fire but talk of the railway went on. A long interval in Arthabaska provided no relief from it; it loomed as the first business of the session of 1880. Tupper rose in April to admit that the hope of Imperial support had been given up, but he came with another plan. This time the government would build the railway and a hundred million acres of land would be sold to provide the money. By June, as charges of frauds and frauds-to-be filled the air and every estimate of cost soared above the last, the work on the second project ground to a stop. Yet it was only a pause; Liberals might watch and carp but there would be another proposal, this session or the next.

3

BLAKE CAME BACK, by way of a by-election, for the session of 1880. Laurier knew him better now, and welcomed him. Yet once again the great grey man with the tired eyes and the firm and gentle mouth brought a sense of strain coupled with the sense of power. He returned, as he always seemed to return, reluctantly, dreading the work that would be thrust on him. That was the way of Blake and like many of his ways it was often boring and irritating. Yet few among even the seamiest politicians of the party doubted his sincerity. Laurier certainly did not. Blake was back because he felt he was needed, because

SIR CHARLES TUPPER, DRAWN BY HENRI JULIEN

he was convinced that the government's plan for the Pacific railway would destroy all hope for the orderly development of the country.

He was hardly in his seat before the manoeuvres began around him. The ailing Mackenzie, bitter and remote, was now a stranger who met his leaders only on a basis of cold formality. He had not called a caucus since the beginning of the session. He sat with Blake at his side, fully aware that most of the party wished to have Blake in his place, aware too that for once Blake was willing. He had no doubt himself as to who was the better man; he had offered the leadership many times but now his sick stubbornness would not permit him to make a move. When the move came, on April 26, it came from the party whip.

Laurier spent that day in his room at the Russell Hotel, sick, and glad to be sick. He had no stomach for the caucus called without Mackenzie's authority and less for the business that would have to follow. Yet he was quite as involved as the other leaders and quite of their mind. Three of them called on him that evening, with Cartwright at their head, to report that a resolution had been passed asking Mackenzie 'to consider the question of the leadership'. The next morning he went with a delegation of five to Mackenzie's office in the House of Commons.

One of the five, the genial Pelletier from Quebec, always dreading unpleasantness, detached himself from Laurier's side at the doorway. The other four went in, greeted the tall Scot standing grimly at the desk, and fumbled through some uneasy commonplaces. Burpee of New Brunswick brought the conversation around to the business at last. The party, he said, had held a caucus yesterday.

It amounted in itself almost to an act of deposition. 'Yes.' Mackenzie's voice was gruff. 'I heard about that.'

In the pause that followed, the reluctant Pelletier edged into the room. Mackenzie turned to him. 'Pelletier,' he said, 'is this not simply a conspiracy to put Blake in?'

'No, Mr. Mackenzie,' Pelletier stammered, 'we thought that in your state of health —'

'There is nothing the matter with my health. It is all a conspiracy of a few men.'

There was another pause, lengthening out painfully. Laurier broke it at last. 'As a sincere friend of yours, Mr. Mackenzie, I must tell you that it is not so. There is a general movement. We have been defeated, you have been defeated. It is only human nature', he went on lamely, 'that a defeated army should seek another general. There is not a man who has not a high regard for your services, but there is a general feeling –'

'Very well,' Mackenzie broke in. 'If that is so, I shall very soon cease to lead the Liberal party.'

The House sat late that night and it was two in the morning before adjournment approached. Just as business was nearing conclusion Mackenzie rose in his place. 'Mr. Speaker,' he said, 'I desire to say a word or two with regard to my personal relations to the House. I yesterday determined to withdraw from my position as leader of the opposition and from this time forth I will speak and act for no person but myself.'

The first Liberal of the Dominion had withdrawn to the status of a private member, never again to attend a party caucus. The next morning Blake accepted the leadership. He had not sought it this time any more than he had sought it in the past. He was to speak of it as 'the crown of thorns' and crown of thorns it would be. Cartwright, for all he had done to make him, would never accept him. 'Master' Blake, always the indispensable, would be always the stone in his path, somehow blocking the way. There were many, for many reasons, who would sympathize with Cartwright's impatience if not his ambitions, who would share his angry derision of this soul-searching intellectual, this man of icy logic, who could never quite come down to the level of party politics.

Laurier was not yet close to Blake, but he was close enough to assess the shortcomings. Politics, for a man so utterly conscientious and so often sick, was strain and drudgery. He was thin-skinned and difficult to approach. There was kindliness and a real hunger for friendship under the cold mask, but it was all too rarely communicated. There was little of humour, none of the easy *bonhomie* that linked disparate men into a party. There was something instead that went beyond all that. This man approached his work utterly incorruptible in pocket and mind.

One felt genius here, and more than that, devotion; politics became what politics should be. Laurier was invited to take the desk beside the leader's on the front benches. He accepted with pride, alacrity, and a curious sense of excitement. He was coming into his own; the years with Blake had begun.

4

THE SESSION ended with the battle of the railway still uneasily suspended, waiting the next proposal. 'I have thrown myself so completely into my own business', Laurier wrote to Mackenzie from Ottawa on June 12, 'that I can scarcely give any thought to politics of late.' Politics was a painful subject to the old leader, with whom he was still on good terms, and the words were kindly meant. They were only true, however, if they were true at all, in relation to the wider scene. On the slippery local ground he had to be forever on the watch.

He seemed to be two men, exchanging identities at the dividing line of the Ottawa. In the federal House and in the federal caucus he was the leader for Quebec, speaking with the voice of French-Canadian liberalism. At home he was all too well aware how little the title meant. In Ottawa only Langevin the Conservative, sitting at Macdonald's right hand, was the great protagonist. Here at home there was no man who was quite an enemy or quite a friend, and it was here that whatever claim he had to leadership rested.

Chapleau was premier of the province now, officially Langevin's supporter, officially Laurier's enemy. Yet Chapleau disliked, despised, and envied Langevin. He was as bitterly at war as any *Rouge* could be with the ultramontanes of his own party. He fought the effects of the Catholic Program with the blunt honesty of Cartier, but he fought it as leader of an almost bankrupt province with the threads of corrupt promotions tangling his feet. Successive *Bleu* governments had generously supported Adélard Sénécal in building part of the North Shore Railway which ran along the bank of the St. Lawrence linking Quebec, Montreal, and Ottawa. Malodorous with jobbery and defects, it was the money-devouring monster from which all troubles stemmed, but Sénécal stood at Chapleau's right hand, managing the whole to his profit and convenience. At the premier's left stood Dansereau, the invaluable journalist and organizer who was beginning to be known as 'Boss' Dansereau. The province snickered and groaned now at the doings of the 'Holy Trinity', and the ultramontanes, who were at least honest, fought it for once on other grounds than religion. Chapleau, harassed by dour churchmen and clinging to unsavoury friends, was groping for a way out. If he could abandon his ultramontanes and align his remaining *Bleus* with provincial *Rouges*, he would be in a totally new position. He was prepared to consider an alliance.

Laurier was not. He had no desire to deliver Chapleau from his troubles by making new enemies. Ultramontanism, cut away and isolated, would be bitterer than ever before. There would be a drift of honest men from anyone sheltering the 'Trinity'. The *Rouges*, linked with Chapleau, tainted with the taint of Sénécal, and still at war with the Church, would have no ground to stand on.

On the other hand Honoré Mercier was tempted, and that official friend was looming taller. Mercier, like Chapleau, was a year older than Laurier. Unlike Chapleau, he had turned away from Cartier at the time of Confederation. He had all Chapleau's flair and Cartier's thirst for bigness, but the strain of Papineau nationalism ran in him confusingly. After a brilliant start as a *Rouge* in the first parliament of Canada, he had gone into temporary eclipse as a lawyer and journalist. He was now ready to emerge and Chapleau's hand was beckoning. The marriage, if made, would be a powerful combination in which two ruthless politicians each looked confidently to superseding the other. It would be a combination of expedience, however, and it would omit Laurier. It might well be the end of Laurier, for either man could step to the federal stage. Chapleau was better as an enemy and Mercier could be trusted as a friend only to the moment when he decided to become a rival.

For this summer, beyond the watching, there was only one positive step. In July Laurier, with a group of his friends in Quebec, started another newspaper on its perilous way. It was to be a longer, stormier way than anyone dared predict, and it was to be marked with more achievements. Laurier would never be quite proud of *L'Electeur,* but it would be his staff and spear-head in the province. The choice of editor, hardly a matter of doubt, had been settled by the Conservative government that ejected the Prothonotary of Three Rivers from the dreary sine-cure provided by Liberal friends. Ernest Pacaud, as he joyfully forsook his rubber stamps and came to the new chair, had settled to his life's work.

With September came the announcement of the federal gov-ernment's third railway plan. A syndicate of private capitalists headed by George Stephen of Montreal was to raise the money for the work. Soon to emerge as the breezy genius in charge of it was the builder William Van Horne. The agreement with the syndicate was concluded in October, subject to the ratification of parliament. In December, two months earlier than usual, the House was convened and Laurier was back in his seat. On December 14 Tupper rose to present the government's two resolutions for the building of the Canadian Pacific Railway.

It was one of the times when parliament came into its own and men seemed a little bigger than they were, clothed with the dignity and weighted with the burdens of government. Every-where along the crowded benches there was the feeling that the country stood at a crossroads. Few men in the House had much respect for Tupper, the man who had bludgeoned Nova Scotia into Confederation, the eternal egoist and self-seeker, the politi-cian's politician who had none of the grace, none of the saving humour that won Macdonald forgiveness for so much. Yet they sat impressed and subdued by the greatness of the project he unfolded and the burly confidence with which he advanced it. There was, for once, conviction and sincerity here and they wove through even the turgid phrases of his peroration. 'I can only say in concluding, after some five-and-twenty years of pub-lic life, that . . . if I have no other bequest to leave my children after me, the proud legacy I would desire to leave is the record that I was able to take an active part in the production of this great measure by which, I believe, Canada will receive an impetus that will make it a great and powerful country at no distant date.'

When Blake rose there was silence of a different kind, in

which respect for the man was mingled with the sense of a losing cause. There was little doubt as to how the vote would go, but if Blake was right it would leave a bitter legacy. He was mordantly sarcastic as he directed his first stinging words at the men of the Pacific scandal who were again before the House with a railway project. Every man on the benches was affected by the passionate force he brought to bear against it. 'If I did not believe, as I do in my heart and conscience believe, that the proposal of the administration is not merely fraught with danger to the country which they say it is designed to serve, I should be glad to give it my support. It is because I entertain the conviction that the measure is not merely dangerous but ruinous that I oppose it at the very outset.'

They listened for a time, still respectfully, as he launched into a vast and detailed analysis of the plan, subsiding only gradually into apathy, as they did too often while listening to Blake, under the deluge of facts and figures that only he could marshal and only he grasp. 'The cost of the railway in cash $88,500,000 . . . from Thunder Bay to the Red River $17,000,000 . . . Pembina Branch $1,750,000 . . . Red River to Jasper House Pass $13,000,000 . . . Jasper House Pass to Kamloops $15,500,000', and on, and on. 'To construct the Pacific Railway . . . a plan which does not relieve us from the burden of its construction . . . which obligates us to go on spending our money for years to come . . . which would involve . . . the total cession of twenty-five million acres of our choicest lands and which hands over to a private corporation the whole profit of that expenditure and a vast monopoly.'

Laurier rose to speak on December 21, echoing Blake, commenting sardonically on the succession of plans and proposals that had been introduced and withdrawn, 'withered as the flowers of summer'. The government 'had created a monster that threatened their own destruction. What was to be done? They went to Europe. They offered their white elephant for sale in the markets of Paris and London, but no one would accept it even as a gift. Finally they had to take the beast home.'

His objections were Blake's objections, his fears were Blake's fears. His only additional service was to put a point on the vast and cumbrous argument of the leader. 'The contract now before us is the last and crowning consequence of the principle laid down ten years ago by the government then in power – that the railway should be built immediately and without interruption until its completion. I have never heard expressed here the opinion that the Canadian Pacific Railway should not be built, but the policy of the Liberals is that it should be built gradually as the wants of the country require and its resources permit. I hold that the adoption of this contract would be a great calamity to the Dominion at large. Twenty-five million acres of land are to be given to this company and are to be locked up at the option of the company. The company have the privilege to hold these lands and like the dog in the manger to prevent anyone using them except themselves. It must be evident to every dispassionate observer that it is a monstrous monopoly and one that will make the company landlords of the Northwest. If the road had been gradually and step by step constructed there might in a few years have been a few less millionaires in this country, but there would have been a much greater number of happy and contented homes.'

He had slipped, perhaps unconsciously, into the past tense. All the resistance was to no purpose: the railway was going to be built to the government's plan. On February 1, 1881, after six weeks of desperate manoeuvring and powerful debate broken only by the Christmas recess, the bill was passed. 'The C.P.R.', wrote John A. Macdonald from the sick-bed to which his exertions had sent him, 'is a fixed fact.'

'THINGS MUST BE TAKEN AS THEY ARE'

1881-1884

BLAKE HAD failed, and Laurier had failed at his side. All the tides in the country seemed to be rolling the wrong way. Beyond the next session loomed the prospect of another general election and an almost certain defeat. The National Policy was in its first bloom and the building of the railway would soon be pumping millions into the country's veins. There would be no standing against this flood of easy prosperity. Ahead there were long years of waiting and opposition while the fixed facts of the nation grew in the Tory mould. Yet all this, in the company of Blake, had its dignity and compensations. Politics in Quebec was quite another matter.

Chapleau's position remained what it had been, and the threat of provincial bankruptcy was hovering over his head. Yet he only grew more dangerous. His overtures to Mercier, continued, well in the open now, and many of the *Rouges* were weakening. The party was dividing into factions for coalition and factions against, into Laurier men and men who wavered with Mercier. In the subterranean gropings where nothing turned on principle there was a constant threat of division and a constant reek of corruption.

The only principles lay with the ultramontanes and they, rigidly upright and grimly wrong-headed, stood for a renewal of religious war. For the rest the struggle turned on power, money, and the North Shore Railway. The sale of the road was Chapleau's one hope of restoring the provincial treasury, and Chapleau's prospective purchaser was Louis-Adélard Sénécal. As administrator of the road Sénécal had disposed of contracts, tariffs, and jobs to his own sweet will. Now, with a view to buying the line cheap, he was running its value into the ground, multiplying costs, overloading the staff, and generally wrecking the property. The scandal was so open that the vocabulary of the people had been enlarged to include 'Sénécalize' as a synonym for 'steal', yet the author of it all had played his cards so well that few politicians and no party were quite free either of involvement or temptation. The member for Quebec East had returned from Ottawa to a treacherous provincial swamp. He might well go down in it if Chapleau should capture Mercier with Sénécal blessing the union.

He had not been home a month before *L'Electeur* came into its own. On April 20, 1881, the forewarned and delighted Ernest Pacaud received an envelope with a bulky enclosure. That evening, spread across most of his editorial space, appeared a long anonymous article headed 'The Den of the Forty Thieves'.

It would hardly have been believed in Ottawa that the diatribe could have come from the pen of the mild-mannered Laurier. For long weeks it was not believed in Quebec. Having decided to strike, he struck with a venom enriched by old associations. 'The Den of the Forty Thieves', said the article, 'is not in the heart of a forest. The robbers who seek refuge in it are not obscure bandits, hidden by day and prowling by night. They strut through the streets, they drink at the public bars, the smoke of their cigars is found everywhere. This den of robbers is the administration of the Northern Railway, and the name of the chief of the band is Louis-Adélard Sénécal.'

He went on to itemize corruption so thoroughly that the letter presented an inescapable challenge to the *Sénécaleux*, an open threat to the government, and a warning to any *Rouge* who might have thoughts of joining it. Then he waited, at peace with himself in Arthabaska, while in Quebec Pacaud fended off the first desperate attempts to establish the author's identity. On May 27, having given up hope that the writer was small fry who could be easily silenced, Sénécal swore out a warrant instituting a $100,000 libel suit against the business manager of *L'Electeur*. The comedy of the law began in Montreal a few days later when Laurier, appearing as counsel to the business manager, announced that he knew the real author, but would not divulge the name. It was hardly necessary by now; his appearance in court had been enough for the 'Holy Trinity'. He engaged in some legal sparring intended to force a change of venue from Montreal to Quebec where the climate was more favourable to a Liberal, and when this failed he named himself as the writer. The learned counsel became the accused, the hearing adjourned till autumn, and the hapless accusers faced a long, uneasy summer.

Laurier himself went off with Pacaud for a first tour of Nova Scotia in the company of Blake. The enlargement and refreshment provided by new territory and a month of close association with the leader were immensely welcome, and he was glad on his return that he had removed Pacaud as well as himself from the superheated atmosphere of Quebec. That summer had not been a time for the little man's valiant indiscretions.

The scramble of politicians was frantic now. Chapleau, face to face with the necessities of a provincial election, still tugged at Mercier but could not abandon Sénécal. The thought of the votes those muddy hands controlled figured in all calculations. It was soon clear, however, that Mercier's choice was made, or had been made for him. While the contents of that letter still reverberated and were still to be aired in court there could be no thought of any link with Chapleau. In September Mercier took to the stumps at the head of the provincial *Rouges*, free of entanglements, virtuous and indignant. Laurier followed, echoing the same note. 'It would dishonour the name of government', he said, 'to call by that name those who govern us. The name they deserve is that of organized rapine and pillage.' Two months later, well prepared and still in a fighting mood, he entered the Court of Queen's Bench to be tried for libel.

Mercier came as his counsel and was assisted by two other distinguished members of the bar, George Irvine of Quebec and C. A. Geoffrion of Montreal. It soon developed, however, that the plan of defence involved the participation of Laurier. He had not been half an hour on the stand before the defendant became the attacker, reading out from a prepared brief a long list of Sénécal's misdoings. It was a shattering and detailed charge and Monk, the presiding judge, whose affiliations were all *Bleu*, became distinctly irritable. He had been taken off guard by the manoeuvre but he was not to be caught again. Three days later, after a lame development of the prosecution's case and a slashing defence by Mercier which transferred the election campaign to the courtroom, the time came for the summing up. Irvine, who was to deliver it, became suddenly bashful over his ability to speak in French. Mercier had been taken ill; Geoffrion was absent for unannounced reasons. It would be best, proposed Irvine, if the defendant were to be allowed to speak for himself.

'The Court', said Mr. Justice Monk, 'desires you should address the jury.'

'I cannot express myself sufficiently well in French to have the courage to address the jury in a case like the present,' protested Irvine. 'We have the right, admitted by the Court, to address the jury –'

'Address it.'

'Will the Court allow me –'

'I invite you to address the jury.'

After a few minutes more of it, punctuated by the remarks of opposing counsel who pointed out that for many years Mr. Irvine had done very well in French before Quebec courts, Laurier rose to ask permission himself.

'You make an appeal which touches me very much,' said Monk acidly, and turned to Irvine. 'I call on you, Mr. Irvine, to reply. If you will not, the counsel for prosecution may proceed.'

Irvine sat down and folded his arms. Opposing counsel proceeded, uneasily aware that the defendant's summation by silence had been as effective as speech and was hardly necessary in any case. The verdict bore him out. Nine of the jurors were for Laurier's acquittal, three against, and there was no prospect that the hung trial would be resumed. Sénécal, at least as a political force, had been whittled down forever.

The high constable and all his staff could not silence the

cheers in the courtroom. There was a great procession to Mercier's house and more cheers for Laurier, who spoke from the veranda. The party was saved in Quebec, at least for the moment. The fall of *Le Défricheur* and the defeat in Drummond-Arthabaska had been well avenged. Yet three weeks later a hardened Quebec electorate returned Chapleau to power. 'Corruption', wrote Laurier to Blake, 'pervades every tissue of our society.'

2

THE GENERAL election was six months away and he went to the last session of the fourth parliament expecting only the worst. He was not disappointed. Echoes of the Confederation debates came back, faintly and ominously, as Macdonald intervened in the old dispute over northern boundary lines between Ontario, Quebec, and Manitoba. It turned formally on the interpretation of a maze of treaties and an arbitration award that Macdonald refused to accept. In the view of the opposition, however, it was part of the ancient quarrel between Macdonald and his former law student, Oliver Mowat, who was a Liberal and premier of Ontario. Macdonald's aim, ran the argument, was to cut down Mowat by cutting down his territory.

Laurier, as a federal Liberal, was forced to the side of Mowat. Under the glare of a land-hungry Quebec he had to come out four-square for Ontario's case. He had to plead that 'the eternal principles of justice are far more important than thousands of millions of acres of land', and in doing so, if he had strengthened the party in Ontario he had certainly weakened himself in Quebec.

It was not going to matter greatly so far as the election was concerned, for Macdonald had made assurance doubly sure. As a new census brought the need for a redistribution of constituencies the hand of the venerable politician, now edging into his sixty-eighth year, had moved with cynical skill. He had 'hived the grits', lopping off Liberals from doubtful seats, huddling them together in their few sure strongholds, leaving his Tories everywhere reinforced. Yet his change in the electoral map had merely broadened the smile of a country already smiling on him.

Manufacturers were growing into rich and convinced Conservatives on the fruits of the National Policy. The end of steel for the eastern section of the railway was only 965 miles from Winnipeg and the western section was four miles short of the summit of the Rockies. Sixty thousand settlers had poured into Manitoba and the street-stakes of Winnipeg were reaching out for miles into the surrounding prairie. There was no withstanding such a boom and on June 20, 1882, the Liberals went down as crushingly as before.

It was three weeks after the election before Laurier could bring himself to write to Blake. He wrote still as member for Quebec East and clothed in a new dignity as Mayor of Arthabaska, but his words came from an exhausted and depressed campaigner. 'I had not and have not yet the heart to speak of what has taken place. Elsewhere . . . there is cause for hope, but we in Quebec have nothing to hope.'

Blake, sitting amid the wreckage of Ontario, asked for the causes of defeat in Quebec. There were all the old ones, said Laurier, still operating and hardly changed. The bribed politicians bribed an ignorant electorate. The clergy browbeat them. 'The great mass . . . never read, and remain as much in the dark as to what is going on in this country as if they were residing in Europe.' The educated men still came from the Catholic colleges, trained by Conservative priests. 'Very good men they are indeed, but prejudiced, biased and, except upon those branches of which they have made a specialty, very ignorant. Very ignorant especially are they of modern history . . . they have imbibed a horror of the very name of liberalism . . . their pupils, when they leave the school, are ignorant but fanatic conservatives.'

With the exception of a half-dozen sheets like *L'Electeur*, there was no Liberal press in the province and, though he did not say it to Blake, there was almost no Liberal party. For that matter there was hardly a recognizable Conservative party. Chapleau, restored to power, had sold the North Shore Railway, and the section that Sénécal coveted had gone to him. But the money from the sale was spent; Chapleau was once more facing provincial bankruptcy and still groping for allies. His ultramontane enemies were becoming a party in themselves, with the beaver for an emblem and Castor for a name. The Liberals, fragmenting into smaller and smaller groups, had played almost no part in the general election, and Mercier was edging away again in the direction of Chapleau. The party of *Rouge* and *Bleu,* the party 'all for Quebec' was once more in the air.

Laurier was painfully clear as to the course that this movement would take, at least in its preliminary stages. Quebec, with its chronically empty pockets, would move into the federal arena demanding 'better terms'. Like every other province she had legitimate enough grievances, but the first claim would not be among them. The story of the North Shore Railway was far from ended yet. Sénécal and his two blossoming soul-mates, the brothers McGreevy, had now re-sold their section and it was being restored to something like working order as a part of the eastern network of the new Canadian Pacific Railway. But it was the credit of the province of Quebec that had largely built the line in the first place, and the C.P.R. was a national undertaking. Quebec, as the politicians would soon make clear, had contributed to the national undertaking several years in advance. The first descent on Ottawa, if and when it came, would be with the demand for a retroactive subsidy. Every other province would be furiously opposed and Quebec would stand once more in surly isolation.

The dismal prospect brightened a little in July. Chapleau, exhausted, sick, and still unable to bring Mercier to terms, gave up the fight at last. It was a surrender ultimately to be fatal in its consequences for him, but well disguised at the moment, since he went to Ottawa as Secretary of State in Macdonald's cabinet. For Liberals the balance of many confused forces was now shifted, and rather hopefully. Chapleau's protégé, Mousseau, who succeeded in Quebec, had been a long-time target for Laurier in the federal House. He was distinguished mainly for genial avoirdupois and would not be likely to dominate any coalition in which Mercier was involved. Coalition, if it came now, might result in a general *mêlée* out of which a real provincial Liberal party might emerge. In Ottawa Macdonald, who had long wanted Chapleau, might have rather more than he bargained for. There was certain to be trouble with Langevin and there might be more with Caron, the ultramontane-tinged politician who ranked as second of the French Canadians in the cabinet. Even the faintest prospect of a crack in that strong wall of Tory power was welcome, and Laurier left for the opening session of the fifth parliament with less reluctance than he had expected.

There was the usual contrast, during the ceremonies of opening day, between Macdonald in his cocked hat and Privy Councillor's uniform and Blake in his rumpled tweeds. It was rather more painful this time, even though the Prime Minister obviously considered himself a little ridiculous in the finery and Blake did not notice. The reign of Macdonald extended now into an indefinite future. Blake, discouraged by failure, sick of politics, and troubled with all the old doubts of his fitness as a party leader, was talking of resignation. Laurier had known for three months that the intention was more than talk and he had written long letters of dissuasion. Now, as the two met face to face, he was more than ever convinced that the tired man would be held to his post with difficulty but that he must be held. With Blake, the party – weak, dejected, and rejected as it seemed – had dignity and stature. Without him it would simply dissolve into quarrelling politicians. 'Who else is there?' was the always-repeated question and among all the ambitious, able, jostling men, rankled by defeat, there was no claimant. Even Cartwright would not look to a future without Blake. The main business of the session, so far as Laurier was concerned, was to keep him, strengthen him, and ease his way.

It was work he had already begun in previous sessions and it was to continue for several more. Sitting at the next desk, he began to be regarded almost as the leader's secretary. Most of the debates went on without him. Blake spoke while Laurier kept his references in order, handed him Hansards and Blue Books, brought the page-boys running to clear the litter on the desk and keep the water-glass filled. It had all come about quite naturally and it was all a pleasure. To respect for Blake's powers had now been added a warm intimacy with the man himself. They both read incessantly, often the same books, though Blake read more. Laurier, whose days seemed full enough, was often appalled and mystified at the flow of volumes on every conceivable subject that went to Blake from the parliamentary library.

He was more aware than ever of Blake's failings as a party man. The little word or the easy laugh would never come. Blake was never found with his hand on a member's shoulder. Always chilly and self-conscious, he was sometimes a bore as well. And yet, in the presence of that wide-ranging intellect, that broad and tolerant understanding, the heroes of so much of Laurier's old reading in the study at Arthabaska seemed to come alive again. This was the political Englishman at his best, this was a man who could stand with Burke and Fox, with the younger Pitt and the later Bright, with all those who had cut the channel for the stream of liberty that flowed today, guarded by the forms and facts of parliamentary government. One could never doubt, with such a man, that it would flow equally for the French as for the English. With Blake Laurier did not feel himself a politician of Quebec, perpetually suspicious and on watch; he was a partner, engaged on the business of a nation. He was a Canadian with Blake, sometimes a little envious of those high qualities, sometimes a little imitative. There were even times, especially when the reports came in from Pacaud, that one turned to Blake with an angry shame over the ceaseless bickerings and squalid turmoil of the home province.

He was hardly concerned at all by the fact that he himself seemed to be fading as a public figure. He knew that he was sometimes glanced at curiously as one of the bright young sparks of parliament who flare and flicker out. He was 'the lazy Laurier' to the newspapers when they noticed him at all, 'the tall, elegant, and gracious Mr. Laurier', and he rather fostered the impression of the political dilettante. He had got himself a good tailor and elegance was becoming habitual, though he still wore the horseshoe scarf-pin chosen by Phoebe Gauthier. His constant bouts of sickness often left him so weak that he could hardly force himself from bed, and physical frailty was one of the sides of himself that he hesitated to reveal to the English. It was better to be known as lazy, and the lazy man was liked. Friendships came easily and held and grew, because friendship in him was effortless. He had been blessed with sympathy for men and their concerns, and it lay in him deeper than race or party dogma. There were few desks on either side of the aisle where he was not welcome for a chat, and on the dull days in the House when Blake was not involved there was always a sunny alcove in the parliamentary library where he could uncoil his long legs, bury himself in a book, and let the nation go on without him.

It seemed quite content to do so through the sessions of 1882 and 1883. Little that Blake and nothing that Laurier said could have any effect on prospering Tory fortunes. Chapleau was duly at odds with Langevin in Ottawa, Mousseau was a failure in Quebec, but the state of the provincial Liberals was worse. Even Pacaud seemed lost amid the confusion and Laurier was constantly rapping the editorial knuckles. Scolded from Ottawa or Arthabaska, pulled about by all the conflicting factions of Quebec, the little man was converting *L'Electeur* into more of a liability than an asset. Loyal as Pacaud was, his heart lay with the local faction and he was zigzagging in the wake of Mercier while still begging Laurier for guidance. 'Why should I take it upon myself to lead the party', Laurier answered him at the end of 1883, 'when my views are not those of the party? I know that my conception of the duties of a public man appears too rigid and too naïve. I am not entering into any controversy on these points for it would be to no purpose. My views are very definite and I could not change them.'

The letter was written as he was getting ready to leave Arthabaska for the session of 1884, and some of the righteous irritation came from the failure of many attempts to hold Mercier in line. More of it came from worry as to what lay ahead. The C.P.R., now bucking its way through the worst of the wild country, was achieving miracles of construction at appalling costs. It was going to need more money, and above all things else for the moment money was in demand at Quebec. Laurier's old broodings on the North Shore road came back to haunt him. Quebec politicians would have a loud and perhaps deciding voice on the subject of the C.P.R.; they would not be likely to forget the other railway.

The session opened on January 17, and on Friday February 1, Tupper rose in his place. Droning through eleven long resolutions, he asked the assent of the House to a government loan of twenty-two and a half million dollars to rescue the half-built C.P.R. from bankruptcy.

It was a breath-taking change from the rosy hopes of three years before, sweetened only a little by the promise that if the advance was made the railway would be completed in five years instead of ten. The Liberals moved to the attack and Blake was mighty in the vindication of his first forebodings. Laurier, when his turn came, saw no advantage in the promise of earlier completion. He saw the twenty-two millions as gone forever: 'I would as soon believe that the waters would flow back from the sea to the lakes as that one cent of money will ever come back from the Pacific Railway exchequer to the Dominion exchequer.'

Yet he knew as surely as Blake that the resolutions must pass. For better or worse, the railway was inextricably involved with the country now, and the country could not fail. He listened to the rest of the debate with half an ear, waiting for the move from Quebec. On February 14 it came.

Mousseau and the entire provincial cabinet, supported by Langevin, Chapleau, and Caron, descended on Macdonald with the demand for a retroactive subsidy to compensate the province for the building of the North Shore Railway. Behind the federal ministers in an almost solid block were the forty-eight Quebec federal Conservatives, and behind Mousseau and his cabinet most of the provincial Liberals stood shoulder to shoulder with the *Bleus*. On this question at least the parties had coalesced and they came with the thinly-veiled threat that so far as Quebec was concerned no money for the North Shore Railway meant no money for the C.P.R.

Macdonald, with a crucial vote impending and a club over his head, had only one course. The C.P.R. resolutions were passed with Quebec support and a resolution followed granting the province of Quebec $2,394,000 'in consideration of their having constructed the railway from Quebec to Ottawa . . . a work of national and not merely provincial utility'.

The country had been endowed with another national and not merely provincial quarrel. Blake rose at once, reflecting the anger of all the English provinces. Laurier, when his turn came, had a speech of Chapleau to answer. A hot exchange of correspondence with Pacaud had left him in no doubt as to the state of feeling at home. Quebec might have raided the federal treasury, but it had been a successful raid. It would be political suicide to let Mousseau and his party take all the credit. On this question, for this once, said Pacaud, the *Rouges* must go with the *Bleus*. Laurier had been furiously angry but he was cooler now and he knew what he was doing. He had had a good many years to think it out, and it was at times like these that the prospect of private life became attractive. There was a very good possibility as he spoke, entirely in French this time, lecturing Quebec rather than addressing the House, that he was consigning himself to the repose of Arthabaska.

'It is always a fault, I think, on the part of a minority,' he said, 'and we are a minority in this House, to attempt to throw obstacles in the way of a government to force them to do a thing against their will.' If the Pacific resolutions were just and reasonable it had been Quebec's duty to adopt them; if they were unjust and unreasonable it had been equally a duty to oppose. 'I think that if there is in the Dominion', he added deliberately, 'a body of men who should always adhere to the principles of justice it is the Quebec contingent in this House.'

It had little effect on the vote and less on his own electors. He had cut away more of the ground beneath his feet, and land-grabbing, money-grabbing Quebec was at odds with the English provinces. A month later he was turned in a new direction, facing a different threat. It came, oblique and innocuous at first sight, from a bill designed to give the federal government power to regulate the liquor traffic in the provinces. There was certainly much to be said for uniform administration, and Macdonald said it. To Liberals with their eyes on Ontario, however, it was another attack on Mowat, diabolically planned to rob him of the control of liquor licensing and all the patronage that went with it. To the Liberal from Quebec, who remembered all too well the predictions of the Dorions, it was an invasion of provincial rights.

'The placing of the present law on the statute books is, in my opinion, an attack on the powers of the province.' He was not surprised, said Laurier, that Macdonald proposed the change. 'He is consistent, he is true to himself. Whether acting consciously from design or moved by the unconscious bent of his mind I cannot say, but he is all the time gradually approaching toward a legislative union. I say that every successful attempt made on the floor of this parliament to deprive any province of any power now exercised by that province, however insignificant, is a successful step in the direction of legislative union. We are all aware that the fact of our having the present system of Confederation is largely due to the peculiar position of the province of Quebec. I still submit that the best system, the only system, by which to govern this great territory is a federative and not a legislative union. Our municipal and provincial divisions, our federal system, all these wheels within wheels, constitute a mechanism which is at once elastic and strong. Therefore I say that this system is the best which can be devised and it behooves every man in this parliament, every friend of this country, to see that no attempt is made upon this form of government.'

Again Macdonald won his vote in the House. Two years later the Act would be declared invalid by the Privy Council, and the lawyer could see that coming. Yet the politician could feel the trend of greater forces and see no strength to withstand them. If anything, such strength as remained was diminishing. Blake, in a great attack on the incorporation of the Orange Order in Ontario, had struck a mighty blow against bigotry and intolerance; he had also shaken his Ontario members and alienated perhaps a fifth of the voting strength of the province. Laurier went home to a divided Quebec with new divisions behind him. The years in parliament had done much for him, and the years with Blake more. He believed now, or half-believed, in the strength and value of this Confederation. But its wheels within wheels were meshing in ominous ways.

3

IN SPITE OF it all there was more to life than politics, and life on the whole was good. He was now in his forty-third year. The chestnut hair was thinning a little, the dome of the forehead was thrusting out. The nose seemed more dominant and the firmness of that enigmatic mouth was now as noticeable as the gentleness. He had come to terms with his ailments and he was aging well. He had never been tempted to smoke and his drinking was confined to a glass of wine at dinner. Whatever gestures he had once made toward physical exercise had long since been abandoned, but in all the travelling about the country and amid all the ceremonies and convivialities of Ottawa self-discipline had become necessary as a matter of self-preservation. It was now an easy habit, always reinforced by Zoë's care at home.

Through the jovial, rough-and-ready George Landerkin, who was a doctor in Ontario as well as a fellow member in Ottawa, Laurier had been able for the first time to take out some life insurance. He was, according to the application that Landerkin sent in, a man in good health, sound in body and mind, who travelled a little. His weight was 165 pounds, his chest measurement thirty-eight inches, and he was destined to live long. He suffered from bronchitis, he had even spat a little blood years before through over-exposure in an election campaign, but all this had been overcome. True or not, it was good to know that there were three thousand dollars of additional protection for Zoë.

He often complained that politics interfered with the law practice, as it certainly did; but on the other hand the prominent politician was much in demand as a lawyer and he had his choice of many important clients. The others went to Joseph Lavergne, hard-working, loyal, and dependable. The debts dragged along, but they were going down. Money was sometimes a preoccupation of the future but not a present worry. The Lauriers lived up to their station, and it was a high one in Arthabaska, but they could afford it.

Apart from electioneering and political tours the routine of his life gave him most of the year in this high and pleasant country. The depth of the winters and the worst of the wet springs were spent in Ottawa; he had much of the summers in Arthabaska and the best of each autumn. The place was livelier than ever with the comings and goings of relatives and friends, and it was curious and pleasant to find the political enmities suspended too.

Bleus and *Rouges* mingled amicably on his wide lawn under his growing trees and walked in the garden which Zoë still tended lovingly. There were even temporary political hermaphrodites from Ontario and the Maritimes and the west. The young Joseph Pope, Macdonald's private secretary, had been an accidental visitor to the region five years before and had met Laurier. Four years later, as his chief went on to the summer home at Rivière du Loup, Pope had returned to renew the friendship and to meet Minette, the spritely daughter of Henri Taschereau who was also Ernest Pacaud's niece. This summer the two had been married and were much at the Lauriers', making it still more difficult to distinguish friend from enemy. Even the Church had relaxed a little, though there was still flint in its smile. Father Suzor was several years gone from the parish. Bishop Laflèche the unchangeable still reigned at Three Rivers, but from Father Héroux, the new curé of Arthabaska, there had come a cordial letter to Laurier on his return from Ottawa the year before, wishing him long years of good health.

Behind it all the relationship with Zoë was changing. She was the woman of Arthabaska, of the old friends and the old surroundings. He was the man of Quebec and Ottawa and the country, a little remote now, a little conscious of the difficulties of communicating from the new height. It was easier to communicate with Emilie Lavergne, the ever-present neighbour, the woman of Paris and London who loved literature and knew history and understood politics on its higher levels. He saw a great deal of her, with and without Zoë. It was so easy and so pleasant on a dull morning or afternoon to slip across from the office, usually with a book in his hand, and spend an hour or two in the tastefully furnished drawing-room that Joseph Lavergne was still paying for. Here there was always a great deal to talk about and to learn. Emilie had read much, as had Laurier, of the salons of Paris and the women who made great men. It was work to her taste and he was malleable, or seemed so.

'When I bound myself in friendship to Laurier,' she was to say later on, 'I saw very quickly that this young deputy of the future was still in certain ways only the little greenhorn of St-Lin. His wife was not the person who could teach him even those elements of etiquette which a man of the world should know, above all a political man destined by his talents to enter the highest circles. He did not even know the correct way to eat an orange at table. I made him understand that this lack of etiquette would hamper him among the English élite with whom he would be called to mingle in Ottawa. I taught him then to eat, to dress with taste, in a word, all that a gentleman should know. As he was a man of wit, he understood it.'

He understood, perhaps, a little more than Emilie Lavergne quite realized or would quite have desired. He had learned from many people and would learn from more. Yet the game of king-making had gone on with suave ardency by daylight and candle-light, at Arthabaska's soirées and at Emilie Lavergne's high teas and *à deux*. She had certainly inspired a good deal of the Laurier elegance in dress and manner. With her love of all things English she had been an unseen aid to the unconscious Blake in fostering Laurier's Englishness.

Four years before, she had borne a son, Armand, who was now the little serpent in this Arthabaska Eden. It was a very little serpent, much about the house and in and out of the rooms when Laurier was present. Only the low and smutty-minded *Bleus* took the gossip very seriously. Joseph Lavergne did not. He had grown quite accustomed now to Laurier's way of rising at his desk and departing with a casual 'Joseph, if you will permit it I am going to talk with your wife.' When Joseph's brother, Louis Lavergne, had come to him storming at the talk circulating through the town he had listened with a tired smile.

'What do you want me to do?' he had asked. 'You say you don't believe the gossip, and neither do I. I have a good wife. Why humiliate her unjustly? She admires him as I admire him myself. All things considered I prefer to live in peace and let people talk.'

Emilie Lavergne, for her part, rather encouraged the talk, always with impeccable taste. The defenders were more embarrassing. 'I know for a fact Laurier is impotent!' stormed one loyal partisan, and rumour had its day with that. None of it was very serious, and all of it was undying. Zoë would live with it now, she knew, to the end.

She could despise gossip or ignore it, and there was nothing she could do to ease the deeper hurt. The changing man would have changed in spite of the woman and Emilie Lavergne was a part of their lives now. There was much to compensate. The house of the childless couple was always full of children. The nephews and nieces came and stayed each summer. The neighbour youngsters gathered on the lawn for the *fêtes enfantines* that Zoë was making famous. The uninvited were sent out plates of cakes, and sometimes the master carried them. The Laurier way with children seemed much like his way with men, a combination of amused tolerance and affectionate sympathy.

He became a reader of coloured history books on the shaded gallery of the house, turning up pictures of Queen Victoria or Bismarck for his youthful audience, going on about them sometimes a little too long. He abetted the young thieves who slipped over his fence and climbed his apple trees. 'They had no money – how would they get them else?' he asked once, hinting at murky depths of social philosophy. As a public man he attended school closings, awarded prizes, and requested holidays of the principals.

Also as a public man, he was called on in May of 1884 to attend an elaborate reception in Montreal. It was held in the offices of *La Patrie*, a Liberal newspaper that had managed in four years to become both prosperous and influential. It seemed to defy the pessimism with which he had written to Blake two years ago. One could even find in it the hope of better times. He spoke in a mellow mood with the clink of glasses round him.

'I propose', he said, 'to speak to you of parliamentary life,' and went on to run lightly and satirically over the defects of Ottawa and the more antiquated aspects of parliamentary ceremony. He drew a good deal of laughter with his description of the House on opening day, the members like boys at school and the old senators flirting with young wives as they waited for the coming of the Governor General. He was amusing on the solemn platitudes of the Speech from the Throne and on the entry of Black Rod, coming with three knocks and retiring with three bows.

'John Bull', he said, 'seems to take a perennial pleasure in seeing these bows made by a man paid to make them. Every year you hear the same remark, "Well, it's worth the money." '

All such old forms, he told his hearers, might seem absurd. 'I am not too sure of this. I cherish a respect for these old solemnities.' He was more respectful still of the gift of the English for parliamentary debate. The English, he said, 'know how to listen and be tolerant. It is not in the ardent temperament of the French to respect the convictions of others. What the Frenchman conceives he conceives with so much intensity that he cannot admit the possibility of others thinking differently from him . . . While the Frenchman wants you to have his opinions, the Englishman wants you to have opinions of your own . . . We French Canadians do not know how to bear contradiction like our fellow citizens of British origin.

'For us, sons of France, political sentiment is a passion while for the Englishmen politics are a question of business . . . Take an ordinary man of any rank whatever in English society. He knows the figures of the public expenditure and of the receipts, he can tell you the yield of the customs and excise, and he is conversant with every item of the tariff. Now how many are there among us, even among those who shout loudest at election times, who have ever taken the slightest trouble to post themselves on those heads? We . . . are thoroughly acquainted with all the discussions on the school question, on the relative value of the different forms of government, on the theories of divine right, on the union of Church and State and on a host of other abstract questions which have no application to our politics and which have never been discussed in any of our legislative assemblies . . .

'Although there are about fifty French members in the House of Commons, it is exclusively an English assembly. French is its official language as well as English, but French is being less and less spoken in it. The reason for this is that it is impossible to take an effective part in the debates unless you use the language of the majority . . . Things must be taken as they are. Our parliamentary laws, usages, and customs come to us from England. Moreover, the English are better adapted than we are for that system of government. In no matter what deliberative assembly they may find themselves, they are more at home than are the

French, and where they are in the majority their language must necessarily prevail . . .

'The force of circumstances is such that in America the English tongue will always be the language of the million and our ambition should be to make French, here as elsewhere, the language of predilection, good company, and polite society.'

The hot young *Rouge* of 1864 had come a long way. It was a genial address genially delivered in the mellow glow about him. It was already a little in the vein of the elder statesman. It was the testament of a French-Canadian Whig, comfortably preparing to subside in the arms of time, fate, and the English.

9

RIEL

1885-1886

ON JANUARY 29, 1885, he took his seat by Blake for the opening of the third session of the fifth parliament. His Maytime mood had, if anything, been improved by the developments of the late summer and autumn. Fence-mending had gone well. He was still in some trouble over the stand he had taken on the question of the Ontario boundary and the North Shore subsidy, but he had met his critics head on at a large meeting in Quebec. He had worked hard on his speech, Pacaud's arrangements for the gathering had been elaborate, and it had all been a resounding success. What, Laurier had asked, was Quebec's position in the Dominion? It was that of an equal partner, sharing responsibilities as well as privileges. If Quebec made an unjust demand today what would happen tomorrow when Ontario came with its hand out? The point was well made and better taken after the cooling-off period, and Quebec, as successful culprit, seemed inclined to accept the reproof. Even Israel Tarte had come round so far at least as to admit that Ontario should not follow the bad example.

There were intriguing possibilities for the future in this softening of Tarte, and for the present Mercier was much more amenable. He came for advice, he extended invitations for fishing-trips, and even though the trips did not come off the other angling went on. There seemed every likelihood that in a year or so Mercier would head a smoothly co-operative Liberal provincial government. The state of the *Bleus* was more lamentable than ever. The coalition that had got the railway subsidy had dissolved with the signing of the cheque. Mousseau had been replaced as premier by a successor who was even less effective. The Castors were only achieving the disintegration of the party. Chapleau, restless, ineffective, and intrigued-against in Ottawa, battled the ultramontanes from the stumps of Quebec. On the mingling of priests and politicians he now out-Lauriered Laurier. 'Woe to him who uses religion as a footstool!' The Castors, he said, resembled the beaver only in the fact that they did their work with mud. They destroyed the sluices of good mills to build their dens; they were only useful when their hides were sold.

Langevin was already jealous of Chapleau and afraid of him. So, with more reason and more intensity, was the mediocre Caron. Both were the federal pillars of the ultramontane *Bleus*, and both were being undermined by Chapleau's attacks. Even the last frowning bastion of ultramontanism seemed to be settling a little with the decline of Bishop Laflèche. He stood almost alone now, separated from Archbishop Taschereau by a host of minor quarrels and a great gulf of principle. His recurring trips to Rome had not bridged the gulf but they had wearied Rome of him, and his position was now clear. Unchanged by endless discussion, unrebuked by chill silence, he had found himself with his diocese divided and his domain reduced, while Archbishop Taschereau moved on toward a Cardinal's hat.

On the federal scene there was every prospect of trouble but there were also some hopeful glints. Each session brought a changed perspective and, more importantly, aged an aging government. Some of the venerable ministers were bending under their toils. John A. Macdonald's seventy-year-old stomach, regarded by himself and the party as the barometer of its fortunes, was rumoured to be giving out. Tilley was seriously ill. The indestructible Tupper enjoyed his usual booming health but he had moved from the cabinet to the post of High Commissioner in London. Nobody doubted that he would play politics to the limit there and be on call for a crisis in Canada, but his absence was comforting to all Liberals and the talk of a rift with Macdonald even more so.

One issue promised battle in the Speech from the Throne, but it was an old and familiar question of the franchise. Two others, equally familiar, were still rumour and cloud. Riel was back with the Métis and the muddle of the Red River seemed to be repeating itself four hundred miles to the west on the Saskatchewan. The C.P.R. was in trouble again and its shares were plunging in New York. Yet these bogies seemed family bogies, the fuel for party quarrels. With the country growing together and almost pulled together now by the steel of the railway, no one quite realized the size and malignity of the twin devils perched on Macdonald's shoulders. Certainly Laurier did not, as he settled at his desk in this House of English businessmen who knew how to listen and be tolerant. More comfortable in Quebec, more hopeful in Ottawa, he had arrived with no inkling that the days of his brief content were almost over.

2

MACDONALD faced parliament on January 29, and for three months thereafter, with the private knowledge that any day might bring the affairs of the C.P.R. tumbling in one tremendous crash. The railway, still almost a year from completion, had run out of money and credit. Panicky shareholders, busily selling off, were driving down the value of its stock in all the money markets. Its unissued stock was totally unsaleable because the government loan that had carried the company through the past year had also blanketed its assets with a government lien. The Dominion of Canada had first charge on the hide, hair, limbs, and tallow of its enormous white elephant, and no unsinged investors were willing to queue behind. Dividends were met and pay-cars still went out because the missing of one would mean the end of all, but the money was being found only through the private borrowings of directors who had reached their limit. There would have to be more help from the government; it looked as though the direct involvement of the country would have to rise to something like sixty millions, and Macdonald did not see how he could make the country stomach it.

He was even more doubtful about his dealings with Louis Riel, and here in addition to the worries there must have been a sense of guilt. The Prime Minister had learned nothing from his experience with the Métis on the Red River because he had not troubled to learn. The westward-moving buffalo-hunters, squatting now on farms along the Saskatchewan, had still no title to their lands, were still beset by all the old fears of an advancing civilization that would make no terms with them. Because of the fears they had brought back Louis Riel from the United States. He was the old Riel, a little more tinged with madness, a little more tainted by corruption. He had had longer now to brood on men's ancient hopes, and longer to deform them in the vaults of his own clouded mind. His kingdom of the west, French and Catholic, was now to be free of France and free of Rome, with Louis Riel as prophet and Bishop Bourget as pope. He would abandon it all for perhaps a hundred thousand dollars, perhaps thirty thousand or perhaps ten in hard cash.

It was pitiful enough, and nauseating enough, but none of it could have shocked and none of it excused Macdonald. He had known Riel before and had bribed him before. Riel was back because of Macdonald's own neglect, his own slipshod, almost hostile indifference to these few thousand half-French, half-Indian people of the west. It was still not Riel nor even the grievances of the Métis that had stirred the Prime Minister, one day before the summoning of parliament, to offer some grudging last-minute concessions. It was the thought of the restless tribes on the reservations, also and equally neglected. Now, in about a week, there would be government emissaries leaving Ottawa on the month-long trip to the Saskatchewan. They were going very late and with little enough to offer. It might not be enough, and Riel was threatening Indian war. Macdonald faced the House and the glitter of opening day with that knowledge too.

Yet he had, with the instinct of a lucky general, left both questions in the lap of the gods and turned to another front. Time might yet avert the prospect of a bankrupt railway and of slaughter in the west; for the present he would pull the country together more to his liking. In the coming session, the Speech from the Throne announced, a bill would be introduced for the provision of a uniform federal franchise.

Twice before Macdonald had introduced the proposal into a Speech from the Throne, and each time he had drawn back. This time he was determined to go on, and perhaps more determined because of his other worries. Through all the years since Confederation the members he saw before him in the House had been elected from voters' lists compiled by provincial officers and according to provincial qualifications. There were now seven franchises, each different from each other, each controlled by a province. The provinces set the rules, the provinces controlled their working, and the governing body of the country came as the result. It outraged every principle of uniformity, it ran counter to the whole grain of Macdonald's nature. 'It is impossible of course', he had said fifteen years before, 'that the elective franchise should be at the mercy of a foreign body.'

Not one of the seven foreign bodies was inclined to concur. There was much to be said for a measure that would put all citizens of the Dominion on the same footing as regarded their voting rights. There was as much to be said against an imposed uniformity that would ignore every provincial distinction and preference. The bill, as it was introduced, made tentative gestures toward liberality: property qualifications in some provinces were to be reduced, single women and some Indians were to have the right to vote. There would be trouble enough over this and more over the fact that control of the voting lists was to be removed from provincial officers to the hand-picked agents of the federal government. At the heart of it all, however, was the essence of the old quarrel. Macdonald the centralizer was at work again. Laurier would rise to oppose him, when his time came, with all the cries of the Dorions ringing in his ears.

There was a considerable delay before the parties came to grips. The House was moody and edgy, sensing more than it knew of the clouds overhanging the country. Laurier, like everyone else, began to be aware of trouble brewing in the murk of the Northwest. He had only to note the comings and goings of Van Horne, only to look at the face of George Stephen, brooding in the Russell Hotel, haunting the committee rooms of the Commons, to know that the C.P.R. was hungry again. With it all, as February dragged on into March, came a new and private worry.

L'Electeur, always short of money, was now at the end of its rope. Pacaud was so desperate that he wrote offering to retire if Laurier could find the means to carry on under a new editor. It was characteristically generous and characteristically impracticable. There was no man but Pacaud for *L'Electeur* and without the paper there was no voice that spoke wholly, surely, and perpetually for Laurier in Quebec. Both had to be saved. Three exasperating weeks of work ended in a dribble of new funds and an agreement by which Laurier backed the debts as co-owner. He did not like the arrangement; it destroyed the fiction of the paper's independence and diluted the value of its support. He would have to escape from the connection as soon as he could, but in the meantime *L'Electeur* was shakily on its feet again and Pacaud in his place.

Then, as the telegram from the west reached Ottawa on March 27, the lesser worries fell away. The Métis had attacked the Mounted Police at Duck Lake near Prince Albert, killing twelve of them and wounding twenty-five. This was worse than the Red River: it was open rebellion and the country was already on a war footing. The government that had been so slow to conciliate Riel was moving quickly to crush him. Detachments had left Winnipeg for the Saskatchewan as early as March 25. By Monday March 30, troops were moving to railway stations in all the eastern cities, and on the thirty-first, Caron, as Minister of Militia, telegraphed the westbound soldiers: 'Wish you to travel night and day. I want to show what the Canadian Militia can do.'

Van Horne, the builder of the C.P.R., was to say later that the railway should have erected a monument to Louis Riel. John A. Macdonald might well have been one of the contributors. At a moment when the road faced ruin and while he still shuddered at the thought of going to the country for help, Riel provided the chance for a spectacular demonstration of what that railway meant. Van Horne leaped at it and Macdonald acquiesced. Between Ottawa and Winnipeg lay the wild country around Lake Nipigon and Lake Superior, much of it still unbeaten by the builders. In some of the Superior sections the muskeg had already sucked down six sets of rails. Fully-connected steel ended two hundred and fifty miles east of Lake Nipigon. From there west the gaps began, with stretches of rail, base camps, and temporary depots interspersed by miles of frozen swamp crossed by nothing but tote-roads, telegraph lines, the wreckage of old roadbeds, and the unfinished gradings for new. Everything in the region was mobilized in the face of savage spring weather. The troops were run to the end of the good steel, bundled out of the railway cars and into sleighs to cross the first stretch of woods and muskeg. When rails appeared again sleighs, horses, and men were loaded onto flat-cars, bucketed on to the next gap, and off-loaded to take to another trail. The process was repeated half a dozen times, always in flying snow and always with plenty of food, for Van Horne's commissariat functioned as marvellously as his other arrangements. He was short of locomotives and short of flat-cars, some of the stretches of rail were simply clamped down over snow and ice, but six days after the men for the west left Ottawa they were in Winnipeg with all their gear. There would be no question now of the country's answer to a call for money. The last great debate on the C.P.R. was still ahead but it had already been won in the Lake Superior wilderness.

The first troops from the east arrived in Winnipeg on April 4. Two days before, half a dozen whites had been massacred by Indians under Big Bear at Frog Lake, a few miles north of the Saskatchewan. Two weeks later, while the country was still hushed with the fear of a great Indian outbreak, Macdonald rose in the House of Commons to move the second reading of his Franchise Bill. Laurier rose next day to attack it. If he felt for the first time the sense of unreality and futility that was to come later and in other debates where politicians talked while men died for their mistakes, he did not refer to it. The many-sided business of the country still had to go on.

The only reason advanced by the Right Honourable gentleman in introducing his measure, said Laurier, was that the present franchise was an anomaly. Laurier did not admit it. 'This is the mistake in this bill; it treats this country as a single community and in the plan we find the well-known predilection of the Right

Honourable gentleman in favour of a legislative union. He does not admit that it is right to have seven separate communities. Well, I start on this principle, and it is one which I commend especially to my colleagues from the province of Quebec . . . that we have in this country seven different communities . . . that we have seven independent commonwealths in this country is a truth which cannot be denied . . . It may be wise or unwise . . . but this is the basis of our constitution.'

He paid his respects not only to the centralizing purpose of the measure but to the political possibilities in transferring the preparation of voters' lists from 'the sturdy yeomen of this country' to 'the innumerable army of parasites which feed on the government and whose sole object will be to do the bidding of the government'. Then he went on to deal with the proposal of woman suffrage and to commend Langevin, as the principal Quebec supporter, 'to the tender mercies of the good, pious, conservative French of the province of Quebec'.

'I do not believe the emancipation of women can be promoted so much by political as by social reform. I believe that the action of women must be most influential in politics as in everything else, but I believe that action is most effective if exercised in the circle of the home. If the Right Honourable gentleman is really anxious to do something for the emancipation of woman, let him give her the opportunity for more extensive education, let him open for her more fields of employment.'

He was on sure ground here, aligned with the clergy for once and with most of Quebec's women. The wife of the habitant never thought of the vote. Women like Zoë and Emilie Lavergne were still quite content to pull their delicate threads far from the public arena. He himself was middle-aged now, rooted in the French tradition and grown up in the depths of the Victorian era. He had seen too much of vote-getting. He recoiled as a gentleman from the thought of delicate fingers soiled by such work, and as a politician from the thousand imponderables of the change. There was also a good deal of Victorian fun to be had from the government's gingerly venture. 'This measure', said the member for Quebec East, 'proposes to give the right of suffrage to unmarried ladies only; it is a premium on celibacy. The writers of the past have spoken of the perplexities of a young woman placed between two suitors; the writers of the future will have to show the perplexity of a young woman who has to choose between a husband and the right to vote.'

Such good temper as he had shown forsook the House when he sat down. The honourable members poised on their benches with rebellion in the west, a battle over the C.P.R. ahead of them, and nothing they could do about either at the moment. Here on the table before them, however, was raw red meat. Quite apart from the theoretical defects of the Franchise Bill, every Liberal still smarting from the effects of the gerrymander saw the new measure as a great engine of political patronage and control. Cartwright leaped at it with newly-enriched venom and behind him brigades of Liberal obstructionists formed themselves into round-the-clock watches. For six weeks, by day and night, Laurier sat almost silent through one of the bitterest debates parliament had yet known. The House of English businessmen was no more. Hoarse, unshaven zealots, fiery-eyed from lack of sleep, tore at every verb and comma in the bill, ripping it to shreds with amendments, reading whole books to Mr. Speaker, forcing as many as twenty-five divisions at one sitting. Macdonald, fighting without Tupper and missing him sadly, gave way inch by inch but put up a battle into which all the desperation of his position on other grounds, all the rancorous stubbornness of an old man accustomed to power, and a great deal of real conviction were thrown. Early in June the bill went through. It was clipped, mauled, and destined to prompt extinction when Liberals came to power, but Macdonald in the angry exhaustion of the moment pronounced it 'the greatest triumph of my life'.

There was hardly a break for the House to recover its temper before the resolutions in aid of the C.P.R. were introduced. Blake, crumbling visibly from the strain of the session, was as mighty as ever in attack, but the issue had been decided and overshadowed by victorious troops in the west. By the end of June the C.P.R. was safe.

Rebellion was ended and the railway that had helped to crush it would go on to its linking in the Rockies. The author of rebellion was in Regina jail, and out of it all the first bitter fruit was ripening on the bough. Riel, suggested the Toronto *News* on May 18, should be strangled with the French flag–'the only service which that rag can render in this country'.

3

THERE WAS still to be no cool rest in Arthabaska. On July 6, in this House of seething, bilious, bleary-eyed men who were being held in Ottawa through the worst of the midsummer heat, Blake rose to move a vote of censure on the government for neglect, delay, and mismanagement in the affairs of the Northwest. On July 7 Laurier rose to support him. It was the longest, strongest speech he had yet made in parliament, and there were in it hints of change. The languid, smiling quasi-secretary to Blake was no longer so easily at home among the English. He was more alert and watchful when the French spoke. Everything was vaguely and troublingly reminiscent of his first session eleven years before, and much he had thought outgrown was not outgrown. The long memories were at work and the name of Thomas Scott was in the air again. The past, or at least that part of it, must somehow be divorced from the present; the cause of the Métis must be disentangled from the aura of Louis Riel. Carefully, deliberately, and feeling oddly alone even with Blake at his side, Laurier stood up to do what he could.

'To tell us', he said, 'that Louis Riel, simply by his influence, could bring these men from peace to war; to tell us that they had no grievances, to tell us that they were brought into a state of rebellion either through pure malice or through imbecile adherence to an adventurer is an insult to the people at large and an unjust aspersion on the people of the Saskatchewan.' The Métis had been long settled in the west before the white men came. They had asked for title to the lands they held and they had asked in addition for the right to take up other land on the same terms as white homesteaders. Macdonald had refused; the Métis must either consider themselves Indians and live on Indian reserves or consider themselves white men and take up newly-surveyed homesteads. They could not have both. Why? Was there not land enough in the vast Northwest? Had not this privilege been given to the Métis of the Red River to settle the troubles there? Why were not the Métis on the Saskatchewan entitled to the same small generosity?

When the government moved at all, how did it move? The surveys on the Saskatchewan repeated every blunder of the surveys on the Red River. The river holdings were ignored, the block line survey was run across them, separating farms from river frontage, cutting across fences, sometimes separating houses from barns. 'Could there be any more vexatious tyranny? I say it would have been cheap justice if they had listened to the prayers of the half-breeds and told them: we will respect your possessions. This I do charge upon the government: that they have for years and years ignored the just claims of the half-breeds of the Saskatchewan, that for years and years these people have been petitioning the government and always in vain. I say they have been treated by this government with an indifference amounting to undisguised contempt, and if this rebellion be a crime I say the responsibility for that crime weighs as much upon the men who by their conduct have caused the rebellion as upon those who engaged in it.

'Justice is the same everywhere.' He echoed Blake's words of the day before and then turned with a new seriousness to the point that Blake had not raised. 'There is in connection with this matter another point which I have not heard referred to, but which seems to be in the minds of a good many people. It is not expressed, but I think the feeling permeates the very atmosphere not only of this House but of the whole of this country. I have not heard it stated, but it is in the minds of many that if these men have rebelled it is because they are to a certain extent of French origin. This I say, and I say it coming from a province where less than fifty years ago every man of the race to which I belong was a rebel and where today every man of that race is a true and loyal subject: I say give these men justice, give them freedom, give them their rights, treat them as for the last forty years you have treated the people of Lower Canada, and you will have contentment, peace, and harmony where today discord, hatred, and war are ruining the land.'

He was not reassured as he sat down. There was to be no

reassurance through the rest of the long summer. Blake's motion was duly lost and on July 20 parliament prorogued. On the same day the trial of Riel began in Regina before a jury of English Protestants. With Riel as co-defendant stood Henry Jackson, an English half-breed follower obviously of unsteady mind. The only possible defence for either man was a plea of insanity and both rejected it. On September 18 the verdict came. Riel was sentenced to hang; Henry Jackson was acquitted.

Insulting as it was, the result of the trial had been a foregone conclusion. No English jury, aware of conditions on the Saskatchewan, would hang a dull-witted man who had fought for his rights. And no English jury would forgive Riel. Ontario had moved west. The ghost of Scott clanked through the courtroom pointing its bony finger. 'We tried Riel for treason,' said one of the jurors half a century later, 'and he was hanged for the murder of Scott.'

As yet he was unhanged, waiting in his cell in the Mounted Police barracks on the bare prairie, fingering his rosary, writing his wild memorials. He was still confident, according to the drift of rumour, that 'politics will save me'. The man watching from Arthabaska shared the confidence, with many qualifications. The first reprieve came, and then the second. The medical commission sent west by Macdonald so grudgingly, so reluctantly, so hedged in with dogmatic legalisms, returned with its report: Riel was a man subject to religious delusions but a responsible being able to tell right from wrong. Finally and unbelievably, on November 16, the trap fell.

Almost every newspaper in Quebec was out next day with black bands of mourning. 'Henceforth', said *La Presse* of Montreal, 'there are no more Conservatives nor Liberals nor Castors. There are only PATRIOTS and TRAITORS – the National Party and the Party of the Rope.'

It seemed so. On Sunday November 22, Laurier came to Montreal, one of thirty-seven French-Canadian leaders assembled from all the parties. Man by man, *Rouge*, *Bleu*, and Castor, they followed each other to the rostrums standing on the Champ de Mars in the midst of forty thousand people. Only Langevin, Chapleau, and Caron were missing. As ministers who had remained faithful to Macdonald and acquiesced in the hanging, they were being burnt in effigy all through Quebec. They were being supplanted here. From one of the three platforms the great voice of Mercier came like a tolling bell, 'Riel, our brother, is dead.' From the same platform, when his turn came, Laurier heard himself cry out, 'Had I been born on the banks of the Saskatchewan I would myself have shouldered a musket to fight against the neglect of government and the shameless greed of speculators!'

It would cost him dear in the federal field, but for the moment he hardly cared. Quebec came first. Its patchwork politics had been resolved into one pattern by the blunt fist of the English. Suddenly the anguish of conquest was alive again. Riel was nothing, but Macdonald had made of that death the proof of domination. Ontario had prevailed; Ontario would always prevail while this union endured. One looked to the long future and saw a west, English too. One looked to the Maritimes, cool, well mannered, and remote, but always English. Those tolerant gentlemen of the English parliament were seen with new eyes now, or rather with the eyes of the young student who had listened to Eric Dorion many years before. Even in the thought of Blake there was no reassurance. Blake was in England, nursing that treacherous health. He would condemn Macdonald, but he would once have hanged Riel. Perhaps he would still have hanged him, coldly and justly, not from the pressure of Ontario, not in the search for power, but simply because his Englishness could not give way to the need for one generous gesture, legal or not. Everywhere one felt the hard grip of that Englishness closing in, and it was not to be endured. Not on this Sunday of the forty thousand; not on the Champ de Mars.

'After all our efforts to establish amicable relations with them,' said the Toronto *Mail* next day, 'the French Canadians are now seeking to compel us to recognize their right to suspend the operation of the law whenever a representative of their race is in the toils. But let us solemnly assure them that rather than submit to such a yoke Ontario would smash Confederation into its original fragments, preferring that the dream of a united

Canada should be shattered forever than that unity should be purchased at the price of inequality.'

This was the answer to the shouts of Sunday; Laurier's musket would be long remembered. Slowly and painfully, through the last weeks of the year, he regained his old perspective. There was a *Parti National* in truth now, and Mercier at the head of it was certain to sweep the province. But the province would still be alone, and more alone than ever, with the cry of race drowning the cry of religion. It would be newly divided, for the Church was cold to Riel, the bad Catholic. Langevin and Caron clung on in the face of the storm and Chapleau fought back. Chapleau would never regain his old place, never be the old man. A consumptive now and a desperate politician, the *poitrinaire* faced his hostile crowds as he had done in the old days, shirt-front torn open, breast bare, defiantly shouting them down. Even the cough that racked him became an actor's tool as he doubled up in pain, straightened with the blood-stained handkerchief in his hand, and plunged on in new torrents of rhetoric. He was pitiful and he was magnificent and he could ask the eternal question: if not this union with the English, what then? Laurier had no answer. He must look to the new session and wait for Blake.

4

ONE BY ONE, when Blake returned, the proposals and the hopes went down. 'At the time of Riel's execution,' Laurier wrote to him on December 31, 'I had supposed that it would be possible to unite the whole party in condemnation of it . . . it seems to me that we in this province, in holding the government responsible not only for the rebellion but for all the consequences of the rebellion including Riel's death, were quite right. Of course if our friends in the other provinces cannot support that view, that is an end of it . . . we cannot ask you to commit suicide.'

If there was coolness in the tone, it was not for Blake. Loyalty and respect remained; Laurier dreaded as much as ever the new talk of the leader's resignation. But he came to Ottawa on February 25, when parliament opened, as his own man. He rose as his own man a little before eleven o'clock on the night of March 16 when a rambling, acrid debate seemed to be dragging toward its close.

It had begun on March 11, channelled by a neat Conservative manoeuvre into a straight vote of censure on the execution of Riel. On such a vote, Macdonald knew, he would get a Liberal from Ontario for every Quebec Conservative he lost. Blake had been caught off guard, or he had not condescended to be watchful. 'I do not propose', he had said, 'to construct a party platform out of the Regina scaffold,' and the words were pitched a little high for the facts. There was no possibility of constructing a platform because on this question there was no party. The Liberals of Ontario were united against Riel. They would unite with Quebec on nothing but a general condemnation of the government's policy in the Northwest, and even in this they had been forestalled. The debate was narrowed to the lines of a formal exercise mirroring the state of the country. The French would vote for Riel, the English would vote against him, and the books would be closed.

Through most of this fifth evening Rykert, a Conservative famous for his scrap-book of political cuttings, had droned along emptying the House with each page he read. Béchard, a French member, had followed him gracefully and ineffectually. As Béchard sat down it was time for the summing-up by the party leaders. None seemed in prospect; no one rose. The Speaker looked around at the yawning, stretching rearguard scattered over the benches and prepared to take the vote. It was only then that Laurier stood up, to sarcastic Conservative applause. He had not expected to speak that night; he had been brought to his feet by another Conservative manoeuvre. The purpose, according to the Montreal *Star* next day, had been to force Laurier or Blake to speak first and give the final reply to the ministers. 'But the Conservatives bitterly regretted their tactics. Laurier had hardly begun to speak when almost all the members returned to their seats. During the two hours which followed . . . at certain moments one could hear the ticking of the clock in the chamber.'

A man was emerging here, full-grown, taking the ground he

would hold to the end of his life. He had thrown aside several pleasant illusions. He was no longer 'the lazy Laurier', the genial, Anglified Liberal. Nor had he turned back, as Mercier had, to the old fortress of the *Rouges*. He had recognized once and for all the gulf that ran between the races and the side on which he stood. He was far from convinced that any bridge would hold, yet the building of it, if bridge there was to be, was the real work of the country. He had taken up this trade of politician and he was not ready to set it down. He intended to go on.

More than ever, it would be on his own terms and in his own way. Even between himself and Blake, in the weeks of this session, there had been that veil of separation, that smiling, noncommittal silence which would grow familiar to many others later on. It would baffle the men of both races and separate Laurier from each. It was not habitual, it often seemed dropped and forgotten, but when it returned it was the sign of crisis. At those times, it would be said, Laurier listened to everything, absorbed everything, and gave not a clue to his feelings till he had made up his mind. He had made up his mind now.

He turned first on the Tory press of Ontario, which had been glad enough for twenty-five years of the massive support of the French-Canadian *Bleus*. Now that press was blackening a whole people as criminals and traitors. Yet he had warning words for Mercier too. 'It would be simply suicidal to French Canadians to form a party by themselves. Why, so soon as French Canadians who are in the minority in this House and in the country were to organize as a political party they would compel the majority to organize as a political party and the result must be disastrous to themselves.'

He turned to the administration of the Northwest and itemized again the long catalogue of neglect. 'Blood, blood, blood – prisons, scaffolds, widows, orphans, destitution, ruin – these are what fill the blank in the administration of this government of the affairs of the Northwest!'

He turned to the benches across with a wide gesture, hands outflung. 'I appeal now to any friend of liberty in this House, I appeal not only to the Liberals who sit beside me but to any man who has a British heart in his breast and I ask, when subjects of Her Majesty have been petitioning for years for their rights and those rights have not only been ignored but have been denied, and when these men take their lives in their hands and rebel, will any man in this House say that these men when they have got their rights should not have saved their heads as well, and that the criminals, if criminals there were in this rebellion, are not those who fought and bled and died, but the men who sit on those Treasury benches?

'What is hateful is not rebellion, it is the despotism which induces that rebellion; what is hateful are not rebels but the men who, having the enjoyment of power, do not discharge the duties of power; those men who when they are asked for a loaf give a stone.

'I will not receive any lectures on loyalty. I am a British subject and I value the proud title as much as anyone in this House. But if it be expected of me that I shall allow fellow countrymen, unfriended, undefended, unprotected, and unrepresented in this House to be trampled under foot by this government, I say that is not what I understand by loyalty and I would call that slavery.'

The government had claimed that the trial of Riel was a fair one. Laurier denied it. 'That he was insane seems to me to be beyond the possibility of controversy. When the government sent this so-called commission to Regina to examine the state of mind of Louis Riel it was not with a view of determining whether the sentence should be carried out or commuted, but it was to throw dust in the eyes of the public and enable the government to say afterward: we have consulted specialists and they have reported in favour of sanity.

'Sir,' his voice dropped at the end of a long and blistering condemnation and the clock was heard once more for a few seconds, 'we are a new nation, we are attempting to unite the different conflicting elements which we have into a nation. Shall we ever succeed if the bond of union is to be revenge, if we are to rake up old scores and launch them at the heads of one another?'

Even the weird metaphor did not stir a ripple in the silence. He launched into his peroration. 'The government have convinced all, the half-breeds, the Indians, the white settlers, that their arm is long and strong and that they are powerful to punish. Would to heaven that they had taken as much pains to convince them all of their desire and their willingness to do them justice, to treat them fairly. Had they taken as much pains to do right as they have taken to punish wrong they never would have had to convince these people that the law cannot be violated with impunity because the law would never have been violated at all.

'But today, not to speak of those who have lost their lives, our prisons are full of men who, despairing ever to get justice by peace, took their lives in their hands rather than be treated as slaves. Their sacrifice will not be without reward . . . their country has conquered with their martyrdom . . . we know that more than two thousand claims so long denied have at last been granted. And more – still more. Representation is to be granted to those territories. This side of the House long fought but fought in vain to obtain that measure of justice . . . it came as the last conquest of that insurrection. And again I say that their country has conquered with their martyrdom . . . and there was cause sufficient, independent of all others, to extend mercy to the one who is dead and to those who live.'

It was nearly one o'clock when the last accents of that voice, beautiful and passionate as it had never been before, died in the House. He had spoken on short notice, without elaborate preparation; his grammar had had its rough spots and some of his passages had carried a measure of political freight. He did not change Cartwright. He did not change Alexander Mackenzie, still lingering and grimly alone. With twenty-one other English Liberals they went with the government on the vote. Yet something was changed, and many members sensed it. Macdonald would have sensed it but he had not heard; he had been at home in bed with sciatica gnawing at his leg. The House, said a sardonic Blake three days later, had witnessed 'the crowning proof of French domination', and he had more in mind than 'the finest parliamentary speech ever pronounced in the parliament of Canada since Confederation'.

10

'A HIGH AND HONOURABLE AMBITION'

1886-1887

THERE WAS no turning back now and no hope that parliamentary eloquence or parliamentary manoeuvre would sew up the great rent in the country. The Quebec provincial elections were six months away and Mercier would certainly go in. Just as certainly he would set the province alight with the torch of Riel. For all his passionate brilliance, for all the sweep and scope of his vision and capacities, or rather because of them, he was the baleful man of this hour. The ruthless politician was merged in the angry patriot. Everything in him called him to this opportunity, drove him to this brink. One's thoughts went back to Laflamme, bankrupt and broken now; they went back to Médéric Lanctôt, the wandering drunkard eight years dead and dead at thirty-nine, sheltered for his last years as a stenographer in the House of Commons. Mercier was a greater man than either and a man equally foredoomed. Yet he was still the leader of the Liberal party in the province. He had to be supported and he could not be restrained. He would hold Quebec and turn it in on itself with its pride and wounds, and in six months more he would have his answer from the country.

The general elections were less than a year away. In the present mood, and the prospects were that it would grow uglier, six English provinces would be aligned against Quebec. Every other issue would be dwarfed, deformed, or thrust aside while race became once more the central quarrel of the country.

The hope lay with Blake, the party, and Ontario. For all his cool and subtle remoteness on the question of Riel, the man who had faced the wrath of the Orange lodges two years before was unchanged. The surly, scrambling politicians were still Liberals and to some of them at least Liberalism had meaning as a unifying, indivisible force. The old province of the English was, after all, Liberalism's first home; there had been a Baldwin there before there had been a George Brown. A new voice, even with traces of the still-detested accent, might recall it to the best of itself. Laurier was tempted by the thought at first and then compelled. He had spoken for Quebec as Blake could not and in doing so he had moved out forever from under the leader's shadow. He would never be envied by Blake, he would never be repudiated, but if he stood a little apart he must choose his own way. There was one Mercier, there had been one Papineau, and the road of both led nowhere. Laurier's road, if there was one, led to the Ontario halls and the hundred thousand Orangemen.

He was a long time in coming to the decision and Blake was longer in concurring. The last session of the fifth parliament prorogued in June and even before that Laurier had been called away. Carolus was dying in St-Lin and the end came on May 21. It came as everything had seemed to come for Carolus, easily and cheerfully. 'I am almost certain to get well in spite of my seventy-one years,' he had written to one of the cousins on March 19, and he had probably believed it to the last. There was the business of consoling Adeline and settling family affairs. The four half-brothers and the half-sister turned for help as always to the famous elder son. The son noted the coughs, the slight incipient ailments that would deprive all these, as they had deprived him, of Carolus's easy well-being. Then he left to face his problems again, curiously soothed by the last sight of the handsome old face, pained as always by the gulf that the years had opened between himself and the living, and newly alone.

By July he was out on the stumps of Quebec, fighting in Mercier's campaign and still trying to hold the reins on Mercier. It could not be done. Chapleau was out as well, defiantly facing certain disaster with his party. The torn man who had wavered to the last hour before supporting Macdonald's decision on Riel was now a prisoner of the record, unhappy in Ottawa and sinking in Quebec. Yet he was still a power to be reckoned with and attacked with the new savagery that was the mark of the times. 'You will speak after me but I know what you will say and I will answer you,' Laurier said, turning directly to him at one of the *assemblées contradictoires*. 'For a long time I have known the circle in which the ball chained to your feet permits you to move.'

It was over by the middle of October and Mercier was in power in Quebec. The newspaper storm redoubled in Ontario and editors finished with Mercier only to turn on Laurier. Where was the man of the musket, and when did he intend to shoulder it? Early in December the formal invitation came from the Young Men's Liberal Club of Toronto. The party elders were strongly opposed to acceptance, and Blake was dubious to the last. But he was on hand at the railway station when Laurier arrived to be surrounded by a bodyguard of Young Liberals, and he was on hand at a crowded reception in the Rossin Hotel. The bodyguard had not been needed and there were neither clubs nor muskets at the reception. The great, bleak hall of the Horticultural Pavilion was crowded to its roof that night, with agile youngsters leaning in through the opened windows at its topmost level. A few jeers came down through the frosty steam of their breath as Laurier stepped onto the platform with Blake at his side, but for the most part there was silence. Toronto waited, convinced and hostile, curious and a little intrigued.

Laurier had come to speak to the English in the English way as he conceived it, and he was not quite at his best. The admired English temperance, logic, and restraint were all a little laid on as he ran over the familiar story of the Northwest, and the story itself was growing a little tired. He made a good deal and rather too much of British fair play. He was for a while the politician driving hard at the wedge that now split the Tories of Ontario from the *Bleus* of Quebec. His one moment of severe heckling followed his declaration that 'In politics I am an English Liberal . . . the principles which I profess, such as they are, did not come to me from the land of my ancestors. They came to me from England.' Yet he himself somehow came out full length as what he was. 'I do not regret that we are now subjects of the Queen,' he said in the midst of a respectful silence from these English, Scots, and Irishmen, all of whom had far-off homelands of their own, 'but may my right hand wither by my side if the memories of my forefathers ever cease to be dear to my heart.'

Through the years ahead Toronto and most of Ontario were to grow familiar with that declaration in one form or another and perhaps a little tired of it. Yet on this snowy December night it reached down to touch something deeper than the squalid sores of Riel. So did the metaphor he had found at last to clothe his conception of this country of the two peoples: 'Below the island of Montreal the water that comes from the north, from the Ottawa, unites with the waters that come from the western lakes, but united they do not mix. There they run, parallel, separate, and distinguishable, and yet are one stream, flowing within the same banks, the mighty St. Lawrence rolling on toward the sea . . . a perfect image of our nation.'

When he sat down and Blake rose to move the address of thanks the leader had never seemed so confident, so powerful, and so much on his mettle. This had been more than support; it had been refreshment and challenge for the first Liberal of the country. It was the same at London, Stratford, and Windsor during the following week. There were jeers and scalding newspaper editorials and wooden muskets delivered to the platforms by the hands of small boys, but there was always an attentive audience. At the end of the tour Laurier went home well satisfied. Blake had been strengthened, he thought, the party had been pulled together, and Ontario had been given a new perspective on Quebec. Blake would have concurred, with qualifications. Ontario did not change so easily but it had seen and heard the Frenchman and would not forget him.

The foray had been an important and risky prelude to the general election campaign which was just a month away. Riel would still be an issue but a lesser issue now, and the others rose in proportion. They were almost all hopeful. The government was going into the fight with a reluctance more than justified by the state of the country and its political map. Oliver Mowat and his Liberals were stronger than ever in Ontario. Mercier rode high in Quebec. William Stevens Fielding, the diminutive former journalist whose goatee was said to cover the closest mouth in politics, had just carried Nova Scotia for the Liberals and he had carried it on the renewed cry for better terms or secession. Manitoba, with its wheat crops frozen out, its settlers leaving the country, and still in the hard grip of the C.P.R. monopoly, was also soured on Tories. The steam was going out of the National Policy and there were hard times on the way. Shaken to its roots and fumbling, the government was going down and the arrival of Tupper in Ottawa on January 25 was only another sign of Macdonald's desperation.

Laurier had come back from Toronto with a new status in the party and a new confidence in the country. Ontario had received him well, better than he had hoped for. Quebec was a little mollified and Mercier, safely installed in power, was making magnanimous gestures. With the great rift over Riel healed or healing there was a new zest in politics. With the prospect of Blake at the head of the nation there were limitless and exciting vistas. Laurier went into the campaign with an eagerness he had never known and when the six savage midwinter weeks came to an end on February 21 he climbed from the last sleigh in the midst of the last blizzard, almost completely confident. He was sure of Quebec, Blake had put up the fight of his life in Ontario, and there was a new surge of power in the Liberals of the Maritimes and the west. Yet the old man who had hived the Grits and pushed through his Franchise Bill and built the C.P.R. had been out in the blizzards too. The first results trickling down to Arthabaska over the telegraph wires on February 23 looked promising; by next day came the rumour of a Liberal win. Then as the slow trains and sleighs brought in the figures from the outlying constituencies the swing came. The government edged even, climbed to a majority of three, then to fifteen, and finally to a safe thirty. Macdonald had squeaked through.

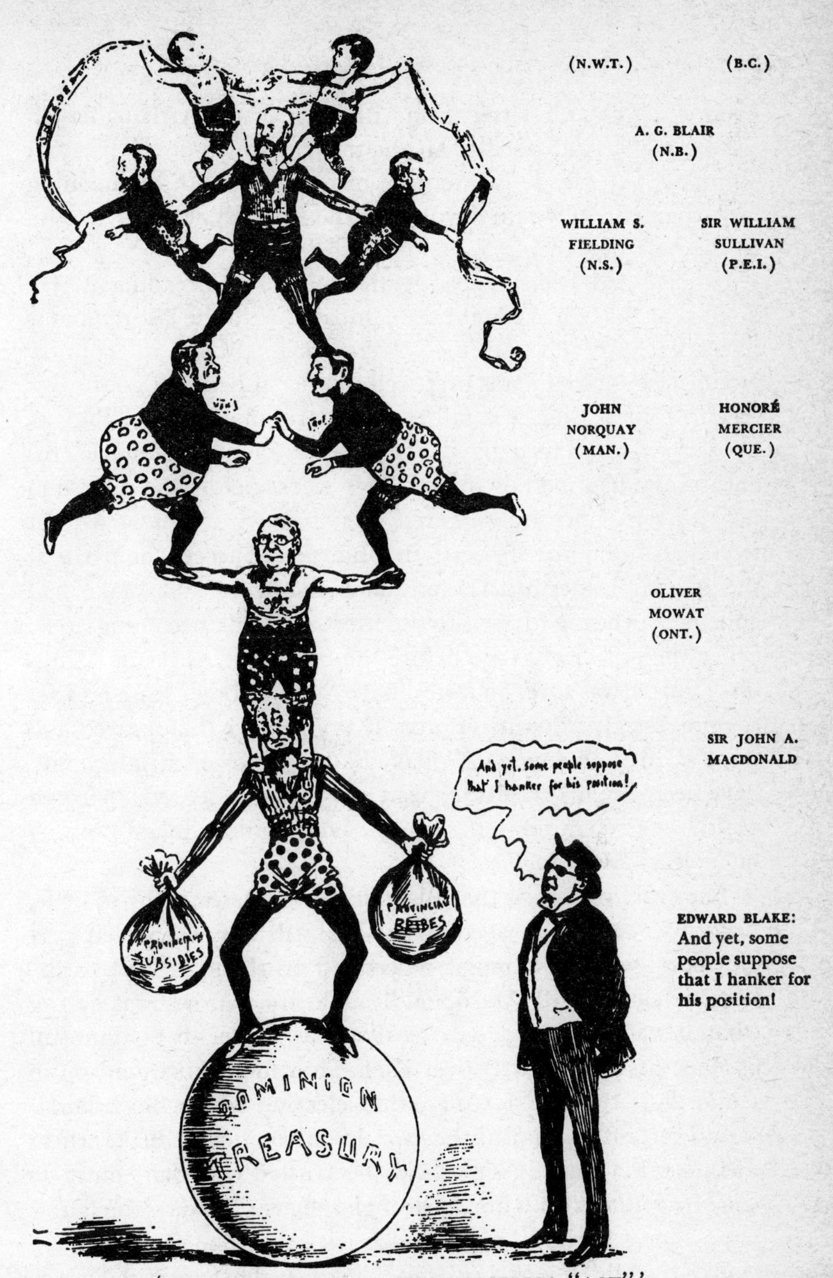

'THE GREAT BRITISH NORTH AMERICA "ACT"'

CARTOON BY J. W. BENGOUGH IN *Grip*, APRIL 16, 1887

2

THE CIRCULAR letter from Blake reached Arthabaska on March 5. Addressed to all the principal men of the party, it announced the leader's intention of resigning with the opening of parliament. It would devolve on the Liberals at once, he said, to choose a new man.

Laurier had been expecting the word and dreading it. He knew that Blake had fought the campaign with the last remnants of his strength and with a cold sense of finality. If the country would accept him he was prepared to lead; if it would not he was free to confess himself a failure as a party man and go. Buoyed up as he had seemed by Laurier's appearance in Ontario, his enthusiasm had soon dwindled. Two weeks before the campaign began he had privately offered to step down if Oliver Mowat would abandon his safe berth in Ontario and accept the perils of the federal leadership. Mowat had demurred and Blake had gone on, spending himself to the limit and even becoming hopeful in the last bright days before the balloting. As Prime Minister, Laurier was sure, he would have taken another lease on life; the old, nagging doubts of himself would have disappeared and most of his ailments with them. Blake in power at last would have been a new man at the head of a nation renewed. Defeated again, the tired mind in the sagging body could think of nothing but release and refuge.

The cruel irony was that Blake had been defeated by so little. According to his dismayed politicians, still busy with their post mortems when the circular descended on them, he had hardly been defeated at all. Macdonald's majority of thirty was half of what it had been and half of that was made up of doubtful Quebec *Bleus*, still surly over Riel. They might turn on him in a month or two and force another election which the Liberals would certainly win. But they would only win with Blake; there was no other man in sight and the trusted confidant must do what he could to hold him. Through the next few days the letters blew in on Laurier like snow, each with the same refrain.

'All I could say was "damn!"' wrote the wrathful Sydney Fisher from Knowlton, Quebec. 'It is simply impossible for him to back out now . . . with Macdonald certainly not the man he used to be, with Tupper clamouring for the lead . . . now is not the time to disorganize our forces. You are probably closer to Blake than anyone else . . . do all you can and spare no pains or argument or remonstrance to make him reconsider.'

'It is simply *impossible* for us to allow his resignation,' snapped J. D. Edgar, one of the leaders in Toronto. He enclosed a copy of his own protest to Blake: 'The whole responsibility of a disgraceful collapse would rightly or wrongly, by friend and by foe, be thrown upon you. There is no other possible leader. In some ways Cartwright might lead, but the French would not follow him . . . I am certainly not going to drudge away at politics as I have been doing unless you are my leader.'

Cartwright's letter came next, acid as always but equally vehement. 'But for his former escapades I would treat this as a mere temporary aberration of mind caused by too much work. As it is, I do not know. I have written to remonstrate very strongly and you had better do the same. He is always much more amenable to influence from men of the other provinces than from us in Ontario and you cannot . . . put the case too strongly. He will be the butt of all sorts of sneers and jibes from the enemy and will get no sympathy from our people, nor will he deserve any.' Then, the rankling bitterness worked out, Cartwright grew philosophical. If Blake went the party must pull itself together. Good might yet come out of evil. 'I think if he retires Sir John is more likely to do so too or to quarrel outright with Tupper who has been giving himself airs.' Cartwright was evidently speculating on the possibility of a Conservative party without Macdonald and a Liberal party with himself at the head of it, but it was a daydream with so little substance that not even he was enthused. Blake was still the man and Cartwright never would be.

On March 16, as rumours began to creep into the newspapers, Laurier gathered together the letters and his own thoughts and transmitted the substance to Blake. 'I have it on my mind that you are disposed to take the blame on yourself if the party did not obtain a full and complete success . . . you alone are of that mind. What measure of success we have had is altogether and solely due to you. In this province the effect would simply be disastrous and we would at once lose all the ground which we have gained during the last few years . . . do not forget this; if you give up the leadership there is no one to take your place; chaos and confusion must prevail and the disruption of the party must finally ensue.'

On the twenty-eighth the sick man, still resisting the pressure, drafted his reply. 'It is plain now that I have not attracted to our side the neutral mass which turns the scale . . . it is then fit that some other man and some different methods should at length be tried. Many kindly tell me that the failure is not due to me . . . but it is largely due to my unsuitability for the place. The ambition to rule a free country is a high and honourable ambition . . . it unfortunately happens that I am by temperament averse to rule. With impaired health, diminished means, vanished business and neglected home affairs . . . I feel that the position has become untenable by me, and that I should be relieved.'

The letter was never sent; the pressures were too great. Laurier, if he was ever to hear the words, would hear them later. The reply that actually went out on the same day was a qualified surrender to the demands of the party, and the surrender was confirmed at the first caucus held after the opening of the new parliament on April 13, 1887. Blake, listening tiredly to the eulogies and sardonically to the confident plans, agreed to continue as nominal leader while a committee from each of the provinces, with Laurier senior for Quebec and Cartwright for Ontario, advised him and did the work.

He had predicted that the arrangement would be 'unsatisfactory as a makeshift, while as a permanency it would be intolerable'. By the end of May it had failed. The leader was the leader for the simple reason that everything must come to him; every paragraph of every piece of legislation, every problem of the party must pass under those exhausted eyes. For six weeks Laurier sat beside him as the great frame shrank under sickness, accumulated fatigue, and the bitter consciousness of failure. Then the chair was empty. Blake was at home, forbidden by his doctors to attend the House again. On June 1 a hushed party caucus received his formal resignation.

3

THE AMBITION to rule a free country . . . a high and honourable ambition'; if Laurier did not have it what was he doing here? The question had always been with him, remote and academic. Now, and abruptly, it was the central problem of his life. There would be no more growing in the shadow of Blake; Blake was gone. There could be no more years as the leisured spokesman of a province and a few constituents, comfortable in the party ranks. There was no leader now whom he could follow; he had grown too tall for any man but Blake. He could turn back if he wished, but the road led all the way to Arthabaska. For fourteen years he had yearned often and audibly for the peaceful practice and the leisure to attempt a history of the country. He could have that now or he could have what Blake had had; there was no other choice. There was, in fact, only the one choice, dictated by all the course of his life, by all his qualities. He would take upon himself the vast, burdening, inescapable tangle of responsibilities that saddled a party leader and he would reach on for the mastery of the nation.

It seemed a wholly private and ludicrously improbable dilemma up to the afternoon of June 1, 1887. Ten days before, he had gone to an evening party in Ottawa and completed a long questionnaire in the hostess's autograph book while the laughter of the watching guests became a little tentative and the eyes glinted curiously. It was a party of English friends, and there were no surprises in the answers. Mr. Laurier's favourite colour was red, the colour of liberty. His favourite flower was the last rose of summer. His favourite object in nature was a child and his favourite amusement 'to read, of course'. He had no opinions on music and none on art and 'alas, no such thing as a favourite occupation'. He would have liked best to live in a small island in the West Indies and his most distinguishing characteristic was 'You know it well – indolence'. The events of the last year or two had changed much but they had not dispelled the myth of the lazy, affable, courtly, delicate lawyer to whom politics was a tiring avocation. He had not allowed it to be dispelled; he wore the mask still and hardly recognized it as a mask. Consciously or not, he played out the game of Emilie Lavergne – the game begun before her in the study at Arthabaska; each year the portrait of the landed gentleman politician, the portrait of the English Whig as seen through the eyes of the French romantic, grew more and more recognizable.

It was the face turned to the English. It could change when he turned on Quebec and the old *Rouge* glared through the mask. It had changed once or twice, more subtly, when he turned back, speaking for Quebec to the English. But those bouts of flaring eloquence, that pride of race, even that anger with the men of his race when they fell short of what the pride demanded, were the stuff of the rare moments and the moments passed. If he had shown any vision of the country as a whole it was a dubious and uncertain one, blurred with rhetoric, tainted with a leaning toward the 'manifest destiny' that led to the American union. In the eyes of many in Quebec he was an Anglified liberal enemy of the Church, not quite to be trusted even by his own party. In the eyes of English Canada he was a French-Canadian politician, cool, knowledgeable, charming, conciliatory, probably a little weak. A good man and a good influence, under the right leader.

Against all that stood what he knew of Blake. Laurier was the chosen companion and the closest friend. There were no masks between them. Laurier was now the first one turned to in the weighing of every problem. Through seven years he had come to think as Blake thought on almost every aspect of politics and on most of life, and even in their differences they had complemented each other. He could add humanity to Blake's cold logic. He could reach men; he was the better politician. He was French and Blake was English and it had not separated them; it had enriched the friendship. It would be tempting to a mind like Blake's to speculate on a future when some such enrichment might be transmitted to the body of the nation, drawing it together. Blake would be tempted to make the great and obvious gesture. His offer to Mowat six months before had been made without enthusiasm and he had not pressed it. He was not drawn to the clever politician; his hope would be for a leader to reshape the long future. For every reason Laurier would be the first man to be thought of by this man who thought alone.

Yet for almost every reason he would be the first to be set aside. So far as the decision lay with Blake, nothing but the party and the country would be considered. Neither the politicians nor the country at large even thought of Laurier as a leader. Mowat was thought of, though he had refused once. There was Cartwright, eager for the place now and confident of it. There was David Mills, the Ontario lawyer, as incorruptible and almost as able as Blake, who had stood with Blake in the party since the days of George Brown. There were half a dozen others, all senior to Laurier, all better known, soundly Protestant and English.

There seemed every possibility at the moment that the new leader of the Liberal party might be Prime Minister within a year. The stakes were higher than they had been, and the risks greater. How could a French Canadian be pushed to the head now? How could Quebec, with Riel hardly in his grave, be given the position that had always been Ontario's? Laurier was no Cartwright, moving in a shell of arrogant self-interest and closed assumptions. He was alive and sensitive to the feelings of men. He knew the set of their minds and the drift of the torrent of advice descending on Blake. Every instinct of the politician in him concurred and he was sure Blake must concur. Laurier would be thought of and Laurier would be set aside.

The afternoon of that same day, June 1, Mills and Burpee of New Brunswick came to Laurier in his office. They had been to see Blake. Cartwright was a candidate, they had told the leader, and Mills was willing to consider himself a candidate. There was always Mowat in the background, and several of the other leading men from Ontario would only require a word. The reply had evidently left them a little stunned. 'There is only one possible choice,' Blake had said: 'Laurier.'

That evening, carrying with him from the office the thought of those stonily blank faces, Laurier went to Blake's house. He pressed his refusal with all the strength he had. Nothing could have been a greater surprise to him, he said, and there was the more truth in it because he had weighed the possibility. The objections that had seemed so conclusive grew more forbidding with every word, and new and nearer ones pushed in from the background as he looked at the man who could not work and could not sleep, lying back on a sofa now with his eyes closed and beads of exhaustion gathering on his forehead. Zoë had sat so often as Mrs. Blake sat now beside her husband, with the same drawn face, the same pity, and the same tired resentment. What right had Laurier to throw the health Zoë had watched so carefully into this dismal game? What was to become now of the life and home that offered her little enough? Blake was the greatest lawyer in the country; he was or had been comparatively rich. How was a Laurier from Arthabaska with his income of five thousand dollars a year to meet the endless demands of this post that swallowed every working day, demanded travel, prominence, and hospitality, and paid nothing? The sick man had no answer. He could not go on and Laurier was the only successor. 'Yes, Mr. Laurier,' Mrs. Blake leaned forward at the end; 'You are the only man for it.'

By June 3 Mills had recovered from his surprise and relinquished his ambition. He had had a little sour fun with Cartwright who waited, self-convinced and omniscient as usual, and slightly on the outside. 'He thinks there is no one else who would even be thought of for the place,' Mills confided to his journal. 'I did not express any dissent. I was amused at his conceit, which puts self so well in front as to be repulsive. No one can ever lead successfully who does not possess sufficient sympathy to think of others. Sir Richard thinks only of himself.'

Some of the newspapers, which were now speculating copiously, did not think a great deal of Mills either. 'Mr. Mills', said the Montreal *Gazette*, 'has to commend him industry and wide information, but he is utterly destitute of personal popularity, is a disagreeable speaker and a man of narrow and extremely partisan views.' Both Mills and Cartwright were being handled roughly by the French press since they had approved the execution of Riel, and in addition to that, Cartwright, as the apostle of free trade, was 'unpopularity itself' to commercial Montreal. He divided support with Mowat in Ontario and the name of Edgar cropped up once or twice, but everything seemed to emphasize the gap that Blake would leave. Few papers could bring themselves to believe that he was gone for good, and no paper mentioned Laurier.

There were four days to the party caucus on June 7 and in those days Cartwright learned the facts. He rose brusquely when the members were assembled and the crowding reporters shut away beyond the closed doors, and moved the nomination of Laurier as leader. Mills followed, seconding the nomination. In their subdued voices and carefully expressionless faces the thoughts were clear enough. Jealousy, disappointment, bitterness were certainly there, but they were the least troubling. The doubt was worse. These men had bowed to the will of Blake from helplessness and old habit but they would never be convinced that Blake was right.

There was frank incredulity on many of the other faces, even of the long-time friends, even of the few who had ever thought of Laurier for the place. François Langelier of Quebec sat there; he had written to Blake that Laurier was too frail. Beausoleil of Quebec had a wire from Mercier in his pocket; he was to go for Mowat first, Edgar second, and Laurier only as third. 'Poor, dear Laurier, a more charming fellow never lived. I would stand by him and fight for him . . . but it would be the veriest piece of political Quixotism': that was the opinion of Louis Davies, king-pin of Prince Edward Island. It was almost the best that would be said for Laurier by the best in this room; one had no need to hear the talk or read the letters, it could all be sensed in the air. The nominee rose and declined, sat through an hour of forced and hollow protest, and declined again. But there was no other claimant now, or none who would advance himself here in the face of the whole party. It would be work for the back rooms, if anywhere, and the caucus must dissolve with something. Laurier agreed to reconsider and the doors opened.

He pushed through the crowd of reporters with a set face and a brusqueness they had never known. Not many followed him, but John Willison of the Toronto *Globe* had sensed something, or his editors had. He could not be shaken off. There had been a nomination, he insisted, and he suspected it was Laurier. For once without a smile, Laurier would neither deny nor admit, confirm nor affirm, agree nor disagree. He reached his office but there was no relief there. The caucus had been sworn to secrecy and the oath was kept. The rooms and corridors of the building had never known such a thunderous silence. There was something in that very silence, however, to steer a trained reporter. It was nearly midnight and Laurier was in his room at the Russell Hotel when Willison found him again. With or without consent, said Willison, he was going to wire the *Globe*. He was going to report that Laurier had been named as temporary leader until Blake had recovered his health.

Somehow for a moment all the ruthless pressures of the day and of the week before seemed to be concentrated in that flat and brazen statement. Laurier could summon nothing but a cold civility. 'I do not believe you will be rash enough to send out any such message.'

The *Globe* itself was even more rash. When the dispatch appeared next day it had been pruned and amplified. Blake's resignation, it announced, was final and irrevocable and Laurier had been elected leader.

Few of the other papers believed the statement and official silence continued. On the eleventh Blake left for Toronto and the parting note came: 'I was afraid to visit the house to say good-bye, knowing that I should break down, and indeed was unable to keep up when I saw a few at the station . . . I did or attempted too much and left too little to my colleagues . . . you have not my anxious temperament.'

Laurier had not gone to the railway station with the others for fear of starting more rumour. Now he was alone. For another week he wavered while behind the scenes the party hardened to a mood that had more of surrender in it than of confidence. Mowat was unavailable. Cartwright was unacceptable to too many. Mills had never been seriously considered. The session was nearing its end and it could not be allowed to end with a headless party. The old question appeared with the new name: 'If not Laurier – who?' Members and contenders alike streamed to his room in the Commons and his room in the hotel, genuine now if still cool in their urgency. He had to accept; it might not be for long in any case; Blake might recover and return. On the eighteenth he made up his mind. 'I know I have not the aptitude for it,' he wrote, 'and I have a sad apprehension that it must end in disaster.'

It was not until June 23, the day parliament prorogued, that he formally announced his acceptance. It was conditional and temporary; he was prepared to resign when Blake was prepared to return. He was to have a stenographer paid for by the party; there was a letter from Edgar promising it. The same day came a good-humoured note from Macdonald's office, signed by Joseph Pope. 'Apart from my personal regard for you I welcome it as postponing indefinitely Universal Suffrage which I feared was in the air.' The postscript struck home more shrewdly: 'Minette doesn't think there is anything in the leadership of the opposition because there is no salary attached. She says honour is all very well, but *cash* is the thing!'

The newspaper comment flooded in, incredulous, indifferent, amused, some of it hostile though most had an air of unbelieving goodwill. There was some rejoicing from Quebec that a French Canadian had been chosen as national leader. The *Globe* hoped cautiously that the man whom a great place sought would be the man to fill it worthily. The old enemy *La Minerve* saw 'the replacing of a giant by a pygmy'. His election might gratify the *amour propre* of Quebec but it would assure the Conservatives twenty-five years of power. Ontario grumbled that the right of leadership remained with the province that paid three-fifths of the taxes. The Victoria *Weekly Colonist* predicted that 'the Reform party will be found to have committed a most egregious error. M. Laurier's sentiments on the Riel question are too fresh in the minds of the people to ensure him any great degree of confidence from the English-speaking people of the Dominion.' The Toronto *World* had already expressed its opinion in advance of the formal announcement: 'That his leadership will end with the present session can scarcely be a matter of doubt, for that the Reform party look upon Mr. Laurier as the political Moses who is to lead them out of the opposition darkness no sane man can believe. A great, a magnificent orator, his parliamentary qualities begin and end there.'

There was a week of crowding congratulations, derision, flattery, multitudinous advice. In the midst of it, nagging and insignificant, a problem of home thrust up. All else gave way to concern for the image of Quebec. With a copy of *L'Electeur* and a letter from Pacaud before him, he brushed aside in a line a flood of jubilation.

'I am very pleased that our friends in Quebec find this a cause for enthusiasm. I congratulate you on your article relative to the Salvation Army. The repeated attacks of a Liberal population against this body are unworthy of Quebec City. It is necessary that the processions of the Army, ridiculous as they may appear to some, have full liberty of progress and if need be I am prepared to march at their head to protect them. Under present circumstances I am mortified that the city which I represent should prove itself so intolerant.

'I will be going to Montreal shortly, where we will be able to talk over this matter, and many others.'

11

'I AM CONVINCED OF MY DEFICIENCIES'

1887-1889

'IS IT TIME to endeavour to strike for a bold policy,' he wrote to Blake from Arthabaska on June 30, 1887, 'or shall we abstain, or shall we wait?' Seven days the leader, he was too urgently in need of guidance to be quite considerate or quite tactful. The sick man was in no condition to offer advice. The notoriously thin skin would be pricked by the implied reflection on the policy of the past. Somehow and from somewhere, nevertheless, the spark of a new idea had to be struck. In the same mood of desperation, a few days later, Laurier composed his first circular to the principal men of the party. 'I particularly entreat you', he wrote, 'to make the benefit of your views to me as complete as possible. I have accepted a position of which more than anybody else I am convinced of my deficiencies and shortcomings and I all the more rely on the help and assistance of every individual member.'

The help was soon copiously forthcoming. All through July the mound of replies grew on his desk, conflicting, confusing, and dismaying. Only now, as each man harped on his special theme with all the variations provided by his own region, his own personality, and his own ambitions, did Laurier fully realize the volume of dissonance that he was supposed to reduce to harmony.

His first public appearance as leader was scheduled for August

2 and was to take the form of a picnic at the village of Somerset, a few miles north of Arthabaska. There he would be expected to plumb the depths of the nation's disorders, to strike the keynote for the party, and to set it moving with new unity and sharpened purpose. Nothing could have seemed more wildly improbable as the day drew near. Even the choice of the meeting-place had caused trouble. For all its name, Somerset's English antecedents were remote and fading. It was now much better known locally as Plessisville, and Ontario noted grimly that the new leader would be deep in French territory speaking French to a French audience. Pacaud, on the other hand, was annoyed at the choice of an obscure village rather than the constituency capital of Quebec City.

Laurier had had to answer both objections with the lame and not very candid excuse that he went where he was invited and Somerset's invitation had come first. Actually, he was far from ready to face Ontario, and Quebec City was dangerous ground for a man emerging as the national leader. Mercier was the first Liberal there, ruling with magnificent flair and gusto, and rasping the nerves of the English at every turn. Quebec, speaking with Mercier's voice, seemed rather an allied state than a province of the Dominion. There was every danger that Laurier, making his début in Quebec City, would be overshadowed in the province and newly suspect to the rest of the country.

As an ally, Mercier was more than ever valuable and dangerous now, for he had just made a move big with implications in the federal field. Looking beyond the borders of Quebec, he had decided to join the discontents of his own province with those of all the others. He had invited provincial premiers to meet at a conference in Quebec City in October, the first of such conferences ever to be held. It would be a colourful and potentially explosive affair with only Prince Edward Island and British Columbia, the two Tory end-pieces of the country, avoiding it. Mowat would be there from Ontario with the scars and trophies of his battles for provincial rights. Fielding would come from Nova Scotia with the echo of the secession resolution following him. Liberal-leaning New Brunswick would be represented and so would Manitoba, furious and aggrieved over hard times and over Macdonald's squelching of its plans to build branch railways in competition with the C.P.R. The old centralizer might well be shaken by this gathering of centrifugal force but the new leader of the opposition could only give it at best a gingerly welcome. Provincial politics were not federal politics and a step with Mercier might well be a step into the abyss.

So far as Quebec was concerned, however, Laurier could walk with his old caution around familiar pitfalls. It was on the wider scene and on the issue he could see rising as the practical question of the day that he was almost totally at a loss. It was the tariff again, that detestable enigma. The National Policy had lost its magic and a new depression was on the way. Rural Ontario, the Maritimes, and the west were now clamorous against a policy that shut out their products from the American market and increased the cost of every tool they used and almost every article they consumed. The brief years of reciprocity with the United States, a generation before, were being remembered as prosperous times. Reciprocity was alive again as an issue, supported by Goldwin Smith, the history professor of Oxford and philosopher of Toronto, supported by Erastus Wiman, the barefoot boy from Churchville, Ontario, who had gone to the United States to make his millions, supported by a bevy of congressmen and businessmen in the United States and by most of the businessmen in Canada who had interests on both sides of the line. Each had his own motives and his own view and shading of policy. Each view was supported or opposed or qualified by some members of the Liberal party and each reply to the leader's circular increased the heat and clouded the confusion.

It was Blake's going that had raised the lid of this Pandora's box. Blake had always refused to make the tariff a major issue. So long as the country was what it was, he had maintained, some protection for its manufactures and industry was necessary. He had deplored the building of the C.P.R. but the C.P.R. was built. He had deplored the favouritism and excesses of the National Policy but had never denied its logic. The country that was still a British dominion, the country that was now to grow along the east-west axis of a transcontinental railway, must defend itself from its mighty neighbour behind a rampart of customs houses. Tariffs would be reduced and adjusted if the Liberals came to power, but tariffs would remain.

The grey realism of his attitude, if it was realism, had sent the party into two elections without a cry to answer Macdonald. Now the cry was rising by itself. What seemed to be taking shape, dreaded or wished for by conflicting correspondents, was an idea that went far beyond the modest mutual concessions of earlier days. It had begun with the hope, shared even by the Tories, that the United States could be wheedled into a free-trade agreement on agricultural products while the tariffs protecting Canadian manufactures remained untouched. It had grown with the failure of that hope. The freedom of trade was now to be complete; the border was to know no customs houses. The gates dividing the continent were to be beaten down and against the outside world Canada and the United States were to join hands in raising a common tariff. It was hardly surprising, as the letters poured in, that the question of political arrangements began to intrude on the mighty visions of trade, or that the phrase 'Unrestricted Reciprocity' began to become interchangeable with the more euphonious term 'Commercial Union'.

For a country in the doldrums it would be a departure of breath-taking magnitude. For a leader at a loss it was an almost irresistibly tempting issue. As a spiritual son of the Dorions, Laurier inclined more to the men who thought in terms of a unified continent than to those who wailed of danger to the British connection. Yet he drew back from both with all the old fears and reservations. The broad aisles of policy were obscured by mazes of statistics, by ranting patriotism and raucous Americanism, by a tangle of personalities and party interests. He distrusted the motives of his multitudinous advisers and was far from certain of his own. The hammer of Cartwright drove him against the unresponsive anvil of Blake, and even here he suspected that old antipathies were as much at work as cool judgment.

Cartwright was all for the new departure, the more so as it was a departure from Blake. Yet his tone was convincingly judicious. 'Matters have been moving fast in Ontario,' he wrote on July 8. 'It is doubtful whether any meeting can be held in a rural district without expressing a pretty decided opinion as to Commercial Union and I am beginning to think we may as well face the music.'

There was no rebuttal from the invalid Blake convalescing at Murray Bay. The view represented the considered opinion of the party's leader in Ontario and its expert on fiscal matters, and in any case Laurier inclined to it. For one thing, in addition to everything else, reciprocity was a question of business; it might turn the country's mind from the question of Riel. 'I would judge that Cartwright is right,' he wrote to Blake on the fourteenth, 'and that the time has come to speak.' By the end of the month, however, as the long silence continued, he was painfully aware that the judgment of Blake was otherwise. Added to this came a new and dampening thought from Cartwright himself. 'There is this serious difficulty', he wrote, 'that we have not as yet any authoritative declaration of the willingness of the U.S. authorities to treat with us and we cannot therefore do more than speak very generally on the subject.'

It was time by then to sit down with pens and paper. There was to be no bold policy for this speech. Blake was silent and enigmatic, Cartwright was having the afterthoughts that should have been forethoughts, the Americans were an unknown quantity, and the men who had answered the circular were as fuddled and divided as their leader.

2

SOMERSET, which was just recovering from the effects of a fire two years earlier, had little to offer but pleasant rural surroundings and a fine summer's day. The picnic, according to the sour Tories of the Montreal *Gazette*, 'was not the immense, overpowering, Conservative-pulverizing demonstration which bombastic advertisements foretold. In truth it was a very tame affair.'

There were, nevertheless, some three thousand people assembled in Mr. Cormier's maple grove by two-thirty in the afternoon. Nearly two hundred of the political élite of Quebec crowded the speakers' platform. A good many of the notables had come by special train, they had all been lunched and wined and played up from the railway station by massed bands, and they were in a jovially attentive mood. It was a knowing audience and an important one, come to assess the old acquaintance in the new role of leader. Everything said here, moreover, would be re-assessed by the English from distorted newspaper accounts and garbled translations. It was not a time to be soothed by familiar faces and bucolic surroundings, still less by party panegyrics. Rather it was a time of notes damp in the hand and a sense of chilling inadequacy that grew with every word.

There were familiar things to say, however, as Laurier rose to follow the seventh speaker, and they steadied him a little. He deplored his new eminence and most particularly he deplored Blake's going. He would never be able to replace the old leader. He would have no part in the prejudices of race and creed. 'French Canadians, I ask you one thing – that, while remembering that I, a French Canadian, have been elected leader of the Liberal party of Canada, you will not lose sight of the fact that the limits of our common country are not confined to the province of Quebec . . . that our country is wherever the British flag waves in America.'

He ran over the country with the eye of a leader of the opposition. Corruption in government was notorious and rampant. He held in his hand the documents that proved that Conservatives had spent $58,000 to carry the single constituency of Digby, Nova Scotia. 'Carry your gaze from east to west and from north to south and everywhere the prevailing feeling will be found to be one of unrest and uneasiness, of discontent and irritation . . . the present government will last as long as Sir John Macdonald and when Sir John Macdonald disappears, after him the deluge.'

He paid his respects as usual to the nefarious work of the centralizer and then turned with a graceful gesture toward the most imposing of all the figures on the platform behind him, electric with genial vitality, immaculate and of the mode in dress, yet somehow with the flashing eyes and the sweeping moustache conveying the effect of cavalier and pirate. 'My friend, Mr. Mercier,' he said, 'is on the point of calling an interprovincial conference. Without knowing exactly what his program is, I trust that he and his colleagues will suggest an amendment to the constitution which will once and for all put an end to the abuse of the veto power and close the door forever to the tyrannical acts which Sir John Macdonald's government is so prone to.'

It was the first public move away from Blake, and if it was opportune it was also sincere. The disciple of the Dorions still yearned, as Blake did not, for provincial governments free as American states from the central power. But this was an old argument on a question still remote. He came now to approach the nearer problem. The reaction to the National Policy had come. 'Ontario farmers are clamouring for Commercial Union with the United States, that is to say, the suppression of all customs duties between the two countries.

'For my part, gentlemen, I am not prepared to say that the advocates and adepts of Commercial Union have as yet very clearly defined their views. What lies at the bottom of the idea, what we see clearest in it . . . is the conviction that any kind of reciprocity with the people of the United States would be to the advantage of Canada.'

Reciprocity had always been the policy of the Liberal party. Macdonald's government had admittedly been willing to allow reciprocity on agricultural products alone, but, 'for nine years now this bait has been dangling in the water. Gentlemen, having thrown out their bait the Government have since that time folded their arms and refused to make any other move.

'We know that there is today in the United States a group of men determined upon giving us Commercial Union. I may say that for my part I am not yet ready to declare that Commercial Union is an acceptable idea. But I may say this – and it is my actual policy – that the time has come to abandon the policy of retaliation, to show the American people that we are brothers, and to hold out our hands to them with a due regard for the duties we owe to our mother country.'

He was not specific as to the duties owed to the mother country. He did not indicate how the extended hands would accomplish what the folded arms had not. He was similarly pious and similarly vague to the end and concluded his argument with the resounding declaration in the flawless voice, 'I submit to all my fellow citizens that it is time to strive for the establishment of a policy which will make all the inhabitants of Canada feel happy to belong to the country.'

When it was over the picnickers cheered loudly and began to gather up their hampers and look for stray children. The greater dignitaries shook the speaker's hand and moved sombrely away from the platform in search of refreshment and consolation. Blake's place had been taken over but it could hardly be said to be filled.

3

THERE WAS to be no joy this year in the late and lovely summer of Arthabaska, nor in the golden autumn. There were to be no briefs backed by the comforting thought of substantial fees, and none of the clean wrestling with facts and logic before a judge in court. All this had to be set aside for the problems of the party. Each day the morning's mound of mail demanded answers and each urgent, self-important correspondent had usually to be put off with polite evasion. The answers, as yet, were simply not forthcoming.

The new stenographer, installed as the gift of the party, waited on a man who did not know what to write. Even Joseph Lavergne sat in a new relation to his partner and provided new distractions. He was now federal member for Drummond-Arthabaska, having returned the constituency to the fold at the general election. Saddled with constituency problems as well as the weight of the law business, he was inclined to share both with a man who had time for neither. The office was crowded with people and nothing was being accomplished. Practice and party alike seemed going to pot.

There were now few days when Laurier could slip across the street for a chat with Emilie. Even when there were he sometimes let them pass. He was reading no books, he was too distracted to welcome new ideas; the old mood of detached, philosophical serenity was gone. Emilie, a graceful success as the wife of a new member, was a little formidable as the companion of the new leader. She was thrilled by Laurier's advancement and even more by what she conceived to be her part in it, but he found her view of the limitless horizons opened to him a little naïve and more than a little irritating. Somehow at this moment Zoë was the one he turned to. She certainly was not happy at the enlargement of his sphere but she was resigned and acquiescent. She was practical and shrewd, she had acquired the habit of seeing political problems in terms of men and votes, and even though the problems were wide as the nation now, they still turned on those aggravating necessities.

Less than a week after Somerset came resounding defeat at Renfrew, Ontario, in the first by-election under the new leader. On September 28, more painful and nearer home, came a beating at many-memoried Charlevoix in Langevin's home territory. Langevin was or should have been merely the ghost of his old self. Somehow, however, the shadow had defeated all the substance that Pacaud had thrown against it. Laurier was inclined to feel that the little man had not tried hard enough; something seemed to be missing from the old days of undivided loyalty. He knew himself to be in an irritable and carping mood and probably unfair to Pacaud, but he felt the hand of Mercier pulling in the background. *L'Electeur* seemed to speak with two voices. Pacaud was being smothered with the work of preparing not only for Mercier's provincial conference but also for a provincial exhibition organized on Mercier's grandiose scale. Laurier's errands were sometimes left undone. Laurier's letters were not answered with the old promptness and sometimes the replies, when they came, were distracted and a little evasive. He had no doubt of Pacaud's intentions but he questioned Mercier's. At best, since he himself had always saddled Pacaud with two men's work, Mercier's would be too much. Some would be left undone or all would be half done. It seemed to Laurier that just at the moment when he most needed a secure base his Quebec organization was getting out of hand.

For the moment there was no time to do more than snap by mail and soothe and encourage at the occasional face-to-face meeting. The party, and Laurier as leader of the party, had to be newly established throughout the country. The question of the issue, the battle-cry, the direction in which to move, overtopped everything else. Liberalism, released from the massive immobility of Blake, was adrift and floundering, and it was all doubly agonizing because the Tories should have been in worse case. Almost beaten in the general elections and stretched out now on the rack of hard times, they had only lived through the last session because of the paralysis of the opposition. In Quebec a whole generation of Conservative leadership had foundered on the rock of Riel. Rural Ontario was growing more hostile to Tory protectionism every day and Manitoba was gone. Tupper, the lone bulwark of Macdonald in the Maritimes, was off to London again as High Commissioner. Yet still the beleaguered old man went on with his corrupt and decaying government, growing not a little weaker each day but a little stronger.

By the end of the summer Blake, still convalescing at Murray Bay, had broken his silence once or twice. The rare letters, however, were about equally dreaded and welcomed. There was no mistaking his cold distrust of Commercial Union and especially his distaste for it as merely a party issue. There was no doubt that he bristled at the thought of Cartwright thrusting in the background. It seemed clear too that he was writing other letters, for two of his innumerable law partners, James Edgar and William Mulock, came down heavily against the plan. Edgar's opinion could perhaps be discounted a little as he was always inclined to lean with Blake against Cartwright, but it was not quite so with the other man. William Mulock was just beginning to make his presence felt in the party, and without being unduly drawn to him Laurier was coming to recognize him as a considerable force. He commanded a flow of profanity said to be the most picturesque of any man in the smoking-rooms of parliament. A lawyer who had had a large part in the organization of a bank, connected with one of Toronto's oldest, staidest, and most wealth-encrusted families, he was yet politician enough to be known on the hustings as 'Farmer Bill'. The views of Mulock, particularly when reinforced by Blake and Edgar, were hardly to be ignored.

There was Mowat to be considered also, and Mowat's cautious reserve was sobering even Cartwright. The chunky little man with the twinkling eyes behind the steel-rimmed spectacles had held Ontario in the palm of his hand for fifteen years. Cartwright was an irascible knight-errant forced to wander off at each election in search of a new constituency. It had to be remembered, and Mowat remembered it well, that some Ontario manufacturers as well as many Ontario farmers contributed to Liberal campaign funds. Faintly in the background too sounded the bugles of the Imperial Federation League, two years old now, built round a core of ultra-English patriots who had risen to condemn Riel, and dedicated to the consolidation of the Empire. There could be no charm for an Imperial Federationist in any closer connection with the United States. The evidence of this led Cartwright during the course of the late summer to suggest that Unrestricted Reciprocity, after all, might be a better term than Commercial Union.

In the view from Arthabaska these mountains gradually became molehills. The Maritimes and the west were all for free trade under whatever name. Rural Ontario stood with them and rural Quebec would certainly outweigh commercial Montreal. Laurier was indifferent to the hair-splitting and impatient of the doldrums. The one clear fact was that the party had to move. 'I am afraid', he wrote Cartwright after the Renfrew by-election, 'that we are doomed to defeat following defeat unless we come out fair and square in favour of Commercial Union.'

He dismissed the hesitations of Mowat and the Ontario provincial cabinet with irritation. 'They are in power,' he wrote 'and they do not want to see a question raised which might disturb the smooth surface of the waters in which they sail. They can afford to rest where they are; we must move onwards and gradually we can, I believe, bring everyone to fall in.'

It was prodding at the point where prodding would do most good. By the early autumn Cartwright was confident again, speaking in military terms and characteristically belabouring the men around him. Ontario leaders, he complained, wanted to wait until success was sure and then step in and reap the fruits. 'Now this will not work. This is a case in which the instincts of the rank and file are much more likely to be right than the prudential objections of average politicians.'

Laurier concurred and the prudential objections were whittled away in further correspondence that did not include Blake. There was considerable talk of moving forward, unfurling the flag, and firing the first gun, a privilege that Cartwright assumed for himself. He would speak out in favour of Unrestricted Reciprocity, though his views would be presented as a personal opinion that did not commit the party. On October 12 at Ingersoll, Ontario, one week after the opening of Mercier's interprovincial conference, the gun went off.

The response in some quarters was easy to anticipate. Alexander Mackenzie, sick, aging, and alone, had already expressed himself. By some unhappy blunder Laurier had forgotten to send the old man a copy of his party circular and the result had crackled back to Cartwright two weeks before his speech. 'I infer from this', Mackenzie wrote, 'that I am to be cast out and ostracized by this new leader.' Commercial Union he saw as an annexationist plot. 'We are to raise a barrier against English trade and so commence a downgrade political life. My feelings revolt at the proposal.'

Nor was James Young, the old friend and correspondent, any less emphatic. He considered the Commercial Union movement 'one of the stupidest mistakes ever made by any section of our party . . . a dangerously anti-National and Americanizing policy'.

It was the unexpected voice, however, that rose loudest and with most effect. Speaking first from three thousand miles away at Belfast, Joseph Chamberlain announced that if Canada wanted Commercial Union with the United States 'she must be made to know that it means political separation from Great Britain'. Two months later, on December 30, 1887, Chamberlain was in Toronto, the towering trumpeter of John Bull.

Out of his speech rose the theme he was to make his own. 'The idea is the greatness and the importance of the destiny which is reserved for the Anglo-Saxon race – that proud, persistent, self-asserting, and resolute stock that no change of climate or condition can alter, and which is infallibly bound to be the predominating force in the future in the history and civilization of the world . . . I am an Englishman . . . I refuse to make any distinction between the interests of Englishmen in England, in Canada, and in the United States. Our past is theirs. Their future is ours. You cannot if you would break the invisible bonds that bind us together. It may yet be that the federation of Canada may be the lamp lighting our path to the federation of the British Empire.'

At the head table as he spoke sat D'Alton McCarthy, the handsome, dashing fifty-year-old lawyer of Barrie, Ontario. Member of parliament, member of the Conservative party, member of the Orange Order, McCarthy was also president of the Canadian branch of the Imperial Federation League, under whose auspices Chamberlain spoke. One thing was clear to Laurier as he read the account of the speech on the last day of 1887 and his skin crawled at the tone. The Liberal party under its French-Canadian leader had somehow managed to link trade with race. Anglo-Saxondom was astir again.

4

PARLIAMENT opened on February 23, 1888, and the first business of the first Liberal caucus was semantics rather than policy. Cartwright's decision as to terms had not been accepted by his opponents. To its enemies Unrestricted Reciprocity was still Commercial Union, burdened with all the weight of pro-Americanism it could be made to carry. Laurier was not yet and never would be impressed either by the distinction or the danger. Cartwright, newly enthused since his own speech in October, had written on January 2, 'We *must* make a new departure and there is nothing which will fill the bill half so well as unrestricted reciprocity.' Laurier, echoing the sentiment to Blake, had been quite satisfied with the old term. 'We must try to make a new departure,' he had written. 'There is a universal desire for a change. Commercial union would afford relief and commercial union must be popular. It is the general desire that we should make it a party issue.' He now found that he had both over-estimated the general desire and under-estimated the importance of a name.

Mulock, Edgar, and the other Ontario members who had been making difficulties would have nothing to do with Commercial Union as a phrase. They could accept the idea of reciprocity since time had made it more or less respectable and both parties had given it lip-service in one form or another. They could be pushed on to unrestricted reciprocity since it could be represented as only more of the same and in any case as the one way of obtaining anything. At that point, however, a shadow barrier of distinctions had to be raised. It was bound to be vague since there was no specific plan and since there had been no discussion with the great potential partner. It was likely to disappear completely under the frosty eye of an economist, but in the meantime it made talk possible. Commercial Union, ran the argument, would involve a joint tariff set by Canada and the United States against the outside world, including the mother country. Unrestricted Reciprocity would not. If the tariffs of the two countries rose and fell together, as they certainly would, that could be blamed on the eyeless obduracy of world trade. Commercial Unionists spoke of the abolition of customs houses along the Canadian-American border; under Unrestricted Reciprocity the customs houses would remain, presumably to fly the flag since they would have nothing else to do. It was not much of a distinction, but it was the best the eager lawyers of the party could devise and political necessities were urgent. One by one the tall men of Ontario fell in line for the forward move, hedging themselves to suffocation with avowals of loyalty to Crown and Empire.

It availed very little when Cartwright came to introduce his resolution on March 14. He was at his powerful, brilliant best as he pointed to the state of the country and the need for new directions, and moved 'that it is highly desirable that the largest possible freedom of commercial intercourse should obtain between the Dominion of Canada and the United States'. He was not long, however, in meeting with the cry of disloyalty, and he was soon snapping back that Canada owed England nothing more than Christian forgiveness for the blunders of her diplomats. Every Liberal who followed him made laborious efforts to separate trade from the flag, but every Conservative hammered the implications home – Unrestricted Reciprocity with the United States was Commercial Union with the United States, and Commercial Union was the first step to political union.

For two weeks the leader of the opposition was an abstracted listener. His thoughts were with Blake, who had now gone off to Italy, and he unburdened himself by letter while the debate was still going on. He had told the principal men of the party, Laurier wrote, that he wanted to resign the leadership at the close of the session. 'My determination is not a matter of choice . . . I have no taste for the position . . . I find no pleasure in it', and – most compelling reason of all – 'The fact is that I have not the financial means.'

The demands on his time in Arthabaska were doubled in Ottawa. Every expense grew. He had to maintain a position he could not afford and there was nothing to look forward to but the prospect of more expense. He could not lead a party from Arthabaska and he would not lead it from a hotel room in Ottawa. He must entertain, he must travel, he must learn to know the country, always on behalf of the party and always at his own expense or on humiliating dribbles from the party treasury. The debts had dwindled in the good years and without politics they might have been gone by now. Instead they were piling up again and the dismal, mutinous preoccupation with them poured out into the letter. 'I have never done with my profession one half or one fourth of what I could have done . . . I now find that I must seriously exert myself or that I will have to face at no distant date serious embarrassment.'

He did not intend to float about the sea of politics awash on the raft of sessional indemnities and contributions from party funds. Cartwright, who had wasted a considerable estate in what he was pleased to call the public service, was one example of what that could come to mean, and there was many another like him. Laurier had done what he could in Blake's absence and that was enough. He suspected that he had not pleased Blake, he was sure that most of the party would welcome Blake's return, and there had been hints that the leader was at least recuperating and considering. Laurier renewed the old urgings more vehemently than ever. 'My dear friend . . . remember this well: there is only one man in the party who does not believe that you are a natural born leader of men, and that man is yourself. You say that you have failed but tell me, pray, where you have failed who could have won?'

Almost perfunctorily he added his report on the political scene. 'We have adopted unrestricted reciprocity. We are still engaged in the debate. So far we have every reason to believe that we have made a wise movement in point of tactics and that we are making headway in the country. We have narrowed the issue to the mere commercial aspect of the question and we intend to keep it strictly on that line. There are political aspects that will spring up, but for the present it is far better to leave them out.'

He was, to say the least, putting the best possible face on a situation that neither he nor Cartwright nor even John A. Macdonald could now control. A year before, Macdonald had expected the talk of Commercial Union 'to blaze, crackle, and go out with a stink'. After Chamberlain's speech in December he had written jubilantly to Tupper, 'Commercial Union is a dead duck.' Now, finding the bird in changed feathers but raucously alive, he was busily equating the Liberal version of reciprocity with a move toward annexation. That was enough in his view, but it was not enough for the favourite protégé whom he had occasionally thought of as a successor. D'Alton McCarthy was now rising under the aegis of the Imperial Federation League as an uncontrollable maverick preaching the Anglo-Saxon Empire and demanding as a first step a wall of imperial preferential duties.

Laurier, when his time came to join in the debate on April 5, had to deal with political aspects whether he wished to or not. He was opposed, he said, 'by those ingrained Tories who imagine themselves bound to rule. On the other hand I have no reason to doubt the sincerity of those prophets of evil who, at every forward step taken by this young country, never fail to see an impending rupture of the British connection.' Argument was useless with Tories whose supreme end in politics was to enjoy the flesh-pots of office and whose loyalty sprang from their stomachs. But he asked those who honestly feared change, 'Are you [so] satisfied with the condition of the country that nothing is to be wished for its advancement?

'We have been told we have developed an interprovincial trade between the east and the west. I deny it. What trade we have between the east and the west is not a natural trade but is due entirely to the fact that the country has to pay the freight. You cannot legislate against nature.'

He went on, moving steadily onto more dangerous ground. Reciprocity with the United States would give access to a market of sixty millions of the wealthiest people on the face of the globe, 'with not even a molehill to separate us. To pretend that our colonial allegiance demands from us that we should be deterred from the spirit of enterprise . . . I deny. I would say this is not loyalty, but that it is mere flunkeyism . . .

'Colonies are destined to become nations as it is the destiny of the child to become a man. No one, even on the other side, will assume that this country, which will some day number a larger population than Great Britain, is forever to remain in its present political relation with Great Britain. The time is coming when the present relations of Great Britain and Canada must either become closer or be severed altogether . . . but this is not the question of today.'

He had done his faintly defiant best, larding it with as many loyal protestations as anyone else. Cartwright's resolution, hammered down by a thumping Conservative majority, went to the records. Across the border Grover Cleveland's Democrats were moving toward a defeat by high-tariff Republicans which would sweep all hope of reciprocity into the dustbin. But the Liberal party was committed, the Imperial Federation League waxed strong, and D'Alton McCarthy was soon to be provided with a new and congenial issue.

5

MERCIER'S provincial conference had been a success, and a success on a high level. The five premiers had met and deliberated almost as the heads of autonomous states. They had resolved that the veto power over provincial legislation, the central buttress of Ottawa's authority, should be returned to the Colonial Office in London where it would be practically a dead letter. They had passed other resolutions aimed at the curtailment of federal power. Everything that Laurier had hoped for at Somerset had come to pass and in addition there had been a resolution endorsing Unrestricted Reciprocity. It should all have been a shrewd blow to Macdonald, and it passed with the touch of a feather because Macdonald chose to ignore it. There was no federal machinery for making deeds out of the words of provincial premiers. Mercier had created an important precedent and intervened broadly in the affairs of the country but the country hardly noticed. It was to be a very different matter when he turned to the settlement of a strictly parochial affair.

The problem of the Jesuit Estates was exactly as old as the conquest. The lands, farms, schools, and dwelling-houses of the Order had passed to the British Crown at the capitulation of New France. General Amherst, Wolfe's superior in the campaign for Canada, had made greater efforts to obtain the properties as a gift in reward of victory than he had ever made to obtain the victory itself. He and his heirs after him had all been disappointed. The British government, benign in victory, had refused to eject the Jesuits until the last of their priests in Canada was dead. History in the meantime passed the Amhersts by, half-promises were forgotten, and all claims obscured. When the properties were taken over, control went first to the old province of Canada. At Confederation it passed to the new province of Quebec, with the provision that rents and revenues were to go to the support of education. Revenues went steadily down, however, amid a confusion of new claimants. The Jesuit Order, suppressed throughout the world in 1773, was reinstated in 1814 and asserted a right to compensation. Quebec evaded the claim but never quite denied it. A party of the Church in Canada disputed the claims of Order and province alike and demanded the revenues for some of its own dioceses and for Laval University. Meanwhile some two million dollars' worth of magnificent lands and splendid old grey stone buildings were going to pieces and yielding a fraction of their worth because no one was prepared to take the risk of buying, selling, or improving them.

Mercier had been educated by the Jesuits and had never lost his affection for them. He was not in the least averse to raising an issue that might embarrass Macdonald, he was a good lawyer and administrator who disliked loose ends, and he was in any case quite within his rights. In June of 1888 he introduced in the Quebec House his bill to settle the problem of the Jesuit Estates. A sum of $460,000 was to be appropriated by the province for the settlement of all claims. Of this, $60,000 was to go to Protestant schools that had been partly supported by the revenues. The balance was to be paid over to the ecclesiastical authorities of the province and was to be shared in due proportion by the Jesuit Order and the Church.

It was a thoroughly reasonable settlement and a good bargain for the province. Laurier, who had been well aware that the question of the Estates stood high on Mercier's agenda, might have breathed a sigh of relief except for one fact. The division of the money between Church and Order had to be arbitrated and the arbiter chosen by Mercier, after a good deal of correspondence which was faithfully reproduced in the preamble to the bill, was his Holiness Pope Leo XIII.

The Quebec House, though sprinkled with a few English and Protestant members, acquiesced in the purpose of the bill. The matter of the Pope's intervention in Canadian affairs was mildly questioned but Mercier replied with equal mildness that it was not an intervention in Canadian affairs at all. His Holiness had merely been invited and had agreed to superintend the division of the fund after it had passed into the Church's hands. If he did not, who would? If honourable members could suggest a more competent authority Mercier would be glad to agree. Honourable members could not, and the bill went quietly through. It was doubtful, however, if Mercier wanted quiet and there was soon evidence in Ottawa, in Arthabaska, and above all in Toronto, that quiet was not what he would get.

For the moment it was one of the unripe worries of the future. The all-consuming question was the party platform and the party leadership. As the session came to an end on June 23 it was apparent that Unrestricted Reciprocity had had a very restricted success. Many of the half-convinced seemed anxious to escape from the issue. The leader was certainly anxious to escape from his post, but all were entangled in the same commitment. No member could formally renounce a matter of party policy, and the leader could hardly abandon the party in the position to which he had brought it. Determined as ever to resign, Laurier found it always a little more difficult to choose the right moment. Haunted by the neglected practice, harried and torn and irritated by problems with which he could not cope and men he could not draw into unity, he was yet enjoying the best health he had known in years. He had no time to brood on his ailments and he was growing a little stubborn. He would not abandon the idea of some arrangement with the United States simply because Macdonald had managed to entangle it in the old disloyalty cry. Still less would he give way in the face of McCarthy and the ranting Imperialists. He could not change course and he could not resign: either or both would be an outright confession of failure.

The obvious escape would be to return the party to Blake, and this now began to seem vaguely possible. Blake was back from Italy and it was obvious from his latest letters that he was in better health and feeling the old call. Self-consciously, in May, he had refrained from offering any political advice, 'the intrusions of an absent invalid being worse than useless'. To Laurier's complaint of financial woes, however, his answers had been so utterly vague and impractical that he almost seemed to assent to resignation. 'A man not only has the right but is bound to preserve his independence and avoid degenerating into a political hack dependent on office for maintenance . . . I cannot look forward without the greatest apprehension to your resignation and trust that calamity may be averted; but *not* at the cost of an embarrassment to you which no friend has the right to impose.

'But is there not an alternative?' went on the letter. 'Can you not . . . explain frankly the impossibility of your giving all your time to the lead? My opinion is that our party would gladly accede to this view.' To what view? What could it all mean but a return to the system of committee that Blake himself had found intolerable, and what could be the outcome but a new crisis and a new leader who would have to be Blake? Why would the man never speak out? Why could he not be pinned down? By the time the master was installed again for the summer at Murray Bay Laurier wrote him in irritable hope. He would go down the river to see Blake, he would urge him to take the leadership again and to take with it, as the one gift of the man who had briefly replaced him, the plank of reciprocity.

The answer was a cordial invitation and an unmistakable warning. Blake would be delighted to see him and the one subject about which he was very anxious to talk was Commercial Union or Unrestricted Reciprocity. 'On this you know I hold views not shared by our leading friends so far as I can judge, and my extreme anxiety not to say anything indicating divergence in any respect leads me to long for an interview and for some solution of my difficulties, failing which I can only hope that I may be allowed to keep silence for a while.'

For a while. It was the old Blake, with all the tortured, tortuous uprightness, with all the burdening sense of his own importance which one had to forgive because it was so genuine and so justified, and with his mind unchanged. He had kept his seat in parliament because it represented to him – empty or not, and whether he admitted it or not – the one safe anchor of Liberalism. He did not hope but he did not doubt that sooner or later he would be called to the rescue of the party. It was not a call he intended to heed, however, while policy remained as it was. Laurier returned from Murray Bay with his pallid skin roughened by the fresh breezes of the St. Lawrence, depressed by long hours of massive argument, and still the party leader.

One duty that could no longer be put off was a progress through Ontario. The arrangements were in the hands of the brisk and efficient Edgar and for the first time Zoë was to be included. Laurier was not surprised but he was newly impressed by the ease with which she adapted herself during the short preliminary holiday with the Edgars at their home in Muskoka. She was still diffident and unsure in English and it was obvious to him at least that her thoughts often wandered back to the garden in Arthabaska, but she was alert, composed, and infallibly charming. Few conversations ended without leaving her in possession of a new friend or some nugget of useful information. For a woman who did not like politics, Zoë was converting herself into a remarkable political asset.

She did not come along on many of the speech-making forays, and it was as well. Shepherded by Edgar, often joined by Mulock and Cartwright and the other leaders, and with John Willison always prominent among the train of reporters, Laurier climbed to the platforms of Bracebridge, Port Carling, Orillia, Cannington, Lindsay, Sturgeon Point, Guelph, Mount Forest, and

Wingham. At Parry Sound he attended a Methodist camp-meeting and at St. Thomas he went to service in a Presbyterian church, duly horrifying the ultramontane press of Quebec. He had discounted this in advance as part of the price of the trip, but if the damage at home was minor it was not balanced by any gain in Ontario.

'I cannot say that his speeches made any great impression on our stubborn rural constituencies,' was Cartwright's judgment. The new leader was here to establish Unrestricted Reciprocity as the theme of the party, but it was equally necessary to justify himself as a French Canadian and his people as dutiful subjects. Interspersed with his trade statistics and his attacks on the National Policy came the avowals of his never-to-be-forgotten origin and his never-to-be-relinquished loyalty. 'May my right hand wither if I forget' – 'may my tongue cleave to the roof of my mouth' – the phrases grew to be habitual but they came with little warmth. He felt no particular ill will in the audiences that faced him; there was only curiosity. But he could not exert himself to satisfy it and turn it to his account. He could not reach out with the charm and ease so readily at control elsewhere. He was on foreign territory with a dubious title to the place he held. He was lukewarm and hoping for release. He was stirring no one and establishing nothing. Only once, when from somewhere at the back of an audience an irate Protestant divine leaped up with a slur on Roman Catholics, did he rouse to a cold, clipped intensity that whipped the heckler to silence. After that, for the evening, he returned to his subject with a release and fluency that brought a surprising burst of cheers at the end. As he was turning away from the platform John Willison came up to him, grinning. 'You should hire that preacher for all your meetings.'

Laurier laughed and was almost his old self through the reception that followed. Yet his next night's performance was as dull and lacklustre as the rest. Toronto had been carefully avoided on this trip and he thanked his stars for it. He knew that the party notables and party contributors who sat on each platform and staged the receptions afterward were beginning to look at him with sceptical coolness. He did not particularly care. 'A man has the right to avoid degenerating into a political hack.'

Trailed by the debts and worries of Arthabaska, entertained in lavish homes he could not aspire to himself, the floridly honoured guest was in reality the half-hearted servant of men who could buy and sell him twenty times over. The time would come, if he went on, when he would be the guest with the extended hand, doing the work at bidding. The tour of Ontario had been a failure and it would be the last failure. One more session, perhaps, and then it must be Blake again. He was almost sure that Blake wanted it; he was certain the party wanted it.

6

THE DETERMINATION was reinforced by Zoë's relief and delight as the quiet of Arthabaska settled about them again. The view of his wife in strange surroundings had brought back much of the old closeness and given him a new respect for her. Always herself, always with a vigilant eye for his comfort and well-being, she was never diminished to drabness by the little concerns. She carried his money and watched over his diet and saw to his dress, but she also moved gracefully and easily at the side of the party leader. She had little experience in the English sphere of public life and less taste for it, but she had the shrewd and simple conviction that most men are more or less the same. She could find the link that made the public figure human; she was soon talking with him of his wife or with his wife of the children. She responded to new personalities and she could sense the core of new ideas. She had grown with the tour, though she had liked it as little as Laurier, and she would not shrink again. As the neighbours called on their return home and the evening gatherings began once more he was a little amused, and a little disturbed and guilty, at the change in the attitude of Emilie that reflected the change in Zoë. Mme Lavergne had stayed at home, the wife of the obscure partner, and she had not liked it. Zoë, as she dissected the events and personalities of the trip, seemed to emphasize with every matter-of-fact word that hers was the first place.

As indeed, he told himself, it was. There had never been any doubt of that and he owed her more of his life than he had given. Now that his own inclinations ran so strongly in that direction, the life of the quiet lawyer and devoted husband, the life of books and the study and perhaps the pen, became irresistibly attractive. There was no reason why he could not aspire, as the practice grew, to an establishment as gracious as any of those he had seen in Ontario. Certainly, at least, he could have freedom from this nagging, squalid concern for debts. A long autumn and much of the winter lay ahead of him before the next session. It would be his last as leader and perhaps his last as a member of parliament. There would be time to make plans, time to work free of the entangling preoccupations and prepare for a graceful departure.

Instead there were the continuing repercussions of the bold forward step. There was the enigma of Blake, more exasperating with every exchange. There was Cartwright on the one hand, wholly committed and urging him on. There were the loophole-seekers on the other, wilting under the loyalty cry and seeing the new Republicanism of the United States as a heaven-sent chance of escape. There could be no hope of a reciprocity agreement, they argued, while high-tariff men were in the saddle below the border; therefore the issue had been removed from the sphere of practical politics. It was true enough for the moment. But what was emerging now was a question for the long future, a matter of the whole orientation of the country. Laurier, with all his old resentments irritated and all his old predilections reinforced by the imperialism of Chamberlain and McCarthy and the loudly loyal Britishers, found himself hardening steadily in favour of Cartwright's North American continentalism. Without reciprocity as an issue, moreover, he was the bankrupt leader of a bankrupt party. He would not go back, he was in no condition to go forward, and he could not get out with dignity. Nor would Blake say a word to assist him or to free him. With every courteous involution of rhetoric the letters from Murray Bay declined the leadership, declined to support the official policy of the party, declined to propose an alternative.

With all this came the troubles of Quebec. Pacaud was raising money for federal and provincial by-elections indiscriminately and fighting them in the same way; he seemed at times to be fighting with himself. He was indignant over the establishment of a new Liberal newspaper in Quebec City. He had to be quieted, he had to be kept working, and he had to have his activities sorted out. Mercier had to be watched, assisted, and evaded all at the same time. He made amicable gestures toward Laurier and sent more invitations for fishing-trips which Laurier found it inconvenient to accept. At the same time he stoked the fires that were beginning to glow over the Jesuit Estates settlement by appointing Curé Labelle as a deputy in his colonization ministry. The man was a beloved and venerable pioneer of Quebec's movement onto new lands but he was nevertheless the first Catholic priest to be appointed to public office since the conquest. It was another regally autonomous gesture under the banner of Quebec Liberalism and the reaction was quite predictable. French-Canadian settlements west of the Ottawa began to be viewed by the high Tory press of Toronto in a new and sinister light. Editors who had been grumbling over the intrusion of the Pope on the Canadian scene now found it necessary to sound a warning against a priest-led invasion of Ontario.

By the end of the year escape from the leadership seemed farther away than ever. Blake wrote in late December that he was not even going to attend the next session of the House. If he could not help, he said, he would not hurt; Laurier could be sure of that. There was the usual obliquity, the usual sense of injury, and a hint that he was allowing the party a little longer to stew in its own juice. But if the strain was growing and Laurier's irritation mounting he tried to smother both in his reply. The presence or absence of Blake for this session was in any case almost irrelevant. Reciprocity, for the French-Canadian leader of the Liberal party, was not going to be the issue. Mercier had made sure of that.

Parliament opened on January 31, 1889, and a long debate on the eternal fisheries dispute with the United States provided Laurier with an opening through which he managed to herd the shaky party. At an agitated caucus a resolution was adopted proposing Unrestricted Reciprocity as the policy that would end all such intracontinental quarrels. The motion was duly presented and lost and then on March 26, as Colonel William Edward O'Brien rose to move the disallowance of the Jesuit Estates

Act, all other issues disappeared from the newspapers.

O'Brien, who had commanded the York-Simcoe Regiment during the second Riel Rebellion, was the loyal spokesman of D'Alton McCarthy. McCarthy was the real leader of the debate and about him as it went on gathered the group of eight Conservatives and five Liberals henceforth to be known alternatively as the Noble Thirteen or the Devil's Dozen. Macdonald, it was quite apparent, inclined to the latter phrase. He knew there was no legal basis for upsetting Mercier's legislation, he was in no position to antagonize Quebec, and he was now witnessing a direct revolt against his authority in Ontario. All this was quite clear as he spoke against the motion, and it was equally clear that McCarthy, if he was fighting a lost cause here, was looking far beyond it.

Laurier spoke on March 28, with five Ontario rebels in his own camp. He supported Mercier's arrangement and he made what he could of Macdonald's troubles. They stemmed inevitably, he said, from the vicious policies of the past. Macdonald had always tried to interfere in provincial affairs and now his chickens were coming home to roost. The mask, moreover, was being torn away from the party that had always worn two faces, 'a rigid Protestant face turning towards the west and a devout Catholic face turning towards the east'.

Yet he was all too conscious, as he spoke, that the real enemy was not Macdonald nor even McCarthy. The old evil genius of the nation was rising again on both sides of the party line. McCarthy reminded Quebec that the fortunes of war had made Canada a British country. Charlton, one of the leading Liberals of Ontario, considered that it should be a country of one race. Listening to them both Laurier felt himself alert and angry and alive as he had not been in three years. 'I tell this to the honourable gentleman,' he answered McCarthy; 'I am of French origin but I am a British subject.' He turned on Charlton with defiant challenge. 'Well,' he asked, 'what would that race be? Is it the British lion that is to swallow the French lamb or the French lamb that is to swallow the British lion? There can be more than one race, but there shall be but one nation.'

The noble thirteen were easily voted down but neither the

end of the debate nor the end of the session brought relief. The issue moved out from the restraining atmosphere of parliament into the wider arena of the nation where new contestants could enter and no holds were barred. Orange Ontario lined up behind McCarthy to form the Equal Rights Association which would guard the country against invading Frenchness and rampant Catholicism. The Toronto *Mail* warned its readers of the French migration creeping west from the borders of Quebec. 'Ontario will not be safe . . . our eastern gate has already been opened . . . Catholic invasion is already streaming through . . . to detach eastern Ontario from the British and Protestant civilization of which it now forms a part and annex it to the territory of the French race, which is also the dominion of the priest.' McCarthy, at the head and heart of it all and riding the whirlwind with zest, called for a buckling on of armour. The 'bastard nationality' must be redeemed in spite of itself for the safety of the nation. 'This is a British country, and the sooner we take in hand our French Canadians and make them British in sentiment and teach them the English language, the less trouble we shall have to prevent. Now is the time when the ballot box will decide this great question; and if that does not supply the remedy in this generation bayonets will supply it in the next.'

Mercier's answer was a magnificent rally at Quebec centred around the Feast of Saint-Jean Baptiste, patron of French Canadians. There, at ceremonies that began on June 23 and went on through June 25, a monument was unveiled to Jean de Brébeuf, greatest of the Jesuit martyrs. French Canadians, not only from Quebec but from all parts of the continent, gathered to hear the reply to imperialism, Protestantism, and Anglo-Saxondom. The Imperial Federation League, said Mercier, proposed to fasten on the nation 'a political régime which through conscription could scatter our sons from the icefields of the North Pole to the burning sands of the Sahara'. To McCarthy and the Equal Rights Association he answered with a new vision that went far beyond the boundaries of Quebec and did much to confirm the fears of the Toronto *Mail*. 'We are now two millions and a half French Canadians in America. We care little for the threats of our enemies. When we vanish we shall say to the generation called to succeed us: We are Catholic and French, and when you, our successors, vanish in your turn, you must say to the generation which will replace you, "We die Catholic and French." This will be our testament and theirs; the supreme last will of a heroic people, transmitted from father to son, from generation to generation until the end of time.'

By contrast Laurier's words when he rose at the glittering banquet table seemed almost pale. He was paler than usual himself. 'I have often thought', he said, gracefully noting the presence of visitors from far-off parts of the continent, 'that Quebec should be for the French Canadians what Mecca is for Arabia, the city *par excellence,* the holy city among all.' But he sounded no echo to Mercier's heroic cry. He spoke of the conquest as a thing complete. He found in Confederation a decree of Providence that the two races should henceforth live in peace and harmony and he tried to bridge the gap between them with two names, English names. He spoke of Blake as he always spoke of him and he dwelt for once on the greatness of Macdonald. 'The man from whom I differ *toto coelo* . . . but it must be acknowledged that in his long career Sir John Macdonald has displayed such eminent qualities that he would have made his mark on any of the world's stages and that, with the single exception, perhaps, of Mr. Mercier, no one on this continent has excelled as he has in the art of governing men.'

He sat down to mild applause. He had not outshone Mercier and he had not intended to. He was beginning to feel himself the leader of a national party and he knew what he must do.

12

'THIS MAN WOULD BE A GIANT'

1889-1891

ONCE MORE, as in 1886, Toronto would have to be the fighting-ground. This time, however, the Tory stronghold was guarded by more than the enemy. It was also ringed round against the French Canadian by a watchful picket-line of his own friends. The invasion of rural Ontario, made at a time of comparative quiet and with a moderately docile party behind him, had been at best a disappointment. To appear in Toronto now, with race and religion an issue and with every prominent Liberal bending under the assaults of the Orange Order and the Equal Rights Association, would be an outright invitation to disaster. It was the opinion of Cartwright, Edgar, and Mulock, expressed with varying degrees of evasion and tact. It was probably the opinion of Mowat. What Blake thought Laurier did not know because he did not intend to ask.

There remained, more rash than the party elders, the party youth. John Willison was a leader among them and he arrived at Arthabaska for a long-promised visit in early August. He was now chief editorial writer of the *Globe*, president of the Young Men's Liberal Club, and at odds with the policy of his newspaper as it gyrated wildly round the issue of the Jesuit Estates. He was certainly no Jesuit-lover and his distrust of Mercier was profound, but the friendly interest with which he had first approached Laurier had warmed and strengthened in the past few years. If the Englishman's understanding of the French Canadian was not as complete as he assumed it to be, his support up to the present had been consistent and he was prepared to go further. He was the man of the moment at the house in Arthabaska, and its charm, for a few quiet days, was allowed to envelop him completely.

Zoë was herself in surroundings that she had furnished to her unassuming taste. They were gracious now, within doors and without. If debt had returned to hover over the rooftop it was not yet oppressive. The house sat comfortably in the midst of a broad lawn, looking down to the street of the church and across the road to the little office. The red brick walls with their white facings had mellowed in ten years and were settling into the landscape as trees climbed and leafed about them. The gardens had grown well. The rooms were the rooms of Queen Victoria's day but homeliness intervened where overstuffed elegance threatened to oppress. The bust of Blake and the portrait of Mackenzie were balanced by a multitude of family pictures. The piano that had come from Dr. Gauthier's by way of Dr. Poisson's was still prominent in the drawing-room and much in use. There were flowers everywhere. The book-lined study delighted the bookish visitor. There were always children about in the daytime and most of the evenings were enlivened by good and witty company. There were one or two evenings, however, on which the guest and his host sat alone, looking out from the screened gallery at the back of the house toward the darkening maples climbing the slopes of Mont Christo.

The conversations ranged over the problems of the party and veered gradually, without seeming direction by the host, toward the problem of Toronto. He would like to go there and present his case, Laurier confided, but it was impossible. Every senior member of the party was against it. There would be riots and violence; he would be humiliated and discredited. Willison scoffed. He had no patience with the party elders and not much with Laurier. There had been no trouble three years before and there would not be this time. The Young Liberals would organize a meeting in a week if Laurier would say the word. The leader was politely incredulous but allowed himself to be persuaded and eventually dared. Willison left with a firm commitment that Laurier would address a meeting if a meeting were arranged. Laurier sat on in Arthabaska, armoured and anchored by the same promise against the coming storm of advice.

By the end of August Willison's confidence was confirmed. The Horticultural Pavilion in Toronto had been engaged. The Young Liberals had the bit in their teeth and the older men were bracing themselves for trouble or looking for escape. 'I find it rather difficult to make the suggestions which you invite about your Toronto speech,' Edgar wrote crisply on September 1. 'If you sought to please the ordinary Toronto public you should not talk politics at all. They are busy with real-estate speculation, trade, education, and a great deal of what they suppose to be religion. The latter is strong enough to make them hate one another cordially, but not true enough to make them love one another.'

Edgar would probably be on hand to face the music but he was hardly inclined to be helpful, and Cartwright was even less so. He was afraid, he confided on September 18, that he would have to be in Boston at the time Laurier was in Toronto. Only from Pointe-au-Pic on the St. Lawrence, where Blake was finishing out the summer, came a word of restrained cordiality. 'I see you are to be in Toronto on the 27th September – we hope you will be able to stay with us.' Laurier would not, and he could hardly expect that Blake would appear with him since he had left Blake to learn of the meeting through the newspapers. This time, and in good earnest, he was on his own.

The loneliness was more or less concealed on the evening of September 30 when he faced the crowded galleries of the Horticultural Pavilion for the second time in his life. The Young Liberals had provided a rousing reception in Toronto and the only hint of violence had come from the Tory press. A good number of the leading federal Liberals had been dragooned onto the platform and Oliver Mowat had decided to attend with every member of his provincial cabinet.

None of it, however, was as reassuring as it looked. Laurier had been made all too well aware of the party's grim suspense, and the speech that Mowat had prepared in his support lay locked in the files of the *Globe*. It was not to be printed, Willison had been enjoined, unless Mowat chose to deliver it. The French Canadian was here to reply to Mercier as he had not replied in Quebec, and he would not be thanked for it. He was here to reply to Ontario, and it would be a hard answer. But his bleak conviction that the work was necessary had been powerfully reinforced even before his manoeuvrings began with Willison. 'It is probable', Cartwright had written him on August 9 after a trip to Winnipeg and an interview with Greenway, the provincial premier, 'that Greenway and his people will move to abolish separate schools and the French language in Manitoba.' McCarthy's field was widening. His work was being taken up by other hands and the hands would soon join.

Willison was chairman of the meeting and got through his introduction with only a few subdued hisses when he mentioned the Jesuit Estates and the *Globe*. Totally unfair, he grumbled afterward, as his damned newspaper had boxed the compass on the issue. Laurier, when he stood up, was almost taken aback by the wave of applause that greeted him. But it was the old applause of 1886; he recognized it as the undernotes came through to him. This iron-bound Tory multitude was prepared to acknowledge courage but it was waiting for him like a watchful gladiator. The speech got under way, he mentioned D'Alton McCarthy's name for the first time, and received his answer. From every section of the hall came a spaced, rhythmic cheering that met him and rose over him as he tried to go on. It was not prearranged, it was not a wild outburst, and there was no venom in it. There was almost a quality of respect about it and it was the worse for that because it was spontaneous and deliberate. It spoke for this city, this Anglo-Saxon capital of the country. It was the voice of the convictions that McCarthy had put into words and for a while it was too much for Laurier.

He was nearly five minutes in regaining control of the meeting and he was not sure by the end of that eternity that he would be able to speak at all. Standing impotent under the steady beat of sound, with his hands beginning to shake and his whole body damp with sweat, he looked out over the silent spaces of the hall for the sympathetic faces, the unspoken support that had balanced the uproar of hecklers at so many other meetings. It was not there. Toronto might respect the man but solidly and adamantly the genius of Toronto resented and opposed the French Canadian. It seemed in that moment that it always would, it always must. Yet, when the cheering gave way at last, he found his voice again.

He answered McCarthy with the theme of Confederation, the Confederation he had once opposed. The years had brought him round; he might have been speaking with Cartier's voice now, almost with Macdonald's. 'The great task we set ourselves twenty-two years ago seems to be no more advanced than it was twenty-two years ago. The causes may be summed up in one word – distrust. Distrust of race against race, distrust of creed against creed, distrust of motives, distrust of intentions; distrust which engenders hostility, the consequences of which are most appalling.'

The imperialists and super-Protestants of Ontario had warned against the ultramontanes and the *Parti National* of Quebec. He had sounded the warning himself often enough and he sounded a warning again, for both sides. He would not predict the destiny of Canada but there could be no imperialism that submerged one race. Neither could religion hope to set the course, any religion. 'I shall be asked, what will you do if the ultramontanes of the province of Quebec make an attempt against our liberties and free institutions? Why, sir, we shall do as in the past. We shall fight them.' And he answered the ultra-nationalists as he answered the imperialists: 'If any there are amongst my fellow countrymen of French origin who have ever dreamed of forming themselves into a small community of Frenchmen on the banks of the St. Lawrence, I am not one of them.'

The matter of the Jesuit Estates was already dwarfed in his own mind by the looming of greater problems, but he was here to deal with it. He defended every aspect of Mercier's settlement and ended with a resounding slap at the underlying intention. 'I believe the whole of that Act would have passed without any trouble . . . but for the fact that the name of the Pope was prominently introduced in it.' He knew enough of English history, he said, and enough of English literature to be aware that the British heart was touched in its most receptive chord 'when Shakespeare put into the mouth of King John the proud words which he made him address to the Pope's legate:

> No Italian priest
> Shall tithe or toll in our Dominion.'

The words rolled out on the swell of the magnificent voice, hardly accented now. They said nothing but they would reverberate through Quebec for too long. Here, in this moment, the hall came alive with cheering and the crisis of the speech was passed. He could go on to speak of reciprocity as a matter of money rather than the flag and to predict that Macdonald would attempt to steal the Liberal's clothes before the next election. Mowat, when his time came, spoke to an audience that seemed to have settled back into the mood of any political meeting. But he spoke from no manuscript, he was frostily non-committal on Laurier, and so utterly vacuous on every other point that his listeners, who knew and enjoyed the ways of the old fox, began to laugh at him. The eyes behind the spectacles twinkled back and as he sat down he leaned over and whispered something to the grim-faced Willison. It was easy to guess what he had said. The speech in the files of the *Globe* was not to see the light of day. For the gladiator of Quebec the thumbs in this arena had been turned down.

Yet the next day even the Tory newspapers were soberly restrained in their judgment. No one was quite sure what had happened but if it was not the best it was certainly not the worst. At a luncheon in the privacy of the Reform Club Mowat was demurely effusive in his tribute to the Liberal leader. Laurier listened without gratitude and with growing irritation, and leaned over to Willison in his turn. 'Damn him,' he muttered. 'Why didn't he say that last night?'

He left Toronto, still resentful. 'Our friends were too intimidated', he wrote Pacaud, 'to give me the support which I had every right to expect.' Nevertheless, he added, 'I confess, without false modesty, that my speech had a very great effect.' He could sense a change in the attitude of the men about him and he could feel the change in himself. Out of a confusion of limp expediencies the hard edge of at least one purpose was beginning to emerge. It was beginning to be recognized. The judgment of Willison, it seemed, might yet become the judgment of the party. 'He is not viciously aggressive,' Willison had written. 'He is not unwisely pugnacious. But he is very, very firm; a calm, strong, steadfast man who will not be turned from his purpose. He cannot fight well except his heart be in it. This man would be a giant in some great national crisis.'

2

CARTWRIGHT saw no great crisis brewing and he was not alive to changing attitudes. He still regarded himself as the doctor who prescribed for the party, and his principal worry was the return of Blake for the session of 1890. In December, as the question of policy rose, his prescription came. Reciprocity, he thought, must sleep while the Republicans of Benjamin Harrison ruled in the United States. Liberals must bide their time, making what hay they could. They might let the Throne Speech pass without debate and tear into the budget when it was presented. They might make it a 'farmer's session', pointing out the effects of the tariff and the general extravagance of the government in depressing agriculture and loading up farms with mortgages. 'Make this our pièce de résistance and garnish a bit with lively attacks on the Inter-Colonial, on Tupper's jobs in Oxford and a variety of minor malfeasances.'

Laurier's mood was considerably different and by no means so relaxed. Parliament was to meet on January 16, and a few days before he left for Ottawa he delivered his farewell injunctions to Pacaud. *L'Electeur* was to provide a reliable correspondent for the press gallery; he anticipated a very strenuous session and he wished to be well reported in Quebec. 'Were our troubles to come only from the government the outlook would be agreeable enough. It is the McCarthy group who are going to set the tinderwood aflame. I see clearly and precisely the position I shall take, but I am not sure whether my views will be accepted by everyone.

'I have asked one or two journalists from Ontario to meet me in Ottawa on Saturday the 25th,' he added. 'Can you also be there on that date as I particularly wish to see you. Promise that you will come.'

These were unusually careful arrangements. By Saturday the twenty-fifth the session would be nine days old. He could hope by then to have shaped the mood of the party and he wished to make it clear to the press. He was equally concerned to prevent Pacaud, perhaps under the influence of Mercier, from going off on one of his disastrous tangents. He was planning as a leader now, and he was taking the reins of the party in hand not the less firmly because of the expected presence of Blake. Blake would be back, but not at the desk beside Laurier; that was Cartwright's position. Blake had made it clear that he was taking his seat as a lowly private member expecting no special consideration. It was clear to everyone else that he must compel and receive consideration at every turn. 'Where MacGregor sits, there is the head of the table,' quoted one of the Toronto papers. The new leader would be spared the incongruity of finding the old at his left hand but he would not be spared much else. Every move he made would be under the weight of that presence, and at least on one issue, under its massive disapproval. Laurier agreed with Cartwright that reciprocity would not be a lively issue in the coming session and he did not share Cartwright's outspoken hostility to Blake's second coming. He welcomed and resented it, however, in about equal proportions since the sceptre that he offered to return with each letter was still declined with each reply. If he was not conscious of any weakening in his own desire to abdicate he was at least more on his mettle. With the work immediately ahead he could deal as well as Blake or better, and somewhere in the depths, perhaps, the vague suspicion was growing that Blake's time had passed him by.

Neither the press conference nor the presence of Pacaud cleared Laurier's field of the minor irritations. Reciprocity, it developed early in the session, was coming in by a side door. Nothing was less desired by the Ontario men than any form of action on the main issue. They did demand, however, with Mulock as their principal spokesman, that a party shelter be erected against the drumfire of the Imperial Federation League. It took the form in their minds of an address of loyalty to the Queen, not, as Mulock said, to reassure anyone in Canada or Britain about the sentiments of Canadian Liberals but to make it clear to the Americans that the country was on the verge neither of independence nor of annexation. The pious vacuity of the resolution as it finally emerged from caucus commanded the tongue-in-cheek support of Macdonald and the entire Conservative party and was passed unanimously. Blake, however, walked out of the House before the vote was taken, angrily declaring in the corridors that he would not be party to a sham. *L'Electeur*'s new correspondent in the press gallery then helped things along by fully reporting the incident with a sardonic commentary of his own on the loyal sentiments.

Laurier had regarded the whole episode as a byplay to appease Ontario. The framing of the resolution had taxed his patience and frayed his nerves. He had supported it in the House irritably and with reservations. 'Our connection with Great Britain cannot forever remain what it is,' he had said; 'I do not expect that Canada will remain forever a colony.' With the deed done, however, and with Blake out of control he was in no mood for *L'Electeur*'s nonsense. 'If he was paid to harm us he could not do any better,' he wrote Pacaud after he had had the correspondent in his office for an hour's scolding. 'What he did regarding Mulock's motion irritated me beyond words. God knows what difficulties I had to encounter to get our friends to accept it; and now it has all been to no purpose.'

The lecture to Pacaud began on February 8 and overflowed into a second letter on February 9. A week and a day later Laurier rose to attack the real business of the session. It had been introduced as expected by D'Alton McCarthy, once more to the discomfiture of John A. Macdonald. The Northwest Territories were now the ground on which the Noble Thirteen, with a clutch of additional supporters, chose to give battle. It was a battle, however, that they quite evidently hoped to expand. McCarthy's motion proposed that the use of the French language should be abolished in the legislatures and courts of the territories but its preamble took a wider view. 'Whereas it is expedient', it began, 'in the interest of the national comity of the Dominion that there should be community of language among the people of Canada . . . the enactment in the North-West Territories Act allowing the use of the French language should be expunged therefrom.'

McCarthy, speaking in support of his motion, had been as always brilliant and hard and narrow. Macdonald had spoken for tolerance with a genuinely moving sincerity, all the more so, perhaps, since his party was cracking under him. Langevin, Chapleau, and all the Quebec members were bitter and aroused. The French language, they maintained, had been official in the courts and assembly of the territories since 1875 and could not now be abolished. The law supported them but the law could not change facts. The great prairies between Manitoba and the Rockies were still largely empty, but they would have little use for French. Wherever settlement came, the English-speaking arrivals were in a ratio of twenty to one to the French-speaking. To the English members of the House, though most stood apart from McCarthy, a law outmoded was a law that should be changed.

As he watched the familiar gulf opening on both sides of the aisle Laurier had been grateful for the intervention of John Thompson, Macdonald's Minister of Justice. The former judge from Nova Scotia had been a rising man since 1885 and he had first made his mark in a powerful, slashing defence of the Riel execution. If it had not endeared him to Laurier it had at least imposed respect. Thompson was a big man and he was growing. He was a convert to Catholicism and since a question of language could never be divorced from a question of religion in this House he was well equipped in spite of his record on Riel to moderate with the French of his own party. On the other side of the aisle sat Blake and for the first time in the session Laurier had been wholly glad of his presence. The Catholic Conservative had reached out a hand to the English Liberal whom every Frenchman trusted, and Blake had taken the hand.

Between them two great lawyers had produced the only practical amendment to McCarthy's bill. In effect it granted what McCarthy asked while defeating the purpose of his asking. The people of the Northwest Territories, it provided, should be allowed to decide the language question for themselves and there was no doubt as to what the decision would be. The amendment emphatically denied, however, that uniformity of language was expedient throughout the Dominion.

From this ground Laurier spoke. He knew the amendment would pass and he supported it, almost carelessly. But he had no intention of stopping there. McCarthy would not, and the time had come to meet McCarthy and McCarthy-ism head on. 'I can find nothing in this bill, I must say, but the old, old spirit of domination and intolerance which, in this land and in other lands, has always characterized the course of pure, undiluted Toryism . . . it constitutes a declaration of war against the French race.

'If this measure of the honourable gentleman were not to be followed by any other, if it were to remain as it appears here, a measure for the proscription of the French language confined to the Northwest Territories alone, where the French population is small, I would be inclined to say: let the measure pass and let us return to those measures of practical usefulness which demand our attention. But . . . this is only a preliminary skirmish, soon to be followed by a general onslaught upon the whole French race in Canada. The French Canadians are to be deprived of their language, not only in the Northwest Territories but wherever their language exists. They must be deprived of everything which constitutes their distinct individuality and this must be done by legislation now; but if not done now by legislation, in future it will be done by force and violence, by bullets and bayonets.

'The honourable gentleman coldly proposes that one and a half million of Canadians – in order, as he says, that they should become good Canadians – should renounce their origin and the traditions of their race. He proposes that the humiliation of one whole race in this country should be the foundation of this Dominion. Does he believe that to subject one whole section of our population to the humiliation of renouncing its origin, of turning its back upon its history, would make them proud of the country?

'We are here a nation, or we want to be a nation. The honourable gentleman will revert to the cold, dry argument that after all a duality of race will produce friction and that friction will produce danger. But where is the remedy? The true remedy . . . is mutual forbearance and respect.'

McCarthy had complained of Mercier's policy and speeches, and of the domination of the priest over the lowly habitant. 'This is what he claims his fellow countrymen and my fellow countrymen of English origin have to bear. Well, I tell him that the French Canadians have also something to bear. What we object to is the meddlesome interference of certain men in Ontario in our domestic politics; what I object to is the whining pity bestowed by some over-zealous and over-good men in Ontario upon the poor, downtrodden, prostrate French Canadians. If we could make a compact between the English and the French, each to mind his own business and not meddle with the business of the other, we would get along tolerably well, not only tolerably well but perfectly well.'

He held up a newspaper quoting one of McCarthy's speeches against the French-language schools in eastern Ontario. ' "As a citizen of Ontario," ' he read deliberately, ' "as a citizen of the Dominion, I heartily endorse the sentiment that we ought, and ought at once and for all time, to put an end to the teaching of our children, either French-Canadian or English, in any other language than the language of the country in which we live." ' Then he turned on McCarthy. 'Is this really the measure of my honourable friend? Can it be that an honourable gentleman possessing the attainments, power, and ability of my honourable friend should stoop to things so low? It is a thing low and vile and contemptible to say that the people of Ontario, whatever be their creed or their origin, shall not have the right to teach a second language to their children if they choose.'

He had dealt with McCarthy, but there remained McCarthy's opposites. Langevin and the ultramontanes stood fast on the settlement of 1875. The guarantees to the French language and the institutions framed for the Northwest Territories, they claimed, were permanent. Chapleau for once stood with them. Laurier disagreed flatly. The institutions of the Northwest were not permanent; they were exceptionally temporary. 'When the time comes I hope we shall all be prepared, without party differences, to deal with this question on the broad principles that apply to this constitution . . . the true principles which are only an emanation of divine truth.'

It was a faint hope and he called in his peroration on 'an eternal Providence who, even when all seems lost, still guides everything for the greatest good'. He had the feeling that events were outrunning him, the sense of an avalanche poised above him and stealthily preparing. The French language was silenced in the Territories and its few rights in Ontario were already threatened. Nor was this more than a beginning. Less than a month after the debate ended McCarthy was in Winnipeg urging the Manitobans 'to make this a British country in fact as in name', and in that same month of March the Manitoba legislature abolished French and Catholic denominational schools.

They had been guaranteed as a right at the time of the erection of the province, buttressed by every constitutional guarantee. The act of the provincial legislature would most certainly be fought in the courts and the courts might well decide in favour of the minority. But where was the judge whose fiat could be made to stand when every fact of growth and population was against it? In Manitoba as in the Territories it was the English and not the French who had filled the empty lands. The interpretation of an old law could not change the will of a new province and the attempt to stand on the law would bring the whole basis of Confederation into question. The attack was shaping and gathering weight against the last citadel.

There was only one defence. Laurier tried to make this clear to Pacaud amid the uproar over his yielding in the Northwest Territories. 'There was no other solution for this question. I wish you would point out the necessity for the people of Quebec province to maintain inviolate the principle of local autonomy. There are circumstances when it may tell against us, but it is the only protection that we have under the constitution, and if we want to apply it in our own behalf we must be careful to apply it also when it is contrary to us . . . I am as sure as I am living that the course which I took will be found the most beneficial when the cause of Quebec comes before the House, and that may be at no very distant day.'

3

It was to be a year of provincial elections and all the omens were good. New Brunswick had gone Liberal in January. Fielding in Nova Scotia and Mowat in Ontario would go to the electors in May and would almost certainly win. June was the month for Quebec and Mercier had never seemed more securely in the saddle or more arrogantly confident. At bay in the provinces, Macdonald tottered down the slope of an aging parliament at the head of a corrupt and inert government. The nagging persistence of hard times was driving him away from the National Policy to look for some form of partial reciprocity. If he folded the flag and turned to the United States the loyalty cry would be silenced. He would be left, on the question of tariffs, in the old dilemma of Blake. The McCarthy group was an indigestible lump in the party's middle, a wedge splitting the ultramontanes of Quebec from the high Tories of Ontario. Every woe of the nation and every factor of policy seemed to point to the old man's going at the next general election.

It was a prospect so strange after a dozen years as to seem almost incredible. It was hardly welcome when one thought of the trials beyond it. And it was difficult to know, as the spring wore on, whether it was obscured or brightened by other factors that lay in the noisome depths well below the level of policy.

Scandal was brewing in Quebec and somewhere at the heart of it all was J. Israel Tarte, who was now publisher of the newspaper *Le Canadien*. Always a *Bleu* of *Bleus*, he had long sided with Langevin in the eternal quarrel with Chapleau. He appeared now to have changed sides and to have drawn Caron with him into an alliance against Langevin. A Liberal, from one viewpoint, could only welcome the change and what it promised. Tarte, Chapleau, and Caron seemed to be stirring together, out of the affairs of the brothers McGreevy, the ingredients of an explosion that could wreck the Conservative party.

Thomas and Robert McGreevy had succeeded to the backstairs throne of Adélard Sénécal and had greatly widened his empire. Thomas was now a large contractor with heavy railway interests. Robert, the younger brother, was a partner in the firm of Larkin,

Connolly and Company, which seemed able to bid very successfully on most of the federal government's public works contracts. Thomas, in addition, was treasurer of the Conservative party in Quebec and brother-in-law to Sir Hector Langevin. During the months of each session in Ottawa he lived cozily *en famille* with the minister, and all had gone swimmingly until the brothers McGreevy quarrelled. At that point a gap had opened in the laced and interwoven system of Tory defences. Robert, vengefully angry at his brother, had come to Tarte with a long and horrendous tale.

Tarte had absorbed the story and shared it with Chapleau and Caron, and by the end of March the facts had reached Macdonald. Robert McGreevy had held, up to the time of the quarrel with his brother, a thirty-five per cent interest in the firm of Larkin, Connolly and Company. The interest had been acquired for him by Thomas, and no money had changed hands. The consideration had been the flat promise that all Thomas's influence would be used to get government contracts for the firm, and that promise had been faithfully kept. Every tender that Robert submitted had been approved in advance by Thomas. Thomas's word had been law in the execution of a contract. Thomas had seen to the arrangements with sub-contractors, to the hirings and firings of men, and to the provision of equipment and supplies. On each transaction he had collected his share of profit and of party patronage and all had been done, according to Robert, with the full knowledge and authority of Sir Hector Langevin.

Macdonald was well acquainted with scandal, but not quite on this scale. He sensed the presence of Chapleau in the background and was appalled at the thought of a rupture in his shaky cabinet. Langevin was one of his oldest friends and the man he had named as his successor. Both were familiar with the passage of large sums of money through devious channels but most of it had always ended in the party chest, devoted to the righteous work of crushing the Grits. Macdonald assumed this to be the case now, as in fact it was. Langevin and Thomas McGreevy, summoned before him, flatly denied all charges. He accepted the denial with whatever private doubts, sent home his Quebec informants, and devoutly hoped that the lid was clamped on Robert.

It was not. Robert was an Irishman and still vengeful. Tarte was at work, delicately and skilfully. Chapleau and Caron stood behind him. In *Le Canadien* attacks began on McGreevy, with hints of more to come. On May 5 Tarte was charged with libel and on May 14 suit was entered against him by Thomas McGreevy for $50,000. He appeared, ominously, to welcome it. He had not told much but there was plenty more to tell and Robert McGreevy was daily adding proof. Under Langevin and the Conservative party the bomb still ticked.

So far so good, in the view of a federal Liberal. But the view changed when it widened to include the provincial party in Quebec. There was another aspect to the range of McGreevy interests. Thomas, despite his involvement with federal Conservatives, was a heavy contributor to Mercier in funds and influence. He was interested in the public works of Quebec as well as of Ottawa. In co-operation with Sénécal he had had a part in building the North Shore Railway and a large part in creating the confusion that surrounded its affairs. He had emerged from them with a claim for $1,500,000 which was at best shadowy, at worst baseless, and which in any case had long seemed quiescent and abandoned. Now, in spite of Tarte's charges, and with a provincial election in the offing, he was advancing the claim again.

All this Laurier knew. He brooded in Ottawa over information that was less specific than Macdonald's but with a full knowledge of the ways of Quebec, and with almost equal disquiet. Always as each election neared the provincial capital became a turmoil of enigmas to which Pacaud was usually a reliable key. He was less so than usual. He was fighting Tarte with all his ancient venom. *L'Electeur* blossomed with praise of Thomas McGreevy as *Le Canadien* bristled with innuendo. McGreevy's hirelings would still be wanted as voters; McGreevy's funds would still be needed for the campaign treasury. Mercier and Pacaud, quite oblivious of the overhanging storm, were still going on in the old way.

At the end of March a letter had come from Mercier, delicately recalling old favours from the hand of Thomas McGreevy. Then a second had arrived, asking for Laurier's help in squelching Robert. Robert's charges, said Mercier, might damage the federal Tories but 'the evil which it would do him would be a poor reward for the services which Thomas McGreevy has done us and perhaps will do in the next struggle'.

The letters were enough to indicate Mercier's mood. When a hint of his actions came it did not come from Pacaud. 'I have just been informed', Laurier wrote to his strangely silent editor on April 19, 'that the local government intend to pay to Thomas McGreevy a large sum of money for his old stale claim on the North Shore Railway. I have good reason to believe that the payment of any amount, large or small, to McGreevy on such a claim would be a very dangerous mistake. I hope you will warn Mercier . . . I could say more than I do now upon this subject but I hope what I say will be sufficient at this moment.'

It was not sufficient. By the end of May a cheque of the provincial government for slightly less than one million dollars had gone to Thomas McGreevy in settlement of his claim on the North Shore Railway. Tarte's libel trial, postponed to the fall sittings, was five months off and Robert McGreevy's brief-case was hardly tapped. On June 17 the Liberal party of Quebec, never so confident, so buoyant, and so prosperous, swept to a brilliant victory in the provincial elections.

The victory dinner was held on July 2 at Le Club National in Montreal. It was more than a local celebration; it had been sponsored jointly by the four victorious Liberal provincial premiers. As the toasts were about to commence, Mme Mercier and other of the attendant ladies rose in the gallery and unfurled before themselves a great tricolour flag. It was French, said their spokesman at the table below, to recall the origin of a people, it carried the British ensign to recall that people's allegiance, and it carried the arms of Canada 'to affirm that we are Canadians'.

Once more a pallid Laurier rose to make a pallid speech. Parliament had prorogued in mid May, he had had six weeks to rest and observe and reflect, and he did not look the better for them. He was replying to a toast to Canada; his theme was provincial rights and he linked the names of the four premiers as their champions. The absence of any special congratulation to Mercier was pointed. Mercier had won his election. He was off on a triumphal tour of Europe which would take him to all the capitals, including Rome. He expected to return with a loan of ten million dollars for the development of Quebec. He very well might, Laurier reflected, but he would find the sequel to McGreevy's million waiting on his doorstep.

4

MACDONALD had pledged himself to hold another session of parliament before the next general election. Steadily, as the summer and autumn went on, it became less likely that the pledge would be kept. McCarthy's disruption of the party continued. The downward slide of the economy continued. The McKinley Bill had been fought through the American Congress and if another year were allowed for its murderous tariffs to take effect the last props would be knocked from under the National Policy. Macdonald could not ignore the hovering threat of McGreevy. With a party corrupt, distracted, tiring, and bankrupt of new ideas, it appeared to be now or never for the aging chieftain.

Laurier's suspicions grew with every week. By September he was warning Pacaud as of old to prepare to go to work. Around Pacaud too the thought of McGreevy hovered, but it was no time for righteous probing. The affair of the claim appeared to have been silenced by the ballots of provincial voters; whatever had been done was done. It was time now to mobilize the grimy cohorts of electioneers. It was time to appease Blake and shape a platform. It was time once more for the bold forward step.

In Cartwright's view the first and essential preliminary was a convention of Ontario Liberals. It would mean the presence of Blake and a new look at reciprocity, on which Blake remained unchanged. After a session through which the old leader had moved remote as the stars from the general run of the party and sometimes on collision courses with Laurier himself, there had been the usual dialogue on the subject of resignation. It had ended as usual and Blake, in a letter to the *Globe*, had answered the prophets who predicted and the critics who desired his return. 'My only wish', he had said, 'is that the confidence and affection of Liberals of all shades of opinion may induce Mr. Laurier to hold the place he so admirably fills.' It was all very well and as usual it solved nothing. Confidence and affection depended on party unity, and Blake's attitude was a principal source of disunion. Cartwright would have been glad to be rid of him, but it was as unthinkable to lose Blake as to abandon reciprocity. He had to be brought somehow into the bed that Laurier and Cartwright had made.

The matter of the convention had hardly been raised when another problem intruded. Overtures began to come from J. Israel Tarte. The move had, on reflection, a kind of lunatic inevitability. Still with McGreevy's secrets and still determined to use them, there was no hope for Tarte on any of his old horizons. Macdonald's dearest yearning was that he be stricken with dumb forgetfulness and vanish in the earth. The *Rouges* of Mercier were Tarte's nearest, deadliest enemies. The provincial *Bleus* were a powerless and defeated rump. Tarte was nearing bankruptcy and faced with a libel suit for $50,000. If he were to go on and survive, and he meant to do both, there remained for him only the camp of Laurier and the federal Liberals.

To a leader with a Blake on his hands the prospect of this recruit might have seemed alarming. Ontario Liberals regarded Tarte as the blackest of black ultramontane politicians. Pacaud bristled at his very name. Mercier feared and detested him for excellent reasons. He had behind him a long record of corrupt and devious electioneering, and it was more than probable that a good deal of McGreevy money had passed through his hands in days gone by. If he was a refugee now, the argument would go, he would most certainly prove to be a Trojan horse later. Yet for Laurier there was not much choice, and he understood Tarte.

The dapper little man with the beard and the sharp eye and the stutter was an Indian fighter of politics. Knowing no rules and few scruples, he lived for the scalps and victories and fought with the weapons at hand. He used money and he used priests, but the priests did not control him and the money did not interest him. In his own unfathomable way and by his own queer lights he was wholly incorruptible; he could not be bought or changed.

He would hold to the course he was set on and it happened to be the right one, with risks for all concerned. As friend or enemy he was almost equally dangerous, but he had to be accepted. He would be strong medicine for Ontario and poison to much of Quebec, but as a federal Liberal he would be a legion of tomahawks.

It was also clear, as the careful discussions advanced, that Tarte was a journalist on the track of the greatest story of his life. He might well have had Mercier in mind as his first target, but his scope had hugely widened as Robert McGreevy's relentless unveilings went on. He now meant to destroy Langevin if it meant the tearing-down of the whole Conservative party. He was not to be turned back by friend or enemy, libel suit or the threat of jail, and there was only one channel into which this vengeful energy could be directed.

The entrance lay by way of the courts. On October 1, 1890, Wilfrid Laurier, now in possession of all the evidence, appeared as attorney for the defence in the libel suit of *McGreevy* v. *Tarte*. It was a clear announcement to the watching political world that Tarte was now a Liberal. Nothing else was accomplished, since the trial was immediately postponed, but in *Le Canadien* the hints of McGreevy misdoings began again. On November 19 the name of Langevin crept into the grisly recital for the first time. The attack was launched, the new recruit accepted, and Tarte would stand as a Liberal in the next general election.

Election talk was so strongly in the wind now that Laurier had already authorized a warning circular from party headquarters. By the end of the year there were rumours of trade negotiations between Ottawa and Washington and before January was out the rumours had been confirmed. The confirmation was not official but the source was Ned Farrer who shared a desk with Willison at the *Globe*, and that was enough for Laurier. A one-time priest or seminarian whose religious convictions had changed and whose political convictions were known only to himself, Farrer had an uncanny knack of being everywhere, knowing everything, and writing with equal force on any side of a question. At the moment he favoured reciprocity if not annexation and he had secured an interview with James G. Blaine, the American Secretary of State. Without exactly invading ministerial privacy his dispatch managed to convey a strong impression of what he had learned. Macdonald was putting out feelers in the direction of reciprocity; and if Macdonald was preparing to steal the Liberal's clothes he was preparing for an election.

It gave new force to all of Cartwright's arguments for a convention of Ontario Liberals and arrangements were under way. Invitations had been sent early in January and the date was set for February 17 and 18 in Toronto. The arrangements, however, had been largely in Cartwright's hands and they had been made without Blake. On January 30 Laurier received an urgent telegram from Willison that brought him into the private offices of the *Globe* on the following morning. For nearly a week Willison, his publisher, and all the directors of the *Globe*, with the support of Mowat and of Blake's brother, had been bottling up a letter from the master. It was for publication, and if it were not published in the *Globe*, Blake had warned peremptorily, it would go on forthwith to the Tory Toronto *Mail*.

Willison's telegram had been delivered in Montreal. Laurier had received it just as he returned from New York where he had addressed the Board of Trade in support of reciprocity. He had probably said a good many things for which he would have to answer in Canada. During the course of the evening the American Secretary of the Treasury had dropped dead. All this, plus two nights on the train, was behind the leader of the party as he walked into Willison's office. He was hardly in a state or mood to deal with what confronted him.

Blake's letter was a full-throated attack on every aspect of the Liberal reciprocity plank. Blake himself, when Laurier met him an hour later, was a wounded lion who had had enough of Cartwright and nearly enough of Laurier. The convention had been arranged without him; therefore he would act alone. He would publish the letter. If he attended the convention he would speak as he wrote. If he entered the election as a candidate he would do the same.

Obviously there could be no convention and Laurier emerged from the interview with that plan abandoned. He had Blake's promise to suspend publication of the letter till the election was over. On February 12, nine days after the election had been formally called, he learned that Blake would not be a candidate and would not speak during the campaign. 'I die dumb,' he was reported to have said. At that moment it seemed a consummation devoutly to be wished.

5

WITH MY utmost effort, with my latest breath, will I oppose the "veiled treason" which attempts by sordid means and mercenary proffers to lure our people from their allegiance.' Macdonald's manifesto was out; the dickerings with Blaine were ended; he had given the back of his hand to the United States. Tupper was back from England for the battle, the Tory machine was grinding through the snows of February, and the seventy-six-year-old chieftain moved at the head of it with all the fire and flair of twenty years before. 'The question', he said, 'resolves itself into this: shall we endanger our possession of the great heritage bequeathed to us by our fathers, and submit ourselves to direct taxation for the privilege of having our tariff fixed at Washington, with a prospect of ultimately becoming a portion of the American union? . . . As for myself, my course is clear. A British subject I was born – a British subject I will die.'

It seemed enough but it was not all. On February 17 at the great election rally in Toronto that really opened Macdonald's campaign, he unveiled a gift of the gods. The redoubtable Ned Farrer had presented it to him, all unknowingly, by way of a thieving proofreader. It was a half-dozen sheets taken from a small pamphlet in which Farrer, viewing the affairs of the continent from the American side, outlined a few measures for bringing the Canadians to their senses. Nova Scotia fish might be taxed out of the United States, bonding privileges might be suspended, the southerly connections of the C.P.R. might be cut at Sault Ste. Marie. Trade with England could be made more difficult and expensive, and finally, with the disappearance of Macdonald, a great movement for annexation would spring up by itself in Canada. The pamphlet had been written 'for an American friend' by a man who wrote for anyone who was prepared to pay. There were only a dozen copies, all in proof, and until the sheets were stolen no eyes had seen them but the eyes of Farrer, the printer, and the proofreader. But Farrer was of the *Globe*, the *Globe* was for Laurier and reciprocity, and what was writ was writ. John A. Macdonald stood up with the sheets in his hand, the nation's champion as of old against the sordid means and mercenary proffers of the arch-traitor.

Up to that night Laurier had been sourly confident. With or without Blake, he was facing a crumbling government that had gone to the country in panic and against its pledge. Away from Blake he moved in a buoyant Quebec. Tarte was a candidate in Montmorency, filling the air with the clouds of scandal to come. Mercier, who had been making hard terms for his support in January, was now tamed. He had come home from his progress through Europe with the decorations of the French president and the Belgian king. He had been made a papal count by Leo XIII. But he had come home with a loan of four million dollars instead of ten, and he had found an opposition newly aroused. If Tarte was no longer attacking Quebec's 'Caesar', other hands were busy. Mercier was aware now that he might have need of Laurier and had thrown his weight behind him. Pacaud was jubilant and confident. Indispensable as always and fully in favour again, the little man filled the air with flattering expectations which Laurier had been inclined to share. The thought of becoming Prime Minister, he had written ten days before that night of February 17, 'makes me somewhat uneasy as there is nothing in my possible advancement that can flatter me. The position, so far as I am concerned, would have value only because it would enable me to do some good for those who are close to me and you, my dear Ernest, are in the front rank. All goes well, I think.'

He knew better as the reports from Toronto began to come in on February 18. Torydom might be bankrupt and the country restless and dour, but John A. Macdonald remained the presiding genius. Reciprocity would not be left where it lay with the Liberal party, an unshaped hope for an indeterminate future. It would stand out as the main issue of the campaign and the great threat to the nation. Quebec might not be much interested and Ontario only half convinced, but no Liberal could stand on a platform now without his answer. That answer in all its fullness, and with all the questions it bred, lay locked in the desk of Blake. It could not be given; it was a major preoccupation through all the campaign that it not be given and without it there was only defensive rhetoric and half-thought-out evasion. Laurier could only deny that reciprocity meant discrimination against England. Even if it did, the interests of Canada came first. There was no need for joint Canadian and American tariffs, there was no thought of political union, and in any case the allegiance that could be bought or held by trade was a poor thing.

March 5 brought the verdict. Explaining and explaining away had not been enough against the magic of the old man and the stark vehemence of the loyalty cry. Macdonald had held the Grits to a draw in Ontario and Quebec while Tupper in the Maritimes and the C.P.R. in Manitoba had given him the election.

It was a majority scraped up from the 'shreds and patches' of the Dominion, as Cartwright was to blurt out later in a savage indiscretion. Macdonald had collapsed a week before the polling and the returns on the night of March 5 had come to the sick-room of a man too tired to care. But he had won and he was to win more.

Two days before the election Laurier had sent his last entreaty to Blake. It had been preceded by others all through the campaign: 'As you admit yourself,' he had written earlier, 'it will do harm all around, and now let me ask you to what person or to what cause will it do any good? Not to you, not to me, not to the country, nor to the party, nor to the cause . . . Now, my dear Blake . . . you should never publish such a document . . . above all remember, that though you may discern here the voice of the official head of the party, it is before everything else the voice of your sincere friend.' The last note was colder. 'I am given to understand that it is your intention to publish your letter on the sixth of March . . . do you not believe that it would be preferable to wait until angry passions have settled down and until the public mind will be better prepared?'

He had received his answer by the time he knew he was beaten. 'I am very sorry to find myself unable to adopt your view,' Blake had replied on the fourth. 'The only doubt I have is whether my patience has not degenerated into weakness and my loyalty to friends into indifference to the public interest . . . God only knows what I have suffered in these last days . . . but . . . my feeling is that the sooner the last painful stage is over the better for all concerned.'

On March 6 the newspapers came to a seedy, shaken invalid at home in Arthabaska. The headlines blared the word of Macdonald's victory but the meat of the news was almost crowded aside by the four columns of Edward Blake's letter. It was addressed to the electors of his constituency of West Durham. It was the draft that Laurier had seen, and nothing disastrous was lacking. Point by point, paragraph by paragraph, it tore down every prop of Liberal policy. It destroyed Cartwright's arguments and derided Laurier's. It ripped away the shelters under which the loyalists had crouched. Finally, in one climactic lecture, all the gathered thoughts and gathered rancours of the great schoolmaster crawled snakily to a point. 'Assuming that absolute free trade with the States, best described as Commercial Union, may and ought to come, I believe that it can and should come only as an incident, or at any rate as a well-understood precursor of Political Union; for which indeed we should be able to make better terms before than after the surrender of our Commercial Independence. Then so believing – believing that the decision of the Trade question involves that of the Constitutional issue, for which you are unprepared, and with which you do not even conceive yourselves to be dealing – how can I properly recommend you now to decide on Commercial Union?'

The papers fell to the floor, followed by a train of expletives that Zoë had seldom heard. Macdonald's victory was now confirmed; there could be no hope of reversing it in the by-elections that lay ahead. But amputation was worse than defeat and there was worse than amputation. Not only had the legs of the Liberal party been sheared away; the head had been shattered and the brains exposed and they were a pathetic sight.

6

He was kept to his bed for three weeks and emerged to the nightmare month that remained before the new parliament. He would not think of Blake and he left Cartwright to pick up the pieces in Ontario. Quebec was enough for the moment. Bankrupt, dejected, and bitter, the party went about the work of clearing the wreckage and saving what it could. Tarte had been elected in Montmorency but his election was being contested. The Liberals had charges of their own against other candidates and the prosecution of each involved court procedures and money. Laurier was not grateful but he saw no way to refuse when Mercier came to the rescue. Ten thousand dollars went into the empty treasury on the strength of a note signed by Mercier and endorsed by Pacaud, Tarte, and some of the faithful *Rouges*. It was post-election routine, hardly the concern of the leader, and the leader hardly thought of it. If any note of warning throbbed in his aching head it was silenced by greater worries.

'J'y suis; j'y reste,' was Macdonald's greeting to the new parliament and the old opposition. Jaunty and restored as he seemed, the words had every appearance of truth. The only man who might belie them made his appearance on May 11, sitting at his desk in the House with a small black bag between his feet. He had been offered, he said, as much as a hundred thousand dollars for the contents of that bag and it would never leave his possession. J. Israel Tarte was bankrupt, beleaguered, and still not secure as a member of the House of Commons. The enemies who could not bribe him were still intent on invalidating his election. But he was safer than he had been for some time. 'It was a case of parliament or jail for me,' he said; 'I have spoiled the soup for too many.' He was in high spirits, he was determined, he had his evidence, and he was not to be held on leash. He was, in any case, the one hope of the moment. A victorious Liberal government might have ignored old scandal, particularly when its roots ran dangerously close to home. To an angry opposition it was worth the risk.

Tarte rose in a hushed House to make his sixty-three charges against Thomas McGreevy, Sir Hector Langevin, and the Department of Public Works. The matter moved on to a standing committee and hearings were scheduled to begin on May 26. Langevin was doomed and the government was threatened; there was no doubt of that on either side of the aisle. Three days before the hearings began, however, the House was hushed again and for another reason.

Macdonald had gone down Parliament Hill late on the evening of Friday May 22, a little stooped and feeble but his usual affable self. He did not return. There had been rumours of a minor stroke a few days before. They had been true. There was a second attack on Sunday. For five days he lay at home apparently on the way to recovery; then came a third stroke and at four o'clock on the afternoon of Friday May 29, a complete and devastating paralysis. For a week after that, with the McGreevy hearings forgotten, the House waited sombrely as the daily bulletins came.

Macdonald died on Saturday June 6. On Monday June 8, Langevin, as senior surviving minister, made the formal announcement and moved that the body of the Prime Minister should be 'publicly interred and that this House will concur in giving to the ceremony a fitting degree of solemnity and importance'. The old man who had served Macdonald since Confederation and before, and whose time of service was ending amid the reek and rancours of corruption, tried to speak of his master. He broke off and sat down in mid sentence. 'My heart is full of tears,' and the tears were streaming down his face.

Through the tense week of waiting Laurier had had little thought for the dying man. He had been the party leader at a time of critical change. Macdonald was gone but McGreevy lingered; the balance of forces and the balance of dangers was altered. He was worried about Pacaud and Pacaud's attitude; the little man was defensive and protesting again and Laurier sensed trouble. He was worried about the succession. 'There is excitement here,' he wrote cold-bloodedly on the seventh; 'we are still in uncertainty as to the new prime minister. We shall probably have news this afternoon.'

There was no news as he rose on the eighth after Langevin, but whatever excitement he had felt was gone now. The full meaning of that vacant seat across the aisle struck home. 'After him the deluge,' he remembered the words he had said three years before. The thought of a little incident, hardly a month old, drifted into his mind; the story had been passed along to him by Joseph Pope. Macdonald's secretary had remained Laurier's friend, with Macdonald's full concurrence, through all the years in Ottawa. No political secret had ever passed those prim and humorous lips, but this had been a casual comment in the outer office made after one of Laurier's official calls. 'Nice fellow, that,' Macdonald had said as he showed Laurier out. 'If I were twenty years younger he'd be my colleague.' Perhaps he yet might be, Pope had suggested. 'Too old, too old': the words had come with a shrug and Macdonald had passed on into the private office.

That office was empty now and the burdens and the secrets and the sinuous connivings and the threads of purpose that held them all together waited for someone else. Laurier knew only one man who could hope to shoulder them, and from that man he was cut off. He had not written to Blake since the election and he could not. Cartwright had not written; Cartwright and Blake would never speak again. Cartwright could not shoulder the burdens. Those scrambling, quarrelling men on the benches across could not shoulder them. Certainly Laurier could not.

He had been sick over the week-end and the always pallid face was pasty and grey. The liquid voice, rising and falling over the stilled House, spoke for the remotest enemy on the back benches and most of all for himself. 'The place of Sir John Macdonald in this country was so large and so absorbing that it is almost impossible to conceive that the political life of this country – the fate of this country – can continue without him. His loss overwhelms us. For my part, I say with all truth, his loss overwhelms me and it also overwhelms this parliament as if indeed one of the institutions of the land had given way.'

7

IT WAS the sixteenth of June before the tortuous enmities of the Conservative cabinet were resolved and the succession settled. Langevin was now out of the question. Tupper was in

England again and too cordially detested by too many of his colleagues even to wish to return. Charles Hibbert Tupper, his son, wished it for him but that bumptious young man did not yet carry much weight in council. Thompson, the obvious choice, was worse than a Catholic born with the affliction: he was a Catholic convert, or 'pervert' as Ontario chose to call it. The uneasy honour went at last to Senator J. J. C. Abbott, who had been one of the lecturers in law during Laurier's days at McGill. Abbott was to administer the post of Prime Minister from the upper chamber, and he was dryly candid as he took up the cares of office. 'I do not feel at all conscious of any ability to conduct the affairs of this great country,' he told his confrères. 'I am here very much because I am not particularly obnoxious to anybody.'

A few days later the McGreevy hearings resumed and two months later they ended. In spite of vanished documents, torn-out ledger pages, witnesses who refused to testify, witnesses who fainted and wept under examination, and book-keepers who skipped the country, fifteen hundred pages of evidence told the sorry tale. It emerged, viewed as expected in two separate reports. The report of the Liberal minority condemned McGreevy and Langevin. The report of the Conservative majority condemned McGreevy alone. Langevin had already resigned on August 11. McGreevy was bound for a comfortable prison cell where, according to the acid Cartwright, he was watched over with great solicitude by most of the Conservative ministry and could have held a cabinet council in the corridor on any day he chose.

Even before the climax in Ottawa, however, the earth had opened in Quebec. Langevin's going was almost drowned in the newspapers by the crash of the falling Mercier. The facts of the railway settlement had been exhumed by many busy spades and they were worse than Laurier had expected. McGreevy's million had come to him by way of Ernest Pacaud and one-tenth of the proceeds of the operation had gone to the intermediary. Pacaud's percentage had won the Quebec election, it had financed a part of Mercier's progress through Europe, it had no doubt solved the problems of many a Liberal candidate in the general election, and enough had remained to back the endorsement of the $10,000 note. 'Tell me', Laurier wrote on August 17, 'whether there is not some fatality pursuing our party.' There was indeed; it pursued both parties equally, endemic to the machines while money greased them.

Blake was at his summer home in Murray Bay, and there had been no communication with him since the election. Added to the thoughts of Blake, amid the dismal preoccupations of these days, were the thoughts of Emilie Lavergne who was also visiting at the resort. She and the master were acquainted and would be meeting and speaking together, possibly speaking of Laurier. On July 19, confessing by a concurrent letter to Emilie that he had found a pretext, Laurier at last wrote Blake. He wrote 'notwithstanding the apparent estrangement in which we now are' and he was hardly candid in his explanation that 'I did not write . . . and I am all the more sorry for it, that I have no good reason to offer why I did not.'

He hardly knew what to expect or what to hope for in the way of a reply. That shattering epistle to the electors of West Durham, with all it had done to the party and to the hope of reciprocity, was as hard to ignore as it was hard to forgive. On one matter of tactics, however, he was clear and careful. 'I cannot be angry with him,' he wrote Emilie. 'I know him too well and love him too well. I tell you all this because I am sure, when you meet him, I must come in for a share of your conversation, but under no circumstances and for no reason, never show him a letter from me . . . I know his heart too well; it is good. If he had the slightest conception how deeply he can wound, his good heart will only suffer more. You are the only one to whom I have unfolded my thoughts on this subject. I was fearing . . . that your affection for me . . . might impel you to place before that man thoughts which perhaps have never struck him and which make him feel still more miserable; for I am satisfied that he is very unhappy.'

Amid the outpouring on Blake, which was totally sincere, the warning to Emilie could hardly have been delivered with more grace and delicacy. It was nevertheless emphatic. He wanted no perfumed diplomacy in this affair; it was too important to him. Nor was he greatly reassured when Blake's reply came. For all its dignified warmth Laurier was not received back easily after six months of silence in which, said the writer, 'I considered the attitude of my old party friends . . . none of whom since the election have made any more attempt to communicate with me than if I were dead.' Laurier wrote again and was answered again, and still held at a distance. Every attempt to bury old bones of contention brought up aggrieved reminders, and every renewed approach to the principal bone was met with alert dissection.

Yet the tone warmed as the letters went on, and there began to be a pale hope. If Blake was indispensable to the party, politics were indispensable to Blake. The old leader was lonely for greatness, the new was trapped by failure. 'I wish I could see the way to go back to my business,' wrote Laurier, 'though at present it is not to be thought of.' He could confide to Emilie at least that 'the misunderstandings of the last few months are all waved aside. This is a great burden from off my heart. I must now press him to come to the front.' The need was for a new formula, a new forward step, and the two men seemed to be joined at least in the search for it.

In October the test case of the Manitoba schools moved on from the Supreme Court to the Privy Council and one step nearer to the arena of politics. In the same month Tarte, with his election at last invalidated, wrote, 'I am absolutely ruined.' In December a Royal Commission in Quebec found Mercier, Pacaud, and the old friend Charles Langelier guilty of conspiracy with Thomas McGreevy. On the fourteenth Mercier was dismissed from office. Langelier was disgraced with Mercier, and Pacaud was crushed in addition under the weight of a judgment for $100,000. In letters to the *Globe* on December 26 and again on December 31, Mowat turned away. The policy of reciprocity, he wrote, was leading to Commercial Union and on to annexation. 'If that is to be the policy of the Dominion Liberal party I cease to be a member of it.'

So far had the party come in the four and a half years since June 23, 1887. Yet its state was hardly worse than that of the distracted, squabbling, scandal-haunted band that sought to govern. 'I ask myself', Laurier wrote to Blake on December 29, 1891, 'if sometimes you do not thank your stars that you are not in the inner circle of party politics. We have come to a period in the history of this young country when premature dissolution seems to be at hand. What will be the outcome? How long can the present fabric last? Can it last at all?'

13

THE RIPENING WEST

1892-1894

EVERYTHING ELSE, through the first six months of 1892, was dominated by the battle for Blake. Without policy, without health, racked by his winter bronchitis and faced immediately with the prospect of defending the indefensible Mercier in a hopeless provincial election campaign, Laurier began the year with no thought but escape. Yet it had to be an escape with the shreds of his self-respect; there had to be some legacy to the party and the country. More and more as the months went by it seemed that only the master's return could provide it. 'To facilitate your re-entrance in public life', Laurier wrote to him, 'I would be disposed to do almost anything.'

The prospect at first grew steadily more encouraging. Blake seemed not only willing but eager to return. Laurier was now the invalid for whom Tory newspapers shed their droplets of crocodile concern; Blake was the man who wrote the consoling letters. Reciprocity, the issue that had built the wall between them, was crumbling stone by stone into a rubble heap from which each party sorted out the scraps it could use. Cartwright, Mills, Charlton, Mulock, and the rest, content to leave Commercial Union amid the debris, were chipping away at another adjective. 'Unrestricted' reciprocity, they urged, should be interpreted as meaning only the most that could be obtained from the United States without damage to Canadian manufacturers and without discrimination against Great Britain. That move had soon been countered by George Eulas Foster, the cynical and brilliant Maritimer who was now Minister of Finance. Going to Washington at the head of an imposing delegation, Foster had staged a perfunctory show of negotiation and returned to report that nothing at all could be obtained on such terms.

For Laurier the whole performance was an infuriating dance of masks in which each party circled the plain fact. The country was commercially orientated toward the United States, Commercial Union was its obvious economic destiny, and what lay beyond that must be left to the work of time. He was almost certain that Blake in his heart agreed with him, he was almost sure that Blake could be brought to accept the future that Commercial Union promised. All that seemed to remain was to press that future jointly into a suitable mould of words.

They would have to be cloudy words, for what was certainly involved in the long run was some kind of divorce from the mother country. No politician in his senses could present that separation baldly to the great, blind, ranting beast, the public. The quibbling and dilution of slogans would have to be endured, the future left to itself. There would have to be an appeal to the immediate interest – the immediate, legitimate self-interest of the country – and for the rest the country would have to go forward as the politicians went, blindfolded.

It was not good enough for Blake. Week by week, as a dismal session opened and the even more dismal necessities of Mercier's campaign distracted him, Laurier saw the nub of the problem emerge. It hardened in caucuses and conferences and in a long triangular correspondence between himself, Mills, and Blake. Policy, strategy, tactics were the surface stuff of the argument, but the core of it all was character. Blake would not accept the policy made without him and against his judgment. He would accept no watering-down or stepping-up that still retained the essence. He would accept no policy that did not say what it meant and all that it meant.

The party had blundered, Blake intimated, and it had done worse than that. It had presented a program for which the country was not prepared and it had tried to obscure the real direction of that program. Now, with fortunes at 'the lowest ebb' – the phrase crept in so gently that its bite was almost lost – was the time for a frank and open retreat. The party must go back to the ground that Blake had always held: a tariff that provided revenue, gave limited protection to manufacturers who were justly entitled to it, favoured Great Britain, and opened the door where possible to trade with the United States. As a maximum concession to semantic difficulties, he could agree to present the policy as one of 'Limited Reciprocity'.

Laurier pointed out with something like desperation that this was exactly what Cartwright, Mills, and the others now meant. But 'Unlimited' had to be kept at the masthead. There could be no more retreats and revisions. There had been too many already, and none was to Laurier's liking. 'For my part personally – I have told you before – I am not disposed to change at all except to go forward. I would be ready tomorrow to go to the length of Commercial Union, including a common tariff and pooling of the revenue: in fact applying to this continent the German Zollverein. We would undoubtedly raise a storm, but as I am satisfied the future lies in that direction I would not mind the storm at all, nor the consequences. But in this the party would not follow me, and therefore there is no use thinking of it.'

For Blake there was no use thinking of anything else. Party or not, the full depth and direction of the leader's mind had to be laid clear. 'You propose some advance, but what advance I do not know . . . Can you expect to succeed as "men of mystery", the possessors of some charm or recipe of wondrous virtue not to be disclosed to the common herd?' Then he proceeded to strip away whatever mystery there was. 'By the courses which of late years Canadian politics have taken we have been drifting ever nearer to political union with the States . . . to join them on fair and equal terms would be for any Province of this Dependency no ignoble lot. Nevertheless, this is not the goal at which I aim.'

He looked at the goal of the imperialists with an eye as cool and hostile as Laurier's. 'In the main interests and policy of the United Kingdom in an Imperial capacity, and in the complications of its diplomacy, we have none or a very slight interest. It is indeed more an Eastern and Indian and African Empire than anything else.' But neither would he reconcile himself to a befogged and pilotless drift into the arms of the United States.

'I cling to the hope', he wrote, 'of a higher though more arduous destiny for the great Dominion. I look for the regeneration of my own country. I cling to the hope that – sooner or later, and rather soon than late – there may be born into the world an independent Canadian Commonwealth; nerving itself to solve after its own fashion the many racial and religious, moral and political, economic and material problems which confront us; united by enduring links of kinship and sympathy, hope and admiration, with three of the leading nations of the world; advancing more effectively than now our own varied interests as well as the true welfare of the old land, the proud mother of free nations as well as free parliaments; and enjoying under arrangements which a wise and liberal statesmanship on both sides of the Line and of the Atlantic may mature, bright prospects of unbroken peace and absolute security, together with the fullest freedom of trade and the widest measure of intercourse compatible with the provision of our revenue and the preservation of our autonomy. May these things be!'

It was almost his swan song in Canadian politics and it would be remembered, though the man who accepted the vision would never be able to give it so noble a frame. At the moment, for the harried politician at the head of a fractured party, the thought was premature. The tone of the correspondence descended on both sides to one of nervous impatience. 'What I now say', wrote Laurier, 'is a reaffirmation of what I have told you often, that our program of Unrestricted Reciprocity is not, in my estimation, the ideal program but it is just such as the party will accept at this moment.' In any case, he added as a final plea, 'You cannot deprive the country of your great services. If you cannot see eye to eye with us, come out with your own views, just such as they are.'

It was not enough, and the old leader's thoughts were already turning away. Ireland was the home of his fathers, he had had much to say on the question of Home Rule, and Irish politicians had long been aware of and impressed by his abilities. Now they were asking for his help, and the raucous politics of Canada were becoming merely a distraction. 'I have to express my deep regret', he wrote on May 2, with a familiar mixture of petulant self-disclaimer and legalistic hedging, 'for having added to your sessional labours by opening the discussion; and to give you the only amends I can by promising never to do so any more. It only remains for me to say that my quack medicine was prescribed for immediate consumption; and I think it very likely that conditions may so change shortly that I would neither prescribe it for the patient nor take it myself. Therefore I am not to be understood as recommending it for use at any future time or as being committed to it under any changed conditions.'

A week or so later the cable from Ireland arrived and Blake left for London to take his seat in the House of Commons as a member of the Irish Nationalist party. 'The one consideration with me which towers up above all others', Laurier wrote him when he had absorbed the news, 'is that in the Imperial Parliament you will find an arena worthy of yourself. A young country like Canada might and should afford vast horizons, but it has been dwarfed by political debauchery. I verily fear that the great questions to which we might have looked will not come up in our day.'

The emptiness without Blake would be a little awesome, but perhaps it was for the best. 'Practical politics', Laurier had written earlier in the correspondence, 'mean that you must deal with men such as you find them and not such as you would like them to be.'

2

HE NOW TURNED, with a curiously renewed zest, to practical politics. If there was no escape there was at least relief from a nagging inner compulsion. He had done his best to restore the too-big boots to their rightful owner; now he must stumble on in them as best he could. And he saw for a little way clearly. The great questions of the day would simply have to be shelved. The party, the government, and the country itself were at a nadir of confusion and corruption. If anything at all was accomplished in Laurier's time it would have to be an improvement. There was no way to go but up.

The government, led by Abbott from the Senate and in practice conducted by Thompson, was falling apart with the quarrels of jealous and besmirched men. Langevin was gone and Chapleau's star was paling. He was still potentially dangerous but now, white-maned and tubercular, he was a disappointed and disgusted man at odds with all his colleagues. By the end of the year he would have forsaken the cabinet and retired to the safety of Spencerwood as Lieutenant-Governor of Quebec. Caron remained as the last of Macdonald's triumvirate of French Canadians, but he was tainted like all his colleagues by the fumes that rose from the prison cell of McGreevy. Scandal was now the stock-in-trade of parliament and the manoeuvrings of ministers to evade the charges against them were to be burlesqued for posterity a year later in Cartwright's resolution:

> That it shall henceforward be a good and sufficient defence, in answer to any charge of felony or other criminal offence, for the person so accused to allege that he did not commit some other crime or felony; e.g. in the case of any person accused of committing murder it shall henceforward be a good defence to plead that the said party did not commit adultery – or if accused of horse-stealing to plead that he did not commit forgery – or if accused of burglary to plead that he is not guilty of coining false money – and generally it shall be held sufficient in any case for the party accused of any particular offence to show that he did not commit some other and different offence. . . . No member of any Liberal administration, local or other, shall be entitled to the benefit of this Act. God Save the Queen.

Yet these antics could only be enjoyed by the pure of heart, and few Liberals were of that elect. Certainly Quebec Liberals were not. Mercier had been duly destroyed by the provincial elections in March. He was a bankrupt and dying man and whatever he had represented in the way of liberalism was now replaced by an arid, backward-looking ultramontanism that did not steal and could not govern. Pacaud was appealing the judgment for $100,000 and would probably win but would certainly bankrupt himself in the process. Meanwhile he had embarked on a new round of slanderings and quarrels not only with his old enemies but with some of his old friends. The whole Quebec organization that had built and supported Laurier was soiled and in disarray, while Tarte, the new-comer who had brought disruption about, could hardly have been more detested.

Quebec would have to be left for a while to sort itself out. Ontario was the one ground that looked fruitful at the moment, and it was to Ontario that Laurier addressed himself through the summer. He came back from a long, exhausting tour surprisingly refreshed. The air had seemed cleaner on the hustings than it had either in parliament or in the home province. He was reinforced in his conviction that English politics were naturally tidier than French, and if they were not very tidy at the moment they at least offered better prospects.

Liberals in Ontario as elsewhere seemed unable to make up their minds on anything, but Torydom was growing two heads. Thompson became the official leader of the party when Abbott resigned in November. Straight as he was, or would have liked to be, he was in the awkward position of having to lean backward in order to remain upright on a number of sensitive issues. Thoroughly British, he had to restrain the imperialists of his party because the core of his support came from Quebec. A Nova Scotian with a native fondness for free trade, he had to give gingerly support to the battered National Policy. Whatever his private convictions as a Catholic, he was trying very hard to keep the Manitoba schools question in the courts and out of politics.

On the other hand D'Alton McCarthy was still the maverick within the herd. He leaned backward and walked softly for no man, least of all for a Catholic. The heart and soul of the Imperial Federation League, he was advancing the cause of Protestant Anglo-Saxondom on a steadily broadening front. He was a power in the Equal Rights Association, which still fought Jesuits and Frenchness. He watered the soil, if he had not planted the seed, of the Protestant Protective Association, which sought to remove Catholics from public life. He wanted the case of the Catholic minority of Manitoba to be thrown out of court. In addition to all this he was now moving behind the banner of the

Patrons of Industry, who were patrons only in the sense that they were consumers, to what looked to every well-protected manufacturer like a position for free trade. He was a dangerous man to follow, but wherever he was bound he seemed to be taking a large part of Ontario with him. It was certainly well away from Thompson, and in the ground between there was room for Liberal manoeuvre.

The first essential was to make the party manoeuvrable, and on this task Laurier was soon embarked with a vigour that surprised himself. For one thing, his health was better. In January of 1893 he was vaccinated and also applied successfully for another four thousand dollars' worth of life insurance. He reported on his application that he had not been troubled with haemorrhages for twenty years. In answer to the question 'active or sedentary' he described himself as 'active', possibly because so much of his time was now spent in traipsing about the hustings of eastern Canada. To George Landerkin, who was again the inspecting doctor, he appeared 'strong, healthy and of good figure'. His weight had built up to a comfortable one hundred and seventy-eight pounds. His teeth were sound, his pulse, respiration, and other functions normal, and his only complaints were an occasional attack of bronchitis, grippe, or lumbago, not at all surprising in a man of fifty-one. The old friend Laurent-Olivier David, who was now city clerk of Montreal, provided a letter supporting the application and ventured the opinion that Laurier would outlive stronger men because of his rigorous self-discipline. It was all a bit rose-coloured, but there was no doubt that he felt better than he had for several years. With no Blake on the horizon, he had settled into the leadership and even expanded a little. For the work immediately ahead he had no doubt of his capabilities. French or English, high or low, he could draw men to himself and make them work with him.

The idea of a national Liberal convention, the first ever to be held, had been put forward by Willison. It was a large and even risky undertaking for a party fifteen years out of power, perpetually in straits for funds, and very sketchily supported anywhere but in central Canada. But the last election, which had been swung for Macdonald by the Maritimes and the west, had shown the value of the 'shreds and patches', and a party that claimed to be national had now to assess its resources from sea to sea. Laurier, when the six months of preparations were completed and Ottawa filled with delegates in June of 1893, was pleasantly surprised at the result.

Fielding emerged from among the Maritime men, small, crisp, secretive, and limitlessly capable. From the west came Clifford Sifton, brisk and tough, undwarfed by any of the giants of the east, and these two were only the best of many important finds. Quebec and Ontario leaders were encouraged by the signs of strength and sobered by the hint of rivals in the distant places. The party was both broadened and pulled together, and at last found the nerve it could not find for Blake. Laurier listened with mixed feelings as a windy resolution wound interminably backward from Commercial Union and Unrestricted Reciprocity to the old safe ground that any man could share: 'that a fair and liberal reciprocity treaty would develop the great natural resources of Canada'.

The delegates greeted it with an audible sigh of relief. The great issue of continentalism was well and truly shelved and the work ahead was to win the next election. A network of local organizations was sketched out and planned. Alexander Smith, barrister, of Ottawa was acquired as Liberal Organizer for Ontario. Tall, moustached, and taciturn, with a hint of Indian blood, 'Silent' Smith was one man in the party whose concern for the poor but malleable farmer would remain constant and who would never forget the horny, hungry hands of the sons of the soil, particularly in areas where the soil was bad. 'You can always buy votes on the sand' would be one of his most famous campaigning maxims. He was to be a repository of party secrets to the day Laurier died and would carry some of them, fortunately, to his own grave. For the moment he was a sign of changing times. A new political citadel, the Reform Club of Ottawa, was opened on June 19, and the shower of oratory told of a party tightened and toughened for the workaday world of politics. Laurier set the keynote, speaking to an audience that had been electrified by his eloquence and charmed by his personality, an audience that felt mistakenly that it knew him at last. 'It is not enough', he said, 'to have good principles; we must have organization also. Principles without organization may lose, but organization without principles may often win.'

3

IF THE PARTY was now prepared for manoeuvre, it was becoming disturbingly apparent how delicate the manoeuvring would be. The celebrations and deliberations in Ottawa had accomplished much. To the general and always dependable hunger for votes and office, a measure of confidence, leadership, and efficiency had been added. Purpose and direction remained to be considered, not as they were expressed in the wide-ranging eloquence of a party platform but as they actually existed in the hard heads of men responsible to their constituents.

There had been more than enough at the convention, as there was in parliament, to make a man cynical about politicians. But that was an old story, and half the story. Each of those beribboned delegates, high and low, good and bad, was in his way a leader. He had been pushed up or he had climbed up above the ruck of his county or his constituency or his province because he gave voice in some way to the character, mood, and wishes of the people he represented. He could be led by the carrot or driven by the stick, but only a little way; in the long run, like it or not, he would be forced back on himself and his own. The currents running through the life of the country would find their expression. The man at the head of all, if he wished to be followed, must sense the general drift. If he wished to lead for long he must feel that drift in himself.

It was the central worry, underlying the money troubles, the treacherous health, and all the day-to-day abrasions of leadership. Laurier, the French Canadian, had guessed wrong once, at least for his time. He had underestimated, as Blake had not, the strength of the British roots. There would be no easy drift into a continental union with the United States. Trade with the United Kingdom was increasing, while trade with the United States remained strangled by high tariffs. The sentiment for Imperial Federation, for some closer linking of the governments of the Empire, was increasingly vocal. And it was all tinged and tainted by the new, impatient surge of Anglo-Saxon Protestantism which McCarthy embodied and expressed. If it was the main current of the times, then not only the French Canadian but the Catholic stood increasingly apart.

It was not the main current in the new territories of the west, and these had to figure more and more in every calculation. The farmer on the prairies, who saw his wheat shut out from a great market not a hundred miles to the south and who paid the price of protection on every implement he bought, was and always would be for free trade. He had very little interest in Imperial Federation. But the essence of McCarthy-ism, which was born of sentiment and prejudice in the east, was as natural and native as the climate in the west. 'This is a British country,' said McCarthy in Winnipeg, and every implication of the words was received almost without comment. To a steadily increasing majority the country was both British and Protestant. The drift to the prairies, since the days of the C.P.R. and even before, had been a drift of Ontarians and Americans with a scattering of Europeans. British or not, they had all reconciled themselves to becoming British, and most of them were Protestants. They had no desire to preserve two cultures, two religions, two systems of education, and they had no means for it. All progress, even as a homogeneous people, was difficult and expensive enough. It was not to be held back by what they considered to be outworn treaties and vestigial remnants. French-Canadian Catholics in Manitoba, and even more in the territories beyond, were now a static and decreasing minority, and every privilege retained by them perplexed the rights of the many.

The Honourable Joseph Martin of Manitoba had been a prominent figure at the convention, more at home in Ottawa than most. He wore his title by virtue of the fact that he had been Attorney-General in the Liberal provincial government that had abolished Catholic separate schools in 1890. He was now the federal member for Selkirk and the one prairie Liberal in the House of Commons. Willison described him with qualified enthusiasm as 'a natural born politician', and that unquestionably he was. But he had been thrown up as surely as any man by the currents moving beneath him. One meeting with Sifton, his much more formidable successor in Manitoba, had convinced Laurier of that. Sifton spoke like Martin on the question of the Manitoba schools. Both spoke for the west, and the west would not change.

On the other hand, that native politician Joseph Israel Tarte had now opened the battle for Quebec. Thrown out of Montmorency by the invalidation of his election in 1891, he had come back to the House this year by way of a by-election. He had campaigned at Laurier's insistence because he was now indispensable, and he had chosen to campaign in large part on the question of the Manitoba schools. Here was a grievance, said Tarte, that the government must redress. It concerned every French Canadian. The cause of the French and Catholic minority in Manitoba was equally the cause of Quebec.

Against Tarte, aligned with the new west which it had largely made, stood the Ontario of D'Alton McCarthy. Between stood the government, quibbling and indecisive. There was every evidence in its record of weakness and bad faith. Either the Acts passed by the Manitoba legislature were valid or they were not. Even if they were, they clearly infringed on the rights guaranteed to a minority at the time the province was set up, and the federal government had power to intervene. Macdonald had staved off the earliest agitation by promising Archbishop Taché, the venerable leader in the west, that something would be done if there was no commotion before the election of 1891. Chapleau, with Macdonald's authority, had reinforced the promise and made it explicit. Either the courts would declare the Acts to be beyond the powers of the province or the federal government would step in to nullify them. The Catholic schools of Manitoba would be reopened. Now, two years later, they were still closed and Chapleau had left the cabinet, impotent and disgusted. The train of litigation had wound up to the judicial committee of the Privy Council and come back with a verdict. The Acts were within the powers of the province. No good angel in a wig, speaking with a learned British accent, had wiped them from the statute books to save the government the unpleasantness.

The judgment, however, had not pronounced definitely on the power to intervene. It had had no need to. The power resided in the British North America Act; it was as explicit there as any provincial right. Yet the omission provided a loop-hole through which the successors of John A. Macdonald, the centralizer, were now squirming. The cabinet under the Catholic Thompson had started off on a new round of litigation to determine the extent of its powers. As everyone knew, the powers were wholly adequate. The only real dilemma was whether to use them.

In mid March, three months before the opening of the party convention, Tarte had squirmed briskly out of his seat to toss the question into the stagnant waters of parliament. The cabinet, he said, instead of governing, was hiding behind lawyers. In its latest performance, acting in what it was pleased to call a judicial rather than a political character, it had summoned the contending parties before it and asked to be convinced as to whether or not it had the right and duty to act on the appeal of the minority. The minority's lawyers had duly presented their brief and argued their case. The Manitoba government had not even condescended to appear, but the result was that another test case had been sent off on the long road to the Privy Council. The government had given itself a year of grace while the Catholics of Manitoba went without their schools. Tarte demanded action, though he was studiously vague as to what the action should be.

D'Alton McCarthy had been quite clear, and so had Joseph Martin. The Manitoba laws had been declared valid by the highest court in the Empire. The Catholic schools of Manitoba were closed and should remain closed. The lawyers should be called off.

Laurier had risen in the midst of a curious silence to extend one hand to Tarte, the other to McCarthy, and the back of both to the government. He had before him Thompson's declaration that the cabinet could deal with the matter as judges, regardless of their personal views on denominational schools. The leader of the opposition was shocked and derisive. 'How convenient that doctrine, which permits the advisers of His Excellency to pocket at once their opinions and their emoluments.' Tarte and McCarthy, who had nothing in common but courage and convictions, naturally found themselves opposed to a government that had neither. Manitoba claimed that its schools, as operated under the new laws, were non-sectarian. The Catholic minority claimed that they were really Protestant schools thinly disguised. What were the facts? Why did not the government investigate and make up its mind? 'If it is true that . . . Roman Catholic children are forced under that law to attend what are in reality Protestant schools, I say this, and let my words be heard by friend or foe, let them be published in the press throughout the length of the land, that the strongest case has been made for interference by this government. If that statement be true, though my life as a political man should thereby be ended forever, what I say now I shall be prepared to repeat, and would repeat on every platform in Ontario, every platform in Manitoba, nay, every Orange lodge throughout the land, that the Catholic minority has been subjected to a most infamous tyranny.'

'If' – it was another tall hedge, almost as tall as the government's. He was to move behind it for the next three years, a stubborn Macduff with another Birnam Wood. The ground of party manoeuvre was clear now, clear and treacherous. He would not come out in the open till he saw the way to the end, for the party, the country, and himself.

4

By the early autumn Sifton was urging him to come west. The prairies of Manitoba were ripe for the harvest. A Liberal provincial government was securely in power. Wheat prices were down, freight-rates stayed where they were, and the C.P.R. rode the country with a hard, unyielding hand. Immigration and settlement, much as they had transformed the province, were a fraction of what they should be. Outflow was almost as great as inflow, and for ten years the whole of Canada had increased its population only at the rate of fifty thousand a year. The fault lay with a corrupt and moribund government in the grip of the National Policy, or so it could be made to seem. Day was dawning for the party that had fought the battle against the C.P.R. and the battle for free trade, even though it had lost both. Liberalism would sweep the prairies at the next general election. The votes were there to be reaped at the glint of the leader's scythe.

The letter was as crisp and businesslike as Sifton himself. It was predicated on the assumption that the question of the schools was closed. But if Laurier knew nothing of the west, Sifton knew little of the east: the question of the schools was not closed and it would only remain on the shelf until the last lawyer had finished the last quibble. It was insinuating itself slowly and surely into the central problem of the country, and that problem in all its ancient malignity would have to be faced again.

It was not a question of investigating the Manitoba schools; that was as much a quibble as anything else. Everyone knew what the investigators would find. They would find that the schools were starved and inefficient, as they were bound to be in a new country. They would find that the Catholic schools had taught in French and almost entirely in French, and that religion had bulked too large in what passed for a curriculum. They would find that teachers, buildings, books, and every other necessity had been lacking for all schools and that the hope of even one adequate system of education was almost beyond the province. They would find what resources there were concentrated now behind a single system of secular schools, and they would certainly find that the schools were directed with a heavily Protestant bias.

So much for Manitoba. The black-haired, black-eyed Métis moppets and their priests and parents had a cause. They had a cause reinforced for the French Canadian by every tie of sentiment and religion. But how was it to be served? How was it to be served in all honesty and in all justice to the rest of the Dominion? By an act of the central government, legal enough and taken in the name of a minority? That act would be in accordance with the safeguards for all minorities which had been provided at the time of the Dominion's making and which had been extended to Manitoba. It would nevertheless set aside the present will of a province. Where did the rights of minorities begin and end? What limits did that pact of Confederation set on change? One could plead the law and the prophets, one could go back to Cartier and George Brown, but one could not make time stand still. One could not turn back the west. The attempt to do so would call into question again not the rights of a province but the rights of the two races. Ontario Orangemen would set up their howl for French and Catholic scalps. Quebec would give back as much and more than it got, and somewhere in the mêlée the whole principle of the dual nation would go down. Perhaps it was going down already; Laurier was not sure. He was sure only of one thing: compromise had made the nation and nothing but compromise would ever hold it together. He would have to go west soon, and he would talk of wheat and freight-rates and tariffs and keep his mouth closed on the schools. But that would not close the question. Whatever Sifton said or thought, the west was not ready for Laurier nor would Laurier be ready for the country till he had groped his way through the fog toward a means of accommodation.

Thompson, the adversary, was groping for the same thing. It was the real meaning of all the legal shuffling. He was buying time, hoping for miracles – with more faith in miracles, perhaps, than Laurier. It was ironic that the two of them were Catholics. It was likely to be helpful that Laurier, at least, had moved beyond the influence of priests. Religion had been stirred into his politics for so long, and politics had taken up so large a part of his life, that there was left for the faith now only a diluted, tolerant affection. 'I am not a believer,' he wrote to Emilie Lavergne. 'I most fervently believe in the justice of Him from whom we proceed and to whom we owe all. I believe in the justice and mercy of his laws, eternal like Himself; further my faith goes not, and I regret it.'

The discussions with her went on, by letter and face to face, ranging over every subject. She was an accepted part of his life now, and often in Ottawa when the sessions called Joseph Lavergne away from the law practice. The wife of the member for Drummond-Arthabaska was rather more prominent than her husband. Mme Lavergne was usually at the side of Mme Laurier when formal occasions called Zoë to the capital, and she seemed to be accepted and welcomed as a companion. It was a good thing, Laurier could tell himself, that Zoë, who was still lonely and unsure in English, should have a friend from Arthabaska at her side. There was certainly refreshment for him in Emilie's presence. On the lowest political level it was worth the talk it caused, for Mme Lavergne was much too chic, clever, and discreet to be anything but an asset in this town where most mistresses were flamboyant liabilities.

That she was not a mistress in the generally accepted sense made no real difference. It did not dilute the pleasure of the post for Emilie, it did not ease the situation for Zoë, and the public attitude was quite predictably divided. The robust souls who took their pleasures raw pointed to Armand Lavergne, thirteen now and growing up to look more like Laurier every day, in so far as his features would permit it and his mother could arrange it. The more delicate-minded, and those who discounted gossip, could direct their attention to Mme Lavergne's brilliance, her elegance, and her political *savoir-faire*. All, including Emilie, were agreed that she came of that long line of women made to sit, with or without benefit of clergy, at the right hands of the great.

For much of each session Laurier lived out the days in 'dull and detested' Ottawa with wife and friend at home in Arthabaska. It was in those periods that the correspondence with Emilie flourished and he let himself go in the manner of the lover he had never been. He waited and pleaded for the 'welcome, so welcome letters'. He found them 'very good, very kind: good, kind, loving like yourself, and yet good, kind, loving as they are, they make me sad and lonely – sad and lonely because I crave all the more to see you. Do you not believe this, my dear, ever dearer friend?' He longed to be in Arthabaska, 'in those hills where my heart is'. Each letter, he vowed, gave him food to live upon until the next came; he changed not in his feelings and even a trace of such suspicion was unworthy of her, his heart clung to the paper on which he wrote. 'Proud I am of your friendship, lucky of your affection,' he burst out in one lyrical effusion, 'and could I yell it on the tops of houses, prouder yet would I be.'

It did not come quite to that, but Emilie encouraged all. Yet through it all, on both sides, ran a vein of prissy intellectualism that might have proved innocence and would certainly have sent the prurient away with a yawn. These two, discussing the love affairs of the great, stood four-square for seemliness and chastity.

Pompadour, for Laurier, was a 'vile woman'. Louis XV disgusted him. 'Tout était dominé chez lui par la sensualité.' The French was rare – they wrote almost always in English; and for Napoleon's Josephine Laurier had good hard English words. 'She was an inveterate coquette, and had I been in N's place I would have been unmerciful.' Above all, when discussion touched on concerns nearer home, the aching lover became the warmly admiring Victorian quasi-uncle. 'Yes, my dear friend, you have every reason to be proud of your children. You seem to me blessed as no mother ever was, and really there is justice in this, for I know not of any mother such as you are, my dear, dear friend.'

Everything that was playful and affectionate in him came out when he spoke of little Gabrielle, the Lavergnes' daughter. It was Armand, however, who intrigued and fascinated him and filled him with fatherly concern. 'That little man', he wrote, after the boy had visited him in Ottawa, 'is full of magnetism, winning and attractive, and at the same time so frank, so outspoken, so clever and also so ready-witted . . . in a few years, when grown up to manhood, with his naturally refined and reserved manners, with his expressiveness of countenance, and with . . . attention to his person which he now neglects but which will come with age, he will undoubtedly be a man not in a thousand, but in a million.'

Armand astonished his great friend by the lightness and ease with which he disposed of a considerable store of information. 'Quite naturally, quite unconsciously . . . he shoots off a remark here and a remark there which cause you to pause and wonder. What is more remarkable yet is the promptness and aptness of his repartees. This is his mother all over.'

The boy was lazy, and it worried Laurier. He refused to learn English and had learned to make a cause of it, describing himself to his mother as 'your son who will always be a patriot'. Laurier laughed at the sentiment. 'Happy age, is it not, when there can be so much enthusiasm for a cause so little deserving it.' On the practical side of the matter, however, he delivered a strong homily.

'Tell him that above everything else he must apply himself to learn English, that it is absolutely essential for such an intense

French Canadian as he is; that it is the absolute condition which will enable him, some day, to defend the rights and privileges of his race. That ought to fetch him, I am sure . . . I would want him, when he is twenty, to be as familiar with one language as the other. You know and I know the great advantage it would be to him . . . at twenty, could he speak and write English as currently and fluently as French, his start in the world would be immeasurably advanced.'

There was much more about the son in the correspondence, almost nothing about the husband, and Zoë's name hardly figured. The two cool lovers, eloquently attached and a little smug in innocence, made their own world. It was certainly a place of refuge for the man who walked around in Ottawa and 'met not a soul worth remembering' or who sat so much alone in a hotel room looking out on 'a nice day for a walk, but my easy chair was tempting'. He had missed a good deal in life, this sedentary student. At the moment he did not see much ahead that attracted him, and he was not yet far escaped from the foolish forties. He could talk to Emilie Lavergne as he could not talk to Zoë or anyone else. For all her devoted Englishness and all her caustic worldliness, she was still of the faith, she prayed. He respected that, or he respected at least the hungers from which it rose. 'I wish I could pray and have confidence in those supreme consolations, when my rebellious soul throbs at the loss of my cherished illusions.' He could pose a little and not be reproached for it. 'Having neither the faith nor the hope, I try to grow indifferent and to become callous at the blows which all my efforts have not succeeded in averting.'

The private pains of his trade he could share, and did share, with Zoë. Yet he painted them in for Emilie as part of the picture. 'There exists in the great mass of the people of Ontario a conviction sprung from late events . . . that French men are boodlers, and that I in consequence am not to be trusted. I am given the full credit of not being a boodler, but that I would be unable to stem the current of boodlism.' He spoke of Pacaud, one of the principal present sources of Ontario's conviction. 'E. has no friend so absolutely attached to him as I am, but I cannot defend his action in public, nor approve his course in private.

This is a real cause of sorrow to me . . . a perpetual torment.'

He twitted Emilie, as he would have dared to twit no priest, for encouraging Armand in youthful religiosity. 'Would you really be happy if your son became a priest? I have just heard Father Plessis, the Dominican preacher. He is really a great sacred orator. His spirit mounts into the highest spheres, but this monk with the shaven head, the not very clean garments, and many other things showed unmistakably that the priesthood does not refine the man, that it has indeed a very different result. I see your dear Armand clothed in this costume and all my heart rebels at the idea. How much better would it be to make him a man of the world, ready to fight, to love, and to suffer. I wish for him the means of being good, of becoming better, and struggling to be of some service to his family and his people.'

The last words would recoil on him wryly in a few years' time. In all of them, if he was not completely opening himself, he was at least delineating the man he felt himself to be. His 'dear friend', his 'Madame de Staël', whose pleasure it was to gather her friends round her 'and then let the mind open its wings and fly about in the arabesques of improvised conversation', was more than a relief from politics. She was the refined essence of politics as he would have wished it to be. She had played her part with Father Suzor and Bishop Laflèche and the Dorions, she was playing her part now with Blake and Cartwright, with Tarte and Pacaud and Sifton and many others, in preparing him for the work ahead.

5

HE HAD taken time, in January of 1893, to set himself straight with Toronto and the imperialists. He was not for a federation of the Empire, he was not for an imperial parliament. He was for something that was already very like the vision of Blake, a young Canada growing up somehow autonomous within a family of British nations. The core of the speech had been genuine enough and sound enough. He felt at home now in this capital of Britishness and Protestantism and imperialism which would never vote for him. He came to a generous welcome and left with added respect, for the very reason, it seemed, that on this as on every occasion he would not knuckle under.

He had clothed what he had to say, however, in suitably loyal terms, and what was suitable in Toronto was hardly ever so in Quebec. Mercier, with almost the last words he was to utter in public, had eloquently rejected the hope that Laurier had raised. 'I admire Englishmen,' said Mercier, 'and I love English women, but England leaves me indifferent, nearly cold . . . I admit that she has done us good but I believe she has done us more harm than good . . . we owe nothing to England and we shall separate from her when the majority, regularly consulted, so wishes, without remorse of conscience, without a broken heart and without tears.' He would never speak again for an official majority and he had not much longer to speak at all, but that voice would not be stilled with the passing of Mercier. It had to be answered; it had to be answered while the drums of the Protestant Protective Association were thumping in Ontario and the problem of Manitoba loomed beyond. A year after the Toronto speech, on January 4, 1894, the time for the answer came.

It was given to a gathering in Quebec much the same as the one that had faced Laurier when he had spoken out for political liberalism seventeen years before. The footing was quite as treacherous. Whatever the Ottawa convention had done to pull the national party together, the leader's relations with what passed for the provincial party had seldom been worse. Neither had the state of that party. Pacaud, mortgaging his house, selling off scraps of his printing equipment, and still adding libel suits and judgments to a back-breaking burden of trouble, could think of nothing but the release of McGreevy and a return to the old days. Correspondence and conversation with Pacaud seemed now to be one long quarrel. Like him, most of the old guard were sore and savage at the rise of Tarte, who was 'Judas Iscariot Tarte' and 'Black Tarte' to as many *Rouges* as *Bleus*. The wrecked régime of Mercier was settling in mud, while ultramontane *Bleus* steered the province on a direct collision course with everything that was growing in Ontario. Around Laurier, precisely at the moment when strength and skill and cool, uncluttered heads were most required, there was the swirl of old rancours and vindictive confusion.

Once more he spoke from an elegant rostrum with a sorry mess behind him. The desk in Arthabaska was cluttered as it had been seventeen years before with warnings of division and counsels to prudence. Everything was drearily reminiscent of the earlier night, and everything was changed. He himself was changed. He was no longer the rash young adviser, he was the man who made the decisions. If he was more at home in Toronto, he was less at home in Quebec; already the taunts had begun that he spoke 'broken French'. He spoke, at any rate, as a man who had fixed his course and settled into it.

To the enemies of 1877 he addressed almost the same words he had used in that year. The Church was still used as a crutch and club by Conservative politicians. 'The moment politics are in question they become terribly religious. Discuss any question with them of protection, free trade, finance, or railways, and immediately their great argument amounts to this: "Ah, we are religious men, we are; but those fellows opposite have not much religion." We have in our midst intolerant and extravagant Catholics who understand neither the times, the country, nor the surroundings in which they live. I mention these things because if we have amongst us men who try to prostitute the Catholic religion to the ends of politics there are also men in the province of Ontario who are endeavouring to play the same game with the Protestant religion.'

He was as French as Mercier and as proud of it, but, 'I also recognize the position in which my race has been placed by the battle which was fought on the Plains of Abraham. There are some amongst us who forget this state of things, who affect to believe that a small French republic or monarchy – I hardly know what they want – should be established on the banks of the St. Lawrence. Those who use this language speak like slaves who would break their bonds if they dared, but who do not do so because they are cowards. For my part I believe myself to be a free man.'

Much of the rest was in the old vein, for the old problems hung on. But the new man grew through it all. He took at last an open and affectionate farewell of Papineau, the Dorions, and his old *Rouge*-ism. He did not forget the wrongs that Papineau had tried to right, but he did not forget either that it was an Englishman who had led the rebels at St-Dénis when Papineau had forsaken them. Lafontaine had feared the union that followed rebellion, but Lafontaine had served it and made it serve the cause of the French. The Dorions and the *Rouges* had feared and fought Confederation, but Antoine-Aimé, at least, had accepted the work of Cartier and Macdonald in the spirit of Lafontaine. For Laurier himself now, 'I believe that I shall continue the work of Mr. Lafontaine and Sir George Etienne Cartier and that the result will be all to the advantage of French Canada.

'You are aware', he went on, as the silvery, slurring voice with its haunting mixture of accents rose toward the peroration, 'that in the eleventh century certain men started out from Normandy, Anjou, Brittany, and Angoulême to capture England. In the sixteenth century men started from the same provinces of Normandy, Anjou, Brittany, and Angoulême to colonize the fertile lands on the banks of the St. Lawrence. In the next century the men of both races met face to face here, and you know what happened. Well, is it not permissible to hope that a day will come when, instead of facing each other on hostile purpose intent, the descendants of the Bretons, Angevins, and Normans who invaded England in the eleventh century and the descendants of the Angevins, Normans, and Bretons who peopled Canada in the sixteenth will meet together, not to fight, but to hold the grand assizes of peace and commerce? I may not live long enough to see that day but if my career should be sufficiently extended to allow me to take part in these assizes it will be a happy day to me. I shall attend them bearing with me my Canadian nationality.'

In all vicissitudes, in all pains, he concluded, as he was to conclude the last speech of his life, love is better than hate and faith than doubt. Then it was time to try what love and faith might do with the next session and, beyond the close of parliament, with the waiting west.

6

BEGINNING in the March blizzards and dragging on as usual into the steamy, mosquito-infested midsummer heat of Ottawa, the session of 1894 came to an end in late July. It had changed little and improved nothing. If debility, corruption, and McCarthy still ate away at the vitals of the Conservative party, Thompson was threatening to restore to it some of his own guts and fibre. The new strength of Liberalism was a matter of spirit and organization, invisible in a head-count and hardly visible in the discussions of policy. The schools question, once more *en route* to the Privy Council, hung fire. The government had set up a commission to study western freight-rates; the Liberals could only point out that the commission was doing nothing. Tariffs had been reduced on lumber and farm implements, and the only answer to that was 'not enough'. The National Policy was dying but Unrestricted Reciprocity was dead. All that remained to the crusaders of either party was a battle with rubber swords under the grim eyes of eastern manufacturers and western farmers.

Laurier had lived out the whole five months of the session harried by the local interests and local quarrels of his distracted party in Quebec. 'It is impossible to make you see reason . . . I feel very disposed to send them all to the devil,' had been the refrain of his correspondence with Pacaud, and though the tone always settled back to one of cool politeness the tincture of acid remained. 'I am but partly satisfied with the results of our session,' he wrote when it became time to shuffle off his eastern concerns and prepare for the trip to the west, 'and am far from accepting the compliments you so kindly pay me.'

It was August 22 when the private car hooked onto the rear of the Atlantic Express started out of Toronto on the long, bleak run to North Bay. On board was a sizeable party of political dignitaries, with Zoë in company, and one other wife. Once again Emilie could be present only in spirit, for Joseph Lavergne was not of sufficient political stature to be helpful. In any case, the arrangements for the tour, which were in the hands of James Sutherland, the party whip, and Joseph Martin, the western expert, had kept French-Canadian representation to a minimum. There were Maritimers, Ontarians, and English Quebeckers, and of the other race only Choquette, an old and unobjectionable friend, in addition to Laurier himself. The aim was to show the west that Liberalism was sound and English sea to sea, dedicated to lower freight-rates, dedicated to lower tariffs, dedicated to the cause of wheat, and grouped round a leader who was almost as good as English.

There was a day in North Bay for Laurier, and another day each in Mattawa, Sault Ste. Marie, Sudbury, and Port Arthur. Then he was round the lakes, with the scrub pine and the sulphur fumes of the smelters and the loom of the grain elevators behind him. The blackened stumps and the wide gash of the road allowance were opening out on prairie and the real work was ahead. From the window of his car the country flowed by, almost empty yet, raw and tremendous, strange and unseizable. He could not be sure either of his own impressions or of the impression he had made. At the jammed railway station in Winnipeg, however, the crowd's wild and well-staged jubilance and its honest curiosity were the prelude to a real triumph.

On the night of September 3 six thousand people looked up and down at him from the seats, aisles, galleries, and window ledges of Brydon's skating-rink. He rose on the wings of a new sensation and a new promise. Here there was neither the sardonic understanding of Quebec nor the intrigued hostility of Toronto, but the fresh and open interest of men who had nothing in particular against foreigners as such. Immigration had made this country, he told them, and must make it, but had it done a tenth of what it could? Was there anything wrong with the climate, the soil, the institutions? Perhaps some of the institutions were not what they might be, but the real root of all Manitoba's troubles lay in the vicious policy followed by the government for the past fifteen years.

Liberalism, which in the past, in the new world and the old, had won every freedom enjoyed by man, was accused by the government of being hostile to the west. Why? Because it had fought monopoly and exploitation? Because Blake had opposed the way the C.P.R. was built? Was it not plain to every man that

Blake's fears of those methods and their results were being borne out?

Sixteen years before, when the first and only Liberal government of the Dominion left power, wheat had been selling at a dollar a bushel. It had risen to a dollar forty for a while, yes, but where was it now? Manitoba Hard, known everywhere as the world's best, was selling at less than fifty cents a bushel. The farmers of the Northwest, still too few, still throttled by C.P.R. monopoly, were growing too much wheat for the old markets and they were shut out from a market of sixty million people a hundred miles to the south of them. They were ground between the millstones of high protection and high freight-rates while the sugar barons and the cotton barons and the railway barons gorged themselves in the east. The C.P.R. had to make its allotted profit; the government had seen to that. It had to make its profit on too small a volume because there was not enough traffic moving over its lines. And how to increase traffic? In the first place, increase immigration. In the second place, and all-important, release the strangling death-grip of the National Policy. Open up the markets of the United States to the growers of the Northwest.

He returned for a moment recklessly and whole-heartedly to the mood of three years before. 'I denounce to you the policy of protection as bondage, yes, bondage, and I refer to bondage in the same manner in which the American slavery was bondage . . . Manitoba is a young giant manacled.' The cheers rose and his voice soared over them while some of his eastern listeners squirmed on the platform behind him, 'We shall give you free trade!'

He was thoroughly at home with the latest examples of corruption in government, he was vague but promising on the question of a railway to Hudson Bay, and when he came inevitably to the matter of the schools he took off on a flight of rhetoric that swept his audience with him and deposited everyone fifteen minutes later at the point from which he had set out. He would not be worthy of the name of man if he were unable to speak his mind to his countrymen on this question – but what of the government? They had shifted and evaded and promised everything and done nothing. 'I said to the government, here is a simple question of fact . . . prove to me that the complaint of the minority is true . . . that Catholic children have been forced to attend Protestant schools . . . and I will be prepared to go before the people of Manitoba and tell them that such legislation should not stand.' But the government of Manitoba – 'I speak in the presence of the members of the government' – had denied the statement *in toto*. What were the facts? Until they were determined, 'I have nothing to say in Winnipeg [beyond what] I have said on the floor of parliament, in Quebec, and elsewhere.' From which point he glided gracefully on into the dream of peace and harmony for which John A. Macdonald and George Brown had composed their quarrels twenty-seven years before.

Three days later an impromptu reception in the study of the private house at which he was staying was somewhat less successful. He had just dealt with a delegation of Indians and handed over a ten-dollar bill to the chief when a group of the leading Catholics of the city was shown in. Joseph Martin, the ubiquitous compère of the tour, sat by, supervising a rather strained discussion. The Roman Catholics of Winnipeg, said the spokesman, had resolved to lay bare to Mr. Laurier the oppressive conditions under which they now laboured. The Acts of 1890, in so far as they gave the appearance of non-sectarian education, were a fraud. The board now in control of education did not include one Catholic member. The certificates of Catholic teachers had been revoked, and the request that Catholics might be permitted to teach in one of their own buildings under the supervision of the Protestant board 'had been treated in a very cavalier manner'. Catholics were taxed for the support of Protestant schools, and even the apparent right to set up schools of their own at their own expense did not exist because it was in practice unworkable.

Mr. Laurier listened and fenced. He desired to hear the views of others in the delegation. The delegation responded vigorously. Textbooks were in effect Protestant textbooks. There was religious instruction that was entirely Protestant in tone, and the Catholic child had to unlearn at home much of what he had learned in school. Even if the parents were able to tax themselves twice and set up schools of their own, they would gain nothing because they would still be forced to use the books prescribed by the Protestant board.

It was all new to Mr. Laurier. He had heard no such definite complaints before. He thought it might have been better procedure to lay them before the government than before himself who had 'no influence in the matter at present, nor power to act'.

The spokesman did not agree. The Catholics of Winnipeg had no faith in the government, but they did hope that the leader of the opposition would devote himself to the restoration of the rights and liberties of the subject. 'You honour me very much,' said Mr. Laurier, 'but as the question is evidently a political one, I must ask you to excuse me now from dealing with a question which would take us into politics.'

It was a weird and wonderful argument from a man on a political tour, and he was not yet off the griddle. 'Supposing', came the next question, 'that Sir John Thompson favourably regarded an appeal to him, would you as leader of the opposition join with him in giving your influence to the redress of our grievances?'

'If, after careful consideration of both sides of the argument,' came the mellifluous reply, 'I find that Catholics are compelled to send their children to Protestant schools, and that injustice is being done them, I think that this Catholic school question would be as favourable a case for discussion as any that could be brought before parliament.'

It was none of it very satisfying, except perhaps to the Honourable Joseph Martin. Laurier, in spite of the generally bracing air of Winnipeg, was glad to be once more safe in the train and heading west. There was reassurance in the rough, angry, confident Liberals who greeted him in Portage la Prairie and Brandon with their talk of hard times and grasping eastern manufacturers. These men were selling their wheat for less than it cost to grow and paying sixteen, seventeen, and even twenty-four per cent interest on the price of their implements. They were ripe for a redeemer, even though he spoke with an accent and veiled himself in Delphic mists on the question of the schools. The question did not arise in the territories beyond the Manitoba border, not yet. As the line of the steel wound on across the hot, brown miles of grass and emptiness toward Regina and Moose Jaw, and on again by the lonely sod huts and the little clusters of shacks around the tall, angular bulk of grain elevators, Laurier was in the almost-virgin country where any educator, priest or not, was still welcome. Then the foothills of the Rockies were lifting over the horizon and with Calgary and Edmonton left for the homeward journey he was climbing into the mountains and winding breathlessly down to the other sea.

The magnificence could be enjoyed here, and the ten days on the Pacific and inland were in a way carefree. British Columbia, the land beyond the mountains, the province that Blake had been willing to relinquish if it meant the cost of the railway, was not yet ready to forgive. But at least it was in the grip of hard times and under a Conservative government. A Liberal could harp on that, pointing to the obvious remedy, and anything won by the missionary would be something in place of nothing. Like all before and after him, he responded gratefully to the polite and enigmatic Englishness of Victoria. The huge, complaining, westward-looking bustle of Vancouver shook him with a sense of power and destiny, and when he returned at last over the mountains to the ranchmen of Calgary and the bewildering variety and promise of Edmonton he had seen and heard more than he could take in. Westward and eastward, outward bound and home, the clack of the wheels, the lonely shrill of the whistle had set the mood of the journey; he was engulfed by haste and bigness. The country dwarfed its men. The nation outraced its leaders: defying plan, reckless of ordered growth, tumultuous, not to be stayed. He returned in early October to the flaring maples of Arthabaska, to the deathbed of Mercier and the troubles of Pacaud, and eight weeks later to the brief and breathless prospect of standing at the head of it all.

14

'I ASK THIS PARLIAMENT NOT TO PROCEED ANY FURTHER WITH THIS BILL'

1894-1896

THOMPSON had gone to England in late November to be made a member of the Privy Council. On December 12 came word of his sudden death in Windsor Castle. It was almost as much of a blow to Laurier as to the members of the Conservative party, and on neither side of the fence were all considerations political. The big man with the cold, commanding exterior that could break open in gusts of flaring anger and rare, revealing moments of gentleness and charm had wanted to remain a judge and would certainly have been a great one. He had left a promising career to come to Macdonald in a time of need, and he had stayed on after Macdonald because a steadily decaying ministry would have gone down without him. He had had to cloak his views in policy but he had never sacrificed conviction. He had had to live with and defend corrupt men but he had despised them, disciplined them, and never imitated them. He had had to accept the snubs that Ottawa society administered to a wife who had once been a shop-assistant, even though she was sufficiently well-bred to charm a Governor General's lady. In a place where money flowed with almost automatic ease into the hands of the willing, he had lived on his nine thousand dollars a year and deprived his family of much. He had gone alone on his trip to England because he could not afford the expense of taking his wife. He had had one overcoat in the winters and one pair of gloves, he had gone without lunch when he could not get home for it, and he had walked to save cab fare, all for the privilege of spending sixteen hours a day in the public service.

Few of his surface qualities were congenial to Laurier, but each man had touched the core of the other on more than one occasion. Now, for the survivor, there was a sense of real dismay. 'The death of poor Thompson', he wrote Edgar, 'is a most shocking event. It has strangely affected me. He was a gentleman and an able man, and there was a genuine pleasure in a fight with him. Who is there now on the other side who can maintain the contest on the same level?'

His private answer was, no one; but he saw no advantage in that. The seventh parliament had still over a year to run and the government had a comfortable majority. It was not called upon to rush into a general election and it would certainly not be inclined to. The elder Tupper, still High Commissioner in London, loomed in the distance, and it now seemed altogether probable that he would return to take over. It was not unlikely that Tupper would draw Chapleau from his retreat at Spencerwood, and the two of them together, while they would not raise the level of any contest, might very well make it rougher than before.

Within a day of the news, however, Laurier sat in his Ottawa office with all calculations upset. The Conservative cabinet, with the exception of Charles Hibbert Tupper and one or two minor figures, did not want the father back. They wanted him as far away as possible. The once-great ministry of Macdonald was now a cluster of aging remnants and assorted enemies, but the vacant throne beckoned and opportunity lurked in the very mediocrity of the available candidates. 'Here we are,' said Foster, who was not mediocre but who was almost completely ruled out because he was married to a woman who had been divorced, 'twelve of us and every one of us as bad or as good as the other – Jack as good as his master.' The words had soon escaped from the council chamber and gone flying about the city, and they were thoroughly revealing. It was almost incredible but it seemed definite by the afternoon of December 13 that the principle of seniority was to prevail. Mackenzie Bowell, the old Orange henchman of Macdonald, who held the portfolio of Trade and Commerce from the Senate and who was the cabinet minister of longest standing, had been sent for by the Governor General.

The picture grew confused and irritating an hour or so later when Sir Frank Smith, another venerable senator and member of the cabinet, was seen hurrying into Government House. Laurier angrily assumed that it was merely a Tory manoeuvre in support of Bowell. Smith was surely an impossible choice, but he was a Catholic and he could be used to allay any fear the Governor General might have of an Orangeman as Prime Minister. The leader of the opposition, however, was not yet on the track of events. It was only in the next few days, as the arrangements for the state funeral went on and the first tentative gestures toward a subscription for the penniless Lady Thompson were made, that the real potential of the situation leaked out.

The government was still headless and locked in crisis. Bowell had been first called by the Governor General merely to discuss the situation. He had assumed more and had been willing and eager to form a government, but he had not discussed his qualifications with his colleagues. He had carefully avoided doing so. When he returned from a second visit to Government House, duly commissioned and highly elated, the first of innumerable tempests broke about him. Charles Hibbert Tupper, sore already at the general rejection of his father, would not even think of serving under Bowell. Foster was vastly amused at the idea. Haggart, the Minister of Railways and Canals, who might have been a strong man if it were not for weak women, was resolute for himself. No one could agree on anything but the incapacity of Bowell. On that point, however, cabinet solidarity was almost total and at least six members were ready to enter a protest with the Governor General.

Through a week of dignified mourning and deceptive quiet the wrestlings in the cabinet found their way to the outside. The very stones of Ottawa oozed rumour. Sir Charles Tupper remained in London, remote, avuncular, apparently disinterested. He was supervising arrangements for the return of Thompson's body, to the agonized disgust of Lady Thompson who shared her husband's opinion of 'the old tramp'. Without Tupper and apparently without an alternative, the party counted the heads of private members and tried to guess what was in them. Liberals did the same. To Conservatives, their comfortable nominal majority began to seem very nominal indeed. Even under a strong hand the government had been riven with dissension. Under a weak hand or none it was threatening to fly apart. Was it worth while, for the sake of another year, to try to hold it together?

It would be eminently worth while to the cabinet, Laurier knew, and he did not permit speculation to carry him on to optimism. He was far from sure that optimism was called for in any case. But the possibilities hovered. Government could not remain headless, and the Liberals were blessed with a leader. He could form a government. He might even peel away enough disgusted and dissentient Tories to command a majority for a time. If not, there would be dissolution and an election and the election would probably be won.

Late that week, when an aide to the Governor General entered Laurier's office, the sleek young man bore all that cloud on his shoulders. It was amusing if deflating to find that his errand was above politics. It concerned the subscription for Lady Thompson and the generous proposal by the leader of the opposition that it should be a national affair rather than one originated by Conservatives and bearing the stigma of party. The matter was discussed and agreed on and the aide departed. He had, however, precipitated events. A newspaper reported that evening that an emissary of the Governor General had made contact with Mr. Laurier, and next morning His Excellency was informed in some haste that the cabinet would loyally accept Mr. Bowell. 'We all turned in like sheep into the fold,' Charles Hibbert Tupper was to record later. 'We thought it quite on the cards that H.E. would say, "Well, you have had nearly a week – you evidently cannot form a government. I will send for someone who can." '

On December 21 the ministry of Mackenzie Bowell was sworn into office. On January 3, 1895, the body of Sir John Thompson was laid to rest with solemn and affecting ceremony in the Catholic cemetery at Halifax. And on January 29 the judicial committee of the Privy Council declared that the federal government of Canada could, if it wished, intervene in the matter of the Manitoba schools.

2

THE GLIMPSE of power had been fleeting and insubstantial, but two facts emerged. Laurier stood alone on the Canadian landscape as a potential and respectable leader, and he had been measured as such from on high. To the Governor General, and even more to the Governor General's lady, the future was clear and inviting 'if only Laurier proves to be big enough'.

John Hamilton Gordon, 7th Earl of Aberdeen, and Ishbel Marjoribanks, Lady Aberdeen, were Gladstonian Liberals and social crusaders who had been received with much misgiving by a Tory Canadian government. A long record of private charities and public political service in the old country had been capped by a term in the viceregal lodge at Dublin, and wherever they went the Aberdeens had left their mark. Ishbel, who had founded or inspired such societies as the Onward and Upward Association, the National Home Reading Union, the Homes for Working Girls, and the League for the Provision of Seats for Shop Assistants, and who had often been seen prowling the Strand in search of prostitutes who might be rescued by her Rescue Mission, was a warmly regal humanitarian impatient of official restraint. The Earl himself, though he sometimes looked in public 'as if he expected to be hit with a brick', was nevertheless a handsome, extravagantly wealthy Scot who supported his wife in everything. The two worked as a team. They came to Canada hedged round by official protocol and formally neuter in politics, but Gladstone looked down from their walls. For the Aberdeens, life in Canada as elsewhere was a sphere of Christian endeavour, and Liberalism in politics was the secular arm of religion.

The formidable possibilities of such a combination had been obscured for a time by the character of 'my dear Sir John Thompson'. Ishbel had fallen in love with him at once in a regal and platonic way, and the Earl had followed suit. They had sympathized with him in his trials as a man at the head of 'a crowd of commonplaces' and they had above all shared his abhorrence of Sir Charles Tupper. Never, if they could help it, Ishbel had assured the widow at the time of Thompson's death, would Sir Charles Tupper return to Canadian politics.

Now, however, if Tupper's past was shady, Bowell's future was nil. That became steadily clearer as the weeks went by. Intrigue and the rumour of intrigue came thickly and quickly from the cabinet councils to the study at Government House. The Prime Minister was a fussy, self-important septuagenarian, swamped in petty problems and faced with another that big men had found too much for them. He was reeling from the impact of stronger personalities and contradictory interests. He was a one-time printer's devil who could not write a respectable letter and preferred to put nothing on paper because he might be held to it. He had been unable to make up his mind, as Ishbel scornfully noted, even on an inscription for Thompson's wreath from the cabinet – 'only do not put – with kind regards'. He was flabbily honest and vaguely well-willing, in the sense that he put office before prejudice; but if he was not a twister born, power was making him one. His power, in any case, was a pathetic fiction. It would certainly not be supported, beyond the bounds of duty, by a Liberal Governor General.

To a Liberal politician this might have seemed grounds for hope. From the first time he had dined with the Aberdeens, early in 1894, Laurier had found the atmosphere of Government House warm and congenial. He and his views were frankly admired and shared. Lady Aberdeen had enveloped Zoë's shyness in an all-embracing charm, and had talked with her in more than passable French. She had sensed the loneliness and sadness of a childless life, and if she had sensed anything more when her acquaintance widened to include Mme Lavergne, it had only deepened her sympathy. 'Dear Madame Laurier' and her tall and distinguished husband were soon received with more than official welcome.

Always the talk, discreet, immensely well-informed, fed by a hundred sources that were not open to the leader of the opposition, was valuable and heartening. Laurier had friends here in a high and strategic place. Yet duty cut both ways and so did friendship. The same Ishbel who was kindness itself to Zoë was also the dearest support of Lady Thompson. Her Excellency had fought a long battle against precedent and the views of Ottawa society to have Mrs. Foster, the guiltless party in a divorce, admitted to Government House. His Excellency was charming and exuded the aura of Gladstone, but Governors General no longer governed. Only in remotely possible and very obscure circumstances could they even tilt the scales. For a realist, the warmth from above politics promised little but restful contrast to the gloom and chaos below.

The transactions of early spring went far to confirm this view. By mid March the fifth session of the seventh parliament had not been called. There was talk of dissolution and an election. Bowell's government, however, confused on everything else, was clear on one point. It could face neither the House nor the country now until it had made some pronouncement on the subject of the Manitoba schools. The latest decision of the Privy Council had pushed the question squarely into the centre of politics. The cabinet hung pinioned and divided on one awesome sentence delivered by the presiding law-lord of the judicial committee: 'They may legislate or not as they think fit.'

For nine days, between February 26 and March 7, the cabinet had postponed decision with one more hopeful charade. Lawyers of the Catholic minority had been summoned to go over the grounds for redress. D'Alton McCarthy had opposed them as counsel for the Manitoba government. He had been able as always in the presentation of his case and caustic in his scorn of the reluctant ministers who sat as judges. The hearings had made it clear that there was every ground for reluctance but none for further delay. Action was called for and suddenly action came, with a stark and surprising bluntness.

It had been inspired by Charles Hibbert Tupper, who was Minister of Justice for one thing and the son of his father for another. He believed that the minority had a case and that Quebec was aroused behind it. He was ready to face Ontario with the proposition that politicians could support the letter of solemn agreements without being personally in favour of Catholic separate schools. There was a comforting certainty in the back of his mind that Catholics would not get far in any case against the wishes of an aroused province. Above all things else he was sure that the last hour for dithering had arrived, and on March 19 he carried his colleagues with him. An Order in Council, drafted in the brusque and unmistakable terms of a Tupper, ordered the Manitoba government to restore the full rights of its Catholic minority. The denominational schools were to be reopened under the threat of remedial action by the federal government.

'They are in the den of lions!' exulted Tarte, and Laurier was inclined to agree. Tarte had changed his footing since he first opened the question of the Manitoba schools. He had not yet been to the west, but he had absorbed the western attitude by political osmosis. He was not yet welcome in Ontario but he had taken Ontario's pulse. He was just back from New Brunswick where Liberal strength was building. He had the feel of the country as few in his province had, and he had not lost the feel of Quebec. He was aware of the power of bishops and aware of their limitations when it came to the work of the polls. He could have told young Tupper much about the habitant and his vote.

Bowell had been manoeuvred somehow into a clear and definite stand. The Orangeman had defied his Orangemen and defied Manitoba; he had given his hand to Quebec. One could imagine the pressures that had moved him and the pressures building now; they were all reflected in the office of the Liberal leader. One could admire Bowell and not envy him. The letters and telegrams and the furious, desk-thumping callers would be descending on him from Ontario, the Maritimes, and the west. They would be descending on the cabinet ministers who had gone along with him and chopping away at whatever support he had had. The next step, obviously, would be dissolution and a general election. The Conservative party would go to the polls on a single deadly issue, united in nothing except contempt for its leader.

It seemed too good to be true, and it was – though the first days that followed promised something even better. By the morning of March 21 Bowell was back-pedalling furiously, showering promises and explanations as he went. The Order in Council could not be recalled, but the answer of the Manitoba government could be awaited. It might, after all, be submissive.

There would be no dissolution. There would be another session of parliament in which, should the answer of the Manitoba government be unfavourable, the whole question could be once more soberly discussed. To go into an election now 'while the political heather was ablaze throughout the whole country would be a piece of political folly inexcusable in any public man'. Whereat Charles Hibbert Tupper submitted his resignation.

He was not a very big man but he was big enough to pull down Bowell. For six days the government was headed into an election not by choice but by necessity. With Quebec newly antagonized, it was certain to be a disaster. The procession of party Solons passing through Laurier's office doubled and quickened, all making jubilant preparations. Then, on the morning of March 27, came word that the younger Tupper had been seen entering Government House. That night he dined there with his lady. Also present that evening, summoned by telegraph from Montreal, were Sir Donald Smith of the C.P.R. and Senator George Drummond, industrialist, important beneficiary of the National Policy, and party treasurer. The next day it was announced that Charles Hibbert Tupper had returned to the fold. The government was saved and the fifth session of the seventh parliament would duly open. Her Majesty's representative had done his duty as he saw it.

3

THE SAME DAY Laurier returned to Arthabaska, and that evening he sat down at his desk. There was the usual crop of bad news from Pacaud; the little man's troubles were getting beyond them both now. Debts, lawsuits, quarrels, illness, general disintegration – old worries and new worries rose like a cloud of gnats from that bristling, plaintive file: 'I understood that you would try to settle this affair . . . I fear you have forgotten me . . . I am sorry you were unable to speak with me very long the other day; I had much to say to you . . . I do not hold you responsible, only to pray that you as chief of the party put an end to the persecutions of those I gorged with money when I had it . . . last Thursday many wounding remarks were passed because I subscribed only $5 to have a high mass sung for poor Mercier

. . . do you not think that the party, instead of organizing to oppose me, would do better to concentrate its efforts to save the veteran of the battle from falling? . . . having lost power we have no more hope of relieving ourselves . . .'

There was a letter from Anglin of Toronto, lawyer and leading Catholic, speaking for the letter of the law in Manitoba. There was a letter from Fielding in Nova Scotia, speaking against it. Willison wrote, a bit pontifical now, always assuming that he spoke with Laurier's mind. There must be no interference with provincial rights: he was very firm on that. Would he never understand that no provincial rights were involved? The federal government had every right and power to intervene. It was the effect of intervention that mattered. It was a question of motives and intentions and ultimately of competing values. Willison could not be brought to see it. He saw bishops in his nightmares. He spoke to Laurier as a reasonable British man, in a reasonable British country. Always, in all his letters, the faintest, slightest shade of patronizing commendation. It was the same with Cartwright. It was the same with John Dafoe, the big, shaggy twenty-nine-year-old editor of the Montreal *Herald* who had already had six years in the west with the *Manitoba Free Press* and was soon to return there. It was the same with many others. Englishmen, stiffening the back of the Frenchman. There would be more of that for Laurier, a great deal more indeed, if he went through the session ahead. And that would be the best and least of it.

There was a letter from Charles Hyman of London, Ontario, the party treasurer. The party leader had much to do with the treasurer, and in one way more than he liked. The cheques came from Hyman, when they came. Hyman paid the secretary who sat waiting now beside the cluttered desk. Hyman's letter concerned a party celebration to be held on Dominion Day. It would have something the same effect, he wrote, as the national Liberal convention two years before. It would pull the party together, strengthen the leader. Somewhere under the letters the bills were waiting, the personal bills, the bills of Wilfrid Laurier. He did not ask Hyman to pay those – not yet. He shoved the clutter away from him, looked at the clear space on the desk for a minute, then leaned back and began to dictate. It was not a very good letter, his head ached more than usual, and he was conscious that he slipped back occasionally into French construction.

'My dear Hyman: I would not advise you to call now, or even to prepare for, the great demonstration which you contemplate on Dominion Day. It is altogether too early to think of it. We may be on the eve of serious complications and it is well for us, before we organize a new campaign, to wait a little the development of events. So, I would advise to wait a little.

'Moreover, I do not know if I will then be at the head of the party. I must once more press our friends in the House to relieve me from that position. Two years ago I wanted to resign . . . we all expected then and we have been expecting ever since that the elections would come off after the fourth session of the present parliament. Matters are now turning differently, and again I am forced to ask our friends to relieve me . . . I cannot go on giving all my time to politics. I must work for myself.

'I have always been of the opinion that an English leader would be much stronger than I can ever be and everything confirms me in that opinion . . . I will do nothing rash . . . but it is a hard task for a man to work for the public when he has no means of his own.

'My health is far from good, I am sorry to say, though I am doing fairly well just now . . .'

The letter went off and Hyman's urgent protests were back by return mail. He was afraid that Laurier was discouraged. He suspected that Cartwright was making things uncomfortable. The thought of another leader could simply not be considered. Laurier resumed the argument, wearily and irritably:

'I am not discouraged at all . . . I have no feelings toward Cartwright but feelings of the sincerest affection.

'I would want to be relieved of the leadership just for one reason, and one only . . . I have no independence of fortune. I must work for my living . . . Before I accepted the leadership I had just a fair professional income, enough to meet all my wants and to have a small surplus at the end of the year . . . I threw myself into the fight, I had to neglect my business and the consequence was that my income was diminished accordingly . . . our friends asked me to go on . . . and that in the meantime they would help me financially. This they have done, and in a very generous manner, yet insufficient to save me from trouble. I see the day fast approaching when I must run into debt, and this I will not do . . . can you blame me?

'Last year I was just once in court, and I have to work for a living!

'Of course I will do nothing rash. The very thought of leaving the party under existing conditions is painful to me. If I thought the general elections would take place in 1895 I could go on. If successful, all right, I would have a salary. If defeated, then my friends could no longer object to my withdrawing.

'The postponement of the elections has been a very severe disappointment to me.

'Again let me assure you, my dear Hyman, that I will do nothing rash.'

Nothing rash. The argument was over and he had lost it as he wrote. It had circled down to the same dismal point. It would call forth the same dreary palliatives.

4

He was still the elegant, courtly leader of the opposition when parliament opened with brilliant ceremony on April 18, 1895. He still returned to rooms in the Russell Hotel. He was as close-mouthed and inscrutable as ever on the question of the Manitoba schools. He called or dined rather more frequently at Government House and he was well prepared when, on June 19, the Manitoba legislature replied to the Order in Council with a flat no.

Greenway and Sifton, the powers in Manitoba, were rather more than firm. The Liberal premier and his Liberal Attorney-General answered the Conservative cabinet in terms of polite defiance. The government, if it wished, might send out commissioners to determine conditions for themselves. The province was aware of conditions and was set on its own way. Beyond that, if the government was determined to force sectarian schools on Manitoba, how would it administer them when the province refused to co-operate?

It was all too evident that the Prime Minister had no idea. For ten days he reeled dizzily back and forth between the angers of Ontario and the pressures of Quebec, between the seven Protestant and the five Catholic cabinet ministers who assailed him in council. He haunted the Governor General's study as a relief from his seething office. The Aberdeens were in touch with Greenway and Sifton. They were in touch with Archbishop Langevin who had succeeded Taché in the west, and with Bishop Laflèche in the east. Politicians and clergymen and assorted intermediaries streamed in and out of Rideau Hall. The Aberdeens were above politics and wanted peace in the land. Somewhere, somehow, something might be worked.

June ran out and Bowell grew a little frantic. Parliament waited and Quebec pressed for the grim remedial bill that would bring Manitoba to heel. It did not come. The disgusted Aberdeens took off from the heat of Ottawa for the cool of the St. Lawrence. On July 6, lacking his stately reed, Bowell collapsed. The government of Manitoba, he announced, would be given time to reflect. There would be no remedial bill this session. Parliament would complete its business and prorogue. If no compromise had been arranged by the end of the year a special session would be called for not later than January 2, 1896.

Three days later Laurier was unsurprised to learn that the Governor General and his wife sat grumpily fanning themselves in a suite of the Russell Hotel. Bowell had summoned them away from the fresh breezes of Quebec. He had subjected them to a hot and hasty journey in a fly-blown railway car, and he could not permit them time even to resume their official residence. They were here to preside at the imminent death of a government. Auguste Réal Angers, Sir Adolphe Caron, and Joseph Alderic Ouimet, Bowell's three Quebec cabinet ministers, had resigned. The private members from Quebec were in open revolt. He faced defeat in the House.

When parliament convened that afternoon Laurier rose to point out that for the first time since Confederation Quebec was not represented on the treasury benches. An explanation by the government was in order. There could be no answer from Bowell, for Bowell sat in the Senate. Foster, the leader of the House, promised a statement next day.

It seemed that the moment had arrived. Quebec Conservatives and Quebec Liberals were fraternizing angrily. A good part of Laurier's night went to the preparation of the no-confidence motion that would bring the government down. Tory potentates and Tory purse-bearers, however, were also using the night, and by noon next day their score was two out of three. Aberdeen was just sitting down in his study to inform the home government of Bowell's resignation when a breathless messenger arrived. Caron and Ouimet were returning to their allegiance. At three that afternoon, pale and crumpled, they were wafted to their seats on the front benches by the derisive chant of the House: 'The cats have come back – the cats have come back.'

The no-confidence motion was duly presented and lost. Quebec Conservative members had swung back behind their returning statesmen. Charles Hibbert Tupper rose amid blistering laughter to assail the wavering uncertainty of the leader of the opposition on the great question of the day. But Mr. Laurier only 'sat and smiled'.

5

THE SESSION came to an end on July 22, with rockets still rising from the patched-up wreck of the government. There was no help for it from Manitoba. Quebec's eyes were fixed on the gaping hole in the cabinet left by the going of Angers, the minister who had not returned. He was the only man who counted for anything with the ultramontanes, and he would have no more of Bowell. Neither would any Quebecker of remotely comparable standing. Bowell had lost the bishops and was leaning again toward the Orangemen. Conservative newspapers in Ontario were assuring their readers that the Order in Council did not mean what it said; there would be no plunge for Catholic schools. Clarke Wallace, cabinet minister and head of the Orange Order, was openly saying as much. Denying its proclaimed policy and facing both ways, the one hope of the government seemed to lie in Laurier himself. If he could be pinned down, Conservatives could swing round. With so little credit to lose, little more would be lost by a complete change of front. From the mouths of Tory guns a volley of crackling adjectives soared up and centred on the leader of the opposition. All the divisions in the country, all the uncertainties of government were caused by his cowardice, his equivocation, his spineless lack of conviction.

The target remained elusive and a little amused. 'I wish that the minority in Manitoba may be allowed the privilege of teaching in their schools, to their children, their duties to God and man as they understand those duties.' But how was the thing to be done? 'If that object is to be attained, it is not by imperious dictation nor by administrative coercion. The hand must be firm and the touch must be soft: hitherto the touch has been rude and the hand has been weak.' Courage? 'My courage is not to make hasty promises and then ignominiously to break them. My courage is to speak slowly, but once I have spoken to stand or fall by my words.'

He had the same answer for Quebec when he went home at the end of the session, and it had become a jovial game by the time he moved over to Ontario. He recalled Aesop's fable of the blustering wind and the warm sun. Which of them had been able to make the traveller take off his coat? 'Well, sir, the government are very windy. They have blown and raged and threatened, but the more they have threatened and raged and blown the more that man Greenway has stuck to his coat. If it were in my power, I would try the sunny way.'

For two months, on fifty-six stumps in Ontario, he held to the position he took with the voters of Morrisburg, where his tour began on October 8. 'Remember that war has to be waged in a certain way. When the Duke of Wellington was in Portugal he withdrew at one time within the lines of Torres Vedras and there for months he remained, watching the movements of the enemy. . . . Gentlemen, I am within the lines of Torres Vedras. I will get out of them when it suits me and not before.'

The tour ended and there were no more crowds looking up at him and no more slyly understanding laughter. There was the silence of the study again and the ministrations of Zoë. There was the endless correspondence with the men who counted, the endless work of probing, explaining, weighing. There was Archbishop Langevin to be thought of, the inflexible man of the west. The ancient, familiar thunder came from the diminished diocese of Three Rivers. There were other bishops, cool or confused or silent. There was Pacaud, shedding his troubles as he scented battle and wanting to have at all enemies in the old way. It would not do: neither the old way nor the old guard. It would be Tarte this time, Tarte with Laurier for Quebec, and beyond Quebec the rest of the country brooded, stormy and enigmatic.

It was too easy to represent this fight over schools as a battle of bishops and Orangemen. It was too easy to see this country in the old way. There was Mills, for example, the hard-eyed Liberal Protestant who had been a friend of Blake, one of the best friends. He represented, perhaps, the strain in old Ontario that Laurier most admired, a dogged, downright, narrow insistence on the right. Mills stood with the Catholic Anglin for the remedial order, because it was law and justice. If those two were wrong, who was right? Sifton? Greenway? Martin? Laurier needed those westerners, though he hardly liked them. He was going to need Sifton in the future, like him or not. All three represented that wave of turbulent change cresting over Quebec. He needed Quebec too.

He was going to need Fielding of Nova Scotia, the always cautious. He would have to dislodge Fielding from a safe provincial premiership. The man who did that would have to be convincing, and convinced himself. By November 5 he was ready at least to give Fielding the best he had. 'It is now evident that the government are going to make a strong bid to capture the Roman Catholic vote by introducing remedial legislation . . . that they will capture it is not at all certain . . . for I know for a certainty that the most intelligent and far-seeing among the Roman Catholics, both clergy and laity, dread the action as likely to conduce not to the establishment of separate schools in Manitoba but to an agitation to abolish separate schools in all the provinces.'

By the end of the month he had received a well-hedged promise that Fielding would support him when a general election approached. It was a heartening sign, reinforced on December 14 by the resignation of Clarke Wallace from Bowell's cabinet. It was not the last of the good news, but news thereafter gradually lost all meaning. On December 15 Her Majesty's High Commissioner, Sir Charles Tupper, arrived in Ottawa from London. On January 3, 1896, parliament opened with a Speech from the Throne announcing remedial action in favour of the Catholic minority of Manitoba as the principal business of the session. Two days later the Honourable George Foster and the Honourable John Graham Haggart walked into His Excellency's study to inform him that seven ministers of the government, all Protestants, were tendering their resignations.

6

LAURIER had known for two months that 'something is brewing here', and had written as much to Pacaud. From the day of Tupper's return he was sure that the something meant trouble. Everything on the surface continued to run his way. A half-dozen by-elections in Ontario and Quebec had gone well. Fielding had come to Montreal for one of them and had performed admirably. Liberals in Manitoba were certain of a smashing victory in the January provincial elections. Well resolved, and well coached by their federal friends, they would certainly give no ground to a dying Tory ministry.

Bowell could hardly have opened the session in a more hopeless condition. The going of Wallace had meant the last of his Orange support. Quebec's grim distrust was still signified by Angers's empty seat. Yet the Prime Minister had pledged himself, through the mouth of the Governor General, to the restoration of Catholic rights. It was hard to imagine the tangle of hopes and plots and plans that had led him to do it, but the effect was now clear. Bowell had walked out to the very end of a plank which seven of his mutinous crew had promptly sawn off. The brisk, decisive ruthlessness meant only one thing: a ruddy old buccaneer, fresh-come from London, stood in the shadows behind them giving the orders.

There was and would be, of course, an immense uproar over

the treachery of the affair. Laurier was not impressed. It was tough-fisted politics in a time of desperation, and it had little or nothing to do with the issue of the schools. That would be a toss-up for either party under the best of circumstances. Under Bowell, whatever the issue might be, the Conservative party was lost.

Foster's statement to the House on January 7 was cruelly to the point. 'Though with many misgivings we agreed to enter the government under Mr. Bowell . . . we found ourselves face to face with Parliament having a Government with its numbers incomplete, and with no assurance that the present Premier could satisfactorily complete it.' Under these circumstances the seven retiring gentlemen had thought it their duty 'to pave the way, if possible, for the formation of a Government whose Premier could command the confidence of all his colleagues'. Tupper was to rally Quebec, bring back Chapleau, who was worth a dozen of Angers, and lead out the party in form before the lines of Torres Vedras.

It was a bleak prospect for the man behind the ramparts, but it was changing as Foster spoke. Key figures in the plot were not performing as expected. The House received the statement in a stunned silence and then the Liberal dialecticians rose to do it justice. Throughout the afternoon Lady Aberdeen sat in the place reserved for her beside the Speaker, engrossed and treasuring all for the husband who could not appear on these premises. She was always a pleasant sight but this time Laurier was rather more interested in the old gentleman who sat behind her, humiliated, fuming, and despondent. Senator Bowell was also a guest of this House, but still Prime Minister. At the close of debate he rose, came over to shake Laurier's hand, and moved along the row of Liberal leaders with greetings which were heard across the aisle and meant to be heard. 'It is such a comfort to shake hands with honest men, after having been in the company of traitors for months.' It might have been a last ungraceful, heartfelt gesture of departure, but Laurier was already aware that it was not.

The Aberdeens by now had had enough of high neutrality, and one of them had acted. Mrs. Emily Ann McCausland Cummings was a discreet and personable correspondent of the Toronto *Globe* who had supported Ishbel nobly in much of her social work. She was also a friend of Mr. Laurier, who was friendly with all newspaper people. For the past day or so she had been going back and forth between her two friends with a frequency noted by Tories. 'It is well at such a juncture', Ishbel observed virtuously, 'to have some means of communication with the leader of the Opposition.'

Through this channel, as much as through the outward goings-on, Laurier followed events. His hopes rose and his hopes fell and his digestion worsened. On January 4, it appeared, a stunned and indignant Bowell had been plied with soothing offers by the elder Tupper. He could have a post in a new cabinet under Sir Charles. He could have the lieutenant-governorship of Ontario. He could have the relinquished High Commissionership in London. By January 5 he had refused all offers. He would never serve with traitors nor permit traitors to serve him. The seven were out and they would stay out. He would form a new cabinet. A defiant and resolute statesman, he held out for just two days, only to find at the end that collapse was not escape. When he appeared before Aberdeen with his resignation on January 7, it was the Governor General who dug in his heels.

'Put that paper back into your pocket please,' were the words that Ishbel reported. She had been present at the interview by request, for His Excellency now wished to have a trusted witness on hand during any conversations with the Prime Minister. Aberdeen had delivered the Speech from the Throne that had been given him. It had been long and trying and in two languages. He had delivered it with some difficulty, shouting above the babble that always rose from the ill-mannered English when the time for the French version came. At all events, as he firmly pointed out, he had pledged the government, in the name of Her Majesty, to face the House and present a certain proposal. The government, so long as it existed, would not be allowed to back down.

Bowell had protested that it was now impossible for him to face the House. Only Tupper could form a cabinet. The traitors were determined on that. His Excellency, who had lost none of his old aversion through closer contact, would not summon Tupper. Never, under any conditions.

With that certainty Bowell had gone back refreshed and stiffened. He could inform Tupper that there would be no summons to Government House. Bowell was the only man who would be permitted to refill the nest vacated by the vipers. Bowell was in or the government was out.

On January 8 a delegation of the dismayed 'bolters', led by Charles Hibbert Tupper, arrived to put themselves straight with Her Ladyship. They had warned Bowell, they explained, at least a month earlier, that they would not go on if he could not find a suitable man to replace Angers and make sure of Quebec at least. He had fussed and promised and not done it and by the time the Throne Speech was delivered they had come to realize that it never would be done. Therefore they had resigned, standing to their word as upright men. Her Ladyship, who had come to have a grudging respect for the filial loyalty of the young Tupper, was not unimpressed. Nothing was changed, however, in the viceregal attitude toward the father, and nothing was changed for Bowell. His pleas for cabinet timber fell on deaf ears or none. Some men he hoped to persuade he could not even get to see. Potential ministers, summoned from out of town, were met at the railway station by pickets of grim-faced bolters and spirited away. By January 9, hapless and hopeless, the Prime Minister was again at Rideau Hall, resignation in hand.

Once more the resignation was refused and Bowell returned to the gaping wreck of his government. Around the city the roar of rumour went on. By Saturday morning, January 11, Laurier was in bed with a cold. By Saturday noon he was shuddering at the prospect of attending a skating party. It had been arranged by Her Excellency and was to take place on the grounds of Government House. At such an innocent function the appearance of Mr. Laurier could hardly be questioned. It was indispensable in view of the latest developments. Bowell was expected hourly in a third attempt to resign. This time he would succeed. He had been given every chance and he could not assemble a cabinet. Tupper would not be allowed to. Torydom toppled on the brink. Government House was ready for action, and it was necessary now and at once to decide on procedure.

Duly dressed and muffled, the leader of the opposition set off to confront falling snow and hordes of healthy skaters. He had not long to endure them. Her Ladyship appeared, pink-cheeked, buoyant, and ingenuous, to present Captain Sinclair of the household who was, she explained 'a confidential friend'. She considered it likely that the two gentlemen would enjoy a walk about the grounds and, likely or not, Mr. Laurier politely agreed. During that walk the shape of the future emerged. Mr. Laurier, if called, could form a government in three days. He would dissolve the House at once. He would go to the country and he would sweep the country if he went as head of the government. If he went to it still as the leader of the opposition, faced by Sir Charles Tupper, it would be a very different affair.

There could be no question of Tupper; Captain Sinclair was emphatic on that. The walk concluded and Laurier returned to the hotel to nurse his cold. Through Sunday and most of Monday there was no word from Government House. The invalid was aware of the tormented Tory procession that passed through its portals on the Sabbath but he remained fairly confident. Monday the waiting was a little worse, but with good reason. A subplot had injected a note of hysteria into the high concerns of government. Sir Adolphe Caron, the Postmaster-General, was one of the few remaining ministers who clung to Bowell. He had recently been accused of corruption in a series of anonymous letters. Tender of his reputation, and with good reason, he had good reason to suspect that the author of the letters was the Honourable Walter Humphries Montague, one of his bolting colleagues. Montague, though he did not deny the contents of the letters, furiously denied the writing. The quarrel had boiled up at this moment with the Aberdeens at the centre of it. 'The whole day from 11 to 6', recorded Her Ladyship, 'has been employed by H.E. in patching up the quarrel between Caron and Montague . . . finally after many interviews and H.E. and Captain Sinclair going backwards and forwards between the two rooms where the two disputants were separately caged, and words being altered and erased and added to, a compromise was arrived at.'

The day, however, was not ended; there was still to be news for Laurier. The debris of the scuffling ministers had hardly been cleared from the desk at Rideau Hall when Bowell arrived. He had not come to present his wrinkled resignation. He was strangely, shiftily, sulkily at peace. Sir Charles Tupper had wished to accompany him, he explained, but he had said no. His Excellency, once more in the presence of Ishbel, agreed heartily but blankly. Why on earth should Tupper have thought of coming? The explanations were voluminous and the fact devastating, at least to Her Ladyship. Sir Mackenzie – the title had come with a recent honours list – had taken back to his bosom the late vipers of the cabinet. 'And this after all his protestations!' Only one Tupper remained out because one Tupper in was quite enough. Charles Hibbert was now merely the honourable member for Pictou, with the post of Solicitor-General, which was not of cabinet rank. His father, always responsive to the call of duty, had been prevailed on to accept the portfolio of Secretary of State. Government was whole again, the ship drove on. The glorious captain still retained the helm, quite certain to be pitched overboard the moment an election loomed.

7

'WE ARE HERE', said Cartwright, rising suavely in the House on January 15 and addressing himself to the replenished treasury benches, 'in the presence of the Ottawa Low Comedy Troupe, and should be grateful for the amusement they have afforded us. What we have been listening to, after all, has really been a series of rehearsals. We had number one rehearsal (because I can hardly count the little episode of the Honourable Member for Pictou as one) when three members of the cabinet went out and two came back. Then we have had what I may call a full-dress rehearsal when seven members went out and practically seven came back. Now, these honourable gentlemen being nearly letter-perfect, we can have the rest of the performance, which will not be long delayed, when all of them go out and none come back.'

It went on in the best Cartwright vein. For the moment Laurier could lean back, watching the flick of the whip and the wincing across the aisle. He had had his fun himself with this 'band of plotters and schemers and conspirators whose bond of union is the cement of office'. He had not said much, and he had made a point of that, quoting Disraeli: 'I am loath by word or deed to take anything away from the lamentable exhibition the government is making of itself.' It was all very well and it did not change the fact. Tupper, still to be confirmed in office through a by-election, was the real head of the government.

By the end of the month he had been elected for Cape Breton, and on February 10 he returned to Ottawa. At seventy-five he emerged from this campaign much as he had emerged from his others, much as he had emerged from the fight for Confederation and the fight for the railway. The same rank cloud of rumour came along with him; he had blustered and bribed and lied and promised and threatened and misrepresented, he had used every shoddy tool in the political kit. Perhaps he had, but he had won and he was here now, his old, burly, over-groomed, blandly truculent self. One did not have to like a Goliath to recognize his strength, and reluctantly admire his hardihood. Even the lady in Government House went that far now. Some of the old discouragement of the days with Blake came back. In Tupper's presence, even at fifty-five, Laurier was inclined to feel himself a raw, uncertain David.

Not everything was running Tupper's way, however. He was not going to get Chapleau as his man in Quebec. That was becoming clearer, and it was due to Tarte. The two old *Bleus* spoke to each other in a language of their own and played by their own rules. Chapleau was, and felt himself, deeply involved in the promise to the Manitoba Catholics. He had never been a man to shrink from a fight, and he was not now. If he was tired or sick or sceptical of the party's chances even under Tupper, that was one thing. It would be another and better if Tarte had really convinced him that the bishops asked too much.

It was a straw, and a man was grasping at straws now. One was counting bishops, and there were a good many of them outside Quebec who were still silent. Even in Quebec they did not all speak in the tone of Langevin and Laflèche. But there was the new note in the Maritimes, struck in Tupper's campaign. It had been a letter, supposed to be a letter from Cameron, a Highland Scot, Bishop of Antigonish, damning the 'hell-bound hypocrites, many of them Catholics' who held back from the remedial bill or dared to ask for further investigation. Genuine or not, it had been circulated freely and well read. From Quebec, from the west, and now on the far fringe of the Atlantic coastline, the cancerous quarrel was growing.

There had also been the letter that came to Laurier himself, not from a bishop but from Father Lacombe, the beloved and gentle old priest who was 'man of the beautiful soul', 'man of the good heart' to everyone on the prairies of the west, white and Indian, Catholic and Protestant. 'If, which may God not grant, you do not believe it to be your duty to accede to our just demands, and if the government, which is anxious to give us the promised law, is beaten and overthrown while keeping firm to the end of the struggle, I inform you with regret that the episcopacy like one man, united with the clergy, will rise to support those who may have fallen in defending us.'

The man of St-Lin, with each day pushing him a little nearer to the ground of D'Alton McCarthy and Clarke Wallace, could only have sympathy for Père Lacombe. He could echo the old man's cry. 'O Tempora! O Mores! Where are we? Where am I? Do I dream?' Père Lacombe had found himself the emissary of the Orangeman Bowell to the ultramontanes of Quebec in the desperate search for a cabinet minister. Well, he had failed, and whatever Tupper might get would be stop-gap and second rate. Père Lacombe's letter had been allowed to go to Tarte and on to John Dafoe and from there to the newspapers. The bellowings at priestly influence had duly risen. If the clergy were going to be enemies it was well that the Orangemen be friends. Laurier had made up his mind.

8

THE SEVENTH parliament of Canada, first assembled on April 29, 1891, was required by law to terminate on or before April 26, 1896. Bowell, in calling a sixth session, had given himself just one hundred and fifteen days to complete the business of the House. By March 3, the day that Tupper opened the debate on the Remedial Bill, Manitoba, sixty-one of those days had been consumed. There had been the preliminary antics of the changing of the guard, there had been the business of Tupper's election, and the rest of the time had been spent in the attempt to pull the Conservative party together, strengthen it in Quebec, and soften up the attitude of the Manitoba government. Somewhere before the session came to an end at least two weeks would have to be found for the passing of estimates and the provision of essential funds. It left the new leader of the House with approximately forty days to carry out the promise of the government, pass the Remedial Bill, and go to the country with an issue.

That Tupper was determined to do so was unmistakably clear. Behind the scenes, as he rose ponderously with his bulky fistful of notes, there was all the hurrying and scurrying that had filled Bowell's days. Emissaries, volunteered and commanded, official and unofficial, were still rushing out to Winnipeg with new suggestions for compromise. Tupper gave them all the most perfunctory attention. Whatever else he might be, he was a realist. He knew the political force of a political commitment, and he expected no relief from a Liberal provincial government. He exuded an optimism he did not feel, but he had been in tight spots before and he had got out of them. He was not unaware that, in spite of recent appearances, a sizeable proportion of the men on both sides of the aisle sat there with convictions. There were men of conviction across from him, French Catholics and Irish Catholics, devoted to separate schools. Whatever the strength they represented, and to whatever extent he actually shared their views, he was the man to make the most of it.

'The question of separate schools', he said, 'is not an issue at all. It is a question of the Constitution of the country – that all the rights guaranteed under it be sacredly guarded. Within this wide Dominion you have got over forty-one per cent of the population Roman Catholics. Are we to leave rankling in the minds of over forty-one per cent of the people of this Dominion the sentiment that a Roman Catholic cannot obtain the same just consideration that he would if he were a Protestant?'

There in a nutshell, compact, undeniable, deadly, lay the

whole force of the argument. The bill itself would be torn to pieces by Cartwright when his turn came in the debate. It was 'certain to breed an endless train of litigation – rival authorities utterly and bitterly opposed . . . it threatens what it cannot perform, promises what it can never implement . . . an imposture, a parliamentary scarecrow – a bill, in one word, for the purpose of disturbing everything and settling nothing.' Perhaps it was all of that, but the argument was not answered. The fears of many a Liberal were not quieted. Forty-eight hours before, as Laurier's intentions grew clear, some of the chief men of the party had come to him, swept by a wave of panic.

It would be suicidal, they argued, to oppose the bill directly. Laurier must not rise, as he proposed, to give the first reply to Tupper. Leave that to McCarthy's group. McCarthy was ready to support Laurier, in so far as it meant getting rid of the government. Let Clarke Wallace, the head of the Orangemen, move the six months' hoist of the bill as he intended. Catholics on either side could vote as they liked; the measure would still be killed. The party would not be committed. Laurier had heard them out and had refused.

He stood up now to commit the party and commit himself. He would have the Orangemen; Père Lacombe had helped to make sure of that. He was going to have less of Ontario and more of Quebec than he hoped for. He intended to make full capital of the fact that he spoke neither as a Catholic nor a Protestant but as a leader responsible to the nation. But it was not quite the point. A French Canadian would have to make the point, at a cost and with a tangle of emotions known only to himself. This Tupper who sat across from him appealed to the fact of Confederation. He had a right to; he had helped to make it. It was a good work and a great work, done with a hard hand. But it was a living, changing thing which had left behind old hopes and outgrown old methods. The man and the club that had bludgeoned Nova Scotia were part of the past now. In one interminable, intricate, exquisitely balanced sentence Laurier rejected them.

'Mr. Speaker,' he said, 'if in a debate of such moment it were not out of place for me to make a personal reference to myself – a reference which, however, may perhaps be justified, not so much on account of the feelings which may not unnaturally be attributed to me, being of the race and of the creed of which I am, but still more in consideration of the great responsibility which has been placed on my shoulders by the too kind regard of the friends by whom I am surrounded here – I would say that, in the course of my parliamentary career, during which it has been my duty on more than one occasion to take part in the discussion of those dangerous questions which too often have come before the parliament of Canada, never did I rise, sir, with a greater sense of security; never did I feel so strong in the consciousness of right, as I do now, at this anxious moment when, in the name of the constitution so outrageously misinterpreted by the government, in the name of peace and harmony in this land; when in the name of the minority which this bill seeks or pretends to help, in the name of this young nation on which so many hopes are centred, I rise to ask this parliament not to proceed any further with this bill.'

9

FROM THE afternoon of March 3 to the small hours of April 16, by daylight and lamplight, sometimes with sessions a hundred and thirty hours long, the debate ground on under the relentless Tupper. He himself was only to be seen in his place at strategic moments, always ruddy and refreshed. The pallid Laurier was absent days on end, but it was not so with the underlings. There was one six-day break, a daily hour for dinner, and an occasional half-day gap brought on by sheer exhaustion or the need for the chars to sweep out. For the rest the House was a cage that threatened to become a zoo.

Cabinet ministers, always on instant call, slept in their offices. Private members, herding in halls and corridors, spread blankets where they could. All too many of them, having said what they had to say and heard more than they could bear, went on a liquid diet. Indian war-whoops and the crash of breaking glasses were heard from the caucus rooms by envious corporal's guards still under the eye of Mr. Speaker. The grey dawns found the chamber of the Commons of Canada unswept, littered with crumpled paper, stinking of sweat and whisky, and still plagued by the acrid drone of yawning, unshaven statesmen.

At five-thirty on the morning of Friday March 20, Laurier, with his face swollen up from toothache and for once far from elegant, saw the second reading passed and the bill head in for committee. The unbearable prospect now was a clause-by-clause dissection and a vote on every clause. It was suddenly relieved when Tupper, who had grudgingly consented to send a last commission west, asked for an adjournment of debate. Even more grudgingly he asked Laurier to be a member of the commission. The first request was promptly and magnanimously granted. The second could hardly be refused, but it could be hedged round with conditions. The invited commissioner would act only if he were allowed to see all the correspondence that had passed between the government of Canada and the government of Mr. Greenway. When Tupper declined to place his cards in the hands of the leader of the opposition, Laurier retired to his bed while the commission went off without him. It would not accomplish anything and the prospect of six days' rest was very heaven.

It ended all too soon when the commission reported failure. The government of Manitoba was unmoved; the government of Canada had exhausted its hopes of compromise. Debate resumed with an angrier Tupper now, and longer hours. Mr. Speaker's eyes drooped and his deputy reeled with boredom as books were read, lifetime histories recounted, division followed division, and every device of obstruction came into play. The filibusterers and the time-fillers and the back-bench ultramontanes and the no-popery addicts took over as sensible men gave up. Lady Aberdeen forsook the House in disgust and ministered impartially to casualties of both persuasions. She treated Mr. Laurier for his indigestion and supplied Mr. Foster with tablets for his throat. At two o'clock on the morning of April 16, with only fifteen of the hundred and twelve clauses yet passed in committee, a private member rose, concerned for history. 'There is one statement', he said, 'that ought to be put on the Hansard, and that is that the opponents of this bill while on the floor of the House were not drunk. That ought to be put in for the simple reason that when future generations come to read the debates on this question it will be very hard to convince them that these honourable gentlemen were sober.'

There followed hard on his heels a burst of lunatic irrelevancies that fully confirmed the fear. The clock stood at two-thirty when Tupper, warned by the Governor General that money would be hard to come by if he did not pass his estimates, rose and gave up. The debate was closed, the Remedial Bill withdrawn. On April 24, two days short of the deadline and with most of the estimates left over, parliament dissolved. The date of the general election was set for June 23, and the newly-elected parliament would convene on July 16.

The last of the planned manoeuvrings were completed by the end of May. Sir Mackenzie Bowell, in tendering his resignation, had no advice to offer as to the succeeding Prime Minister. None was needed. The Aberdeens, like it or not, would have Sir Charles Tupper at the head of public affairs. Graceful as always, they concealed their private fumings, and five days before the happy accession Ishbel stood with the elder Tupper as godparent to the young Tupper's son.

10

LEAVE QUEBEC to Laurier and me,' Tarte had said, and that was the way it would be. There were Sifton and Martin for the west and there was Fielding in the Maritimes now, already towering over the party veterans. In Ontario there was always Cartwright and at last there was Mowat as well. The man who would not come out for Blake had come at last for Laurier and it was a good sign, one of many. Mowat would be badly needed; they would all be badly needed, preaching Laurier to the English, drawing their English picture of the man who was still half-known. They all applauded his stand on Catholic schools, they seemed confident, and he wished he could share that confidence. He wished he could share the confidence of Tarte, preaching and pleading, angling and whispering in Quebec. The old *Bleu* made much of the glories and benefits that would come to French Canadians through the first Prime Minister of their race. That, too, Laurier would have liked to believe.

He had carried his fears with him from the time he took the leadership. Just two months earlier he had offered, like Blake before him, to step down if Mowat would take his place. How could a French Canadian be strong in Ontario? Where did he stand now even on his home ground? 'How can I be strong in Quebec?' he had burst out in one of the late-night meetings before the campaign began. 'I am an old Rouge – I have been fighting priests and bishops all my life.' The old friend George Landerkin had been listening and had dined well. He had swayed over, brought a pudgy hand down in a great sweeping gesture on his chest, and delivered the answer. 'I am an old Rouge too, but I am not such a damned fool as to fight bishops.'

That was the fight now, in Quebec where Laurier counted. At the end of May, midway in the campaign, he had found himself home in Arthabaska. There was a blessing of bells for the new church; Laurier had sponsored one of them and it was expedient to be there. Father Suzor had returned for the occasion too. He had seemed older and gentler, a little less comic in age, almost a regretful friend. The impression had passed with the day, the tour had resumed, and Laurier came exhausted a night or two later into neighbouring Mégantic county. Archbishop Bégin, the successor to the liberal Taschereau, had been there just before him. He had made his pastoral progress through the county, 'mitre on head, cross in hand', denouncing the Liberal betrayer. At that news the courtly Ottawa leader on whom English Liberalism depended became for a sudden moment the country *Rouge*, bursting out in a flow of good, harsh *Canayen* profanity that amazed his hearers and took them back in spirit to twenty years before. And why not? Was anything changed?

The night of June 23 came and in Quebec a great illuminated board set up by *L'Electeur* provided the answer, or at least an answer. In the darkness of Dufferin Terrace, discreetly apart from the crowd, the Aberdeens watched too. They were in Quebec for a great round of ceremony that was to culminate on July 1. On June 24 all ceremony gave way to the march of the thousand carriages in Mr. Laurier's victory procession. Charles Hibbert Tupper was with Their Excellencies, urging them frantically against any hasty conclusions. His father was sending them telegrams peremptorily demanding their instant return to Ottawa. Their Excellencies could not return; the long-planned ceremonies of Dominion Day in Quebec held first priority.

By June 25 the last of the doubts was ended. A train was awaiting Laurier, telegrams were descending. He had Mowat to see, and Fielding. The other cabinet certainties were waiting and the uncertainties were fidgeting, all demanding his attention. He wanted to be in Arthabaska, he had to be in Toronto and in Montreal and Ottawa. He was a little peremptory himself in warning the Governor General against last-minute appointments. There were four vacant senatorships and many other plums. He would need them all.

It was July 2 when the Aberdeens returned to Government House. At three in the afternoon, recorded Her Excellency, Sir Charles Tupper appeared. 'The plucky old thing came down blooming in a white waistcoat and seemingly as pleased with himself as ever. He did not at all appear as the defeated Premier come to render an account . . . not he! . . . Down he sat and harangued H.E. . . . showed conclusively to himself that Laurier had no majority on any one point of policy . . . then he announced his intention of waiting till the 7th . . . then came some discussion as to whether he should recommend Senators and judges' – and the six-day battle began that was required to dislodge Tupper.

By the ninth it was over. The final figures were in and unmistakable. The long list of appointments that Tupper had submitted with urgent demands for approval had been turned down. The request to destroy the correspondence concerning them had also been refused. The grandfather who was never again to speak a civil word of the godmother had taken his final leave.

Laurier was on the train for Montreal when the word reached him. He arrived at the Russell Hotel that same night. This time, when an aide from Government House made his appearance, the newspaper men who watched him were correct in their speculations. He came with an invitation that was accepted for the following morning. When the call was completed Laurier left the study of the Governor General commissioned to form a government. On the morning of the eleventh he returned to be sworn in. The eighteen years in opposition were over. The age of John A. Macdonald had dwindled to its close. He was Prime Minister of Canada.

15

'IS IT NOT A CONSIDERABLE TRIUMPH?'

1896

LAURIER had said he could form a government in three days, and he was one day better than his word. The cabinet, with a single gaping vacancy, was sworn into office on the thirteenth of July. Even so, the date of July 16 for the opening of the new parliament obviously could not be met. It was Thursday August 20, with Ottawa sweltering in the last of its midsummer heat, when he walked into the Senate chamber at the head of the Commons of Canada to hear the Speech from the Throne.

It was to be a short speech for a short session, and all other rites, at his suggestion, had been duly maimed. There was to be no state dinner and no drawing-room: one or two garden parties would be enough to enable Their Excellencies to meet the new members. Lady Aberdeen, with Zoë's hearty concurrence, had even hoped for some modification of the dress for opening day, but convention and tradition had been too strong. The hall on its masculine side glowed with the usual array of uniforms and the usual scarlet and ermine. Laurier himself, not being as yet a Privy Councillor, enjoyed the comparative comfort of formal morning dress. It was not so with Zoë and not so with Her Ladyship. They had survived the glittering procession of carriages and the haze of heat and dust and now wilted among the flower-like ranks of the ladies sharing the private reflection that 'it is too ridiculous to be driving through this very colonial town dressed up in diamonds and evening dress in full daylight'.

Her Majesty's representative, speaking for Her Majesty's ministers, apologized for bringing the members together at an inconvenient season. He explained that it was done because of the necessity of making provision for the expenses of government. He promised careful consideration of the tariff during the recess at the close of the session and expressed every confidence that by the time the following session began the controversy over the Manitoba schools would have been satisfactorily adjusted. He then rose, the Commons returned to their domain, and the eighth parliament of Canada took up the work that the seventh had left undone.

The estimates crawled through with much incidental wrangling over the wave of firings and hirings that was Liberalizing the public service. It was certainly going on and it was just as certainly inevitable after eighteen hungry years. By comparison with earlier days it remained at a decent minimum and well below the notice of the Prime Minister. There was little else that demanded much of him in the work of this first session. The housekeeping and house-cleaning could be left to other hands. He had a breathing-space in which to assess his position and the instrument he had forged.

So far as numbers went the position was comfortable enough. He had a safe majority of twenty-three. The country had accepted him. Nothing in the electoral map, however, as it had shaken together after the final tabulation of results, gave any very clear reading of the country's mind. Quebec, in spite of the bishops, had gone Liberal by forty-nine to sixteen. Ontario, in spite of the Orangemen, had divided its support almost equally between Tupper and Laurier. So had the Maritime Provinces. The Northwest Territories and hostile British Columbia had trooped into the Liberal camp by a majority of six to three, yet Manitoba, the very heartland of the schools issue, had gone to the Conservatives by four to two. From winners and losers alike the letters flooded in, each with its own explanation of what had happened. The more he studied them all the less they told him. Constituency by constituency and candidate by candidate, an infinite variety of reasons drove him back on the old fact: people voted for men and not policies. Elections decided everything and answered nothing.

He had moved nevertheless with a sure and ruthless hand in his first act of government. For the making of his cabinet he was only beginning to pay the price in uproar behind the scenes, but he had the men he wanted. Tarte, with Langevin's old portfolio as Minister of Public Works, came as head of the Quebec delegation and the new power in the province. He was more than vastly capable; he was the spearhead of an election battle that had reduced Quebec Conservatism to a powerless Castor rump. Tarte had won over Chapleau. He had drawn the teeth of Dansereau. The renegade *Bleu* had beheaded his old party; every ancient alliance, from the time of the Forty Thieves, had been turned to Laurier's account. In effect he had brought about the coalition dreamed of in Mercier's days and it was black and bitter medicine to Pacaud and the tribe of *Rouges*. But the pyramid of power was broadened at the base and neither the old enemies nor the old friends had any hand to look to but the hand that controlled Tarte. They, and no doubt Tarte, would be one of the later problems.

It had cost the promise of a senatorship in addition to a cabinet portfolio to draw Mowat from the shelter of Queen's Park. He had both now, and was well worth the price. The old man, a half-dozen years before, had composed the quarrels of Ontario over its French and Catholic schools. In him Laurier had the Minister of Justice who could deal with Manitoba. He had Fielding in Finance, as the one man who could hope to find a course through the snarled-up maze of the tariff policy. He had the tough New Brunswick politician Andrew George Blair for the battles that lay ahead in the Railways ministry. Mowat, Fielding, and Blair had all been provincial premiers, new to the federal field. Laurier had elbowed aside a crowd of loyal veterans to make way for them, and was still hearing the complaints. He had Mulock as Postmaster-General and he was holding off Joseph Martin from the all-important Ministry of the Interior. That would be a ministry of the west, and it was reserved for Sifton when the question of the schools was settled. He had had to relegate

Cartwright, who wanted Finance, to the lesser portfolio of Trade and Commerce because the long shadow of Commercial Union could not be allowed to fall across a new fiscal policy. In filling the lesser cabinet posts he had balanced ability against the demands of geography, religion, race, and party expediency, more or less to his own satisfaction and much to the displeasure of many. J. D. Edgar sat elevated to only partial contentment in the chair of Mr. Speaker. Cartwright would still have to be soothed, Martin would have to be dealt with, and the others who howled in darkness would have to howl for a while.

It was curious to find how quickly one hardened to this work of granting and withholding, curious to feel what power really was. One had to look over the heads and the outstretched hands, the old friendships and the old loyalties, to the goal of the public interest. One was all too well aware that the feelings of the private man obscured the view. There might come a time, he suspected, when the interests of man and nation would seem to merge, to the danger of both. In the meanwhile he had done the best he could. There were at least a dozen among the angry and unrewarded whom he liked better and to whom owed more than the men who sat in cabinet.

It was a relief sometimes to run his eye along the back benches and speculate on the new-comers who had no claim as yet. One of them was Henri Bourassa, the member for Labelle in Quebec, twenty-eight years old and the grandson of Papineau. A man to watch for that reason alone, but also for many others. Handsome, slight, composed, a bearded D'Artagnan of words rather than swords, Bourassa was the aristocrat born and bred, a product of libraries and tutors, perfectly at home in English and in French. A little spoiled, perhaps; Laurier had known him from boyhood and had watched the spoiling. A man, perhaps, who liked books rather more than men and understood them better, but that was a commonplace of youth. There was a brilliant, incisive mind here which seemed to have the balance that the grandfather's had lacked. Bourassa liked the English and was rather like the best of them, yet he was the best flowering too of roots deep in Quebec. One thought of the long past and warmed to him as to few others; one thought of the long future and warmed again. No grandson of Papineau would enter this House without the thought of one day taking the highest seat. It would not be in Laurier's time but it could be by Laurier's help. Papineau's grandson Prime Minister of Canada: it would be a good closing to a long and bitter chapter. It would mean that much had been done by the man who paved the way, and there had been stranger twists before in this strange country.

He did not have time for many such random musings and he was too wryly knowledgeable to give them much rein. Young Bourassa was promising and he must grow as the other men grew, skirting the pitfalls or dropping out of sight. He had much to offer and he would come as everyone came sooner or later to ask for something in return. Something for something; from the lowest transaction in a country store to the cabinet council and the heights, the rule held. There was no changing it and Laurier himself had benefited by it. On June 24, one day after the election, the letter had come from Mulock, crisp and clear as always.

'What the country requires is clean government . . . I think steps should be taken *now* to raise a fund that would protect you from want the rest of your days and if you have no objections I will quietly inaugurate such a movement . . . we shall raise from $50,000 to $100,000.'

He had had no objections. There were no strings. It was an open and honourable arrangement and the same thing had been done for Macdonald by his friends. Mulock, quite certain of his cabinet post, had had no particular axe to grind and the wealthy contributors would ask for nothing specific. At worst it was partial assurance that the head of the government would not be easily bribable. At best it was a formal acknowledgment of success and power, and it was not the only one. There was to be a new house for the Prime Minister as the gift of a grateful party. Having delivered the goods, Mr. Laurier was now to be freed from the long, drab worries of the past ten years. He was reminded acridly of Doctor Johnson and Lord Chesterfield and that other offering which 'had it been early, had been kind'.

2

THREE DAYS before the opening of parliament and three thousand miles to the north-west of Ottawa, a prospector by the name of George Carmack had filed a mining claim on a stretch of water known as Rabbit Creek in the wild recesses of the Yukon territory. Within a matter of weeks the word of gold was spreading across the continent and the rush to the Yukon had begun. Nothing was known of the country, no one was there to administer it, yet it was a part of Canada and would soon be an inescapable problem.

On September 12 Shaughnessy of the C.P.R. wrote to Laurier renewing his proposal to Tupper for a railway to be built from Lethbridge or Fort Macleod through the Crowsnest Pass and the Kootenay Valley as far as Nelson, British Columbia. It was necessary, he said, if Canada was to keep the business of the new gold, copper, and coal mines that were opening in British Columbia. The Prime Minister should see that it was proceeded with immediately before the Americans got in.

Immediately. It seemed to be the word that leaped from every paper crossing his desk. New industries and new territories were suddenly clamorous for attention. New railways were in the making. East and west – Grand Trunk, Intercolonial, C.P.R., those new men Mackenzie and Mann on the prairies – they were all nursing expansive plans. And these, for the moment, were the least of the problems. The Yukon bordered on Alaska. Southern British Columbia bordered on Washington, Idaho, and Montana. It all gave new dimensions and new urgency to the ancient bickerings with the United States. Boundaries were still unsettled. American and Canadian fishermen were still wrangling over rights in Atlantic waters. American and Canadian sealers quarrelled in the Bering Sea. The tariffs stood and slept not. Everywhere and at once the enormous country seemed to be astir, and everywhere it stirred it rasped its mighty neighbour.

There would have to be adjustments with the United States. There would have to be a dike built against the climbing wave of imperialism that washed from the other side. Somehow and soon this North American nation, British and French, would have to find its place in the great triangular relationship that held the key to the future.

He had come to power at a lucky time for the country and a lucky time for himself. The nation of five millions, with its clusters of settlement beaded along the endless line of the railway, had seemed to sit on its haunches since the great days of Macdonald. Now conditions were changing. The farmers had developed earlier-maturing wheats to cope with frost, the bane of the prairies. They had scraped together the money for better implements and mastered new methods to get more wheat from their land. Wheat itself was in steadily growing demand as industrialization quickened the older world. The farmers of England and Europe were becoming factory workers ordering their food from abroad. They were paying more for it as the gold of California and Australia and South Africa, soon to be followed by the gold of the Yukon, pumped money into the trade streams and buoyed up prices. The American east was becoming a land of industrial consumers and the great wave of settlement that had washed in from the Atlantic for over a hundred years had now filled the farmlands of the American west. Above them lay Canada with its millions of empty acres. The hundreds of thousands of the land-hungry would still be coming from Europe and they would have to turn north now. The younger sons and the dispossessed of England would soon be on the way. Thousands of American farmers, seeing the price of their farms rise to fifty and a hundred dollars an acre, would sell off and make for the cheap land north of the border. Slowly and silently the channels that direct the streams of migrant men had cut their way to the Canadian prairie. There was good land for all who would come and a world-wide demand for their product. Give them good treatment, brace them and build on them, and the illimitable future dwarfed the imagination.

The Yukon, the east, the west, America, the world: the problems swarmed like flies and yet there were trumpets in that stir of wings. This was the nation; he was the head of it. The thought was sometimes overpowering, often vastly exhilarating, and every plan must wait. He had the six bishops of Quebec and the running sore of the schools to deal with first.

3

SIX ONLY, out of the twenty-nine Roman Catholic bishops in the country, had come out flatly against the Liberal party in the general election. There was much to be made of that and Laurier would make the most of it, but the heart of the problem remained. The twenty-three who had held their peace would accept a measure of justice, they would make a truce with change. The six flinty enemies, all men of Quebec, stood for the irrecoverable past.

There was no possibility that any could be fully satisfied. The day of the Church in Manitoba, as the guide of a French and Catholic state within the state, was ended forever. Whatever this might bring of danger to the faith and race must be accepted. Whatever it might mean to Quebec must be accepted. The nation and the peace of the nation were above all.

Laurier had not made the necessities that grew from the fact; they had made themselves. But he had asserted them with all his strength and he was utterly determined that they should be recognized. There was no alternative and in his present mood he desired none. He had never been so bitterly attacked and had never been so bitter himself against the blind, reckless, backward-looking absolutism that seemed to inform the ultramontane mind. It was cold comfort to know that it was not the whole mind even of the Church in Quebec. It was cold comfort to find the ecclesiastics of English Canada a little more patient and tolerant; their attitude merely emphasized the deepening rift between the races. Once more a section of the hierarchy, isolated though it was even in the body of the Church, was turning Quebec against the nation. The elections had settled nothing and would not be allowed to. Langevin went on, Laflèche went on, and the other four followed with all the pastors of their flocks. French as he was, Catholic as he still professed himself to be, Laurier was inclined to forget the real agonies behind that anger, the real loss that no statesmanship could quite repair, the real predicament of churchmen floundering in politics because they were utterly convinced of right and driven by duty. He had always been the politician and he was the government now. The possible and the attainable were his sphere of action, and the more the tumult rose the more that sphere contracted.

He would get what he could for the Catholics of Manitoba. He had said that, he had meant it, and he had always been sure that he could do as well or better than any other man. He believed that the long future would bear him out. It was bearing him out now, so far as the political side was concerned, but that was the lesser matter. No compromise would heal, no settlement would hold till the body of the ancient Church and the body of the new nation were brought to move in step.

Whatever the arrangement, it could only be the signal for a new outburst, but it had to be made quickly. Sifton was already in Ottawa with two or three others of the Manitoba cabinet. They were anxious to come to terms now, and for a variety of reasons. With a Liberal government in power there was nothing to be gained by further recalcitrance. They were in need of federal grants. Politically they rode a subsiding wave, as the results of the election had shown. Tupper, though he was vastly aggrieved at Quebec and vowed that he would never touch the issue again 'with a forty-foot pole', had made a great fight in Manitoba. Whether because of that or from simple weariness the extremes of anti-Frenchness and anti-Catholicism were tapering off. The Catholics, if left alone by their bishop, would probably be tiring too. For everyone the fifteen hundred children going without schools were a troubling, hurrying fact. The time was as ripe as it ever would be for those 'sunny ways' which were now a byword in every newspaper.

As the talks began with Sifton and the other western men, Laurier brought in Tarte. Mowat, however, was the principal federal negotiator. The Prime Minister sat by a little aloof and for once Tarte was an admiring listener as the canny Protestant Ontarian steered his course among the bristling shoals of legalism and prejudice. By the end of August the Manitobans had gone home with the frame of a settlement to lay before their cabinet. It was not much better and no worse than Laurier had hoped for. In outline the most that could be given and accepted had been clear for years and the talk of commissions of inquiry was simply laid aside. Tarte would go west for the final work when Manitoba was ready for him, and in the meantime there was much else to do.

Rome had quieted Quebec in 1877, and Laurier was turning to Rome again. In September he decided on the first move, and he made it tentative enough. The forces against him had to be measured before he risked everything and his first emissaries, if they did not do much good, would probably do no harm. The Abbé Proulx of St-Lin was a shrewd old friend from the parish nearest his heart. He combined much learning and considerable independence of mind with a way of collecting allies and information. The Chevalier Drolet, who had earned his title thirty years before as a Papal Zouave, was at least a notably good Catholic and anxious for a trip to Rome. The two went off together with instructions to learn, listen, and if possible convert, while the Prime Minister composed himself for waiting.

By the end of October Proulx and Drolet were back with word that most of ecclesiastical Canada had been there before them. The air of the Vatican was ominous. Canada was half-known and known mainly from the reports of bishops. It was considered to be a preponderantly Catholic country. The decision of the Privy Council, with its hedge of ifs and buts, had been totally misunderstood. The impression was abroad among the cardinals of the Curia that the Queen had granted justice to her Catholic subjects and that Laurier, anti-clerical, atheistic, and possibly a freemason, was withholding it. There appeared to be no disposition to send out a papal legate to investigate Laurier's side of the case, and it was clear from the Abbé Proulx and from other sources that the Chevalier Drolet had been no help at all. The involutions of high Church diplomacy had been too much for him, he had been lost amid the great corridors and the rustle of rich vestments. He had gone to the wrong people, antagonized those he had seen, and insisted on reading out to all and sundry a long list of the faults and indiscretions of the bishops of Canada. At home now, rebuffed and embittered, he was hinting darkly of bribery and sinister influences. The first mission had been a failure.

By this time Tarte was in the west and Henri Bourassa was with him. It was curious and it seemed of good augury that these two were congenial. No one without courage and no one who was not wholly sure of himself could either bear Tarte or be borne by him. Many with both qualities still found Tarte impossible, but it had not been so with Bourassa. He was devoutly Catholic and he had not been easy in his mind on the question of the schools, yet he had been willing to learn from the tough little politician who had routed the bishops. According to Tarte the young man had not had much choice: he had been kept locked up in Tarte's house for a week until he was convinced that Laurier was right. Laurier was already sceptical about the ability of any man to hold Bourassa against his will, but he was delighted at the result of the sojourn. In a long and careful memorial Bourassa had stated the position of Catholic Liberals on the schools question and the position of Catholics generally in the public life of the country. Laurier had promptly transmitted the memorial to Rome, signed by himself and his supporters. Whatever its influence there, it had convinced him that Bourassa was the man to help Tarte in presenting the case to the west. He had suggested to both men that they go on to the Pacific when the work was over and see the rest of the country.

On November 8 and again on November 9 came letters from Tarte. The settlement was made. Tarte had discussed not the terms, which were still secret, but the general position with leading Catholics and with the Archbishop himself. He was optimistic. Everyone was agreed that the closed school-houses had to be reopened. It seemed that the worst settlement, which this was not, must be preferable to more years of hopeless agitation. Everything depended now on conciliation and good faith. 'If the proposed amendments are put into effect in a spirit of friendship and good will,' said Tarte, 'all will go well. If, on the contrary, they are enforced in a niggardly spirit, nothing good will come of them.'

The right of the Church to organize school districts, to segregate Catholics within a framework of separate education, was as flatly denied as ever by the terms of the agreement. The right to Catholic teaching and to teaching in the French language was precariously established. In each town school of forty pupils and in each village school of twenty-five pupils there could be one duly-qualified Catholic teacher. Religious instruction could be given by a priest during the last half-hour of each school day, and from this period children of other faiths would be excused. There could be no further separation of children by religious denominations. Nor could there be special privileges of language for the second of the partner races that had made Confederation. The language clause put the French on the same basis as the Germans who were already sprinkled through Manitoba. They would be on the same basis as the coming hordes of the future that Sifton foresaw. 'Where ten of the pupils in any school speak the French language (or any language other than English) as their native language,' the clause provided, 'the teaching of such pupils shall be conducted in French (or such other language) and English upon the bilingual system.'

These were the regulations that the provincial cabinet was ready to put into effect and beyond them, unwritten, was the understanding that Catholics should be given reasonable representation on school boards and advisory councils and exercise some influence on the selection of textbooks. It was little enough and vague enough, but it was all that could be had. Much indeed would depend on the good faith and conciliation that Tarte hoped for. On November 19 Laurier released the agreement and prepared himself for the storm.

It broke over him, as expected, from both sides, and amid the uproar there were reassuring voices. Tarte had been right about many of the Catholics in the west; they were at least willing to give the agreement a trial. Much of Catholic Ontario was inclined to accept the concessions and much of Protestantism was inclined to grant them. D'Alton McCarthy, whatever it might prove, was one of the first to declare that Laurier had worked out a reasonable and satisfactory compromise. The Grand Orange Lodge of Manitoba, however, was prompt to denounce the betrayal of national schools and the insidious restoration of priestly influence. It was answered with equal promptness. On both sides the torch-bearers reached for the brand and carried the cry east, while the voice of Archbishop Langevin came with them. 'I tell you there will be a revolt in Quebec which will ring throughout Canada, and these men who are today triumphant will be cast down. The settlement is a farce. The fight has only begun.'

In the last sentence, at least, he spoke the truth. For Quebec, in the dioceses of the bishops who fully supported Langevin, it was 1877 again, with all the terrors of pulpit and confessional, with all the damnings by bell, book, and candle, and with all the savage retorts by the reddest of the *Rouges*. By the end of December, according to Tarte, no Catholic in the diocese of Chicoutimi was allowed to receive the sacraments if he subscribed to the newspaper edited by Tarte's sons. Laurent-Olivier David was under the ban for a mild and reasoned pamphlet he had written criticizing the attitude of the Church. On Saturday December 26, Pacaud's *L'Electeur*, silenced by official decree, published its last edition. On the following Monday it appeared as *Le Soleil* and Pacaud was chortling over the fact that he had gained four thousand new subscribers. There was no time to heed him and no comfort to be taken from the fact that the war went on. Either the war would come to an end or the days of the Catholic were numbered as a co-equal citizen.

By December 23 Laurier had decided on another mission to Rome. His man was Charles Fitzpatrick, a useful Quebec politician whom he had made Solicitor-General. Fitzpatrick was a lawyer and an Irish Catholic who had been one of the defenders of Riel. His piety was as flagrant as Drolet's, his ability was greater, and he would not be going alone. In advising the Governor General of the mission Laurier had suggested that the support of the British ambassador in Rome would be welcome and Aberdeen had come back with a better suggestion. Charles Russell, son of the English Chief Justice Lord Russell and a long-time familiar of Rome, could be persuaded to go along. With the two, and perhaps as persuasive as either, would go another of many gifts from an old friend. Blake, in London, had prepared the last brief for the Manitoba minority and had argued it before the Privy Council. He approved the terms of the settlement, he was now preparing a memorial in support of it for the Vatican, and if any man's words could move those subtle Italian minds they would be the words of Blake.

The session had closed on October 5, and free of the distractions of parliament Laurier had given his time to the defence of the settlement. Anxious and interminable, the correspondence with churchmen who would listen and with laymen who could influence them went on. Pacaud, with his infinite ability to inflame, had to be scolded and watched and taught. He was fumbling the matter of McCarthy and the accusations of *Bleu* newspapers that Laurier had made a disgraceful capitulation to bigotry. The truth of it, wrote Laurier, was quite the other way. 'Instead of explaining and defending McCarthy, show the great triumph it has been for the Liberal party to have been able to convert this bitter opponent of former days . . . No longer than six years ago, on the floor of the House of Commons, McCarthy was waging a relentless war against the French language and predicting its ultimate disappearance from British America. Today the same man approves legislation which embodies, as one of its principal clauses, the teaching of this language in the schools . . . is it not a considerable triumph to have brought about this state of things?'

In the tortuous manoeuvrings of the past six years he had won over first Mowat and then McCarthy. It opened up vistas he was not yet prepared to discuss with Pacaud, but already it meant much. He felt, Laurier wrote, that he had duplicated Cartier's feat in the conversion of George Brown and that was how the settlement in Manitoba should be regarded. 'I flatter myself that there is not a man in this country who could have obtained what I did from that Province . . . I do not wish to blow my own trumpet,' but he wished the trumpet blown and he gave instructions accordingly.

In his correspondence with churchmen he dwelt endlessly on the 'two principles perpetually in antagonism in our system of government – the principle of centralization and the principle of provincial autonomy'. He was eloquent and defiant when he came before Le Club National in Montreal on December 30, with the storm at its peak. 'I have taken the work of Confederation where I found it when I entered political life, and determined to give it my life. Nothing will deter me . . . it may be that the result of my efforts will be the Tarpeian Rock, but if that be the case I will fall without murmur or recrimination or complaint, certain that from my tomb will rise the immortal idea for which I have fought.'

With it all, he was changing curiously in his own depths. 'What blindness!' he wrote to David on November 28, as the first furies of the clergy were released against the settlement. 'What fatal aberration! It is a strange thing that these violences, this ignorance of things of our time, this war to which we are exposed, far from separating me from the church has drawn me nearer. I feel that it has made a singular travail in me. Faith is strengthened rather than diminished. I have not the time to analyse this interior travail, but I state it and above all I feel it. I feel above all how much religion is superior to all that is done in the name of religion.'

He was a weightier and more troubled man now than the brisk decrier of priests who had twitted Emilie Lavergne. Yet he was still sure of his course. He wrote to no one else as he wrote to David but he had crisp words for Angers, the old, proud ultramontane enemy who was troubled and wounded too. 'You wish to maintain the dignity of the French race and the supremacy of the Catholic religion in the sphere where it exists. So be it. I am in accord with you . . . Does it not seem to you that the French race will be able to maintain its autonomy only by keeping up with the races with whom we have to struggle? . . . We live in an atmosphere and in a place where practical education is absolutely indispensable. Have we not come to a point where you yourself deplore the fact that you do not speak English as you speak French? . . . For me the safety of the French race is not in isolation but in the struggle. Give our children the best education possible, put them on a footing of equality with those of the other race, and give them the legitimate pride which they will have in such a struggle. There is safety – there is autonomy.'

16

'LET THE BUGLE SOUND, LET THE FIRES BE LIT ON THE HILLS'

1897

As the new year began the government was complete. On November 17, two days before the formal announcement of agreement on the schools, Sifton had entered the cabinet as Minister of the Interior. Joseph Martin, finally rebuffed, had gone back to Manitoba only to pull up stakes and move on to British Columbia. He was looking for new fields, he was not in a good mood, and he would probably be heard from in the future.

Sifton, for his part, had not been pleased with what he found awaiting him. His department, concerned above all with western settlement, was 'a department of delay, a department of circumlocution, a department in which people could not get business done, a department which tired men to death who undertook to get any business transacted with it'. Mountains of red tape, accumulated over a dozen years, had to be unsnarled before real work could begin and in addition to that the multiplying problems of the Yukon lay piled high on his desk. He had plunged into the mass, however, with a grim and silent efficiency that was more impressive than words. For over a year he would scarcely be heard in parliament yet every man in government would feel his presence. Perhaps it was his very affliction – that growing deafness in a man of thirty-six – that shut him into himself and gave such an impression of concentrated, relentless purpose.

The first thing Sifton meant to do was unlock the Northwest. The C.P.R. and the smaller railway builders had now earned in land grants something like twenty-four million acres. They had taken title to less than two million because as soon as they took the title they were liable to taxes. The whole amount, huge as it was, represented only a fraction of the land available, but the companies' field of choice had been so wide that they had staked off every tract remotely fit to settle. In effect the whole of the prairies, from the American boundary to nearly a hundred miles north of Edmonton and from the borders of Manitoba to the Rocky Mountains, was a closed railway preserve. Sifton proposed to open it. The railways would select the land they had earned, take title, and pay taxes on it. Everywhere else their hold would be released and there would be no more grants of land. Henceforth the Dominion of Canada would be landlord of the Northwest. Some blocks of land in the more settled regions would be marked out for sale at a price set by Sifton. Apart from those areas the only cost of a farm for a man who came to work would be his sweat, his time, and his courage.

The free homestead of a hundred and sixty acres was the backbone of the plan. It was not a new thing, but Sifton's methods were. He knew what it meant to a man with little or nothing to come to a bare patch of prairie and turn the sod and sometimes live in a cave made out of the sod until his three years of back-breaking work were finished and he owned the land. He knew the tangle of regulations and conditions, all rigid and out of date, that baffled both the men who had to obey them and the men who administered them. He was determined to sweep them all away. He would set the policy in Ottawa, and the policy was to fill a vacant empire in the shortest possible time. His satraps on the ground would be given the widest possible discretion. There would be every possible latitude for the man in the sod hut. Everything would be directed to the end of putting John Doe on his hundred and sixty acres, keeping him there, making his life tolerable, and multiplying the process by the hundreds of thousands.

Sifton was going to advertise in thousands of American newspapers. He intended to advertise in England and to comb the continent. He was going to establish missions and bureaus abroad, he was going to send publicists after them and bring publicists from Europe and England and the United States to see the prairies for themselves. The steamship lines and the railways, with special rates for settlers and their effects, would be drawn into the plan. He was going to use fairs and exhibitions and public displays around the world. Wherever a restless man looked up Sifton intended him to see the great sheaf of wheat and the beckoning gateway to the golden west. His energy was a little frightening and the possibilities of trouble were limitless. This ruthless, close-mouthed man was asking for all but absolute control over four hundred million acres of land. He was asking for the power and the money to exploit them and he was going to take what he could get in the way of humankind. One looked at those unyielding agate eyes, burning resentfully as deafness closed around him, and wondered for the future. But Sifton got what he wanted.

Fielding's days and nights were given to the deputations and the briefs and the cloud of hopeful hungers that circled the question of the tariff. It was the central problem of the moment and it reached into every phase of the country's life. Cartwright was back from England after discussions with Joseph Chamberlain, who was now Colonial Secretary. From the long-time evangelist of imperialism the one-time proponent of Commercial Union brought a new and weighty idea. Why should not that suggestion of a North American *zollverein*, utterly unacceptable, be transformed into a *zollverein* of the Empire? Why not indeed? It was the logical expansion of the idea of preferential trade between the colonies. It led on, by the simplest and most natural transition, to proposals of common defence and an imperial federation. Cartwright was studying all the proposals now. They were Fielding's problem too. They would become Laurier's problem when the colonial premiers assembled in June for the Queen's Diamond Jubilee and the conference that was to follow.

Blair was busy on plans to extend the Intercolonial from Lévis to its natural terminus at Montreal and on other plans to deepen the navigation channels of the St. Lawrence. He was also busy with Sifton on the proposal for a railway through the Crowsnest

Pass, and out of their interlocking concerns was growing the framework of an agreement big with promise for the west. The C.P.R., in return for a building subsidy and for the increased traffic it would draw from the line, was to reduce freight-rates on eastbound grain and flour and on westbound settlers' effects. It was easy to see that the Crowsnest Pass agreement would be a hinge and pivot-point on which all future relations with the prairie railways would turn. An immediate saving of several millions to the farmers already on the land would be multiplied by tens of millions in the years ahead.

Some of Blair's work impinged on Tarte's field, and Tarte was busy at everything. His public works and his politics always went hand in hand; but there was drive and vision too, and he was beginning to command the uneasy respect of men who had long detested him. He saw as clearly as anyone the need for ports and elevators and terminals and all the enormous apparatus of grain-handling facilities that a growing west would bring, and he was determined to meet it. He was not so clear as to the boundaries of his domain. He was preparing, he wrote to Laurier from Montreal, 'to assure the solid friendship of the Grand Trunk and the Pacific at the same time. With these two great railway companies behind us we could stand up to the fury of the clergy.' It betokened energy and was thick with strategy, but it was hardly a letter that the Prime Minister could show either to his clerical correspondents or to his Minister of Railways.

Mulock, probably the best administrator in the cabinet, was revolutionizing the moribund ways of the post-office, planning for penny postage, and pressing for a fast steamship service to England. Sydney Fisher, the perennial bachelor and gentleman farmer from Knowlton, Quebec, was promoting a similar revolution in his department of Agriculture and he was working with Louis Henry Davies of Fisheries on plans for storage plants and shipping facilities that would get Canadian cheese, butter, and fish out to the markets of the world. Everything came to Laurier for discussion and decision, everything had to be fitted into the loom of the greater problems, and somehow amid the real work the side issues seemed to blow up by themselves. The Prime Minister, in an unwary moment, had been lured into promising a national referendum on prohibition. Now even that bleak and innocent subject seemed to be shaping up as a quarrel between Ontario which wanted it and Quebec which would not have it, between the Methodist view of life and the Catholic view of life.

The demand for posts and patronage was a steady roar in his ears, and too many of the claimants were deserving. His handful of senatorships and judgeships had long since dwindled away and the line of the disappointed seemed endless. He was well aware that to many an old friend he was 'a tool in the hands of intriguers', surrounded by clannish French, a man who had betrayed his colleagues in opposition 'with an indifference no Turkish sultan could have surpassed' and one who now employed 'the cut-throats of the Liberal party, ambitious, vain, corrupt, and too ignorant to know how incompetent they are'. It was as bad or worse with the small fry on each of whom in two or three years the fate of some crucial constituency might hang. It seemed that every day and word and action of the long past came back to haunt him. 'We'll never forget you,' he had told some flushed party organizer at a forgotten by-election. He had clapped a hand on a young man's shoulder somewhere and given him that lustrous smile. 'You're the type of fellow we need,' or 'Come and see us when we're in power.' They were all here now, either in person or by correspondence, with every tone and shading of those bygone utterances still fresh in their minds. 'I have decided', he wrote wearily to one of the rejected, 'never to make another promise.'

In every cabinet meeting he had to deal with the clashing opinions and ambitions of driving, hard-headed men, intent on their own projects and jealous of their own precincts. He could already see the promise of trouble between Tarte and Blair. Sifton went his way, but woe to the man who got into it. As a question grew and ramified, reaching out into department after department, Laurier was sometimes so strained and wracked by the mere work of peacemaking that the issue itself was obscured for him. Yet he was satisfied that he had brought together a powerful team. They were politicians as they had to be, yet they were not afraid of their constituents. Sifton, the western free-trader, was flatly opposed to duty-free implements for his western farmers. The Canadian manufacturer, he saw, could not stand the competition, and if he went out of business the man on the prairie would be left at the mercy of American industry. Tarte, the parochial politician of Quebec, was vastly intrigued by Chamberlain's idea of imperial free trade and was studying it with Fielding. They were tough men all and they would never be easy to handle, but they saw beyond their noses and they were working together.

As the time for the session neared the news from Rome improved. Fitzpatrick's reports were awed but optimistic. He was endeavouring to outdo the cardinals in piety and he thought he was winning friends. The opinion that Blake had submitted had impressed all who read it. Even more encouraging were the light-hearted letters of Charles Russell to his father, some of which filtered back through high and private channels and ended on Laurier's desk. On his arrival at the Vatican, much more knowledgeable than the earlier men, Russell had taken Fitzpatrick directly to the apartments of the Cardinal Merry del Val, the Pope's companion and attendant. Just thirty-two years old, and the son of the Spanish ambassador in Rome, Merry del Val appeared to be a very unusual cardinal. By the morning following the visit he had read and digested all the papers left with him and arranged for the Canadian emissaries to have a private audience with the Pope. So warmly did he appear to support their case that he would almost like, he had said, to come himself to Canada as the papal legate.

This, at first glance, was hardly to Laurier's taste. He remembered Bishop Conroy of earlier days and hoped for a man of British birth and aura. In later reports it became a little less hopeful that there would be any legate at all. Leo XIII was very old and in failing health. The audience had been difficult. He had been warmly welcoming, had insisted that Fitzpatrick and Russell sit down one on either side of him, and had listened attentively and sympathetically. It was difficult to know, however, whether the frail old man with the faltering voice and the cares of a world-wide church competing for his attention had been won from the views that had been pressed on him for so long. Laurier, with a long experience of hopeful beginnings and dismal endings in such negotiations, began to be pessimistic.

A week before the session opened one of his doubts vanished. An official letter from the Vatican informed him that an apostolic delegate would be leaving for Canada shortly and that the man would be the Cardinal Merry del Val. Much of the country would bristle at the name, nothing in any case would be solved merely by his coming, but it was at least a first step. The other problems were crowding in as the time for action approached. Speculations on the new tariff and reminders of old promises filled the newspapers. The nearing of the Diamond Jubilee and the Colonial Conference had sharpened the urgency of all imperial questions. For Laurier an irksome personal question was the matter of the title that would certainly be offered him, and Edgar was beforehand with a letter of righteous injunction. He could not believe that Laurier would accept. It was not worthy of him. Brown had refused, Mackenzie and Blake had refused. Laurier should allow himself to be made a member of the Privy Council and a Right Honourable, but nothing more. All of it was sound advice from the standpoint of Grit Ontario. It was equally so when one thought of *Rouge* Quebec. It went with Laurier's own weary distaste for many of the knighted gentlemen who moved around him. He was on record as scorning titles, as being 'a democrat to the hilt', and he felt no inclination to change his view. Yet the problems of refusal began to mount. A Jubilee was a time of showering honours. Most men went expecting and demanding them. If Canada refused, what of the other premiers?

It was one more thing to lie awake with, but he slept reasonably well. The Speech from the Throne was ready. He had his answers for the speculating newspapers and probably for Chamberlain too. The mercurial Edgar could be easily spun round and probably would be by the time the session ended. There were time-honoured and time-tested methods for accomplishing that. A papal legate was coming, and hopes went with the doubts. He was quite sure, Laurier wrote Abbé Proulx on March 22, 'that the number of mortal sins in this country will be reduced by one at least after his departure'. He was not as sure as he sounded but the question was out of his hands. With a move in train to settle religious war he could turn to the country's business.

2

PARLIAMENT convened again on March 25 and there were hard words, as expected, for the Manitoba schools settlement. The railway programs also took their battering. Bowell, immured in the Senate now and still nursing his grievances, was nevertheless leader of a venerable Conservative majority that intended to throw a roadblock into the path of the Intercolonial. In the House itself, however, Tupper had little to fight with and was hardly the man he had been. He did not like the wrong side of the aisle, he was inclined to ramble interminably among the great days of the past, and he still seethed with resentment over Aberdeen's handling of him after the general election. Nothing stood for long against the momentum generated by the new government and the peak of the session arrived on April 22 when Fielding brought down his first budget.

It was apparent by the end of his speech that the country had a great finance minister. The mood he evoked was that of nineteen years before, when Tilley had introduced the National Policy. For the first time since that historic evening there was a feel of buoyant, throbbing energy, of new life in every department of the country's business. Yet the central exhibit, the tariff, might have seemed, with one crucial exception, the drab, old-maidish sister of Tilley's flamboyant beauty. Fielding, Cartwright, Tarte, Sifton, and Laurier had all had a hand in its making, but over it all the hand of Blake still hovered. It had to recognize, as Blake had recognized, the inescapable necessities. It was a 'tariff for revenue' now, not a 'tariff for protection', but all Fielding's skill could hardly support the argument that the change in philosophy had changed much else. The customs duties, which were now only for revenue, somehow managed to protect most of the manufacturers who had enjoyed protection before. 'We will give you free trade,' Laurier had promised the cheering farmers of Winnipeg and free trade was now given them, but it was confined to a half-dozen painfully modest items such as fence wire, cream separators, and binder twine. The government clung to its principles but the stubborn facts remained; the industrial east contained three-fifths of the population of the country and the east had to live. For years, commented Foster, the Liberals had been cursing the principle of protection. Now 'they have lifted up their voice, and behold! they have blessed it'.

It was not from the raking of old ashes, however, that Fielding had struck his fire. It was from a new departure, growing out of Chamberlain's suggestion and beautifully introduced. There would be, said Fielding, maximum and minimum tariffs: 'One tariff for countries which are willing to trade with us and a different tariff for the countries which are not.' Canada was now prepared to grant a reduction of one-eighth, to be increased in a year to one-fourth, of the duties on imports from any country that admitted the products of Canada on terms equally favourable. It could apply to no country of any importance except Great Britain, which admitted the goods of all the world free of duty.

In the opinion of Tupper, as he pored over the delicate phrasing, it could not even apply to Great Britain. She had trade treaties with Germany and Belgium, for instance, both of which countries had high tariffs. The treaties bound her colonies equally with herself and they provided that Germany and Belgium should receive the benefit of any reduction made by any of the colonies. If these two foreign countries would not reduce their tariffs, and they certainly would not, how could they accept the Canadian offer? And if they could not, what would be the position of Great Britain? She must either refuse the offer of Canada or denounce her treaties with Germany and Belgium. The imperial mother was being invited to change her trading policy at the disguised dictation of a colony. Quite so, replied Cartwright, but 'we were not born yesterday'.

It was high-handed generosity and it had moved very far from the idea of a closed Empire trading within itself. The colony that had been asked to join in the rearing of new walls was breaching the old instead. Yet the manner if not the matter was that of a dutiful daughter asking for nothing in return. For the moment at least, as Laurier was careful to point out, 'we saw only one nation in a position to take advantage of that tariff, and it was

Great Britain'. The mother would find it hard to refuse her chick, and there were no first indications of any intention to do so. Instead, as the idea of an imperial preference caught fire in Canada, there was a lighting-up of sympathy in newspapers across the Atlantic. 'For the first time in my experience,' wrote the London correspondent of the New York *Times*, 'England and the English are regarding Canadians and the Dominion with affectionate enthusiasm. . . . The spirit of preference for the Mother Country appeals to the imagination here. This change will make Mr. Laurier when he comes here in June far and away the most conspicuous and popular of all the visiting premiers of the Empire.'

The views of a newspaper correspondent were not necessarily the views of Chamberlain. There had been no British reply when Laurier left parliament in the closing days of the session and sailed with Zoë on June 5. He was nevertheless not going empty-handed, and he left with a lighter heart for other reasons. Exactly a month before, the Cardinal Merry del Val had arrived in Ottawa. He had been prevailed on with difficulty to accept a private car from New York for the last lap of his journey. He had been formal, cool, and remote, utterly reserved on the matter of the schools and emphatic in his insistence that he had come to inquire and report, not to make pronouncements. Within a day of his arrival, however, he had been moving heaven and earth to get in touch with Greenway, who happened to be travelling somewhere in Ontario. He had had Fitzpatrick continually on the run, locating knowledgeable laymen who could state both sides of the case. He had been to Manitoba and he had been to Quebec, he had been to Toronto and he was now back in Ottawa with hardly a bishop or a cabinet minister or a leader across the country who had not been drained of his opinions. Several times the lithe young form in the rich vestments had settled down across from the Prime Minister in a study chair. Laurier had told everything and learned little, but he had learned enough to content him. A sense of opening vistas had come with this 'most truly prince-like man I have met'. The verdict on Laurier's work, and he believed it a good work, lay now in hands he trusted.

3

JUNE 22, the first high day of lovely English summer, had been chosen for the Diamond Jubilee of Queen Victoria. As the *Lucania* ploughed eastward and the horrors of seasickness gave over and the problems of Ottawa grew more remote, it was impossible to avoid excitement. Zoë shared it, the nation behind him shared it, it was running around the world. In London a multitude of officials had been busy with plans for a year. Their letters and their sub-officials had been going back and forth over every sea and into every corner of the Empire. Now, from the remotest fringes of the great red splotch on the map, thousands of troops, hundreds of contingents, deputations, and dignitaries were streaming toward the centre.

London was preparing itself for a million and a half visitors. Speculation in tickets for seats along the route of the Jubilee procession had become an international business. To feed the expected multitudes London hotels, a year before, had blanketed hundreds of acres of land with options on garden crops that were only now ripening. Beef from the Argentine and mutton from New Zealand had been ordered in such quantities, it was said, that the rates for ocean freight had climbed by thirty per cent.

Official invitations for the more important ceremonies had reached Laurier early in February. His worries had begun some time before. The Jubilee was to be a great affair, and Chamberlain was at the heart of it. The heart of all would be the conference of colonial premiers. For the third time in ten years, and this time in a hugely impressive setting, the hopes and claims and duties of the Empire were to be examined and the future shaped.

Laurier did not think that that future would emerge in a pattern acceptable to Chamberlain. He did not, in fact, believe that there would be much shaping. Little as he yet knew of the other colonies, there was always Quebec to remind him that this bustling Anglo-Saxon who considered himself a businessman was really an imperial romantic. Chamberlain had not changed one of the ideas put forth in Toronto in 1887. He was developing and expanding them and he had taken the post of Colonial Secretary to do it. The imperial *zollverein,* which he was not likely to get, was in his mind only the first step toward an armed Empire, one in peace and war.

There was an ugly side to this empire-building now in the business of South Africa and the Boers. The flag seemed to be going ahead of trade there in good earnest, and it was hard to see that raid of Jameson into the Transvaal as the heroic failure it was touted up to be. It had made the Dutch more stubborn and more Dutch, and it would create a new wariness at the conference table. There would be men there like Laurier who were not interested in making the Boers British, even for the gold and diamonds of the Transvaal, even for the prospect of the Cape-to-Cairo railway. They would be repelled rather than attracted by the dream of total Englishness, alarmed rather than inspired by the thought of iron-bound unity and complete submergence in a fate ultimately to be determined by the lords of the little isle.

Yet Laurier had learned enough from Blake and had been sufficiently battered in the days of Commercial Union to leave his dogmatism aside. The future shaped itself while men lived from day to day, dealing with things as they were. Certainly in this huge agglomeration of disparate peoples there were limitless possibilities. The French Canadian, Prime Minister of Canada, was proof enough of one of them. He was going to Chamberlain with the free and embarrassing gift of a new trade policy, which might open a door on other gifts, even if they were not such as Chamberlain had in mind. For the rest he was going to England for the first time, he was going as head of the first colony, and he meant to make the most of it.

The ship had hardly docked when the mail-bags came aboard with the first of the invitations. The presence of M. and Mme Laurier was desired at Liverpool where the Duke of Devonshire was giving a luncheon in the cause of Imperial Federation. M. and Mme Laurier, as they settled down in the most palatial of the palatial suites provided for colonial premiers in the Cecil Hotel, seemed to be desired in every city, banquet hall, and stately home of the British Isles. On June 12 came a note from Chamberlain informing Laurier that he was to be made a Privy Councillor, effective on the day of the Jubilee. The matter of the title came up in one of the talks with the Colonial Secretary that punctuated a whirl of sightseeing, speech-making, and festivity during the next ten days. Laurier had long since abandoned himself to his fate and arranged for others to share it, including the once-reluctant Edgar. Mr. Speaker, who had deplored the prospect of Laurier's knighthood, was now accepting his own, 'yielding to the urgings' of his friends and 'solely as an honour to the House of Commons'. In the case of the Prime Minister of Canada everything had been long arranged and Chamberlain was aghast at the hint of a refusal that would offend Her Majesty and throw the whole schedule of Jubilee honours awry. June 21 was the last evening of life as simple Mr. Laurier and on that evening, with Zoë beside him, he entered the audience chamber of the Queen Empress for the reception that followed the state dinner at Buckingham Palace.

He came at the head of the colonial premiers and by that time he was almost at home among the fifty princes, the half-dozen kinglets, the archdukes and grand dukes, the innumerable host of peers, and the generals, marshals, and admirals who surrounded the state chair. He was accustomed to approving eyes. The great homes had opened to him, imperial statesmen had hung on his words, vast audiences had cheered him to the echo, and the most eloquent of his loyal phrases had shone forth in the newspapers like gems. Britannia's arms had enveloped him and the Jubilee was about to overwhelm him.

It had been a deceptively gradual process, starting with disappointment. The old city, when Laurier first arrived, had not looked as he expected it to look because it hardly knew itself. It was alive with strange figures in outlandish tribal dress and with smart troops in familiar khaki whose black, brown, and yellow faces spoke of a thousand far-flung training camps around the world. Its dark walls and doorways stood scrubbed to scaly whiteness, its ancient statues were emerging stark and almost indecent from the hands of workmen clawing away centuries of grime. Great lines of stalled traffic surged in the streets with shouting carters, indignant coachmen, and cursing gentlemen on horseback inching their way around uprooted safety islands and lamp-posts felled for hauling off. London pedestrians skittered through the confusion damning it all, and above it all, blotting out much of the city's face, rose the great, gawky scaffoldings on which the Jubilee watchers would sit. They lined both sides of streets along the route of the procession. They reached out over balconies and climbed from rooftops. The greatest business houses and the staidest clubs sprouted their timber frameworks. Churches had rented out the cemetery space beside their walls, and over the tombstones long stepped rows of planks climbed high as the steeples, each row to be parcelled out in eighteen-inch sections and each section to be sold for a pound. The rattle of hammers and the scrape of saws was everywhere and the smell of fresh-cut pine drowned out the sooty reek of the city. John Bull was preparing to turn an honest imperial quid but his ancient home at the moment was less reminiscent of history than of a mining camp in the west.

The raw spadework of ceremony had been about completed, however, by the time the Lauriers arrived. In a day or two the saws and hammers were disappearing and the last holes in the pavement had been neatly patched. Cables began to swing out over the streets, hung between ranks of tall pylons marching down either side. Flags blossomed from rooftops. *VR* symbols appeared in doorways and windows, first of cardboard or coloured glass, then multiplying and competing with each other in size and elaboration until the larger buildings were banks of scarlet and purple and gold with giant emblems picked out in metal and brilliants. A wave of red cloth rippled gradually over the unsightly bareness of the wooden stalls. The stalls looked down on roadways cleared of their impediments and now becoming splendid vaults as evergreens and palms and bunting covered the overhead wires. The flood of traffic had increased, if anything, for new sightseers swarmed hourly to see the preparations. Thousands of vehicles still choked the streets and spewed off into the lanes and alleys. The weirdly garbed dignitaries of the far-off possessions and the black and brown and white and tawny soldiers still stood and gaped, but order and magnificence were coming.

It was all there as the morning of June 22 broke dull and cloudy. The last workmen hoisted the last flags, polished the last pylons, and hung the last flowers of this Empire to which every flower, tree, and shrub on earth was somewhere indigenous. Still uncertain of its weather, the city glowed and glimmered like a theatre and garden. Quite clear, quite empty, already lined with thousands who had taken their places through the night, and cordoned off by good-natured police, the route lay carved like an eccentric figure eight on the face of London. By seven o'clock, as Laurier's carriage rolled along its prescribed way to the Victoria Embankment, every side-street rippled with humanity and bubbled with casual cheers for the glittering detachments of troops and the notables like himself who were moving to their places of assembly. Zoë sat beside him, shivering a little with excitement and the damp and glad of the cloak with which it was still permissible to cover the regal pearl-grey silk of her gown. It was not yet necessary to assume a full processional stateliness, but she was stately enough and diamonds sparkled in her greying hair. He himself wore the cocked hat, gold lace, and white silk stockings of an Imperial Privy Councillor and the seven-pointed star of a Knight Grand Cross of the Order of Saint Michael and Saint George gleamed on his chest.

The whole area of the Victoria Embankment was alive as the assembling contingents of the Colonial Procession flowed in. The Colonial Procession was to form the first section of the whole. The units of the Royal Procession were now deploying around Buckingham Palace and the centre of the city throbbed to the stamp of fifty thousand soldiers, sailors, marines, and cadets who were to align themselves shoulder to shoulder with the police along both sides of the six-mile route. Along the Embankment here, down the length of half a dozen converging streets, flowed bristling streams of colour, clanking with sabres, thudding with hooves and boots, spiked with bayonets, cavalry carbines, flags, and pennoned lances. Over the shifting blur of uniforms, the stamp of horses, and the bark of orders in a dozen tongues a single question hovered. Would the old lady's luck hold? By eight o'clock it was answered. The sun came through the clouds, the last murky fringes drifted away toward the horizon, and the royal weather that Victoria had enjoyed for every important ceremony of her life broke in a great smile over London.

Five minutes later a bugle sounded. Field Marshal Lord Roberts of Kabul and Kandahar, the beloved little 'Bobs' of all the Empire, cantered out ahead of his escorting staff on a white Arab pony. White-plumed, scarlet-jacketed, and ablaze with orders, he was followed by a gorgeous troop of Life Guards and he was, as usual, impatient to get on. There was a kind of flustered, good-natured gaiety about the first swirl of movement. Then the band of the Royal Horse Guards swung in behind the Life Guards and struck up. As the blaring instruments sparkled in the sunlight and the drummers began to sway rhythmically between the silver kettle-drums hung on each side of their saddles, the Governor General's Guards moved out as the leading section of the escort for the Prime Minister of Canada. He followed in his carriage with his lady and behind him came the towering busbies of the Toronto Grenadiers and the swinging kilts of the Royal Canadian Highlanders. The bare knees and the sporrans gave way to hooves again and the scarlet to khaki as the big, bronzed troopers of New South Wales rode into the stream, their carbines slung on their backs and their wide slouch hats pinned up on one side with a black and white feather. It was still khaki and still carbines, with a blaze of pennons and steel, as the New South Wales Lancers followed. After them – a mile of magnificent men astride magnificent horses, interspersed by the carriages of their premiers and borne along on the blare of massed bands – came the troopers of Victoria and New Zealand, of Queensland and the Cape of Good Hope, of South Australia, Natal, and the lesser crown colonies, and, drawing the loudest cheer of all, the cocky Rhodesian Horse who had ridden on the Jameson raid.

There was a last mounted band, a deliberately spaced interval, and then, swarthy under their fezzes, a river of blue and gold, the Zaptiehs of Cyprus rode out at the head of the colonial infantry. The Dyaks of Borneo followed, bayonets fixed, rifles at the perpendicular, little brown men who still hunted heads when they were at home on leave and wore the shrunken trophies of enemies neatly sewn to their belts. The massive, bearded Sikhs flowed into the stream whitening it with their immaculate turbans, and the Zouaves of Jamaica came on billowing in red and blue. They were followed by the Haussas from the Gold Coast who had never marched in shoes until they felt these pavements, by the Chinese from Hong Kong in pointed, enamelled caps that sparkled pagoda-like on their pig-tailed heads, by the Maltese and the Singhalese and the Malays and by men from all the continents and from islands of all the seas. Each unit in the rich and swaying confusion of garbs and gear spoke of a conquered territory and a conquered race. Each man marched now with Her Majesty's rifle shouldered and Her Majesty's bayonet fixed, the men with the brown and black and white and yellow faces, the round-eyed men and the slant-eyed men, the squinting desert men and the wizened jungle men who kept the peace of her Empire.

The parade filed up the length of the Mall in just under an hour. It came into the cleared square before the gates of Buckingham Palace, took the salute of the household troops and naval detachments cordoning the square, and passed on down the length of Constitution Hill. As the cheers from the Mall subsided the cheers from the hill became a steady, rolling roar billowing over the sound of the massed bands.

The formal procession was only now beginning. As the Northwest Mounted Police, the last unit of the Colonial Procession, filed past there was a short, expectant pause. Then, towering on a huge bay, a blaze of scarlet and gold under his white plume, Captain Ames of the 2nd Life Guards, the tallest officer in the British Army, cantered out through the palace gateway. Behind him as he turned for Constitution Hill came an escort of four troopers and after them, squadron by squadron, regiment by regiment, battery by battery, with its fanlike files of bluejackets hauling brass naval guns, its platoons of aides and equerries, its staff officers and Field-Marshals and sheriffs and gentlemen-in-waiting, its ambassadors and legates and its twenty carriage-loads of princes, kings, and bishops, came the full flood of the Royal Procession.

At eleven o'clock a lone cannon boomed from Hyde Park.

The Queen was on her way. A moment later Field-Marshal Lord Wolseley, Commander of the Forces, emerged alone from the gateway. As he rode on, the eight white horses of the state carriage appeared, each ridden by a red-jacketed postilion, each with a running footman pacing beside it. By the wheels of the carriage rode the Prince of Wales, the Duke of Cambridge, and the Duke of Connaught, the three royal princes, and around the Queen as she moved toward Constitution Hill glittered the Captain of the Escort, the Field Officer of the Escort, the Master of the Buckhounds, the Gold Stick of Scotland, the Gold Stick in Waiting, the Master of the Horse, and twenty equerries. She sat in the midst of it all under a white parasol, a familiar huddle of black, facing her two favourite daughters. Five minutes before, as she stepped through the palace doorway, she had pressed an electric button and by five cable routes spanning the seven seas her message of greeting had started round the world. 'From my heart I thank my beloved people. May God bless them. Victoria, R.I.'

By this time the head of the Colonial Procession had passed down Constitution Hill, into Piccadilly and St. James Street, and along Pall Mall and the Strand to Temple Bar. At the entrance to the ancient City, Field-Marshal Lord Roberts had drawn up in salute, the troops had reversed arms and passed through, and the procession had come at last up the length of Ludgate Hill to the vast, canopied pavilion before the entrance to St. Paul's.

At this point it had halted and deployed. With the other colonial premiers and their ladies the Lauriers had stepped from their carriage to the seats reserved for the guests. Here in all their medieval splendour, with a great bank of pink-cheeked, white-surpliced choir boys in their midst and the Prime Minister of Great Britain and his cabinet sitting humbly on the steps, were the most noble and most ancient of the peerage and the most honoured of the visitors.

They sat facing Ludgate Hill as Captain Ames appeared towering on his bay horse and the scarlet wave of the Royal Procession flowed toward them, thundering with bands, glistening with plumes and lances, drowned in the cheering that rolled out over the city from three million throats. They rose as the Queen stepped from her carriage and was handed to the rostrum. From the great tribune and the red-covered balconies and the tens of thousands who surrounded them the *Te Deum* climbed to heaven in thanksgiving for the glory of this Empire that the sixty years of Victoria had rounded to its peak. The National Anthem followed and finally the Doxology. 'Praise God from Whom All Blessings Flow,' sang the Archbishop of Canterbury, and threw up his surpliced arms at the conclusion calling for three cheers for the Queen. The guns boomed, the soldiers whirled their busbies on their bayonets, and amid the thunder and blaze about her the little old lady was seen to wipe away a tear.

The procession re-formed and moved on in reverse order with the carriage of the Prime Minister of Canada moving at the head of the Colonial Procession behind the carriage of the Queen. It passed by Cheapside and King William Street, by London Bridge and Westminster Bridge and Parliament Street and the Mall to the palace again. It was a route that had provided, by happy design, a glimpse of the great mnemonics of British history. At the top of Constitution Hill the man from St-Lin, who had pored over a thousand volumes of that history, had passed the figure of Wellington frozen in bronze. As he came down Piccadilly and St. James Street he had passed the windows of White's and Boodle's from which Fox, Pitt, and Sheridan had once looked out. He had come through the 'sweet, shady lane' where Nell Gwyn had leaned over a garden wall to exchange her naughty talk with Charles II. He had gone by the statues of the soldiers of the Crimea and the lions of Trafalgar Square and he had looked up to Nelson on his column. He had passed Temple Bar where Elizabeth was met by the Lord Mayor when she rode into the city to celebrate the destruction of the Armada, and the crooked haunts where Falstaff had heard the chimes ring at midnight and the Temple and the Law Courts and Fetter Lane and Fleet Street and the Tabard Inn of Chaucer. He had passed the houses of parliament where the heart of the Empire beat and the abbey where the great dead lay at rest; and still, as he went by the Horse Guards in Whitehall where Charles I had lost his head, there were grim-faced living troopers rigid as stone sitting their saddles in the gateway.

It would have been enough merely to see it all, more than enough to share in it as a lowly participant. But he had ridden with his wife at his side in the highest place of any man of the Queen's dominions. He had been cheered as few others, after the Queen herself, were cheered on that day. The days before it had been filled with gracious welcome, and a long calendar of glittering occasions waited in the days ahead. He had been more than merely fêted, he had been liked and admired for himself. Great audiences had hung on his eloquence and imperial statesmen had eagerly sought him out. Wilfrid Laurier of Canada, at glistening banquet tables, had become Sir Wilfrid Laurier of the Empire, giving back only a little of what he got. He did not regret a word of it, certainly not on that day. Certainly, and with all due reservations, 'it would be the proudest moment of my life if I could see a Canadian of French descent affirming the principles of freedom in the parliament of Great Britain'. Quite as certainly, if those principles were ever truly threatened, Canada would be the first of the colonies to rally to their support. 'Let the bugle sound, let the fires be lit on the hills,' had been his injunction to the imperial mother, envisioning such remote, unthinkable catastrophe. If the attendant qualifications had been lost in the billowing applause it was hardly the orator's fault.

4

TWO DAYS after the Jubilee the eleven colonial premiers, all Right Honourables now, sat down with Joseph Chamberlain. For the five sessions that occupied the next two weeks, surrounded, enhanced, and harassed by engulfing festivities, Laurier sat at his right hand. He stood at his right hand when, as one meeting ended, the delegates moved out to the steps at the dour old entrance to the Colonial Office. A photographer appeared, a chair was discreetly brought, and Chamberlain's grouping froze his conception of Empire for posterity.

He sat in the centre, gloves in his left hand, top hat cradled in his right. The men of the subject peoples stood about him, as rigidly at attention as sedentary statesmen could be, and one step behind. It would be almost the last of such photographs, though the autocrat of Birmingham, passing sixty now and still with the black hair, the boyish face, and the monocle screwed in his eye, could not have been brought to believe it. It might well have begun to dawn on him, however, that this Frenchman come from Canada, so eloquently responsive under the chandeliers, was a cold fish in the mornings.

Laurier was obviously the leader among the colonials and the pillar of all plans. In the way he filled the role, however, he was an irritating enigma. One of his favourite banquet themes had been the value of the imperial connection. He had been emphatic in making the point that that connection could not remain static. Either the relations of the mother country and her colonies must grow closer, he had said, or they must break entirely. Yet he seemed now to be prepared to leave the decision, with its horrid possibilities, to the coming on of time.

Australia had been expected to bristle, and did bristle, at the proposal of an imperial council that should grow into an imperial parliament overriding the authority of all Dominion parliaments. Sir Wilfrid treated the project with a cool vagueness that was just as damaging. The idea, he admitted, was an old one and impressive. He himself was stirred by it and was on record to that effect. Yet when one came to study the position of a colonial member standing in the House of Commons at Westminster many questions arose. What exactly would he do there? Whom would he represent? How would he vote, and for how much would his vote count, if the interests of his colonial constituents clashed with imperial interests? The proposal raised great difficulties; it might perhaps be considered at some time in an indefinite future.

He was even less helpful in the matter of imperial defence. While other premiers wavered on the question of contributions to the imperial army and navy, Laurier's answer was a flat, if polite, no. Colonial money was needed for colonial development; he did not see that armies and navies were. The colonies lived and throve under the great shield of Britannia, but a few colonial battalions or a few colonial sailors would not greatly strengthen that shield. Instead they might call up the question of autonomy. Colonial governments might have to ask by whose command and for what these men were to die. It would be an embarrassing question, for it was quite obvious that in many of the quarrels of the Empire Canada had no part. Certainly a great emergency would be another matter entirely but who, with the picture of that Jubilee fresh in his mind, could see a threat around the horizon?

It was all very discouraging for Chamberlain and when the question of trade arose the shoe was on the other foot. His imperial *zollverein* had been talked out before the conference began. It would mean a reversal of policies too drastic to be considered for free-trade England and tariff-protected colonies to band themselves together against the world. The Canadian proposal was very different. Canada was here with the free gift of imperial preference, asking nothing in return. If it involved difficulties, what great change did not? If the mother country could only accept it by denouncing her treaties with Belgium and Germany, which came first, the colony or the foreigners?

The colonial premiers were unanimous for the colony and the English press was of the same mood after the conference ended. To some few sour and disgruntled observers, notably Germans and Belgians, it seemed a piece of rash impertinence for a colony so to direct, however softly and suavely, the trade relations of the motherland. It seemed so to Sir Charles Tupper, who arrived in London on July 30 denouncing the proposal as 'a declaration of independence, an insult rather than a compliment, an absurd scheme'. Whatever their deepest thoughts, however, Chamberlain and the British government did not appear to agree. Sir Charles was deflated on the same day he delivered himself when formal notice was given that the treaties with Germany and Belgium would be denounced and the preference accepted.

'For the first time on record,' declared the London *Daily Mail*, consciously patronizing and unconsciously enigmatic, 'a politician of our New World has been recognized as the equal of the great men of the Old Country.' A new flood of invitations descended, and the politician of the New World was off with his

"HOME, SWEET HOME."

CARTOON BY J. W. BENGOUGH, SEPTEMBER 1, 1897

wife to Edinburgh and Glasgow and the universities and Windsor Castle and once more to Buckingham Palace. But the other homeland remained. France was in a black mood with Great Britain over Egypt and the Sudan, and Paris was hardly welcoming, but Paris had to be seen. The Lauriers crossed the Channel and found the old tongue sweet on their lips again. A frigid official atmosphere was soon warmed by two happy speeches, and after banquetings came a glimpse of the French countryside and the home of ancestral Lauriers. There were a few days in Switzerland and a few days in Rome, where the Cardinal Merry del Val, just returned from Canada, was on hand to greet them. A cordial audience with the Pope hinted at least at a partly favourable report. Then it was France again, England for brief farewells, a short stay in Ireland, and the Lauriers were aboard the *Labrador* and bound home.

There was a thunderous reception at Quebec when the ship docked on August 27, and more welcoming crowds as it moved up the river. There was a piano for Zoë as a gift from the ladies of Quebec, and other gifts poured in on her until she exclaimed that she would have to have a new house to hold them. That would be attended to; the new house was ready. Montreal, Ottawa, and Toronto all echoed the cheers of Quebec; so did the newspapers of the Maritimes and the west. Everywhere the reports on Laurier had been devoured as eagerly as the reports on the Jubilee, and he seemed to have done all things well. He had been devoutly loyal, yet he had not succumbed to Chamberlain. He had had his way in the matter of trade, yet it had been a graceful, filial way. He had stood at the head of all the premiers of the Empire. He had been a great figure in England and he had made his mark in France. He had spent an hour with the Pope and a day with Gladstone. As he came up the river he carried in his pocket a letter that had been delivered to him at the ship, urging a railway to the Yukon. All the old problems would be waiting piled high on his desk. He was not quite ready for them. On the night of the great reception in Montreal he sat late, as he often did, with the old friend, Laurent-Olivier David. 'It seems to me', he said in one reflective, expansive moment, 'that to sit in the House of Lords would be the supreme end of ambition for a public man.' He was abruptly conscious of a quick, intent glance and the crackling of the fire seemed louder in the sudden quiet of the room.

17

'THE TIMES OF SAINT-FRANÇOIS DE SALES'

1897-1899

'I AM NOT SURE whether the British Empire needs a new constitution,' he had written from London, 'but I am certain that every Jubilee guest will need one.' He had a fortnight in Arthabaska to attempt to restore his own, and then he was back in Ottawa with the crisp forewarning of autumn creeping into the air. This time he was to be spared the dismal return to the Russell Hotel. Its brown old corridors and overstuffed lobby, never quite free of the smells of food and drink, would not know the Lauriers as residents again. At 335 Theodore Street, which was one day to be known as Laurier Avenue, the new house awaited them, spacious and welcoming, the gift of a grateful party.

The faithful Mme Lavergne was at hand to advise Zoë during the work of settling in. She was also present, and not greatly elated, when the curé called to inform his distinguished new parishioners that the first pew on the right-hand side of the aisle would be reserved for them. They would be sitting, Emilie pointed out, with their backs to the entire congregation. 'One does not, of course, go to Mass to see the hats, but so long as we are there why may we not be allowed to see them?'

It was not to be so great a problem for her as it might once have been. The long relationship, always graceful, was now in graceful decline. On August 4, while the Prime Minister and Lady Laurier were still abroad, Joseph Lavergne had been elevated to the bench as a judge of the Superior Court in Quebec. His duties as a member of parliament were relinquished and his sphere of action would henceforth be removed from Ottawa. At about the same time, as Emilie prepared to accompany him, she received from the Prime Minister's secretary a packet containing all the letters she had written to Wilfrid Laurier. If it was intended as a gentle suggestion that she should return the letters she had received it was not responded to, but she was far too discerning not to perceive the hint of finality. She would always be the friend and often the guest of the Lauriers, but now the friend at a distance.

2

IN THE LAST week of September Sifton and a sizeable party left Ottawa burdened down with quilts, moccasins, and sleeping-bags, each man carrying a Colt .45 on a strap slung over his shoulder. The Yukon gold rush was in full flood and the tumult in the Klondike was almost out of control. With the Alaska boundary still unsettled no one yet knew whether Lynn Canal, the end of the sea route up the Pacific coast, was American or Canadian water. Seattle and Vancouver were at war for control of the traffic. Beyond the head of Lynn Canal lay the height of land and the passes and the wild country leading to the gold-fields. Skagway, Dyea, Whitehorse Pass, and Chilkoot Pass were all names in the news and little more than names. There was going to be trouble with the Americans over access routes by sea, there had to be an attempt at administration in the roaring mining towns, and the clamour for an all-Canadian railway into the country would soon have to be dealt with. Sifton went off distrustful of gold rushes, impatient with the Yukon as a distraction from his greater concerns on the prairies, but resolved to see for himself. He was back early in November with his distrust changed to that hard, driving enthusiasm that no one in the cabinet could withstand. He had walked in by one of the passes and out by the other, he had seen the gold-fields and been swept by the mood of the country. There were tens of millions still to come out of the Yukon and they had to be kept by Canada. A railway was a necessity.

With a new railway problem, all the old problems with the United States cried louder for solution. There could hardly have been a worse time for the wide-ranging general adjustment that Laurier had in mind. The Cleveland Democrats, usually pacific and always for lower tariffs, had precipitated a savage quarrel with England over a question of Venezuelan borders in 1895. It had simmered down, but the truculent mood of the country had not been improved by the election of 1896 which returned McKinley's Republicans. Trumpeting the Monroe Doctrine and damning Chamberlain for his high-handed tactics with the Boers, the Americans themselves were developing an ominous concern over Spain's treatment of Cuba. This new-world imperialism that was eyeing Cuban sugar would also be alert to gold and it did not promise well for discussions on the Alaska boundary. The question of the fisheries could be relied on to produce its rasping disputes and, as always with a Republican administration, higher and higher tariffs were the order of the day.

Nevertheless in November Laurier decided on a visit to Washington. It was made with as little ceremony as possible, merely to feel out the ground, and he found McKinley surprisingly cordial. The Americans were prepared to talk, though it would obviously be talk on their terms. 'We have had a warm welcome and some cool proposals,' he reported, but he did return to Ottawa with an agreement to form a Joint High Commission which would meet to discuss all questions in a few months' time.

The head of the Canadian delegation, he decided, would be Chapleau. It would put an able man in a position to do useful work and it would solve one of the knottiest of the thousand patronage problems. Chapleau's term as Lieutenant-Governor of Quebec expired in January of 1898 and, whatever Laurier's inclination, it simply could not be renewed. The *Rouges* of Quebec were threatening open revolt if that plum went to the ancient enemy. Tarte, on the other hand, proclaimed the value of Chapleau's more recent help. Tarte, after all, had won it. Federally and provincially, Quebec was now a solid Liberal stronghold and Chapleau had done much not only to make it so but to drain away the political malignancy of the times. He had cowed the Castors so thoroughly that they had not dared to revive the question of the schools as an issue in provincial elections. He had presented the Liberal case to the Cardinal Merry del Val, and he had done it with more effect because he spoke as a converted man. The last of the great old *Bleus* was now safe in the camp of Laurier and he should be kept there. He could not be treated as 'a common valet', said Tarte, and as usual Tarte was right.

With Chapleau provided for there would still be many to appease, but affairs in Quebec went well. Laurier had been considerably heartened in September by a long meeting with Louis-Joseph Paul Napoléon Bruchési, the new Archbishop of Montreal. Forty-two years old and just returned from Rome, where he had quite evidently had some brisk discussions with Merry del Val, this was a man of the old school in Quebec who had now been made to share the vigour, the forthrightness, and the broad outlook of the young cardinal. He was quite as firmly of the Church and for the Church and he gave no clue as to any pronouncement from Rome, but there was a general sense in him of a changing mood.

Ontario, the other side of the coin, seemed changing too. For several months Laurier had been tempted to try a risky experiment. His thoughts hovered over D'Alton McCarthy as Mowat's failing health made a change in the cabinet necessary. McCarthy had approved the schools settlement, he had approved the new tariff, and he was happy to see his idea of an imperial preference become a reality. He had not renounced his Anglo-Saxon attitude; he was convinced that Laurier had adopted it. Once in harness in the cabinet, however, his judgment in this respect might be beside the point. He might run as well as Sifton while the leader did the driving. McCarthy would be a strong man for Ontario, a brilliant Minister of Justice, and a seal of conciliation.

The cloud across this prospect was David Mills, the old comrade of opposition days, who was also a power in Ontario. Dogmatic and consistent to the end, Mills had stood out against Laurier on the question of the schools and had gone down to defeat in his own constituency. He was not soothed by the fact that a crucial number of ballots, clearly for him, had been improperly marked and had been thrown out because of new electoral regulations that Laurier had supported. He was not grateful for his leader's forgiveness on the matter of the schools nor for the senatorship that had been given him, but rather aggrieved because no seat in the Commons had been vacated in his favour. He was rankled by what he considered to be neglect, by what he considered to be a triumph of hypocrisy in the dealings with Manitoba, and by a number of lesser sores. It was really hard to know all that was in Mills's mind. Somehow and obscurely he seemed to blame Laurier even for the unofficial red pencils that had been used in polling booths and the check marks that had strayed into the black sections of ballots to cheat his voters of their franchise and leave him out in the cold.

Mills wanted the portfolio of Justice, and only Justice. He still had friends in Ontario who could blow up a storm too dangerous to be resisted. To a first offer that he enter the cabinet and accept the post allotted to him when the shuffle came, he returned a sharp refusal. The inference was plain that he distrusted his prospective colleagues and was not too sure of Laurier. There seemed nothing to do for the moment but give in gracefully, and on November 18, as Mowat left, Mills became Minister of Justice. He was in his seventies and not strong; McCarthy's turn would come. In the meantime, however, little had been gained in Ontario and the sessions of the cabinet were less comfortable than before.

Everything went on and everything waited. Neither the hour with the Pope nor the talks with Merry del Val nor the meeting with Archbishop Bruchési had reassured Laurier as to the outcome of the mission. There had been friendliness and sympathy and a measure of understanding, but the minds had not met. There would always be a gulf between the secular and the religious view of the place of Catholicism in the nation; that much was recognized. The question was how deep and whether a bridge could be built. The decision would be basic and it could be disastrous. Until it was settled nothing was settled.

There was renewed proof, early in December, that one mind at least had grasped the nub of the problem. Charles Russell had gone back to the Vatican, where the pronouncement of the

Pope was almost daily expected. He had had hopes of cabling the contents but gave them up; it would be improper for the news to reach Laurier before it reached the bishops. Merry del Val had warned him against the publication of extracts, which would probably be garbled. He had no knowledge of the text or tenor as yet, but Merry del Val seemed cheerful. More than that, he had delivered himself in words that seemed to Russell to merit verbatim report. 'The worst of all is', the Cardinal had said, 'that these good bishops are perfectly right in all their arguments. The Catholics of Manitoba *have* been done out of their rights. The central parliament *has* the power under the constitution to pass remedial laws. The Church *does not sanction* mixed schools when the faith of the children may be lost. But the bishops seem incapable of grasping the situation as it is, that as a matter of practical politics the central parliament cannot pass (no matter which side is in power) a remedial law and that the Church cannot allow generation after generation of children to grow up without any education at all, waiting until there is a Catholic majority in Manitoba which may never be.'

On December 18 the papal encyclical *Affari Vos*, dealing with the Manitoba schools, was issued in Rome. It was to be read in all the pulpits of Catholic Canada one month later. Laurier read it in the study of the Abbé Proulx in St-Lin, where he had gone to be with Adeline and the family for the Christmas holidays. The Act of Confederation, said the encyclical, had secured to Catholic children the right of education in public schools in keeping with their conscientious convictions. The parliament of Manitoba had abolished this right by a contrary law. The bishops had done right to oppose this law, for 'By this law a grave injury was inflicted . . . it is not lawful for our children to seek the benefits of education in schools in which the Catholic Religion is ignored or decisively combated, in schools where its doctrine is despised and its fundamental principles repudiated. If the Church has anywhere permitted this it was only with reluctance and in self-defence, and after having taken many precautions which, however, too often have been found unequal to parrying the danger.'

The compromises embodied in the Laurier-Greenway settlement were 'defective, unsuitable, insufficient'. Bishops, in working for further amelioration, 'have our concurrence and approbation, for the things which you sought and still seek to protect and defend are most sacred'. Yet it was possible to differ on the question of tactics, and it was essential never to lose sight of the principles of moderation, gentleness, and mutual charity. Until Catholics should obtain their full rights they should not refuse partial satisfaction. 'If, therefore, anything is granted by law, or custom, or the goodwill of men, which will render the evil more tolerable and the dangers more remote, it is expedient and useful to make use of such concessions. As concerns intellectual culture and the progress of civilization one can only recognize as praiseworthy and noble the desire of the provinces of Canada to develop public instruction and to raise its standards more and more . . . there is no kind of knowledge, no perfection of learning, which cannot be fully harmonized with Catholic doctrine.'

He read it again and again, tiredly envisioning the months that lay ahead, reaching on into years. 'Partial satisfaction' – 'defective, unsuitable, insufficient' – they were still to be fought for, those most sacred things. There was no end yet, there never would be an end. Yet – 'moderation, gentleness, and mutual charity' – 'the goodwill of men' – 'it is expedient and useful to make use of such concessions'. The poison was drawn, the climate altered; the *Rouge* could walk before his bishop again, freed of the horns and hooves. Somewhere in this bare little study with the crucifix on the wall, somewhere among those files of wrinkled letters, lay one fulfilled prediction. The number of mortal sins was reduced by one.

3

THE COUNTRY was on the move, Laurier had survived the Jubilee and escaped Chamberlain, and the schools were out of politics. He could congratulate himself on all this as he sat down in January of 1898 to work on the Speech from the Throne. Sifton was ready with his new measures for the Klondike and his plans for the Yukon railway. On these projects Laurier was prepared to accept the judgment of the cool man of business.

They were in any case almost routine items among the nation's expanding affairs. The great work of the year, when a few loose ends were tied, would be the adjustment with the United States.

The loose ends began to entangle him, however, even before the session opened in February. The Pope might accept an imperfect compromise with a prospect of gradual improvement for the schools of Manitoba, but Archbishop Langevin would not. The broad formal framework of the settlement he now had to endure; there was no alternative. What he would not endure were the thousand rasping details unsettled within it. The choice of textbooks, the setting of curricula, the training and qualification of teachers still opened every door to an all-pervading Protestantism. They all had to be closed. Everything, to the uttermost rim of the vaguest promise for the future, must be settled at once and in writing, on his terms.

He broke out regularly from the pulpit or in the Catholic papers, duly inflaming his host of Protestant opposites. He bombarded his correspondents across the country and across the ocean, and even Archbishop Bruchési weakened under the assault. Should not Laurier, he wrote, at least outline some proposals for improvement of the settlement in the Speech from the Throne? It was the last thing in the world Laurier would consider. He had as firm a grasp as Tupper on the forty-foot pole and never, if he could help it, would the contentions of Manitoba again invade parliament.

He made it an issue and a warning in his letters to the churchly warriors. He impressed it on Langevin in two face-to-face meetings that Bruchési arranged in Ottawa. The Church and the state had composed their public differences. If they became embroiled again it would be at the peril of the Church in Canada and the peril of Quebec. The settlement was not final but the course was fixed. Improvement now was the work of time and the conference room in the hands of patient men.

Bruchési was uneasily convinced, but not Langevin. The man who faced Laurier at the meetings in Ottawa heard his mother tongue dwindling toward silence in Manitoba and was haunted by the thought of the souls for whom he was responsible to the uttermost generation. He could not be reconciled. He went home from the last meeting to fling himself on his knees and ask God to deliver him from the charm of this statesman who was so utterly convincing and so wholly wrong. His prayer was answered; he would never succumb and never be wholly silenced. The interminable months of agitation, discussion, and correspondence, with Laurier always at the centre, were only beginning. But the schools were open and the schools went on.

Laurier's hope was to spend a month in the west himself, but that hope soon died. Sifton was magnificent in his first major performance on the floor of the House of Commons, but his bill for the Yukon railway was stopped dead in the Senate. Bowell and his Tory relics were having their way while the Tuppers, father and son, manoeuvred behind them. To Laurier's heated mind the obstruction was 'very much akin to a crime against Canada'. In all the flush of his third year at the head of a confident majority, he was determined to have no more of it. Nor would he wait for Liberalizing time. The Tory ancients would change their views while they lived, or he would change the Senate.

He found himself becoming steadily more involved in the snares of Senate reform, while at the same time an inward disquiet added to outward fury. The storm that had blown up about the railway bill centred quite as much on Sifton's administration of the Yukon. Single-handed and all but absolute, the Minister of the Interior controlled the roaring wilderness of shacks and mining camps and brothels and saloons that made up the bonanza region. His police kept what order there was. His officials allotted claims and collected royalties. It was hardly surprising that disappointed gold-seekers and sensation-seeking newspaper men should come back with lurid reports of maladministration or should hint of fortunes made by Sifton and his friends. Nothing was confirmed, everything was certainly exaggerated, yet the thought of the Yukon brought the thought of the greater west. Those prairies would bear the stamp of the man in charge of filling them and the wrong man there could mean a real national catastrophe. He was not the wrong man; Laurier would not believe it. He could not afford to believe it.

By March there were cabinet problems and another snag in

his plans. Fitzpatrick, always inclined to snuggle under the wing of his Catholic leader, was making trouble with Sifton. Tarte was now habitually at odds with a half-dozen of his colleagues, and Mills was providing a new note of dissonance. This, at least, Laurier did not propose to endure much longer. He had wanted McCarthy in the first place and now he intended to have him, but it might mean a bad break with Mills. Added to all this came the latest letter from Chapleau, now duly retired from Spencerwood and replaced by a faithful *Rouge*. 'Excuse the numerous erasures . . . I have dictated painfully from my sick-bed and my new secretary is not yet accustomed to this work, nor have I time to teach him.' It was a rather pathetic postscript to long memories of a spectacular old enemy and it cast disturbing doubts on the plans for the High Commission.

By the end of June everything had to be thought out again. Chapleau was dead and, stunningly, McCarthy was dead too, killed by a fall from a running horse. The cabinet planning was stalled and Laurier could find no man to his taste for the post of High Commissioner. He would have to shuffle aside whatever could wait and take on the work himself.

The meeting of the Joint High Commission had been delayed by the outbreak of the Spanish-American War in April. Now, with the war nearing its end, a date had finally been set. Sessions were to open on August 23 in Quebec and continue later in Washington. For the first time an international meeting dealing with Canadian affairs was to be held at least in part on Canadian soil rather than in the American or imperial capitals. It was one sign of the country's emergence as a nation. Another evidence of escape from imperial tutelage was the fact that only one British representative, Lord Herschell, would be present to represent the mother country. Canada would speak quite clearly for herself through Laurier, Cartwright, and Sir Louis Davies. John Charlton, another old Liberal, who was not of the cabinet, would also be included because he was a large dealer in lumber with interests on both sides of the line, and lumbering was one of the problems. The invaluable Joseph Pope would be one of the two secretaries and for the other secretary Laurier turned, with what each recognized to be a kind of inevitability, to Henri Bourassa.

Preparations for the meetings went on in a mood darkened a little by another impending change. The Aberdeens were leaving Canada before their term was out, and though it had been their own decision Laurier suspected the hand of Chamberlain somewhere in the background. To that high Tory empire-builder the appointees of Gladstone were as uncongenial as they were to the unforgiving Tupper, and transatlantic relations had been strained for some time. The move, for Laurier, would mean not only a change in the political atmosphere but the end of a warm and easy neighbourliness with the dwellers in Rideau Hall. The kittens he liked to play with and the dogs that Zoë fancied all came to them from the kennels of Lady Aberdeen. Teacup talk with the Governor General had ranged widely, intimately, and openly over national and imperial problems. There was not likely to be any such casual closeness between the Prime Minister and the new incumbent.

In the middle of August, for the first time and the last, there was a pleasant, sunny week-end with the Aberdeens in Arthabaska. Then it was time for Quebec, and after a day of ceremony that proved to be unexpectedly cordial the members of the Joint High Commission settled into their work. It was soon apparent that the genial Lord Herschell was to be a blessing rather than the curse that British negotiators had usually turned out to be in dealings with the Americans. Cartwright was magnificently well-informed and clear in his thinking and displayed unusual resources of tact, which Davies supplemented. Charlton, totally preoccupied with lumber and pressing for his own interests, was a dubious asset in the debates, and Henri Bourassa had occasionally to be convinced that he was secretary and not leader of the delegation. But the Americans remained friendly and conciliatory. The dreaded high-tariff Republicans proved to be men like other men, balancing conflicting interests. The representatives of a nation that had just won Cuba by a successful war were less inclined to become worked up over the issue of British imperialism. No question on the agenda seemed to be as thorny as expected once it was taken in hand, and Laurier's hopes rose.

The commission sat at Quebec from August 23 to October 10 and adjourned for a month before the sittings in Washington.

For Laurier the first series of meetings had been interrupted by many recalls to Ottawa, and there had also been a sombre week in Arthabaska. Ubald, the frailest of the half-brothers, had been sick for several years. In September Henri, another of the brothers, brought him home to die in the house on Mont Christo. As he looked at the assembled family, more prosperous and better provided for now that the great brother held the keys to many kingdoms, Laurier was oppressed by the same sensations he had felt at the death of Carolus. None of them was strong; the old spectre still stalked, and Ubald was only the first to be overtaken.

The commission resumed in Washington on November 9 and Laurier was much there as the year ran out. He was pleased with his delegation and pleased with the Americans. There seemed to be a real desire to live at peace on the continent. All the differences between the countries were being widely and deeply explored. The sealing and fisheries questions were well on the way to settlement. There were amicable gestures on the tariff and a compromise was being worked out on the all-important question of the Alaska boundary. Canada was likely to gain at least enough sovereignty over the dreary waste of Lynn Canal to permit access by sea. A Christmas mood seemed justified by the time Christmas came, but it did not last the year.

The cold wind came from the west, where Tacoma had joined with Seattle in the war for the Yukon trade. As they felt the chill the American delegates began to stiffen on the question of Lynn Canal. By January of 1899 it was clear that they spoke with the voice of the American Pacific coast. No agreement was going to be made that gave ships from Vancouver free access to the Yukon, and with that word the negotiations on all other points collapsed. Quite as huffy as the rest of his delegation, Laurier declined an offer of arbitration on American terms, with its foredoomed result. The main prize had been snatched from his grasp and he would not return with crumbs. If there could be no agreement on Alaska there could be no agreement on anything.

He was back where he had started with the Americans and there was not much else on which he could congratulate himself as he prepared to face parliament in the session of 1899. His casual view of the liquor question was going to cost him a few nights' sleep and the reading and writing of a thousand arid letters. The Prohibition referendum had been held and the one-third of the electorate that had troubled to vote had pinned him on the horns of a dilemma. Ontario was for prohibition by 154,000 to 115,000. Quebec was against it by 122,000 to 28,000. The whole country was for dryness by a total majority of just 13,000 votes. Short of pitting Quebec against Ontario again, there was only one possible position to be taken: the majority was too small to be a reliable indication of the country's will. That position Laurier took and would hold, but there would be no more off-hand referendums.

The Aberdeens were gone now, and it had been a gracious parting. Before leaving Ottawa they had defied politics and precedent by dining cosily *en famille* with the Lauriers, sending Zoë beforehand into an unaccustomed tizzy of preparations. But the sucking-pig cooked in French-Canadian fashion had been a great success and the Aberdeens' gift of a silver loving-cup had been passed round and drunk from standing while all admired the inscription, 'Oublier nous ne le pouvons'. There would certainly be no forgetting this warmly regal friendship, and at the dock-side in Quebec first impressions of the successor had shadowed final farewells. Lord Minto strode like a soldier, talked mainly of horses, and his Conservatism bristled like epaulettes. As the last gift of the Lauriers was carried aboard the ship and Ishbel exclaimed over it – 'one of those dear little red Quebec berlots sleighs' – the Prime Minister had felt a little chilled by the wind of changing times.

The project of the Yukon railway was dead, and he was not sure that he was sorry. Chamberlain was cooling the hope of Senate reform, and here again Laurier was beginning to have his own doubts. Those elderly gentlemen sat behind stronger ramparts than he had thought. Of many suggestions for change, none very promising, the one he had finally advanced was that of throwing Commons and Senate together in case of a dispute and having them vote in a 'congrès of the two houses'. Chamberlain had replied soberly and politely that that would be a grave matter. It would call into question the whole 'pact or treaty between the self-governing colonies which now constitute the different provinces of the Dominion'. Which was quite true, and more than enough to give pause.

Apart from greater affairs, one member of the cabinet had now been tamed. Laurier, however, was not proud of the way it had been done nor very sure of the result. Mulock, the efficient Postmaster-General and the innocent of Ontario, had taken it upon himself during one of the Prime Minister's absences in Washington to dismiss the Montreal postmaster. He certainly had the authority, he had done it with ample cause, and if he had considered politics at all he could point to the warm approval of Quebec *Rouges,* since the postmaster was a notorious former *Bleu.* He happened, however, to be Dansereau, the old schoolmate of L'Assomption, nesting in shelter since the decline of Conservative fortunes. Chapleau had got him the appointment, and now Chapleau was dead. Dansereau remained as the linchpin of the alliance with quiescent *Bleus* and the right hand of Tarte. He was about as good a postmaster as could be expected of any hard-drinking newspaper man who spent all his time at politics, and the Montreal post-office was undoubtedly a shambles. That, however, was nothing compared to the shambles that Dansereau's going, sore and disgraced, might make of politics in Quebec. Always a restless adventurer, always able to whip up a powerful following, and with no Chapleau to rein him in, Dansereau might be the spark to revive a lifeless party. Laurier, when word of the dismissal reached him in Washington, had acted with a dispatch that left Mulock breathless. Dansereau was to be restored forthwith, said a first letter, without question, without delay, and with apologies. Mulock had acted rashly and without authority. A second letter hammered the instructions home; in effect Dansereau would come back or Mulock would go out.

Dansereau was reinstalled now, mending his ways for a time, and supported by a brace of assistants who did his work. A much-subdued Mulock, wiser in the ways of Quebec, had apologized for haste and presumption. His master, in turn, had apologized for an over-hasty rebuke. The papering-over was done, but the cracks remained. Mulock had retreated a little into his Ontario shell. Dansereau's thoughts were straying toward the newspaper world again. He would go sooner or later and the days of his manageability would go with him.

Yet if it had been a poor enough year in many ways, there were still compensations. The country throbbed with confidence and growth. The long quarrel of the schools was simmering down. Laurier seemed to have impressed on everyone that finality was out of reach on that question. 'There is still much intemperance of language,' he wrote to Archbishop Bruchési, 'but can it be otherwise while men are men?' Little by little, through endless conferences and interminable correspondence, the settlement was being improved and made to work, always with a door still open for further change. Time was bringing its own changes. Bishop Laflèche had passed to his reward from Three Rivers, still firm in the convictions of his youth, still brooding on his differences with the liberal cardinal of Quebec who had gone ahead of him. 'I am in much haste to be taken to the other side', he had confided to an attendant, 'to learn if it is Taschereau or I who is right.'

For Laurier, his presence in the funeral cortège of the old warrior was less incongruous that it might have seemed a year or so before. On a long road one turned many corners, and some of them led back. There was still not time, there never would be time to analyse that deep travail of spirit about which he had written to David. But the association with Merry del Val had done much. The growing friendship with Bruchési had done more. 'You know how to make religion loved, Monseigneur,' he wrote in one of his many letters to the Archbishop of Montreal. 'It seems to me that we are returned to the times of Saint-François de Sales. The men of my generation and my school have all been excellent citizens; they would even have been excellent Christians if anyone had known how to appeal to their hearts and speak to them as you speak.'

18

'SIR WILFRID LAURIER IS TOO ENGLISH FOR ME'

1899-1900

THE STORM over South Africa blew up on the Canadian horizon with deceptive quiet. There were warnings enough but the problem, as always, was to assess dangers and to act only when they had emerged in their real shape. Laurier would never be sure, when the two years were over, that his timing and his judgment had been right. He would never again, in fact, be quite as sure of himself.

The dispute with the Boers was obviously moving in the direction of war. He was not prepared to say whether it would be a good war or a bad one; he did not know. It was clear that Chamberlain had embraced the dream of Cecil Rhodes; South Africa, in one way or another, was to become British. Certainly a great deal of rich territory, a great deal of imperialistic planning, and some huge financial interests were involved. On the other hand the Boers, trekking always a little farther away from territory shadowed by the Union Jack, seemed to take with them nothing but their slaves and a brutal reluctance to submit to the ways of civilization. The Transvaal was the heart of the trouble and even in the Transvaal British subjects were fast becoming a majority. It had to be acknowledged that they had followed the Boers across the grassland and intruded on their last place of refuge. Many of them, no doubt, were merely gold-seeking, self-seeking transients serving imperial interests and disturbing the tranquillity of a Boer state. It was nevertheless quite intolerable for any liberal, much less a liberal who had ridden in the Jubilee, to accept the idea that an Englishman should have to live for fourteen years in a territory and be forty years old before he could acquire the common rights of a citizen.

There would have to be an adjustment, and if it was to stop short of war it would probably be by a federation that would embrace the Transvaal and all the South African territories. Naturally the Boers would be reluctant acquisitions but their rights would be guaranteed along with those of their fellow British subjects. If their submergence was also guaranteed, the process would still be gentle by comparison with the imperialism of other European powers. Undoubtedly, in the long run, it would make for the general advancement of civilization. A man on the fringes of the quarrel should not be expected to probe much deeper than that. Laurier could permit himself to hope that a matter so obviously within the competence of British diplomacy and the power of British arms would be treated as a strictly British affair.

The difficulty was that Chamberlain had no such intention. When war came, little or great, he was determined to treat the world to the spectacle of all the colonies rallying with their money and their men to the side of the imperial mother. He was still convinced that only a few obscurantist leaders, notably the evasive Frenchman in Ottawa, stood in the way of the great dream of a federated Empire. They would be swept along or swept aside as the call to a righteous struggle opened the flood-gates of pride and loyalty.

Long before the session of 1899 opened in March there had been signs of what was in the wind. The Canadian military had been restless ever since the changing of the guard at Government House. Minto himself was proving to be a pleasant surprise, very much the soldier, very much Chamberlain's man, but a great deal more sympathetic and alert to Canadian attitudes than he had at first seemed. The genial General Gascoigne, however, who had commanded the militia in the days of the Aberdeens, had gone with the Aberdeens. He had been replaced by General Hutton, who quite evidently considered his appointment to

Canada as a mandate to prepare for war. He bustled with plans, bristled with authority, and his ideas of the relationship of the military to the government seemed to antedate Cromwell. On the home side, and vigorously competing with Hutton in nuisance value, there was Sam Hughes, a startlingly handsome, frenetically military Ontario Orangeman who was also a member of parliament for North Victoria. Hughes had been a subaltern in the days of the Fenian raids and had never forgotten it. He had been one of the Noble Thirteen in the days of McCarthy and had swung round with McCarthy to support Laurier on the question of the Manitoba schools. His fiery friendship was now one of the embarrassing fruits of that victory and he wrote incessantly, evidently with an eye on South Africa, begging to be allowed to raise a body of troops 'to go anywhere – on a day's notice'.

Early in February came a warm and disarming personal letter from George Wyndham, the new Under-Secretary of State for War in London, suggesting imperial willingness to incorporate a special Canadian regiment in the forces of the Empire. It was followed in March by an inquiry from Minto on behalf of the War Office and the Admiralty. In case of war in South Africa what would be the position of Canada? Were Canadian troops required by the Militia Act to serve abroad? Canadian troops, Laurier replied after a discussion in cabinet that gave him a disturbing foretaste of what might come, could be required to serve anywhere so long as it were shown to be in defence of Canada. South Africa, however, obviously did not come within the scope of such a definition.

By April the South African League Congress, one of Cecil Rhodes's inspirations, was cabling the Canadian branch of the British Empire League asking for a resolution in support of the British case against the Boers. Within another month a pamphlet of the Imperial South African Association, 66 Victoria Street, Westminster, was on Laurier's desk. It contained 'handy notes on South Africa for the use of speakers and others' and its frontispiece was a map of the prospective Cape-to-Cairo railway. The propaganda campaign was mounting as the dispute went into its last stages in South Africa, and Ontario newspapers were responding vigorously.

In Montreal Hugh Graham, an indomitable imperialist and proprietor of the *Star*, was doing all he could to set English Canada alight. Over the rest of Quebec, however, the silence was ominous. It was apathy as yet, but an alert and hostile Tarte was a sign of warning. Imperial trade was one thing, imperial wars were another; Tarte would have nothing to do with any war. The business of the House went on with every debate sharpened by the old underlying sense of cleavage. The sessions of the cabinet were short-tempered and close-mouthed, with a new bristling of Englishness at Tarte's stuttering Frenchness. Always difficult, he was nearly unmanageable now because he was a sick man. It was just as difficult for the Prime Minister to rein in the war-horses on the other side. To Minto's urging that Canada guarantee troops in the event of a war in South Africa Laurier could be evasive and legalistic. To the newspaper pressure and the pressure in the House daily pumped up by new injections from English and South African imperialists, he could afford to yield a little.

On July 31, seconded by Foster from the other side of the aisle, he moved a resolution expressing the sympathy of the country with the efforts of Her Majesty's government to obtain justice for the British in the Transvaal. The object, he said, was to assure fellow subjects in South Africa 'that our heart is with them and that in our judgment they are in the right'. Perhaps the effect of the resolution might also be, he added piously, 'that this mark of sympathy, of universal sympathy extending from continent to continent and encircling the globe, might cause wiser and more humane counsels to prevail in the Transvaal and possibly avert the awful arbitrament of war'.

The resolution passed unanimously and the House rose as one man to sing 'God Save the Queen'. But the Boers in the Transvaal continued their stubborn, infuriating resistance to British demands and whenever they gave the least sign of weakening the demands increased. The loyal indignation of Ontario and of the Montreal *Star* increased with them. Minto, prodded by Chamberlain, renewed his urgings for the 'spontaneous' promise of a Canadian contingent. Hutton, with or without the promise, was busily preparing the contingent. With all the British military man's genius for pouring oil on political flames he announced in the hearing of Tarte that once war was declared public opinion would force the government's hand. At the same time, rebuffing Sam Hughes with the remark that no colonial officer would be fit for service abroad without three years' training, he roused that parched glory-hunter to frustrated and wrathful vehemence.

The session ended in mid August and the House at least was stilled. But the cables and the mails and the newspapers continued their work. By September General Hutton had had his eyes discreetly opened to one fact of Canadian life and had privately offered a battalion command in his South African force to a French-Canadian officer. On October 3 the *Canadian Military Gazette*, officially without Hutton's knowledge, published full details of the contingent that would be sent.

Laurier saw the article in Toronto, with Willison close at hand. He had been touring Ontario for a month and he knew the mood of the province. He also knew what awaited him at home and he took the occasion to meet it. Toronto typesetters were busy with his response when he stepped from the train in Montreal next morning. Tarte was the man on his mind but the first inquirer to greet him was merely Henri Bourassa, looking very stiff and very young.

There was no doubt as to the sentiments of Tarte's disciple, and no difficulty in waving them aside. 'My dear Henri,' was the tolerant response to the first protest. 'You are very impatient. Buy the *Globe* this evening and you will have my answer.'

The Prime Minister on this occasion, reported the *Globe*, had set aside his long-standing rule against newspaper interviews. The article in the *Military Gazette* was pure invention. There had been no offer of a contingent because it was impossible to make one without a grant from parliament, and parliament was not in session. 'Though we may be willing to contribute troops, I do not see how we can do so.'

It was a soft enough answer for Ontario, yet the ribs were there for Quebec. There could be no official contingent without a full debate in parliament. Bourassa was silenced, Tarte was satisfied, and there was still no war. Ontario and the *Star* were shouting 'treason' but that shout might die if the object of all the clamour were briefly removed. There was a long-standing invitation from President McKinley to attend a series of official gatherings in Chicago. The President of Mexico would also be on hand and continental goodwill would be the theme. The settlement of the Alaska boundary question could be made a part of that theme. Meetings and banquets would be a poor substitute for the promised reconvening of the Joint High Commission, but any forum would help in presenting the Canadian case. There would be a relief from present thoughts and just possibly a return with something to divert the thoughts of the country. On October 7 Laurier took the train for Chicago.

He was back in haste on the eleventh, leaving behind him an atmosphere chill with righteous disapproval. He had spoken well for Alaska but the American heart beat for the Boers. On October 9 the Boers had sent their ultimatum to Great Britain. On October 12 the first shots were fired and war was a fact.

Chamberlain, busy with the mobilization of a dozen colonies, had not paid too much heed either to the movements or the words of the Prime Minister of Canada. He appeared instead to have pounced with hearty eagerness on the statement of the *Military Gazette.* Minto had now a cable and a letter to display in which imperial authorities gratefully acknowledged an offer that had not been made and stipulated their terms for acceptance of the contingent. Troops were to be armed, equipped, and transported by the colony. They were to embark not later than October 31 and proceed direct to Cape Town. Four units of about a hundred and thirty men each would be sufficient and no colonial officer should hold a rank higher than that of major. Sam Hughes, who had been frantically cabling Chamberlain, was not desired. Neither was the regiment or brigade he had offered to raise at the usual moment's notice. 'We do not want the men,' Chamberlain had written Minto on October 4, 'and the whole point of the offer would be lost unless it was endorsed by the Government of the Colony.'

The Prime Minister of Canada, through the columns of the

Toronto *Globe*, had taken the position that there could be no official contingent without the authority of parliament. The meetings of the cabinet through October 11 and October 12 were a grim microcosm of what debate in parliament would be. Even the mildest of the French-Canadian ministers resented Chamberlain's tactics. The least imperial-minded of the English bristled at Tarte. The little man's power had long since gone to his head while sickness gnawed at his middle. His stutter was growing worse and his English had not improved. For months his entrance to council, usually late and usually for effect, with his cane winking in his hand and his pointed beard bobbing defiance, had been the signal for disruptive argument. It was more so than ever now and there was no gainsaying his premise.

Quebec would not support a war in which she had no interest. She would not submit, blindly and voicelessly, to a tax in money and blood. Tarte made that abundantly and offensively clear. It was equally clear that Ontario and the rest of English Canada would not refrain from the war at Tarte's dictation. The field might be remote and the cause dubious but it was still an English war. The call of the blood might not be as loud as Chamberlain thought but it was loud enough. It was quite as much a reality as any of the sentiments of Quebec. If parliament were called, a divided government would face it after a month in which all the bad blood of the country had been brought to a boil. The parties and the nation would be torn apart in a new quarrel and this time one that went to the very depths. The cabinet meetings hovered at the brink of that prospect and began to draw back. The shape of the compromise emerged.

There could be no official offer of troops by the country. The word 'contingent' should not be used. But neither could the government discourage men who wished to serve, and surely it would be a small enough thing to pay a portion of the cost. The recruitment of a thousand volunteers would be authorized. 'The Prime Minister,' ran the Order in Council as it was drafted on October 13, 'in view of the well-known desire of a great many Canadians who are ready to take service under such conditions, is of opinion that the moderate expenditure which would thus be involved for the equipment and transportation of such volunteers may readily be undertaken by the Government of Canada without summoning Parliament, especially as such expenditure, under such circumstances, cannot be regarded as a departure from the well-known principles of constitutional government and colonial practice, nor construed as a precedent for future action.'

The cabinet was still together, though hardly united. Tarte, the realist, had succumbed to political realities. Fighting to the last ditch for the 'no precedent' clause, which he still despised as a fiction, he had given the little at last to this English Canada which could take all. He was unforgiven and unforgiving, unchanged, and impossible to silence. He would never again be anything but a political liability in English Canada. But he was indispensable in Quebec and he would carry Quebec with him, sullenly acquiescent. That much of the coming battle, it seemed, was won.

There remained Ontario, loudly dissatisfied with grudging half-measures. Laurier's thoughts were already turning in that direction when some of the principal Quebec members arrived in Ottawa on the evening of the thirteenth. They had been summoned by Tarte as a last angry gesture and Laurier had not protested. He had no need to be shown the mood of Quebec but it would soothe Tarte a little and change nothing. The men who came would be presented with an accomplished fact and they would yield to it.

He was not surprised when Henri Bourassa walked in on him, accompanying distinguished elders. The meeting in Montreal had been a forewarning. Tarte's protégé would be difficult but he was still a young member. The Prime Minister's eyes were on the faces of the older men as they read the Order in Council. He could measure every emotion and share it, so far as he was left with any emotion at all. The matter had been decided, he told them, and the Order would be promulgated tomorrow. He was not surprised at the shrug and the weak little joke with which one of them passed it along to Bourassa. Since the wine was already poured there was nothing to do but drink. He was quite prepared for the stiffening in the younger man, and for the question: 'Mr. Laurier, do you take account of opinion in the province of Quebec?'

He smiled and shrugged. 'My dear Henri, the province of Quebec does not have opinions; it has only sentiments.'

There were more questions then, all from Bourassa, sharp and probing to the point of insult. He parried them restlessly, hardly knowing whether to be amused or annoyed. This gosling parliamentarian assumed the role of grand inquisitor as if by right and with rather too obvious relish. No, he denied, he had not said that troops could not be sent without the authority of parliament. He had said that he did not see how it could be done. A way had been found. The men were going as volunteers, not as an official contingent. The distinction was narrow, yes; certainly the intention was to avoid a debate in parliament. But a debate, in view of the mood of Ontario, might do irreparable harm. 'My dear Henri' – he stirred a little irritably as more questions followed – 'the circumstances are difficult.'

'It is because they are difficult that I ask you to remain faithful to your word. To govern is to have the courage, at a given moment, to risk power to save a principle.'

He found himself on his feet, not quite sure for an instant that he had heard correctly. The indrawn breath of the older men had been quite audible. He might have explained with some heat that he had been quite faithful to such words as he had uttered, that he had chosen the words with painful care. But for this sprig of Papineau, in spite of the smug self-righteousness, he still could feel only sympathy and affection. It was the business of a Prime Minister to be above anger and above these stinging platitudes that came so easily to the young and irresponsible. He walked round the desk and put a hand on Bourassa's shoulder. 'Ah my dear young friend, you have not a practical mind.'

The shoulder moved from under his hand. Bourassa could not straighten to the height of Laurier's six feet, and one had the suspicion that he resented it. Nothing else was lacking either in the manner or in the reply; a mantle was being assumed. 'If you decide on intervention, Mr. Laurier, you decide at the same time on the attitude which you prefer me to adopt; either to resign or to speak and vote against the ministry.' Five days later the resignation came. Tarte had advised against it as bad politics.

Perhaps it was more than that. The disciple seemed to have moved beyond the master. One had the uneasy impression that a new force was abroad.

2

ON OCTOBER 30, one day before Chamberlain's deadline, a force of 1,150 volunteers, already known officially and unofficially as the Canadian Contingent, sailed for South Africa. It was more than had been asked for but it was not going to be enough. Two months of fighting proved that the advance on Pretoria would be something other than an easy route-march. General Buller, the British Commander-in-Chief, would not eat his Christmas dinner in the Boers' capital. He and some of his fellow officers were revealing an incompetence worthy of the high days in the Crimea and they were facing men who knew their country and loved their well-oiled rifles. Kipling would soon be writing of the 'big men, gross men, heavens how they shoot!' and a somewhat subdued Empire entered the twentieth century with a serious war on its hands.

By January of 1900 a second Canadian contingent was on its way and Sir Donald Smith, now Lord Strathcona, was using some of the ample resources accruing to him from the C.P.R. to finance a troop of mounted infantry. Chamberlain's tone had changed from that of a man organizing a parade to that of a man who needed help, and Canada, at least, was calling some of the tune. Her contingents were not simply absorbed into the imperial forces but served as distinct units. Her volunteers were welcome. Sam Hughes was now blissfully fighting the Boers where he could find them and conducting his own war by correspondence against the never-to-be-forgiven General Hutton. The General was soon to join him, having made himself sufficiently obnoxious in Canada for the government to demand his removal. Either he would go, Minto had been informed, or the government would resign. The Prime Minister faced parliament, when it convened on February 1, relieved at least of the presence of Hutton and Hughes.

It was to be a war session and an election session; that much was sure. Laurier would have to go to the country in the fall and there were a good many clouds over the prospect. Tarte had accepted the policy on South Africa only to the extent of remaining in the cabinet. That spiked and thorny blessing was more than ever essential since Dansereau was at large again, earning six thousand dollars a year as editor of *La Presse* compared to the annual four thousand he had received as postmaster of Montreal. The new newspaper was powerful and well financed, officially independent, but slanting ever more definitely against participation in the war.

Only the thin partition of cabinet responsibility divided Tarte from Dansereau and held the spectre of a new *Bleu* alliance chained in the realms of nightmare. Nothing at all could prevent Tarte from expressing himself or allay his bitter vehemence. His *La Patrie* seemed to be at war with all the newspapers of English Canada, he was regularly burned in effigy in Ontario, and a more serious result had been the defection of Manitoba in December. There Hugh John Macdonald, the personable son of John A., had led the provincial Conservatives to victory over the diminished Greenway government. Tarte, the Liberal Empire-hater, had figured largely as a whipping-boy in the campaign and it was not reassuring to know that Joseph Martin's friends, always on the trail of Sifton and trumpeting new charges against his administration of the Yukon, had also played their part.

There was Bourassa in addition, still abetted by Tarte but moving in an orbit more and more his own. He seemed the man that Tarte would like to be if politics were not politics. Once resigned, he had acted with exemplary correctness. Presenting himself to the electors of Labelle as an independent candidate who opposed Laurier on nothing but participation in the war, he had been re-elected by acclamation. Laurier had made it a point to see that he was unopposed. He had noted the size of the crowds drawn to Bourassa's meetings, admired the quality of the speeches, and endeavoured to laugh them off. 'If you were twenty', he had told some of his worried Quebec elders, 'you would be cheering him.' It was true but hardly comforting when one thought of the leaven at work in that on-coming generation.

Nevertheless he felt himself sound in the country. War or not, prosperity was becoming a byword and prosperity made men reasonable. Quebec seethed but Quebec would accept the sending of the contingents. Ontario would only complain that Laurier had not done more, that he had been half-hearted. He had indeed, but the half of his heart had been given freely, at great risk and against great difficulties. The man who bestrode French Canada had gone to the utmost limit on behalf of English Canada and much should be given in return. Ontario, with the old Grit bedrock of fair-mindedness under the sound and fury, would see that. He intended to make her see it.

The occasion came on the afternoon and evening of March 13, after a worse six weeks in parliament than Laurier had expected. Reasonableness had been the one thing absent from the savage debates. Tupper had plunged for high Tory loyalism on the question of South Africa and his party had followed him in with all guns blazing. Laurier, first in the Jubilee parade, had been last in the Empire's time of need. Foster's long finger had pointed across the aisle and his beard had waggled at Tarte's. Tarte had eagerly responded. Gasping and grey, hardly able to keep his feet, stuttering in his broken English to make sure that every poisoned barb found its mark, he had had many Liberal colleagues squirming as angrily as Tories.

Bourassa, the newly-elected independent, had been ushered to his seat on opening day with the Minister of Public Works as his principal sponsor. The Speech from the Throne had hardly been read when he was on his feet demanding the immediate tabling of all correspondence between Laurier and Chamberlain. It had been produced benignly by the Prime Minister in response to 'my young friend's impatience', but the young friend had only returned to the attack. Canadian troops in South Africa were paid at imperial rates and parliament proposed to adjust them to the higher Canadian rates. Bourassa denied the right; these were imperial troops sent in despite of parliament. Legalistic, hair-splitting, adamant, and infuriating, he had held to his point, always in excellent English, while the shouts of 'small-mindedness' rose about him. When he stood up later to make an interjection in French the shouts changed to 'speak English' and he was launched on another tirade in defence of his right to use his mother tongue. The country outside was responding to the mood of parliament and French students and English students had been rioting in Montreal. Nothing had been omitted that might build up the tension of the House as the galleries began filling on the afternoon of March 13.

The motion before the members was Bourassa's motion, and it had been born of Tarte. It proposed that parliament, insisting on its sovereignty and independence, 'refuses consequently to consider the action of the government in relation to the South African war as a precedent which should commit this country to any action in the future. That the House further declares that it opposes any change in the political and military relations which exist at present between Canada and Great Britain unless such change is initiated by the sovereign will of parliament and sanctioned by the people of Canada.' A draft of the resolution had been lying in Laurier's desk for some months now and he had been expecting this day. It would result, he hoped, in considerable enlightenment to the country and the return of a chastened friend.

Bourassa had come to him fresh from Tarte, hot with anger at Chamberlain and contemptuous of the flimsy safeguard provided by the 'no precedent' clause in the Order in Council. By sending troops to South Africa under any pretext whatever Laurier had 'capitulated' – the word was to become wearily familiar – to imperialism and Ontario. Henceforth the door was open to every increasing demand made in the name of an all-embracing Empire, to that taxation without representation, that spending of money and blood in far-off wars, that had been a haunting fear in Quebec since the days of Mercier. The door must be slammed shut and bolted. A parliamentary statute must deny the poisonous precedent, stop Chamberlain in his tracks, and assert once more that Canada was her own mistress. Laurier had invited a draft of the resolution and Bourassa had complied. He had returned for his answer after a week of simmering eagerness, and the answer had been no. The resolution, said Laurier, where it was not redundant seemed likely to be inflammatory. As Prime Minister he could not propose it. It was of course Bourassa's privilege to propose it himself, and the way would be paved for him if he wished to do so. In that case, however, it was quite

CARTOONIST'S COMMENT ON BOER WAR POLICY

possible that Laurier would speak against it.

As Bourassa rose that afternoon to launch himself on a three-hour speech that would extend into the evening session, he was serving a purpose that would not be revealed to him until he was considerably wiser in the ways of politics. Not through any Machiavellian forethought, but simply from the way things had come about, he was cast in the role of lightning-rod and sounding-board for the Prime Minister. For all the speech-making and all the columns of print, Quebec's case had not yet been presented to the nation in a way the nation would heed. The Prime Minister could not do it because he was the Prime Minister, the man of all Canada. Tarte could not do it because he was Tarte, enmeshed in the old alliances and the old hostilities, with all the past clanking at his heels and all the fury of the present boiling about him. He would never represent to the English anything but the worst of Quebec. Bourassa was the best of Quebec, a Gallic Galahad clear and clean, free of all ties to the point of ostentation. The country would listen to him and hear the authentic voice of French Canada. It would not be changed but it might be sobered a little. It would know at least what a Prime Minister faced in his task of holding the nation together and if the worst came to the worst the young man was still expendable.

Not a vote had been changed by the time Bourassa sat down and Laurier rose. But the young man had emerged as a new presence in the country. Cool, dogmatic, and provocative, echoing and enlarging on Tarte yet always himself, clothing his mordant Frenchness in immaculate English, he had drawn the shape of the future out of the unchangeable past. Papineau was still here, but it was a saner, unbruised Papineau. This man accepted England, he accepted the household built on conquest, islanded in the new world. Yet he demanded of it with passionate hope and conviction the thing that had never been, an equal acceptance and embracing of the families of the two roots.

Not once during the three hours that Bourassa was on his feet had the House stirred or interrupted him. In and around the speech had hovered all the themes of Tarte, the parochial isolation, the dread of far-off wars, the resentful, legalistic demand to be called to the councils of an Empire that demanded money and blood, the unmistakable inference that such a demand would not be answered. No clause in an Order in Council, nor even his own resolution, would wipe out for Bourassa the effect of what had happened. 'The precedent, sir, is the accomplished fact.'

All the self-importance of the spoiled young politician, all his relish of the stir he was creating, was apparent. He was searing on the reasons for the war, on the purpose of colonial contingents, on the manoeuvres by which they had been obtained, and on the weakness of a government that had yielded to the pressure of Tory 'yellow journals'. Yet none of this was the heart either of the speech or of the man. 'I am a liberal of the British school. I am a disciple of Burke, Fox, Bright, of Gladstone.' This grandson of the old rebel stood on the premise of Confederation, he welcomed it, and he wished to share in all its fullness the union of the two peoples. But union it must be, with all that was implied or promised, free of the pressure of that other force always and forever drawing toward the imperial centre, seeking to tighten the Anglo-Saxon grip. 'I do not ask for independence now nor for a long time to come. It will be asked, then, what do I wish? I wish that the constitution of my country be respected as it is. . . . Mr. Chamberlain and his frantic disciples, and his unconscious followers both English and Canadian, are leading us toward a constitutional revolution the consequences of which no man can calculate. If new propositions have to be laid down touching the policy that is going to govern this country, neither the Colonial Secretary nor any member of a British government nor any representative of the imperial government in this country has the right to say what shall be the course of a free people. It is our duty as a free parliament representing the free opinion of the people to say what is going to be the policy of the people.'

Several hours of the evening session remained when he was finished and the Prime Minister made the most of them. It had been a long time since the House had heard such a challenge and it would be a long time again before it would hear such a reply. 'I put this question to my honourable friend,' said Laurier: 'What would be the condition of this country today if we had refused to obey the voice of public opinion?' The question remained unanswered and the argument seemed to prevail. At the end it was generally conceded that Laurier had won, and the vote bore him out. But the last echoes of the Jubilee had died in his ears as he sat down. Sir Wilfrid Laurier was Laurier of Canada again. And the man of all the nation was no longer wholly sure that he bestrode Quebec.

3

ON THAT same night of March 13 Tarte left for Europe, mainly to restore his health and nominally as High Commissioner for Canada to the Paris Exposition. Since the lofty title involved very little in the way of work he hoped to return refreshed for the election campaign in the fall. In the meantime, as the session dragged on with electioneering becoming steadily more open and vituperation more bitter, his absence was a blessed relief.

Bourassa was hardly stilled after his great day in court when Chamberlain renewed the pressure. The turn of the war had come and the end seemed to be approaching. Would Canada, he inquired through Minto, desire to have a voice in the post-war settlement? And would it not be opportune, at the close of such a war, to reconsider the proposal of a Colonial Council? To both suggestions the reply had a new coolness. Canada would not ask to take part in a peace conference, Laurier said, though she would attend if invited. As to the Colonial Council, if it were viewed principally as a measure for imperial defence, 'my conclusion is that the time has not come for any disturbance in the relations now existing between England and the colonies'.

The cold douche was administered through secret dispatches. In the House he stood up on June 7 to propose a resolution congratulating the Queen on the entrance of her troops into Pretoria. Tupper duly responded and all seemed to be going well when Bourassa rose to part the sea of loyal eloquence. He could not associate himself, he said, with congratulations to Her Majesty on an unjust war in which two hundred thousand troops had crushed a population of about the same number of poor peasants. 'I acknowledge the power of England, I admire the might of England, I admire many and many of the deeds that England has done throughout the world but, sir, this war will not add an ounce to the glory of the English flag.'

The cries of 'Shame!' reverberated from every wall. Foster leaped up to lead them and after ten minutes of complete uproar the whole House, except for two members, was on its feet drowning out Bourassa with 'God Save the Queen'. The Prime

Minister remained sitting to demonstrate his disapproval of conduct that defied the rules of the House and the authority of Mr. Speaker. Fielding sat staunchly beside him, though it was easy to see what he thought of Bourassa. Amid it all and for what it was worth Laurier could hold irritably to one crumb of comfort. The young man would sooner or later destroy himself because he did not know where to stop.

A week later another man, not so young, was stirring up quite irrelevant trouble at the other end of the country. It had been going on for some time but it was now rising to the point where it had to be dealt with. Joseph Martin, still rankled, still alternately bargaining and blustering for a federal appointment and always exploiting his nuisance value, was now leader of one of two deadlocked provincial parties in British Columbia. As governments tumbled and rose he seemed to be getting McInnes, the Lieutenant-Governor, into his toils and creating a situation of mild anarchy. All politics in British Columbia revolved at the moment around the exclusion of Japanese immigrants and it was not a question to be toyed with for the benefit of Joseph Martin. In May, under the Lieutenant-Governor's authority, he was governing through cabinet ministers who could not obtain election to the House. When a provincial election went against him and the McInnes-Martin alliance still showed a disposition to remain in control it became time to act. On June 19 Laurier pulled a telegraph blank from his secretary's desk and scrawled out in his own hand a message to the Honourable Thomas McInnes, whom he had promoted from the Senate three years before. 'It is the opinion of the government that the result of the appeal to the people of British Columbia makes it impossible for you to remain Lieutenant-Governor of British Columbia and that you should telegraph your resignation today.' It was a hard-handed solution by the man who had kept so jealous an eye on Macdonald the centralizer, but it was the end of McInnes and the end of Joseph Martin.

On July 18 the session came to its conclusion. On October 9 the eighth parliament was dissolved and the general election called. Sifton, who had been in Vienna through most of the year consulting an ear specialist, was now back. He was resigned to deafness, equipped with an ear trumpet, and assailed with new and more damaging charges over his administration of the Yukon. His position in the west was threatened and a threat to Sifton was a threat to the whole party.

Tarte was the threat in Ontario. He was back too, thirsting for the fray, with newly-renewed quarrels buzzing round his ears. Any hope that absence and illness would keep him out of trouble had soon gone by the board. He had lectured Paris on his view of imperial relations and had managed to sound, as his speeches came back duly garbled and mistranslated, like a new Lafayette on his way to war with the British. He had not liked his work, he had not been pleased with the exposition, and he had not liked the Parisians. He had grievances against Chamberlain and Chamberlain's 'English understrappers' and no one on either side of the Channel, according to Tarte, had treated him as the representative of a self-governing country. The French President Louvet had set out on a visit to the colonial pavilions without even informing Tarte and had presumed to come into the Canadian section by a side entrance leading from the Australian pavilion. 'I am not in the habit of receiving by my kitchen door,' Tarte had informed the advance guard and the President of France had been turned round and brought in by the front. All this had been heard and noted in English Canada. If Tarte's health had been improved by his voyage abroad, his public image had not.

In Laurier's correspondence with the member for Labelle the salutation 'My dear Henri' had now been replaced by 'My dear Bourassa'. The young man who read everything read the parliamentary reports from England and there had been a suggestion in the British House that Canada might take part in a peace conference with the Boers. Bourassa had leaped on it as proof that Laurier was engaged in new intriguings with Chamberlain. The Prime Minister had tartly denied it, and had added to his letter a faintly ominous postscript. Bourassa's attitude, he wrote, seemed to amount to 'a declaration of war to be held in reserve and launched at an appropriate time'.

The reply, on September 4, denied the allegation loftily. 'I have not yet contracted the habit of such opportunistic machinations.' It was far from being a gesture of forgiveness or a declaration of friendship. 'I wholly maintain the attitude I have adopted since your capitulation . . . my thoughts are clear, my convictions profound; I have fortified them by reflection and study; I reveal them completely as I hold them, without reticence and without exaggeration. I have therefore no fear of departing from the way on which I have set out. It will lead me nearer to you or farther away from you as you resist or submit to Chamberlain and his school. Exterior circumstances do not affect me, neither the insinuations and complaints of your valets who accuse me of combating you from ambition and spite, nor the temptations of Conservatives who urge me to make war on you, nor the violence of young hotheads who wish to cry "down with the English", nor the stupid fanaticism of the English who accuse me of stirring up a war of races. . . . Believe me if I open my heart to you it is not for the pleasure of making a display of virtue. But I detest ambiguous situations. It is so painful for me to dwell on the differences of opinion and principle which separate us that I at least wish to dissipate and prevent useless misunderstandings. If a complete political rupture must come I should wish that nothing had passed between us which two Christians and two men of honour would be able to regret.'

It was all clear enough, as was everything he wrote. It was all offensive enough, if one wished to take offence. As Prime Minister Laurier could hardly relish this state of well-watched tutelage that was offered rather than support. As a man who had spent most of his life among the snares of politicians, the violence of young hotheads, and the stupidity of fanatics, he was sceptical of any man's ability to stand so confidently free. Sooner or later Bourassa would lean and then plunge. The question was, which way? The young man who detested ambiguous situations had indeed created one.

In spite of everything, as the familiar election stir quickened about him, Laurier was not deeply concerned. On October 16 he dashed off a crisp note to Mulock. 'My brother, A. C. Laurier, who is our candidate for L'Assomption county, will send in his resignation as postmaster of Laurentides. I wish you to appoint in his place his son, Wilfrid Laurier.' Then, with the family's

'SIR CHARLES HAS A SHOCKING DISAGREEMENT WITH THE MOST EMINENT STATESMAN OF HIS ACQUAINTANCE!' CARTOON BY J. W. BENGOUGH IN THE TORONTO *Globe*, OCTOBER 17, 1900

importunities stilled and the Prime Minister's share of the patronage disposed of, it was time to embark on the campaign.

In French Canada he had Tarte, still mutinously loyal, utterly absorbed in the work of winning votes. To English Canada, in spite of Tarte, he stood at least as the imperialist *manqué*; Canadians had fought the Boers. 'Sir Wilfrid Laurier is too English for me,' Tupper was declaring in Quebec, while he reversed the coin in Ontario. The same game worked the other way and Tupper's time was over. There was the imperial preference to please the imperialists and there was prosperity to please everyone. The revenues were buoyant and Sifton's immigration policies had already settled seventy thousand new families in the west. The war in South Africa was decided if it was not ended, the country's thoughts were turning back on itself, and the country had been well governed.

By the small hours of November 8 the verdict was in. The loss of fourteen seats in Ontario was a little more than Laurier had expected but less than he might have feared. In Manitoba Sifton, fighting the battle of his life, had silenced his enemies on the Yukon charges and put a permanent crimp in the career of Hugh John Macdonald, who had stepped down from the provincial premiership to oppose him. Fifty-eight of the sixty-five Quebec seats had gone Liberal and the Maritime Provinces had not only rejected Foster but put an end to the political career of Sir Charles Tupper. With that great bulk removed from the scene only an innocuous lawyer, Robert Borden of Halifax, stood up as the leading Tory. One surveyed a clear horizon, almost too clear. There was Bourassa still to be thought of and there was *Les Débats*, the new Quebec newspaper, edited by half a dozen brilliant young men and openly Bourassa's champion. But Quebec was still Quebec and its young men did not change. How could a man who hoped to build for the future ever wish them to change? The newly-confirmed Prime Minister could only chuckle approvingly as he heard that the busiest distributor of *Les Débats* in the halls of Laval University was the twenty-year-old Armand Lavergne.

19

FORESHADOWINGS AND DEPARTURES

1901-1902

ON FEBRUARY 8, 1901, two days after the opening of the first session of the ninth parliament, Laurier stood up in the House to salute the closing of an age. Victoria had died on January 22 and, for good or ill, the world would no longer be the same. With the passing of that dowdy little symbol dikes seemed to fall away and walls crumble. One was suddenly conscious of the rushing rivers of change, long gathered and in full spate.

A month later the battle over the Boers, still dragging on in South Africa, was more or less brought to a close in the Canadian parliament. Bourassa, after a brilliant, scathing analysis of imperialism and all its works, moved a resolution requesting the British government to conclude an honourable peace on the basis of independence for the Boer states. Since nothing was more certain than that the Boer states would be annexed at the close of the war, the speech was merely another exercise in irritation and the speaker's accumulating rancours carried him on to the verge of imbecility. The war that had discredited and weakened the Empire had shortened Her Majesty's days. Bourassa had opposed it, he still opposed it; he refused to be 'an accomplice of murderers of the Queen'.

The House by this time was equally weary of Bourassa and the Boers. It was remarkable, Laurier could point out, that a man who had been so unready to send help to the British government should be so ready to send advice. A parliament newly in order under a restored government went on to deal with the affairs of a prosperous country. Robert Borden, now installed as leader of the opposition 'for one year', was as uncertain in his new place as he appeared to be temporary. On May 23 the short session came to a tranquil close and the Prime Minister faced a long summer brightened by the thought that Bourassa would be several thousand miles away. Later on, when reports from Dublin indicated that the young man's zest for speech-making had not been dulled on his first tour of Europe, he could comment tolerantly, 'Our friend Bourassa is a little skittish just now.'

There was a royal tour to prepare for, and the problem of Alaska returned to haunt July and August. By mid September, as Laurier went to Quebec to meet the Duke and Duchess of York, he was in a mood of irritable pessimism. The Americans had closed the door to settlement of the boundary question on his terms. The best he could hope for now was a treaty drawn in Washington. He did not like the look of the first draft and he liked still less the British readiness to accept it. Some of the terms would obviously have to be changed, they would all have to be arbitrated, and a stiff-necked board of arbiters fighting to the last ditch might save at least a way of ingress to the Yukon. He could find the men in Canada but the crucial voice as always would be that of the imperial mother. He was far from hopeful that in her present chastened condition, tarnished by war and hungry for American friendship, she would fight very hard for a strip of frozen coastline.

At Quebec he took up his duties as shepherd to the royal pair and moved on across the continent with them. Most of his correspondence for the next month went out 'from the Royal Train', and there was more than enough of it amid the daily harassment of thumping bands, ceremonial occasions, and loyal oratory. The tour had been clouded by shock even before it began, as an assassin's bullets brought down President McKinley. On September 19, five days after the President died of his wounds, there had to be a pause for a day of national mourning. The aggressive and unpredictable Theodore Roosevelt was now at the head of

American affairs. It was a new factor to be dealt with as the royal train turned back from Vancouver in early October. Laurier was assessing the change as the last salutes and the last fulsome farewells sounded in Quebec. He was still assessing it under the maples of Arthabaska when another strain arose.

Bourassa, bristling and refreshed by travel, had returned to an assault both on British imperialism and on American continentalism. He or his friends had hired the largest hall in Montreal for the occasion and the hall had been filled to overflowing. All too obviously, from now on, Bourassa would not be cramped within the walls of the nation's parliament.

The address had been prepared with more than his usual care, and was certainly destined to appear in printed form. Much of it was masterful and scholarly. It was firmly based on a real and poignant love for the best in English history and the best qualities of the English nation. 'To all those who, few though they be, were, out of a pure love of liberty, instrumental in securing and preserving to us political freedom our admiration and our gratitude are due without stint.' In the list of statesmen eulogized he included that very Gosford who had sent out a warrant for his grandfather sixty-four years earlier. But the fair-mindedness became single-mindedness, savagely vitriolic, crushingly and one-sidedly documented, when he turned on the new England of Chamberlain and Rhodes and the Boer War. Rampant imperialism had involved Canada, to its eternal danger and discredit, in an unjust struggle, and though the Prime Minister was exempted from much of the responsibility the exemption was hardly flattering. Laurier had really opposed the sending of troops, however weakly. His yielding had been the result of promises he had made during the excitement of the Jubilee, and 'to my mind it never occurred to the Prime Minister that in doing so he was going beyond a hearty acknowledgment of England's generous hospitality'.

He turned from that, another and different Bourassa, to examine his own nation. Canada was threatened on the one hand with an endless drain of money and men to support imperial adventures. She was threatened on the other by a creeping tide of pan-Americanism. Where was the refuge? It was not in independence, for the two races were not yet ready to live together. Freed of the restraining hand of the mother country, unfettered by the British North America Act, a domineering English majority would drive French Canadians into the arms of the United States. Bourassa did not wish for that. Neither did he wish to live as a French North American; the vision of his grandfather had no charms for him. He wished to live as a British subject under a constitution granted by an older, better England, and he wished for a new spirit within that constitution. 'A mutual regard for racial sympathies on both sides and a proper discharge of our exclusive duty to this land of ours, such is the only ground upon which it is possible for us to meet so as to work out our national problems. There are here neither masters nor valets; there are neither conquerors nor conquered ones; there are two partners.'

Who could quarrel with a word of it? The best notes of Papineau and Cartier and the Dorions and Mercier and of Laurier himself were all to be heard amid that stinging eloquence. Yet so was the other all-pervasive echo. 'There is nothing more unhistorical', said the newly-travelled philosopher who demanded a mutual regard for racial sympathies, 'than the legend which attributes to the Englishman an inherent aptitude for colonization and maritime pursuits. Owing to his stay-at-home propensities and his love of comfort, he feels a reluctance to go and settle abroad. From his slow temperament and uninventive mind, as from his insularity, he cannot adjust himself to the social and economic environments of other nations, unable as he is to understand them. Feeling uncomfortable abroad, he makes himself disliked. Is there under heaven one single spot where a born Englishman has endeared himself to his neighbours and reciprocated their love? This remark I make in no spirit of disparagement, those characteristics of the stock being a mere result of atavism. When you meet him in his proper environment at home, the Englishman evinces qualities political, social, and individual which make of him a most affable and estimable man. To sum up, I might say that as a host he proves the most charming, and as a neighbour the most execrable of all men.'

'If you were twenty you would cheer him.' The words came

wryly back, still true. But the cheers were all French, the men who cheered were younger than the speaker, and Bourassa had returned from Europe more himself. The eyes still looked on history through the lenses of the parish pedant and the view was still delivered in the tone of the parish boor. This was unquestionably a voice of the future and the twentieth century came on, still to be lived in company with the execrable neighbour race. The Victorian gentleman in Arthabaska, now moving toward the close of his sixtieth year, read the speech several times and shook his head.

2

WITH NOVEMBER 20 came the birthday congratulations. He received them in Ottawa, for Arthabaska was now little more than a place of rest and recuperation, to be come to and departed from with inescapable commotion. There was always a great stir when he arrived at Victoriaville station and another stir when he left. Everywhere he moved now he seemed to move amid a great running-about of officials and under hundreds of staring eyes. It was all very fatiguing, it all required a certain composed posturing; and, probed to depths he did not trouble to search, he might have confessed he liked it.

Distinction he had always had and now authority was settling on him familiarly and gracefully. The wavy hair was whitening and giving back around the wide dome of the forehead. The prominent nose thrust out, oddly reminiscent, like much else in his manner and gestures, of John A. Macdonald. The mouth was all his own, masterful, firm, and smiling, always a little enigmatic. When he sat in council men looked into the clear directness of those wide-set eyes and saw only what they wished to see; the eyes themselves told nothing. When he walked the corridors of the House or rose beside his desk, tall and still slender, with the immaculate elegance speaking a little of the past, it was always an occasion for the watchers. He was quite aware of it, not displeased by it, and never allowed it to change the easy familiarity with which he moved from desk to desk during breaks in the sittings, dropping down for a chat here, flinging an arm over a member's shoulder there.

The rhythm of the sessions had become the rhythm of his life, and in a sense at least the Commons of Canada was his real home. He left exhausted at each prorogation and returned for each opening with an undiminished relish. Quizzical about everything and cynical about much, he yet moved through the ceremonial observances of parliament with respectful grace and was wholly devoted to the realities. There were few junior members more regular in their attendance than the Prime Minister. During long, somnolent hours while back-benchers filled up Hansard for the benefit of their constituents at home he sat patiently in his place, not always listening. Page-boys watched alertly at such times for the snap of his fingers which would send them running for the dictionary. When it came he would open it and settle back to run a finger down the pages, tirelessly absorbing the riches of that English language that was now, according to some of his French-Canadian enemies, more familiar to him than his own.

When debate sharpened he would look up alertly and set the book aside. A man on his feet in a remote corner of the House would often be flattered to see the Prime Minister lean forward with a hand to his ear to hear better. Sometimes annoyance would corrugate his forehead into barely perceptible wrinkles. It was the one sign that every member recognized.

The dangerous moments and the late-night sittings always brought Zoë into the gallery above him. To older members she was almost as familiar as he was, a devoted wife knitting her way through the calms, a shrewdly knowledgeable politician ready and watchful at the first sign of a storm. In calm or storm, as the Speaker rose and the benches began to empty at a sitting's end, she was always at Laurier's side to help him on with his coat, see to the knot in his scarf, and sometimes persuade him to a walk home.

Her sight was failing and she no longer read easily. Because of that the Laurier household, equipped now with cook, butler, maids, and a valet for the master, had acquired another member. Yvonne Coutu, the daughter of Emma Gauthier who had been married at Zoë's side, now served as quasi-secretary to Sir Wilfrid and companion to his lady. She would be for both of them throughout the rest of their lives a happy link with a past that neither had relinquished.

Because the Prime Minister wished to know every side of everything he was always approachable in his office, and the weekly 'at homes' were already becoming famous. For all but the irreconcilable, on those Sunday evenings, party divisions were forgotten and even politics seemed to retire to the background. Tories and Grits, *Rouges* and *Bleus*, and people of no opinion from the length and breadth of the country gathered in the salon, mingled at the card-tables, and sang round Zoë at the piano. The host moved among them, usually with children at his heels, stimulating the course and absorbing the gist of every conversation. By the time he retired for his nightly hours in the study he had taken away much and left behind a glow that softened the harsh light on parliament hill. There was even more powerful magic in the small and intimate dinners with which every cabinet minister was familiar and which every private member enjoyed at least once a year. Through all of it and on every occasion, the hovering interests swarming at the door met with a frosty welcome if they crept in. The urgent adviser or the aggrieved petitioner, snatching at a precious moment, received short if smiling shrift. The matter was certainly important and would be discussed at the proper time. 'I promised you that? Oh well, I promise it still.'

He had moved inevitably into a new phase of the relationship with Emilie Lavergne. She pouted now because Joseph was not being advanced in the judiciary. More importantly, she worried about Armand and expected her illustrious friend to share the worries. The boy was indeed a handful, as Laurier discovered after one of the long avuncular talks which were now becoming rarer. The affectionate adolescent had become the graduate law student, difficult, critical, and embarked on a course of his own. His mother's Englishness seemed only to confirm his Frenchness. If he had now been moved grudgingly to acquire the second tongue it was merely to use it as a weapon. His solution for the questions of the day was to 'throw the English into the St. Lawrence'. At the same time he was not to be divorced from the cloudy radiance hovering over his antecedents. He shouted for Bourassa but he combed his hair like Laurier. He was undoubtedly brilliant, certainly destined for politics, and certain to be a problem when his day arrived.

Zoë's days were as crowded as Laurier's now, and if the first oneness of youth had never quite returned it was replaced by an unscarred acceptance of their different roles. Graceful under her title, Lady Laurier accumulated chairmanships, addressed women's meetings, and encouraged good works. In her home the great and the little were as much at their ease as the visitors of long ago had been in the three rooms at Dr. Poisson's, and some of them were still the same people. She followed the interplay of politicians with an ardour and a truculence that Laurier could never quite equal and with a female point of view that he sometimes deplored. A supporter was a friend and an opponent an enemy, to be treated as such. She had a good old-fashioned view of power and patronage; it was meant to be used. No cabinet minister was safe from her urgings in support of a friend and most of them submitted, usually at small cost to the country. Most of the importunings were concerned with would-be clerks, stenographers, or postmistresses, all burdened with the aging mothers, invalid relatives, or ne'er-do-well husbands about whom one heard so incessantly in this place. Lady Laurier, rampant in support of them, was a formidably persistent suppliant.

At home in her writing-room, with the little dogs and kittens climbing over her knees and Yvonne Coutu beside her to read through the quiet hours, she was still the Zoë Lafontaine who had left St-Louis street for Mont Christo. 'If we do not see each other as often as before,' she wrote to Yvonne's aunt, the Hannah Gauthier of the old days, 'it is because I belong to everyone and to no one in particular. I would rather be the wife of a simple avocat in Arthabaska. It was the best time of my life.'

Laurier himself often spoke and wrote in that vein. Yet it was merely the nostalgia of a busy man relaxing for a moment and conscious of the swift flow of the years. He would not have changed the past and he felt no drawing back from new horizons. Life for the last five years had been almost as good as life could be, gracious and gracefully lived on the highest pinnacle. He had had health, the best health he had ever known. He had had a richness and breadth of experience that made it hard to recognize the man of five years before. He had had power and had used it with purpose. The new lease on power seemed proof that he had used it well. He moved and manoeuvred men with easy sureness and under his hand, as the sum of all manoeuvrings, the country grew to his mould. In spite of incessant drudgery and the drabness behind the façade it was a good life, a life of work that promised to have value. He was wholly committed to it now, utterly absorbed in it.

From among the mound of birthday congratulations the letters of the old favourites were singled out first. Pacaud wrote as always, a more prosperous Pacaud now, freed of his debts and judgments but changed in little else, certainly unchanged toward Laurier. 'Yes,' Laurier replied: 'Here I am at sixty. My health is good. There probably remain some worth-while years to me, though evidently it is the beginning of the end.' He said the same to David, with a glance at the pitfalls round him. 'To how many reverses I am exposed! Perhaps I may regret having lived too long.'

It was Willison's turn next day, the Willison who had been twenty years a friend, who was now writing his friend's biography, and who still somehow possessed the gift of striking the wrong note. 'I have no desire to live to "a good old age",' Laurier replied to that wish. 'So long as my health continues as it is now, and that I can work, I am quite willing to live even as long as Methuselah. But at the first sign of weakening let Providence, which has ever been kind to me, take me away. Nothing so sad as to survive oneself.'

3

ELEVEN MONTHS later he came home on a ship from Europe as the walking ghost of his fears. The ship was stopped at Rimouski to spare him the rest of the river and he took the train for Quebec. He stepped to the platform there, leaning on Zoë's arm in the crisp afternoon sunshine of October 18, 1902, and a soft, dismayed murmur ran through the watching crowd. At the first sight of him in Ottawa a few days later Robert Borden, the friendly and admiring enemy, 'was so greatly shocked that I averted my gaze'.

From the beginning of the session in February of that year Laurier had felt, and had tried unsuccessfully to conceal, the premonitions of decaying strength. He had been inclined to blame them on the ordeal that lay ahead. The accession of Edward VII meant a coronation in June, and the coronation meant a colonial conference. He would be facing a Chamberlain ever more urgently bent on the old plans while behind him Bourassa's oratory steeled a new Quebec. The resentments of the speech in Montreal had now spilled over onto Canadian politicians, corrupted by imperial honours, all playing the imperial game, competing in the English provinces for 'the prize of loyalty' while they claimed in Quebec to have done as little as possible. 'Of sole devotion to Canadian interests we hear no more . . . the only point in real dispute between both parties is which will eat the biggest piece of the jingo pie. All this, of course, does not prevent them from selling Canada wholesale to American railway magnates.'

Faced with this and much more, Laurier had delivered some flat statements before he left for England. Canada had no suggestions to offer for the conference's agenda. On commercial matters and trade she was prepared, as always, to negotiate. She did not consider that any political reorganization of the Empire was called for. As to proposals for imperial defence: 'There is a school abroad, there is a school in England and in Canada, a school which is perhaps represented on the floor of this parliament, which wants to bring Canada into the vortex of militarism which is now the curse and the blight of Europe. I am not prepared to endorse any such policy.'

'For us,' Dansereau had written in *La Presse*, 'this is the end of militarism.' Even Bourassa had been reduced to a watchful silence. Yet once in London, where everything was dragged out and confused by the attack of appendicitis that delayed the King's coronation for six weeks, it was as if Laurier had never spoken. Chamberlain remained convinced that the Boer War, just victoriously concluded, had drawn the colonies together in a surge of martial enthusiasm. It had certainly damaged the reputation and strained the resources of the Empire. 'The weary Titan' staggered 'under the too vast orb of his fate' and every lightest word from the days of the Jubilee was to be called in as a promissory note. Far more directly than in 1897, with the army and navy at his side, Chamberlain renewed the pressure not only for his imperial *zollverein* but for the establishment of an imperial council and for definite pledges of military and naval contributions.

He had, from his viewpoint, good and compelling reasons. The Victorian Empire, radiant, righteous, and omnipotent, seemed already a part of the past. There would never again be a Jubilee like that of 1897. Britannia had wrestled the Boers to their knees with no credit to herself and at staggering cost. The world had glared as she fought and the world had not stood still. The United States, raucous and hostile, always on the move, was threatening to change the very shape of the map with its plans for a canal through the Nicaraguan isthmus that would link the Atlantic with the Pacific. There would be new streams of commerce to compete with the imperial flood that rolled through Suez. Signor Marconi, in Canada and Newfoundland, was negotiating for a station at which to test his wireless signalling device. It had been successful in Europe and if it succeeded in a wider field the ancient barriers of time and distance, breached already by the telegraph and the railways and the fast steamship lines, would be breached again. All the affairs of earth were moving at a quickened pace and the mood was not benignant. Europe's imperial colonizers were seeking to outdo England while they reproached her for her successes. Their climbing tariff walls were threatening to silence her boast of free trade with all the nations. The Germany of the new Kaiser, trumpeting and belligerent, had launched itself on a shipbuilding program that in half a dozen years would pose the ultimate threat to British naval supremacy. Everywhere about him, as the world's clock ticked on, Chamberlain's vision of armed imperial unity acquired in his eyes a new justification and a new urgency. Yet at the same time it was becoming less and less attractive to the peoples he hoped to recruit.

As the meetings began, the plan for an imperial council went down first. For colonies whose local parliaments were absorbed in their own problems and who fretted at the last light touch of imperial reins there was no attraction in the thought of 'a new government with large powers of taxation and legislation over countries separated by thousands of miles'. The imperial *zollverein* fell next. Neither Canada in North America nor Australia in the Pacific nor any of the lesser colonies was prepared to shut itself off from the rest of the world's trade behind the tariffs of a closed Empire. The hardest battles came on the question of defence, and it was through these interminable sessions that Laurier, suave, elusive, growing greyer each day, stood frequently alone and always in the same place.

The smaller colonies were gradually wheedled out of a little money. Australia, already pledged for contributions to the imperial navy, reluctantly agreed to continue them. Canada would give nothing. She would be on hand, Laurier said as he had said before, in a time of great and common emergency. She would soon have to establish a small naval force for the protection of her own coasts. But she would not contribute either in ships, money, or men to the imperial flotillas and the imperial striking forces that were to be available for any cause, at any time, anywhere in the world.

Chamberlain expressed a lofty surprise at his attitude. Laurier was surprised at Chamberlain's surprise. In the Boer War, as in a host of other little wars, the Empire's interest had really been Great Britain's interest. Canada, like Australia and the other colonies, had interests of her own. She reserved, in all loyalty and duty, the right to judge and act on them.

It was the middle of August before the King was crowned and Chamberlain had given up. The coronation ceremonies had been as lavish as those of five years before and some of the marching regiments had worn new battle honours, but much of the magic was gone. Laurier had refused a peerage and evaded every commitment. His banquet eloquence had had a cooler, more guarded note. The manner of the Colonial Secretary had grown chill as the 'icy wind from Canadian snows' reached him. Chamberlain did not read the French-Canadian press, he did not see the mail that poured into the suite of the Canadian Prime Minister. He looked into that tired, unyielding face and saw only the stubbornness of an unassimilated foreigner. He was not notably changed to find, at a private discussion arranged by Laurier, that Fielding and three other English-Canadian colleagues who happened to be in London were all of Laurier's view. The courteous Frenchman was still a slippery customer. 'I would rather do business with a cad who knows his own mind,' Chamberlain confided to Lady Minto. To Jameson of the Jameson raid, also fuming in London, 'the damn dancin' master' had 'bitched the whole show'.

By that time none of it seemed to matter. The carriage with its footmen in royal livery still drew up at the door of the Cecil Hotel. Laurier could hardly walk to it unaided. There were the last days in London to be lived through and formal engagements in Paris and in Rome. He fulfilled them gracefully and effectively but he lived with gasping weakness in a blur of pain. He went on to the Channel Islands and to Switzerland but the search now was for rest and for the doctor who could put a name to his ailment. The weeks of harrying negotiation had been worse than he feared. There had been the delay of the King's illness and the unrelenting round of the functions arranged to fill it. Now, from Canada, had come a barrage of letters, cables, and newspapers to deliver the final stroke. The six good years had ended, for the government and the man. For the moment he could think only of the man. It seemed that all his functions were threatened with collapse together, and not from the old enemy always lurking in the shadows. The word 'cancer' now haunted the consultations.

It was six weeks before he could face the voyage home and there was no rest to be looked for there. Government must be thought of now. For all his efforts the secret of his condition had not been kept. It had been suspected in London, rumoured in Canada, and to one alert ear it had been the call for action. The Ontario newspapers had called Tarte 'master of the administration' at the last election, and Tarte had rather liked it. 'Shall Tarte rule?' had been a hackneyed cry of the stumps. It was now a real question.

Even before he left Canada Laurier had seen the question

taking shape. The more he responded to the tug of the wide country the more Tarte dragged him back. The hectoring Frenchness that had barked down the English cabinet ministers had begun to be applied to the chief. Tarte's eye ranged as broadly as Laurier's, but it was still the eye of the party politician with the weight of Quebec behind him. He was jealous of Sifton and half resentful of the settlement of the west itself. The country was spending millions 'to fill Manitoba and the territories with foreigners of whom a good part are not worth much'. Why should there not be more for the colonization societies of Quebec, whether or not they accomplished anything? 'I assure you that if I were in opposition or even a private member I would force your government to share a little more.'

The letter had followed Laurier to London in June. It had not unduly disturbed him. The theme was only one of the little man's varied complaints and the tone was becoming familiar. It was the tone of a politician who had reached his limits and was chafed by them. Neither colonization nor Quebec had brought the final break, but simple opportunity. Late in July, as the rumours came from London, Tarte seemed to have convinced himself that Laurier's end was near. He had leaped for the emptying chair with the ruthless, one-eyed directness that had marked him all his life. He commanded Quebec, he intended to win Ontario on a program of high protection. Ontario was the province of the great industrialists who knew no flag but money. Their cheque-books would wash Tarte clean of the stains of the Boer War and their weight would swing the rest of the country to him. 'Laurier is better loved, but I have the great interests behind me.'

There was, as usual, a gritty core of conviction at the base of his motives. As Minister of Public Works he travelled from coast to coast, dealing with big men, often respected by them, chafed as they were by American competition. He had sat as a mutinous high-protectionist in a low-protection cabinet. He had always preferred smoke-stacks and machines to wheat-fields, always seen big business as the final arbiter in the country. Now, with demonic energy and dismaying success, he had ranged big business behind him. The headlines of every newspaper told the story.

The furious protests of Cartwright and Sifton and Fisher and Mulock and Fielding reinforced it. Thousands of workers everywhere in industrial Ontario had poured out of their factories to hear Tarte's speeches. Hundreds of manufacturers had cheered him at their banquets. If he were master of the administration, ran his theme, he would build a tariff wall as high as the Americans'. He would outbuild the Americans in canals, harbours, ships. He would 'save to Canada the profit of the exportation of her resources and build up a nation here'. J. Israel Tarte, assured that the captain was gone, saw the helm of government swinging within his grasp. He was out to embark alone on a new National Policy.

On October 18 the man with the ghastly face limped across the railway platform at Quebec and took the train for Ottawa. The next day he went to Tarte and a day later it was over. He would hear nothing of the tariff, nothing of the danger from Ontario, nothing of his own position. The one question at issue was the responsibility of ministers within the frame of cabinet government. 'My dear Tarte,' ran the letter that closed the exchange; 'Having expressed to you my well-settled opinion upon the consequences of your recent attitude, my first duty was to wait upon His Excellency the Governor General to inform him that I was obliged to demand the resignation of your portfolio.'

It was clean and sharp and costly, and time would present the bill. 'So long as I have Tarte and Sifton with me,' Laurier had once said, 'I shall be master of Canada.' He now had Sifton alone.

20

'WE CANNOT WAIT BECAUSE TIME DOES NOT WAIT'

1902-1903

THE AFFAIRS of the country rushed on and the tangled reins were waiting. For three weeks they seemed too heavy to take up. Tarte was gone but the damage that Tarte had done was not repaired. Tariffs and protection were buzzing in the air again. The question of Alaska remained, with prospects steadily darkening. There were hints from England that the European powers hoped for a boundary dispute that would open a new rift between Washington and London; it must be avoided, and avoided in all probability at the expense of colonial claims. The western prairies could no longer be emptied of their wheat by the boxcars of the C.P.R. They were 'a hopper too big for the spout'; there would have to be another railway. The sick man thought of the giant struggle that had built the first and the thought overwhelmed him. The whole weight of government overwhelmed him. He had spoken of resignation on the voyage home, and he still spoke of it.

Zoë was not deceived. Fielding, the chosen heir, was quietly and incisively firm: Laurier could not be replaced. The torrent of paper still flowed over the study desk. The stream of visitors came to the huddled form in the study chair. Government went on.

By November 11 the genial party whip James Sutherland had moved into Tarte's office. J. R. F. Préfontaine of Montreal had been given Sutherland's place. Neither alone nor both together quite filled the gap. Sutherland was the party organizer and the vote-getter of Ontario. Préfontaine was a lesser Tarte, with all the little man's weaknesses and none of his strength. There would be less force in the cabinet now but there would be less trouble. These men were manageable.

It was no longer the cabinet of the first days. Fielding, the unchangeable, remained but Mowat and Davies were gone. Mills had been gracefully eased from the ministry of Justice to the Supreme Court bench and Charles Fitzpatrick had taken his place. Cartwright was aging, Mulock was cooling and stiffening, and Blair had become a dangerous enigma. No less than Tarte, he had always allowed his politics to confuse policy. With a new railway looming there could be no such confusion now.

Even of Sifton Laurier was no longer sure. Sifton had wanted the ministry of Justice and the aura that surrounded it; he detested the man who had got it. Fitzpatrick made a profession of Catholic piety and he had dealt with the Pope on the schools of Manitoba, from the wrong side of the question. To Sifton, Fitzpatrick's appointment was the reward for his work in Rome, a new knitting together of powerful co-religionists. Tired of the west, tired of his reputation as a political hatchet man and a maker of dubious deals, he still went on with his work, efficient and indispensable. But there was a new edge to his manner and a new strain in council. The barbed scraps of the smoking-rooms came drifting to the leader's ear. 'As long as Sifton is in the cabinet,' Fitzpatrick was said to have said, 'we are sitting on a powder keg.' 'I have always known', came the rumoured reply from Sifton, 'that Fitzpatrick carries a knife in his boot for me.'

There had been strength enough for the patching up of the ministry, but it failed as the work was finished. Laurier, the doctors decided, was not threatened with cancer, but asthma came instead, leaving him breathless and gasping at the slightest effort. On November 12 he left with Zoë for Hot Springs, Virginia. There was an amicable note from Tarte, sending him off, and he replied in the same vein. 'I believe there is nothing gravely wrong with me, but I am absolutely certain that there is something which doesn't go properly.' The first mail to Hot

Springs brought several pages of advice from Sam Hughes, temporarily a friend again and this time, happily, concerned with the body of Laurier rather than the body politic. 'My dear Sam,' he replied, 'I am not dead yet, nor do I intend to give up the fight. I have tried everything that you suggested except buttermilk.'

To the last remedy he could not steel himself, but by mid December he seemed stronger. Roosevelt and Hay, the American Secretary of State, were pressing in their wish for an interview on the subject of Alaska and he risked the trip to Washington. He returned to Virginia chilled by the conversation and exhausted by the effort. A week later, still unable to face a Canadian Christmas, he took the train for Florida.

'I see with relief the passing of this year,' he wrote to Pacaud from St. Augustine on January 2, 1903. 'I have really been very sick and at one time I believed it was all up with me.' The asthma remained with him and henceforth every graceful move would be made with elaborate care. The smiling apology, 'I'm a lazy dog,' would become familiar. But he was anxious now to be home and in one respect at least the climate at home had altered. He had passed along to Bourassa the full report of proceedings showing the attitude he had taken at the colonial conference, and he was no longer suspect as a secret ally of Chamberlain. 'Now that the procession of boot-lickers has passed,' the young man wrote in his inimitable vein, 'permit me to say that I become again your firm and sincere supporter. And so long as you maintain this attitude I shall support you with all my strength.'

It was a good note to come home on and the snows of Arthabaska did not change it. 'I am now in very good health,' he reported to Willison on January 13. 'Happily there is before me now no burning question, no irritating problem. The only thing to do is push forward as fast as possible the development of the country.'

2

He formulated his plans with no such clear horizon nor in any such glow of health. It had become politic now to put the best foot forward with Willison. The editor of the Toronto *Globe* had crossed to the Toronto *News*, and whatever the reason for the change it was a step away from Laurier. Officially independent, and always leaning in a crisis toward stout British conservatism, the *News* was now owned by the millionaire meat-packer Joseph Wesley Flavelle, whose record matched its own. Willison at the new desk, while he would certainly not be inclined to make capital of his old friend's physical or political ailments, would be steeped in a Tory atmosphere and supported by Tory money. It would no longer do to tempt him.

Yet if the optimism was a little forced the plans were real enough. The very problems were for the most part only the fruits of success. The filled-up lands along the line of the C.P.R. were producing more grain than the C.P.R. could handle. In 1901 Manitoba had harvested fifty million bushels of wheat. Within five years that figure would probably double. The territories to the west of Manitoba were becoming another granary. The flood of immigration was rippling out into new country along the patchwork of branch lines that William Mackenzie and Donald A. Mann, those incredible westerners, were putting together as the Canadian Northern Railway. Nor did the seeping wave of humanity stop where the branches stopped. There were homesteads far from steel and there were thousands of would-be farmers who had been dumped into the west and were still idle, not from lack of land but from lack of means to move the wheat they wished to grow. Obviously and clamorously, the answer to all this was another railway.

It was going to be built and Laurier intended that it should be begun this year. Every consideration seemed to heighten the urgency. The west could not be allowed to choke on its own riches. Idle men in such a country were not only a tragic absurdity; they were a labour force on the ground ready and eager to lay the steel they needed. The country could not grow ribbon-thin along the spine of the C.P.R.; it had to be given breadth as well as length. There was the United States to be thought of, the same uncomfortable neighbour it had been in the days of Macdonald; and more and more now Laurier thought of it with the same resentment and fear.

The Americans were probably going to have their way on the question of the Alaska boundary. They certainly had things all their way with trade. While their own tariffs shut out Canadian wheat and manufactures they were still infuriatingly ready to threaten reprisals at the least suggestion of expanding the preference with England. It was railways, moreover, that gave them their best club. The Canadian Pacific now operated 1,500 miles of subsidiary lines in the United States and emptied much of its traffic through Boston or New York rather than Montreal. It was dependent on 222 miles of line crossing the state of Maine to reach the eastern seaboard. The Grand Trunk crossed 175 miles of American territory to reach its terminus at Portland. Even the Canadian Northern, which ran for 45 miles through the state of Minnesota, operated to that extent by courtesy of the Americans and at the mercy of the bonding privilege. It was only the trains of the Intercolonial, badly managed, badly routed, rambling down to the sea from Montreal, that could not be stopped somewhere along their way by an American customs officer.

All this Laurier was determined to change in the changing of the west. Nor was he thinking of the west alone. There was good farmland in northern Ontario, hardly touched yet. There were interminable stands of fine timber, and prospectors were bringing in more than hints of immense mineral resources. Pulpwood, water power, ores, everything that now figured in the new calculations of businessmen demanded rails to serve it. Ontario had to be thought of and, even more, Quebec.

Quebec's northland was bleaker than Ontario's, but it was also less explored. Who was to say what the prospectors might find? Beyond that and above it were the other considerations. Quebec, in the building of the C.P.R., had been an acquiescent partner. The benefits were apparent in the great homes on Mount Royal and the enrichment of Montreal, but there was another side to the picture. The opening up of the prairies had shifted the balance of population against French Canada. Quebec's hopes for the colonization of her own raw territories had faltered or stood still, while her resentment grew. Tarte's voice was not the only one raised against the vast spending in the west on foreigners who were not worth much. All this might be answered now, and answered with the new railway.

Quebec had had its own plan for something like eight years, promoted by a syndicate of local capitalists. A new transcontinental, in opening up northern Canada, was to open up northern Quebec, redressing the old imbalance. The project appealed to the politician, it appealed to the colonizing clergy, it had many attractions for the gambling man of business. Not many such men had invested their money yet; the plan was almost at a standstill but it was far from dead. No new plan, if it was to have the support of Quebec, could afford to ignore the old. The first maps from which Laurier acquired his picture of a route were those of the old Quebec project.

They were impressive enough, and they had impressed Van Horne of the C.P.R. as well as Sir Sandford Fleming, greatest of railway surveyors. For every reason they impressed Laurier. The line of the route climbed from Quebec City westward into the timber and clay lands of northern Quebec and northern Ontario, running along to touch the southern end of James Bay and the northern end of Lake Winnipeg. It crossed the Peace River district, drove up through the Rockies at the Peace River pass, and dropped down to the Pacific at the harbour of Port Simpson on the British Columbia coast, just at the head of the Queen Charlotte Islands and five hundred miles north of Vancouver. Such a line would be much more than a second spout to empty the prairie hopper. It would not duplicate the C.P.R. but complement it. It would make Quebec City a seaport terminal rivalling Montreal. It would open up the hinterlands of northern Quebec and northern Ontario. Following westward along the highest limit of arable land, pulling new cities from the northern soil, it would broaden the country along the whole of its length by something like three hundred miles.

The Prime Minister was well enough aware that trains do not run on maps, even when the maps are accurate. Much of the route was only roughly surveyed, all of it was wild and difficult, and there might be drastic changes. There was also the question of a leg to reach the Atlantic. When one looked eastward from Quebec City the difficulties were more with politics than with topography. The best and most direct line from Quebec to the sea was that of the Grand Trunk, but its terminus was Portland, Maine. A port on Canadian soil was of the very essence of any new plan. The Intercolonial was Canadian end-to-end and wandered eventually into both Saint John and Halifax, but nearly a fifth of its length was political mileage that had been piled on as handouts to the lucky constituencies of thirty years before. There were surely other routes and better routes, and justification for them. Laurier, with his imagination fired by the prospect to the west, was soon and easily convinced that a new, more direct line should complete the transcontinental from Quebec to the sea.

The air was already thick with building proposals. Not only Blair but every other cabinet minister seemed to have his plan. Of the existing railways only the C.P.R. stood watchfully aside, ruled out by the fear of monopoly. So far as Laurier was concerned there was one obvious plan and two companies to be considered. The Grand Trunk, with three thousand miles of well-built lines in the east, had pushed westward as far as North Bay. Mackenzie and Mann's Canadian Northern, already linked up from Edmonton to Port Arthur, was feeling out around the Great Lakes at one end and toward the Pacific at the other. The two companies should be persuaded to join hands and out of the merger build the complete line.

There would be much to justify to the country, notably that northern routing through the barren Quebec wilderness. It made no sense to the English businessman always on the search for easy territory and quick profits. But the English businessman took the support of Quebec for granted. A Prime Minister, particularly a Prime Minister from Quebec, could not. Quebec's support would have to be earned and paid for by the prospect, however remote, of the development of her own north.

In addition to that there would be every other difficulty inseparable from railways and politics. Members from coast to coast would be shouting the claims of their constituencies for a share of the mileage. Each railway would be out for itself with every form of pressure, and there would be politicians to help them. One politician, Laurier was determined, would not be given the chance. He did not like Blair's connections in the Maritimes and he did not trust Blair's friendship with Mackenzie and Mann, the most inveterate political manipulators in the country. Laurier would have to deal with those two because they were also miraculous builders, but he would deal alone. However outrageous the procedure and however embarrassing the result, the Minister of Railways on this occasion would be left to stand on the sidelines and await a *fait accompli*. The experience was no longer rare in the Laurier administration.

If he was to be a Macdonald without a Tupper, Laurier intended also to be a Macdonald without a Pacific scandal. He would listen to Sifton and Fielding and to Cartwright and Mulock and the other men he trusted. He would listen, for that matter, to Blair. The negotiations, however, he intended to handle himself. Before the bill was introduced he intended to establish the Railway Commission that had been demanded for a long time as the controlling authority over all rates and services. He intended to set up another commission, completely impartial and preferably with Van Horne at the head of it, to report on all the transport needs of the nation, by road, rail, and water. But the railway bill would be passed and the survey parties out before either commission was functioning. The need for a second transcontinental was after all clear, paramount, and immediate; details could be changed later. If the cart seemed before the horse in the parliamentary procedure there were good and sufficient reasons. Part of a Prime Minister's business was to assess moods, seize opportunities, and win elections. With seven fat years behind him and a mighty project ahead, he intended to go to the country.

3

IN MID FEBRUARY, a month before parliament opened, his growing fears for Alaska were newly confirmed. Washington's original treaty, a little improved by revision, had had to be accepted. That done, everything depended on the arbiters who were to interpret its maze of clauses and translate them into an actual boundary line. There were to be three Americans, two Canadians, and one British member on the board of arbiters. The prospect of deadlock was obvious and was only a little relieved by the condition that each arbiter 'should first subscribe on oath that he would impartially consider the arguments and evidence presented'.

As usual, Washington had negotiated direct with London in the setting up of the board, and Chamberlain had gone too far before Laurier could dissent. Little as he liked the arrangement, he had agreed to it in January and had put on a hopeful face for the benefit of its critics. 'It is suggested', he had written in January, 'that the American jurists will never agree to any decision which would cause loss of the disputed territory to the U.S. That may be, but this is no argument against the treaty itself. It is rather an argument against the honesty of the American jurists, and I can only hope that it is a slanderous insinuation.'

He could not sustain the mood when the names of the Americans were announced. Elihu Root, though his views were known, had to be accepted as a great lawyer who might be susceptible to argument. The other two men, however, were open enemies who had already declared their positions. To Senator Henry Cabot Lodge the Canadian claims were 'baseless and manufactured'. Senator George Turner was a man from the state of Washington, the source and centre of the Yukon trade, and was openly opposed not only to any concession but to arbitration itself. 'I consider that their appointment', Laurier wrote hotly to London, 'would be a direct violation of the treaty which says that impartial jurists shall be appointed.'

The letter left Ottawa on February 19, already two days late. London had accepted the appointments on February 17. President Roosevelt, came the bland and regretful explanation, 'had got his back up' and would have to be humoured. Short of a judicial miracle, or short of war, the hope of a Yukon coastline could be written off.

Meanwhile it had become apparent that there was to be no neat marriage of eastern and western ambitions in the building of the railway. Not only was the cabinet utterly divided on the plan; the Grand Trunk and the Canadian Northern seemed to be broken up into four competing camps rather than two. Sir Charles Rivers Wilson, president of the Grand Trunk in London, dreaded the vast westward expansion of his business and was approaching the whole project with great reluctance. Charles Hays, his thrusting American manager in Canada, approached it with burly zest and was eager not only to expand the Grand Trunk but to devour the Canadian Northern. Rivers Wilson, if he entered the west at all, was inclined to enter it in co-operation with Mackenzie and Mann. Mackenzie, for the Canadian Northern, seemed to agree. On the other hand Donald A. Mann, who was much of a pair with Hays, was quite as determined as Hays to swallow the competing railway and take all. Each company seemed to speak with two conflicting voices. Both, whenever they could be brought to negotiate, were magnificent and unaccommodating in their demands. Neither would work with the other, one had to be refused, and for Laurier that one became the Canadian Northern. He could never quell his suspicions of Mackenzie and Mann. The cloud of lurid politicking and dazzling high finance still hung thickly, as it always would, over the magnificent achievements of the prairie railway. It would have to be left to follow its own course. The Grand Trunk, dubious, divided, and still shifting its ground, remained at the bargaining table, and in place of Mackenzie and Mann its prospective partner was now the Dominion of Canada.

The sweeping simplicity of the original conception was breaking up in a tangle of cross purposes. The Canadian Northern, fighting for its life in the west and with more subterranean strength in the east than anyone realized, was now out to destroy the whole project. Hays of the Grand Trunk, indifferent and hostile to any eastern expansion, was interested only in invading the west with sufficient help from the government to wipe out Mackenzie and Mann. Sir Charles Rivers Wilson, still dreading the west, had closed his eyes to most of the other essentials. He was not interested in the development of Quebec City and he was appalled at the cost of running steel through empty northern hinterlands. He saw no reason why the rich traffic of the prairies should not be drained eastward for the enlargement of his Portland base. All thought of the building up of Canadian seaports and terminals he waved off as 'mere claptrap' and 'the silliest piece of false patriotism conceivable'.

At the same time everything Sir Charles dismissed was standing out more and more as a political necessity. Sifton, who spoke for the west and thought for the whole country, would not have prairie wheat poured through to the sea to fatten an American port. Quebec would not support a plan for another railway that ignored its own ambitions. The Maritimes by now were quite as emphatic both in their demand for the Atlantic terminal and for the new direct line that would supplant the Intercolonial from Quebec to the sea.

Out of it all the alternatives emerged. If there was to be a railway either the government must go it alone or it must go with the Grand Trunk. Sifton, who had once been inclined toward working with Mackenzie and Mann, was now inclined to plunge for government building, but Laurier drew back. A government that built the railway might have to operate it and the Intercolonial, as a commercial disaster and a political morass, was an example of the result. Blair, the guardian angel of the Intercolonial, maintained a silence that was as dangerous as it was dignified. Left out of the negotiations though well aware of them, his views were ready on demand but they were seldom demanded. He was a hearty enemy of the Grand Trunk and would give them nothing. He was too much the friend of Mackenzie and Mann. He wanted to extend the Intercolonial westward to an eventual linking with the Canadian Northern, and he wanted the first link to be a water link by way of the Great Lakes. He was in no hurry to fulfil Quebec's hopes, he saw no need of a second line from Winnipeg to the Pacific, and he would have no new leg to the Atlantic competing with the Intercolonial. He was plausible in everything he urged and suspect in everything, and he stood alone. The other principal ministers, each from a different ground, shifted gradually to the support of a plan that reversed the original thinking and would certainly be opposed on almost every point by the Minister of Railways.

The first step in the arrangement, still only half complete by the time the session neared, would be the incorporation of a subsidiary of the Grand Trunk, to be known as the Grand Trunk Pacific Railway. With partial support from its parent and partial support from the government for the bonds it would have to float, the Grand Trunk Pacific would build westward from North Bay, above the Great Lakes, across the prairies, and over the mountains to Port Simpson. Eastward from North Bay to the Atlantic the government itself would build a line that would be known as the National Transcontinental and would be turned over on lease when completed to the Grand Trunk Pacific. The terms were not yet defined, the route of the National Transcontinental remained a matter of eager rumour, and the Grand Trunk in England was already seeking escape from some parts of the bargain. But at least a plan was on paper.

When parliament opened on March 11 Robert Borden rose in his place and congratulated the Prime Minister on his improved health. The Prime Minister responded affably, trusting that 'though we may be divided upon many questions yet we can be united upon one, and that is a mutual respect for each other'. On March 20 Blair introduced the bill for the Railway Commission, which no one opposed. On March 31 a second bill was presented for the incorporation of the Grand Trunk Pacific, and as that went into committee the session's amenities were over.

The Prime Minister's health was no longer a subject for congratulation. He was not seen at his desk in the House so often, and each time he appeared he was a greyer, more harried man. The doubts of Rivers Wilson, the blustering and conniving of Hays, the still unresting manoeuvres of Mackenzie and Mann had all descended on him in a thick smother of feuds and competing interests. He emerged from it three months later with little left as intended and everything left to explain.

The Grand Trunk Pacific would not be building the long western section around the Great Lakes from North Bay to Winnipeg. The government had agreed to assume that extra burden. All the way from the Atlantic to Winnipeg, therefore, the government was building a railway that the Grand Trunk would not build, and turning it over to be operated under lease. Why would not the Grand Trunk build it? Because it was considered uneconomic. Why build it at all? The Prime Minister answered that the road was indispensable. It was 'the key to the transportation problem from the prairies to the ocean', and the leasing agreement kept it in control of the government. In the west Laurier was giving the Grand Trunk Pacific the fruits of the rich grain traffic of the prairies, the real goal of the whole operation. Why, if the fruits were so rich, should the government not have them? He answered that no government body would be flexible enough and alert enough to meet all the demands and seize all the opportunities of a great railway in a new country. Yet the Canadian Northern was already on the ground and it was certainly alert and flexible. The only answer to that, spoken or not, was that the Prime Minister of Canada did not think much of either Mackenzie, Mann, their methods, or their resources.

As to costs, there would be a government guarantee partially supporting the bonds of the Grand Trunk Pacific. The government would bear the expense of building the eastern section of the railway, but would gradually recover it all through the leasing agreement. Assuming that the guarantee on the bonds would never be called, Laurier could show on paper that except for a picayune $13,000,000 in interest charges there would be no ultimate cost to the government at all. 'Whatever we give with one hand', he could say, 'we shall receive back with the other.'

He could no longer picture the line as brushing the tip of James Bay or running along the northern fringes of arable land into the rich country of the Peace River. Everywhere, as now projected on the map, it showed a tendency to sag down toward easier country, crowding the C.P.R. This feature was disturbing and disappointing, but the necessities had been explained to him by men who should know. He had, after all, to trust the men who knew. Quebec's hopes would still be served and the new, direct line would run as planned from Quebec City to the Atlantic. That Atlantic leg would certainly be assailed as boodling duplication, but Laurier could show that its route was a hundred miles shorter than the route of the Intercolonial and he could almost claim that it opened up new territory, since the two lines ran nowhere nearer together than thirty miles and much of the way with a mountain range between them. The Atlantic terminal port was not quite on the Atlantic, but this also was explainable since it would have been political suicide in the Maritimes to choose either Saint John over Halifax or Halifax over Saint John. Sleepy little Moncton, on the Petitcodiac River at the head of the Bay of Fundy, would be waked up to hear the call of destiny.

By early July the railway bill was ready. With one crucial exception Laurier had marshalled the cabinet behind him. The plan had been endorsed in caucus. It was not the plan he had set out with but he was sure the essentials were there. He was turning back to the mood of 1885, with himself in Macdonald's place. There had, after all, to be a controlled recklessness, there had to be leaps in the dark. There might be staggering mistakes but in the end the long strings of boxcars, heavy with prairie wheat, always on Canadian soil, would roll to the Atlantic coast. They would roll to the Pacific too when the time was ripe, perhaps when that canal of the Americans had changed the world. East and west, broadening and building on the great stream, the country would draw together and reach up into the empty barrens of the north for still-unguessed-at riches. The time had passed for protest and dissent, change and delay. He meant to have his railway.

On July 13 Blair handed him the resignation he had been holding since July 10. On July 16, a private member now, Blair tabled his correspondence with the Prime Minister up to the last protest he had entered 'before you finally determine that you will perpetrate what I cannot help regarding as one of the most indefensible railway transactions which has ever taken place in this country'. On July 22, with all this still in the headlines, Laurier acknowledged with regret Van Horne's refusal to accept the chairmanship of the transportation commission. On July 30, with the galleries packed and every seat in the House filled, with no Minister of Railways and the transportation needs of the country uninvestigated, with the party and the country still vibrating to the shock of Blair's resignation, and for once too much in haste to be courteous, Laurier rose to present his bill.

There had been no time to supply Borden with a copy, and

Borden was resentful. The Prime Minister, for his part, seemed a little ill and a little flushed. He had a great many more notes than usual, and he fussed with them. He climbed quickly and impatiently into a high and edgy key. There were those, he said, who urged the policy of tomorrow and tomorrow, who advised the government to wait, to pause, 'to consider, to reflect, to calculate and to inquire'. He would have none of it. 'We cannot wait because time does not wait. We cannot wait because in these days of wonderful development time lost is doubly lost; we cannot wait because at this moment there is a transformation going on in the conditions of our national life which it would be folly to ignore and a crime to overlook; we cannot wait because the prairies of the Northwest, which for countless ages have been roamed over by the wild herds of the bison or by the scarcely less wild tribes of red men, are now invaded from all sides by the white race. They came last year one hundred thousand strong and still they come in greater numbers . . . our duty is not of tomorrow but of this day, of this hour and of this minute. Heaven grant that it be not already too late. Heaven grant that while we tarry and dispute an ever-vigilant competitor does not take to himself the trade that properly belongs to Canada.'

He could not communicate such fervour to the House. The tarrying and disputing went on for two months and it was September 29 before the bill passed its third reading. He rose to the occasion with another salute of the same nervous shrillness. 'A new star has risen upon the horizon, a star not in the orbit of the American constellation but a star standing by itself resplendent in the western sky, and it is toward that star that every immigrant, every traveller, every man who leaves the land of his ancestors to come and seek a home for himself now turns his gaze.'

The railway was launched. It would never pay for its axle grease in any years he would know, and it would haunt the rest of his own and many more. He had made the project himself and he would never escape from the trap. He would never find a Tupper, still less a Van Horne. He had made the wrong enemies and the wrong friends. He would see his thirteen millions breed a mountainous burden of debt. The monumental blunders would rise higher than his own monument, only settling a little as time and the Canadian northland bore him out. The hopes he had seen as only a leap away were still a century ahead. 'Those young men', he was to say a year later, pointing to the roaring galleries of a crowded hall in Toronto, 'if they live to old age will see this country with at least sixty millions of people.' They would not; many of them would not see even middle age. Most would see war, depression, paralysis – a vast and swirling reversal of all the streams of progress. He was planning in the mood and seeing with the eyes of his times, though there was more he might have seen. The long knives of Mackenzie and Mann were sharpening for him in the west. In the east an eminent former colleague, now a Conservative journalist, had already pronounced an epitaph. Ten transcontinental railways, wrote J. Israel Tarte, builder of canals, apostle of Montreal on the St. Lawrence, would not change the facts. From the lakehead to the sea the wheat cargoes of the future would be moved by water.

21

NEW PROVINCES

1903-1905

A WEEK AFTER the railway debate concluded, the chill wind of Alaska blew again. It had, in fact, been blowing throughout the summer, and every breath had increased rather than allayed the irascible anti-Americanism of Laurier's mood. It had played its part in hurrying him on with his railway and it had not, on the other hand, added anything whatever to his filial respect for the Empire.

Chamberlain, after accepting the American arbiters, had compounded the felony by hinting that perhaps there should be two Britons on the other side instead of one. The hint had been brusquely ignored; Laurier had named two Canadians and Lord Alverstone, Chief Justice of England, had meekly become the third member. The three arbiters for Canada had been flanked as the Americans were by an imposing body of counsel, and both sides had begun the proceedings by submitting elaborate briefs.

In September the whole tribunal of arbitration had been assembled in London for the oral argument. Sir Louis Jetté, the lifelong friend of Quebec, and A. B. Aylesworth, one of the coming men of Toronto, were the Canadian arbiters, with Lord Alverstone presumably supporting them. Blake had been one of the counsel till his health failed him, and Sifton was now on hand. They were all able men and they were faced by able men, with a fascinating case between them. To both sides the opposing briefs had been impressive and to Laurier at least there had been a kind of encouragement in the very strength with which the Americans presented their case. If they were disposed to argue so hard and skilfully, perhaps after all the best arguments would decide.

George Vancouver, just a century before, had surveyed and named this wild coastal region fronting on the north Pacific. England and Russia had quarrelled over it for thirty years and finally come to an agreement on the line dividing Alaska from the Yukon. In 1867, as the Dominion of Canada became a fact in North America, the United States had bought Alaska from Russia without being very sure of what she got for her seven million dollars and accepting the fence staked out by diplomats who had never seen the country. The fence was now in question and for almost every yard, where it twisted along the coast, there were claims and counter-claims. The intentions of the original treaty-makers had to be unravelled. Geographical features, carelessly described or not described, had to be identified while place names varied from chart to chart. Intricate, elusive, utterly charming to a man of law, the argument ran back through reams of parchment and dockets of yellowing maps to the very deck of Vancouver's ship, the very state of his mind, and the direction in which he might, perhaps, have been facing when he looked up such and such a channel to describe such and such a headland, island, or mountain. It seemed for a time that the arbiters, courteously absorbed in their game, would play it out by the rules.

Over it all, however, hung the imperatives of statecraft and the big stick. Roosevelt saw to it that his own view was put abroad in London and the word came back to Ottawa. The Canadian claim for access to deep water along any part of the Alaska coast was 'just exactly as indefensible as if they should now suddenly claim the island of Nantucket'. The American President wished 'to exhaust every effort to have the affair settled peacefully and with due regard to England's honour', but it was to be settled his way or he would obtain the authority from Congress to 'run the line as we claim it, without any further regard to the attitude of England and Canada'.

The words were not official and fortunately did not require an official answer. But the judicial atmosphere began to drain away from the tribunal and the balance shifted. Lord Alverstone, the cool interpreter of treaties, began to seem rather the anxious diplomat, less inclined to discuss points of law with his colleagues, more inclined to suave consultations with the Americans in side rooms. On October 8 the cable came from Sifton: 'I think that Chief Justice intends joining the Americans, deciding in such a way as to defeat us on every point.' The British seemed determined, he added, to avoid trouble with the Americans. Jetté and Aylesworth had had enough and were thinking of withdrawing from the commission.

Law was being thrown overboard and imperial necessities were once more taking control. Yet even at that there was still a good card left. If the Americans were interested in Alaska they were still more interested in the Nicaraguan isthmus, where they were acquiring the strip of land for the new canal by old and familiar methods. British support, in the face of world opinion, would be valuable to the United States and with a little resolute bargaining it could be made to command a price. It had to be tried, even if it meant a deadlocked tribunal and an angry Roosevelt. The question was no longer only a question of the Yukon; Laurier was resigned to the loss of most of his case there. But the loss would have to be explained in terms the nation would accept. Something had to be saved. Everything could not be blandly tossed away by this imperial hand that dealt in colonies as it dealt in goods. The Prime Minister by this time had become more than an angry statesman and an outraged lawyer; he was an infuriated Canadian. 'Our commissioners must not withdraw,' he cabled back. 'If we are thrown over by Chief Justice, he will give the last blow to British diplomacy in Canada. He should be plainly told this.'

The telling had no effect. The decision of the tribunal, four to two against the Canadians, was recorded on October 20. It reached Canada just in time for a one-day debate on October 23, the day before 'this interminable session' came to a close. Borden was outraged, Bourassa pointed out that nothing more could be expected from the British connection, and the grim-faced Prime

Minister sat silent under a barrage of angry questions. Why had there not been three Canadian commissioners? Why had there been an even number on the whole board, when it meant deadlock at best? Why had he not insisted that the Canadian parliament be given the right to ratify the findings?

All the answers lay in the letters exchanged with Chamberlain and, quite as angry as his questioners, Laurier promised to table the correspondence at the next session. Even without exploring the mechanics of imperial negotiation the basic trouble was clear. Laurier made it clearer in his words to a surly House. 'We are only a small colony, a growing colony, but still a colony . . . we have not in our own hands the treaty-making power which would enable us to dispose of our own affairs.' The country would have to obtain from the British parliament the power to deal with other nations as a nation herself. 'So long as Canada remains a dependency of the British Crown the present powers that we have are not sufficient for the maintenance of our rights.'

He had moved on, with Chamberlain's help, to pass another milestone. It was noted by the alert *Manchester Guardian* with a slight shudder of surprise. 'This is indeed a remarkable passage,' the newspaper commented. 'The demand for control over foreign affairs strikes at the very root of the imperialist position and if pressed must lead to a complete overhauling of the ordinary conception of imperial and colonial relations.'

2

THE THIRD SESSION of the ninth parliament had been the longest ever held and it was not, after all, to be the last. The interminable negotiations on the railway had been concluded and the debate won, but the Grand Trunk remained the Grand Trunk. Bartering and bickering to the end, it had finally subscribed to an agreement that it now could not fulfil. Before the year was out it began to be evident that the English financial houses who would have to float the bonds for the Grand Trunk Pacific did not like the prospect. By the beginning of 1904 there was clearly trouble ahead.

The government's guarantee was based on a fixed maximum as the cost for the mountain section. Builders and financiers were now pointing out that no one could set a maximum on the cost of building through mountains. The experience of the C.P.R. was darkly recalled. Every estimate had been torn up, every cost had doubled and redoubled as selected routes proved impracticable, rock slides thundered down over roadbeds, and spring torrents washed out the work of months. There could be no roof on the government's guarantee if the bonds were to sell at all, and there could be no change in terms till parliament sat. There was at the moment, therefore, no firm agreement, no firm prospect of the railway, and no election issue.

On the greater stage there were also changes and doubts. Laurier was not, after all, going to table the correspondence with Chamberlain regarding the Alaska tribunal. It might be satisfying, but it would butter no parsnips and change no facts to show that the real weakness lay with the imperial authorities. He had given Alverstone a sizeable piece of his mind, and he had done so on the full swell of his own and the country's anger, but he had done it in secret. Publicly he had turned to the quelling of a fruitless commotion that could lead nowhere. The question of the Yukon was decided, the importance of the Yukon was dwindling, and there were other questions now.

Even while the policy of the United States defeated and repelled him a new kind of pressure was mounting from the other side. Chamberlain had come to the Colonial Office to weld a solid empire. He was leaving it now, but only to approach the goal from another direction. He was embarked with all his formidable energy on a campaign to reverse British tariff policy, abandon free trade, and make imperial preference a rallying cry for the colonies. He had been handicapped before in his attempts at promoting a *zollverein* by the fact that British markets lay open to all the world. He intended to close them; free trade would go. He could then offer the colonies private and preferred entrance to an enormous protected market. He could demand as his price that they set up reciprocal tariffs against the outside world. It was good bait and a heavy club, but the penalty for Canada would be new reprisals from the United States. Of the two clubs Roosevelt's was the bigger and the man still tingling from Alaska stood in the shadow of both.

There were other and nearer shadows. 'I am now fully restored to health,' Laurier had written to Pacaud in September, 'and feel alert, fresh, and well. I believe I have turned a dangerous corner and that now the way is safe for at least a few years.' It had been true enough but the cheerfulness had been a little overdone because Pacaud, ill and far away in Florida, had been in need of cheer. 'Now, old friend,' Laurier had gone on, 'courage and patience. Courage has never failed you, but I can hardly say the same for your patience. That was never one of your favourite virtues.' The little man had not responded to the rallying. The tangled affairs of his newspaper and his estate were now descending on Laurier's desk and Pacaud would soon be on the way home to die. That dingy, bustling, memory-haunted office in Quebec was already emptied of his presence. The friendship of thirty years was in its last months. One did not like to think of it.

Adeline Ethier Laurier had died during the past year, and St-Lin would never be the same. Mowat had died. Tarte, now an unsuccessful *Bleu* and a busy adviser of Borden, was dying on the political vine. There was small satisfaction in that, less in the fact that Bourassa was responsible for the withering. Tarte, as everyone seemed eventually to do, had become unworthy of that prickly friendship. A sinking enemy of the rising man, he had left the platform of the last *assemblée contradictoire* wry, humiliated, and broken. It was more than enough; when political ghouls had begun to rake up his past Laurier had stopped them with a firm hand. He and Tarte still wrote to each other as cool and seasoned realists too wise in the game for rancour. The times that had changed for one would change for the other. Change was everywhere. To one man at least change had been good. David the faithful, of the long and hard-up years, was now a senator. It was one of the rewards of power, and it was a heart-warming pleasure to be asked for advice on small investments now rather than on debts.

Blair was gone from the cabinet, but not far. He had too much ability and he was too dangerous while the railway hung in the balance to be summarily disposed of. He had, after all, done much to form the Railway Commission, which was a non-political body. He sat as its chairman now, a non-politician who would still have to be watched.

A great many would have to be watched, even Sifton. The westerner who was no longer so close to his chief and had once been rather close to Mackenzie and Mann was souring on the Grand Trunk. He was turning away from the fight to save the agreement and talking of change. 'You know what was once said to be a safe rule in politics,' he wrote on February 21; 'Find out what you would not like your opponent to do if he were in your place and do that. If I were Borden the last thing I would want you to do would be to take hold of the railway as a national project, put it under a strong commission, and push it through.'

There was the old brisk tone to the advice, and it was tempting. But there would be no change in the plan because there could be no more delay. The Grand Trunk Pacific must be kept, the increase in the guarantee must be forced through. The country wanted the railway and it would pay the price and get it. Beyond the railway there was an election to be fought and beyond the election was the carving out of provinces. It had been a growing issue in the territories for years and could not be postponed much longer. Neither could it be dealt with by a government in its late days. The territories had schools, the new provinces would have schools, and the spectre of Manitoba glared from the past. Laurier intended to face it with a new, confident administration fresh from victory.

He would certainly face it with a new Quebec at his back. Bourassa, never far from his thoughts, spoke now with reason of his 'young army'. He spoke amicably, but he spoke as general to general, and he was engaged by early February in enlisting a new recruit. The constituency of Montmagny was preparing for a by-election and Armand Lavergne was twenty-four. 'Get your disciple elected,' said the old general to the younger, 'though when he reaches the House under your auspices he is going to be another thorn in the flesh.'

Even before nomination day at Montmagny there were glints of the intriguing future. The young candidate, handsome and Laurier-like in dress and gesture, was summoned before the party elders for a pledge of loyalty which he refused to give. He was threatened, in writing, with the consequences and turned to Bourassa for advice. When Bourassa refused to be the keeper of his conscience he found his own course, and it was wholly characteristic. He would not sign the pledge and he would not return the warning letter. He would wave it up and down the length of the country and he would win the nomination and the election on the strength of it.

He had done exactly that and the hint of the bar sinister, raised at some of the *assemblées contradictoires*, had been quite as neatly dealt with. Lavergne, who had been known in enemy quarters as 'the bastard' for most of his twenty-four years, saw no reason to deny the title now. He seemed to have learned already that a great part of politics is the art of becoming discussed. 'Whether I be the son of Laurier or Lavergne,' had been the only answer drawn from him, 'I have good reason to be proud.'

On March 10, as the fourth session of the ninth parliament got under way, the new member for Montmagny was introduced to a rather more than usually curious House. One sponsor was his Uncle Louis Lavergne, now the member for Drummond-Arthabaska; the other was the Prime Minister. The time came for the maiden speech and Lavergne, lacking a livelier quarrel, stood up in vigorous defence of the right to smoke. A luckless private member from Ontario had varied the usual mournful resolutions on liquor with a bill to prohibit cigarettes. The House was bored with the subject but it was not bored with Lavergne. His English was not very good and he apologized for it, but the sparkle of the man came through, restless and dangerous. The glamorous enigma still persisted round him; the thorn was not yet fleshed but it was sharp.

3

TEN DAYS before the session opened Laurier had made known the new terms he proposed for the Grand Trunk Pacific. Borden was ready with a variety of excellent ammunition and the attack rose to its climax in mid April. It was bad enough, said Borden, that the agreement should have to be altered even before it came into operation. It was worse that the government's liability for costs in the mountain section was now in effect unlimited. He quoted the inmost thoughts of Blair and revealed the heart-searchings of Grand Trunk shareholders, all from copies of confidential documents that emptiers of wastebaskets had somehow placed in his hands. He pointed out that there had still been no general inquiry into the transportation needs of the country. There were still no adequate surveys of much of the proposed route. There was no demonstrable need for great sections of the proposed mileage. The government was in guilty, headlong haste because it knew its plan was bad.

Borden was for throwing out the entire agreement and the Grand Trunk with it. He was for lopping off the whole length of the proposed National Transcontinental. He was for government building of a few lines on the prairies and a line west to the Pacific. He was for expansion of the Intercolonial in the east and a linking of rail and water. Beyond that he was for new surveys and new investigations and for waiting while these were completed. He was for reconsideration, gradualness, and the look before the leap.

It was prudent talk but hardly a plan, and the operative word was 'wait'. There was to be no more waiting. A Sifton newly convinced by a newly impatient country gave a powerful answer to Borden and the amended agreement went through. Flawed plans could be amended, objections met, mistakes repaired; anything could be tolerated now in this Canada of the twentieth century, except delay. The election theme had been struck, powerful and eloquent, and even the supporters of Borden echoed its lower notes. The railway, one of them told him, 'will give us good times for at least ten years, and after that I don't care'.

It was high time for the hustings now but balky Tories lingered, hoping for an issue of their own. In June it threatened to crop up when Major-General the Earl of Dundonald, Commander-in-Chief of the militia, burst out in public over 'a most flagrant instance of political interference'. Gross enough it was from the standpoint of a commanding general, for Sydney Fisher, Minister of Agriculture temporarily functioning as Acting Minister of Militia, had drawn his pen through the name of an officer just entered on the roll of a new squadron of dragoons.

Generals, however, whatever their private thoughts, could not be allowed to denounce the civil power in public. Dundonald was no Hutton and had done good work during his two years in Canada. He was nevertheless a political innocent who had been unable to accept Laurier's advice that 'you must not take the militia seriously'. He had now precipitated a situation in which heads would have to roll and the only possible head was that of the general. His resignation must be demanded at once, Laurier informed a protesting Minto, and when there was delay at Government House Dundonald was dismissed by Order in Council.

Newspapers blossomed in headlines and debate thundered in the House but the government's ground, which was civil control of the military, was ultimately unassailable. Fisher's explanation of the practical details was quite simple and thoroughly familiar to every politician. The new militia unit had been recruited in Fisher's constituency and officered by his favourite enemies who were attempting 'to turn that squadron if not the whole regiment into a Tory political organization'. In spite of the bellowings of Sam Hughes, there was a somewhat hollow sound to the whole affair until the Prime Minister made his irritable contribution to the debate. He rose, impatient and abstracted, to pay his tribute to Dundonald as a soldier and point out his ignorance of conditions in the Eastern Townships, which were Fisher's territory. He doubted if Dundonald had ever been there. Dundonald was, he suggested, with the French equivalent, *étranger*, hovering in the back of his mind, 'a foreigner – no – I had withdrawn the expression before honourable gentlemen interrupted. He is not a foreigner, but he is a stranger.'

There was only a breath between the word and the withdrawal, but it might have been enough. The loyal leaped for the breach as in the good old days and the quarrel precipitated by the English politician of the Eastern Townships threatened for a while to become the quarrel of the French-Canadian Prime Minister. Robert Borden, however, was not among the leapers and his presence commanded silence when the Prime Minister stood up at the end of a long debate. 'Sir,' said Laurier, 'I have been told today on the floor of this House, twice, that when I used the word "foreigner" there was in my heart a sinister motive, there was in my heart a feeling which found expression. Sir, I have only this to say. If sixty years of what I believe to be, after all, an honourable life, a life which has certainly been one of loyal devotion to British institutions, is not a sufficient answer to such an insinuation, I will not attempt to make an answer.' From across the aisle Dr. Thomas Sproule, the latest head of the Orange Order, had a remark or two to make but beyond that there was a stillness to be broken later only on the rare Tory husting. Dundonald toured the haunts of the military in Ottawa, Montreal, and Toronto, enjoyed his choleric martyrdom, and was gone with a hot July. The Canada of Wilfrid Laurier and of Robert Borden, it seemed, was not quite the Canada of the old days.

4

THE SESSION closed in August and there was better than a month of rest under the maples of Arthabaska. Then it was time for elections. Vigorous and refreshed, Laurier opened the campaign with a great and glowing meeting at Sorel on the St. Lawrence. For two weeks afterward his progress through Quebec was an uninterrupted triumph. There was no Tarte beside him but that was rather a relief. He had no Pacaud but he was resigned to that. Getting Cartwright elected, the ever-recurring problem of each campaign, had now been solved. Aging and rusting a little, burdened with honours and hard-up for money, Cartwright had been glad to accept a seat in the Senate. He would still be a member of the cabinet for as long as he liked. Perhaps it would be a little longer than Laurier liked, but young men could wait. There would be room enough for the young, and work enough, in the years beyond the election.

He looked forward to those years with a confidence and an excitement that he seemed to communicate to his audiences as never before. He had been irritably amused when the always wayward Bourassa had spoken of leaving politics and had suggested with a barbed smile that he might be named postmaster of Montreal. How could he think of such a thing at such a time? For once there was peace in Quebec and Bourassa was a power there, and well knew it. He stood with Laurier now and there would be work ahead for both of them when it came to the erection of the new provinces. The schools question this time was to be solved in the spirit of Confederation. 'There will doubtless be fanatics to criticize and I shall have need of men of character among the French-Canadian wing of the party as a counterweight. In any case it would be a crime to shut yourself up in a post-office. Do you want to spend your life cancelling stamps?'

1904 ELECTION. CARTOON BY FERGUS KYLE

There was no real fear of that, though neither was there much hope that the schools question would be settled with the off-hand simplicity that Laurier had suggested to Bourassa: 'it is only to apply Section 93 of the Act of Confederation'. Willison, ever a little more the Englishman and less the friend, had his own view of the Act of Confederation and his suspicions of Laurier's plans. He was endeavouring now in the *News* to smoke them out. The creation of the new provinces, he suggested, had been delayed until after the election because the Roman Catholic hierarchy was determined to have separate denominational schools there and was likely to get them.

The man who had stood out against the hierarchy on the question of the Manitoba schools and stood out against Quebec in the South African War replied with the more heat, remembering that. 'Why in the name of patriotism', he snapped, 'attempt to resurrect the now dormant school question? Why, when we have profound peace, attempt to prejudge public opinion? The school question will come up again all too soon. It will come in a very different form from what it was in 1896, but with the same bitter passions on both sides, and again it will be my lot to fight extremists and to place and maintain the question where it has been placed by the British North America Act . . . let me tell you that I see my way clear before me.'

It was close to an acknowledgment that the break with Willison was near, but nothing was changed for Laurier in Toronto. He came there on October 14, after the great weeks in Quebec, to speak of the Canada of the in-flooding thousands, the Canada of the new railway and the provinces-to-be, the Canada of limitless horizons. 'You cheer for me but you don't vote for me,' he cracked the old joke to thousands of affectionate enemies who knew they would lose their votes and still thundered for him from the seats and aisles and galleries of the Horticultural Pavilion. The foreignness seemed gone; the bridge was built. His railway would cross the wilderness above them, feeding its wealth down. His theme was now their own: 'The twentieth century shall be the century of Canada and of Canadian development!'

It was four days later and he was out on the Ontario stumps when the telegram came from Blair that brought him back to Ottawa. The next day he was in Montreal, hardly as appalled as his supporters but with much to be sorted out and quickly. Blair's telegram had now been supplemented by an announcement published in the Saint John *Telegraph* which was or had been Blair's special organ: 'I authorize the announcement that I have resigned my position as chairman of the Railway Commission and have notified the Premier that beyond reaffirming my strong objection to the Grand Trunk Pacific scheme, I have no present intention of re-entering political life.' It was followed that same day by another announcement in the same paper. Mr. Blair's intentions had been revised. He would very shortly be entering the election campaign against the government.

It was not Blair but the shadowy figures behind him who had to be dealt with. The abilities of Mackenzie and Mann, it seemed, had been badly underestimated. They had a railway in the west. They had scraps of railway in the east, and options and secret agreements with the owners of other branches. They had always had access somehow to millions of money. They seemed to have made a friend of Hugh Graham, Laurier's old and inveterate adversary of the Montreal *Star,* of Dansereau, who was usually available to men with money, and of many others. Now, from what could be determined amid the haze, a rich and wonderful plot was under way. Laurier was to be defeated and the Grand Trunk scheme was to be defeated with him. Mackenzie and Mann, with Borden as a tame Prime Minister and Blair as Minister of Railways, were to build what they wished of the transcontinental line and unload their unprofitable properties on the government at their own figure.

One of the prime movers in the affair seemed to be David Russell, a promoter of Saint John with the cheerful conviction that every man was for sale. There were tantalizing rumours about 'a stout man with red hair and wearing blue glasses', who could only be Mr. Lukes, the accountant for Mackenzie and Mann. He had usually been seen carrying a bulging black bag. The C.P.R., no friend of the Grand Trunk, seemed to be standing aside in well-apprised neutrality, waiting for a piece of the Intercolonial as its share. Somewhere at the centre of things was Hugh Graham, 'cool-headed enough in his own business but in politics excitable, almost hysterical'. Graham had no need of railways or of money, but could 'be made to believe anything that promises to bring the Conservative party into power'.

Money supplied through Russell had first bought the *Telegraph* and the *Evening Times* of Saint John, the papers behind Blair. Blair, it appeared, had then engaged in some stock-market speculations on joint account with Russell. The Honourable 'Sweet William' Pugsley, Attorney-General in the New Brunswick cabinet, had next moved noticeably close to Blair, for what reason the present tangle of information did not make clear. What was painfully clear was the role and success of Dansereau.

On October 11, a week before Blair's resignation, Dansereau had met Treffle Berthiaume, owner of *La Presse* and another of Laurier's valued friends, at a concert in Montreal. After enjoying the music they had proceeded to the home of J. N. Greenshields, solicitor for Mackenzie and Mann, who also happened to be entertaining David Russell and a brace of lawyers. Conversations had gone on until six the following morning, a good deal of champagne had been drunk, and a day or so later a very cheerful Dansereau had left for Europe. He left in luxurious accommodations provided for him by David Russell, he expected to be gone a year, and he carried in his pocket, said rumour, a copy of a contract providing among much else that he was to receive an income of a thousand dollars a month for ten years whether he worked or not.

Dansereau, according to Laurier's panicky informants, had persuaded a reluctant Berthiaume to sell *La Presse* to the agents of Mackenzie and Mann at a price of slightly over one million dollars. The paper was now to reverse its editorial policy and turn against Laurier and the Grand Trunk. As its first thunders rolled and Blair took to the stump, another quarter of a million dollars was to go to work. Scandal was to break over the heads of cabinet ministers and force their resignations. At least twenty of the Quebec Liberal candidates now standing were to be bribed to give up 'in disgust'.

Many of the details were not clear to Laurier and would not become so until the redoubtable Edward Farrer, still as busy as ever, concluded an investigation some months later. It all sounded 'like the program of a parcel of lunatics' but some of it was real. By midnight of October 20 Laurier had decided how much, and he went for the jugular with suave and practised skill.

It would be most regrettable, he conveyed to Berthiaume, and unprofitable to all concerned, if the rumour were true that *La Presse* had been sold to Mackenzie and Mann. A newspaper, after all, was not like a railway or a piece of real estate. Its value in the ultimate analysis rested solely on the subscribers who supported it. Its influence remained only while it was trusted.

What would its value be when Laurier came out, as he would be forced to, with the announcement that the chief newspaper of French Canada had been sold to a group of English speculators for purposes that he would not fail to make clear?

Blair, in Ottawa, was the next to enjoy an intimate talk. A day later Laurier resumed his campaign in Montreal, where a good many cheering thousands made it clear to *La Presse* what their views were likely to be. On that same day Borden, who had heard his share of rumours, announced that campaign contributions would have no influence on any policy he directed and that contributors who thought otherwise might have their money returned. The policy of *La Presse* remained unchanged. Blair returned to New Brunswick with no comments for any newspaper. Day after day the stumps waited him in vain. No scandals broke. No cabinet ministers resigned. No candidates forsook their candidatures. The campaign soared to its climax and on November 3 the government of Wilfrid Laurier was returned with a majority of seventy-four seats, the greatest it had ever known. It was two months before Hugh Graham, sufficiently recovered to approach a forgiving enemy, negotiated on behalf of his embarrassed friends the agreement that saved and caged their million-dollar white elephant.

'It is distinctly understood', ran the undertaking signed at the St. James Club on January 18, 1905, 'that the paper *La Presse* is not to be a Tory organ, that it is to be independent, and that it is to give Sir Wilfrid Laurier a generous support. Mackenzie, Mann & Company. (Signed) Wm. Mackenzie, President. D. D. Mann, Vice-President.'

5

BY THAT TIME the new parliament had been sitting for a week and an expectant House was awaiting the great work of the session. A region of some half million square miles, with a population of less than a head per mile, was to be separated from the Northwest Territories and enrolled in the Dominion of Canada as the provinces of Alberta and Saskatchewan.

There had been argument over the names and the scholarly Joseph Pope had pleaded with Laurier that the rolling, Homeric tones of Assiniboia be preserved in one. He had been unsuccessful; the decision lay with the people of the west. There had been some argument in favour of creating one province instead of two, but the area involved had been considered too large for that. There was argument now as to whether the public lands should be owned by the Dominion or the provinces and there was the inevitable debate over subsidies. Finally, and crucially, there was the question of education and the right to separate schools.

There was no question of language. D'Alton McCarthy had settled that long before; Alberta and Saskatchewan would speak English. The people of the prospective provinces were not unhappy about it, for the immigrants who were now filling the lands almost all spoke English or came expecting to speak it. Even among the original inhabitants there had been time for a generation to grow up accustomed to the one tongue and largely forgetful of the other. Nor was there any great concern about the schools. In districts where French lingered instruction in French was tolerated during the last hour of the school day. The priest was entitled to the last half of that hour for instruction in the Catholic religion if enough of the ratepayers wanted it. The price of the privilege was high, for such schools were separated from the general system and had to be supported separately by people who already paid the general school tax. All schools, separate and secular alike, worked from the same textbooks, were governed by the same standards, and were under the same largely Protestant control. It was hardly an ideal arrangement from the standpoint of the priest or the French Canadian, but this was the Protestant west.

Section 93 of the British North America Act, which Laurier had mentioned to Bourassa and which governed the four original provinces of Confederation, had provided very differently. So had the Act that, eight years after Confederation, Mackenzie and Blake had set up for the government of the Northwest Territories. Under each of these statutes a minority of either religion had had the right to its own schools, regulated by authorities of its own faith and equitably supported by the general school tax. The days of such privileges seemed very far off indeed now.

They had begun to go down with the beginning of McCarthy's crusade, they had been finished off by the Territorial Ordinances of 1901, and there was no possibility whatever that Protestant provincial authorities would wish to revive them. Yet they were the privileges enjoyed equally by Protestants in Quebec and Catholics in Ontario under the terms of the compact that Cartier had wrung from George Brown. They were of the essence of the spirit in which Confederation had been made. A sovereign Dominion parliament, creating provinces where none had been before, had every right to revive them.

The act incorporating the provinces was to be known as the Autonomy Act and the clause dealing with education turned out to be Clause 16. As Laurier worked on its framing the newspapers were already busy with speculation, a good deal of it in the old hostile Ontario tone. He could not help that; there would be an uproar in any case. Fielding was away in Europe and Sifton, who was now troubled with arthritis, was enjoying the murky lithia baths of an Indiana retreat bearing the haunting name of Mudlavia. The two giants of the administration were not on hand, but Laurier had their views on most of the questions with which the act would deal. Only on the matter of Clause 16 had discussion been a little strained and vague. It would be a case, Sifton had thought, of maintaining the status quo. The territories would become provinces with the same educational arrangements they now enjoyed.

Even this, for Sifton, represented a considerable concession. The whole stream of his feeling ran to secular schools. He favoured complete provincial autonomy in matters of education and he knew that in the west it would mean the end of priests in classrooms. The compromise of Manitoba had been a compromise with federal authority and the weight of Quebec. He had not liked it even though he had helped to make it. In the case of the new provinces he would be compromising again for the sake of Quebec, a little more grudgingly. He was growing tired of Quebec.

The man in Ottawa worked with the thought of Quebec too. He had made Quebec give way on the schools of Manitoba. He had sent troops to South Africa in spite of Quebec. He had yielded to D'Alton McCarthy fourteen years before on the floor of the House of Commons: 'If this measure . . . were to remain as it appears here, a measure for the proscription of the French language confined to the Northwest Territories alone, where the French population is small, I would be inclined to say: let the measure pass.' It had passed, and the yielding had gone on, in this country where there was no divorcing the French language from the Catholic religion nor the question of schools from either. It had gone on in the hope of peace with the English, peace with the Protestants, in the hope that somewhere, somehow a turning-point would be reached and the old spirit that had made the Confederation would assert itself again.

The schools of the west hardly mattered. The French were too few, the Catholics were too few; they would change nothing. But the great gesture, the turning back to the spirit of Confederation, could mean everything to Quebec. It had been a Laurier ten years younger who had fought the last great battle with the bishops. Some who sat in the seats of those bishops were now his friends, dear friends. Quebec was dearer to him, as the ground of home becomes to aging men. Power was dearer to him, and he possessed it now as never before. Only Quebec could threaten it, Quebec and its young men.

Of some of them Laurier was sure. In that on-coming generation there were strong and steady currents running with him. He could count on Rodolphe Lemieux, caustic and cool-headed, who had learned journalism from Pacaud and law from Mercier and come to parliament with the victory of 1896. Lemieux was now Solicitor-General, a step from cabinet rank. There was young Ernest Lapointe to balance young Armand Lavergne. Each of them had won his by-election in the same month and it was reassuring to see how often the mutinous flair of one was met and doused by the wide-minded, good-humoured loyalty of the other. Youth was as always the incalculable enigma, but there was good hope in it.

There remained Bourassa, always the uncertain figure and now a little more so. That talk of leaving politics and taking postmasterships had sprung a little from irked vanity. Bourassa had entered parliament at the same time as Lemieux. He had eyed the post of Solicitor-General and had not been given it. He had made it known that he would accept the post of Speaker and had not got it. Apart from considerations of the restless past, either position would have been a waste of Bourassa. Those abilities, once safely directed, called for more than sub-cabinet rank or the stately impotence of the Speaker's chair. It was now time to use them. Bourassa could be a pivotal figure in this question of new schools, and it was policy to make him feel it. There were other pivots and the Church was one, represented now in the person of Mgr. Sbaretti, residing in Ottawa as the papal delegate for Canada. Bourassa was soon drawn in on the work of the day and much in the company of the papal delegate. The suggestions of both men were valuable and persuasive. Fitzpatrick was doubly valuable as the shaping of the clause went on beneath his skilful hand.

On January 22 Sifton wrote from Indiana that he was feeling the benefit of his treatment and was much interested in the progress of the bill. 'You do not say anything about the schools question. I assume that you have not as yet discovered any serious difficulty in dealing with it.'

He had not, Laurier replied on the twenty-sixth. He was slowly working it out. 'I am satisfied with the progress which we have made on it, though everybody dreads it.'

It was nearly a month later, and one day before the introduction of the bill, when a telegram from Ottawa and a telegram from Mudlavia crossed. 'Bill will be introduced tomorrow,' was Laurier's message. 'I shall be home Friday morning,' came the telegram from Sifton. 'If any serious difficulty it might be well to postpone final action till then.'

There was to be no postponement now. On the morning of February 21 Laurier's reply went off: 'Important bill should be introduced immediately . . . public opinion being worked against us though not injuriously so far. Do not hasten your return. First reading today but cannot come up for discussion for at least a week.'

That afternoon, a tired, tense man, Laurier came before the House to introduce the bill creating the new provinces. Clause 16, drafted by Fitzpatrick 'with my own hand, clause by clause, line by line, word for word', under the authority of the Prime Minister, returned the schools of Alberta and Saskatchewan to the régime set up in 1875 by Blake and Mackenzie. The work of D'Alton McCarthy was wiped out.

SIR WILFRID LAURIER. PEN-AND-INK SKETCH BY HENRI JULIEN

There was no such suggestion in Laurier's calm and reasoned words. Yet something snapped as an interjection came from across the aisle. It came out of a taut silence, and once more as in the old days it was from a Grand Master of the Orange Order. Laurier turned on Dr. Sproule almost too quickly, as if expecting it.

Then he turned to the Speaker, dropping his notes on his desk. 'In everything that I have said I have refrained from saying a single word upon the abstract principle of separate schools. I approach the question upon another and a broader ground. I approach the question not from the view of separate schools, but I approach it upon the higher ground of Canadian patriotism. Having obtained the consent of the minority to this form of government, having obtained their consent to the giving up of their valued privileges and their position of strength, are we to tell them, now that Confederation is established, that the principle upon which they consented to this arrangement is to be laid aside and that we are to ride roughshod over them? . . . I have no hesitation in saying that if I were to speak my mind upon separate schools, I would say that I never could understand what objection there could be to a system of schools wherein, after secular matters have been attended to, the tenets of the religion of Christ, even with the divisions which exist among his followers, are allowed to be taught.'

There were five minutes more of it before he sat down, and it had all been too much. The old politician knew it and the old man hardly cared. There were to be no concessions here to that Quebec that 'has no opinions, only sentiments'. The perfunctory comments of a first reading were duly made and honourable members received their copies of the bill for study. Five days later Sifton arrived from the south and the next day he resigned. The eight years of power had mightily enlarged the country. They had not changed it.

6

ON MARCH 1 Laurier informed the House of the resignation of Sifton. There were strong hints by now that Fielding would resign on his return. Laurier did not know how many of the western members would follow Sifton nor how much of Ontario would fall in behind Sam Hughes, Dr. Sproule, and the Orangemen. It hardly mattered. Three months after a triumphant general election he was faced with the disintegration of his cabinet and complete disaster.

For a while his stunned resentment centred on Sifton. The

man who hated Fitzpatrick had seen his chance to destroy Fitzpatrick's work. The man who had never quite freed himself of the charges bred in the Yukon was now pursued by charges rising in the west. There was talk enough that he was glad to be out of the cabinet, that any pretext would do. Jealous and hard, bigoted and unforgiving, he was still the prairie politician who had set out with Joseph Martin to destroy the Catholic French. Then Fielding returned, who was none of these things, and still stood with Sifton. It was not Sifton Laurier was fighting, nor Fielding, nor even the ghost of D'Alton McCarthy. He stood opposed to the settled course of the nation.

He had tried with too much confidence and rather too little candour to return to the old dream of Confederation as he had grown to share it with Blake. He had hoped for too much from the goodwill of an east that had changed only toward himself. He had thought too little of the changing west which Sifton was filling with his thousands of English, Americans, Germans, Russians, anything but French. The French-Canadian Prime Minister might resign and go with dignity. He threatened it. Sifton was unmoved. Still Prime Minister, the man of Quebec might stand his ground and fight. It would be Quebec against the nation and Quebec would lose. There was only the other course, the old course, the search for a compromise.

Before he quite yielded Laurier turned to some of the old Protestant friends. 'Can you doubt', he wrote to J. R. Dougall, editor of the Montreal *Witness*, 'that if the provinces of Alberta and Saskatchewan had been admitted into the Dominion in 1867 instead of 1905, they would have received the same treatment as was given to Ontario and Quebec? Why refuse what has been done for the minority of Quebec and the minority of Ontario? If this be refused, the minority of the Northwest Territories will smart under a sense of wrong and injustice. They will believe that the public faith of the country is violated against them and to their prejudice, and who will pronounce their complaint unfounded?'

He tried again with Willison, and the answer closed a door that was not to be reopened. No one called Willison a Tory yet, but he was aging and returning to his roots, even as Wilfrid

Laurier. 'I am very sorry', his reply came, 'that I cannot accept your view of the constitution. I have no opinion to offer beyond those which we express in the *News* and therefore I will not argue the question here. I have tried always to allow for the natural race feelings of Quebec and not to make capital out of racial issues, but while I have all this respect and consideration for the natural race sentiments of French Canadians no man could be more strenuously opposed to clerical interference in state affairs, and from Confederation down the plain meaning of the constitution has been deliberately perverted to serve the ends of the Roman Catholic hierarchy. Further, the hierarchy have never touched education except to check, embarrass, and prevent the free play of human intelligence.'

Willison, as often before, was skirmishing somewhere in the woods, apart from the real battle. Whatever the feelings of the hierarchy, Mgr. Sbaretti had agreed by the middle of March that compromise was necessary. Compromise was under way, and it was humiliating enough. The Prime Minister had accepted the necessity and so had all the Quebec members except two. Bourassa, with Lavergne beside him, was outraged and adamant. The two were alone in the House, but unseen behind them were the new Quebec newspapers, the new Ligue Nationaliste, which spoke with Bourassa's voice, and the new Catholic Association of French Canadian Youth, frequently inspired by his eloquence and taking as the basis of their action the belief that 'the French-Canadian race has a special mission to fulfil on this continent and should, to that end, maintain its character distinct from that of other races'. The war, if it came, was not to be with old bishops or even with old politicians but with angry young men who spoke for a beleaguered people.

The amended Clause 16, which Laurier presented to the House at the second reading of the bill on March 22, had been drafted by Sifton. It had been discussed with Fitzpatrick only through a third party and presented to the Prime Minister as a tacit ultimatum. Nothing would induce Sifton to discuss with Fitzpatrick the 'ambiguities' of the original clause; it had to be thrown out root and branch. There was no possibility of Sifton returning to the cabinet. Only on his own terms, as the terms were embodied in the amendment, would he support the bill at all.

The new clause was about the same length as the old, but the references were to statutes since McCarthy rather than before him. On this question it was to be McCarthy's Canada. Instead of being lifted from the separate schools of the new provinces, the fetters would be clamped a little tighter. Alberta and Saskatchewan would have not quite what Manitoba had; and for much of the House, much of the country, even for the reluctantly acquiescent Fielding, it was still too much. The image of the Confederation as Cartier and Mackenzie and Blake had seen it was consigned to the past. The capitulation was complete, Bourassa would say. The way had been paved anew for the suppression of French and Catholic education.

Laurier did not believe it, not quite. But he rose with a new loneliness to make his skilful, supple speech, beating a retreat from the old amendment to the new. Sifton spoke as a private Liberal member, making no attempt to disguise his changed attitude to the party leader, and making much of the danger from which he had saved the country. The debate went on, cool and moderate for the most part, as quietly inflexible men spoke from positions they would not change. Even Bourassa struck fewer sparks than usual. It was no longer in the House but in the halls of his home province that he sounded the old, passionate note, and more and more it was becoming passionately French. Some of his words in the Commons, long before the debate was ended and the acts passed in May, had had a note almost of farewell. 'I regret every time I go back to my province', he said, 'to find developing that feeling that Canada is not Canada for all Canadians. We are bound to come to the conclusion that Quebec is our only country because we have no liberty elsewhere.'

7

PARLIAMENT prorogued on July 20 in an atmosphere of general amiability heightened by the fact that sessional indemnities had been increased and a salary voted to the leader of the opposition with Laurier's cordial support. The crisis of the schools was resolved and the parties were glad to forget it.

By October the administrative framework of the new provinces was complete and election campaigns were under way that promised to return strong Liberal administrations. The preliminary work on the new railroad was getting under way, money was on the flow, and the figures for immigration continued to climb. Gratefully returning to business, the country went on.

Laurier was not deceived as to his own position. 'I believe that I shall pull through this difficulty,' he had written in April, with the schools debate at its height, 'but I am not sure that I shall pull through stronger than at the beginning.' The long withdrawal had begun. He would never recoup the loss of Sifton in the west, and in Quebec the 'young army' of Bourassa was on the march away. It was hardly surprising in the late days of October to receive a copy of a newspaper article, ascribed to the pen of Armand Lavergne, hinting that a prestigious old man, now distinguished mainly for a habit of capitulating to the English, might retire to his trees and books in Arthabaska.

In the chilly twilight of the first day of November Laurier answered the correspondent who had forwarded the clipping. The suggestion of retirement came, he commented inelegantly, 'like a hair in the soup', but, 'you know what I think of this insubordinate child for whom I have a great affection in spite of his vagaries'.

Beyond that, he had only the familiar answer. 'I assure you that it would not be disagreeable to retire to Arthabaska "under my great trees, with my dear books", but my health is good now, there remain for me important matters to finish and even to commence.'

22

A TIME TO GO

1906-1908

HE LOOKED BACK now on ten years of government, and there was cause enough for complacence. Prosperity, under Laurier, had become not only a matter of statistics but a habit of mind. The country thought large, and there seemed no reason to do otherwise. A half-million immigrants, most of them bound for the prairies of the west, had come in since the turn of the century and the flood was still mounting. The money of foreign investors, most of them English, came as generously and easily. In Manitoba, Saskatchewan, and Alberta, as the ploughs of the homesteaders turned the inexhaustible acres of dusty brown grass into fallow land, the wheat yield had climbed from an annual eighteen million bushels to nearly a hundred and eighteen million. Wheat was transforming the country and making it the mecca of the world's land-seekers, yet wheat itself was merely another beginning. The prairies saw only a part of the great and golden commotion.

Ontario and Quebec, the old twin heartlands of the nation, had still a rich and steadily diversifying agriculture. Industry was booming, growing, and ramifying as it had never done before. Pulpwood, child of the lumber industry, was outstripping a parent that was still enormous. The northern frontiers of the old provinces were opening on a wealth of minerals and of water power that was work for a nation in itself. Yet British

Columbia's promise was equally rich and was being as eagerly exploited. Even the provinces by the Atlantic, deep in the sulky doldrums since the last of their great square-riggers left the sea, were now astir with the impulse of new methods and the taste of new money. With improved fisheries and more modern mines, Confederation was becoming bearable. Tupper could thank Laurier that his picture was found less often turned to the wall.

The foreign trade of the country had almost exactly trebled in the ten years. The outflow of population had been slowed to a trickle, and while the inflow grew there was movement within the movement. Maritimers were crossing the country to British Columbia rather than southward to Boston. Quebeckers turned to their own northland rather than to the mills and machine-shops and stony farms of New England. There was hardly an Ontario family that did not have a son or a brother or a cousin farming somewhere on the prairies. While the country rose in the world it was weaving together as a nation.

Everything about the picture made doubts seem niggling and delay criminal. As the curtain was lifted daily on the riches of the country, horizons broadened beyond it. Canada, fronting on two oceans, could look to the east and the west for its trade and traffic. There were no limits, for there was no measuring-stick; the world-wide vista seemed to justify all predictions. When such a man as Van Horne could picture the C.P.R. with one terminus in Euston and the other in Hong Kong or Sydney, it was not for Laurier to doubt the future of his new transcontinental. 'This great project did not come one hour too soon,' he told an audience of cheering Liberals in Toronto on February 20, 1906. 'It came at the right time. It is easy to see that before many years a third and perhaps a fourth railway will be necessary through the interior of the country to the coast.' Nor did his vision stop at the coasts. There were the markets of China and Japan and India to think of, and all the European traffic with the east which now went by way of Suez. 'Sir, we have a better route over the Pacific. Mark my words, and by and by we shall see train upon train carrying over Canada passengers from the Orient to Europe and from Europe to the Orient.'

Thirty-four survey parties were out in the northern wilderness, tracing the roadbed for the National Transcontinental. The broad scar of the Grand Trunk Pacific had been cutting its way across the prairies for six months. Mackenzie and Mann, busy and devious as ever, were fitting together the jigsaw of a third transcontinental. The plans that rode on all this lacing of steel were imperial in their scope. Laurier was a convinced and ardent enthusiast for the 'All-Red Route' which would link the British Isles with Australia and New Zealand by means of fast steamships and direct rail connection across Canada. He saw it as one of the principal items of business for the 1907 Colonial Conference, of which he had received notice just the day before he spoke in Toronto. Not only would it place Canada at the very heart of a world-wide communications network; it would also lessen with every passing year the country's dependence on the United States.

More and more, even as he stood out against the pressure of British imperialists, this freedom from continental domination was becoming an obsession with him. Canada's position was still not delineated; it had not yet established a firm and positive identity within the great triangular family of the Anglo-Saxon peoples. Nor was it yet prepared for the twentieth century at home. The west coast seethed with troubles over its Chinese and Japanese and Hindu immigrants. The thousands of the foreign-born on the prairies were still unassimilated. In-flooding money had given financial and industrial buccaneers their head. The rights and relations of working men and their employers had hardly begun to be investigated. There had to be social reform, financial reform, industrial reform, while all the time old channels had to be kept clear and new channels opened for the surging thrust of the country's growth.

There were indeed important matters to finish and commence. The Prime Minister faced them with enormous personal prestige, with restored health, and with an impregnable majority in parliament. Yet he stood more nearly alone than ever before, at the head of a government that for all its bristling strength was in process of decay. The little flaws were accumulating, the little rifts were opening, and there was never time to mend them.

Mulock was gone now, the latest of the departing giants. He had left for the Ontario bench with all the usual flourishes, but the parting, if amicable, had been a cool one. Sir Wilfrid Laurier had been slow in procuring a title for Sir William Mulock. The Catholic of Quebec and the Protestant of Ontario had grown apart rather than together in the ten years, and the all-pervasive strength of the leader had come to be rather too much for a man who was strong-willed himself. It was only another of many warning signs.

Quebec was drifting with Bourassa and away from Laurier. No election would return to Laurier the cabinet he had once had. If there were young men about who were the equal of the old, he had not found them. He hardly wanted them any longer, for strong men meant trouble. The great questions he now decided for himself; in lesser matters he was prepared to put up with weakness for the sake of peace. Confident power permitted him the luxury of loyalty to old friends, and he had seen too much of men and too much of politics to demand a rigorous purity in either. It was all reflected and it all recoiled on him as his third administration faced the second session of the tenth parliament.

The session opened on March 8, 1906, and it was one of the nastiest he had ever lived through. When it closed on July 13 he knew it was only a prelude to worse. The attack had centred not on policies but men and all of the men were vulnerable. He had known it for a long time, ignored it for a long time, and now would have to face it. The party of Wilfrid Laurier was going the way of the party of Macdonald.

Around Frank Oliver, the new Minister of the Interior, all the old scandals of Sifton's day had been released in a stinging swarm. The sudden death of Préfontaine had lifted the lid on a noisome mess in the department of Marine and Fisheries. Hyman, the old friend of London, Ontario, and the new Minister of Public Works, had offered his resignation in the face of charges of corrupt electioneering. Talk of women buzzed around Frederick Borden, the cousin of Robert, who had been Minister of Militia since the first days of the régime, and there was more and worse of the same about Emmerson, the Minister of Railways.

Even Fielding the incorruptible had sat through the session in the House certain of eventual ouster. A long investigation into the practices of his campaigners in 1904 was still under way, but the result was a foregone conclusion.

Wherever one set his foot it seemed to be in a swamp. There had been thirty separate attacks on the administration and more were certainly preparing. All formal charges had been put into the slow-grinding mills of official inquiry and ministers were loud in defence of their personal conduct. But Frederick Borden was a shaken and worried man, Hyman was almost gone though Laurier still declined his resignation, and late in March the affairs of the Minister of Railways had approached a climax.

Emmerson was a personable widower whom Laurier had often urged to marry again. Zoë urged it too, as she did with Sydney Fisher, the Minister of Agriculture, and with William Lyon Mackenzie King, the young man who was becoming prominent in the Labour department. Emmerson had most need of the check-rein and least inclination for it. Very frequently missing from his desk and sometimes visible in less reputable spots, he had prolonged one absence beyond the usual limit. During the course of it a letter had come to Laurier from Emmerson's sister lamenting his latest 'downfall', blaming it on the company he kept, and begging the Prime Minister to make it possible for her to come and nurse him. Laurier had replied warmly, called on Emmerson the same day, and conveyed the message. It had developed in a subsequent letter, however, that the presence of the lady would only be possible if her husband were appointed a solicitor to the Grand Trunk in Ottawa. With this condition, much as he desired to retain a knowledgeable politician, Laurier had been unable to comply. The correspondence had been dropped, Emmerson had emerged repentant, and at his next fall and rising another method had been tried.

The files of the Prime Minister now contained a declaration in his own firm handwriting but completed by the shaky signature of the Minister of Railways. 'I hereby pledge my word to Sir Wilfrid Laurier that I never will again taste wine, beer or any other mixed or intoxicating liquor, in token of which I place in Sir W.L.'s hands my resignation as a member of the cabinet and Minister of Railways with the date in blank, leaving it to him to fill in the blank and act upon it should I fail in my promise. Henry R. Emmerson.'

It had been high time for Fitzpatrick to ascend to the bench, and rather a relief to see him go. The contrivings of that comrade of Quebec had usually been in favour of Laurier, but not always, and they had seemed to become more intricate as he grew older. Aylesworth of Toronto had come as Minister of Justice in his place. Fifty years old and growing deaf, the brilliant arbiter of the Alaska board was rather too brilliant a lawyer for the purposes of the House. In a savage counter-attack he had permanently damaged Foster, one of the leading scandal hunters on the other side of the aisle. That old enemy, who sat now at Borden's right hand, had been barred by divorce from the chance of the leadership in 1892 and was doubly barred now. He had been the administrator of an insurance company and no one had proved that he had been dishonest. But he had been perilously clever, and less than clever in his defence. Laurier himself had come to his rescue at last, for it had not been pleasant to watch the merciless probing of Aylesworth. Neither had it been particularly reassuring. Laurier admired Aylesworth, trusted and respected him, and was sure of trust and loyalty in return. But the venom turned on Foster had been that of a man already aging under infirmities, doubly embittered and solitary in the grip of the same affliction that plagued Sifton.

The new blood in the cabinet had hardly refreshed it and outside the cabinet there was always Bourassa, contemptuous of grimy office-holders. The session, which had seen a government-sponsored Lord's Day Act, had given him a new *cause célèbre*, and the by-election occasioned by Fitzpatrick's going had been an opportunity to promote it. In framing the Lord's Day Act Laurier had responded a little to pressure from Ontario, but more to an obvious need. Archbishop Bruchési himself had approved the bill as a bar to commercialization of the Sabbath and as the guarantee of a day of rest for exploited workers. Bourassa, however, had leaped at it as a new invasion of French Canada by the puritans of Protestant Ontario. The blue Sunday of Toronto was to be fastened on Quebec. In parliament and outside, always with Lavergne at his heels, he had squeezed the uttermost venom from the new grievance. Nor had he stopped there. It was disturbing to discover Bourassa's changing view of the nation. The man who had feared that Canada was no longer Canada for all Canadians now spoke of the new-comers to the western prairies as 'those thousands of strangers who have contributed nothing to the building of the country, who have made no sacrifices for the cause of national unity, and who, if we ever had to pass through some fearsome test, would not associate themselves with it'.

It was a strange charge to go out from a comfortable study against the men who were staking homesteads and fighting the prairie winters. The answer was obvious. 'I should like to see', Laurier told Quebec, 'a good number of young men of talent, lawyers or doctors, go and pitch their tents in the English provinces and there make a good position for themselves by their work and virtue. Nothing would contribute more to destroy the national barriers of prejudice and to create precious sympathy for us in all parts of Canada.'

It was not the answer that would appeal to Bourassa, still less to Lavergne. Laurier was beginning to lose the hope that there was any answer. 'Having known Mr. Papineau, I can in some measure understand Mr. Bourassa. Having known Mr. Bourassa, I can in some measure understand Mr. Papineau.' Down through the years from grandfather to grandson, always a little clearer as the years passed, ran that linking strain of brilliant, bitter futility.

Fielding, unseated in August, was duly re-elected in October with the largest majority he had ever had. It was one of the few rays of light in the gloom that oppressed Laurier as he prepared for the reopening of parliament on November 22. In September in Arthabaska, without warning, a heart attack had carried away his half-brother Henri. Another brother, Romuald, had been lingering on for months in a Montreal hospital, expected to die. Laurier went through the first weeks of the session awaiting this second blow. On December 28 it came.

'The year 1906 has been for me a year of trials. Two brothers have been taken from me, the one struck down in a moment, the other by a slow malady which prolonged his agony for days and weeks. This is what life is. How fragile it is and how tenacious.' He was writing again to Bruchési, that rock of comfort in the restless sea about him. 'And', he added forebodingly, 'what sufferings it reserves even for the happiest.'

2

THE SESSION, adjourned for the Christmas holidays, resumed in January 1907. By the end of the month there had been another break with the young army of Quebec. Whatever Laurier might feel, the party veterans had had enough of Lavergne. In the by-election in Fitzpatrick's constituency, with the Lord's Day Act as his text, the burgeoning Armand had come out full voice against the government. He had helped the official candidate to a sound defeat and was now trumpeting it about the province as evidence that the party of Laurier was no longer the party of Quebec. If Bourassa, the font of all, was still above discipline, Lavergne was not, and on January 28 discipline was applied. In all matters of patronage, Laurier informed a deputation from Lavergne's constituency of Montmagny, the government could only be guided by the members who supported it.

It was, in effect, expulsion from the party and the twenty-seven-year-old seized on it as the occasion for some wildly discursive eloquence during the sitting of February 5. By the twenty-fifth he had gone on to move for the adoption of bilingual currency and bilingual postage stamps. The climate he had managed to create, however, was totally against concessions. Lavergne was well on the way to becoming the Quebec equivalent of Sam Hughes, one of his principal hecklers. He was still cutting his teeth, commented Dansereau, who was once more back with *La Presse* and restored to the fold. Dansereau, replied the new *enfant terrible*, was still on the bottle.

Labour legislation, tariff revisions, and the first steps toward social security measures all waited for the attention of parliament, but it was scandal that held the floor. Commissions were busy investigating the workings of the Elections Act and the workings of the civil service but they had not yet reported. In the meantime the mud flew, dredged up from both sides. Foster, still bleeding from his own wounds, attacked with the savage brilliance of another Cartwright. Duller members, often squirming for shelter, traded threats. The 'nasty, dirty, mean insinuations' of a Liberal enemy were worthy of 'the sewer which takes the place of a mind with him', declared a wrathful New Brunswick Tory. If matters of his private business were discussed he would retaliate in kind. 'I shall discuss the characters of honourable members opposite whether they be ministers or private members, and their connection with women, wine, and graft.'

Silence from Bourassa in such a situation was too much to expect. Irreproachable and irresponsible, he rose on March 26 to deliver a flawless lecture to the evil-doers of both parties and to move for 'a strict and impartial inquiry as to whether any Ministers of the Crown or members of Parliament have improperly made use of their positions . . . or have otherwise been guilty of personal misconduct.' It was easy to answer the proposal, which the author had advanced without submitting himself to the drudgery of obtaining evidence. It was based, Laurier said, on the 'insinuations and tittle-tattle of the street'. Hyman's resignation had not been accepted because nothing had yet been proved and Hyman had solemnly denied all charges against him. It was the same with other men whose reputations were being attacked. Bourassa repeated gossip and threatened what he would do if he had the proof. 'If he has not the proof, why does he mention it at all? The rumours which have been floating in the air at last fell into the gutter, and the honourable gentleman gropes in the gutter and brings those rumours into the House.'

There were limits, nevertheless, even to the protection provided by constitutional procedure and an unshakable majority in the House. The springboard for Bourassa's oration had been a pamphlet dealing with the latest indiscretions of the Minister of Railways. The pledge had not held and the time had come to fill in the date on the letter of resignation. On April 1 Laurier informed Earl Grey, who had now replaced Minto as Governor General, that Emmerson's departure was imperative. On the next day, bowing to circumstances and admitting nothing, Emmerson bade farewell to his portfolio. 'I have never been,' he said, weightily bequeathing another jewel to the annals of parliamentary debate, 'mark my words, Mr. Speaker, and I make them with the full knowledge of the solemnity of the occasion and the dignity of my position – I have never been in a hotel in Montreal with a woman of ill repute.'

3

THREE DAYS later came a grateful change of air. Sailing with Zoë on April 5, Laurier arrived in London a week later to prepare for the opening of his third Colonial Conference. The welcome was as warm as ever, the arrangements as lavish, and it now seemed that all of high society had been mobilized to promote the consolidation of the British Empire. Much else, however, was changed and the change was almost startling when the conference opened on the fifteenth. Joseph Chamberlain was a hopeless invalid now, struck down by a paralytic stroke the year before. The Liberal government of Campbell-Bannerman was in power, dividing much of its strength between the imperialists of the new day and the traditionalists of Gladstone's Little England. General Louis Botha, once the commander of a Boer army with a British price on his head, was now here from South Africa as the Honourable Louis Botha, Prime Minister of a British Dominion. The Earl of Elgin presided as the new Colonial Secretary, happily remindful of that other Elgin who had brought responsible government. Asquith and Lloyd George sat in on some of the sessions, and a bumptious young under-secretary by the name of Winston Churchill had a good deal to say. It was Sir Wilfrid Laurier of Canada, however, who had become the dean of the conference and around whom debate revolved.

Some aspects of his position he made clear at once. The dominions and the home government met as equals. 'We are all His Majesty's governments.' It would be better, he thought, to change the name of the gathering from Colonial to Imperial Conference, and the change was duly made. Laurier came with no chip on his shoulder and he was deeply warmed both by the friendship that he instantly struck up with Botha and by the very fact of the presence of this former rebel Boer. Such a change, so quickly brought about, seemed justification for much. Whatever Chamberlain had represented in the British ethos, there was evidently side by side with it a constructive, creative, and conciliating genius. Yet there was still the inheritance from Chamberlain to deal with. Busy and secretive, determined and high-placed, the promoters of empire went on much as before. To their propositions Laurier gave short shrift.

Once again and decisively, so far as Canada was concerned, there would be no Imperial Council overriding dominion parliaments. In the matter of trade there could be no question of excluding the rest of the world. Too much had been excluded already. So far as the United States was concerned, 'We have said good-bye to that trade. If we were to follow the laws of nature and geography between Canada and the United States the whole trade would flow from south to north and from north to south. We have done everything possible by building canals and subsidizing railways to bring trade from west to east and from east to west, so as to direct it into British channels.' With the best will in the world there was no more to be done on that score, and in the case of defence there was less.

For five days, from May 2 to May 7, Laurier sat silent as discussion circled the old dreams of imperial armies and navies. Deakin of Australia, slowly wearing down, irritably parried the thrusting importunities of the already all-knowledgeable Churchill. 'Most of your propositions', he snapped at last, 'seem incontestable to you, but our experience refutes many of them.' On May 8 Louis-Philippe Brodeur, present as Minister of Marine and Fisheries, quietly re-stated the old Canadian position. The Canadian government was against naval or military contributions of any kind. Brodeur quoted Tupper to show that Canadians of all parties supported the position. On May 9, briefly and decisively, Laurier closed the issue: 'I have said all I have to say on the subject.'

There remained his own proposal of the All-Red Route, and the last days of the conference were devoted to it. Many of the details Laurier had worked out with Sifton, who had come to London on business of his own and who was as clear and resourceful as ever in the face of a large undertaking. Out of the work came a new enthusiasm for the project and even a hope of closing the breach with Sifton. In the late hours of debate

Laurier was not disposed to accept quibbling even from British ministers. 'I dislike the word "inquiry",' he told Lloyd George, who wished to investigate the possibility of alternative routes. 'An All-Red Route *must* cross Canada.'

The Prime Minister of Canada had dominated the proceedings of the conference, and outside the walls of the Colonial Office his writ still seemed to run. Everywhere he spoke with mellow warmth and authority, with an affection deeply responded to, and with a finality that appeared to be accepted. 'Some years ago,' he told a dinner of British parliamentarians, 'under the sway of sentiments which the traditions of English parliaments inspire in every British subject, I thought a moment that I might be able to have a seat at Westminster. I have since come to the conclusion that it was a fine dream all the same. Always we return to our country more convinced that imperial unity should be based on local autonomy.'

There was a month in Italy and Switzerland, enjoyed this time in the glow of good health and with a sense of triumph. 'Thinking of all that has passed,' he wrote David, 'I am surprised at the results obtained. I have escaped all the dangers. All my ideas have been accepted all along the line. My policy has carried the day. It seems to me certain that this perilous voyage has in sum turned out well. But this is between us for I do not wish to seem to beat the big drum.'

There were drums enough when he returned late in July. Quebec and Montreal gave him two of the mightiest receptions he had ever known. This time, however, there were no congratulations from Bourassa and at the other end of the spectrum there was only a hostile apathy. The crowds of Montreal, according to the Tory *Gazette*, had been 'cheering for a negation'.

4

He had been exhilarated in London by the new rapport with Sifton. Never quite liking the man and never expecting now to plumb the depths of that mind, he still responded to its clarity and vigour. The man with the lugubrious ear-trumpet, always haunted by scandal, was still one of the great forces in the country. Laurier needed him, still wished to use him, and three thousand miles from Ottawa it had seemed that the prospects were good. As the work on the All-Red Route brought the two men together the memories of schools had receded. It had seemed possible to dismiss as a minor undertone that sense of growing antipathy to Quebec and its French. When at last and definitely Laurier came out with the proposal that Sifton re-enter the cabinet he had not been quite refused.

Sifton was still considering in August, and one hesitated to guess what those cold considerations could lead to. Nevertheless, if the price could be paid, everything but purity would be restored to the battered ministry and there would be new strength everywhere but in Quebec. For both those shortcomings there was one obvious remedy and in the first month at home, still hopeful and refreshed, Laurier set himself to attain it.

Armand Lavergne, officially in disgrace but still regarded with an amused, avuncular eye, became one of a number of emissaries from the Prime Minister to Bourassa. He was warmed and flattered by the work, and it seemed for a little while that he might be successful. Lavergne's idol was restless between crusades and looking for new directions. The teeth of the Lord's Day Act had been drawn by a Senate amendment which gave provincial Attorneys-General complete discretion in its administration. There was no fault to be found with Laurier's attitude toward British imperialists and the matter of the schools was settled. Old quarrels slept, there were no new ones immediately on the horizon, and so far as the cabinet was concerned it was now or never for Bourassa. Obviously he realized it, and for a few weeks he seemed inclined to resist the steady, secret pull that was drawing him back inside the shell of Quebec.

On one point, however, he was adamant, and it was enough. He would not serve in any cabinet with Sifton, and Laurier would not forgo the prospect of Sifton even for Bourassa. Hardly had that been settled when Sifton's answer came. He would enter the cabinet, but he would enter it only in company with two other members named by himself, and the result would be that he held control of policy and control of the succession. It was too much. The succession was reserved for Fielding and Laurier intended to be master while he remained. On August 29

William Pugsley was sworn to the ministry of Public Works, bringing with him all the rich and ripe aroma of New Brunswick politics. On August 30 George Perry Graham, a lively Ontario Protestant, editor of the Brockville *Recorder*, became Minister of Railways and Canals.

Graham was a hard, clean fighter and Pugsley was clever. There was still Fielding. There was the immovable, always capable Sydney Fisher, who had held the portfolio of Agriculture from the beginning. There was Rodolphe Lemieux in Quebec, who gave Bourassa as good as he got. There was the venerable acerbity of Cartwright, the undoubted stature of Aylesworth, and there were half a dozen other men who were far from being weaklings. Laurier was quite capable as yet of meeting anything that might develop from the direction of Robert Borden. But he had found no new strength and he had passed a turn in the road that would be final. Sifton remained as the enigmatic private member, neither out of the party nor of it. By the end of October Bourassa was gone.

Early in the month he came to Laurier with his resignation. Always above the drudgery of work and discussion in committee, he had freed himself months before from the bonds of party. 'The future and the fate of either political party, as at present constituted, is utterly indifferent to me.' He was now abandoning hope of the federal parliament. He intended to turn to Quebec provincial politics and his target would be Gouin, the Liberal Premier – Gouin and all that he represented in the way of entrenched loyalty to the policies of Wilfrid Laurier. Bourassa did not say that; it was merely implicit in everything else he said. He had been challenged to run for a provincial seat and he intended to accept the challenge. It was Bellechasse, a stubborn rural constituency where he was certain to be defeated, but that did not make much difference. There would be other elections and wherever he went the young intellectuals, the young clerics, the young men of the cities would read what he wrote and hear what he said and follow him. Bourassa, with all that he represented of Quebec and all that he might have meant to the country, was lost. There was not much left to say between the man of sixty-five and the man of thirty-nine, and Laurier said what there was in two pithy sentences. 'I regret your going. We need a man like you at Ottawa, though I should not want two.'

In November, as a final gesture when Bourassa was defeated in Bellechasse, Laurier offered him an uncontested return to his federal seat. It was significant enough that the Conservative party was equally accommodating. But neither offer was accepted. The captain had turned his back on the old leader and the young army followed. Laurier could only watch, still with a touch of incredulity. 'They should be my natural allies.' Always a little more, almost insensibly, he was leaning on Ontario. Or rather, he was leaning on the name of Laurier in Ontario, the Maritimes, the west, and in Quebec too. Only the strength of the legend stood opposed to the new forces, and the strength of the government resided in one man.

He came to the end of his sixty-sixth year with 'my health, perhaps, better than at any previous period of my life'. On November 28, a week after his birthday, the tenth parliament convened for its fourth session. Louis-Philippe Brodeur, struggling with the mess bequeathed him by Préfontaine in the department of Marine and Fisheries, was immediately under attack. A week or so later it was Pugsley; and while this latest Minister of Public Works was defending a speckled record in New Brunswick word came that Israel Tarte was dead. Frank Oliver's department of the Interior would be next in line for attack and Aylesworth's irascible failings were making him a liability. Occasionally there was word of Blake, but the reports now were only of a hopeless invalid who had returned from England to die. Always a little grimier, always a little lonelier, the work went on.

5

THERE WERE amicable stirrings in Washington and it was beginning to be apparent that a Republican government, under bitter attack for its policies, was thinking of gestures toward Canada. Elihu Root, the American Secretary of State, made most of them and Laurier reciprocated, without warmth. Talk went on, circling the fisheries, the boundary waters, the movement of warships on the lakes, and all the perennial problems. There was certainly a groping together and James

Bryce, the new British ambassador in Washington, was helping it on. So was Grey, the amiable, well-willing imperialist in Government House, whose liking for Laurier and for all things French-Canadian took the bite from his bark. The Prime Minister, however, remained stiffish and difficult, querulous of every proposal and flatly rejecting some. He remembered Alaska too well to be lured by Root into any wholesale 'clearing of the slate', particularly under British auspices. When a proposal of Root's came to him through Grey, suggesting that Lord Alverstone of the Alaska Commission pay an official visit to the United States, he threw up his hands in amazed irritation. Alverstone could not visit the United States without visiting Canada, and there were few Englishmen whose presence would be less desired. Was Grey not aware that ever since the boundary decision the word 'Alverstonize' had acquired as permanent a place in the Canadian political vocabulary as the word 'boycott' in the English?

So far as trade was concerned Laurier meant what he had said in England. The country had been rebuffed at every turn by the United States and it was now doing very well under the tariff administered by Fielding. Better relations with the United States were certainly desirable and Laurier was uneasily conscious of his promises to the Canadian west, long unfulfilled. But he would bargain seriously with the Americans when the Americans were seriously ready, and not before. He was in no great hurry. With every day and with every advancing mile of the new transcontinental he felt his position growing stronger. The Roosevelt administration was in the last year of its life and the Laurier government could do with refreshment and a mandate. The work for 1908 was to patch up, paint up, and pull the party together for an election.

'The opposition will of course put their faith in scandal and extravagance,' wrote Hyman from retirement in Florida. 'Are we again going to be fortunate enough to counteract by arousing the interest of the country in some great national scheme?' The answer was no. The great schemes were under way, the country itself went on magnificently, but there was still the debris of Hyman's day to be faced. January and February went to a bitter, dogged defence of the department of the Interior, with Oliver bearing the brunt and Sifton's name dragged in to haunt every transaction. Under the administration of these two men millions of acres in homesteads and ranch lands and railway grants had passed from the Dominion of Canada into the hands of private owners. Fortunes had been made and it was beyond belief that all of them had been made honestly. Sifton's fortune was rumoured to be one of the largest and no one would ever be satisfied with the explanation that he was merely a lucky speculator, that every dollar had been made independently of his public office. He stood up to defend himself by defending Oliver on February 6 and once again the cold, hard, fearless strength of the man left his enemies gaping. But he had proved nothing except that Sifton was unassailable.

At the end of March Fielding brought down the report of the commission that had investigated the civil service and there was rich material in that. 'It is practically impossible', said the report, 'to fix the responsibility on anybody. The Deputy is supposed to shoulder responsibility for everything, but that means he speaks for the Department and the Department, like the King, can do no wrong. There seems to be a huge redundancy of work which proceeds in a slumbering, haphazard way, giving rise to constant blundering and confusion. There is no visible sign of a single directing head or an intelligent purpose, unless it be that of spending as much money as possible. Politics enter into every appointment and politicians on the spot interest themselves not only in the appointment but in the subsequent promotions of officers.'

Through April the skeletons of patronage leaped from every closet and no minister was safe. May and June brought a savage battle over a new franchise bill, forced on Laurier by the toughest and most worried of his politicians and all too obviously designed to elect Liberals. It went through, mutilated, after a series of conferences with Borden which grew steadily more acrimonious and in which all matters agreed on had finally to be reduced to writing. On June 17 Fisher introduced a bill to reform the civil service, and it passed a cynical House which welcomed the close of the tenth parliament a month later. There was to be an election but there was no issue. The ins clung on, the outs hoped only faintly to get in, and neither held out much prospect of improvement. 'There is not only a lack of efficient organization and method,' the report on the civil service had concluded, 'there would seem also to be a lack of conscience.' It seemed to apply as well to the men above the clerks.

6

ON JULY 20 the great twelve-day festival began in Quebec celebrating the three-hundredth anniversary of the founding of the city. It had been planned for months and no magnificence was lacking. From England with a British naval squadron came the Prince of Wales. The Marquis de Lévis and the Comte de Montcalm came from France with French warships. The Vice-President of the United States was on hand. As usual there were the sour undercurrents of gaucheries and resentments. The English spoke too much of Wolfe at a celebration for Champlain. The French waved too many tricolours to suit the taste of visiting imperialists. Clerical Quebec seethed with the rumour that the principal envoy from Paris was a freemason. All was harmony, however, at the great public occasions and Laurier found it good, after the dismal preoccupations of Ottawa, to ride that glittering swell. Once more he declined a peerage. Once more, and more explicitly, speaking as a weathered pilot in his home port, he defined the course he had plotted for the ship of state. 'We are reaching the day', he said, 'when our Canadian parliament will claim co-equal rights with the British parliament and when the only ties binding us together will be a common flag and a common crown.'

Then it was time to think of retaining the helm. As the dog-days of August came on there was a curious calm, deepened by the absence of Bourassa, who was away in Europe. Bourassa had not been greatly pleased by the plans for the tercentenary, and he had earned a holiday. In the ten months since his retirement from Ottawa he had shaken many citadels. Surrounded, as a nervous Liberal press described it, by 'the choir boys of the new pontiff', he had nevertheless spoken little more than the truth when he told a great meeting in Montreal on May 25 that 'two or three young men, supported by men still young, having at their disposal neither money nor newspapers nor places nor patronage, but having feeling, thought, and principles, have succeeded in arousing the province'. On that same day Armand Lavergne had resigned his federal seat and gone to campaign with Bourassa in the provincial elections. Both had been elected. Bourassa's rebuff in Bellechasse had been more than made good by his defeat of Gouin himself in Gouin's own constituency. Quebec's long, easy days of impregnable Liberalism were over. Bourassa, Lavergne, and youth, much more than the handful of *Bleus* who slumbered on in their seats, were the real opposition.

The solid, stolid, clear-thinking Gouin, though he had been easily reinstalled as the leader of a powerful majority, was clearly in for trouble at the next session. One could read another warning in the fact that Bourassa had chosen to begin his provincial campaign with a powerful speech at St-Lin. His purpose, as he proclaimed it, was the salvation and not the destruction of St-Lin's most famous son. The mantle of Laurier should not be used 'to wipe the floor of the Legislative Assembly, soiled by intriguers'. Bourassa did not look, for the moment, beyond the boundaries of Quebec. 'We are going to spread throughout the province the ideas of independence, honesty, and patriotism.' The intriguers he had marked down, however, were the buttresses of Laurier's strength and it was hard to imagine Bourassa, still less Bourassa with Lavergne at his side, proceeding coolly toward that 'equilibrium between the two races and equilibrium between the federal and provincial powers' that he announced as his goal.

He returned from Europe at the end of August, however, concerned only with Quebec. Contact with republican France had made him more the Catholic. Rest had refreshed his ardour for reform. He intended, he said, to replace party spirit by public spirit and to launch Quebec on a program of economic, moral, and intellectual development. Then, and only then, would he turn to the question of autonomy and the proper place of the province in Confederation. For the two begrimed parties now disputing power he had only equal contempt. In the approaching general election, except where it was necessary to root out the occasional corrupt candidate, he would make no choice between Laurier and Borden. The calm, it seemed, was real; Quebec was safe.

1908 ELECTION. CARTOON BY FERGUS KYLE

7

ACROSS THE REST of the country the well-oiled machine was already under way. There was still Fielding in the Maritimes. The giants were gone or fading in Ontario and the officials reported the party 'in an extremely apathetic and comatose condition', but there was still money. There was still Silent Smith, the party organizer, silently at work. In the west Sifton had made his declaration: 'The policy of Sir Wilfrid Laurier', he told his nominating convention at Brandon, 'represents the completion of the National Transcontinental, the building of a

SIR WILFRID LAURIER AT SOREL—THE PREMIER AND SOME OF HIS SUPPORTERS ON THE PLATFORM.

SKETCH BY GEORGE E. MCELROY IN THE MONTREAL *Star*
SEPTEMBER 7, 1908

line of railway to Hudson's Bay, and the development of the natural resources. Negation, criticism, and scandal are offered by the opposition.'

On September 5, once more under the flaring maples of Sorel, Laurier opened his campaign. He was the issue and Sifton had given him his theme. 'Let Laurier Finish His Work', the banners and broadsheets bellowed as thousands crowded closer in under the platform to hear the silvery voice that no longer carried quite as it once had. 'Not many years now remain to me. The snows of winter have taken the place of spring,' he told them, tossing his white head; 'but however I may show the ravages of time my heart is still young.'

At Montreal a few days later the cheers billowed deafeningly again. 'One task finished but calls to a new task . . . so much done, yet so much to be done. I dream of all that I wish to do to complete my task, yet unhappily the years pile on my head. It is probably the last time that I shall appeal to my compatriots.' He dealt with scandal, and the issue remained Laurier: let Laurier judge, let the great work go on. 'There have been abuses . . . there was a Judas among the twelve apostles; there may well be one or several black sheep in our flock, but if there are it is for us and not for the Conservatives to rid ourselves of them. We have been twelve years in office and these years will be remembered in the history of Canada. In them Canada has been lifted from the humble position of a colony to that of a nation. In 1896 Canada was hardly known in the United States or Europe. In 1908 Canada has become a star to which is directed the gaze of the civilized world. That is what we have done.'

Later a wrathful Willison was to say of the campaign, 'There never was in Canada a more flagrant misuse of public works and public appropriations.' Religion leaped from the vestry as Orangemen published a pamphlet attacking marriage decrees of the Church. Sharp-eyed Liberal organizers seized on the material joyfully and broadcast it through Quebec as the opinion of Robert Borden. Laurier noted the tactic, disapproved of it, and failed to stop it; he was too busy with scandal. There was much else to trouble the mind of a man whirled from constituency to constituency, smiling and shaking hands, slapping the backs of a thousand muddy minions. 'The indications are that we will win handsomely,' he wrote to Grey on October 20, 'but I am not altogether pleased. I do not think there was sufficient justification for the nasty fight which has been put up by the opposition, but it has brought to light some things which are not pleasant and which must be gone into with a severe hand when the issue is settled.'

Settlement came on October 26. Laurier had won, but hardly

THE COUNTRY:—"I think it would be cheaper to get a new housekeeper and new linen, than to let Laurier take another five years to clean up."

CARTOON BY N. MCCONNELL IN THE TORONTO *News*
OCTOBER 10, 1908

handsomely. Fielding had been unable to hold the line in Nova Scotia. Sifton had been a liability in the west. In Ontario and Quebec the government held the same number of seats as before, though many of the constituencies had changed. Across the whole country the total majority of seats was reduced by only fifteen and still stood at a safe forty-seven. But without Quebec it would be reduced to four, and out of the 1,150,000 Canadians who had voted there was only a majority of 25,000 who preferred Wilfrid Laurier.

8

I AM CONFINED to my bed by a stupid disease vulgarly known as the "shingles",' he reported to Grey on October 30. The usual mountain of congratulatory messages lay piled about him but he was not much deceived by them. His instinct was to go.

Two weeks later, on a dismal, foggy November morning, he came into his office, dismissed his secretary, and sat down alone to write out a letter in longhand. It was his resignation, addressed to Grey and advising that Fielding be called as his successor. His appointment with Grey was for one o'clock. He sent for Fielding and was told that the Minister of Finance was in conference with a deputation and would be available about noon. He got up and stood for a moment warming his chilly hands in front of the grate fire.

It would be half an hour or so before Fielding could arrive, and among the callers waiting in the ante-room was a thirty-four-year-old Montrealer by the name of Cameron. Kirk Cameron was a familiar now, a well-to-do businessman whose affairs grew with the pulse of the country. Fifteen years before, at the Liberal convention in Ottawa in 1893, Cameron had been a young school-teacher with a zest for politics. He had shaken Laurier's hand at the convention. Or he said he had; Laurier did not remember. He knew only that from that day forward he had had an enthralled friend, ready at any time for any errand. This time Cameron had been sent on a mission of inquiry to one of the constituencies and would be back with news. Laurier asked for him to be shown in.

When he came and the business was disposed of Laurier pointed to the letter lying open on the desk. He watched as the other read it with consternation. Years before the Scot had refused an invitation to stand for parliament. He would never do it, Cameron had said, until he had the means to be above political favours. He had the means now but the time had passed by. He was one of the young men who had not been gained, and there were hundreds of them. One was not sure, this grey morning, if it was not for their good.

Yet there was something warming in that shocked face as it was raised to him. This man had nothing to gain or lose by his going, and still could not conceive of it. That name, Wilfrid Laurier, still meant much to many. He was still respected, needed. It seemed to dispel the gloom a little and weaken the resolve.

'I will make you a bet, Sir Wilfrid,' Cameron said softly, 'that Fielding will talk you out of this.'

The Prime Minister shook his head. The elections had been a bitter disappointment. There was a time for every man to get off the stage and he felt his time had come. He looked forward to retirement. He looked forward to writing a political history of Canada.

Cameron went out and Fielding came in. The arguments piled up one on the other, all familiar, all in the end decisive. There was no question of health at the moment; Laurier was well. It was Laurier who had won the election rather than the party, and his going would be a deadly blow to the party. Fielding had sided with Sifton on the question of the schools; how could he hope to hold Quebec while that grievance was still fresh? Finally agreement came. He would carry on, Laurier said, through the sessions of 1909 and 1910. Then, with two healing years behind him and two years to settle into the leadership before the next election, Fielding would take over.

The appointment with Grey was cancelled and the letter of resignation torn up. The old routine resumed and government went on. Taft was now President of the United States, and the eternal missions coming and going between Ottawa and Washington seemed to be accomplishing something. On Christmas Day Laurier was forced to concede that the Bering Sea question seemed to be approaching settlement. A treaty on boundary waters was almost ready for signature. The Atlantic fisheries dispute had gone to the World Court at The Hague and in that too there seemed a good possibility of agreement. But Root's latest proposal, that the two countries negotiate for free trade in coal, had been met with a flat refusal. The Americans would have to talk of more than coal if they wanted an agreement on trade, and they were not likely to do so. Even if they did come round, tariffs would be more in Fielding's sphere than Laurier's. There would be no reason for a retiring Prime Minister to change his plans. The road seemed clear to the end.

23

SHIPS AND MEN

1909-1910

THERE WAS ONE considerable decision still to be taken. It had hung over Laurier from the days of the first colonial conference, and it remained his decision. It could not be left for Fielding. On March 29, 1909, with the first session of the eleventh parliament two months old, Foster put the point.

He rose to move 'That in the opinion of this House, in view of her great and varied resources, of her geographical position and national environment and of that spirit of self-help and self-respect which alone befits a strong and growing people, Canada should no longer delay in assuming her proper share of the responsibility and financial burden incident to the suitable protection of her exposed coastline and great seaports.'

The question of a navy had now reached the floor of the House. Laurier was surprised only at the mildness of the resolution and of Foster's accompanying speech. He knew that both had been delayed for two months because of the opposition of Monk, the leader of Quebec's federal Conservatives and the son of the judge who had presided at the libel trial in the case of the Forty Thieves. Monk was certain to be difficult; any such proposal in Quebec would have to run the gauntlet between charges of militarism and charges of imperialism. Laurier had nevertheless expected that both the state of the world and the temper of English-Canadian Tories would force them to stronger measures.

Only two weeks before Foster spoke a great shock wave had reverberated from London as Reginald McKenna, First Lord of the Admiralty, announced that the shipbuilding program of a truculent Germany was overtaking the British. By 1912, at the present rate, he had said, German and British strength in dreadnoughts would be equal. Since the great armoured battleships were the only units that counted in the thinking of naval planners, the result would be that British supremacy was ended and the seas no longer safe. Instantly from London there had gone up a mighty cry for more ships, and it was echoed in Canada by all the varied voices that had opposed Laurier's 'negations'. The voices were a good deal louder now and a good deal more effective. The high-placed gentlemen in England who had been busy at the time of the Imperial Conference were extending their efforts to Canada. Even the usually Liberal Toronto *Globe* had come out on March 23 with the shout that Canada 'fling the smug maxims of commercial prudence to the winds' and place dreadnoughts or the money for dreadnoughts at the disposal of the British government.

Foster did not ask this. He pressed for no reversal of the policy that Laurier had established. Regular contributions to an imperial navy, he agreed, would smack of colonial tribute. Any gift, either of money or of dreadnoughts, should be considered only if it were established that a naval emergency existed. The immediate recommendation was for a limited, local, independent Canadian force.

It was all a little less than Laurier had prepared for and a great deal less, he knew, than many Tories wanted. But it had to be taken at face value. The time had come to redeem the promises of London, always expressed or implied. The other side of the coin was now presented. Laurier had refused, in the name of autonomy, to contribute to imperial navies. How, in that same name, could a country with great coastlines open on both oceans, a country that lived increasingly by sea-borne trade, refuse to provide what was necessary for her own defence?

Laurier was not impressed by the rumblings of imperial crisis. Still less did he like the backstairs methods of British imperialists in Canada. In spite of that, it was now necessary that the Prime

Minister define the position of the Dominion within the Empire. He did so in words that might have been Foster's or Borden's, almost in the words he had used at the first imperial banquetings twelve years before. 'If the day should come when the supremacy of Britain on the high seas will be challenged, it will be the duty of all the daughter nations to close around the old motherland.' He went a step farther, with his eyes on the faces of his Quebec opposites. In such a day, he said, 'I would deem it my duty to devote what might be left of my life and energy to stump the country and endeavour to impress upon my fellow countrymen, especially my compatriots in the province of Quebec, the conviction that the salvation of England is the salvation of our own country.'

He found Foster's speech admirable and denied only the implication that Canada had not carried her share of the burdens to date. The resolution itself he criticized only for the vagueness of its wording, and he worked in complete harmony with Borden and Foster to repair that fault. At the end of a long day the amended resolution passed by a unanimous vote. 'The House', said the operative paragraph, 'will cordially approve of any necessary expenditure designed to promote the organization of a Canadian naval service in co-operation with and in close relation to the imperial navy.'

Three days later, as the last dregs of scandal were stirred again, Laurier was face to face with another Foster. Why, demanded the man still savage from the cloud on his own name, was the Prime Minister not taking action to recover money stolen from the public treasury? 'Is it because you share in it – for party interest and party advantage?' The reply came after the dinner recess, unsoftened by the hour of reflection, from a grim and white-lipped man. 'I take this occasion to observe to my honourable friend that there is no man so ready to make insinuations . . . and no man who will wince and whine so much when he receives a return blow. I have to say to my honourable friend that I never manipulated other people's money, I never manipulated trust funds.'

The words were as unforgivable as the words that had drawn them forth, and the Prime Minister was compelled by an abashed

Speaker to withdraw them. He had reduced Foster but hardly enhanced himself. Two weeks later he had to come before the House with the first demand of the Grand Trunk for another ten million dollars and listen to Borden putting the worst possible face on the railway project. 'As far as the whole road is concerned,' said the man who now stood in the place of Blake, 'the probable cost will be about two hundred and eighty millions. Of this the country provides in cash contributions or in bond guarantees about nine-tenths.' It was a far cry from the thirteen millions Laurier had spoken of five years before, and much else was not marching to plan. All this and more was duly pointed out. The session he still thought of as his next-to-the-last came to its end on May 19 with more than its usual quota of bruises and resentments and frustrations.

Yet the naval decision had been taken and the last of the dangerous corners, it seemed, was turned. Quebec was moody but Quebec was quiet. Bourassa, immersed in provincial battles, had hardly deigned to notice the talk of ships. Archbishop Bruchési, writing to the Governor General about the prospect of navies and wars, had been immensely reassuring. 'When the bell rings,' he had said, 'we shall all go.'

2

LONDON still throbbed with the fear of the Kaiser's dreadnoughts and the call had gone out for a conference on imperial defence. In conjunction with this an imperial press conference had been arranged and there was no doubt that some of the best brains of the Empire would be devoted to chilling the blood of colonial newspaper men. Robert Borden was also going to London and though the visit was unofficial he would certainly be the target of every Admiralty strategist and every imperialist politician. It seemed to a man who was unconvinced of crisis and intended no change in policy that that would be enough. Brodeur, the Minister of Marine, and Frederick Borden, who still lingered on in his mightily-mustachioed splendour as Minister of Militia, would attend the defence conference but they would be safely anchored by the resolution of the Canadian parliament. Laurier, through June, had domestic fish to fry.

For part of the past session, with electioneering ended and scandal growing stale, parliament had acted more like what it was, the responsible custodian whose decisions affected billions of the country's wealth and millions of future lives. On a motion of Borden, and with Laurier's full support, a committee on natural resources had been set up to control the development and prevent the wastage of the country's fisheries, forests, mines, waterways, and water power. The effect would be to end a pioneering, buccaneering era in which haphazard, uncontrolled grabbing, stealing, and destroying had been of immeasurable cost to the nation. In a debate that struck no sparks and made few headlines a step of enormous importance had been taken, and it was equally important now to find the man to head the committee. In Laurier's mind there was no doubt as to his identity. Once more and in spite of everything he intended to make use of Sifton, and the first overtures were under way. Always a little more difficult now, they moved more slowly than expected and it would be September, as it turned out, before Laurier had his man. Even in June, however, he had little doubt of the result. He could not count on friendship and Sifton was beyond flattery. He was beyond money-hunger and contemptuous of power that he felt he could have for the taking. The one thing remained that had never failed to move him, the perennial fascination of the big job.

On June 1 Laurier had the pleasure of installing Charles Murphy of Ottawa, a vigorous, one-armed Irish Catholic, as Secretary of State for the newly-established Department of External Affairs. For a department dealing with diplomats it was a rather odd choice; Murphy was much like Tarte in his love of parochial politics and his affinity for enduring feuds. Laurier, however, did not yet give the new department much importance. 'I think', he had said in introducing it to the House, 'that at this time we should have what every other government has, a department . . . where everything relating to our foreign relations may be found and that instead of being scattered as at present in the various departments they should be concentrated in one where we can get at them at a moment's notice.' Over such duties Murphy could preside as well as anyone, and his function as an Ottawa Catholic would be rather more important.

It was mainly along the borderlands of the Ottawa that French-Canadian settlement had 'invaded' Upper Canada. Toronto and Quebec might quarrel at long range but here there was actual mingling and confrontation. In the process the overgrowth of dispute was stripped away and the roots laid bare to hint of future trouble. Orangeism and ultramontanism made much of religion but the real battleground was race, and the quarrels of French and Irish Catholics were opening rents even in the seamless garment of the Church. Bishops with brogues, even though they were carefully chosen for their ancestral French names, were no longer acceptable to French Canadians. The Irish were discontented with the shortcomings of French schools. The tug of Bourassa was growing stronger, dragging up the inevitable reaction, and there was only one way to meet it. 'Some of the French people are leaving us,' Laurier advised Murphy, 'and you should make every effort to win over the English clergy and the English-speaking Liberals.'

One day after Murphy's appointment Rodolphe Lemieux, who had been carrying the weight of two portfolios, vacated Labour and the ministry was occupied by William Lyon Mackenzie King. The grandson of William Lyon Mackenzie was thirty-five years old, and few men could have seemed more improbable as the descendant of a great rebel. Hopelessly condemned to stubby rotundity, nervously correct in dress, in the social amenities, and in everything he did, he seemed the apotheosis of the ordinary. He was, however, a formidably educated young man who had acquired nothing without intending to make use of it and who achieved nothing without carefully making it known where it would be appreciated.

He had already covered the country and a good deal of the world as a special commissioner for immigration and as deputy in the Labour ministry. There was nothing visible behind him but success. 'A promising young man,' wrote James Bryce from Washington, 'if he keeps his health and his modesty.' A warmly oozing humanitarian who had made a special study of the problems of labour, King was something new in the government of the day. He bled for the trials of the working man, but under the gush, Laurier had reason to suspect, that blood ran cold enough for any politician. King was his mother's blatantly adoring son, and the ice in the maternal veins had come to the Prime Minister's notice a year or so before when he had been the unwilling recipient of a stream of letters from several young ladies living at a Y.W.C.A. in the United States. They were seeking his intercession on behalf of King's aunt, the mother's estranged sister, who was being left to die alone, penniless and without help.

One was inclined to admire King's ability rather than to like King, but he was not a man to lose sight of. It would have been impossible in any case; King had pushed himself up with a trembling suavity that almost masked enormous impudence. Or enormous self-confidence; in spite of everything the man was impressive. He had been largely responsible for the Industrial Disputes Investigation Act of 1907, one of the first government gestures toward the heading-off or settlement of strikes, he had proved himself an amazingly skilful arbiter in many of the disputes, and he had done much more than any man before him to equip the department of Labour with modern statistical methods and a modern outlook. Laurier had procured him the Cross of the Order of Saint Michael and Saint George in 1906 and absent-mindedly recommended him again in 1908. He was now ripe for more than decorations and one saw him into the ministry with the sense that here at least was a man of the new day.

July Laurier allotted to a short foray in the west. The usual drift of news came after him but did not greatly disturb him. It was evident that an imperialist campaign was developing and that Willison, for one, was helping it along. The extent of the German menace was daily magnified and the scope of Canadian planning set against it, with loud outcries over the shortcomings. Hugh Graham of Montreal, whom Laurier had made Sir Hugh without greatly changing him, demanded dreadnoughts and more dreadnoughts for the motherland. A Dominion Day speech, reported from London, gave a hint that Borden was weakening under pressure. Out on the dusty prairies, however, there seemed little interest in warships and less to fear from them. Laurier saw instead his first year of crop failure and it was somehow curiously exhilarating rather than depressing. 'I knew before but I never realized as I do now', he wrote to Grey from Somerset, Manitoba, 'the enthusiasm of this western people. There is no crop whatever in the southern part of Manitoba, Saskatchewan, and Alberta – everything has been devoured by intense heat and drought. The people are not at all discouraged – far from it – they are as buoyant as ever and say this is part of the game.'

When he reached home in August Quebec was astir in its own incalculable way. Bourassa had been a brilliant force in provincial politics but not an unqualified success. Some of the corrupt had gone down before him but the righteous had stood fast, and between the extremes ordinary men had been irked by his usual assumption of inviolable authority. He had descended on the Quebec legislature as one bringing it the tables of the law and had been met by a steadfast Gouin who had taken two stiff drinks in an ante-room and marched out to answer the first speech of the oracle with stunning effect. 'These are the people', he said of Bourassa and Lavergne, 'who all their life have thought only to hate and destroy. At Ottawa they worked only to destroy the men who undertook something for the country – Laurier, Brodeur, Lemieux, Fielding, Sifton.'

It was a measure of Gouin's courage and confidence that he included the last two names. The solid core of Quebec remained unshaken. In later mighty orations Bourassa had held the House far into the night and left it gaping, but beyond reasserting his powers he had not accomplished much. He seemed to be moodily aware of it. He was yearning now for a newspaper of his own and for the support of substantial men, but the goal seemed far off. Always withdrawing a little more into himself, yet always surrounded by the terrible young, he had no appeal for the comfortable middle-aged.

It seemed to be Lavergne now, 'straight as a sword, lively as a flame', who was the more effective politician. He had done as much as Bourassa to make the session in Quebec one of the liveliest ever held, and he had not abandoned any of his Ottawa interests. To his demands for bilingualism and his complaints about western immigration he was now adding the question of the navy, which he had instantly pounced upon as an imperialist machination. He would never serve in any of England's wars, he declared, but he was always at the disposal of his country and he had his gesture ready. With the stars of a captain blossoming inexplicably on his shoulders, Armand Lavergne emerged as a member of the Canadian militia. 'I have been much edified', Laurier commented dryly, 'to learn that Armand has become one of the recognized defenders of the country. I hope that he will not be called to pour out his blood for it and I expect that in uniform he will learn that thing which is called discipline.'

He was writing to Lavergne's wife, his 'little Georgette'. Before long he was responding again, without amusement, to the bond that he never could and never wished to break. 'I write you a word on the subject of my father-in-law, M. Roy,' came a letter from Armand himself on August 12. 'His doctor is of the opinion that he is mad. Bienvenu, the liquidator of the Banque de St-Jean, is equally convinced. My wife is desolated and making herself sick. I ask neither favours nor privilege, but justice. It is why I address myself to you.'

The little Georgette was involved in a family tragedy. The failure of the Banque de St-Jean had dragged down Roy, her father, and sent him, an overwrought wreck charged with a share in the collapse, to the penitentiary. Instinctively and automatically, with all the confidence of many remembered claims granted before, Lavergne had turned to Laurier.

He was asking, with his usual urgent pomposity, to have Roy declared insane and transferred to a mental institution. He quoted chapters of unsound law, he had no medical proof, and he was totally assured and peremptory as to the powers of the great man. For once, in this last respect, he was mistaken. Laurier could only study the case, study the law, and convey the result of his probings. Until a prison doctor could be prevailed on to supply a certificate of insanity nothing could be done. The rest for a while was silence, and the thought of the heart-broken wife and the troubled husband had to be shelved. The Imperial Conference in London had ended and the Canadian delegation was home with its report. On September 18 it was made public.

The Admiralty, as usual, had pronounced itself in favour of a single imperial navy under centralized control. The Canadian delegation had been unable to agree. The next suggestion had been that the Dominion create a fleet unit 'capable of being used in its component parts in time of war'. This proposal too, which would have made all ships subject to an instant call from the Admiralty, had been rejected. What the Canadian delegation desired was advice as to the building of a Canadian fleet and they had asked the Admiralty to submit alternative plans. The first was to be based on an annual expenditure of about three million dollars, and the second and smaller one on about two million. The Admiralty had reluctantly agreed and was now preparing the plans. Whichever plan was accepted was to form the basis for the Canadian navy bill.

3

'THE YOUNG are coming up and taking the place of the old fellows,' Laurier wrote on that same day, September 18, to a disgruntled veteran who had lost a nomination. 'That is what has happened to you in your county, and that is what will happen to me before long in Canada. Let us submit with good grace.'

He was preparing for his final session in a mood of benign resignation. He saw trouble ahead for himself over the navy bill, but a good deal more for Borden. Monk, the leading Conservative of Quebec, was already withdrawing the grudging assent he had given the naval resolution. Never 'a man to break windows', he had had several months to absorb the atmosphere of his province. He was now talking of the enormous expense of a navy, of the need for a national referendum on the question, and hinting at the imperialist designs that lurked behind it. On the other hand, both in Ontario and the west, Borden was feeling the surge of hard-core English Toryism. A 'tinpot navy' made in Canada would never be enough. The emergency was real and called for immediate action. It was scandalous ingratitude to expect the overburdened British taxpayer to go on any longer carrying the whole cost of imperial defence. There should be an instant offer of ships and money to the mother country, and it should be made with or without the approval of the present Conservative leader.

By the middle of October it was clear that a movement had begun to oust Borden. On October 23 a Vancouver paper reported that Foster was favouring McBride, the premier of British Columbia, as his replacement. Three days later Foster, who was now all for dreadnoughts, had moved on to increase the clamour in Winnipeg. 'So far as the Conservative party is concerned,' said Borden in a statement on October 29, 'the question of Canada's participation in imperial naval defence rests today exactly where it did when the unanimous resolution of parliament was passed on the twenty-ninth of March last.' It was pleasantly clear, however, that he was whistling in the dark.

For his own part, Laurier was sure that he was asking of the country generally about all it was prepared to give. A great deal of rural Ontario had even to be convinced that it was not too much. 'I am aware', Laurier wrote to one of his leaders there, 'that there is among the farmers no enthusiasm for the organization of naval defence. You do not believe in armaments, but in this you are ahead of the times. Your policy may perhaps be appreciated in the twenty-first century but not at this date.' Farther west the dreadnought-givers were also coolly received. A cash subsidy from Canada to the imperial navy, proclaimed Frank Oliver's *Edmonton Bulletin*, would be simply 'a donation for the relief of distressed Dukes'. Let the ten thousand people who really owned England be properly taxed and Canada would not need to give a defence contribution.

In Quebec the storm warnings were up but the wind was still fitful. Bourassa now was quite obviously gathering in not only the provincial Conservative party but Monk himself. The two were appearing at banquets and sitting on platforms together, always with Lavergne as a third, while a sprinkling of grey-haired *Bleus* stood out incongruously among the legions of hot-eyed youth. Yet Bourassa, for all his successes, seemed more and more the admired ineffective. His discontents with the present were turning him back toward the past. He was moving nearer to the position still held in the seminaries, where Bishop Laflèche was unforgotten and Laurier unforgiven. In contrast with Papineau before him he was growing closer to the Church and it was separating him from some of his restless intellectuals, while Gouin and the Liberals, for whom the old chapters were firmly closed, stood up to him as steadily as ever.

His hopes of building a third party based generally on righteousness and himself received a stunning setback in November when of three provincial by-elections two went to the government. In spite of all Bourassa's efforts Gouin was returned to the seat he had lost a year before. The constituency of St-Sauveur was the one success, and it was Lavergne rather than Bourassa who had led the fight there. A gleeful Liberal press was proclaiming the end of a legend. 'The legend is that which people sought to weave around Bourassa, the superman, the redeemer, the flaming word whom nothing could resist. Finis the legend. Finis the comedy.'

On all this the affairs of the family Lavergne were once more intruding, with what effect it was difficult to gauge. In October, painfully aware of what he was likely to bring down on himself, Laurier had made it known that he intended to appoint his old and distinguished friend Sir Louis-Amable Jetté as Chief Justice of Quebec. In the minds at least of Emilie and Armand, the position had long been reserved for Joseph Lavergne, and reaction was instantaneous. He could not understand, Armand wrote on October 22, 'the humiliation done to my poor father'. By the end of November, recalling the result of the St-Sauveur campaign, he had interpreted events to himself all too clearly.

Neither by letter nor in personal interviews was the Prime Minister able to convince this dedicated politician that the father was not being made to pay for the sins of the son. The question of relative fitness for the office of Chief Justice was brushed aside. Armand Lavergne had beaten Laurier's candidate in St-Sauveur; therefore there could be no advancement for Joseph Lavergne. There only remained the satisfaction of revenge taken and a hint of revenge ahead. Armand's thought was clothed in suitable obfuscation but it was still plain enough. 'You tell me that you do not see the relation between the nomination of Sir Louis and the election at St-Sauveur. Here it is: it is that, if I endanger the advancement of my father by my political attitudes, I am able at least to ratify this same attitude in the most Liberal constituency in the Dominion. I see by the papers that Sir Charles Tupper supports your naval policy. Should I congratulate you? I feel myself still too Liberal to come to that.'

He was back with another letter on December 6, still cherishing 'my certainties', but writing in a different, more appealing mood. The flush of St-Sauveur was almost gone. 'No, you are right, do not wish me success in politics. Why do I desire it? I do not hope for it. Only one thing pains me; it is that you should believe I love you less and that the past does not count. No. It counts always. It is above all when I fight you that I feel how strong it is, since each time when duty calls in a loud voice the sweet past murmurs, "et tu Brute". I appear an ingrate to you. God is my witness that I love you, but forgive me, I love my country too.'

It was painful and self-important and overblown. It was still youthful. It called up the smiling memories of Arthabaska and made one wish for the time to explain, convince, recover the admiring confidence of the old days. There was no time and there was little hope. For that matter, when had this wayward sprig, so facile in his straddling of the fence between principle and self-interest, ever given or deserved confidence? Yet there was this much to be thought of. If Bourassa was floundering and Lavergne adrift, what was there left but Laurier as the home port?

The plans from the Admiralty had been received by the time the session opened on November 11 and through December Laurier was immersed in the framing of the naval bill. Borden was still in deeper trouble than himself, and there did not seem much to fear from the debate. 'The only effect that I foresee', Laurier wrote in a businesslike vein to one of his advisers, 'is that it is going to consolidate the opposition in the province of Quebec and probably divide it in the Dominion. I believe that on the whole all the sane elements will stay with us, and if so we have nothing to fear.'

He mused more philosophically with another correspondent. 'I ask you to consider this. Our existence as a nation is the most anomalous that has yet existed. We are British subjects but we are an autonomous nation; we are divided into provinces, we are divided into races, and out of these confused elements the man at the head of affairs has to sail the ship onwards. If you were in the position in which I am you would have to think night and day of these different problems. On every occasion I have had to disappoint scores of my friends on some point or other. I do not expect that the task will be as heavy in the present instance; still it will be of such a character as to give me many troubled hours. It is some consolation to think, however, that it will probably be the last one.'

4

ON JANUARY 10, 1910, the first issue of *Le Devoir* appeared on the streets of Montreal. After eighteen months of hard canvassing Bourassa had his newspaper, and he had it on his own terms. Almost all of the money had come from small investors. A holding of fifty-one per cent of the stock gave him comfortable assurance of editorial freedom. He had the choice of the best writers from the smaller nationalist papers and he had a host of supporters, distributors, and promoters in the universities, the seminaries, and the parish rectories of the province. He rode the tide of a genuine revulsion from political graft and apathy. He had youth, brains, an adequate supply of money, and all that part of the Church that had not accepted the results of the lost battles. The spent force of Ottawa and the shattered legend of Quebec were vibrantly alive again. Epitaphs had been premature.

'Duty' declared itself in its first issue. It would support honest men and denounce rascals. It favoured the provincial *Bleus* because it somehow saw in them 'probity, courage, firm principles, great largeness of views'. It was weary of both federal parties who since the days of the South African War had connived to sacrifice the national interest to opportunism, party intrigue, or mere cupidity. *Le Devoir*'s purpose was to awaken the whole people and above all the ruling classes to their religious, national, and civic duty: 'Thus the title of this journal, which has astonished some people and caused some colleagues to smile.'

The first issue removed what little doubt there was as to Bourassa's attitude on the navy, and the second bared the knife. At the very hour of *Le Devoir*'s appearance, declared the opening manifesto, Canada was threatened with a new episode of the imperialist movement. The man who proposed the navy, said next day's issue, was the man who had sent Canadian troops to South Africa and abandoned the cause of separate schools in Alberta and Saskatchewan. Laurier had 'veiled in golden clouds the betrayals, weaknesses, and dangers of his policy'.

On January 12, Laurier rose in the House to introduce the naval bill. The larger of the Admiralty's plans had been accepted. A naval college was to be established, a naval board set up, and a force recruited that would be under the control of the Canadian government. In time of war that force might be placed at the disposal of His Majesty through an act of the Canadian parliament. In an emergency, if parliament were not sitting, the cabinet might do the same, subject to later ratification. The Canadian government would build, or would have built in England, five cruisers and six destroyers, and the annual cost of the whole naval establishment would be about three million dollars. In one important aspect the navy would be much less formidable than the militia, which Armand Lavergne had entered so light-heartedly. Under the provisions of the militia act any male citizen of Canada from seventeen to sixty could be compelled to serve anywhere in the world so long as it could be shown to be in defence of the country. The naval bill specifically excluded compulsion of any kind; there would be no man in a Canadian ship who was not a volunteer.

With that clause, Laurier hoped, he had silenced the fears of conscription. Beyond that he could only point to the position of the country as he conceived it, in time of war as in time of peace. He had never believed there was any emergency that demanded special contributions; he believed it less now. Even London was simmering down, even Asquith was beginning to question the calculations and the information of Reginald McKenna. Certainly the big-navy men would continue to thump their tubs and certainly the imperialists at home would take advantage of it, but they could be ignored. Canada's problem was a long-range problem and Canada's way, as always, was the middle way.

He said it on January 12 when he introduced the bill. He said it at the second reading in February, with Bourassa an avid listener in the press gallery, scribbling his notes for *Le Devoir*. He said it again at the third reading in April, when Bourassa had dragged himself off reluctantly to attend the session in Quebec. Other questions intruded and Laurier brushed them aside. Between debates on the navy he was attacked for the Grand Trunk and its building methods. The Americans were wheedling with one hand and threatening a tariff war with the other. He

'FOR CANADA AND THE EMPIRE': THE NAVY PLAN
CARTOON BY FERGUS KYLE

sent Fielding to deal with them and he flared up at Grey when the Governor General pressed for assent to already pending treaties. There was certainly progress in Washington, there were shifts and changes of mood that might be the prelude either to great trouble or to great opportunity, but for the three months between January 12 and April 20 the question of the navy overrode all others.

The Prime Minister ridiculed the dreadnought-givers 'who

carry abroad upon their foreheads the imperial phylacteries, who boldly walk into the temple and there loudly thank the Lord that they are not like other British subjects'. He had the same treatment for those who wished to live forever with their pockets closed behind the shelter of the British navy and the Monroe Doctrine. Did they forget that Canada was a country with two sea-coasts and exposed coastal cities, with a large ocean trade and great revenues that depended on it? 'You might just as well tell the people of Montreal, with their half-million population, that they do not need any police protection.'

There was no need or question of a referendum. The government's policy had been clear since the Colonial Conference of 1902 and its mandate had been twice confirmed at general elections. It accepted no responsibility for imperial policy, it gave no promise of unvarying support, and it had refused contributions to imperial forces. It simply recognized the position of the country so long as it remained within the Empire. 'If England is at war we are at war and liable to attack. I do not say that we shall always be attacked, neither do I say that we would take part in all the wars of England. That is a matter that must be determined by circumstances upon which the Canadian parliament will have to pronounce.'

On the other side of the aisle there was heartening cacophony. Bourassa's voice came clearly through the throat of Monk. The bill had now become a surrender of Canada's autonomy, a victory for Chamberlainism. Arthur Meighen, the rising prairie Conservative, stood up to denounce Monk. The Orangemen of the far right shouted for 'One Fleet, One Flag, One Throne', and Borden swayed with uneasy dignity in the middle of a split party. Canada must have her own navy; to that point he held with the resolution of the year before. But the weeks in London and the prodding of Foster and his Tory rebels had changed much else. Borden was now for an imperial defence committee, the first step in the direction of an imperial council, and he was now ahead of the Toronto *Globe* in flinging the smug maxims of commercial prudence to the winds. 'I say to the Prime Minister, go on with your naval service, but do not forget that we are confronted with an emergency which may rend this Empire asunder before the proposed service is worthy of the name. We have the resources, and I trust the patriotism, to provide a fleet unit or at least a dreadnought without one moment's unnecessary delay. Or, and in my opinion this would be the better course, we can place the equivalent in cash at the disposal of the Admiralty.'

The issue was fully joined when Bourassa spoke for himself, first in *Le Devoir*, then to the usual packed and roaring meetings. The bill was 'a national capitulation'. It was 'the most complete backward step Canada has made in half a century. It is the gravest blow our autonomy has suffered since the origin of responsible government.' The fact that a Canadian parliament would control a Canadian navy made no difference to Bourassa. The provision for voluntary enlistment was brushed aside in one sentence a paragraph long, echoing Honoré Mercier, bristling with geography, and venomous with by-passed history. 'Let the notion occur to a Chamberlain, a Rhodes, a Beers, to gold-seekers or opium merchants, of causing a conflict in South Africa or India, in the Mediterranean or the Persian Gulf, on the shores of the Baltic or the banks of the Black Sea, on the coasts of Japan or in the China Seas, we are involved, always and regardless, with our money and our blood.'

Wars, he appeared to assume, were fought by legislative enactment, and ships should be confined to the national three-mile limit. The naval bill did not limit the navy to the defence of the Canadian coast. It did not augment Canada's security: it decreased it. Mounting armaments in Canada might even induce the United States to fortify the border. 'We Canadians owe all our blood, all our effort, all our consideration to the country that Providence has given us. Not in my name but in the name of your sons, in the name of those who will bear the weight of this political crime, in the name of those who will pay the taxes which will weigh more heavily on us, in the name of those who perhaps soon will embark in these vessels to go and perish upon far-off seas, I have the right to ask you to unite with me in making known to Lord Grey, Sir Wilfrid Laurier, and Mr. Borden, that before setting us upon this path they ought to explain their designs, make them known to the people, and obtain approval of their policy.'

He ended always on the hedge of a referendum; the country might have its navy if it wished. That queer ambivalence ran through every argument. It was not imperialism, it was not militarism he attacked as the real enemy; it was a treacherous Prime Minister. He did not appeal to race, he said; he spoke with equal voice to French and English, Protestant and Catholic. Yet the armed men sprang up where the dragon's teeth fell, and the passionate implications were wholly clear. The time had come to undo the work of Wilfrid Laurier. Bourassa could no longer endure it.

On April 20 the naval bill passed and on April 21 Kirk Cameron was again a visitor to Ottawa. He had met Bourassa on the street in Montreal, said Cameron, and the man whose black hair and beard were now flecked with grey had taken his arm and walked along with him, unusually eager and discursive. 'Let me tell you, my Christian friend,' Bourassa had said, 'Laurier has now driven not one nail in his coffin, but many. On Sunday I speak at the church door in Sorel. The next Sunday I speak at another church, and it will go on till he is finished.'

The warning was hardly needed. Other warnings, in the other vein, were multiplying from Ontario. The half-forgotten voice of Bishop Langevin was loud in the west again. Already the plans for retirement had been quietly and definitely shelved. The winning of the latest battle had revived the oldest war.

24

'GOVERNMENTS ARE BORN TO GROW AND DIE'

1910-1911

FIELDING, though he was not yet to be Prime Minister, was more than ever the kingpin and pivot of the administration. Under his policies prosperity had come and stayed. With his tariffs the trade of the country, firmly orientated toward British markets, had also increased with continental Europe. He had held the interests of the manufacturing east and the farming west in uneasy equilibrium and if he had not solved the problem of the United States he had achieved for the country, for the moment at least, a kind of independence. With or without the help of the mighty neighbour, Canada was getting along.

She was getting along, in fact, rather better than the Americans. Sixteen years of high-tariff Republicanism had begun to produce their reaction below the border. There was a great clamour from consumers for lower living costs, from manufacturers who wanted cheaper raw materials, and from exporters who were finding that other nations, too, could impose prohibitive duties. Taft had come to power in 1908 as a Republican, but he had a country that was growing a little tired both of big business and the big stick. It wanted a freer world so far as trade was concerned, and it wanted friends.

Even in the late days of the Roosevelt régime the changing mood had been felt. Laurier had recognized it and been prepared to profit by it but he had not been prepared to be taken in again, least of all with the help of benevolent Britons. 'We have suffered on the Atlantic, we have suffered on the Pacific, we have suffered on the lakes,' he had told an audience in Toronto in 1907. 'We have suffered wherever there has been a question to be discussed between British diplomats and foreign diplomats.' That phase, at least, of imperial relations was ended.

Root, the American Secretary of State, Bryce, the British Ambassador in Washington, and Grey in Government House were still a familiar triangle whose deliberations went on over Canadian heads. When their proposals came up for decision, however, they found themselves faced by a Prime Minister with a long memory who was dealing from a position of strength. He had a great respect for Root, a greater for Bryce, and he liked Grey. But he was not to be hurried or cajoled. As the problems that had faced the High Commission of 1899 were brought up again he had been obdurate and difficult. He had rejected, he had quibbled, he had refused for months on end even to discuss some of the proposals, and he seemed to have found the secret of dealing with the Americans. Much had been settled, and a great deal of it on his terms. Three weeks after parliament closed in May Laurier was still lashing himself into a fury, for Grey's benefit, over one of the clauses in the endlessly-amended and still-unsigned boundary waters treaty. By June both that difficulty and another more important had been resolved. The World Court at The Hague had disposed satisfactorily of the ageless fisheries question and a new permanent High Commission manned by both countries was to deal in future with all disputes over boundaries and boundary waters. 'We are setting up', said Root, 'a Hague tribunal for North America.'

There was more than that in the wind now. Ever since Taft had come in, and all the while his diplomats had been labouring to recover friends, the zigzag course of American politics had been creating new resentments. The liberal-minded Taft had found himself the prisoner of a Republican old guard who met the demand for tariff changes by whittling out a new and larger club. Any country that refused to American products the lowest tariff it granted to any other country was to be met with a flat increase of twenty-five per cent on all its exports to the United

States. No concessions were offered in return and no account was taken of the reciprocal arrangements by which other countries earned the reductions they granted each other. The United States was to get the best that was going or its markets would be closed.

The act had been passed in 1909, to come into effect on March 31, 1910. One by one, groaning and protesting, most of the countries around the world had given way. Canada remained, tied to the British preference by a host of solid advantages and flatly refusing the same preference, for no advantage, to the United States. Through the fall of 1909 and on into January and February of 1910 the thought of a tariff war had mingled with the preoccupations of the navy bill. It had not sweetened Laurier's mood, and he had been ready in November for some hard-handed retaliation. If the American act came into force, he told Grey, he would immediately impose export duties on Canadian pulp and the first result would be the closing of some twenty paper mills in New Hampshire.

Fielding had gone to Washington in March to find Taft embarrassed and unhappy. Taft admitted that American demands were outrageous, but he could not escape from the provisions of the law. He had no objection to the British preference and he made no claim that his own country was entitled to it. If he was not to apply the act, however, there had to be Canadian concessions, or at least something that looked like concessions. 'Both of us', Fielding reported to Ottawa, 'are searching for a decent excuse to help each other.'

The excuse, when found, had been beautiful in its simplicity. Out of the categories to which Canada gave preferential entry, thirteen insignificant items ranging from photographs to prunes had been selected and the preference on them had been granted to the United States. The United States had accepted and the threat of a twenty-five per cent super-tariff had been lifted from Canadian exports. The Canadian parliament had then dropped the duties on photographs, prunes, and the rest to the same level for all the world and everything had gone on as before. Or rather better than before. In Laurier's files there was now a letter from the American Secretary of State dated March 26 and expressing the hope that trade relations between the two countries might be adjusted on 'broader and more liberal lines'.

Republicans were changing or Democrats were growing stronger. In any case the air from the south was sweeter. There was no doubt that the thought of reciprocity hovered. The issue Laurier had chased so painfully from 1887 to 1893 might now be offered to him as a gift. It would dwarf every other issue, including the navy. The question was, did he want it?

He was not unduly anxious or unduly optimistic. Americans gave little and Canadians were now in a position to demand a good deal. Nothing, he had said a dozen times, would be allowed to upset the trade with the United Kingdom. Yet as the old quarrels with the Americans were cleared up his old resentments were lessening. One of the first of his goals had been a reasonable adjustment to the facts of continental life. If that could be achieved now it would be a good bequest to Fielding and a better to the country.

As the session closed Laurier was already preparing for a wide-ranging tour of western Canada. Quebec still seethed and it had to be left seething. *Bleus* and Bourassa men were almost indistinguishable now. The youth and the young clergy distributed and devoured *Le Devoir* and it was the only lay newspaper permitted in Catholic colleges. Bourassa, Lavergne, and Monk swept from meeting to meeting, a restless, relentless trinity, stirring into the naval cauldron all the remembered potions. Out of it rose the fumes of the quarrel on the schools, the quarrel on the Boers, the quarrels on immigration, bilingualism, freemasonry, and Anglo-Saxon domination. There was never a lack of cross-winds to lift them higher. On May 6 Edward VII died and on May 9 George V was proclaimed King. With a coronation ahead, Catholics lifted a mighty outcry over the form of the King's declaration in which he was required to assert among much else 'that the invocation or adoration of the Virgin Mary or any other saint or the sacrifice of the Masses as they are now used in the Church of Rome are superstitious and idolatrous'. There was an equal outcry by Orangemen a month later when Asquith published a new declaration from which the offensive statements had been removed. At the height of it all Michael Francis Fallon, the Irish Catholic Bishop of London, Ontario, chose to burst out in print against the shortcomings of French-Canadian schools and the politics of French-Canadian priests. The Prime Minister who had lived out the age of Victoria and now the age of Edward saw nothing but new division and fragmentation. Lemieux was going to Europe and would spend some time in Rome. Laurier moodily entrusted to him a letter for Merry del Val and turned his eyes west.

Bourassa's third party was becoming a Catholic party. Ultramontanism was on the march again for the old cul-de-sac. It had been headed off before by a younger, stronger Laurier in a newly-booming country. Perhaps if the older Laurier could find a new issue, a great and thrilling prospect, he might turn the trick again. It would be for the last time, it would have to be soundly based in the country's needs and will; he did not know as yet if it was possible or desired. The answer, or a part of the answer at least, lay on the prairies.

2

IT WAS TO BE the greatest of all his tours. Behind him the talks with the Americans went on. The stir in Quebec went on, eating away his footing. As the train edged up into the scrub pine, however, and roared along around the Great Lakes, he began to see what he had helped to build, what he was still building.

He opened the tour on July 9 at Fort William and Port Arthur, the warring twin cities, 'the key to the western situation'. He urged them to join, pool their strength. 'We will help you. For every step you take we will take two; for every dollar you spend we will spend two.'

Manitoba was Tory now, solidly in the grip of a dirty provincial party. In spite of that there were ten thousand waiting to cheer him at the railway station in Winnipeg and show him what wheat and railways and immigration had done for this hub of the west. He passed on by Ste-Anne, Selkirk, Brandon, Birtle, Minnedosa, and Rapid City to cross the border of the first of his new provinces and stand under a mighty arch of grain sheaves at Yorkton. He came by Melville, Lanigan, Humboldt, and Prince Albert to Saskatoon, with the cheers of Germans, Frenchmen, Italians, Scandinavians, Poles, Armenians, Galicians, Doukhobors, and Russian Jews ringing in his ears. Saskatoon, the village of a hundred people five years before, was now a city of fourteen thousand, an Athens along the Saskatchewan, building its own university. Under a forest of bunting Laurier laid the cornerstone and told the crowd of a lad he had met that morning by the name of John Diefenbaker. 'You have some remarkable newsboys here. This one talked to me for half an hour at the railway station and then said, "Well, Mr. Prime Minister, I can't waste any more time. I have to deliver my papers." '

Over the maze of steel that now latticed the prairies he came down through Regina, Weyburn, Yellow Grass, Lang, Wilcox, Rouleau, Pasqua, and Moose Jaw, and turned north again toward Battleford. A shunting freight train brushed his car near Pense and he was shaken for a day but did not miss an engagement. Then it was Davidson, Hanley, Langham, North Battleford, Lloydminster, and on into Alberta to Fort Saskatchewan. Vegreville, Edmonton, Calgary, and Red Deer were all familiar yet vastly changed, scores of the towns were wholly new to him, and racing ahead of the map-makers, still unnamed, were other lonely elevators with their clustering tar-papered shacks. There was rest at Banff the magnificent, nesting among its mountains, and then it was Vancouver and the sea. A huge reception at Victoria was arranged by the Tory McBride, the rumoured successor of Borden. The party man forgot party for the occasion, as party had seemed to be forgotten all along the line. This was Laurier who came, bettering all legends and creating new as he went. The tall, top-hatted, exquisitely garbed figure had been discovered behind a station as the train stopped on its way, tossing a ball with a youngster. Standing magnificent and electric on an open-air platform at Edmonton, he had paused suddenly with his hand upraised. Thousands of eyes had followed his eyes as he looked across the street to the upper floor of a building where a child was leaning from a window. 'Is that little one safe?' The thread of his argument might have been resumed after that, but no one remembered or cared. The words had been enough. The legend was enough.

Or so it seemed from the train. The mail and the newspapers and the telegrams that followed him were less reassuring. To Bourassa now these cheering westerners 'have done nothing to make our country what it is, while we, descendants of those who thrust back the forest, hunted wild beasts, loyally defended New France, then fought for the English flag against the revolting colonies, have not the right to say to Laurier and Borden who have cancelled with a pen-stroke all our dearly-acquired liberties, "You are only cowards and traitors." ' He too had once loved Laurier, served him, and believed in him. Now, 'I say that when a man, whatever his personal qualities, so despises the confidence and love which a people has given him – such a man is more dangerous to his religion, his country, and even to the British Crown than the worst of Orangemen.'

With this from Bourassa, it was painful to imagine the trend of the uninhibited Lavergne. Nor was Quebec the only cloud in the prairie sky. From July 18 to August 2 the tour, which had been carefully routed to pass over the lines of the Grand Trunk Pacific wherever possible, had to be shifted to the C.P.R. Obdurate, high-handed, tight-fisted, and deaf to reason, Charles Hays had driven the Grand Trunk men to strike. 'I am deluged with telegrams asking me to interfere,' Laurier wired to Mackenzie King on July 28. The Minister of Labour was planning a tour of Europe, but he was the one man in the government alive to the mysteries of unions and labour relations. He would have to forgo his tour and mediate with Hays.

Five days later the strike was over. On August 5, while Laurier was at Moose Jaw, a twenty-eight-page single-spaced typewritten report arrived from King, giving an almost breath-by-breath account of the negotiations. The drama and detail were wearisome, King's 'usual aspect of conscious merit' breathed from every line, but there was no doubt that a smoothly determined young man, quivering with nervousness at every step, had backed an irascible old tycoon into a hopeless corner. Nor had he shrunk from risk as the last chips fell. King had given the union a pledge, on the faith of the government of Canada, that all striking workers would be taken back, even though he knew that Hays would twist and turn to avoid it.

Hays, according to King, was fighting the labour battles of American railway magnates who were prepared to reward him richly, and would rather have seen the Grand Trunk go down than lose face himself. There was not much left of his countenance now, however. 'We have saved him from himself,' was King's pious comment. Laurier was more concerned with the enlargement of government intervention in private business, and for six days the report and its implications simmered in the back of his mind. By the eleventh, however, he had accepted it. He remained troubled by King's undertaking, he wrote, but 'nothing could be better than the way in which you forced Hays from position to position until the final conclusion'. He still was not wholly sure of his tiresome little minister, but under the chubby flesh there was sound steel.

On September 2 the tour came to an official close in Medicine Hat, and Laurier was homebound. At Winnipeg next day a Catholic delegation was on hand to remind him that Archbishop Langevin was very much alive. His Grace was journeying east almost by concurrent trains to attend the Eucharistic Congress in Montreal. He would not be the only problem awaiting Laurier there. The city, on the verge of this greatest of all Catholic public ceremonies, was an empurpled political morass. Bishop Fallon of London, who had once taught in Ottawa, was leading the Irish prelates in a war with the French of Bourassa. *Le Devoir*, supported by most of clerical Quebec, fought back with all the thunder if not the authority of the Church. The woes of Charles Murphy, the cabinet minister on watch, filled almost every mail.

Montreal, according to Murphy, was hardly safe for an Irishman or a Liberal. He had appealed to Archbishop Bruchési to moderate the storm, without much effect. Bruchési was not omnipotent and he was, after all, French. He could hardly be expected to lean to Irishmen, even men of the cloth, who opposed the teaching of French in Catholic schools. Bourassa was to be one of the principal speakers at the Congress and it would certainly be made the occasion of a great nationalist demonstration. Murphy was aghast at Laurier's unwillingness to compete, and there were still friends of the cloth who urged his appearance. Finally and reluctantly he agreed to be present and speak. He was a Prime Minister of Orangemen as well as Catholics but the risks would have to be accepted. 'It is evident', he wrote to the Rome-bound Lemieux, 'that we face a new campaign, so-called religious. It is always the same. Those people wish to learn nothing and they do not know how to forget anything.'

He was plunging into the old troubles, but it would be with a refreshed spirit. He had stood at Prince Rupert on the Pacific and told of his dream of the day when he would pass coast to coast over the new railway. At Regina a great blond German farmer had promised him many strong sons for his navy. Everywhere around him in a babble of many accents the voice that was always Canada gave Bourassa the lie. 'I return ten times more Canadian,' Laurier had said in farewell. 'I have imbibed the air, spirit and enthusiasm of the west.' He had done more than that. Everywhere he went, on platform after platform, in railway stations and in halls, on street corners and in stubbly fields, the sun-burned deputations of the Grain Growers had come to him, recalling the old promise, demanding the opening up of that mighty market to the south. He was coming back with his issue.

3

ON SEPTEMBER 7 he reached Ottawa and on September 9 he went to Montreal to keep his promise. The Twentieth Eucharistic Congress was the first ever to be held in North America and the great city in the loveliest month of its year offered a magnificent setting for the ceremonies. Its population had been nearly doubled by the influx of pilgrims from all over the continent and from abroad. There was a cardinal legate from Rome. There were high Church dignitaries from England, from the United States, from most of Europe, and from much of South America. The French genius for warmth and splendour and grace in decoration had never been more in evidence.

It was nevertheless a politically depressing scene. Opening on the sixth, the Congress had divided itself into a French-speaking section meeting in Notre Dame Cathedral and an English-speaking section meeting in St. Patrick's Cathedral. Only the tact of Archbishop Bruchési had prevented the Irish from further confirming division by arranging separate banquets for English and French bishops. Nothing Bruchési could do had warmed the coldness toward Laurier or soothed the resentments of Murphy, who was in charge of Laurier's arrangements. It was unthinkable that the Prime Minister should come and not be suitably received. It was equally impossible for Bruchési or any prelate of rank to offer a formal reception without appearing to take sides.

Eventually, after desperate manoeuvrings by Murphy, Laurier arrived to take lunch with high foreign prelates at the home of Shaughnessy, the Catholic president of the C.P.R. From there he went on to a reception in the Windsor Hotel given by the Catholic Club of New York. In the evening he came with his party to Notre Dame Cathedral, from which the Holy Sacrament had been removed for the occasion. With French, English, and papal colours brilliantly aglow about him, he was presented to a sizeable audience by Archbishop Bruchési and delivered an address in which, as the Protestant editor of the Montreal *Witness* reported, 'There was nothing which I, as a Methodist, am not ready to accept.'

He had been brief, pallid, and ineffective, and his reward came next day. In the afternoon twenty-five thousand of the Catholic Association of French Canadian Youth met in the open to hear Archbishop Langevin speak of his struggles for the faith in the west. In the evening Bourassa was to speak and the crowd in Notre Dame was far greater than it had been for Laurier. Bourassa was preceded by Archbishop Bourne of Westminster, who produced from the height of his Irishness and Englishness the one match required to set the gathering alight. Since Canada was growing and peopling itself with those of many different origins, he said, the Church must not give the impression that Catholicism was linked with the French language. In the future it must be linked with the English language.

He sat down amid a murmurous hush and while two succeeding speakers toyed with platitudes Bourassa, with Langevin at his elbow, had a chance to revise his notes. When he stood up at last he threw away his manuscript and the full power of the man flowed out over the huge audience to join them and lift them with him. 'From this province of Quebec, from this minute

French colony whose language, it is said, is doomed to disappear, have come three-quarters of the clergy of North America. Let us beware, yes, let us most carefully refrain from extinguishing this fire which with its intense light has illuminated a whole continent for three centuries.

'But, it is said, you are only a handful. You are destined inevitably to disappear. Why persevere in the struggle? We are only a handful, it is true; but in the school of Christ I did not learn to estimate right and moral forces by numbers and wealth. We are only a handful, but we count for what we are, and we have the right to live.

'For nineteen centuries there has not been a Hebrew pope, a Roman pope, an Italian pope, a French pope, but the Pope, father of all, the great Catholic family. Let us go higher. Let us go to Calvary, and there on that little hill in Judea which was not very high in the world let us learn the lesson of tolerance and of true Christian charity.'

Reading it next day in Ottawa, one was not surprised to be told of the moment of utter silence at its conclusion, nor of the rejoicing storm that followed. The legate, who had remained stiffly in his place as Bourne concluded, had risen to cross the platform and shake Bourassa's hand. The crowded pews had blossomed with waving hats and handkerchiefs, bishops with hands held still by decorum had applauded with their feet, and the Place d'Armes later that night had been a solid sea of jubilation. The next afternoon, as one hundred prelates, ten thousand priests and members of religious orders, and fifty thousand laymen paraded through the streets in the closing procession of the Congress, Bourassa was cheered as no one else, legate or bishop or priest. From wherever he was, one imagined, the grandfather who had lost the Church and lost his struggle with it must have smiled a grim smile.

4

THE SESSION was due to open on November 17. There was time first to see what political manoeuvre could do. Willison in the Toronto *News* was already scenting reciprocity in the air, and bristling. He had good reason. By early October Fielding had resumed his negotiations with Washington. The omens read well. The capitals were growing closer.

Borden seemed hopelessly at sea and had twice threatened to resign. His big-ship Tories refused to consider the question of the navy closed and were still out for his head. He could not even pretend to control his *Bleus* of Quebec. Nor did there seem to be any chance of improvement. He had been forced to cancel the call for a national Conservative convention. The presence of his Quebeckers in any party council would mean a certain disaster, while their absence would make it a farce.

Laurier was in worse case, and better. His English-Canadian Liberals had accepted the navy decision. Quebec was no mystery to him as it was to Borden. He was the first enemy of Bourassa but he was not hampered by the formal allegiance of Monk. He knew the extent and depth of clerical enmity but he had his friends too, as Borden had not. His sheep were clearly distinguishable from his goats. He was not immobilized. There was nothing to lose by full and open attack.

On October 10 he went to Montreal, a very different man from the meek and pious pleader at the Eucharistic Congress. The hall this time was secular, the crowd satisfactorily overflowing, and the target clearly defined. 'This violent section – you know it – comprises the Pharisee end of Canadian Catholicism; those who have constituted themselves the defenders of a religion which no one attacks; those who handle the holy water sprinkler as though it were a club; those who have arrogated to themselves the monopoly of orthodoxy; those who excommunicate right and left all those whose stature is a little greater than theirs; those who seem to have only hatred and envy for their motive and instinct; those who insulted Cardinal Taschereau when he was alive and who, now that he is dead, attack his memory; those who made Chapleau's life bitter; those whom the people with their picturesque language designated Castors.'

Behind the words there were thirty years of memories and they all sprang to life with the revival of the old term. He went on to pay his respects to Monk, the captive of Bourassa, and to Bourassa, the captive of the past. Clause by clause he dissected the naval bill. On what ground did these two stand in opposing it? The fear of conscription? Conscription was ruled out, clearly and specifically. On the grounds of militarism? Imperialism? It was Laurier who had given the answer to the demand for military and naval contributions in 1902, and Bourassa had applauded it. 'The Canadian ministers who were in London – and I was one of them – opposed this demand of the imperial government in a categorical refusal, respectful in form but absolute in meaning. We did more than that; we placed before the Conference our own policy, which we intended to follow. We declared our intention to sustain the obligation incumbent upon all nations of defending their own territory.

'I defy contradiction when I say that the present naval law is in complete accord with the policy of 1902, as approved by Messrs. Monk and Bourassa. It simply decrees that the Government of Canada should organize another naval service, and that this service should remain entirely under the control of the Government of Canada. Outside of this there is not a single word which would give to Great Britain that which she demanded in 1902 – the organization of a war service to be put at the disposition of the War Office – not one word.'

He returned to Ottawa and a deluge of heartening mail. The speech had been effective. 'What you said about Bourassa', wrote François Langelier, the old *Rouge* comrade, 'recalls a memory of youth. In 1862 when I was studying in Paris I saw Sir Louis H. Lafontaine almost daily. One day, having asked him why he left politics when he was still young and when his government had a solid majority, he told me it was from disgust. "Papineau, on his return from exile," he said, "claimed incessantly that I had sold out to the English. I scorned these accusations at first but I saw that they took hold among the young Liberals, who believed them. I could not hold on and I resigned." Bourassa, it seems to me, follows the same line of conduct, but I am happy to see that you are not disposed to do as Lafontaine did.'

Laurier had no such intention, and was pondering quite other affairs. Once more the family Lavergne occupied his thoughts. Ten months before, he had had a heart-breaking letter from the little Georgette, still on thc subject of her father. He had immediately ordered another medical examination, but hampering legalities still held the old man fast. It was only on October 12, after a petition from all the notables of the father's home district, that Laurier was able at last to send a telegram: 'Order issued for the release of M. Roy.'

Two days later a letter arrived from Armand. 'Useless to tell you what joy has been brought to the heart of my poor wife. We thank you from our hearts. I see by the papers that your meeting in Montreal was a great success. Permit me to add the congratulations of an adversary to those of your many supporters. Although politics separates us my great affection for you makes me always personally rejoice in your triumphs.'

There was greater bounty in store of which Armand was not yet aware. Neither was he aware of surrounding considerations. Louis Lavergne, Joseph's brother and Armand's uncle, was now the member for Drummond-Arthabaska. He was ambitious for a senatorship, as who was not, and a senatorship was now vacant. The results of the appointment, if it were made, should be at least interesting.

The constituency, according to Louis's vehement assurances, was solidly and safely Liberal. There was no question that the candidate who replaced him would be easily elected. Yet Drummond-Arthabaska had every association with Laurier himself. No party that claimed to be fighting Laurier on all fronts could possibly allow a by-election there to go uncontested. Bourassa, Monk, and company would have to come forward, and to certain defeat. In the process the naval issue and all of Bourassa-ism would receive a good airing and quite possibly a decisive check. It would be all the more decisive if the candidate should stand high under the wing of Bourassa. Joseph Lavergne had held the seat, and then Louis. It was quite possible, and quite in character, that the spectacular Armand should leap to be the third. There would be the pride of family and the pride of a forlorn hope; there would be, of all things, panache. If it meant the end of Armand there was not much lost to the Liberals; if it meant his eventual conversion, all the better. In either case the party would be strengthened in Quebec. On October 13 Louis Lavergne, resigning as federal member for Drummond-Arthabaska, became a member of the Senate.

'I learn with joy', came word by the next mail, 'the news about my dear uncle.' Armand had forgotten resentment on the subject of his father. He was still brimming with gratitude for the release of his father-in-law, and still eloquently regretful of the differences that separated him from his great opponent. 'The love of country is a jealous love, which will not share me.'

He was equally eloquent, but a little cagey, on the subject of Drummond-Arthabaska. There was no doubt that he was considering and no doubt that he was attracted to the candidature. He was not sure, however, if he was justified in imposing on himself and his poor wife the hardships of such a struggle. 'I pray God to reveal to me what is my duty. In any case, if I make the struggle you know that it will be honourable and that, conquering or conquered (above all, conquered) I shall not love you the less.'

On October 17 Laurier went to Arthabaska, somewhat belatedly, to sniff the wind for himself. By the eighteenth it was clear that duty had released Armand. He would not be a candidate for the vacant seat. He would lead the fight in the constituency, but he would lead it on behalf of a not-very-promising farmer by the name of Gilbert. Liberals laughed as the word came to the crowded committee room. The organization was functioning smoothly and the Liberal candidate, Perrault, was a sound and personable lawyer who could make a speech. Laurier left, however, for the first time uneasy. He had caught the scent of trouble in the country districts and, as always, there was no time to track it down. Once again and for the thousandth time he breathed a regretful sigh to the memory of Pacaud. The thought came back disturbingly of that not-very-promising 'big Burgundian' who had won the shattering victory of 1877.

5

THERE WOULD BE just two weeks for the campaign, and it was already under way. It was not to be fought in the obscurity of the Bois-Francs highlands; Bourassa made that plain on October 20 at a huge meeting in Montreal. Hordes of students headed by brass bands flooded into the Ontario Rink with a mammoth portrait of Bourassa going before them bearing the legend 'Country before Party'. Flanked and supported by Lavergne and Monk, the leader renewed the always-expanding tale of Laurier misdeeds, the threat of conscription and war, imperialism and national extinction. All was to be met and countered at Drummond-Arthabaska. The thousands who would have no vote were unrelenting in their cheers and still unsatisfied when Bourassa sat down. Armand Lavergne took over and was still in magnificent voice as the whole audience, parading from the hall to the streets, stopped twice along its way for more speeches.

There was no possibility that Ontario would ignore the commotion and within a week every Tory newspaper was breathing the ancient flames. Dominion and Empire stood at the cross-roads in Drummond-Arthabaska. The time had come to apprise the French again of the facts of conquest. With the supporters of his own candidate proclaiming among the hills that 'our fathers had to pierce the British flag with bullet holes to breathe the air of liberty', Robert Borden in Ottawa retired to dignified shelter. He would not take sides in the contest; voters must vote according to their consciences. Out of the thick of the fray came a wire from Lavergne to Laurier, followed in haste by a letter. He had not said, as a Liberal paper had reported, 'If I am a Castor, Laurier is a skunk'.

Laurier was quite prepared to believe him on that, but everything else was said in due course. Much of it was powerfully answered as thirty-five Liberal parliamentarians, some of them cabinet ministers, poured into the county to meet the opposing influx. 'It is they', said Brodeur, pointing at Bourassa during one of the *assemblées contradictoires*, 'who would belittle Canada . . . They are rousing French Canadians against English Canadians. You are not accustomed', he added, turning more directly on the idol, 'to be denounced as I denounce you now. I appeal to all Canadians, French as well as English, to have nothing to do with men who would lead us to civil war.'

There was no evidence that the appeal had much effect. The reports of the party organizers came, still confident. Laurier no longer believed them. At best he had precipitated a nasty, dangerous outbreak; at worst he had called down disaster. He had certainly stimulated his enemies to new and ingenious methods. During the last week there was word of men in uniform driving the back roads, stopping at farm-houses, taking a census, they said, of able-bodied men, 'merely to have the lists ready when the Laurier Naval Act goes into force'. On the night of November 2, against the protestations that his presence was not required, he went down to Arthabaska.

He was there next day, sitting in the old office as he had been thirty-three years before, when the results came in. The candidate of Wilfrid Laurier had been defeated by 207 votes. On the evening air from Victoriaville came the sound of jubilant enemies, their voices raised in song. 'Veni, Creator Spiritus' saluted the Holy Ghost which had guided minds aright. The strains of 'O Canada' floated across the Gosselin, but the words were unfamiliar. It was now 'O Bourassa'.

In Montreal in the offices of *Le Devoir* printers were distributing back into the case the type of an editorial, which had already been written and set, explaining that the Liberal party had once more won an election through 'drunkenness, debauchery, tumult, and appeal to the lowest passions. This dirty work has been done under the serene eye and with the tacit and complacent connivance of the Right Honourable Sir Wilfrid Laurier, P.C., G.C.M.G., K.C., D.C.L., LL.D., etc.' As a great crowd gathered in the street outside Bourassa appeared in the doorway. 'I say to you French Canadians that we have today done a great work. We have taught Sir Wilfrid Laurier that he is not omnipotent, and that he cannot plunge Canada into the responsibility of supporting a navy without first consulting the people.' It was revealing, anti-climactic, and completely characteristic. The man who had denounced the navy as the tool of Machiavellian imperialism and the destroyer of Quebec's sons, the bone of contention between a beleaguered minority and an arrogant oppressor, now climbed back on the fence. The people should decide.

6

LOUIS LAVERGNE was a disconcerted senator, but his explanation was simple. 'The nationalists made the farming community believe that their children would all be taken to the wars and blown to pieces.'

Another Quebec senator, J. P. B. Casgrain, went a little deeper. 'The truth is the French clergy are educating the youth of the province to be anti-English, making the plea that if they lose their language they will lose their religion. That is the whole story.'

Neither was quite the whole but there was no changing the fact. Borden recognized it, without enthusiasm. He refused to congratulate the victorious candidate and scolded his chief whip for having done so. There would be another man on the opposition benches but it added no strength to his party. It brought no hope of any discernible policy. There were no winners. The only loser was Laurier.

Laurier was busy for a few days ruefully replying to rueful correspondents. 'Drummond-Arthabaska is an ominous constituency,' he wrote to one. 'I was defeated there thirty-three years ago and defeated again this time, but there is no reason to be discouraged. This is the fate of war.' He was apologetic to another. Apology was called for; he had been very late in sensing the mood of the county. 'I took the word of Mr. Lavergne and Mr. Perrault. I should not have been deceived – I should have looked more closely. Moreover I wanted to reward an old and faithful friend, even if a very indiscreet one. I am too old now to mend my ways in that respect. I am sixty-nine years old and I have been fourteen years in office. Governments cannot live forever for governments are born to grow and die as well as men, and if I fall by the roadside not a murmur will pass my lips. But mark my words, whoever takes up the reins of power will have to have a navy.'

To Louis Lavergne himself he was a good deal less mellow. 'You have said, assured, and repeated that the county was ready, that Perrault would be elected by a great majority. I took your word; you know the result.' He felt, he said, recalling a saying of Lincoln to another English friend, like a boy who had stubbed his toe; he was too big to cry and it hurt too much to laugh. Yet as November 17 and the opening of the session came he began to recover his perspective.

Since the night of November 3 the nationalist cheers and challenges had begun to take on a notably hollow sound. Bourassa offered to meet Laurier on the ground of any city constituency 'to see whether the Canadian people is the slave of a man or whether it is in the service of a principle'. Beyond that, however, he seemed to be hauling his wind. He had vindicated, he said, 'only the equal rights of two great races'. Lavergne went off to address the students of the University of Toronto, asking that he might take home with him 'a message of peace between the two provinces'. On his home ground again he blossomed out once more in his captain's uniform to declare that 'if Canada were attacked the French Canadians would be the first to rise against the enemy, even if the enemy flew the French flag'.

The theatricals failed notably to appease or convince Ontario, but there was some balm in them. 'Mr. Bourassa and his friends', Laurier wrote, with a strain of returning truculence, 'have got scared of their victory and especially of the manner in which they obtained it, and from that day to this they have been very meek.'

It began to seem in December that the worst had passed and that before long the clatter of shipyard hammers might replace political invective. *Niobe* and *Rainbow*, two old ships of the British navy, were already in service as stop-gap training vessels. Twenty-one successful candidates passed for entrance into the new naval college at Halifax. On December 6 Quebec Liberals in caucus determined to stand fast for the navy and embark on the work of recovering support in the province.

In the meantime the news from Washington had been good enough to justify a strong hint of reciprocity in the Speech from the Throne. A great deputation of farmers arriving in support of the hope had refreshed the Prime Minister with a heartening breeze from the west. He was here for another session and did not regret it. It might be a memorable year.

7

THE SESSION adjourned as usual for the Christmas holidays and resumed in January 1911, with the gentlemen on the left of Mr. Speaker irritably tense and the gentlemen on the right tensely expectant. Through most of the month Fielding's seat was vacant and everyone was now certain that when the small, chubby gentleman settled in his place again he would bring important news.

Sifton, for one, had anticipated it. Still a Liberal and still a private member, he had hardly figured in politics for the past year. His private affairs were large and all his remaining energies went to the work of the Committee on Natural Resources. As chairman he had justified his choice thrice over. He was, as always, the brilliant public servant utterly absorbed in the work at hand. It was beyond doubt, however, that recent events had hardened his attitude toward Quebec, and Quebec and Laurier to him were indivisible. There was no reason to consider Sifton a friend.

It was a little ominous but it was difficult to be alarmed by his speech in Montreal on January 9. In his own fathomless way Sifton was preparing some kind of ground on the question of reciprocity with the United States. If it came, he said, 'Must not our trade, our business, our very way of life become intermingled so that we shall become dependent on them? What must follow in the natural course of events but political union?' Well in advance, he was resurrecting the old argument, yet when one went into his history it was hard to believe him serious. The files of Silent Smith reported Clifford Sifton in favour of reciprocity during the campaign of 1900. Sifton had told Grey in 1905 that if there were free trade between Canada and the United States the value of all Canadian land would be increased. He was now asking troublesome questions and he was now privately involved with railway interests that were likely to favour the status quo. On the other hand, though he owned and controlled the *Manitoba Free Press,* he was making no effort to damp down the ardour of John Dafoe, its editor, who was loud for reciprocity. Above all, he did not know, as Laurier did, what was preparing.

The word from Washington was almost incredibly good. Taft and his progressives had shaken free of the Republican old guard. 'I am profoundly convinced', the President had said in a message to the Canadian people, 'that these two countries, touching each other for more than three thousand miles, have common interests in trade and require special arrangements in legislation and administration.' It was an emphatic and formal welcome to Canadian negotiators, and they had found it more than confirmed when they entered the private offices.

There had seemed to be a mood not known between the two countries since the first reciprocity treaty was denounced at the close of the Civil War. Red tape had been swept aside, hostilities had been forgotten, and everything had given place to a large-minded, businesslike concern with the best arrangement possible. Fielding and William Paterson, the Minister of Customs, had met with better proposals than they had dared to hope for. What was shaping up, as the coded messages passed back and forth between Ottawa and Washington, promised free or almost free entry to the United States for Canadian grain, meat, cattle, dairy products, lumber, pulpwood, minerals, and fish. American duties would be lowered on a sizeable list of Canadian manufactures, and little or nothing was asked in the way of return. The tariffs protecting Canadian industry were hardly to be touched. The imperial preference was to remain and all the United States was to receive was a general lowering of Canadian tariffs to the levels enjoyed by other countries of the world. The mighty sister was opening her own gates and was not demanding, for once, the key to her neighbour's house.

Everything appeared to be granted that had been asked for by both Canadian parties since the days of John A. Macdonald. Even in the heyday of the National Policy, even during the hottest battles over Commercial Union, no one had denied the hope or the desirability of obtaining the American market for raw materials. The fear had been of the flood of returning manufactures that would close Canadian factories and turn workmen into the streets. With that fear removed, what was there left to fear? What argument was possible against a free flow of trade, against an adjustment that every fact of history and geography made natural, and in which the needs of the smaller partner were still recognized?

There seemed to be none to the Canadians, but behind the negotiators loomed the American Congress. From past experience it seemed altogether likely that recalcitrant senators would wreck so glittering a bargain. Yet Taft and his advisers were confident and that confidence left nothing for the men across the table but to take all they could get. Day by day the expected snag, the old, familiar stumbling-block, failed to make its appearance. On January 17 Fielding wired that negotiations were moving well. On the twentieth, as if still a little doubtful himself, he reported, 'Negotiations seem to be concluded.' On the twenty-first came the flat statement, 'Negotiations concluded today.'

He thought it best, Fielding said, that he and Paterson should not turn up in parliament until the arrangement could be announced, which would probably not be before Thursday, the twenty-sixth. Until then the Americans would not be ready. He suggested that he should arrive in Ottawa on Wednesday evening and that a cabinet meeting should be held that evening or at the latest on Thursday morning. 'Then on Thursday, soon after the opening of the House, we could make a statement.' He believed, he added, with the nearest approach to excited complacence that he ever permitted himself, 'you will come to the conclusion that we have not made a bad bargain'.

More than that was apparent as Fielding finished his speech in the grey twilight of the afternoon of January 26. The gentlemen to the left of Mr. Speaker filed out in solemn melancholy as the House rose. Everything was better and everything was far worse than any of them had expected. 'I just don't dare to vote against it,' one of them was heard to say. Foster's 'heart was in his boots' and some of the western Conservatives had even applauded with the Liberals as Fielding spoke. Right and left, east and west, there seemed to rise up a great sigh of acceptance. Trade and geography had ended their long war. The obvious was at length manifest, the inevitable had come to pass. The country was wheeling ponderously into its place in North America.

8

IT WAS the moment to go to the country, as the wise men of Laurier would tell him when the moment had passed. For a week Borden faced a distracted and dejected party not even disposed to fight. The Quebec Conservative wing, apart in everything else, was one with the English in this. Even Bourassa, who had just returned from another trip to Europe, inclined to reciprocity. He was not much on economics, the measure was tainted beforehand by the fact that it was Laurier's measure, but the obdurate honesty of his mind held him captive. Reciprocity for him meant 'Canada for the Canadians'. He did not believe it would lead toward annexation by the United States, and whatever it did to lessen imperialist hopes was all to the good.

He had included Rome and the Vatican in his visit to Europe, and had found it somewhat deflating. The welcome for the hero of the Eucharistic Congress had been disconcertingly cool. Rodolphe Lemieux had delivered Laurier's letter. To a forewarned Merry del Val, still the power by the chair, Archbishop Bourne might be a fool and Bishop Fallon all too characteristically Irish, but Bourassa called up the memories of Langevin and Laflèche. He had not been encouraged in his course and it might be some time before he once more convinced himself that he knew better than Rome. It seemed for the moment that Bourassa, above all Bourassa as an opponent on reciprocity, could be left out of the calculations.

Against a plunge for the polls, however, was the very magnitude of the issue. It was too large to be offered to the country without exhaustive discussion. It seemed too good to be afraid of, too obviously and certainly acceptable to be cheapened by a quick election. There was all of February, all of March, all of April before the coronation of George V and another Imperial Conference would demand the Prime Minister's presence. In the meantime nothing was more important than reciprocity and nothing more obvious than reciprocity's merits. The nation and the nation's parliament should be allowed to have their say.

The first ripples of opposition seemed the usual party froth. It was no surprise to have Monk demand another referendum. Hugh Graham was his familiar self when he wrote on February 3 enclosing a front-page editorial of the Montreal *Star*. It was properly admiring of Laurier and flatly against his policy. Laurier, as the country's great man, should save Canada from an entanglement with the United States that would mean the end of the British connection and the end of Canada as a nation.

Laurier replied on the sixth that it would mean no such thing. 'It is almost word for word the tariff agreement which was offered to the United States by Sir John Macdonald.' On the same day he also answered the financial community of Toronto. It was a little disturbing to find that the principal complaining party was Zebulon Lash, a Liberal and one of the partners in Blake's old law firm. It was probably significant that Lash was the genius who had created the bewildering financial structure upon which Mackenzie and Mann based the Canadian Northern. But Lash, after all, was a reasonable man and a friend, surely open to conviction. What earthly objection could there be from Ontario manufacturing interests, Laurier asked. 'The whole of this treaty is practically confined to agricultural products.'

Sifton was the next man to be dealt with, and Laurier sent for him. He was opposed to reciprocity. Why?

'Because I do not believe in it.'

'You did once.'

'Yes, but conditions have changed.'

'No, it is you who have changed. Your opposition is personal. What is it?'

The answer was a shake of the head and a retreat into depths never probed through all the years of shouting down that ear trumpet. Sifton, for better or worse, was an enemy again.

Debate in the House resumed on February 9, and there was no doubt that the ripple of opposition was becoming a swell. Borden, refreshed from the old fonts of Tory strength, was preparing for battle on high ground. Canada had had one reciprocity treaty with the United States and had been years in recovering from the effects when that treaty was abrogated. When she had recovered, however, she had found markets, created a national spirit, provided transportation by rail and water from coast to coast, and made herself practically independent of the United States. Was all that process to be reversed with no certainty of permanent gain? What would happen if the United States, after having made the agreement, decided to revoke it once more? And what if the agreement endured? The ultimate result of the government's policy would be commercial union. That would be to abandon the purpose for which 'our fathers who founded this Confederation' had made so many sacrifices. 'Loyalty to their memory and to the ideals which they consecrated demands that we should continue with firm heart and unabated hope upon the path which we entered nearly fifty years ago.'

Beneath the oratory the hard facts began to emerge, none of them surprising in itself, all of them together accumulating formidable weight. The old British loyalty remained, flag-waving but deep-rooted. No one could be convinced that increasing orientation toward the United States would not mean a move away from Great Britain. The preference would be tampered with, even though Laurier said not. Manufacturers and industrialists expected to be hurt later if not now. To the railways a swing of trade to the south meant breaks in their long and profitable east-west hauls. The banks and the money interests, linked with all railways and all manufacturers, spoke with their voice. Out of it all Van Horne's voice rose in a flat command, 'Bust the damn thing.'

On February 15 Laurier gave up with Lash. 'Your views and mine are so far apart that I scarcely hope it will be possible to reconcile them. It may be my own fault, and I suppose it is, but I still persist in believing that reciprocity in natural products cannot injure any vested interests and cannot be a bar to our national development.' The answer to this, on the twentieth, was not addressed to Laurier but to the public. It came jointly from Lash, Sifton, and sixteen prominent Ontario Liberals and it formally denounced the Liberal policy on the issue of reciprocity, 'believing as we do that Canadian nationality is now threatened with a more serious blow than any it has heretofore met with'.

On February 28, in the House, Sifton spoke for himself. It was a deadly speech, and an odd one. One could only blink to hear this tight-lipped solitary, this most secret of secret negotiators, express his shock that 'four or five gentlemen who . . . are in control of the affairs of the dominant political party can suddenly of their own motion, without discussion, without debate, without the knowledge of the country, commit the country to a radical change of fiscal policy'. It was strange to hear that this man who had combed the world to build the west, and who knew as well as any man what the west would yet produce, was content with its present outlets. 'Everybody knows that there is a perfectly good market for all that our farms produce.' Sifton was afraid of geography as he had never been afraid before. Reciprocity would lead to commercial union. It would not bind the provinces together. 'It binds, but it binds the other way. It binds British Columbia to Oregon and to Washington and to California; it binds the provinces of the Northwest to the states immediately to the south of them; it binds Ontario and Quebec to the states south of us, and it binds the Maritime Provinces to the states of New England.'

There were many other reasons, but never the whole reason. The Canadian meat-packing industry would be destroyed. Canadian flour millers and Canadian fruit and vegetable growers would suffer. The inflow of American capital would be checked, because American factories would no longer build branches in a country that sent them their raw materials free of duty. The gain in American markets would mean the loss of British markets. Reciprocity would make the country dependent on the United States. American interests would capture control of the cattle business of the Northwest. 'Sir, we are putting our heads into a noose . . . the best years of my life were given to the settlement of that country, and I cannot tell you how I feel about that great country being made the back yard for the city of Chicago . . . these resolutions, in my judgment, spell retrogression, commercial subordination, the destruction of our national ideals, and displacement from our proud position as the rising hope of the British Empire.' It was over-eloquent for Sifton, and curiously unconvincing. But the breach between Sifton and the party was now 'absolute and irreparable'. It meant, Laurier reported to Grey next day, 'the accession to the opposition of an active, clear-sighted strategist and organizer'.

Sifton was now Borden's or Borden was Sifton's, and somewhere behind both were the heirs of Joseph Chamberlain. The propaganda of Empire, intricate and incessant, was now developing as a recognizable force. Its manifestation in Canada was the Round Table Group, which Willison had helped to found with the support of affable gentlemen from beyond the seas. Laurier had watched the assembling with distaste and distrust, not the less because it was done very privately and very quietly, reaching out always toward those in strategic places in the life of the country. The purpose obviously was to recruit the susceptible and influential in support of the imperial dream, and with that dream the prospect of reciprocity would hardly accord. There was no measuring the strength of the group as yet but once more the imperialists and Willison, for what he was worth, could be counted on as enemies.

Laurier spoke for himself on March 7, powerfully and confidently. The arguments against him were based on self-interest or they were based on fear, fear for the future of the country, fear for the British connection. There were grounds for neither. If the Americans hoped for annexation they were hoping in vain, but there was something better offered. 'There may be a spectacle, perhaps, nobler yet than the spectacle of a united continent, a spectacle which would astonish the world by its novelty and grandeur, the spectacle of two peoples living side by side along a frontier nearly four thousand miles long, with not a cannon, with not a gun frowning across it on either side, with no armaments one against the other, but living in harmony, in mutual confidence and with no other rivalry than a generous emulation in commerce and the arts of peace.' If such a thing could be accomplished, he assured the Canadian people, 'Canada will have rendered to old England, the mother of those nations, nay to the whole British Empire, a service unequalled in its present effects and still more in its far-reaching consequences.'

Still the debate dragged on. In April the American Congress was called into special session to approve the agreement, and the heat from below the border added to the heat above. There were warnings from rural Ontario that reciprocity was not catching on as it should; the interminable ramblings of parliament were confusing the issue, not sharpening it. The weatherwise Alex Smith, silently going out from his Ottawa office to sniff the air of the back concessions, reported on April 10: 'Hon. W. S. Fielding said that this agreement was entered into at a psychological moment which may never occur again. This may be true, but the psychological moment for getting out the information to the public is rapidly passing.'

There was certainly force in his words, but the House could not be silenced. The issue was a caught tiger that would not let go. Debate was stiffening the opposition rather than weakening it. Tory money was pouring into the coffers or promising to pour in, and the tubs of loyalty were thumping. It seemed to be the Tory back-benchers, quite as much as the leaders, who had somehow taken heart. Some stubborn wind was blowing from the constituencies, feeding the winds here. The talk droned on with all estimates blocked and business piling up. The veiled treason that barters its birthright for the gold of the kings of the south was heard of again. The treaty-makers who had gone to Washington in secret and returned in secret 'had opened up this Pandora's box and out pranced the Trojan Horse'. On April 24, to Borden's proposal that the House turn for a while to another subject, Laurier replied irritably that it would be 'reciprocity or nothing this session'. By April 28 he was rejecting an elaborately generous proposal that debate be adjourned and resumed when he returned from the Imperial Conference. A threat of unlimited debate followed and he gave it his own stiff answer. 'If such be the temper of the opposition, I think it will probably make it necessary for me to resign my determination to go to England, and stay on in Canada.'

The bluff failed, but he was still more irritable than alarmed. There was really no great hurry; he could always dissolve parliament and call an election. He was sixty-nine years old and he did not like dramatic reversals of plans. He felt himself sure of the country; a pause for reflection could only strengthen him. On May 5, in spite of his refusal of the week before, he tamely allowed a party caucus to accept the offer of adjournment. Parliament would recess for two months while the Prime Minister attended the Imperial Conference. That night jubilant Tory leaders gathered for a dinner at Borden's house. If it was a celebration of sorts it was based on confidence for which Laurier still saw little ground.

9

ON MAY 12 he sailed for London, this time without Zoë. She was an ailing old lady now and the old gentleman, for a while at least, was the stronger. He guided her when she walked, and sometimes he put a gentle hand on her arm when increasing deafness caused her to raise her voice: 'Not so loud, Zoë.' She spent much time with her kittens and her dogs and birds, 'Lady Laurier's menagerie'. Often in the afternoons she drove out with Yvonne Coutu in the big English car which was always breaking down, to stop along the way for ice-cream cones which she shared absent-mindedly with her pets. Yet her mind was as clear as his own, her memory as long, and nothing political escaped her. London, without Zoë, would be a sadly different place.

There was nothing there in any case to which he particularly looked forward. Bob Edwards's *Calgary Eye Opener* was not his favourite publication but it had been close to the mark in one of its latest comments. 'Sir Wilfrid Laurier is taking hold of the approaching Imperial Conference as if it were the handle of a syrup pitcher in a second class restaurant.' The thought of another coronation oppressed him and none of the imperial business could distract his thoughts from Ottawa. On May 23, the day the Conference opened, he wrote Murphy and ordered him to see to the printing of electoral lists. 'In view of the tactics of the opposition it may be quite within the range of possibilities to have a dissolution this fall.'

By contrast with the situation in Canada, however, the negotiations in London were crisply decisive and final. The ghost of Chamberlain walked and the Round Table Group was hard at work behind the scenes. An 'Imperial Council of State' was the new reincarnation of the old idea, and Sir Joseph Ward of New Zealand was its somewhat inadequate prophet. He appeared with his neatly typed speeches, evidently composed by other hands than his own, and was immediately at sea when he reached the last page. One by one Australia, South Africa, Newfoundland, and even Asquith himself bore his arguments down. 'The proposal seems to me to be utterly impracticable,' said Laurier, and it said all.

The last of the hampering strings on Dominion trade were untied. Even the right to advise the mother country on the effects of foreign commitments was declined at Laurier's insistence. Advice in the long future might mean support of that advice, perhaps with force. 'We have taken the position in Canada that we do not think we are bound to take part in every war.'

As the conference ended it was clear that Dominions and mother country would go forward into whatever the future held, linked by the Crown but each speaking for itself. Laurier had imposed his conception, which was still the conception of Blake and, for that matter, of Macdonald and Tupper, on the imperial union. He had been long himself in coming to it and he had no illusions that he had said the last word. But he had moved as firmly as he could as far as he could see the way, and he had carried many with him. Even in this mighty London, always so perilous yet always so warming and exalting, he found strength and warmth and trust.

A few days after the coronation of George V he passed through the crowded streets on the way to the thanksgiving service that was to be held in St. Paul's. Once more he rode in an open carriage in full levee uniform, with two coachmen in royal scarlet on the box before him. There were the same massed ranks of faces behind the same glittering lines of police and soldiers. There was the all-pervading air of good-humoured curiosity, mixed now with a touch of familiarity. One could imagine that many of those who cheered today had cheered him before. He reached the cathedral area and ahead of him the lines of dignitaries, lesser than himself though still very great, moved around to go in by the side entrance. The carriage of Wilfrid Laurier, however, rolled up to the crimson-carpeted royal entrance, where the Bishop of Ripon stood waiting in the doorway to greet him. He walked up the steps, tall under his plumed cocked hat, slender still in his uniform slashed with the blue band, glittering with the star of his Order, and turned for a last instant to survey the crowds of London.

It was a good farewell, a satisfying end. Somehow over these nearly fifteen years, as master of Canada and counsellor of the Empire, he had brought into synthesis all that he loved in the ancient British tradition and all that he clung to from his own roots. 'We are making for a harbour which is not the harbour I foresaw twenty-five years ago, but it is a good harbour. It will not be the end. Exactly what the next course will be I cannot tell, but I think I know the general bearing and I am content.'

10

He sailed from Southampton on Dominion Day, and on July 10 he was in Quebec. He had one week before the opening of parliament and he had been away too long. The air of his constituency told him that and Montreal confirmed it. He looked out on the eleventh over a great crowd gathered in the Champ de Mars and heard the cheers of the faithful. But they rose from a mass speckled with hostile silence. His cry was a war-cry and it came late.

'Henry of Navarre at the battle of Ivry said, "Follow my white plume and you will find it always in the forefront of honour." Like Henry of Navarre, I say to you young men, "Follow my white plume".'

He took just ten days after parliament resumed to get his bearings and to make his decision. The country had come alive with his return, his followers told him, but it was only a measure of their own failings. The party without him was a dull and lifeless mass, unable to quicken to a rising challenge. Business and money, Bourassa and Borden, Orangeism, Catholicism, imperialism, nationalism, had all coalesced against him. Ontario Torydom, under the British flag, stood fast for no truck or trade with the Yankees, for dreadnoughts instead of tinpots, for Old England against the Frenchman Laurier. The Quebec of Bourassa, Lavergne, and Monk, the Quebec of the colleges and seminaries, stood for the Catholic schools that had been lost, against the militarism that Laurier was to fasten on the country, against the hordes of strangers who had filled the west, and now even against truck or trade. Reciprocity, too, was the work of Laurier, and Bourassa had discovered its flaws. *Le Devoir* was now sharing in the flood of money that poured out as Sifton steered a growing political organization and Hugh Graham's battalions of writers filled the white space of the country's press.

Every extreme had met, every rankling remnant from the wars of the past had surged up in one impossible, ludicrous combination. It was good, perhaps, to meet them all at the end, upon such ground. On July 29 Laurier dissolved parliament and called a general election on the issue of reciprocity. It was an issue, said Fielding at the last caucus, 'to fight upon, to win upon, and even to fall upon'.

The American portions of the agreement had been fought through both houses of Congress with disastrous side effects. Taft had declared that reciprocity would 'make Canada only an adjunct of the United States'. Champ Clarke, Speaker of the House of Representatives, had jocosely announced that 'we are preparing to annex Canada' and had followed that with the hope that he would see the day 'when the American flag will float over every square foot of the British North American possessions, clear to the North Pole'. Repentant now, with his own measure safe, Taft was writing Laurier for advice on his later speeches, but the harm was done.

Both Canadian leaders issued their manifestoes on the day parliament closed. Neither had a word about the navy. For Borden, Quebec and all that the navy implied to Quebec was forbidden ground. For Laurier it was a separate war, dearest and deadliest. He expected painful losses but he still expected to win, and Ontario was the key to recovery. He had leaned long on Ontario now, and he had paid much for the privilege. It was heartening on August 2 to receive a letter from Leighton McCarthy, nephew and political descendant of D'Alton, promising that 'no stone will be left unturned to bring North Simcoe back into the ranks behind you'. That much the years had brought. He had neglected British Columbia and complaints came now of 'the stupidity of western ministers' that had disrupted the party there. Manitoba's dismal Tory machine was quite likely to defeat Manitoba's wish for free trade but Alberta and Saskatchewan were safe, and surely the Maritimes too. Throughout the country the lethargy of the party annoyed him in the face of the great issue, but the issue itself would win. He could not doubt that, and would not.

On August 16 Borden went deep into the rich heartland of Ontario to open the campaign at London. On August 17 Laurier began. He chose Three Rivers this time, across the river from Sorel and almost as storied a centre as Quebec itself. If he was battling long memories he was part of a greater memory, and no one would be allowed to forget it. 'I am branded in Quebec as a traitor to the French and in Ontario as a traitor to the English. In Quebec I am branded as a jingo and in Ontario as a separatist. In Quebec I am attacked as an Imperialist and in Ontario as an anti-Imperialist. I am neither. I am a Canadian. Canada has been the inspiration of my life. I have had before me as a pillar of fire by night and a pillar of cloud by day a policy of true Canadianism, of moderation, of conciliation.'

In seven crowded meetings through the next week he tried to undo the results of the lost summer. Bourassa, Lavergne, and Monk had used it well and everywhere he came, it seemed, their meetings had been before him. They still went on, larger than Laurier's, but he drew his crowds too and hacked with all his powers at the combine that opposed him. 'Bourassa – Borden – Sifton – Monk. What a salad!' 'If I had to bet, I should bet on the old gamecock who for fifteen years has led the Liberal party to victory.' The charge of conscription was a monstrous and baseless lie. The facts of the navy had been utterly misrepresented; not only Quebec's duty but Quebec's interests were bound up in it. 'The day when England's supremacy on the sea is destroyed your national and religious privileges will be endangered.'

There were vigorous lieutenants still, and Bourassa was not spared. Bourassa was not a candidate; he was merely everywhere, speaking, inspiring, writing. *Le Devoir* was ubiquitous too. Prosperous Tories bought tens of subscriptions each. A Tory campaign committee was distributing the paper free to the farms of the Eastern Townships. The reason was not ignored; not by Rodolphe Lemieux, not by Ernest Lapointe. 'If I were given to the bitterness of the nationalists,' said Lapointe, 'I should say that M. Bourassa has opposed reciprocity since the capital of his paper has increased by $200,000. I should say that M. Bourassa has been bought.'

If it was so, the money had gone where it was not needed.

Bourassa was unchanged, indifferent to his associates, exultant. The goal of a long six years was now in sight. 'The power of the man of the golden mean, of the honourable compromises, of false "conciliation" solutions, evaporates like morning mist under a hot sun.'

The battle for Ontario began and the old man at bay was still powerful and confident. He warned the manufacturers, as Fielding had, of those great deputations of grizzled, red-necked farmers, of the cloud building in the west. If they denied this measure of reciprocity that the west so clearly wanted, 'They are preparing for themselves a rod which will one day fall across their own shoulders.' John A. Macdonald was the Moses of reciprocity who had failed to reach the Promised Land. 'I am the Joshua who will lead the people to their goal.' The cheers remained faint; there were old friends absent from the meetings and old fighters no longer at Laurier's side. Every word of Bourassa and Lavergne followed him across the Ottawa, clanging in his ears, clanking like chains about his neck. He denied the words, he would not deny himself; he was still of that soil and people. He had become once more to Ontario the Frenchman annexationist, withholder of dreadnoughts, servant of the Pope.

Ontario was being lost, but Quebec was almost gone. He hurried back for a last sweep along the length of the river, into the familiar heartlands. From Montreal to Rimouski far down the St. Lawrence the special trains carried their hordes of partisans like a great nomadic swarm, doubling and trebling for a day the populations of little towns. At each meeting's end came the reports of Bourassa's meeting or Lavergne's meeting, sometimes a town, sometimes a county away, always a little larger. On September 15 at Rimouski Laurier saw his crowd begin to melt in mid speech; Lavergne was there too, and there were fights in the streets that night.

Bourassa, suddenly discovered by the Tory press as a man 'of great moral energy, a sincere admirer of English institutions', was much demanded in Ontario. He yielded only to the extent of a quick visit to the many French of Sudbury and was back by the first train. On the next night, September 19, at the Ontario Rink in Montreal, came Bourassa's final meeting. For three hours the cheers for him drowned every other speaker, and once more at the end the crowd flowed away in a body, breaking in shouting rivulets at the corners of narrow streets. Along one street came the car of the Prime Minister, bound for the railway station. Laurier was passing through for his last meeting in Quebec. Suddenly the automobile was engulfed by jeering youth, pounding at the sides and windows, kicking at the wheels. Stones rattled as the chauffeur spun the wheel, backed off, and squirmed away through the crowd. Ten minutes later in Place Viger station, as Laurier's aides hurried him to the train, the chorus of 'O Bourassa' swelled over him, defiant, deafening, and conclusive.

He had conceded weeks before that the cities of the province were lost, and had hoped to make up for it in the country districts. On the night of September 21, sitting in a bleak committee room as returns reached Quebec, he learned that he had not. He had lost twenty-seven seats in Quebec and seventy-two in Ontario. He had lost Manitoba and British Columbia. He had swept Alberta and Saskatchewan but had barely held the Maritimes. His majority in the House had become a minority of forty-five, and the total vote of the country was against him by forty-seven thousand. Seven of his ministers, including Fielding, had gone down in the general disaster.

He rose tranquilly when the night's work was over and went to bed. The next day he left for Ottawa. Some of his oldest friends met him at Montreal; Zoë had telephoned them to be sure to do so. Still calm and good-humoured he accepted their condolences and went on. Zoë was waiting for him when he arrived late in the evening at the house on the street that was now called Laurier Avenue. Dim-eyed now and very tired with a long vigil, she was still the strong staff. It was after all Providence, she said, which was taking him a little from his country and giving him back to his old wife.

He smiled, patted her shoulder, and persuaded her to go to bed. His secretary was waiting and a servant brought in a cold supper for both. It was a silent meal, quickly cleared away, and the secretary soon left. There was nothing that night that required Sir Wilfrid's attention. As the door closed he put his face in his hands. Then for a long time the tears came.

25

'I WILL STAY WITH THE BOYS FOR A WHILE'

1911-1914

ON MONDAY September 25, after a blessed Saturday and Sunday of partial seclusion, he faced the newspaper reporters in the office of the Prime Minister. They found him, as he was pleased to note when he came to read their accounts that evening, 'bright, erect, and firm'. He stood as usual with his back to the familiar fireplace, but he was now a tenant on notice. The shucking-off of greatness had begun. It was with a new and nearer intimacy that he referred to those so often white-bearded and paunchy companions in misfortune as 'the boys'.

'I will stay with the boys for a while at least,' he said. 'It would be like desertion to leave them now.' The meetings of the lame-duck cabinet would begin that afternoon and there was a flavour of irony, duly noted, in the fact that one of the first duties would be to set a date for Thanksgiving. 'You'll come and see me sometimes in the other office, won't you?' he called after the reporters as they filed out.

Borden had returned to Ottawa without fanfare on Sunday morning, already pursued by hordes of the hungry faithful. On Tuesday evening he emerged from the shelter of his home to pass through the streets of the capital in a mud-splashed carriage hauled by a hundred men and followed by a drenched procession three miles long. Neither Ottawa streets nor Ottawa weather had changed much in thirty-four years. The fireworks and lanterns and dripping banners were all poignantly reminiscent of those that had once brought a triumphant Minister of Inland Revenue to the doorstep of Alexander Mackenzie. Laurier, however, was not compelled to view them. Borden, with his usual dignified courtesy, had vetoed the suggestion that Laurier Avenue be made a part of the route.

The winding-up of affairs went on for nearly two weeks, a leisurely phantasmagoria through which the ministers moved with outward dignity and dazed inward rankling, quite unhurried by the besieged and bewildered cabinet maker in the other camp. Laurier faced his council for the last time on Friday morning, October 6. It was about one-thirty when the final transactions were disposed of and the moment of silence came. He leaned back, put his hands on the desk in front of him and stood up. Cartwright sat near him, Senator Cartwright now, the companion of thirty-seven years, the one unbroken link with the first day in the first parliament. Yet the two men had neither spoken nor glanced at each other when they entered the room. There had never been friendship between them and there was nothing at all now. To that crabbed, stooped, arthritic solitary, always thrust aside at the peak of the game, 'Master' Laurier had come to be as bitterly resented as 'Master' Blake.

Fielding sat there, defeated in his own riding. Sydney Fisher, the elegant, aging bachelor who had resisted all Zoë's matchmaking for fifteen years, was another casualty. So was George Graham. So was Mackenzie King. They were indispensable men and Laurier had assured them, for what the assurance was worth, that he would try to find them other seats. They all knew the uncertainties of that prospect, and there were three other defeated ministers to whom he had given no assurance at all. He could offer nothing now to any man around the table but a lean sharing of the rough side of politics under a leader who was old and infinitely weary. The instrument of government was about to dissolve into a cluster of dubious loyalties; power was gone. 'Well, gentlemen,' he said, not looking at anyone in particular, 'that is all.' His voice dropped a little on the last three words, he turned rather quickly but erect as ever and walked from the room.

That afternoon he went to the Governor General with his resignation, and four days later Borden's cabinet was announced. The Montreal *Star* was vastly dissatisfied and spoke of 'sinister influences'. Certainly the hand of Sifton had been powerfully felt and would be from now on. Quite as certainly the ineffable Bob Rogers, late of Manitoba, would add nothing of stature or virtue. Sam Hughes as Minister of Militia was a guarantee of trouble. Toronto had firmly rejected Foster as Minister of Finance and he had been relegated, like Cartwright before him, to the portfolio of Trade and Commerce. It was the position of Quebec, however, that reflected most clearly the new state of affairs. Of the gaudy triumvirate that had defeated Laurier only Monk emerged as a minister. Bourassa had been asked and had declined. Lavergne had declined though no one was very sure that he had been asked. The work of the pair was done, and well done. Of Quebec's sixty-five members thirty-eight were now on the opposition side of the aisle. The remaining twenty-seven sat with the lugubrious Monk, dissident, powerless, and distracted in the grip of Protestant Ontario.

According to the newspapers, Bickerdike, one of the English Quebec Liberals, had been quite clear as to the identity of the mighty shade called up to defeat his party. 'I don't know his name – he's dead long ago – but he's the man who wrote Rule Britannia.' The half-truth represented half of a process that was not likely to stop. The Orange banner, 'One Fleet, One Flag, One Language and One Throne', had flapped wetly over the victory procession in Ottawa. By the time the first session of the twelfth parliament opened on November 15 the Duke of Connaught had replaced Grey as Governor General, and there was no doubt that the son of Queen Victoria would stiffen up the easy-going imperialism of Rideau Hall. Dr. Sproule, Grand Master of Orangemen, presided as Speaker over the sittings of the new parliament, and though he was an estimable and dutiful man who read the prayers of the day in French after two weeks of hasty coaching, Monk's face was a study as he listened. Monk's dictum soon came down the corridors to the new office: 'I have no doubt that God Almighty understood him.'

On November 20, as Laurier reported to Marie-Louise Pacaud, 'all that is left of our Liberals in parliament gathered together to celebrate, alas! – my seventy years'. The formalities of the first caucus and the proffered resignation were over; there was no doubt that he was still the only leader. In his own mind there was equal certainty of complete and crushing failure. Quebec he could understand if not forgive; he could regain Quebec. But Ontario, the Ontario he had fought for all his life, faced him again blank-eyed, hackles erect, flexing its British muscles. He was still the rejected foreigner. 'It was not reciprocity that was turned down, but a Catholic premier.'

Every newspaper, friend or enemy, had some word of praise for his magnificence in defeat, his serene determination to go on. The façade was effortless, but façade it was. Behind it he sat for a while with his familiar pains and aches, with the new misery of infected teeth, not expecting to live long nor wishing to. Zoë had had to calm his old man's fears about money, about the cluster of friends and relatives and deserving cases and causes that year by year had received their dribble of cheques. None of them would suffer, she told him, everything would go on as before. 'I shall make my little economies.' He found himself more concerned about Hannah Gauthier, with whom the years had dealt hardly, than about the importunities of Mackenzie King or the wrecked affairs of the party. It was blessed routine, the only routine he knew, that came to his rescue at last.

George Graham seemed to have the best chance of an early return to a seat. That matter would have to be dealt with. Mackenzie King, for whom nothing could yet be found, was agonizing over an invitation to become the leader of the provincial Liberals in Ontario. He would have to be saved for the federal field. Alex the Silent Smith was clamouring for repairs to the party machinery, and in that pungent realist there was the best balm of all.

Smith did not believe that religion or race had defeated Laurier in Ontario. 'You were not defeated by these cries. The cries got the start of you because you had no organization. We had nobody in charge. It was like playing marbles with marbles made out of mud. Warnings, directions, and offers of assistance were all resented, and the result was that you had not the support of the lineal descendants of those who were proud to see you elected in 1896. The two main causes of your defeat were, first, fifteen years in power and, secondly, no organization.'

He did not wholly believe it, and never would. He was irked by the charges of Smith and other realists that he had let a tired Old Guard fence him off from the youth of the party. But it was a healthy irritation and a healthily practical problem. By the turn of the year he was wholly involved in it, the politician again.

2

BY THE END of February 1912 George Graham had been elected for South Renfrew and Mackenzie King was installed in modest discontent as director of the Liberal Information Office in Ottawa at a salary of $2,500 a year. The Chief was at work again, and he had been powerful on the stumps in behalf of Graham. 'I am prepared to remain at the head of the Liberal party', he told a victory gathering in Ottawa on March 2, 'so long as you want me and so long as God spares me and blesses me with the perfect health that he is giving me today.'

Outwardly at least he was completely adjusted to his new state, restored, truculent, and almost cocky. Reciprocity was dead but he refused to bury it. 'O men of little faith,' was his taunt to the Conservative party, 'that seed will still germinate.' He was enjoined to give up his naval policy. 'No sir, I will not give it up.' Before he was asked to reconcile his views with Borden's, he suggested, let Borden, Bourassa, Monk, and the others reconcile their own.

It was a cruelly well-aimed thrust. While the issue of the navy sat like a fused bomb under the table of the new cabinet, the facts of life were already asserting themselves. On February 19 the pet measure of the Honourable Robert Rogers, providing for the annexation of the territory of Keewatin to Manitoba, came before the House. In the matter of schools, at least, the views of the Honourable Robert ran with Sifton's and were vigorously supported by Sam Hughes. It was hardly surprising, therefore, to find that the bill contained no provision for the separate denominational education that the people of the Northwest Territories had always enjoyed. The old fires flared, with all reactions predictable. Monk, at the head of his powerless French delegation, refused to renew the battle of 1905. The hierarchy of the Church demurred and gave way as before in return for a promise of concessions. Lavergne charged down to Ottawa and found only one senator and one young private member in any mood for war. Bourassa, always himself, waited till the issue was decided and then spoke.

When he was finished the alliance that had won the election hung in shreds. He had reproved Monk, rejected Borden, and scolded even the bishops. 'It is not the business of bishops and priests to make law.' He now rejected even the Laurier settlement in Manitoba which he had helped Tarte make, sixteen years before. There could be no more of such compromises. The speech in the great crowded gloom of Le Monument National in Montreal went on for the usual three hours, and as usual it was not enough for his cheering audience. 'If the Canadian constitution is to last, if the Canadian Confederation is to be maintained, the narrow attitude toward the rights of minorities which increasingly manifests itself in the English provinces must disappear and we must return to the original spirit of the alliance. We are not British by blood and language, but we are British by reason and tradition. We are not submissive dogs, we are not valets. We deserve better than to be told, "Remain in Quebec, continue to stagnate in ignorance, you are at home there but elsewhere you must become English." We are Canadians before all, we have the right to be as British as anyone, and we have the right to enjoy those rights throughout the whole expanse of Confederation.' There was all the old bitter clarity in his arraignment of facts, all the old love for his ideal of British institutions, all the old blank contempt for the processes by which they moved. Above the drudgery of persuasion, above friendship, above the give and take of parliaments, for fifteen vocal years he had gone his way and now stood still, anchored and impotent in vanity and resentment. It was heart-breaking as always and pointless as always to protest. Bourassa, it seemed, had arrived at his final position.

Nor was there much comfort, two months later, to find him dourly admitting in *Le Devoir* that Laurier was 'still the great figure of Canadian politics'. Whatever Bourassa's regrets, if regrets there were, events moved on and he would be found in his accustomed place with the other familiar actors. In June, during the week of Saint-Jean Baptiste, Archbishop Langevin proposed that the three million French of the North American continent should form a great union for the protection of common rights and religion. 'If we have remained French it is because we have remained Catholic; it is by guarding our religion that we guard our race.' In the same month Ontario's department of education, loudly applauded by that Catholic Fallon who had once been a priest in Ottawa and now was an Irish bishop, took steps to eliminate French as a language of instruction in Ontario's primary schools.

The new measure, soon to be famous as Regulation 17, rose largely out of conditions in the Ottawa region, wrathfully observed by Bishop Fallon when he had taught there. Here, as in other areas of French settlement throughout Ontario, an arrangement prevailed that had been made by Mowat almost a quarter of a century before. 'French Canadians', he had said in 1889, 'cherish their own language lovingly. Proscribe French, their mother tongue, and they will hate you and have nothing to do with your schools. Permit their own language to receive attention, and they are glad to have their children learn English also as soon and as fast as it can be imparted.' It had been his answer to the rising D'Alton McCarthy and to those sentinels in the watch-towers of Toronto who feared invasion from across the Ottawa, and it had seemed to be moderately successful. Supposedly bilingual teachers had taught young children in the language most familiar to them, supposedly proceeding in due course to the study of English. In practice, particularly in the country districts, many of the teachers had been very sketchily bilingual, and out of the seeds borne on the wind through recent years had grown a proportion who were openly unwilling to teach English. English and Irish fathers, living as a minority in such districts, had found their sons referring to the beast that pulled the family buggy as 'le cheval' while being only dimly acquainted with it, if at all, as 'da 'orse'. It was hardly Mowat's idea or Mowat's fault, but the cure was now to be rigorous. Henceforth, under Regulation 17, children who entered school speaking only French might be taught 'where necessary' in their own tongue, but only during their first year or two and only in schools 'where French has hitherto been a subject of study'.

The effect of the blow was still padded by quarrels over the interpretation of the wording but the intention seemed clear. A provincial and Protestant department of education, not a local school board, would decide where the teaching of French was 'necessary'. There would be no provision at all for the teaching of French in schools established after June 1912. 'This is a British country.' Ontario had gone back to the cross-roads and turned to the way of McCarthy, with all the familiar results. By July Bourassa was informing Ontario that French Canadians no longer feared annexation to the United States. As for English Canadians, he told them pleasantly, they were American already, 'by your language, your nasal accent, your common slang, your dress, your daily habits, by the Yankee literature with which your homes and clubs are flooded, by your yellow journals and their ranting, by your loud and intolerant patriotism, by your worship of gold, snobbery, and titles.'

The new cloud was one of the ugliest yet, but Laurier watched it for a while almost indifferently. Regulation 17 had still to thread the usual maze of protest and litigation; he did not believe that it would be allowed to emerge in its present form. At the end of the session he had gone to Virginia for a rest, with Zoë for the first time a reluctant companion. 'With all my infirmities,' she had written to Hannah Gauthier, 'I fear to be an embarrassment. In the old days I should not have borne to be parted from my husband, but today it is much changed.' The two weeks in the south had not done much to refresh either of them and for himself, as the summer wore on, the premonitions of death returned so strongly that he could not quite drive them from his mind or keep them from his conversation. He was sure that Zoë would outlive him, he was anxious about her and anxious to tidy up his affairs in a new will. Yet the clearing of the decks, when it was done, seemed to bring new assessments and new energy. He wanted to return to power, he would want that for as long as he lived and could work, and he did not need his urgent crowd of lieutenants to assure him that the prospect was good.

The issue, if he wanted it, was already taking shape. Borden was in England framing his new proposals for the navy. They would be less palatable to Quebec than ever; the men around Borden, the tone of the Tory press, the influences that would work on him in London made that certain. If he could be shaken in Ontario and the west before the battle began there was every chance that he could be forced to the polls and beaten. It was time for a sampling of the country's mood, and on August 15 the announcement went out from Liberal headquarters that the Chief would make a tour of the west. Two weeks later, as western reports of good crops and good prices indicated a benign apathy toward the ruling party, the guns were retrained. 'You may say', Laurier told the reporters, 'that we have changed our plans. I will make a tour of Quebec and afterward proceed through Ontario.'

He started on September 7, and one week was enough to reassure him on his position in Quebec. Lemieux was still at his side, and Jacques Bureau and Ernest Lapointe and Henri Béland, the pick of his old fighters. Gouin held the provincial citadel, totally unshaken. The towns that had shouted for Bourassa now listened with a new thoughtfulness and a new respect to Laurier. He swung up through northern Ontario and found it boisterously friendly, boisterously responsive to his ridicule of that 'salad' that called itself a government. September 21, the anniversary of his defeat, was celebrated in North Bay and it was a triumph. Graham, Charles Murphy, and Mackenzie King were with him, all elated and alight with the changing mood. By the first of October he was into older Ontario, the heart of his hopes and troubles, and it was easy indeed to believe that defeat had come through nothing but a slipshod accident. Even Toronto seemed warm, welcoming, and repentant. 'I don't feel ripe for

POST-ELECTION COMEBACK. CARTOON BY FERGUS KYLE IN THE *Globe*

heaven yet,' he told a crowd in Woodstock that was fattened by delegations from a dozen towns around and made noisy by seven visiting bands. 'At all events, I want another tussle with the Tories.'

At Mount Forest on the eighth an enormous mass meeting overflowed the streets and surged about him with Union Jacks and the banner 'Ontario Is Returning to Laurier.' It was all electrifying, all alive with new beginnings, colourful with new and renewed men. Graham was once again his genial, vigorous self, King was smoothly effective, Murphy was the fighting Irishman as never before, and Frederick Pardee of Sarnia, who had been quietly moving up in the old régime, was suddenly in full flower. The sense of strength, of full and powerful recovery was all about him, and he had hardly returned to Ottawa when the news came that Monk had resigned from the cabinet.

The issue was the navy and the sign, Laurier told a meeting at Sorel on the twenty-second, was for the government 'the beginning of its disruption and downfall'. Scarcely a year old, the impossible combination had now cracked and Borden's first firm step, it seemed, was likely to be his last.

3

'Mr. Borden should know', Bourassa had written in *Le Devoir* on July 24, 'that all participation in imperial naval affairs is distasteful to French Canadians, and if he has forgotten it we have only to remind him of the vote in Drummond-Arthabaska.' With this gracious injunction and with Monk already gone, Borden introduced his naval bill on December 5, 1912. There seemed to Liberals a noble augury in the fact that as he finished his introduction he missed his chair, sank to the floor with a heroic bump, and broke his glasses.

'O ye Tory jingoes,' said a sardonic leader of the opposition a week later, 'you give England two or three dreadnoughts to be paid for by Canada but to be equipped, maintained, and manned by England. . . . You are ready to furnish admirals, rear-admirals, commodores, captains, officers of all grades, plumes, feathers, and gold lace, but you leave it to England to supply the bone and sinews. You say that these ships shall bear Canadian names. That will be the only thing Canadian about them. You hire somebody to do your work; in other words you are ready to do anything except the fighting.'

It was not quite as bad as that, but it could be made to seem so in spite of the fervent choruses of 'God Save the King' and 'Rule Britannia' that rose from the other side of the aisle. Prodded on by the big-ship Tories, driven back by a flinty Quebec, and basing everything on the premise of a great naval emergency, Borden had resolved his policy into a simple attempt to buy time at a cost of thirty-five million dollars. There would be no Canadian navy until some way had been found for the Dominion to participate in the shaping of British foreign policy. Laurier's act would be wiped from the statute books. In the meanwhile, however, as a contribution to the imperilled motherland, Canada would provide the funds for what Winston Churchill, now First Lord of the Admiralty, grandly described as 'the largest and strongest ships of war which science can build or money supply'.

It was very much Churchill's plan, offered at Borden's invitation and supported with memoranda in the First Lord's own imperial style. Since he intended to build the ships in any case, and since Canadian money would be welcome, Churchill had leaped with hearty haste to take advantage of the changing climate in Ottawa. He continued to write as the debate went on, indicating to the colonials with disastrous clarity that he did not think they could build ships or man them or maintain them. Likely young Canadians might be permitted to train with the Royal Navy as officer candidates, some few tankers and small craft might be started in Canadian shipyards, but beyond that and the money all should be left to Admiralty.

'That document', said Henry R. Emmerson, referring to one of the memoranda in the liveliest speech he had made since his far-off fall from grace, 'is calculated to cause more irritation, to undermine more seriously our constitutional freedom than any that has come from authority in Great Britain since the days of Lord North.' Quebec echoed and re-echoed him in its reaction to the whole bill, quite unsoothed by the prospect of giving money instead of men, quite unconvinced that the first gift would be the last. Behind Borden his nervous Quebec nationalists, most of whom had been elected on platforms similar to that of Drummond-Arthabaska, sat forsaken by Monk and scourged by Bourassa. They might be held to a party vote in the House but they shuddered at the thought of a dissolution that would turn them out naked before their constituents. It was clear to Laurier, as debate rumbled on through December and took up with mounting acrimony in the new year, that the great opportunity beckoned. He grew less sure through February and March, even with the party solid and hungry behind him, that he wished to take advantage of it.

The debate had become, with his help, another swamp of words. It dragged on into the small hours of interminable sessions, with exhausted men belabouring each other when they had spent their arguments. There seemed every justification for blocking, delaying, and driving Borden to the polls. To a man who had dealt long with Joseph Chamberlain everything was wearily, exasperatingly familiar. The old, undying imperialists were manufacturing another crisis for all the old reasons. The navy bill was the first long step toward everything Laurier had avoided: imperial squadrons, imperial councils, the whole apparatus of centralized control. How, he asked the House, did Borden propose to exercise that 'voice in all questions of peace or war' that was to precede a real navy. 'The Foreign Office, only last year, had to deal with the question of the division of Persia. Are we to understand that Canada and all the other dominions would be invited to discuss such a question? A few years ago the Afghan boundary was a burning question. Within the last year, when the German Emperor sent warships to Agadir, the Foreign Office had to take immediate action. Would the Dominion of Canada also be interested and be consulted upon this question?'

The 'tribute' that Borden and Foster had shied away from in 1909 was now to be imposed, and it would be self-perpetuating. The thirty-five million dollars would change nothing in the naval situation, and the situation itself had been luridly misrepresented. British politicians themselves were emptying much of the wind from Churchill's sails. 'Do any of us really believe that there is danger, any vital danger?' asked Bonar Law. 'There has never been a moment and there is not now', said Asquith, 'when we have not been overwhelmingly superior to any combination which can reasonably be anticipated.'

Fielding, infinitely missed in the House, was still a supporting echo of these British voices. Fielding was in London, a private gentleman for the moment, busy on his own affairs but much sought out and listened-to and listening. Many of the politicians there, he wrote, 'feel that the German war scare is being overworked by the jingo elements and tend to ridicule what they consider the extravagant and dangerous tendencies of the Admiralty. They are letting the ministers understand that the Churchill-Borden arrangement is very obnoxious.' Even Churchill, said Fielding, had sent for him and admitted that the approach to the Canadian public through Borden had perhaps been a mistake.

With it all, Laurier sat in the House at the head of a boisterous party, privately wavering as the liverish nights and days dragged on toward the Easter recess. The navy was hardly the project nearest his heart. He had fought one election on it and did not relish the thought of another. Far as he stood from Monk and Bourassa, he would be hived with them by the Tories and hived in Quebec. Much of that good month's work in Ontario would be undone. 'A sudden dissolution with the waving of the flag', he wrote Fielding, 'might make us lose the ground we have gained. I believe that a campaign upon the high cost of living would be far more effective.'

It was a strange, drab note to be sounding amid the imperial cacophony about him. Yet there was no doubt that the days of Laurier prosperity were on the ebb. That hope of a population of sixty millions was seen now as what it had been, the grotesque optimism of boom times. Immigration, business, industry, and the inflow of money were all falling off. The new railway struggled on, still uncompleted, always in deeper trouble, while the bitterly competing Canadian Northern matched its woes and multiplied them. The country was worried and anxious, uninterested in battleships or navies, and it could turn irritably on the man who roused it. 'I am thinking of these matters night and day,' Laurier added to Fielding, 'and I never felt as I do now the loss of so many friends whose presence at this moment in parliament would be so valuable.'

He was still thinking when parliament resumed after the recess, but a grim-faced Borden who had had enough was about to resolve his problem. On April 3 and again on April 7, as the prospect of more all-night sittings stretched away endlessly, Borden charged Laurier with that obstruction and delay so frowned on from the government side of the aisle. Laurier was unrepentant; the Conservatives had obstructed reciprocity in 1911. On the ninth, Borden, a dismally unhappy figure with his neck swathed in bandages to conceal a mass of boils, arrived in the House with a curious air of portent. Laurier felt it but was not warned. The bill was in committee, he was still in a position to offer fifty amendments if he wished. Apart from dissolution there seemed no visible process by which debate could be brought to an end.

Abruptly and stunningly the prospect changed. Laurier rose to speak and across the aisle John Hazen, the Minister of Marine and Fisheries, also rose. The leader of the opposition turned for the routine decision from the Speaker that would ordinarily have given him the floor. Instead he found another Conservative, Northrup, on his feet, moving that the Minister of Marine and Fisheries 'be now heard'.

Since the rules prescribed that such a question should be put without debate, the government majority promptly gave Hazen the floor. Just as promptly Hazen moved for the power to apply closure to end the naval debate, adding the motion 'that this question be now put'. The magic formula provided for sharply limited debate, not on the navy but on the power to apply closure. Five minutes of very fast footwork had given Borden control of the situation and Laurier, for almost the first time in his life, found himself in full cry at the head of a band of outwitted and enraged warriors.

Afterward he was unforgiving but not sure that he was sorry. Borden's mournful countenance above the bandaged neck was evidence enough that he did not like what he was doing. He persisted with uneasy courtesy, allowing a full two weeks for the debate on the closure motion. It was quite evident, however, that he intended the motion to pass. On April 23 debate simply ran down and the government headsman was equipped with his axe.

There remained, however, the most venerable obstructionist of all, which no government had yet found a way to remove. In mid May the navy bill, passed at last under the threat though without the application of closure, went to the Senate. On May 30 it came back. Henceforth for a while it would be Borden and the Tories who were vengefully dedicated to reform of the upper chamber. The patrician fathers, still largely Liberal and grateful to their maker, had found 'that this House is not justified in giving its assent to this bill until it is submitted to the judgment of the country'. They were the precise words of the amendment that Borden had moved to the naval bill of 1910.

'IS THIS TO BE THE FATE OF THE LAST FREE PARLIAMENT IN THE WORLD?' CARTOON BY FERGUS KYLE IN THE *Globe*

4

FOR THE MOMENT, and for what it was worth, the last word had been said on the question of the navy. On June 6, as parliament was about to prorogue, Laurier inquired with a certain acid complacency as to Borden's next step. There was apparently not to be one. The Admiralty would build its ships and 'eventually' Canadian money would be found to pay for three of them. In the meantime the Laurier act remained on the statute books and the embryo naval service continued a lean and friendless existence. Of the two old training cruisers that the country had to show as the result of four years of savage controversy, *Rainbow* found means occasionally to limp to sea from Vancouver. *Niobe,* which had come to grief on Sable Island in 1911, now lay tied up at Halifax, 'going aground', as the sailors said, 'on her own beer bottles'.

Summer came on and the old man longed for Arthabaska. The party leader could not think of it, did not want to think of it. He was ill much of the time with a general diffused wretchedness that the doctor attributed to his teeth. Sooner or later he would have to gird himself for a painful, protracted session with the dentist. He was ready as any man to delay that, however, and in the meantime his newly-gathering followers lifted him up and pushed him on. For the plaintive Mackenzie King there was at least the prospect of a seat when a general election came. He had been promised the nomination for North York, particularly attractive to him as the old constituency of his rebel grandfather. Fielding was back in Canada, more interested at the moment in returning to the newspaper world than to politics, but that would quickly change. The reports from Ontario, the Maritimes, and the west were all confident. There seemed small reason to regret the missed opportunity. The other election issue was thrusting up. During the autumn Laurier began to broach it at his meetings in Quebec. 'Is it not said,' he asked, 'as it was never said under the Laurier administration, "Money is scarce"? The question of the day is the cost of bread, not of battleships.'

The Conservative party had hardened into warring wings of English and French Canadians. Depressed times were driving another rift between eastern and western Tories. Government was softening at the centre, if the reports that Alex Smith retailed could be believed. For Laurier it was not Borden but Sifton who was the controlling power, and Sifton was no longer a power in the west. Rumour, at least, involved him with every malevolent eastern money interest and the richer he grew the more he was glowered at as a political force. He overshadowed the Canadian Northern and the Grand Trunk, his growing imperialism was suspect, his anti-Frenchness took on a new taint. And the fabric of the man himself, still in his early fifties, restless and driving and driven behind that barrier of deafness, seemed to be giving way. An informant found him, Alex Smith reported, 'rather queer and variable. He thinks Sifton does not know much where he is at in anything as he appears not to be his former self in any respect. He does not look well, his face seems to change each day, and now instead of a firm, strong face it is getting puffy and soft. His face is but a reflex of his mentality, which is by no means what it was. His life is a tragedy.'

It might or might not be true. One grew accustomed now to such reports on the old enemies and the old friends. As he looked round him, Laurier had told the House at the opening of the session in 1912, he saw not one of the men who had started out with him in politics. Cartwright and Blake had both died that year. Of Blake, the greatest leader he had known, Laurier's last souvenir was a pathetic, hardly legible note scrawled unsteadily in pencil. One of his last memories of Cartwright was the sight of him in earnest conversation with Tupper, returned from England to sit by Borden's invitation as a distinguished guest in the House of Commons. One watched the two old heads bobbing together, and looked away. Nothing was forgiven, age had not sweetened either; it had merely emptied them of cause and force. It would empty Laurier, but not quite yet awhile. It was good to have work, worry, responsibility, the thread of purpose. It was something, at least, to close this year of 1913 with a glimpse of refreshing youth and feel, perhaps, that one could still strike a response. In mid December he came before the students of the University of Toronto, presented to them as 'the greatest of all Canadians'. If it was hyperbole it was well cheered and he was well listened to. 'If I were your age,' he told them, 'I would not leave school until I could speak and write in French.'

There had been no autumn parliament in 1913, and he growled at Borden over the delay when the session at last opened on January 15, 1914. On that point, however, he speedily got the worst of it. His own westerners were quite as strong as the Tories in their dislike of the fall sessions that had taken them away at the height of the harvest business. As the House settled down the mood of the country settled over it. It was not going to be a year for 'Rule Britannia' or 'God Save the King'. There was an acrid little debate over a new rash of titles, and it was initiated not by a Liberal but by a Tory back-bencher. Even among the faithful, it seemed, there was disenchantment with the transatlantic loyalties of high Conservatism. The country was tired of titles, bored with Empire, weary of grandiloquence, and worried over money. Hard times and the railways were going to hold the floor.

All men in that House, on both sides of the aisle, would find it impossible eight months later to recreate the atmosphere in which they began the session. That European 'vortex of militarism', it seemed, had been voted away with the navy. There was always Sam Hughes building his armouries, staging his reviews, sounding the alarm. The gentlemen of the Round Table developed the gospel of imperial federation and filled the public prints with it. Their converts spoke from platforms and from board-rooms, all for the iron-bound Empire, all for haste, envisioning Armageddon. They had become accepted sounds, almost unheard. 'The air is so full of a spirit of pacifism', complained Principal Hutton of Toronto University, 'that it is necessary to urge upon the country the duty of national defence.' Nor was it merely a mood of parochial isolation; it ran through the world and the age. The vortex had swirled too long. The power to tear mankind apart had grown too plain, but so had its consequences. They were absurd, incredible, ludicrous in this latest age of reason. The thought of a great war haunted the houses of all governments and all men, but it lived with them like a mad relative shut away in a room apart. The year had opened with a new sunlight of peaceful protestations over Europe. Laurier could quote from a long list of the best British references when he reminded Borden of the talk of crisis a year before and asked, 'Emergency? Who speaks today of emergency?'

There was no reply to any effect and a routine session droned on into May with the government girding itself for the work of saving the railways. The Canadian Northern came first and the needs of Mackenzie and Mann were now to be met by a guarantee of forty-five million dollars. The arrangement was as usual a mighty maze concealing a shocking bargain, but no one denied that the railway had to be finished. No one could deny, either, that it had been a great work. Laurier had never liked Mackenzie or Mann. Those needy tycoons had haunted his railway building and his politics from the beginning, generally with baleful effect. He had given them a good many millions, and given them each a knighthood in January 1911 without securing much in the way of friendship or support. He had no doubt at all that many of his own troubles and many of the troubles of the Grand Trunk Pacific had come from them. Yet they had opened up thousands of miles of the country with their steel and no one had yet proved that any of the millions flowing through their hands had stuck to their hands. Gamblers, builders, and dreamers, reckless and unashamed, they were a part of the great years and had helped to make those years. They could not be abandoned now, and they could not be escaped. Laurier fought hard to have the government, which had become the principal investor in the Canadian Northern, placed in control of the property. He had his own past to contend with and he failed; nothing could pry the railway loose from Mackenzie and Mann. On June 2 the money was voted.

The needs of the Grand Trunk Pacific were smaller but quite as urgent and the situation the same. Much of the planning had gone wrong, much of the money had been wasted, politics had been everywhere. Yet it was the same under the new government as under the old, and the country needed the railway. No one had yet brought himself to doubt that. For the Grand Trunk, by the time prorogation came, there was another sixteen million dollars.

He left for Arthabaska in the middle of June, determined this year to have his summer of rest and quiet. It would be good to relax with the pale hope that railway problems were settled even if the railways themselves were not completed. Of all his politics, in the forty years on which he now looked back, railway politics had been the roughest, the dirtiest, and the least satisfactory in their results. It would be painful to compare the maps of actual building with those maps he had studied when he first began to think of his new transcontinental. Too much of the stark north had still to hear the whistle of its first train, too much of the fat south was crammed with competing lines. Nothing had come out complete, nothing quite as he hoped, but the steel was there and the towns grew up beside it. Much should certainly have been better, yet much had been done.

The maples in Arthabaska had grown well. For two weeks

he sat gratefully under their shade. Across the dusty road the many-memoried windows of the little office looked back at him. The gracious lawn swept round to the looming bulk of Mont Christo, rising behind the house. Zoë, as usual, unfolded like a rose in the beloved garden and it was good to hear her laughing with Yvonne Coutu. It was good to have the relatives and friends come and the children crowd about him, peremptory in their demands for attention. He was still the story-teller who made history come alive with its kings and queens, and some of them now he had seen and talked to himself. Sometimes, still, he went on a little too long. Often he sat smiling while the children sang, the domed head with its nimbus of white hair nodding, the eye-glasses on their black silk ribbon moving gently in time. He was an old man at home, yet somehow not of this place nor quite of this day. The valet, the chauffeur, the huge old English car, the budgets of mail and stir of portentous visitors hinted of greatness still. The immaculate morning-coat and trousers, the elastic-sided shoes, the large cravat with the horse-shoe pin were all of an older fashion, all his own. He was Laurier, familiar enough yet somehow larger than life, man and legend.

Of the Lavergnes, Louis the senator remained a neighbour, uncomfortably mindful of what that senatorship had cost. Joseph in Quebec was a disappointed judge, Emilie a cool acquaintance. Armand went his way, daily enlarging on his handiwork. Now, as Bishop Fallon and Bourassa stoked the fires of controversy over Regulation 17, Armand was ploughing all the fields of history for buried bones. Was Canada, he asked, 'indebted to England because in 1780 she conceded Oregon, Illinois, Michigan, Ohio, and Washington to the United States, or because she gave up Maine and Vermont and abandoned the ports of Alaska and the Yukon in 1904? Is it because she was afraid to take the part of the South in the War of the Secession and thus allowed the United States to become a nation and a dangerous neighbour of Canada? Do we owe her anything because of the Anglo-Japanese treaty which has allowed the west to be invaded by the Japanese?'

One could only sigh. Many of the effusions came from the bottle now, it was said, and that seemed likely. In any case

Armand was no longer a problem or a hope. There were still problems enough, and hopes of a kind. The government seemed unlikely to last another session and it was weakening everywhere. The prospect of power again seemed near, and more oppressive as it neared. The problem, if Laurier stepped down, would be a leader and his thoughts wavered between Graham, King, and Fielding. He doubted Graham's strength. Fielding was out of the House. King, that half-employed, resentful expert on labour, was being tempted by the Rockefellers in the United States, who were having labour problems. He would very likely go, and it would be a pity. There was not much to be done about it by a man out of power. There was not much to be done in any case, for nothing was ripe yet. The party looked to Laurier and it was not ready to look elsewhere. For himself, knowing himself, he had resigned those old ambitions for writing and leisure. Politics was a habit, the quest for power was a habit, probably lifelong now.

The word of the assassination at Sarajevo came on June 28. Another war scare. For almost a month he sat on, absorbing the news as it came, his mind adjusting slowly, opening like a stiff window on the appalling prospect. Then, on August 4, the telegram came and he took the train for Ottawa.

26

'THERE IS IN CANADA BUT ONE MIND AND ONE HEART'

1914-1916

FOR TWO WEEKS, amid the demonic swirl of the capital, he struggled to find a footing for himself and the party. Up to the morning of August 18, the day of the opening of the special session, he was still unsure of Quebec. But he had his own ground as he rose in the silent House next afternoon.

'When the call comes our answer goes at once – "Ready, aye ready." ' 'We are British subjects, and today we are face to face with the consequences which are involved in that proud fact.' To everything the government had done and was doing 'we raise no question, we take no exception, we offer no criticism. It is our duty, more pressing upon us than all other duties, at once, on this first day of this extraordinary session of the Canadian parliament, to let Great Britain know, and to let the friends and foes of Great Britain know, that there is in Canada but one mind and one heart.'

He had no illusions as to what was ahead. 'The war in which she is engaged will in all probability – nay, in absolute certainty – stagger the world with its magnitude and horror. But that war is for as noble a cause as ever impelled a nation to risk her all.' He had no doubt of the central danger to the country, and he struck to avert it with all the power he had. 'If my words can be heard beyond the walls of this House in the province from which I come, among the men whose blood flows in my own veins, I should like them to remember that in taking their place today in the ranks of the Canadian army a double honour rests upon them. The very cause for which they are called upon to fight is to them doubly sacred.' Whatever his doubts and memories, whatever his inmost view of that England and that France he spoke for now, all was swallowed up in his horror at the grey flood of savagery that had broken over Belgium. He withheld nothing, qualified nothing in his total support of the war, and in the four days of the special session he towered beside Borden as the pillar of a united nation. 'The last four days', said Foster as prorogation came, 'have vindicated Canadian public life and parliamentary life for all time to come.'

Foster spoke of a long future, and rashly, but for the moment with much truth. The country, like the world, clanged with outrage at the first blow of the iron Teutonic fist. 'The question cannot be discussed,' said Archbishop Bruchési on August 23. 'We have given England provisions and gold and we will give her men.' Ten days later he was echoed and reinforced by another of the Quebec hierarchy. 'What should be the measure of this co-operation? It should be that demanded by the necessity of conquering.'

Even Bourassa, who had been in France through the summer, was swept briefly by the mood of France. It was Canada's national duty, he said, 'to contribute in the measure of her strength.' The qualifications soon followed. That strength should be determined by protracted study, that duty was sharply limited. Canadian jingoism, British foreign policy, the wider causes of war were acidly dissected as Bourassa returned to himself. At the moment, however, his learning and eloquence had become a little irrelevant even for his fieriest followers. Olivar Asselin had been one of the young leaders at Drummond-Arthabaska. He had no love for jingoes nor did he welcome bishops as recruiting agents. Neither was he prepared to see France fall. 'Mr. Bourassa', he snapped, 'has fallen into his customary error of being erudite when it would have been enough to entrench himself in plain common sense.'

Common sense, like everything else, had come to wear a different face in the lurid glow of the times. Censorship was in force, the markets were closed, banks were in a panic and only shored up by government Orders in Council that made their notes legal tender. To the man in the street, uncertain of his job, his future, even of the worth of his money, every condition of life seemed upside-down. The blazing headlines of one day were contradicted the next; everything was cheered and nothing quite believed. The politician groped, only a little more confused by the little more he knew. There was shouting above and grabbing beneath the surface. Law was elbowed aside. The spy scares came and the talk of the two hundred thousand enemy alien reservists who would have to be caged in the country. While the streets grew speckled with khaki, brokers and businessmen of a month before blossomed inexplicably with the tabs of rank on their shoulders, rushing from meeting to meeting, visibly pleased with themselves and visibly useless. Yet under it all and a part of it all, mastered by the lifelong foe of common sense, ran the huge, authentic drumbeat of assembly.

One day before war was declared Sam Hughes had caused the flag over military headquarters to be whipped down to half-mast because he was afraid the British would 'skunk it'. Within six weeks of the removal of that fear he had filled a huge camp called up from the bald farmland around Valcartier in Quebec with thirty-three thousand men. Dumping overboard every plan that had ever been made for an orderly mobilization, shoving aside his commanders and his framework of military districts, piling men in from the length and breadth of the country by a hundred special trains, he now had 'chaos supreme' but it was in motion.

On October 1 thirty-one thousand men and fifteen thousand horses, in a tangle of units without equipment or with the wrong equipment or with equipment that was to prove utterly useless later on, went helter-skelter onto thirty transports at Gaspé. On October 2 Hughes passed down the lines of ships in a launch, distributing bundles of his valedictory, 'Where Duty Leads'. In six weeks, he informed the bewildered but good-humoured and healthy troops, peaceful Canadian citizens had become 'an army of free men to do duty on the historic fields of France, Belgium, and Germany for the preservation of the British Empire and the rights and liberties of humanity'. On October 3, at three in the afternoon, the twenty-one miles of ships carrying the first Canadian contingent filed down the St. Lawrence.

The arrival at Plymouth would be memorable for a confusion that took nine days to sort out, and behind the departing troops the first clear glow of the home fires was already becoming smoky. While Hughes talked of second and third and fourth and fifth contingents, others of the cabinet were in no mood to waste a war. On October 15, Murphy reported to Laurier, 'Bob Rogers had a meeting with the faithful and told them to prepare for an election in three weeks.'

The prime aim, apart from the saving of some shaky ministers, would be to free the party of its Quebec nationalists. Nothing could be better for the purpose than a wartime election, nothing more certain, it seemed, than that a mighty wave of Britishness would submerge the men who had grumbled about Keewatin and opposed the gift of dreadnoughts. Already two ministers from Quebec who had entered the cabinet with Monk and remained on after him were finding it decidedly uncomfortable. The government, according to Murphy, was 'looking for a crowbar' to pry them out.

On October 19 they went, and the next day Laurier reported to Frank Oliver. There was no doubt whatever that the government had been considering dissolution for a week. There was equally no doubt that the best elements had greeted the proposal with scandalized disapproval. 'But since last Saturday the madmen of the party are making another effort and again beseeching the Prime Minister who, I understand, is again wavering.' He could not quite believe that Borden would yield, but all the pressures were growing and would not relax. Sam Hughes bellowed for men, but they were to be British men or they would be made British. There had been no response whatever to Laurier's pleading for the formation of distinctively French-Canadian units. Recruiting was true-blue British in methods and personnel, with the head of the Quebec district a former Methodist minister. The Honorary Colonels multiplied and the chosen began their reaping among the rich sheaves of the war contracts. The notable J. Wesley Allison, Hughes's favourite middleman, was already becoming a power. The prospects on every hand for Tories newly confirmed by a general election seemed almost illimitable. 'It is sufficient to make us awake and lively, so as to be ready should the fray come.'

The golden mood had passed. By November Bourassa, now saluted in the Montreal *Star* as 'von Bourassa', was delivering himself in his familiar voice. The Canadian contribution, he opined, should have been 'a suitable contingent of soldiers, well-disciplined and perfectly equipped'. The Canadian gifts of food and produce had been nonsense; 'thousands of bags of flour and great piles of cheese – which rot today on the docks of Liverpool because the English do not know what to do with it'. There should have been organization, there should have been planning, there should have been vigilant control of private profit. 'But no, it was necessary at all costs that Canada's aid should take an inflated, noisy, loud form, worthy of the fat-stomached newly rich who dominate high finance, big business, and the high policy of the Canadian nation. Glory to the Empire!'

Nor in the midst of it all did Bourassa forget Regulation 17. On December 16 he went to Ottawa to address a meeting that had been postponed from November because of the prospect of a riot. Nothing had been cooled by the delay. A hostile crowd refused to hear him but he went on with his speech for the benefit of newspaper reporters who sat near by amid the uproar. A soldier climbed from the audience, handed Bourassa a British flag, and ordered him to wave it. Bourassa, totally uncowed, took the flag and laid it on the table. He had upheld the British flag all his life, he said, but he would do nothing under compulsion. As the first few rows of the audience, almost solidly khaki, prepared to surge onto the platform the curtain abruptly came down. Bourassa retired to the Château Laurier and completed his speech for the benefit of a cluster of friends and the ever-faithful reporters.

When he finished he could have demonstrated, point by sparkling point, immaculate clause by clause, that he had nowhere made the participation of French Canadians in the war conditional upon the recognition of their rights in education. But the effect of the speech was much simpler, and would be duly absorbed by the Orangemen. It would be duly conveyed to the English by Bishop Fallon. It had already been conveyed to the French by that master of the forthright phrase Lieutenant-Colonel Armand Lavergne, who now went about in uniform. 'If we are asked to go and fight for England,' he had said on the first day of the war, 'we reply – "Let us have our schools".'

2

THE MOST important thing for the moment', Laurier wrote to Gouin on January 9, 1915, 'is the school question in Ontario. You are on extremely difficult ground.' He was speaking to a provincial premier on provincial problems, but he had no longer much hope that he could speak as an aloof counsellor. Once more, even in the midst of new and savage tumult, the war of schools was swallowing his nights and days.

He had not believed that it would this time. He was not yet quite able to divest himself of that old trust in Ontario, recovered since 1911 as the party rebuilt itself. He knew the Orangemen and accepted the new fact of the embattled Irish. Nothing could be done about them, nothing had ever been done. But he had reached over their heads in the old days to link hands with the taller men, and there were tall men still. He knew them, he could name them, they were of the party. They were not Blakes or Mowats or even Mackenzies but they were in the tradition that began with Baldwin, they were the best of Ontario. They spoke, if they would speak with their whole minds, for those hundreds of thousands of the long and deeply rooted who were not French and were still Canadian, who accepted the essence of the pact of Confederation, who thought of language and race not as prison or fortress, brand or banner, but as facts to be lived and grown with as the country grew together.

He had given much ground, believing that and trusting in it. There was not much more to be given. It was no longer a question of scattered minorities in the west, no longer a question on which religion intruded to confuse everything. This was the central issue: the country as Laurier saw it or the country of D'Alton McCarthy, gradually constricting, tightening in on Quebec, suffocating it.

He had studied the wordings and revised wordings of Regulation 17 with growing resentment, with growing contempt for its heavy-handed grammar, with growing awareness of what it might mean in the hands, for one, of Howard Ferguson, the Ontario Orangeman who was provincial Minister of Education. Certainly there were difficulties to the teaching of French in Ontario, certainly there were poor schools and ignorance and ill will. But the answer to the Bourassas and Langevins and Lavergnes was also the answer to Ferguson and Rogers and Hughes and the others like them. Surely, at this time of all times in the country's history, it lay in improvement and generosity, in patience and understanding and renewed effort. If it did not, if Laurier could no longer command such effort from the men about him, then they were changed or he was. He had overstayed his time.

He began the year and would end it with that thought. The war and parliament and politics went on and all around him there were tumult, bitterness, corruption, and confused tragedy. The strutting, stealing colonels crowded parliament hill. The harsh thunder of British jingoism grew louder each day, to be answered by the rasp of Bourassa and the cockerel crow of Lavergne. Yet out of it all grew the clean, hard body of the fighting country, bleeding now from its wounds. By the end of May twelve thousand Canadians had been killed or wounded, or were missing among the gas clouds and shell craters of St-Julien, Festubert, and Givenchy. The Princess Patricias, first of the battalions in line, had been almost wiped out. One officer and twelve men remained of the original strength and the officer was Talbot Papineau, cousin of Bourassa.

As the scale and horror of the war dawned on the country, the talk of an election dwindled. Even Bob Rogers had been forced to restrict his hopes to an indefinite extension of the life of parliament. In this Borden concurred, and Laurier concurred on conditions. 'I have this to say to the Prime Minister and his colleagues: I do not care for an election. Let the Prime Minister and his colleagues say that there shall be no election as long as the war shall go on, and I will pledge myself and the party that we shall stop all preparations and think of nothing but the war.'

Through the summer, as the total of men dispatched to England rose toward a hundred and fifty thousand and Sam Hughes talked of 'sixth, tenth, or twentieth contingents', recruiting began to slacken. It slackened most in Quebec, and the oldest fear came back. 'I would not have my compatriots of French speech take an attitude different from that of my countrymen of English speech,' said the old man on the stumps, sick in body and sick at heart. 'It is not our cathedrals that the German shells demolish but it is the monuments and treasures of France, and they are French women who are outraged and massacred. I claim for my country the supreme honour of bearing arms in this holy cause, and if I support the government it is because I have the heart to do my duty.' The recruits came at his words in a renewed trickle and French-Canadian officers, building battalions in Quebec, wrote to congratulate him. One of the first was the son of Arthur Dansereau, a boy in his twenties and already a wounded veteran. But the trickle was still too small and the demands always growing. Around Laurier and ahead of him the murmur ran from town to town and field to field. He fought down his own dread to answer it: 'The fear of conscription is as groundless today as it was in 1911.'

By a dozen exhausting meetings, damned by Bourassa, shrilled at by Lavergne, hailed in the Montreal *Star* as 'a great, a potent and a striking figure in our public life', he came on September 2 to Napanee, Ontario, and utter collapse. Infecting his whole body, those aging, aching teeth could no longer be denied. He was carried home to Ottawa for an operation to remove an abscess from the lower jaw. It was only a prelude to worse, and as he emerged from nineteen days of lingering wretchedness in hospital Borden came to call. They spoke together easily and still as friends, equally oppressed by their roles, each unenvious of the other. Borden had just returned from England. The news was bad. It would be at least a year, probably eighteen months, before the full British strength could be mobilized and brought to bear. The story of loss and slaughter was only beginning.

Laurier looked away from Borden and shook his head, looking at nothing. 'I am afraid', he said quietly, 'that this will be a very long war.'

In October he dragged himself again to the recruiting platforms, while behind the scenes the negotiations began with Borden for the extended term of parliament. A quarter of a million men were now called for. They were becoming steadily harder to find and the antics of Sam Hughes were embroiling the government on both sides of the Atlantic. The warlord of parliament hill was much in London, eager to command his armies in the field or at least to instruct the British. He was beginning to be looked at with the same enthusiasm that greeted an arriving Zeppelin. 'His mouth', wrote one of Laurier's informants, 'is always puckered to go to a banquet or to make a speech.' At home, between quarrels with ministers and reviews of troops, he dispensed contracts to a train of shady followers, offended Quebec at every turn, and found time amid his duties to be present and prominent at a meeting of the Orange Grand Lodge where one of his fellow parliamentarians declared that 'Never shall we let the French Canadians implant in Ontario the disgusting speech they use.'

Yet if Hughes was the most aggravating he was far from being the most sinister of the men around Borden. Rogers the indispensable, the 'Minister of Elections', was a perpetual hatcher of plots and threat to Quebec. Sifton had got his knighthood at the beginning of the year, and the word ran that he was after more than that. There was talk of the railways again, linked with Sifton. The Canadian Northern was unchanged and unredeemed by the gift of forty-five millions. The Grand Trunk Pacific was bankrupt. Both would be coming back to the pots of gold and both, it was said, were of lively interest to Sifton. The rumours were all familiar, and the truth as usual impossible to pin down, but the talks with the harassed Borden went on coloured by the thought. He would agree to extend the life of parliament, Laurier said, if he knew the government's program. The government's program, Borden replied, must depend on the needs of the country. Steadily more wary, steadily more frigid, and at last in writing, the negotiations dragged through to November.

They closed as a great bell boomed from the past with the word of Tupper's death. On November 13, still with nothing decided, Borden left to attend the state funeral in Halifax.

There would be an extension of parliament, Laurier had no doubt of that. He could set terms, he could tighten the reins a little but no more. The blank cheque must be issued to this man he still liked but no longer quite respected. Borden, his government, and the war must be used to cloak a squalid railway deal. Blustering Britishness must still be endured, entrenched behind the flag. Laurier must still go on, shouting men to the butchery. He went on, applauded by all that was English in party and country, but the year-long dialogue of defeat went on too.

Quebec was vocal and aflame with the question of the Ontario schools. It was meat and drink to Bourassa and Lavergne. It haunted Laurier. Yet he could not seem even to gain the whole attention of the English leaders of the party. 'Will you permit me to ask if you have taken the trouble ever to read Regulation 17?' If they had they shunned it gratefully; it was a provincial affair, sacredly safe from federal interference. Silence was golden; they congratulated Laurier on his own. Ontario was unchangeable, prepared to slaughter the party that raised the question.

He flared back, the angry Frenchness creeping into his syntax. 'Do not commend me for what I have done or refrained to do in this matter. It has given me more concern than anybody else in the party. I feel quite sure, at least I believe, that it never entered your mind that in a civilized country the teaching of a second language, and such a language as French, could be thus ruthlessly prohibited. If it has come to this . . .'

They brushed it away, soothingly and impatiently. It had not come to that; Ontario educators were merely correcting abuses. French would still be taught. Now, with a war on . . .

Now, with a war on, he persisted doggedly, a war for France as well as England, a rule had been adopted that forbade the teaching of French in any Ontario school where it had not been taught before June of 1912. That was the plain meaning of the words. 'If it has come to this, that the language of the race to which I belong is proscribed . . . I have about come to the conclusion that I have lived too long and that my usefulness has gone.'

Fifty of the party's chief men gathered about him in Ottawa on December 20 for a discussion of the war and policy. They were a hard, angry, confident group with a sprinkling of youth now to enliven and spur the veterans. They were fully aware and eager to take advantage of the government's blundering and corruption, yet there was little of cheap politics. The first Victory Loan of $100,000,000 had gone over the top. The country was becoming a mighty munitions factory as well as a granary. There were two hundred thousand Canadians under arms. The call was now for half a million men. Whether Borden was driven on or driven out the war came first, the war and unity. They were embarrassed in Laurier's presence by the attitude of Quebec, embarrassed and impatient when he raised the question of Ontario. Certainly the schools were a difficulty, but just as certainly provincial. A national party should assume no public attitude. There was much to be said on both sides and it called for persuasion, discussion, for work behind the scenes.

He was not reassured. There was no anger here. There was no Mowat. He had struck no spark of agreement from Newton Rowell, the leader of Ontario Liberals. He did not like that little Methodist teetotaller; he did not trust him. Nor was there any other hopeful glint from Ontario. On every side, on every other question, he was buoyed up by confidence, loyalty, almost a kind of worship. On this he stood alone.

He was almost sure of what he would have to do now, and almost sure of the result. The opening of parliament was scheduled for January 13, 1916. While it was still ten days off he sat down for half an hour of blessed relief. The letters of Marie-Louise Pacaud had now replaced the letters of Emilie Lavergne. 'You who write as the bird sings, send me a line.' The lines had come as always at the New Year, and the old man's vein in reply was that of a fatherly lover. Only for a moment toward the end did the weight of his cold gloom settle on the pen. 'I noticed a few days past how long has been the road I have travelled. I am tired, wearied, and find no joy in work. I sigh for rest.'

3

BY THE END of January the legal life of the government had been extended to October 1917. It was less than Borden had asked for but this much Laurier had given free of all commitment. The war demanded it now, whatever suspicions lingered. All ends and all enmities gave way to the greater fear. 'I speak my whole soul and heart when I say that if Germany were to win I would be thankful that Providence should close my eyes before I saw the sun rising on such a day.'

Each newspaper presented the daily butcher's bill and the daily cry for recruits, always a little more strident. Each day the festering sore of the schools added its drop of poison. 'Not a soldier, a cannon, nor a cent', said Lavergne in the Quebec legislature, 'should be sent from this country for the war.' In Ontario, Regulation 17 was now reinforced by a decision of the Appellate Court. As the new commissions and new arrangements clamped down in Ottawa, bilingual schools closed, teachers went on strike, and three thousand children marched to the city hall. 'The French Canadians of the capital,' wrote seven priests of the city to officials of the Patriotic Fund, 'compelled as they are to bleed themselves to resist the government in the matter of the schools, have very little left to contribute.'

Laurier wrote, pleaded, and recoiled from the velvet obduracy of the party. There was no support from Rowell or any of the Ontario men. There was no support from Fielding. There was no hope in the press. Willison towered and prospered, high in the Tory circles and among the elect of the Round Table; nothing was to be expected of him. The *Globe*, still regarded as a Liberal newspaper, should have been another matter. It was not. It gave Bourassa his theoretical inch. Certainly French should be taught more commonly in the schools and colleges of Ontario 'because that would make for national good will'. The *Globe* did not discuss the effect on good will of forcing the French child to stumble through English in his first years of learning but it was powerfully clear on the point it saw as the main one. 'When Mr. Bourassa declares for "the principle of equality of rights for both races all over the land" he makes a demand that, if pressed, will cleave the Dominion asunder and in the end lead to the sweeping away of many privileges now enjoyed by minorities. Canada is not going to be a bilingual country in the sense in which Belgium is. The electors of Ontario are not going to recede from the position that every child educated in this province, no matter what its racial origin, shall secure an English education.'

It was of no use to protest that all this was agreed to, that it was not in question, that it was accepted as the basis of the argument. Whatever Bourassa might say, all that Laurier asked was the privilege for the child who desired it to be taught French in addition to English. He admitted that he found no right in law, that he had no club to wave. He asked for a concession and was met with silence; he sought to conciliate and the voice of Lavergne rose over him: 'Speak French everywhere.' A French-Canadian educational association advanced to the position that 'Canada is and always has been a bilingual country.' As Ontario hardened Manitoba stirred. The government of Norris, the Liberal, had thrown out the Rogers clique but not all who thought like Rogers. It was now considering restrictions to the Laurier-Greenway agreement. Even the work of 1896 was threatened.

On the night of February 3 Laurier had gone to a concert in Ottawa. He came out from it to a red sky, a tumultuous city, and a macabre addition to the general sense of desolation round him. Fire had broken out in the parliament buildings, just at the beginning of a dull evening session. Hazen of the government had actually been speaking when a messenger burst in with a wild shout. The chambers and offices had emptied quickly but not quite quickly enough. Half a dozen were trapped as the flames raced through the corridors and ate their way to the outside to be whipped by a snowy wind. When Laurier's car drew up on parliament hill the glass roof of the Commons chamber had just splintered and flames were reaching along the front of the buildings. They licked up the base of the tower always ahead of the jets of steaming water which froze as they fell, and by midnight the chamber of the Senate was ablaze and crumpling. By four in the morning the roofs had fallen in and the interiors of most of the buildings were completely gutted. Only the jagged hulks of the outer walls stood up, bearded and gaunt under sworls of blackened ice.

Laurier drove home with the memories of forty years tumbling in a dazed succession through his mind. Among those lost, he was to learn next day, were two young women who had dined with himself and Zoë a night before. He had known them from childhood and had seen, in the days of his power, to their installation as secretaries. He was still shaken as he settled with the rest of parliament into hastily improvised quarters in the Victoria Museum. 'The destruction of this fine building', he wrote on February 8, 'is akin to a personal loss, but the loss of human life is still something like a nightmare.'

By the end of March he had settled his course on the schools. No man who spoke for recruits in Quebec, as he still spoke, could ignore the ferment there. The province was on the eve of another election. Bourassa and Lavergne were already out on the stumps, preaching their new theme. The Boche in Ontario was to be fought before the Boche in Europe. Six hundred thousand names had been signed to a monster petition. Borden's French-Canadian ministers stormed, threatened, and gave way before the adamant wall of Ontario. Doherty, the Minister of Justice, a Catholic Montrealer, sided with his English colleagues. The break was clear and complete.

'We French Liberals of Quebec', Laurier wrote to the editor of the *Globe*, 'are fighting Bourassa and Lavergne. Will the English Liberals in Ontario fight Howard Ferguson and the extreme Orange element?' The answer, it seemed, was no, and he was not prepared to accept it. Provincial matter or not, he intended to broach the question of Regulation 17 in the Dominion House of Commons. By April 6, with Lemieux and Lapointe as helpers, he had prepared his resolution. As its terms seeped out the cool ripple of dissension became a panicky wave in the English section of the party. Murphy, the fighting Irishman, was in Atlantic City for his health, probably happier there. 'I cannot see', wrote Alex Smith a little maliciously, 'that you are getting any assistance from those who during the last twenty years have been exalted over the Liberal party.' Laurier was undeterred. Dafoe charged down from Winnipeg and found him 'stubborn as an army mule'. On May 8 he showed the draft of the resolution to Borden and on May 9 Lapointe rose in the House to introduce it.

It proposed 'That this House, especially at this time of universal sacrifice and anxiety when all energies should be concentrated on the winning of the war, would, while fully recognizing the principle of provincial rights and the necessity of every child being given a thorough English education, respectfully suggest to the Legislative Assembly of Ontario the wisdom of making it clear that the privilege of the children of French parentage of being taught in their mother tongue be not interfered with.' The words, right up to the time of Lapointe's rising, had been much worked over and altered. Now, in as clear, mild, and conciliatory a tone as Laurier could devise, the House of the Dominion of Canada was requested to request of the sovereign province of Ontario that it stay its hand.

Borden, who had said the day before that the resolution would do no good and probably much harm, contented himself for the moment with minor quibbling. That was an expected preliminary to debate. The first significant straw blew from the other side of the House. W. E. Knowles, a Liberal of Saskatchewan, rose to move that the resolution, since it dealt with provincial affairs, was out of order.

The Speaker reserved his decision to the next day and when it came it was against Knowles. Laurier rose to speak, first as the lawyer. According to the terms of Regulation 17 the teaching of French could be continued ' "in schools where French had *hitherto* been a subject of study." Mark the words. What is the meaning of the word "hitherto" here and why has it been introduced? If it does not mean that the tuition of French is to be restricted to schools where it was taught in 1912, then all I ask is that it be removed and we shall have no further quarrel.'

He moved to the other paragraph which provided that ' "where necessary in the case of French-speaking pupils, French may be used as the language of instruction and communication". What is the meaning of these words, "where necessary"? They did not exist before; they were introduced in June 1912. Here is a school in the back concessions and you have to apply to the Chief Inspector to know whether or not it is necessary that the child should be given the privilege of having an education in the French language, in his own tongue and not in English. Why this harsh provision? I ask, why this unnecessary and harsh provision?'

One Ontarian at least was listening with admiration. 'As he proceeded', wrote the correspondent for the Toronto *World* next day, 'his years dropped from him like a garment and he seemed as vigorous and resolute as a man of thirty-five.' The House settled into deepening silence as he turned away from judicial arguments and constitutional arguments. 'I do not here and now invoke the cold letter of any positive law. I rise to plead before the people of Ontario in behalf of His Majesty's subjects of French origin.'

He did not disguise his contempt for those subjects who put the question of schools before the duties of war. He had equal contempt for the subjects who marched to war behind the slogan that now blossomed in Willison's Toronto *News*, 'One Language, and One Language Only'. Heavily, emphatically, repetitively, he built the base of his argument. 'I want every child in the province of Ontario to receive the benefit of an English education. Wherever he may go on this continent I want him to be able to speak the language of the great majority of the people on this continent. No man on this continent is equipped for the battle of life unless he has an English education. I want every child to have an English education.' Finally, with all the bitterness in him battened down, with all the art and power and earnestness at his command, he came to his central plea. 'Now I come to the point where I want to speak to my fellow countrymen in the province of Ontario. When I ask that every child of my own race should receive an English education, will you refuse us the privilege of education also in the language of our mothers and our fathers? That is all that I ask today; I ask nothing more than that. I simply ask you, my fellow countrymen, British subjects like myself, if, when we say that we must have an English education you will say, "You shall have an English education and nothing else."?'

It was another of the speeches that men would remember as a great experience of their lives. It hovered over the next few days of debate, imposing its own character. For once, while the press bellowed, parliament deliberated. On both sides of the aisle there was dignity, compassion, sympathy, and reasoned argument. There was also a kind of academic aloofness. Laurier had touched his hearers but he had not struck through to their depths. He had impressed men once again with himself and his convictions; he had not changed them.

The debate went on to the small hours of May 12, but it was apparent much earlier that the resolution would be lost. In his office on the morning of the eleventh Laurier sat alone as the party caucused by provinces to decide on how it would vote. His old friend Dandurand of Montreal came to him with the results. There was no question about Quebec, and the Maritime members had also fallen in line. The westerners could not be shaken; loyal in everything else, they were against Laurier in this. Then came the word of Ontario. While all the leaders sympathized with the aim of the resolution, said Dandurand, they doubted its expediency, above all at the present time. They would vote for it, however, if Sir Wilfrid wished them to do so.

He stood up at the last words and walked abruptly to the window. 'No. I shall not ask them. They should not expect that after all these years.'

He stood looking out in silence for a while and then turned back to his desk. Everything changed, even that view, this room. He was standing in the last parliamentary office he would ever occupy, and suspected as much. 'I have lived too long. I have outlived Liberalism. It was a mistake for a French Roman Catholic to take the leadership. I told Blake so thirty years ago.' He raised his head, the long, pale hand groping for the eyeglasses dangling on their black cord. 'Yes – but those thirty years –'

For a long minute he was silent again. Then he sat down, drew pen and paper toward him, and scribbled a few lines. 'I shall announce my resignation in the House this afternoon. Please give this to George Graham.'

The instant consternation that followed, the crowding-in on the office, the repentant eagerness of the men who had sent the earlier message, were all persuasive and warming. The Ontario men would certainly vote with Laurier, though it would change nothing. They had not realized, they assured him, that he took his resolution so much to heart. There could be no possible thought of his resigning. That would be the ultimate disaster.

He was still leader as debate closed with the vote heavily against him. 'Let our Quebec friends thoroughly understand the situation,' wrote John Dafoe. 'We shall not allow them to impose their will on the rest of Canada.' To that there was only the question, 'What remains?' And the old answer. 'Nothing but the means which has brought about every reform in British countries and transformed Great Britain itself. That amounts to saying that in constitutional countries it is by persuasion, by moderation that in the end right triumphs. That is the only resource remaining to us.'

It was a frail candle to hold up in the bellowing darkness about him, and his own position was clear. The old Frenchman was loved by most of the men of the party and respected and indispensable. But the things that he took to heart were not English. They would be borne with, rather than supported.

27

'THE ONLY TACTICS OF THE TORIES WILL BE "FRENCH QUEBEC"'

1916-1917

IN JUNE at last the dentist claimed his own. On the first of the month Laurier took note of the latest interview granted to the press by the Honourable Robert Rogers, who was not satisfied with limited extensions to the life of the war parliament and who had smelt opportunity throughout the debate on the schools. 'The slogan', Laurier predicted, 'is to be "No French". I understand that pressure is made upon the government to dissolve immediately and fight on that line before the slogan becomes stale.'

On June 2 he betook himself once more to Le Monument National to beg Montreal for recruits and denounce from a sore mouth and a sore heart the 'bitter, warped, prejudiced little souls' who divided Quebec from the country. Then he returned to cancel all engagements and surrender himself to the tormentor. 'All my teeth are bad, and the problem is to save as many as he can and replace those which have to be removed. It is slow and painful work.'

The dragging misery of the summer was enhanced by the sense of crisis. Enlistments were falling everywhere and most of all in Quebec. The dreadful lists of the casualties still came. In April the battle of St-Eloi had bled away twenty-eight hundred men. In June came word of the battle of Sanctuary Wood and a toll of eight thousand Canadians killed, wounded, or missing. There were four divisions in England and the recruits in training at home brought the total of men under arms to three hundred and seventy thousand. There were another three hundred thousand in the munitions factories. The farms, producing as never before, were starved for men, and women were turning everywhere to the men's jobs. In agriculture and industry, in work, money, and blood, the country had given mightily and was still giving. But it was strained to the limit now, there was no end in sight, and the strain was beginning to tell.

Borden, for all his flaws, had worked with clean hands and a whole heart. There were men in the cabinet with him who had done great things. But there was no escaping the aura that grew around them. There was no escaping the wear and tear of the war. The government was crumbling steadily. Every provincial election of the past four years had been a disaster or a warning. Some twenty seats in the House had fallen vacant and remained unfilled because of the dread of by-elections. Hughes and Rogers imposed their stamp on the politicians. New-made munitions barons and food barons towered among the elect, a little richer, a little more English, a little more patriotic every day, making the war a crusade for Anglo-Saxondom, a cause of the Tory party. Corruption and confusion were inevitable and seemed everywhere. The Ross rifle was at the height of its evil fame. Reports came back from England of great piles of rusting, useless equipment prescribed by Sam Hughes, of tainted grain shipments, bad boots, and dud shells. At home even the new parliament buildings rose from the ashes, under the hand of Bob Rogers, clouded with all-too-likely rumours of fat profits and enormous commissions.

With it all, nothing seemed left undone to rasp the nerves of Quebec. The brash, drill-sergeant Englishness of recruiting methods continued, undermining the best efforts of French Canadians who came back as wounded veterans to spur enlistment. Olivar Asselin, as caustic a nationalist as any, had swallowed his dearest angers to enlist months before. 'If I wish to go,' he had said, 'it is because I should rather die than see France conquered and powerless.' He was shipped off unnoticed, with the battalion he had helped to raise, not to France but to garrison duty in Bermuda. At Valcartier units of French-Canadian volunteers, for all the protests of their own veteran officers, were broken up, scattered among English battalions, and generally treated as second-rate foreign troops.

From either side of the Ottawa Sam Hughes and Lieut.-Col. Lavergne, those dearest enemies, worked in a grisly concert. While Hughes stamped out the last goodwill of the clergy Lavergne talked of the schools. While Hughes snubbed General Lessard, the highest-ranking French-Canadian professional in the service, he offered command of a battalion to Lavergne. Lavergne refused and the point was made: French Canadians would not fight. He could not assume the responsibility, said Lieut.-Col. Lavergne, of asking Canadians to take part in a war that was not for the defence of Canada. He was not afraid, he said, to become a German subject. It would be no worse, he said, than life as a British subject. As his late aunt had said, 'Bitten by a dog or bitten by a bitch, it's all the same.' He asked himself, he said, 'whether the German régime might not be favourably compared with that of the Boches in Ontario'.

Stalking and talking in uniform to his following of country curés and shouting students, he was about equally ignored and deplored by another half of the province. But every word was a war-flag west of the Ottawa. Bourassa was never silent and the suggestions of a rope for him grew more insistent in the English press. Lavergne sprang to his aid unasked. 'Let them come and arrest Bourassa if they dare. I have in my county three thousand farmers ready to protect him with their lives.' The words were broadcast through the Ontario press; the cold, bored silence with which they had been listened to was not.

As the summer grew toward the dog-days even Talbot Papineau added to the smouldering heat. The wounded officer, convalescing in England, remonstrated with his cousin Bourassa in an open letter that was published in all the newspapers. He spoke from experience of 'the time you are within fifteen yards of a German army and know yourself to be holding about one yard out of a line of five hundred miles or more'. He wrote as a man 'determined as you are that we shall remain French as long as we like', but he also wrote as a Canadian soldier in England, resentful of slackers. For the fact and the impression that French Canadians were not doing their share, he told Bourassa, 'you will be largely responsible'.

The letter had reached the press through Andrew McMaster, a Liberal and an admiring senior partner of Papineau in a Montreal law firm. Laurier could well have wished that it had not. Bourassa, after duly questioning the authenticity of the document and its propaganda purpose, replied with cutting respect. The 'gallant young officer' had backed his words with deeds where many had not. He was entitled to his opinions. It should be noted, however, that the bond between the cousins was not so close as it might seem. A Protestant, educated at Oxford, English in his first language and favourite associations, Talbot Papineau was separated from the people of his grandfather by religion, mother tongue, and upbringing. He could not feel as they felt. French-Canadian coldness to the war was the result, not of Bourassa's work, but of 'hereditary instincts, social and economic conditions, a national tradition of three centuries'. Quebec's first generous enthusiasm had been dissipated by English bluster and English profiteering; enlistments lagged because recruiting was now carried on by 'blackmailing, intimidation, and threats of all sorts'. Bourassa was replying, as he was well aware, not only to a hero but to a young Liberal who was anxious to come home to politics. He cut as always painfully near the bone. By the time the newspaper storm died down Talbot Papineau's fear that 'whoever bears a French name in Canada will be an object of suspicion and possibly of hatred' seemed well on the way to fulfilment.

Outside Quebec, swirled in the vicious circle, the war of the schools widened. There was fretful talk in Alberta and Saskatchewan now. From Nova Scotia the same mail that brought reports of a Liberal victory in the provincial elections brought a copy of a 'strictly confidential memo' that had circulated through the Orange lodges during the campaign. 'Orangemen', it enjoined, 'must use their utmost influence to stop the curse of bilingual schools as their brethren have so successfully done in

Manitoba and Ontario.' For a government going down in the stormy sea of the country 'No French' appeared indeed to be an acceptable raft.

The sore suspicions multiplied as the invalid's mouth healed. Laurier returned to the recruiting platforms in August and September. 'My teeth always bother me some, but it is quite bearable.' Saluted now by Bourassa as 'the most nefarious man in all Canada', he saw his response dwindle while his urgency grew. He could only welcome the National Service Board, set up for the registration of the country's manpower. It promised to recognize the demands of agriculture and industry, to hold men at home where they were needed. Yet Conservative politicians, nesting in all its eyries, seemed another threat to Quebec. The antics of Sam Hughes grew beyond endurance and Borden dismissed him from the cabinet, but even that, welcome as it was, could be prelude to an early election. Hughes had become too much for any party to carry. So was Rogers but Rogers lingered, the 'Minister of Elections'. As the government rocked there was talk of a coalition, but Laurier dismissed it brusquely. He expected a dissolution and he expected it to be sudden, probably when the Duke of Devonshire arrived to replace Connaught as Governor General. Truculent and convinced, he tried to impress his suspicions on the English men of the party. On September 28 he quoted an informant deep in government circles: the government 'were clean gone out unless they made a direct appeal against the French, and they are going to "go it bold".'

'There is something in the air,' he wrote on October 4. 'It may be conscription, but I doubt it.' He had little to support his doubts. Conscription in Canada, he argued, would cut off immigration from the neutral United States. The shortages of manpower on the farms and in the factories were as serious as the shortages in the army. National Registration was advanced as a plan to assess the country's resources and apply them to the best effect. If that was so, though Laurier would have no part of Borden's political Board, it pointed away from rather than toward conscription. There were certainly other requirements as urgent as those of the military; R. B. Bennett of Calgary, Borden's unmanageable manager of the work, was insistent on that point. Yet the cry was up for soldiers and there could be no doubt as to the direction of Tory thinking. The move afoot, wrote Laurier, 'will be in the direction of putting a cleavage between Quebec and the rest of the Dominion. With a French-Canadian leader Quebec is our best stronghold. This is so obvious that men like Rogers and others who are controlling the party will make the most of it.'

By October 21 he was in a mood to carry the war to the enemy. There would be no coalition and no second extension to the life of a decrepit parliament. The sooner an election the better. 'The time has come to meet and assail the government squarely. It is not only good politics but it would be criminal, when our troops are being sacrificed at the front, to allow this mismanagement to go further without a firm hand.' He was speaking already a little in the vein of the stumps, to men who would have to climb to the stumps behind him. He was intent on getting in the first blow, on heading the direction of the battle away from Quebec. There seemed some hope in November, as the Pope and the Privy Council combined in their separate ways to take a little of the heat out of the schools question. Benedict XV enjoined his Irish and French to strike a truce. The decision of the Privy Council leaned both ways as usual and confused both sides. But the muttering stillness that followed gave only minor relief in national politics. Quebec was to be the theme, election or not.

December came and high Torydom still hesitated on the awful brink of the polls. Borden embarked on a speaking tour of the country and arrived on December 6 at Montreal, where his first appointment at the Ritz Carlton was with a delegation of Orangemen. After this auspicous beginning he went on to a cool reception from the high clergy and a cooler from his public audiences in the province. He was in the west by December 16 and on that evening, much to his disgust, Sir Joseph Flavelle, who was now Chairman of the Munitions Board, let a sizeable half-grown cat from the party's bag.

Sir Joseph was of the Round Table and of those upper echelons of the party who saw a federated Empire emerging from the fires of the war. He had also a lively awareness of present conditions. Speaking to the Canadian Club in Ottawa, he recoiled from the thought of a general election in which 'a racial cry will be inevitable and English will be pitted against French and French against English and there will follow years of bitterness'. He recoiled equally from the thought that any government 'sustained by the vote of a section of this Dominion which, no matter for what reason or conscience, were unwilling to bear their share in this struggle' should take part in the Imperial Council after the war. The inference for coalition and the purpose of coalition were wholly clear. Quebec, 'not by party guidance or by party methods', was to be excised from its place in the Dominion.

The plan, or at least the talk of it, was premature. Neither coalition nor dissolution was noticeably nearer as Borden returned by way of an unenthusiastic Toronto to spend Christmas in Ottawa. He was an exhausted, irritable man, 'tired and sick of this infernal life', and promises made in Quebec clanked behind him. He had assured the hierarchy, as Bennett had, that National Registration would make conscription unnecessary. On December 26, however, he stood behind a desk onto which many telegrams had descended and around which many pressures had mounted. The delegation which faced him was a group from organized labour rather than Quebec alone, but the question was familiar. The answer had now changed. 'I hope conscription may not be necessary, but if it should prove the only effective method to preserve the existence of the state and of the institutions and liberties we enjoy, I should consider it necessary and should not hesitate to act accordingly.'

2

'THE ONLY TACTICS of the Tories will be "French Quebec".' The old man in the house on Laurier Avenue was unmoved by rhetoric, unchanged by argument, and steadily more alone. On January 19, 1917, parliament met. Three weeks later it adjourned and Borden sailed for England. He was gone till the middle of May, surveying the needs of the war, and with him, as was duly and acidly noted, went that expert on the needs of the party, Robert Rogers. The other companion, though of different stuff, was no more to Laurier's liking: 'When it comes to the task of making the worse appear the better reason,' he had said of

Arthur Meighen, 'few men can do more than my honourable friend.'

On May 14 Borden returned. On May 18 he announced the intention of the government to bring down shortly a plan of compulsory military service. 'The number of men required will not be less than 50,000 and will probably be 100,000.' On May 25 Laurier went to his house to discuss the prospect of entering a coalition. On June 6 he finally rejected the offer. It had been as fair as Borden could make it; the haggard, harassed Prime Minister spoke with the memory of Vimy a month behind him, with the grim demands of the coming months ahead, and with the knowledge that the year's enlistments totalled fifteen thousand less than the year's casualties. Laurier could have the naming of half the ministers, an almost co-equal voice in every policy. But he would have to stand with Borden supporting the pledge of conscription, and on that the decision was made. 'He may change; I will not.'

On June 11 Borden introduced the Military Service Bill. By July 24 it was law. Six weeks of frantic manoeuvre and fierce debate, inside the House and out of it, had scraped the nerves of the country to the raw, exhausted the politicians, and wiped out party lines. But they had not settled the question. A week before, with second reading behind him and the passage of the measure certain, Borden had moved for another year's extension of the life of parliament. He had won, but only by a bare majority of twenty votes, and the next day, angrily defying the pleadings of half his cabinet, had announced that he would not accept the result as a mandate to go on. The government had three months to live and if it went out conscription would be suspended. Laurier had made that clear. He was not yet out of the game and he still held powerful cards.

He intended to play them with all the skill he had, but he was not hopeful. Twenty-two of his Liberals had voted against him on conscription. Some were dispensable hacks but most were his best men, sick as the rest of the country, sick as Borden himself, of this government in which Borden was the prisoner of a clique rather than a leader. They had had enough of Rogers. They were all too aware of Sifton, always at work in the background, always with the smell of railways clinging round him. They wanted a house-cleaning and most of them wanted Laurier. But they stopped there, or rather they went beyond him. The gap that had newly opened with the new war of the schools was wider now. The Chief spoke more often of the need of stepping down.

'The only solution', he had said in June, 'seems to me this: have an appeal to the people, have it right away, either in the form of a referendum or an election.' He himself had refused a referendum on the question of the navy, yes, but he had done so with good reason. He had been the head of a strong government with a firm mandate, executing a policy that had long been declared. This government of Borden's, weak and distracted, was reversing a declared policy on a far more dangerous issue. It could only do so with the fullest sanction of the country. 'Let the people decide.' That done, Laurier would accept the verdict and loyally support it. He would urge Quebec to support it. He had pressed the argument everywhere with all his strength; and everywhere he was failing.

In his files was another letter of Talbot Papineau, ten months old now, passed along by McMaster. 'We judge that Sam Hughes has at length been cast overboard', Papineau had written in November, 'and that the Conservatives are making this change in the hope of saving the party, but the general assumption is that they are too late and that Laurier will be returned. Naturally I hope so. We want improvement. I don't think the people at home quite realize the temper of the soldiers here. They are fighting mad, and will no longer tolerate exploitation by political non-combatants at home. I would say that they are in an ugly temper and likely to cause trouble if political conditions continue as they are.' He had been eager to get back to Canada, eager to get into politics, 'not because I am quitting here or because my nerve is gone. I went through the Somme fighting and I am quite ready to go through it again. Only I am persuaded in my own mind that I can be of more value in another capacity. I feel very deeply that my life having been spared in a miraculous manner, it is no longer my own – no more than those of all my poor friends who have been killed.' Before the letter was many months older Papineau was to join his friends, but that voice, so poignant now, would still speak for hundreds of thousands in khaki. It would have spoken for Laurier, but it spoke first for conscription.

The old friends of the party, the old English friends, spoke almost as movingly. 'I find myself on the present occasion', Laurier had said in the House at the third reading of the bill, 'estranged from friends who were just as near and dear to me as any of my own brothers.' It was true, and small comfort to plead that he had tried to impose his views on none of them, that he respected their consciences, that the estrangement was temporary and only on the single issue. He convinced no one else, if he convinced himself, when he argued in private that 'the question is only a transient one and has no permanency. It will be over in three months, six months or at most a year.' Conscription would pass, the war itself would pass, but the men who had grown with Laurier would be changed. They were changing now. Through the months before the vote they had watched the shabby manoeuvres, damned the Tories, and jockeyed for every advantage. They still jockeyed as August came in and manoeuvres began again, but with a new anger and a troubling kind of dignity. To most of them Laurier had never before felt closer, never more surely loved, more necessary. They were lost men and lost politicians without him, and they knew it. But too many of them riffled through their daily mail now for the letter with the army frank, stiffened at every telegram, turned to the casualty lists before the headlines. 'Since my son left' – 'My boy writes' – it was hard for the childless septuagenarian to answer arguments that began with those phrases. Why not the other man's lad if mine must go? Why not Quebec?

Everything came back to Quebec, pinning him behind those ramparts. He argued with half a heart that better recruiting methods there would bring more men; it was too late even if it was true. He was irritably impatient with the talk of civil war – Lavergne's 'nonsense'. He was equally impatient with those who saw him as all-powerful, able to swing the province if he chose. Borden had climbed to power by way of Bourassa's back, by way of the platform built at Drummond-Arthabaska, and that work was not to be undone now. Laurier had stumped

Quebec on the promise of 'no conscription'; so for that matter had Borden, but Laurier would keep the promise. He would keep it because he must. 'If I were to waver, to hesitate or to flinch, I would simply hand over the province of Quebec to the extremists. I would lose the respect of the people . . . and would deserve it.'

Borden was firm and grim on the needs of the war. There was no doubting him. But the need for food and work was as great as the need for men. The millions of the United States would soon be on the way. Why should this Canada, already so near to its limit, be drained of its last fifty or a hundred thousand? 'The number of men who can be spared from agriculture and industry is infinitesimally small. Conscription will take in a few farmers and school-boys; this will be the supreme triumph of Toryism, but Toryism will once more have asserted its undying spirit of domination.' It was not Quebec alone that opposed conscription. Labour was against it, and farmers were against it, even in Ontario. Yet 'Ontario is no longer Ontario; it is again the old, small province of Upper Canada and again governed from London.' Conscription remained for Laurier what it had been, the malevolent child of shoddy politicians, trading on generous men. 'The attitude which is represented as the attitude of Quebec maddens them. Everyone who is in favour of conscription favours the movement not because he believes it necessary but because Quebec is represented to be against it.'

3

ON AUGUST 1 the government turned from war to the railway question. There was to be another $7,500,000 for the Grand Trunk Pacific. The cost of taking over the Canadian Northern, paying its debts, and reimbursing its shareholders hovered mistily between twenty-five and thirty-five million dollars. Once more the friends of the railways would link their propping-up with the saving of the nation. Once more their enemies would link it with the saving of Mackenzie and Mann and Sifton and the banks that stood behind them. Certainly for Laurier this need of new millions explained much in the wildly unwonted antics of the man he regarded as the real force to be dreaded. They had gone on through June and July and they continued through August with the debate, adding their full share to the dizzy confusion about him.

In June, with the strings from Ottawa reaching out to the ends of the country and every allegiance in doubt, Sifton had come to Laurier apparently a Liberal again. He was disgruntled with Borden, opposed to conscription, and opposed to coalition. But the government should still be kept for another year; there should be another extension. Why? Again there was the old unfathomable, mumbling silence. The chances of the party in an election, Sifton thought, would be better later. He gave no reasons, but by July 3, as Laurier refused coalition and opposed conscription, Sifton had swung hard round. He was now in favour of both, with the year's extension to the life of parliament as well. When that was finally denied he had gone to work as of old, mobilizing Ontario and the west. But he was not the Sifton of old; he was stumbling, and stumbling badly.

The latest and worst of his falls was just ahead. During the first week of August a thousand delegates from the four provinces of the west converged on Winnipeg. The convention had been inspired by Sir Clifford, but his welcome in the west had been so cool that his brother Arthur, who was premier of Alberta, had taken his place as principal promoter. The men assembled were all Liberals, many of them for conscription and many attracted by the proposed coalition which was now advanced under the name of Union Government. Their work, as the Siftons planned it, was to signal the final divorce of the west from the old Frenchman of Quebec. 'It is not for the purpose of having the program of the western Liberals that the convention is called,' Laurier observed sourly, 'but to split the Liberal party.'

The thousand had become twelve hundred by the time of the first meeting on August 7, and it was soon evident that the Siftons had underestimated the strength of the absent Chief. For three days there was savage wrestling in the committee rooms. Laurier's supporters, led by Frank Oliver of Edmonton, had asked for advice from Ottawa and the advice had come. Conscription should be ignored in the framing of a party platform. Delegates should 'confine your resolutions to the broad questions for which western Liberals have long striven and which will still be alive when conscription will be dead'.

To John Dafoe of the *Free Press*, who had put himself at the head of the Sifton forces, conscription was the one question of the day. He was no imperialist; he was as flatly opposed as Laurier to the dream of Joseph Chamberlain and as distrustful of the gentlemen of the Round Table. He had done much for Liberalism and much for the west. 'On many things', Laurier was to say of him a few months later, 'he has the most advanced ideas of Liberalism and even radicalism; on others his horizon is the horizon of the sixteenth century.' He might have said more, of many men like Dafoe. The clearest voice in the west, fiercely determined in his conception of the part Canada should play as a self-respecting British nation at war, Dafoe seemed totally ignorant of the major gap in his premises. One-fourth of this British nation was French-Canadian and without that fourth the nation was not viable; it could not be moved as a whole. That fact the old man in Ottawa must deal with, as he had dealt for forty years. Conscription was part of it, but so were schools and Orangemen and priests and immigrants. Sentiment was part of it, the part most often ignored. 'The Englishman respects your opinions, but he never thinks of your feelings.'

The party, Dafoe urged, must stand for conscription with or without Laurier; it must stand for Union Government. The number of men of his mind was impressive and formidable, yet so was the aura of Sifton in which he moved. He loathed Rogers but could not escape him here. He was confronted by old detestations and by old loyalties. Hour after hour the sweating lieutenants on the floor, without visible assistance from Ottawa, fought the convention away from the brink of a declaration. 'I cannot and will not say anything which would look like seeking endorsation,' Laurier had wired. 'I stand upon my record.' It seemed to be enough. The final resolution asserted the party's 'admiration of the life and work of the greatest of all Canadians, Sir Wilfrid Laurier'. There was no mention of conscription. 'Convention over,' Oliver wired from Winnipeg on the morning of August 9. 'You were endorsed by almost unanimous standing vote.'

Hard on the heels of the telegram came a visibly shaken Sifton, and behind him was Kirk Cameron. It was a bleakly amusing study to watch the younger man's face as Sifton spoke, banging the ear trumpet on the desk for emphasis. Conscription had abruptly become 'the most iniquitous measure ever introduced in the free parliament of Canada'. Sifton was now profanely divorced from its authors. 'We must fight the buggers on it and we'll lick 'em!'

'I didn't get much comfort on that line in Toronto,' Cameron observed sceptically.

'What? What?' The words had to be shouted into the trumpet again, and the response was vigorous: 'Toronto! Toronto! Toronto will do what it's told!'

Cameron was inclined to recall Sifton's old relations with Toronto, but the interview had to be cut short. Both Laurier and Sifton were required at Rideau Hall and shortly after noon another conference assembled in the presence of the Duke of Devonshire. Its gravity was intensified by the fact that the home of Sir Hugh Graham, now Lord Atholstan and Montreal's leading conscriptionist, had just been bombed. Its ramifications were suggested by the fact that in addition to Borden, Foster, Laurier, and Sifton it also included Gouin of Quebec and Lord Shaughnessy of the C.P.R., who was notably aggrieved by the prospect of new millions for his competitors.

The Governor General dwelt for a few moments on the critical position of the war, the dangers of an election, and the need for national unity. He then offered to retire but was invited to remain. Through an hour and a half of grave and dignified argument Borden worked round laboriously to his final offer. If Laurier would enter a coalition government and agree to the extension of parliament for six months, Borden would suspend conscription for the same time.

There was no cause to question the sincerity of the offer or the need for men. Laurier replied with arguments of equal sincerity. He had called Quebec to the colours from the beginning of the war and he promised to redouble his efforts. He promised to support conscription if the country gave it a mandate. He would assist any government that went to the country freely and was freely returned. Coalition was another thing: the one impossible thing. By whatever gate he entered Borden's government Laurier would be facing Quebec side by side with the author of 'the hateful blood-tax law'. There would be no response in Quebec to recruiting under such auspices. In six months, newly embittered, the country would be faced again with the need for conscription. It would be faced with the need for an election in which Laurier would stand for nothing and Borden with English Canada would be pitted against the Quebec of Bourassa and Lavergne. Bourassa would have indeed his 'formal and definitive incitement to insurrection'.

As Laurier left Government House that sultry afternoon he had some reason to believe that he had averted the worst of the dangers. The Liberals of the west were still uneasily with him. 'Whither thou goest I will go,' Aylesworth of Toronto had written, English and Empire-lover though he was, with a son at the front. There were not many Aylesworths in Ontario but there were many friends, Liberal still. The Chief had fought for them with all his charm and guile and skill and earnestness and subtlety. He had released the consciences of the men who were ruled by conscience; they might vote for conscription and be Liberals still, it was not a party matter. He had played on the fears and whetted the ambitions of the men whom such things moved; hold the party together and they would win, conscription or not. The issue would be bad government, corrupt government, government afraid of the country and out to steal a mandate under this trumped-up label of Union. Get out the tribe of Borden and get on with the war. An election was necessary to clear the air, he had told the conference. He did not expect to win, he expected to lose. He expected conscription to come. But it would be enforced by a government with a mandate and supported by an opposition that was wounded but still together. It would be supported by a Laurier who had kept his promise to Quebec.

He stood at the high point of his slim and sombre hopes, and the ebb had already begun. On August 13 Charles Doherty, the Minister of Justice, introduced the Military Voters' Bill which provided the vote to men in the services and added a neat provision that would enable the government to apply all floating votes to constituencies where they were most needed. On August 21 decks were cleared and cleansed by the tossing overboard of Rogers. On the same day the Liberal Tobias C. Norris, Premier of Manitoba, publicly forsook Laurier and declared for Union Government. On August 29, over opposition from its own members as loud as any from the Liberals, the government applied closure to jam through the railway bill. On the same evening malcontents were stilled as the seething party closed its ranks round Borden. On the thirtieth came a wild night of anti-conscription riots in Montreal, heightening all fervours in the English press, and on September 6 Meighen rose in the House to present his masterpiece.

The War Times Election Bill first divided the female franchise of the country into haves and have-nots. 'This bill therefore provides that the wives, the widows, the mothers, the sisters, and the daughters of the members past or present of the actual overseas forces shall have the right to vote in the War Time Election.'

It proceeded next to deal with the foreign-born, most of whom were in the west and most of whom were Liberal. 'This bill disqualifies for the War Time Election those of alien enemy birth or of other European birth and of alien enemy mother tongue or native language, who have been naturalized since the thirty-first of March, 1902. It is further to be noted that whosoever is disqualified from voting by this measure is at the same time exempted from combatant service in the war.'

There was no doubt that many of the German and Austrian peoples in the country were cool to the war, and Meighen made much of it. Yet closure was ready and closure was going to be necessary to ram through this monstrous gerrymander which removed at one stroke the rights of citizenship granted over the past fifteen years not only to Germans and Austrians but to every Czech, Slovak, Pole, Ruthenian, Swiss, or Russian who spoke a Germanic dialect. It was hardly surprising, as one watched him across the aisle and thought of D'Alton McCarthy, to find that the hard, flat prairie voice lacked much of its usual assurance.

By September 10 the War Times Election Act had wiped out

much of Liberal strength in the west. At five-thirty on the morning of September 20 parliament prorogued, facing a certain election. 'Whether we win or lose', Laurier had written the day before, 'is not the primary consideration. My chief preoccupation is to maintain the unity of the party.' The tired words were hollow; the War Times Elections Act had smashed his slender dikes and the drift of politicians had begun to move away. A telegram announcing the completion of the great Laurier bridge over the river at Quebec arrived with ironic impact amid the collapse of everything about him.

'Complications rise right and left,' he wrote on September 28, 'which overturn one day all that was accomplished the last. There is nothing to do but hold on.' There was not much to hold on to. The thunder of newspaper headlines was incessant against him. Ottawa was filled with Liberals and the Chief's office was never empty. The light in the study burned deep into the small hours and there were loyal protestations and sometimes tears mixed with the arguments. But Laurier was never sure whether the men who talked to him had come from Borden or were on the way to Borden. He could not hold ground with the good men against those endless casualty lists. To the others the prospect of Union Government, with all cards stacked in its favour, had become irresistible. There was no money and even the party helpers were disappearing; it was the leader now who sat down with a faithful few to check the constituency rolls and see the vanishing names with his own eyes.

By the first week of October he had no organized party in Ontario or on the prairies. He was all but sure that British Columbia was gone, and the Maritimes were going. He was surprised to learn on October 6 that Fielding had called at the office but had not waited to see him. The crowd in the ante-room, it seemed, had been too great. The diffidence was explained next day when Fielding arrived with a delegation from Ontario, the Maritimes, and the west. The old friends Frank Carvell and Pardee were there and the spokesman was James A. Calder who controlled the Saskatchewan Liberal organization. It was the opinion of the deputation, said Calder, that the party could not win with a French-Canadian leader.

The statement from this man was not surprising; Calder had spent much time in the company of Borden lately. Laurier looked at Fielding, and for a moment Fielding looked down. But he spoke clearly enough when he spoke. He felt that a change of leadership was necessary.

Calder went on to say a little too much. He could not support the proposal of a referendum: there was too much feeling in the west against conscription. He was for conscription. If the party went to the polls with an anti-conscriptionist leader, a French Canadian – he broke off as the flash of anger came. 'Do you mean to tell me that because of my origin I cannot be a Liberal leader? You tell me you will not have a referendum because the people do not want it, and yet you will not allow a man to lead who represents the view the people have.'

On that note the meeting dissolved, and a week later Calder and Carvell were members of the new Union Government. Fielding had returned to the Maritimes to make up his mind there. Yet the word of the proposed abdication, as it seeped out to the streets and Laurier discussed it with his few remaining leaders, seemed only to pull the crumbling party together. There would be no Calder, no Carvell, probably no Fielding. There would be, perhaps, only a loyal rump but it would go down, if it went, with Laurier.

He seemed to be renewed himself. 'Now I am in the fight to face a murderous winter election, even if I have to die for it,' he wrote to the Maritimes. 'There is nothing to do but spit on our hands and prepare,' he wrote to British Columbia. 'What can you do in Vancouver?'

4

HE COULD drop the brave, brisk fighting mask with Aylesworth. 'The racial chasm which is now opening at our feet', he wrote, 'may perhaps not be overcome for many generations.' That same day, October 16, the first of thousands of summonses were going out to conscripted men. The former Liberal leaders of Ontario, New Brunswick, Manitoba, Saskatchewan, and Alberta were members of the Union cabinet. The party organizations, the party rolls, and the party war chests had gone with them. British Columbia was wavering away and Prince Edward Island, seemingly loyal, could affect nothing. Nova Scotia hung fire waiting for Fielding to speak. There could hardly be a doubt, after that last meeting in the office, that he would come out with pain, dignity, and moderation in support of Union Government.

On the morning of October 18 Laurier stepped out to his veranda in the brisk autumn sunshine. A flurry of aides withdrew into the shadows of the doorway as a streetcar stopped at the corner. Bourassa got down, turned into the walk, and climbed the steps. It was confrontation again, a meeting carefully manoeuvred by his own friends and Laurier's. As the old man's pale, veined hands went to each of his shoulders Bourassa stood for a moment looking up. He himself was grey-haired now, a man who took streetcars because he could not afford automobiles, a man of forty-nine with nowhere else to go. 'Bourassa is a man of great ability, but his ability is negative and destructive. He will never accomplish anything constructive or of benefit to any cause which he may espouse.' Laurier had written the words not a year before. They counted for little now. If Bourassa had destroyed himself he had been destroyed also by the ugly accumulations of a hundred and fifty years, prejudice, privilege, hostile power, and greed. There was still nobility in his dreams and detestations, he was still of the heart's core and the heart's blood. The two turned in at the doorway and climbed the stairs together. For the first time in almost ten years they sat facing each other in the study. Nothing was forced between them, nothing was lacking in warmth, nothing was left undone to assuage wounded pride. Nothing remained at the end to complete the rift in the country. For the benefit of the English, Bourassa promised with a smile, he would still 'throw a few boots' at Laurier. They would not hurt and they would not help. He was an ally now in Quebec where none was needed. He was the albatross through all of English Canada.

Bourassa went and collapse came for Laurier. 'Nothing but a severe attack of indigestion,' the doctor said. There was a week of living on pap, huddling in bed, dragging himself to the study to receive his callers. He was alone there, late at night, on the day that Fielding's letter appeared in the Halifax *Chronicle*. It was as expected. As usual, in the last half hour before bedtime, the Bible was near at hand with a pencil beside it. Laurier had formed the habit of jotting down in the flyleaves the numbers of significant verses against significant dates. The well-thumbed, well-scrawled pages were in their way a record of his triumphs and disasters and the moods in which he had met them. Psalm 55, the reference was this night, verses 12 and 13:

> For it was not an enemy that reproached me; then I could have borne it: neither was it he that hated me that did magnify himself against me; then I would have hid myself from him.
>
> But it was thou, a man mine equal, my guide, and mine acquaintance.

5

BY THE END of the month, with disintegration complete, he had set himself to the work of reassembly. The rallying-point would be Liberalism; in effect, Laurier. The man who opposed conscription was the man of Laurier's mind. The man who supported conscription could still support Laurier, for Laurier would impose the measure if the voice of the country spoke for it. A referendum after the election was the first pledge. Conscription was not the issue; it would pass with the war. The issue was the living nation, to be healed of its wounds, to be made autonomous within the Empire, to find those policies that would link the east with the west, the English with the French. They had always been Liberal policies, they had always been Laurier policies. They were the only flag to be raised, if any flag remained. 'The last and only thing which I have left to me now is my own record and consistency.'

In the west and in the Maritimes there remained of the party only guerilla bands, with Oliver and a few like him pulling the pieces together. In Ontario there was Aylesworth, six years out of politics, aging and almost totally ineffectual behind that maddening wall of deafness. There was Hartley Dewart the lawyer, able enough but pushed up through the provincial party mainly because the older leaders were gone. There was Hyman of the earlier generation, who could or would do nothing, pleading his health. There were the others like him to whom one wrote with diffidence mixed with doubt; they were after all old, almost as old as Laurier. 'That you should be a candidate at this juncture would certainly have a steadying effect on public opinion, but I am afraid it is too much to ask.' There were dozens now like Pardee, the declared and regretful enemy, and there were a few like Graham the entangling friend, the lifelong politician and friend of everyone, shifting and straddling hopelessly.

There was also Mackenzie King. That chubby John of Arc, with the voices of destiny and duty always harping at one ear and the voice of the Rockefellers at the other, was hardly the stuff of heroes. His bank account grew and he watched it with anxious eyes. He still yearned for a soul-mate and shied like a wary faun from each prospective woman. He had been more in the United States than in Canada during the past three years, more involved with the Rockefellers than with the war or even politics. The fact was thrown up to him often and he squirmed at attacks that he might have met head on. He was unmarried and he had not fought, but he was forty-three and had more dependants than most. In spite of that name of Rockefeller which clung about him he had done as much as any man of his time to civilize capital and enlighten its view of labour.

King hovered in Canada now, fearful, repelled and fascinated by the stormy political scene. He was relentlessly single-minded, righteous, and almost open in his view of himself as the future Messiah of Liberalism. He could be a maddening bore, yet few who complained of him were in a position, as he was, that would require them to give up an income of twenty-five thousand or a hundred thousand a year for the sake of similar ambitions. Laurier did not complain, Laurier dangled the crown, tantalizingly, maddeningly, always with something withheld. He was still the idol with short-comings, the confidant who never quite confided, but he had the final word. 'You must run,' it had been, and King was at last pinned down. Borden had thought of him and passed him by. The Americans wanted him and would have to want. King inclined toward conscription but he was going to stand against it as a Laurier man in North York. He would not do much for the party; he would be lucky to elect himself; but he would be a man to build on later, probably the one man.

By November 4 the manifesto was ready. On November 9 Laurier left for Quebec to deliver his opening speech. There were hundreds of women this time among the mighty crowd at the railway station, but most of them would be without votes. They were here to welcome the saviour of their sons. In the evening it seemed that the city had moved *en masse* to the Martineau Skating Rink and there was no room under the roof. From the steaming, bellowing hall the words of Laurier went out to shivering thousands waiting in the frosty night. The telegraph keys started them across the country and the work in Quebec was done. There would be Bourassa here, glumly accepting Laurier as the lesser devil, glumly demanding total abstention from the war. There would be Gouin and Lapointe. There would be Rodolphe Lemieux, joined by one aching bond to men who had left Laurier and still himself unchanged. 'I am pleased to see my only son take up arms to fight for ideals of justice, but I would have regretted to see the hand of a sergeant laid on the shoulder of the boy to compel him to fight. Laurier is a Liberal, a Canadian patriot – above all, he is Laurier.'

For a week or so the effects of the opening speech seemed startlingly good. O. D. Skelton, the friend from Queen's University, was enthusiastic. Alex Smith reported the word from Toronto: 'There is an unmistakable tide toward Laurier at present.' Graham, conscriptionist still, begged to be allowed to stand as a Laurier man in spite of it. The answer was yes. From Prince Edward Island came the promise of a solid Liberal victory if Laurier would authorize the repudiation of Bourassa. 'Yes, you may,' he scrawled on the back of the telegram, 'as much as you want.' Conscription itself had stirred up a sullen backwash that played its part in Ontario as everywhere else. By November 19 over fifty per cent of the men called up had filed their claims for exemption. 'It is not impossible', Laurier wrote that day, 'that Ontario in this contest may turn out to be a box of surprises.'

Yet, even as he wrote, the expected was bearing him down.

'Bourassa Fully Endorses Laurier', had been the headline in the Toronto *Globe* on November 13. Willison's opening gun had been a cartoon spread across the eight columns of his front page showing 'The Hindenburg Line', with a malevolently decrepit Laurier flanked by his supporters. The campaign had built from that, with Willison directing it all. Each day the knot with Bourassa was drawn a little tighter. Bourassa would rule Canada if Laurier were elected; a vote for Laurier was a vote for Bourassa, a vote for the Kaiser. In all the country west of the Ottawa River there were now only three daily newspapers that spoke for Laurier.

November 20 was his birthday. On that morning a copy of the Montreal *Gazette* lay on his desk. It was now clear to the *Gazette* that 'Sir Wilfrid Laurier has never ardently favoured Canada's participation in the defence of the Empire, that on the contrary he has regarded the greatest struggle for civilization and democracy in which the world has ever engaged simply with an eye to party advantage.' He read it and pulled a sheet of paper toward him and copied out with his own hand another *Gazette* notice of a dozen months before. It told of his great recruiting speech at St-Lin and congratulated him on the results. He listed down the dates of his sixteen largest rallies of the past three years, all for recruiting. Then, brusquely, he shoved the paper aside. It would be of no use to reply and there was no time.

The other newspapers with the day's crop of abuse lay piled in the outer office. There were endless lists to be checked by exhausted aides; he would have to lend a hand. The desk before him was heaped with the clamorous pleadings of tired old men and anxious amateurs, out in the constituencies with no money and no helpers, squabbling, confused, and desperate. It was the same here at the centre. Across the country the nominations were made and the men stood, for what, exactly, Laurier hardly knew. 'I am a little in a quandary as to whom to endorse.' Some of his public endorsements recoiled with fire and fury; the support of Sir Wilfrid Laurier was not desired. He himself was running in an Ottawa riding as well as in Quebec East, because someone had to fight for the vacant seat. He could not ignore the constituency and he could not attend to it; he could attend to nothing wholly. There were problems everywhere, there had to be meetings everywhere, he was in demand everywhere while the jangling telephone and the ceaseless mail and messengers pinned him to his desk.

He was seventy-six on that November 20 and a thinned-out flow of congratulations came with the other mail. To one letter at least, somewhere in the small hours of the first morning of his seventy-seventh year, he sent an answer. It could hardly have brought much joy to the friend and churchman. 'Accept my sincere thanks for your good wishes,' he wrote to Archbishop Bruchési. 'The years have brought nothing good. I owe only gratitude to Providence for the health which I enjoy . . . and after all health is the greatest good of life.'

The turmoil was worst in the west and the calls from there were loudest. He did not plan to do much. He could manage a trip to Winnipeg, he thought, with a quick return to the east. 'Can go to Winnipeg for not more than two days,' he wired on November 22, 'and not farther west.' He thought of December 3 as the date for the Winnipeg meeting and in three days had changed it. He had to have a meeting in Ottawa, he had to have a meeting in Arnprior; the demands of the east entrapped him. The west grew more strident. The men in Vancouver demanded him. Oliver in Edmonton demanded him. Knowles of Moose Jaw wired that Laurier could bring the remaining Liberals of Saskatchewan 'out from under the bed'. Laurier wired on December 1 that it would be quite impossible for him to visit Vancouver, and frantic protests came back. By Friday December 7, nothing was left of the plan to close the campaign in Ontario. He settled that evening into 'Matapedia', the private car the C.P.R. had provided, bound through to the Pacific.

Hartley Dewart of Toronto was with him and Walter Mitchell of Quebec, Gouin's English lieutenant. J. P. B. Casgrain, another old friend of Quebec, had agreed to come along 'as honorary secretary, not as orator'. Whatever the views of Shaughnessy, Edward Beatty of the C.P.R. had seen to it that the car was comfortable. It seemed almost too roomy. The correspondent

'HI: LET LAURIER IN!' CARTOON BY N. MCCONNELL IN THE TORONTO *News*, DECEMBER 13, 1917

of the Toronto *World* had politely declined an invitation to be aboard. The editor of the *Globe* had answered a similar invitation with the cool reply that the Winnipeg meeting would be adequately covered. No one was invited or expected from the Toronto *News*. To Willison's paper Laurier was now 'a demagogue, a charlatan and a mountebank'. Its artists were preparing a map of the country with Quebec shown in black, 'The foul blot on Canada'. Bishop Fallon had discovered that every anti-war element was anxious to bring back Laurier for its own unworthy purposes. The Supreme Grand Master of Orangemen had asked that day for 'the strongest appeal in my name urging the brethren to drop all other considerations and to unite in support of the Union Government. This government must be sustained or Canada disgraced.' As the clack of the wheels went on through Sunday morning three out of four of the country's Protestant pulpits, and a good many of the Catholic, were echoing the same advice.

It was twenty below zero as the train reached Winnipeg that evening, and a little colder next day. The bustling committees filled the suite at the Fort Garry Hotel and the usual promises ran wild. There would be twenty-five seats won in Manitoba, perhaps thirty. The Chief listened and smiled and shook hands, and his hands were cold. He had seen too many committees, and he missed too many faces. There was nothing to warm the blood in the sight of Dafoe's *Free Press*, rampant and rancorous. A telegram came from Ottawa, cutting more ground away. The government was exempting farmers' sons in Ontario; conscription could be dispensed with where it cost votes. Another wire came for Laurier, trivial and irrelevant now, just as he was leaving to speak. Mackenzie Bowell had died in Belleville that evening. One more gone of the few who still lingered. The Chief came down to the lobby and passed through to the street. The wind that cut at his throat and knifed through to his bones seemed a little icier.

Then it was the big, bleak hall of the Industrial Bureau and the old man was himself. More than himself, it seemed. The breath of the five thousand lined in the street outside was a frosty cloud. The smell of the six thousand jammed in the hall before him was very incense, the smell of the flesh and blood, the smell of the nation. He was here with nothing new, he was here as he was, the tired old Frenchman flaunting the tattered plume, astride of the ancient purpose. He had said it all before and he said it again; nothing would serve, nothing would stand, except for a whole people.

He was heckled a little and cheered more, and at the end the cheers were deafening. They rolled down the street as the crowd poured away, ignoring the following speakers. The thousands had come for Laurier and they had seen Laurier. They were somehow reassured.

He left for Regina in the morning while the *Free Press* blazed behind him. He went that night from the crowd in Regina's Metropolitan Church to the crowd in the Baptist Church to the crowd in the Westminster Church, with a wave for the freezing hundreds who could get into none of them. 'How would the Kaiser vote?' asked John Dafoe. 'Ichabod, O Ichabod,' he mourned on his editorial page, 'So fallen, so lost, the light withdrawn which once he wore. The glory from his grey hairs gone, forevermore.' His front page carried a two-column advertisement of the Union Government side by side with the report of Laurier's speech, refuting Laurier's points. On page after page Dafoe returned like a nervous mosquito to stab with some new dart, to repeat his question, 'How would the Kaiser vote?', and then by some irked compulsion to justify the asking. Still, when Dafoe's reporters came to Calgary they found a town on watch in the midst of a howling blizzard, waiting for Laurier. It was eleven o'clock at night and thirty degrees below zero when the train pulled in, four hours late. It was three o'clock next morning when the fourth of the meetings ended and the old man sought his car.

Oliver was pleading for a trip north to Edmonton but the car went west for the mountains. 'Have engaged Hotel Vancouver ballroom and Avenue and Empress Theatres,' the wire had come from the coast. 'Will also have church near by for the overflow.' Another church was required and still there were luckless thousands cheering outside in the rain. At eight o'clock in the evening, after just nine hours in Vancouver, Laurier turned east.

He had come expecting a love feast, said some friend or enemy, and he had found five of them.

On Sunday evening, December 16, 'Matapedia' passed through Regina. It rolled into Winnipeg at seven-twenty on the morning of December 17, election day. To the surprise of the *Free Press*, which had expected Sir Wilfrid to wait in Winnipeg for the results, it rolled on. It was a little after ten in the evening as it drew up in Fort William. Dewart, Mitchell, and Casgrain ran for the telegraph office, collected a sheaf of telegrams, and hurried back. The 'all aboard' came and the Imperial Limited belched and moved ahead with the darkness of pine and snowdrift closing about it.

There had not been time in the station even to glance at the telegrams. It was the leader's place and privilege to absorb the shock. The returns were incomplete and there was still the soldiers' vote. There would be more to come and worse. But there was enough now. Laurier had taken sixty-two of the sixty-five seats in Quebec. In every other province, except for Prince Edward Island, he had been almost wiped out. Ontario was a complete disaster and it was doubtful at the moment if there would be one Liberal member from any of the provinces of the west. He sat for a moment and looked up, almost too tired to summon the old, tired joke. 'They cheered for me but they didn't vote for me.'

28

'I HAVE NO FAULT TO FIND WITH LIFE'

1918-1919

I PROPOSE to go to Quebec next week to consult some friends on the situation. I have stood up to the fatigues of the trip admirably but the reaction makes itself felt and I am a little tired today. A few days rest will put me on my feet.'

He was two days home and he intended to go on. The war went on. The nation stood, a nation still. 'It will be necessary that the young get to work,' he wrote to Ernest Lapointe three days later. In Quebec the old *Bleu* newspaper *L'Evénement* warned the province that had followed Bourassa, 'You are now really isolated and alone in your corner, unable to do anything for yourself or anyone else.' The New Year's message of John Dafoe came a week later. 'When we demonstrate, as we shall, that a solid Quebec is without power, there may be a return to reason along the banks of the St. Lawrence.' The barbs of the half-truths flew in all directions, answering nothing. The answer as always lay in work renewed, work and youth.

The Quebec legislature was already simmering with a resolution to the effect that the province 'would be disposed to accept the breaking of the Confederation Pact of 1867 if, in the other provinces, it is believed that she is an obstacle to the union, progress, and development of Canada.' Laurier dismissed it impatiently, impatient with the English worriers about secession. 'There is no such movement at all. If you look carefully at the motion you will see that all it says is: "If the other provinces are not satisfied with our company we are ready and willing to go." This is simply an answer to the vicious campaign of abuse which has been carried on by the Tories.' He had an answer for John Dafoe too but he left it to wait on time and Thomas Crerar. That rangy, sun-burned head of the western Grain Growers had led his thousands of farmers into the arms of the Tory east and sat now as Minister of Agriculture. He would not be a happy minister very long.

The year turned and Laurier went on. He was bitter enough and fearful enough too. 'The masses of the people were with us, but effective means were taken to stifle their voice . . . The wrong of the measure is forcing it upon an unwilling people; and by this I do not mean French Canadians alone. All the labour classes protested against it and asked for a referendum . . . in the western provinces our party was simply annihilated by the manoeuvres of the enumerators under the War Times Elections Act . . . what the press failed to achieve the women and the parsons completed . . .' 'Let us take it cheerfully, however, and be prepared to continue the fight for the good cause.'

The injunction to cheer seemed an echo of bygone times. The war was a grey horror that enveloped everything else. An old man, powerless and helpless to change much, he had watched the world and the nation change for four years. They were still changing. The cry of the armed ape seemed the only voice that mattered through the first months of 1918, and there was a new and brutal foreignness even in the air at home. Conscription was failing as Laurier had said it would fail, not only in Quebec but in every other province. By the middle of March, of the hundred thousand called for, there were barely twenty-five thousand men in khaki, untrained, totally unready still. Not one had crossed the ocean. Yet the casualties still came, the need for troops was worse, and harsher compulsion brought more savage resentment. Whatever façade of confidence he maintained for the men about him, Laurier confided darkly to the old English friend who had found the key to the Vatican: 'The peace of the country', he wrote Russell, 'is certainly in real danger.'

The process of recording, counting, and distributing the votes of soldiers overseas was a squalid, squabbling battle of party agents. It was over by the end of February. The soldiers had voted twelve to one for the government and the position was now clear. Eight English Liberals had survived in Ontario, two in the prairie provinces and ten in the Maritimes. The party would sit with eighty-two members, sixty-two of them French. The three Conservatives elected in Quebec were all English, all from the English enclaves around Westmount. Of the hundred and fifty others who would sit for the government with them the only French Canadian was a certain Chabot of Ottawa. He had been opposed by Wilfrid Laurier in the fight for his constituency, and Laurier had been defeated.

The constituency of Quebec East had gone for Laurier as usual. The leader of the opposition was in his accustomed place when parliament convened on March 18, 1918. He had had his quota of preliminary skirmishes with Borden over the details of opening and he looked fresh and truculent. For the moment he was. 'My health is good, but still it is the health of an old man and I cannot but feel that my strength is slowly ebbing away.'

2

HE HAD strength enough for anger as Borden rose on April 3 to give the House the details of the conscription riots in Quebec City. From March 28 to April 1 crowds had run wild among the offices of the administrators of the Military Service Act. Buildings had been burnt, equipment smashed, and files and official documents dumped into the streets. The eight hundred troops in garrison had been called out and by the night of April 1 these were reinforced by another thousand brought down from the west. 'From house tops, side streets, snow banks, and other places of concealment,' ran the official report on that night, 'the rioters opened fire point blank on the troops who, as on previous nights, displayed great steadiness and forbearance under severe provocation. But at length, after several soldiers had received bullet wounds, it became absolutely necessary for the troops to return the fire. Five soldiers were wounded and of the crowd four were killed, many were injured, and fifty-eight were arrested. By 1:20 next morning order had been established and by 5:00 a.m. the troops had returned to barracks.'

On April 4 the Habeas Corpus Act was suspended in Quebec and the city was all but under martial law. The rioters, said Borden in the grim new mood of the time, 'may well be given the opportunity to exercise their warlike spirit on the enemies of the country'. There was no evidence that he intended his strictures to apply to Lieut.-Col. Armand Lavergne, who was now a politician at liberty. Defying Bourassa as well as Borden and Laurier, Lavergne had run as an independent and been soundly beaten. If he had closed what passed for a political career, however, he had not closed his mouth. It ran on, serviceable as ever in the cause of mischief. Bourassa deplored the riots and denied responsibility. 'I never thought the people would have the punch to do it,' was Lavergne's admiring comment.

One no longer smiled and dismissed the young Armand as that March and that April passed into history. The sunlight of Arthabaska was too far off, too shrouded now in the gloom of the seventy-seventh year. There were the trickles of blood in the streets and the rivers of blood abroad. There was the ring of the German U-boats tightening round England's throat. There were the grey millions of Ludendorff punching for the Marne again and the thought for the first time that the war might actually be lost. There was the bleak sureness of all that had been lost at home. It was not a time to endure this still-unbloodied picker and pincher of wounds. The boy of Arthabaska was a man of thirty-seven, a little pouchy and paunchy. Quebec was tired and sick of him; Laurier was tired and sick of him.

It did not draw one closer to those enemies who had made Lavergne and used him. They sat with the power Lavergne had helped to give them and could not command men, not even the men whom Laurier might have brought. 'Yes,' he wrote in one of the bitterest letters of his life, 'it is now felt on the treasury benches that conscription was a failure. There are strong reasons for believing that the government would quietly let the act pass into oblivion, but the blind, the fools, and the miscreants who coerced the government to coerce still hold the whip high over their heads. And now the band of the blind, the fools, and the miscreants is being strengthened by those other blind, fools, and miscreants who at this moment are stirring up the people of Quebec to violence and riot.'

3

On April 17, for the first time in its history, the House held a secret session. The members were told what the public could not be told: the allied armies in Europe hovered on the edge of disaster. The sombre talk changed little, for the country, strained to its limit, had little more to give. It was the armies of the United States now, gathering and on the way, that were the great hope. Debate in this House could release only a new flood of paper and renewed turmoil. On April 19 the exemptions protecting lads of twenty-two were done away with. The exempted sons of farmers were liable now. Every Canadian of nineteen years or more was subject to his call.

The session droned on, giving women the franchise. Quebec members opposed it, Laurier included. He was still the Victorian gentleman and still of the mind of his province, but the mind of the day was changed. The day grew an hour longer with the daylight-saving act. The country edged toward dryness as Sam Hughes, Rowell, and Foster hailed the advent of Prohibition. On May 13, over Laurier's tired protests, much was made of his golden wedding day. Among the flood of calls and messages was a message from the King. Liberals of the Commons and Senate presented a magnificent golden salver to himself and Zoë. Around the church of Sacré-Coeur at the time of morning Mass there were crowds of damp-eyed watchers as the big car rolled up, the chauffeur got out, and the nobly erect old gentleman handed down the beloved old lady.

One day later Ottawa was filled with five thousand angry farmers from Ontario and Quebec, and with armed troops sealing the crowd away from the House of Commons. From eleven in the morning until two in the afternoon, jammed into the Russell Theatre for a meeting that had been allowed as a safety valve, the invaders stormed against the new rigours of conscription. Borden faced them at last and faced them down. Yes, exemptions had been promised to the sons of farmers and exemptions had been cancelled. No, they would not be restored. The needs of the war were paramount. He was speaking, and he knew it, not to a race but a class, and the far-off prairies listened. When the five thousand left, still refused a hearing in the House, Borden had lost the votes of the prairies with them. The first great rift had opened between the men of the eastern factories and the men of the western lands.

A week later the House turned once more to the matter of titles, sourly weary of the rain of stars and parchments that had come with the war. Sir Robert Borden privately shared the mood. Sir Wilfrid Laurier emphasized it and neither man was in a position to be very firm. 'Why I accepted it with the views I hold now', said Laurier, 'will be going into a matter of personal history which I do not care to bring forward. But at all events I may say this: I see here a little class of titled people, knights, commanders of this order or that order. If they will make a bargain with me, I am quite prepared, if we can do it without any disrespect to the Crown of England, to bring our titles to the market place and make a bonfire of them.' The offer was not accepted. Borden put a stop to discussion and the House moved toward adjournment with greater matters in hand. The Prime Minister and some of his colleagues would soon be required in England. The great German offensive seemed to have spent itself and the climax of the war was at hand.

On May 23 parliament was ready for prorogation with most of its business disposed of. The day's sitting, still in the big bare hall of the Victoria Museum, resumed at seven in the evening after the dinner recess. It was a thin House. Borden and most of the ministers were clearing up in their offices, waiting to appear in the chamber when the summons came from Black Rod. Members occupied themselves with the usual last-minutes estimates and the usual wrangling over other loose ends, while Foster presided on the government side of the aisle. He was as lean and acidulous as ever but very white now. Sam Hughes was there, still vocal as a private member. Fielding was in the place he had made his own, on the cross benches, adrift from both parties. He was drifting back toward Liberalism steadily enough. So far as he and Laurier were concerned there had never been a break; the problem was a resentful party. Jacques Bureau and Rodolphe Lemieux slumped in their seats beside the leader, both as tired as he was and glad of the end of the session but looking a little in the mood for a last-minute skirmish.

There was an hour or so of wrangling over an allowance to Fitzpatrick, who was Chief Justice now and had served for a spell as Deputy Governor General. He was entitled to his five thousand dollars for the service. Laurier got up to justify the grant at some length, drifted off into a little historical disquisition on the need for such a deputy, and then bickered amiably for a while with Hughes as to whether the payment should be described as 'travelling expenses' or 'special allowance'.

At eight-thirty Fielding tried to get the House back on the rails. The Governor General was expected at ten o'clock and there were still nineteen million dollars of post-office estimates to be considered. By midnight, with the Governor General patiently in waiting, the estimates had been considered but other matters had risen. Lemieux had expressed the hope that the Prime Minister and his colleagues who would be leaving next day for the Imperial Conference would not jeopardize the interests of Canada by wild imperialistic schemes. Foster had assured him they would not. Who would the colleagues be, Laurier asked. Foster replied that Arthur Meighen, James Calder, and N. W. Rowell would be going. 'Some choice!' said Bureau.

Lemieux was not yet satisfied and around one o'clock, after more desultory byplay, he produced a quotation from a speech of John A. Macdonald. The old ghost spoke up lively as ever from out of that Liberal mouth. 'We are told', Lemieux quoted, 'that we want imperial federation. I will not trouble you with a disquisition on that subject now, but I will tell you imperial federation is utterly impracticable. We would never agree to send a number of men over to England to sit in parliament there and vote away our rights and principles. I am, so far as that question goes, up to the handle a home-ruler. We will govern our own country. We will put on the taxes ourselves. If we choose to misgovern ourselves we will do so, and we do not desire England, Ireland, or Scotland to tell us we are fools. We will say: "If we are fools we will keep our folly to ourselves; you wiil not be worse for it and we will not be the worse for any folly of yours." '

They were embarrassing words to Tories in the mood of these times, but Foster was equal to the occasion. Lemieux, he said tartly, should not consider himself the only guardian of the rights and liberties of the country. 'I would ask him not to spoil his holidays by having any undue anxiety as to what may be done on the other side.'

'You will allow us the privilege of believing', said Laurier, 'that our trust in our missionaries is not unlimited.'

The hour was late and the syntax a little confused, but Foster was piously understanding. 'It is always open for us', he said, 'to become more and more trustful.'

'It is very slow to come.'

Honourable gentlemen yawned, stretched, and looked toward the door. Black Rod was now on the way and the tone of the dialogue was degenerating. Another member hinted at his low estimate of the ministers attending the conference. 'Let them keep away from the booze over there,' added Bureau. 'Preach prohibition.'

'And practise it,' nodded Foster, the lifelong prohibitionist, as the knock came at the door. Black Rod entered with his three bows and announced that His Excellency desired the attendance of the Honourable House in the chamber of the Honourable the Senate. The honourable members rose. Laurier rose with them and walked for the last time from the chamber of the Commons of Canada.

4

NOW WHEN WE are touching on the fatal term of life all that comes from those we love is doubly precious and dear. Ah, those days of Arthabaska, so faint, so remote that they seem almost a dream. Those days of Arthabaska! How gladly would I return to them. I have no fault to find with life for I have been happy in my domestic life, happy in my public life. I have touched the summit, I have reached the heights, and yet my thought goes back in preference to those days of Arthabaska.'

There was time now to answer the latest letter of Marie-Louise Pacaud, saluting the golden wedding. There was always work and there were always friends crowding in on the office at the Museum and the study at home, but everything was easier in June and the friends were less urgent. Politics was a matter of planning, so far as anything could be planned; there was no immediate crisis. The crises had passed, leaving their wreck behind them. Creditors dunned at the door of party headquarters. Deserving and defeated candidates complained in bankruptcy. Frank Oliver's Edmonton *Bulletin,* last of the Liberal dailies in the west, was going to the wall, pushed, as Oliver claimed, by Tory eastern interests. If the *Bulletin* went there would be silence, for the hope of commencing even a small western weekly was beyond the party's purse. On the other hand, from Toronto, Peter Larkin reported that the *Globe* was uneasy in its new allegiance to the Union Government, not the less so because Larkin for once was waving his money as a club. It was quite possible, he had warned, that he would either buy up shares in the paper or set himself to compete with it.

Peter Larkin. 'Aileen and Mrs. Larkin send their love.' The letters had been coming for years with that closing salutation. So had the cheques for the party with their large round figures. Laurier could remember the tall old man from the days when he walked Toronto with a basket, delivering his own Salada Tea. He could remember the fatter days when the title was offered, and he remembered the refusal. 'I am not ambitious. I am for "the house with the narrow gate". Any interest I take in political affairs is, I am sure you will believe me, unselfish. I would be ignoble indeed if I did not with pleasure make my little effort toward lengthening the period of power of the best government Canada ever had or is likely to have.'

The government had gone out in spite of Larkin but defeat had not changed him. He had been the worshipping follower through the years of opposition; he had stood fast for Laurier's stand on conscription. The collapse of the party had only brought from him an offer to make his first bid as a candidate, and he had seemed ashamed of his gratitude when Laurier declined. He still gave, deprecating every return. He still dressed like Laurier, he still loved to be told he looked like Laurier, he still loved Laurier. There were none quite like Larkin but there were many still of his mind and more returning. Graham lingered about, unhappy and repentant. Fielding had never gone far and was now nearer. Murphy had stood through it all. Alex Smith grumbled and grunted loyally. Pardee, Crerar, Carvell, Pugsley, the little and the big, the lost and the recoverable; they might not come back to Laurier but they were not far off. Of them all, Mackenzie King was the man most to be thought of, but that could wait a while.

The long thoughts were good thoughts on the whole. Whatever had been rejected by this party and this country, it was not Laurier. 'I have taken the work of Confederation where I found it and determined to give it my life.' Nothing had been so clear and sharp either in conception or in dedication, yet it was that which had come about in the long shaping. He had taken the Confederation and made it the Canadian nation.

He had established the place of the nation within the Empire almost as Macdonald would have done. Its place in North America and its relation with the neighbour nation were not yet established but neither was defeat final, if it was defeat. Time would have more to say on that question. It could wait on time, it was not vital. The vital thing, always at the heart of all, was the relation of French and English.

That problem Confederation had not solved. Macdonald had not solved it in the almost quarter-century which had been given him for the work. He had left it, at his going, rasped and exacerbated by neglect and evasion, above all by the attitude he had brought with him from Kingston and kept through all his days. The French and Frenchness were to be tolerated and got round, quieted where necessary with minimal concessions. The country was essentially British.

The attitude was more than wrong; it was potentially fatal. It stemmed from the old dichotomy in English thinking; the nation sea-to-sea conceived as a whole, yet conceived of always with the English purpose dominant. There was also a French purpose, equally present at the making of Confederation, not to die with George Etienne Cartier and not to be restricted to the limits of Cartier's vision. To deny it was to deny the nation. To admit it was to concede nothing. To define it was to begin the work of building, and to that work Laurier had been the first to set his hand.

Rooted in Quebec, with all the old hopes and angers hovering over him, he had been confronted by the new facts of the nation's growth and peopling. They meant the relinquishment of much he cared for, much that Quebec cared for, but to define is to set boundaries. He had held to the possible and essential. He had rejected alike the passionate absolutes of Bourassa and the cold pragmatism of a D'Alton McCarthy or a Sifton. The one would have ignored the present, the other the past; and neither could be ignored. They were facts to be dealt with too, and Laurier had dealt with them. The French purpose had shaped itself in him, cleared of its angry myths, yet proud and unyielding still and totally reconcilable with the best of the English purpose. It was simply to remain himself and to walk as a Canadian everywhere, equally partaking of, equally responsible for, the nation's life. From that standing ground and with that measuring rod he had 'capitulated,' 'retreated', 'equivocated,' bartering for time, for peace, dealing with the present as it was, clearing the channels of the future for the flow of the two purposes.

He seemed to have failed utterly. Around him now east and west were at odds, French and English embittered as never before. The old parties were wrecked and the old banalities of the party labels meant less than the little they had ever meant. Yet out of disruption there was a groping back, and it would be to his ground. There was no other while the country remained what it professed to be. 'My one hope is to keep the party together.' He had not done it; he did not believe that a French Canadian should ever lead again. Yet he had saved more than a party and he could not help but know it. There was no Liberalism now but the essential thing of the spirit, the liberalism of Wilfrid Laurier. There would never again be Canadianism that was not stamped with his imprint. Never again would a man stand easily at the head of this nation who did not speak the tongues and share the purposes of the two races, who did not feel in himself the flow of the two rivers, 'parallel, separate, and distinguishable and yet . . . one stream.' The politicians sensed it, the people sensed it. Those last thousands of the bleak December days who would not vote for Laurier had still cheered for Laurier. They had reached out to him though they could not yet reach him. He had stood before them in defeat the living denial of failure, the man that each must become, the first Canadian.

'I make three petitions every day of my life,' he had once told Kirk Cameron. 'O Lord, keep Thou the door of my lips that I say nothing to hurt or harm anybody. O Lord guard Thou mine actions that I do nothing to hurt or harm anybody. O God be merciful to me, a sinner.' There had been mercy for the sinner and there was quiet for the man now even though he lifted his eyes to a great darkness, seeing no more than he had ever seen. 'I was born in the Catholic faith and I shall die in it.' That cool acceptance of a common bond had never been real belief. Mackenzie King, the earnest Calvinist, knew that. Bruchési knew it. Laurier still prayed to darkness, but it was easier again to pray. The scars were healing. The doubts and angers that had haunted the past six months were nearly at rest. No man, said Cameron, had ever left the presence of Laurier humiliated. If true, or near the truth, it had brought its rewards. It would be as good an epitaph as any.

5

TRAIN TRIPS were ordeals to be dreaded now, but on July 15 Laurier took the train for Ste-Agathe in the Laurentians. David had a summer home there, and rest and solitude in the company of that old unashamed idolator would be worth the effort. After the heat of Ottawa the clear, brisk mountain air was tonic and wine. Through a dozen long evenings Laurier sat on the veranda with the lake below in the dark, relaxed, expansive, uplifted by his audience. He had always seemed a little of the god in this presence. He had always shown off a little for David.

Quebec, he mused aloud, had followed Bourassa and had learned some dear lessons. The spirit of conciliation was not opportunism. Quebec was not powerful enough to sway the country. Neither was Laurier. There were limits. There were limits for the English too. Had Laurier been in power he would not have made the mistakes Borden had made in the war. He would have shown England that Canada, in all loyalty, could only go so far. He would have said at the beginning, and the English would have agreed, that the uttermost strain should be avoided. The jingo shout for the last dollar and the last drop of blood had only called up Bourassa's answering shout of nothing at all. Perhaps two hundred thousand men and some hundreds of millions of dollars would have been enough. Laurier's policy had been laid down at every Imperial Conference, and had been agreed to. If it had been followed it would have checked and avoided the new rancours in Quebec and the newly rampant imperialism. Laurier would have held to the policy, he would have held the party to it, and he would have kept the country together. Even now the damage could and must be repaired. But the task would fall to others. 'I have no appetite, no strength. I must not forget that I am now an old man.'

On the morning of the Sunday before he left there seemed to be a good deal of whispering and manoeuvre about him. He was alive to its purpose and not really surprised that afternoon to see the curé of the parish coming up the path with Bourassa. Bourassa also had a cottage in Ste-Agathe and it was hard to be unaware of his presence. The two hours on the veranda went by in good talk, serene talk. One discussed and explained now for the sake of friendship. One no longer sought to convince or hoped to change. Bourassa was warm, nostalgic, and a little wary, obviously responsive to 'that monster of charm', and obviously resistant to the familiar spell. 'Mr. Laurier,' he said as he rose to go, 'the more I know you the more indulgence I have for the politicians.' It was not much but it was Bourassa, and probably the end of that.

The automobile came up from Ottawa for Laurier's return and he motored back with David. This time the route led by L'Assomption. The car turned in through the grey stone gates of the college and stopped in the courtyard. There was a flurry of greetings as the great alumnus got out and then he was standing in the gallery of the priests, bowing low over the hand of the Rector, Canon Villeneuve, with whom he had played and fought as a classmate in the old days. When they walked outside Laurier said a few words to the youngsters hastily assembled on the playground. Dismissed as he finished, they still lingered and he looked at them smilingly. The solemn round eyes in the fresh faces were as inscrutable as the years ahead. His glance travelled up the wall of the old building, so forbidding from the outside. He put out a hand to touch it and the hand lingered a moment. Then he turned with that straightening that was slower now, obviously a little painful, and walked to the waiting car.

6

'IT IS NOT at all impossible that the war may end within forty-eight hours.' He wrote the letter on November 8 and the same day Borden, with Foster and Arthur Sifton, left for England again. Three days later the armistice was signed.

The end had been in sight through the late summer and autumn. There had been time to prepare in a way, yet no amount of time would have been enough. For Laurier the vast relief and release were borne down, almost stifled, by the weight of the fears and questions. The dregs of the agony were all about him. Carvell's son was dead. Graham's son was dead. Lemieux's son was dead. Broken, embittered men, those fathers stood for a hundred thousand like them, mourning their dead, their maimed. They stood for the country itself, warsick, heartsick, dangerous, and divided.

As he came back from the Laurentians Laurier had taken up politics again with the certainty that a new age was approaching and an old man must go. It had set him to work with a startling return of vigour. He had gone to Knowlton for a semi-political week with Sydney Fisher and had deliberately stirred up, among a half-dozen elderly strategists assembled on the wide lawn of the estate, some of the questions of labour and labour relations that loomed in the new era. He had pursued Kirk Cameron to Montreal with the same questions. He had gone to Toronto to make other soundings and on September 17 he assembled in his Ottawa office a group that bore a strong resemblance to his old cabinet.

Fielding sat there, ready to be a Liberal again when the Maritimes had forgiven him. Graham was there. 'If you think I can be of any assistance,' he had written, 'I will try to come back, though to tell the truth there is not much steam in me. I feel more like running away somewhere and hiding.' Mackenzie King was present, wearing the scars of defeat in North York, righteously superior to the men who had not borne the full heat of the battle, righteously indignant, as in 1911, that another seat had not been found for him. With all the strains of the meeting there was a sure sense of renewal, and it remained undampened by the report next day that King had been seen at lunch with Sir Clifford Sifton. 'I am not surprised that Sifton should want you,' Laurier commented when King got round a month later to admitting that overtures had been made. 'He is an able man and knows brains. He would like to have you in his cabinet, for it is his cabinet.'

King would not go, and Fielding and Graham would be back. The tide was running well. Alex Smith still fumed about the Old Guard, damned Laurier for his 'puttering around on organization', and found the party's position generally 'helpless, hopeless, pitiful, and calamitous'. The puttering still went on. There was a monster meeting in Three Rivers to welcome home Henri Béland, once a Laurier Liberal, whose political assets had been multiplied by three years as a prisoner of war. The old man puttered off to attend the gathering, aware of Tory hopes. Three years of Germans might have changed Béland on conscription, on Laurier, on Liberalism; the returned prisoner of war might be the Conservatives' key to Quebec. One hour with Béland was enough to settle that question. 'Béland will be all right,' the Chief was able to report.

Lemieux was bigger than Béland would ever be, and had to be held too. He had grown indifferent to politics, he was sick at heart for his son, and his road to the heights was closed. Laurier himself had closed it. 'No Roman Catholic French Canadian should ever try to lead the Liberal party again.' Yet Lemieux must remain in politics for the sake of the party in Quebec. A hundred others like him had to be soothed and stirred and clamped together once more for the sake of the party in the nation. Only the Chief could do it, and after that he could go. There would be the books for a while, perhaps, and the shade of Arthabaska. The new course would be set by the new man.

Laurier knew the eventual man, and he knew the pitfalls round him, a great deal better than Mackenzie King himself. King complained and prospered. He was back with the Rockefellers again but still returned to Ottawa hungry and unrequited. Politics had been unjust to him, though politics was his first love. The only offer he had yet received, he said, after all he had laid on the altar of loyalty, had come from Sifton, the arch-enemy. Surely a seat could be found of all those seats in Quebec. It could, and it was the last thing King should have. Walled up among those dour sixty-two, he would be lost to the English party. Pushed on too hard, he would be much too expensive. There were other politicians who had their claims also and had served their time. To Zoë, who had watched them come and go for fifty years, the brilliant, unmarriable prig was still 'wet behind the ears'. He was certainly green and young as men went in the trade, and one word of him as leader could shiver the assembling party into new fragments. Fielding, Graham, Fisher, and half a dozen others were all leaders or wished to be regarded as such. Fielding was certainly a leader, and he was still for Laurier a more warming prospect than Mackenzie King. King was tuned to the new times, King wrote books on labour and solved labour problems while old men on lawns fumbled and groped with them. But there were other problems and King would have to wait. He would have to be fed on hope while the party came together. And even when that was done he might find hope deferred.

'No man in Canada has your chances today. The thing is for me to bring you forward all I can.' The promises were dangled but were not entirely effective. The expert of the Rockefellers had returned to the Rockefellers when Laurier went to London, Ontario, on November 19 for the largest Liberal gathering held in the province since the election. King's presence had been much desired but he had not found it possible to attend. There was no doubt, however, by the time the evening ended that he would be an alert and impressed absentee. Enthusiasm had been electric and warming; Liberalism was alive again. There would be a national convention within a year, Laurier announced. It was time once more to go forward.

Implicit and avoided in all public discussion was the subject of the new leader. That could wait for the convention. Laurier came home and saw a birthday pass and watched the turn of the year. There was much to watch. Peter Larkin reported 'a rustle in the hay'. The stirrings of thousands of subscribers were edging Joe Atkinson and his Toronto *Star* in the direction of Laurier again. The government on parliament hill, at least in the opinion of the leader of the opposition, was 'piling up one blunder on top of another' while Borden, much in demand, was refusing to come home. Borden was staying in England, Laurier wrote bluntly, 'not so much for the Peace Conference as to assist in the preparation of a program of protection disguised under the name of British Preference'. As that prospect rose the cloud in the west rose with it. Tom Crerar, reported Murphy, 'says Union Government is so unpopular that he is sick of it and will soon be back on the farm'.

By the end of December a sweet wholeness settled on the Liberal party in the Maritimes as Fielding returned to the fold. John Dafoe had come on a visit to Ottawa, still damning the French but cursing Ontario protectionists with a fiercer voice. He had now discovered that the natural allies of the west were the Quebec farmers. The *Globe* in Toronto was attacking Sifton. The rustles in the hay were good.

7

THE POLICY of the government in the next session, Laurier wrote Aylesworth on January 13, 1919, "will be neither flesh, fish, nor good red herring. It will be a hotch-potch of some kind, but of what kind it would be most rash to venture an opinion.' Parliament was scheduled to open on February 20 and the Chief was preparing himself in familiar mood. He was still in lively form when he spoke next day to a party meeting in

Ottawa, but a trip to Toronto had to be postponed. 'It is not only that time is very precious for me, but I dread the journey as I do not feel just now as strong as I would like to be.'

He had summoned 'those who ordinarily make up my council' to be on hand in Ottawa not later than February 17. It was likely to be a fighting session and he looked forward to it. It would be good to have Fielding back at his side again. It would have been good to have King too, but that unelected butterfly, still on the wing in the United States, was hard to catch when there was neither net nor honey. King's wishes remained unchanged and so did his conditions, spoken or not. He did not propose to give up what he had for the random hurly-burly of politics outside of parliament. He wanted a nomination to a safe seat. He would be in Chicago, he wrote on January 23, for three or four weeks and then would go on to New York 'if there is nothing sufficiently important to take me to Ottawa in the interval'.

'It seems to me', King ruminated piously in his letter, 'that very little is needed to rally the progressive forces around the standard of Liberalism at this time, and I do hope that some of our friends will be bold and brave enough to sanction a course which would surmount local fears, prejudices, and jealousies and make possible the beginning of a real reconstruction, industrially, socially, and politically, in Canada.' To that Laurier could only respond Amen and repeat an old suggestion. 'Your better course is to stay in Canada and deliver as many speeches as you can without waiting for an official candidature.'

The course was too rash for King, but by January 30 he had at least been persuaded to give up a plan of going to England on behalf of the Rockefellers. 'My heart and my will are with my own country and only the lack of opportunity of service there at all comparable with that which lies before me through the connections I have formed here would lead me to take any step which might mean a severance of my life relations with Canada.' It came still from the United States and still with steel in the velvet. The wheedling went on. By February 9 Montreal Liberals were urging King to visit the city and address the Canadian Club. 'This desire', Laurier wrote, 'I share absolutely.'

On February 12 he wrote again. There was a convention of Ontario Liberals planned in Toronto. King's presence was indispensable, so much so that if he could not arrange to be present on the date set the date would be changed. The tone of the leader was becoming a little peremptory, though pleasantly and flatteringly so. Laurier was conducting negotiations that were as delicate as they were urgent. King's book *Industry and Humanity* was now circulating and was much talked of. King's speeches, when he made them, struck with powerful impact on a country plagued with post-war labour troubles. The man would be good for the party and good for the nation, but not quite yet in the role he expected to fill. Sought and besought as he was, even a less eager man than King might be justified in thinking he was sought as the next leader. He had obviously treasured every word of the careful half-promises of the past several years. Yet they remained half-promises.

No one could give more and Laurier, in private, offered a little less. When conversation turned to the question of the leadership and all ears were cocked he was fond of telling the story of the old habitant who had buried two wives and was about to join them. 'Bury me between them,' he had said, 'but cant me a little toward Cécile.' Laurier canted toward Fielding. There would be less strain in the party, fewer jealousies. Now, as one's eyes closed during the long discussions and one's head nodded and the voices grew faint, one thought more often of the old days, more affectionately of the old men. Fielding was seventy. He would lead well but not for long. King was indispensable, the man of the future, but he would be the better for a little seasoning. His time would come.

Politics went on as usual, the real purposes honest enough but lying deep. They were still going on the following Saturday noon as Laurier stepped out of the car in front of the big hotel that bore his name. It was February 15, sunny and pleasant, with that far-off promise of spring that February sometimes offers. The luncheon of the Canadian Club was about as usual and the old man drowsed a little as a guest speaker enlarged on the territorial claims Serbia was likely to make at the Peace Conference. Then he was back in the quiet of the empty office with the papers in front of him. A letter from Peter Larkin. A letter from Pugsley.

He seemed to be a little dizzy and rose from his chair. Then he was on the floor; he seemed to have struck his head against the desk. Everything came right again as he stood up, but he turned carefully and shrugged into his coat. He would be better at home. He made a move to telephone for the chauffeur and changed his mind. There would be questions, commotion, rumour. The streetcar stopped at the corner and he could manage the stairs all right. He closed his scarf round his throat, took up his hat and stick, and in a minute or so was rattling home through the streets of this Ottawa he had never got round to making the Washington of the North.

If he was pale when he got home Zoë was unable to see it. If she suspected anything she said nothing. 'I feel that my strength is slowly ebbing away'; it had lain between them for many months. He could not touch dinner but that was common enough. Sleep was as usual, a succession of dozes linked by the marching memories, nagged by tomorrow's problems. He was dressing for Mass in the morning as the second blow struck.

When he was conscious again he was in bed and the lights were on. It was early evening. Zoë was sitting near by much as usual. Sister Marcelline, his favourite of many nuns who had nursed him, was moving around the room. He smiled at her. 'Well. It is the bride of the Divine Husband who comes to help a great sinner.' Then it was later, with the sense of deeper night. Zoë was looking down at him; did he wish the priest? It was hardly a question. 'Very well,' he said, 'but I am not so sick as you think. Only a little weak.'

The glow of candles and vestments grew about him. He felt the oil on his forehead and listened attentively to the words. How many times had he stood looking down on others, hearing the solemn Godspeed? – Henri, the favourite – the other brothers – Adeline – Carolus – the line reached back to Malvina and the misty face of Marcelle Martineau Laurier. There were living forms in the room, a murmurous hush of waiting. The third blow came, abrupt and suffocating, and his hand moved in Zoë's. The words were a breath from darkness: 'C'est fini.'

For two days, when it was all over, he lay in the house on Laurier Avenue while the friends came and went. Zoë was there to greet them and be greeted. In the lonelier hours she sat with the still watchers, her face grave in the candlelight, biding her own time. It would be nearly three years yet. At five o'clock on the afternoon of February 20, the day parliament convened, he passed to the hands of the government for the lying-in-state and the state funeral. 'Do you think we can trust the buggers with the old man's body?' asked Murphy, out of his black Irish grief.

They could be trusted. The gaunt museum hall that still served as a Commons chamber was heavy with massed flowers and hung with the colours of mourning. Even the floor was strewn with a profusion of petals. One chair and one desk stood in their accustomed places, draped in purple and black. The ranked hundreds of the others had been taken away. There was no aisle of division as the casket was carried in. For forty-eight hours, as the thousands shuffled by, it stood in the centre of the floor. Then it was gone. The chairs came back, the aisle returned as was fitting. Over the wide country the flags climbed on their staffs again, and the man became the memory.

A Note on Sources

THE PRINCIPAL published sources of material used in this work are indicated by the list of books and publications that follows. Of these, the *Life and Letters of Sir Wilfrid Laurier,* written by Oscar D. Skelton and published in 1921, would stand first. The biography by Sir John Willison and the all-too-short memorials written by L.-O. David have been much referred to. Mason Wade's *The French Canadians* has been constantly at hand, as have the *Histoire de la Province de Québec* and other historical and biographical works of Robert Rumilly. Lucien Pacaud's collection *Letters to My Father and Mother,* supplemented by consultation of the actual letters in the Public Archives of Canada, has provided many valuable insights.

I am much indebted to the writings of Professor Frank H. Underhill, and of other scholars, in the learned journals; to the doctoral thesis 'Laurier and a Liberal Quebec' written by Professor H. Blair Neatby, to the graduate thesis 'Laurier, citoyen d'Arthabaska' by Frère Antoine, S.C., and to the paper 'Correspondance Laurier—Mme Joseph Lavergne, 1891-3', read by Professor Marc La Terreur before the Canadian Historical Association in June 1964.

Manuscript and other sources consulted are indicated in the notes, and of these the principal was the large collection of Laurier Papers in the Public Archives of Canada.

Books and Publications Used

ABERDEEN AND TEMAIR, John Campbell Hamilton Gordon, 1st Marquess, and Lady Aberdeen. *We Twa,* Reminiscences of Lord and Lady Aberdeen. 2 vols. London: W. Collins Sons & Co., 1925.

FRÈRE ANTOINE, S. C. (Maurice Carrier). 'Laurier, citoyen d'Arthabaska'. Unpublished thesis, University of Ottawa.

ASSELIN, Olivar. *L'Action Catholique – les évêques et la guerre.* Pamphlet published by the author, Montreal, 1914.

BANKS, Margaret A. 'The Change in Liberal Party Leadership'. *Canadian Historical Review,* June 1957.

———. *Edward Blake, Irish Nationalist: A Canadian Statesman in Irish Politics.* University of Toronto Press, 1957.

BARTHE, Ulric. *Wilfrid Laurier on the Platform.* Quebec: Turcotte & Ménard, 1890.

BÉIQUE, Caroline. *Quatre-vingts ans de souvenirs.* Montreal: L'Action Canadienne-Française, 1939.

BORDEN, Henry, ed. *Robert Laird Borden, His Memoirs.* 2 vols. Toronto: Macmillan, 1938.

BOURASSA, Henri. *La conférence impériale.* Pamphlet. Montreal: Le Devoir, 1927.

———. *Conscription.* Pamphlet. Montreal: Le Devoir, 1917.

———. *The Duty of Canada at the Present Hour.* Pamphlet. Montreal: Le Devoir, 1914.

———. *Great Britain and Canada.* Lecture delivered at Montreal, October 20, 1901. Pamphlet. Montreal: Imprimerie du Pionnier, 1901.

———. *Great Britain and Canada.* Preface to English edition. Montreal: Editions Beauchemin, 1902.

———. *Pour la justice.* Speech at Monument National, March 9, 1912. Pamphlet. Montreal: Le Devoir, 1912.

———. *Le projet de la loi navale.* Speech at Monument National, January 20, 1910. Pamphlet. Montreal: Bureau du Devoir, 1910.

———. *The Reciprocity Agreement.* Pamphlet. Montreal: Le Devoir, 1911.

———. *The Spectre of Annexation.* Pamphlet. Montreal: Le Devoir, 1912.

BRUCHÉSI, Jean. *Histoire du Canada.* Montreal: Editions Beauchemin, 1959.

———. 'Sir Wilfrid Laurier et Monseigneur Bruchési'. Royal Society of Canada, vol. 40, 3rd series, sec. 1, 1946.

BUCHAN, John. *Lord Minto.* London: Nelson, 1924.

BUCKINGHAM, William, and Sir George William Ross. *The Hon. Alexander Mackenzie – His Life and Times.* Toronto: Dent, 1892.

CAMERON, A. Kirk. 'Memorandum of Significant Events and Actions in the Life of Rt. Hon. William Stevens Fielding'. Unpublished note prepared for Norman McL. Rogers.

CARTWRIGHT, Richard J. *Reminiscences.* Toronto: William Briggs, 1912.

COLLARD, E. A. *Oldest McGill.* Toronto: Macmillan, 1946.

COOK, Ramsay. 'Dafoe, Laurier and the Formation of Union Government'. *Canadian Historical Review,* September 1961.

CREIGHTON, Donald. *John A. Macdonald.* 2 vols. Toronto: Macmillan, 1952, 1955.

DAFOE, John. *Clifford Sifton in Relation to His Times.* Toronto: Macmillan, 1931.

———. *Laurier: A Study in Canadian Politics.* Toronto: Thomas Allen, 1922.

DAVID, Laurent-Olivier. *Laurier, sa vie, ses oeuvres.* Beauceville: L'Eclaireur, Limitée, 1919.

———. *Laurier et son temps.* Montreal: La Cie de Publication de *La Patrie* Ltée, 1905.

———. *Mes contemporains.* Montreal: Eusèbe Sénécal & Fils, Imprimeurs, 1894.

DAWSON, R. MacGregor. *William Lyon Mackenzie King: 1874-1923.* University of Toronto Press, 1958.

DE CELLES, Alfred D. *Discours de Sir Wilfrid Laurier.* 2 vols. Montreal: Librairie Beauchemin Ltée, 1920.

DUNDONALD, D. M. B. Hamilton, 12th Earl. *My Army Life.* London: Arnold, 1926.

EAYRS, James. 'The Round Table Movement in Canada, 1909-1920'. *Canadian Historical Review,* March 1957.

FRASER, Barbara. 'The Political Career of Sir Hector Langevin'. *Canadian Historical Review,* June 1961.

FRÉCHETTE, Louis. *Laurier.* Men of the Day, 2nd series. Montreal: Louis N. Taché, 1890.

GRAHAM, Gerald S. *Empire of the North Atlantic.* University of Toronto Press, 1958.

GRAHAM, W. R. 'Sir Richard Cartwright, Wilfrid Laurier, and Liberal Party Trade Policy, 1887'. *Canadian Historical Review,* March 1952.

HAM, George. *Reminiscences of a Raconteur.* Toronto: Musson, 1921.

HARVEY, D. C. 'Fielding's Call to Ottawa'.

HOPKINS, John Castell. *The Life and Work of the Rt. Hon. Sir John Thompson.* Toronto: United Publishing Houses, 1895.

LANDON, Fred. 'A Canadian Cabinet Episode of 1897'. Transactions of the Royal Society of Canada, 3rd series, sec. 2, vol. 32, 1938.

LANGELIER, Charles. *Souvenirs politiques de 1878 à 1900.* 2 vols. Quebec: Dussault & Proulx, 1909.

LA PIERRE, L. L. 'Joseph Israel Tarte and the McGreevy-Langevin Scandal'. Canadian Historical Association, Report of the Annual Meeting, June 1961.

LA TERREUR, Marc. 'Correspondance Laurier–Mme Joseph Lavergne, 1891-3'. Canadian Historical Association, Report of Annual Meeting, June 1964.

LOWER, Arthur R. M. *Canadians in the Making.* Toronto: Longmans, 1958.

———. *Colony to Nation.* Toronto: Longmans, 1946.

LUCAS, C. P., ed. *Lord Durham's Report on the Affairs of British North America.* 3 vols. Oxford; Clarendon Press, 1912.

MCARTHUR, Peter. *Sir Wilfrid Laurier.* Toronto: Dent, 1919.

MACDONALD, Adrian. *Canadian Portraits.* Toronto: Ryerson, 1925.

MCGREGOR, F. A. *The Fall and Rise of Mackenzie King.* Toronto: Macmillan, 1962.

MACMILLAN, Cyrus. *McGill and Its Story.* London: J. Lane, 1931.

MAILHOT, Abbé C. E. *Les bois-francs.* Imprimerie d'Arthabaska, 1914-25.

MOREAU, Henri. *Sir Wilfrid Laurier.* Paris: Plon-Nourrit et Cie, 1902.

NADEAU, Gabriel. 'Le plus illustre de nos poitrinaires'. *Bulletin de l'Association des médecins de langue française de l'Amérique du nord,* April 1944.

NEATBY, H. Blair. 'Laurier and a Liberal Quebec'. Unpublished doctoral thesis, University of Toronto.

———, and John T. Saywell. 'Chapleau and the Conservative Party in Quebec'. *Canadian Historical Review,* March 1956.

PACAUD, Lucien. *Sir Wilfrid Laurier – Letters to My Father and Mother.* Toronto: Ryerson, 1935.

PARKMAN, Francis. *The Jesuits in North America.* Toronto: George N. Morang & Company, 1899.

QUIGLEY, Carroll. 'The Round Table Groups in Canada, 1908-38'. *Canadian Historical Review,* September 1962.

ROSE, George MacLean, ed. *Representative Canadians – A Cyclopedia of Canadian Biography.* Toronto: Hunter, Rose, and Company, 1888.

RUMILLY, Robert. *Henri Bourassa.* Montreal: Les Editions Chantecler, Ltée, 1953.

———. *Histoire de la province de Québec.* 26 vols. Montreal: Montréal Editions.

———. *Mercier.* Montreal: Les Editions du Zodiaque, 1936.

———. *Mgr. Laflèche et son temps.* Montreal: Les Editions du Zodiaque, 1938.

———. *Sir Wilfrid Laurier.* Paris: Ernest Flammarion, 1931.

SAYWELL, John T., ed. *The Canadian Journal of Lady Aberdeen.* Toronto: Champlain Society, 1960.

SKELTON, Oscar D. *The Day of Sir Wilfrid Laurier.* Chronicles of Canada Series. Toronto: Glasgow, Brook and Company, 1916.

———. *Life and Letters of Sir Wilfrid Laurier.* 2 vols. Toronto: Oxford, 1921.

STANLEY, G. F. G. *Louis Riel – Patriot or Rebel?* Ottawa: Canadian Historical Association, 1954.

STEVENS, G. R. *Canadian National Railways.* Toronto: Clarke, Irwin, 1960.

TUPPER, Sir Charles. *Recollections of Sixty Years.* London: Cassell, 1914.

UNDERHILL, Frank H. 'Edward Blake'. Essay in *Our Living Tradition.* University of Toronto Press, 1957.

———. 'Edward Blake, the Liberal Party, and Unrestricted Reciprocity'. Paper delivered to the Canadian Historical Association, June 1939.

———. *The Image of Confederation.* Reprint by Canadian Broadcasting Corporation of Massey Lectures, 1963.

———. *In Search of Canadian Liberalism.* Toronto: Macmillan, 1960.

———. 'Laurier and Blake, 1882-1891'. *Canadian Historical Review,* December 1939.

———. 'Laurier and Blake, 1891-2'. *Canadian Historical Review,* June 1943.

VAUGHAN, Walter. *The Life and Work of Sir William Van Horne.* New York: Century, 1920.

WADE, Mason. *The French Canadians, 1760-1945.* Toronto: Macmillan, 1955.

WALLACE, W. Stewart, ed. *The Memoirs of the Rt. Hon. Sir George Foster.* Toronto: Macmillan, 1933.

WILLIAMS, A. M. 'Conscription, 1917: A Brief for the Defence'. *Canadian Historical Review,* December 1956.

WILLISON, Sir John. *Reminiscences Political and Personal.* Toronto: McClelland & Stewart, 1919.

———. *Sir Wilfrid Laurier.* The Makers of Canada Series. London and Toronto: Oxford, 1927.

YOUNG, James. *Public Men and Public Life in Canada.* 2 vols. Toronto: William Briggs, 1912.

Notes

ix Quoted in John Dafoe, *Laurier: A Study in Canadian Politics* (Toronto: Thomas Allen, 1922), pp. 95-6.

Chapter One

pg. ln.

2 34 Instructions to Governor Murray, December 7, 1763, W. P. M. Kennedy, *Documents of the Canadian Constitution, 1759-1915* (Toronto: Oxford, 1918), p. 27.
5 4 *Oldest McGill*, by E. A. Collard.
14 *McGill and Its Story*, by Cyrus Macmillan.
26 *Ibid.*
6 4 Montreal *Gazette*, May 5, 1864.
7 15 Report of Proceedings of Convocation, McGill, 1864.
8 1 *Ibid.* (translation).
12 Montreal *Gazette*, May 5, 1864.
24 Francis Parkman, *The Jesuits in North America*, vol. II, p. 8.
13 21 *Lord Durham's Report on the Affairs of British North America*, edited by Sir C. P. Lucas.
32 *Ibid.*
14 11 Stephen Leacock, *Mackenzie, Baldwin, Lafontaine, Hincks*, The Makers of Canada Series (Toronto: Oxford, 1926), vol. 5, p. 379.
15 9 Durham Report.
16 26 Letter, Dr. Francis Duquet, September 14, 1855, Musée Laurier, Arthabaska.
17 17 Carolus Laurier, quoted in O. D. Skelton, *Life and Letters of Sir Wilfrid Laurier*, vol. I, p. 27.
29 Charles Laurier, *ibid.*, p. 23.
34 *Ibid.*, p. 24.
18 14 PAC: Laurier, 807-9, 121-37.
26 PAC: Neilson Papers, 5, 317-20.
19 4 PAC: Laurier, 807-9, 38-44.
20 9 Peter McArthur, *Sir Wilfrid Laurier*, p. 11.
26 Skelton, vol. I, p. 30.
22 23 *Ibid.*, p. 35.
30 Sir John Willison, *Sir Wilfrid Laurier*, vol. I, p. 32.

Chapter Two

pg. ln.

29 21 Skelton, vol. I, p. 97.
39 2 Quoted by Léon Trépanier in *La Patrie*, September 19, 1954, and March 31, 1957.
42 11 Translation of lines quoted by Léon Trépanier in *La Patrie*, March 31, 1957.

43 35 *Parliamentary Debates on the Subject of the Confederation of the British North American Provinces* (Quebec: Hunter, Rose & Co., 1865; Ottawa: King's Printer, 1951), February 3, 1865.
44 7 *Ibid.*
29 Mason Wade, *The French Canadians*, p. 350, quoting Bishop Laflèche.
33 Confederation Debates, p. 856, March 6, 1865.
45 26 *Ibid.*, p. 858.
29 *Ibid.*, p. 263.
34 *Ibid.*, p. 863.
46 6 *Ibid.*, p. 252.
15 *Ibid.*, p. 657.
23 *Ibid.*, March 14, 1865.
48 3 Louis Fréchette, *Laurier*.
49 20 L.-O. David, *Mes contemporains*, p. 85.
50 19 L.-O. David, *Laurier, sa vie, ses oeuvres*, p. 6.

Chapter Three

pg. ln.
51 11 Willison, *Laurier*, vol. I, p. 109.
52 7 Abbé C. E. Mailhot, *Les bois-francs*.
26 Frère Antoine, S.C. (Maurice Carrier), 'Laurier, citoyen d'Arthabaska', has supplied much material for Laurier's life in Arthabaska.
55 29 *Ibid.*
56 23 Robert Rumilly, *Mgr. Laflèche et son temps*, pp. 26-7.
37 Willison, *Laurier*, vol. I, p. 109.
57 2 *Ibid.*, p. 111.
58 2 *Ibid.*, pp. 113 ff.
31 Confederation Debates, p. 59, February 7, 1865.
60 5 Willison, *Laurier*, vol. I, pp. 121-2.
37 George MacLean Rose, *Representative Canadians – A Cyclopedia of Canadian Biography*, p. 453.
61 26 'Laurier, citoyen d'Arthabaska'.
36 Abridged and free translation of poem quoted in Skelton, vol. I, pp. 42-3n.
66 30 Part of the account that follows is from Skelton, vol. I, pp. 40 ff; part from Léon Trépanier in *La Patrie*, September 19, 1954; more supplied by Mme L.-H. Gariépy (Jacqueline Migneau), niece of Yvonne Coutu.

Chapter Four

pg. ln.
71 4 Lucien Pacaud, *Sir Wilfrid Laurier – Letters to My Father and Mother*, p. 147.
81 15 'Laurier, citoyen d'Arthabaska'.
28 Wade, *The French Canadians*, p. 352.
82 11 Rumilly, *Laflèche*, pp. 59-60.
84 30 'Laurier, citoyen d'Arthabaska'.
37 *Ibid.*
85 10 *Ibid.*
21 *Ibid.*
86 13 PAC: Laurier, 47-8.
87 10 'Laurier, citoyen d'Arthabaska'.
27 David, *Laurier, sa vie, ses oeuvres*, p. 15.
30 *Ibid.*, p. 13.
88 13 Ulric Barthe, *Wilfrid Laurier on the Platform*, p. 8.
89 29 Skelton, vol. I, p. 119.

90 2 Wade, *The French Canadians*, p. 358.
18 Skelton, vol. I, pp. 131-2n.
94 17 James Young, *Public Men and Public Life in Canada*, vol. II, p. 190.
31 *Ibid.*
95 4 Toronto *Globe*, March 31, 1874.
10 Parliamentary Debates, Library of Parliament, March 30, 1874.

Chapter Five

pg. ln.
98 29 William Buckingham and Sir George Ross, *The Hon. Alexander Mackenzie – His Life and Times*, p. 263.
99 30 Skelton, vol. I, p. 197; Parliamentary Debates, Library of Parliament, April 16, 1874.
100 20 Willison, *Laurier*, vol. I, p. 192.
32 PAC: Laurier, 148400.
101 5 *Ibid.*, 148399.
9 *Ibid.*
21 *Ibid.*, 148407-9.
102 25 Skelton, vol. I, p. 222n.
105 25 PAC: Mackenzie Papers, 1046g.
106 16 Willison, *Laurier*, vol. I, p. 265.
23 Bishop Bourget, Pastoral Letters.
38 PAC: Laurier, 148416.
107 24 Hansard, March 10, 1876, p. 589.
108 12 Willison, *Laurier*, vol. I, pp. 287-8.
19 Skelton, vol. I, pp. 139-40.
24 Willison, *Laurier*, vol. I, pp. 287-8.
109 12 PAC: Laurier, 148420.
17 *Ibid.*, 148423-4.
20 *Ibid.*, 148426.
110 3 *Ibid.*, 148428-9.

Chapter Six

pg. ln.
112 22 Hansard, March 22, 1877.
113 18 Pacaud, *Letters*, p. 6.
116 7 PAC: Mackenzie Papers, 105.
20 *Ibid.*
117 12 *Ibid.*, 1637-8.
118 11 *Ibid.*, pp. 51 ff.
122 12 PAC: Mackenzie Papers, 1693.
27 Wade, *The French Canadians*, p. 369.
33 Rumilly, *Laflèche*, p. 124.
123 18 'Laurier, citoyen d'Arthabaska'.
32 *Ibid.*
124 13 PAC: Mackenzie Papers, 1712.
125 7 Skelton, vol. I, pp. 211-12.
32 PAC: Mackenzie Papers, 1713.
126 4 Skelton, vol. I, p. 214.
20 Ottawa *Free Press*, November 6, 1877.
24 PAC: Mackenzie Papers, 1721.
127 15 *Ibid.*
28 Toronto *Globe*, November 17, 1877.
128 1 David, *Laurier, sa vie, ses oeuvres*, p. 27.

13 Ottawa *Free Press*, November 14, 1877.
25 *Ibid.*, November 23, 1877.
130 6 Skelton, vol. I, pp. 215-16.
29 PAC: Pacaud Papers, 777-9.
131 9 Toronto *Globe*, December 5, 1877.
38 Ottawa *Free Press*, December 6, 1877.

Chapter Seven

pg. ln.
133 28 Skelton, vol. I, pp. 154-5.
36 Richard J. Cartwright, *Reminiscences*, Appendix H, p. 388.
136 36 Skelton, vol. I, p. 242.
141 9 *Ibid.*, pp. 220-1.
16 Hansard, April 27, 1880.
142 10 PAC: Mackenzie Papers, 2360-1.
144 37 Hansard, December 14, 1880.
145 13 *Ibid.*
27 *Ibid.*
35 *Ibid.*, December 21, 1880.
146 19 *Ibid.*
26 Donald Creighton, *John A. Macdonald*, vol. II, p. 310.

Chapter Eight

pg. ln.
148 31 Skelton, vol. I, pp. 241-2.
149 33 Charles Langelier, *Souvenirs politiques*, vol. I, p. 159.
150 30 Montreal *Gazette*, November 12, 1881.
151 8 Blake Papers, Ontario Public Archives, Laurier to Blake, July 10, 1882.
152 16 *Ibid.*
23 *Ibid.*
29 *Ibid.*
156 24 Pacaud, *Letters*, p. 15.
157 14 Hansard, February 19, 1884.
36 *Ibid.*, April 9, 1884, p. 1444.
158 23 *Ibid.*, April 12, 1884, pp. 1539 ff.
159 19 *Ibid.*, March 18, 1884, pp. 945 ff.
160 20 Insurance policy and application at Château de Ramezay, Montreal.
162 8 'Laurier, citoyen d'Arthabaska'.
25 *Ibid.*
32 *Ibid.*
35 *Ibid.*
163 17 Robert Rumilly, *Sir Wilfrid Laurier*, pp. 72-4.
165 6 Barthe, *Laurier on the Platform*, pp. 171 ff.

Chapter Nine

pg. ln.
167 14 Rumilly, *Laflèche*, p. 208.
170 16 Creighton, *Macdonald*, vol. II, p. 407.
171 29 *Ibid.*, p. 419.
174 4 Hansard, April 17, 1885, pp. 1167 ff.
30 Creighton, *Macdonald*, vol. II, p. 427.
175 4 Wade, *The French Canadians*, p. 412.
176 37 Hansard, July 7, 1885, pp. 3119 ff.
177 16 George F. G. Stanley, *Louis Riel – Patriot or Rebel?*, p. 23.

20 Attributed. See R. M. Hamilton, *Canadian Quotations and Phrases* (Toronto: McClelland, 1952), p. 200.
32 *La Presse*, Montreal, November 16, 1885.
178 5 *Ibid.*, November 23, 1885. Also Wade, *The French Canadians*, p. 417.
9 *La Presse*, Montreal, November 23, 1885. Also Skelton, vol. I, p. 314.
179 2 Wade, *The French Canadians*, p. 419.
31 Blake Papers, Laurier to Blake, December 31, 1885.
180 10 Skelton, vol. I, p. 318.
37 David, *Laurier, sa vie, ses oeuvres*, p. 49.
183 21 Hansard, March 16, 1886.
36 *Ibid.*, March 19, 1886.

Chapter Ten

pg. ln.
185 25 Skelton, vol. I, p. 27.
186 9 Rodolphe Lemieux, quoted in Barthe, *Laurier on the Platform*, p. x.
187 19 Barthe, *Laurier on the Platform*, pp. 303 ff.
190 5 Margaret A. Banks, 'The Change in Liberal Party Leadership'.
191 5 PAC: Laurier, 411-18.
13 *Ibid.*, 423.
27 *Ibid.*, 427.
192 5 Blake Papers, Laurier to Blake, March 16, 1887.
16 Banks, 'The Change in Liberal Party Leadership'.
29 PAC: Laurier, 433.
193 32 At Musée Laurier, Arthabaska.
195 30 Skelton, vol. I, p. 341.
196 15 *Ibid.*, p. 342.
24 Banks, 'The Change in Liberal Party Leadership'.
30 *Ibid.*
33 *Ibid.*
197 20 *Ibid.*
198 12 Willison, *Reminiscences Political and Personal*, p. 160.
23 Copy of letter supplied to writer by Professor Frank H. Underhill.
38 Blake Papers, Laurier to Blake, June 18, 1887.
199 12 PAC: Laurier, 460.
19 Banks, 'The Change in Liberal Party Leadership'.
27 *Ibid.*
34 *Ibid.*
200 13 PAC: Pacaud Papers, 103-7.

Chapter Eleven

pg. ln.
201 3 Blake Papers, Laurier to Blake, June 30, 1887.
15 PAC: Laurier, 537.
205 3 *Ibid.*, 460.
11 Blake Papers, Laurier to Blake, July 14, 1887.
18 PAC: Laurier, 208111-13.
31 Montreal *Gazette*, August 3, 1887.
207 33 Barthe, *Laurier on the Platform*, pp. 353 ff.
211 13 PAC: Laurier, 208114-19.
22 W. R. Graham, 'Sir Richard Cartwright, Wilfrid Laurier, and Liberal Party Trade Policy, 1887'.
28 *Ibid.*
36 PAC: Laurier, 208128-32.

212 17 W. R. Graham, *op. cit.*
21 *Ibid.*
26 *Ibid.*
213 3 Toronto *Globe*, December 31, 1887.
24 PAC: Laurier, 208190.
29 Frank H. Underhill, 'Laurier and Blake, 1882-1891'; also W. R. Graham, *op. cit.*
214 27 Hansard, March 14, 1888, p. 144.
215 21 Blake Papers, Laurier to Blake, March 29, 1888.
216 6 *Ibid.*
11 Creighton, *Macdonald*, vol. II, p. 495.
13 *Ibid.*, p. 494.
217 15 Hansard, April 5, 1888, pp. 554 ff.
220 15 Underhill, 'Laurier and Blake, 1882-1891'.
27 *Ibid.*
221 7 *Ibid.*
222 8 Cartwright, *Reminiscences*, p. 275.
30 Willison, *Reminiscences*, pp. 162-4.
226 23 Hansard, March 28, 1889, pp. 897 ff.
37 *Ibid.*
227 13 Wade, *The French Canadians*, p. 425.
22 Willison, *Laurier*, vol. II, p. 53.
33 Wade, *The French Canadians*, p. 423.
228 6 Rumilly, *Mercier*, p. 364.
24 Barthe, *Laurier on the Platform*, pp. 535 ff.

Chapter Twelve

pg. ln.
231 16 PAC: Laurier, 1060.
20 *Ibid.*, 1073.
24 *Ibid.*, 1067.
232 11 *Ibid.*, 1010.
234 4 Barthe, *Laurier on the Platform*, pp. 535 ff.
30 Willison, *Reminiscences*, p. 174.
235 7 Willison, August 30, 1889, quoted in Barthe, *Laurier on the Platform*, pp. xi ff.
22 PAC: Laurier, 1889.
36 PAC: Pacaud Papers, 339-42.
237 16 Hansard, January 29, 1890, p. 133.
23 PAC: Pacaud Papers, 346-9.
38 Bills, House of Commons, 1890, vol. I, Bill 10.
240 38 Hansard, February 17, 1890, pp. 726 ff.
241 9 Skelton, vol. I, p. 445.
35 PAC: Pacaud Papers, 351-2.
245 5 L. L. LaPierre, 'Joseph Israel Tarte and the McGreevy-Langevin Scandal'.
15 PAC: Pacaud Papers, 357.
32 Langelier, *Souvenirs politiques*, vol. II, pp. 43-4.
247 2 Toronto *Globe*, July 3, 1890.
250 3 Frank H. Underhill, 'Edward Blake, The Liberal Party and Unrestricted Reciprocity'.
20 Creighton, *Macdonald*, vol. II, pp. 552-3.
251 2 Willison, *Laurier*, vol. II, pp. 165-6.
30 Pacaud, *Letters*, p. 57.
252 17 Skelton, vol. I, p. 417.

36 Blake Papers, Laurier to Blake, February 2, 1891, and March 3, 1891.
253 6 PAC: Laurier, 1637.
29 Toronto *Globe*, March 6, 1891.
254 17 Langelier, *Souvenirs politiques*, vol. II, p. 91.
18 Creighton, *Macdonald*, vol. II, p. 560.
30 John Dafoe, *Laurier: A Study in Canadian Politics*, p. 105.
255 26 Hansard, June 8, 1891.
36 PAC: Pacaud Papers, 397.
256 14 Willison, *Reminiscences*, p. 176.
33 Hansard, June 8, 1891, p. 885.
257 13 Senate Debates, June 17, 1891, p. 98.
258 1 PAC: Laurier, 1883.
15 Blake Papers, Laurier to Blake, July 19, 1891, and August 1, 1891.
32 Marc La Terreur. 'Correspondance Laurier–Mme Joseph Lavergne, 1891-3'.
259 4 Frank H. Underhill, 'Laurier and Blake, 1891-2'.
14 Blake Papers, Laurier to Blake, August 1, 1891.
17 La Terreur, 'Correspondance'.
23 PAC: Laurier, 1907.
33 *Ibid.*, 2041.
260 4 Blake Papers, Laurier to Blake, December 29, 1891.

Chapter Thirteen

pg. ln.
261 11 Blake Papers, Laurier to Blake, April 13, 1892.
263 22 *Ibid.*, April 29, 1892.
264 21 Underhill, 'Laurier and Blake, 1891-2'. Blake Papers, Blake to Mills, March 23, 1892.
34 Blake Papers, Laurier to Blake, April 29, 1892.
265 13 Underhill, 'Laurier and Blake, 1891-2'.
23 Blake Papers, Laurier to Blake, June 17, 1892.
28 Underhill, 'Laurier and Blake, 1891-2'.
266 29 Cartwright, *Reminiscences*, pp. 389 ff.
268 27 Application at Château de Ramezay, Montreal.
Hansard, March 7, 1911. Quoted by Laurier.
270 3 Quoted from the *Globe*, June 20, 1893, by John W. Lederle in *Canadian Journal of Economics and Political Science*, February 1950.
274 14 Hansard, March 8, 1893, pp. 1997-2001.
276 26 La Terreur, 'Correspondance'.
280 1 *Ibid.*
14 *Ibid.* Also 'Laurier, citoyen d'Arthabaska'.
20 La Terreur, 'Correspondance'.
281 12 Rumilly, *Mercier*, p. 51.
283 29 Willison, *Laurier*, vol. II, pp. 489 ff.
284 22 Pacaud, *Letters*, pp. 75-7.
28 *Ibid.*, p. 80.
287 13 *Manitoba Free Press*, September 4, 1894.
288 25 *Ibid.*, September 7, 1894.

Chapter Fourteen

pg. ln.
290 An important reference for this chapter has been *The Canadian Journal of Lady Aberdeen*, Champlain Society Edition, edited with an introduction by John T. Saywell.
291 12 Aberdeen Journal, Introduction, p. xl.

35 *Ibid.*, p. xlii.
293 33 *Ibid.*, p. xliv.
294 8 *Ibid.*, p. 172.
23 George Ham, *Reminiscences of a Raconteur*, p. 102.
295 15 Aberdeen Journal, p. 172.
296 19 *Ibid.*, Introduction, p. xlv.
297 8 Dafoe, *Laurier*, p. 43.
298 6 Aberdeen Journal, Introduction, p. xlvii.
299 4 PAC: Pacaud Papers, 492-3.
300 25 PAC: Laurier, 3732.
301 18 *Ibid.*, 3733-4.
303 22 Aberdeen Journal, p. 238.
304 19 Hansard, July 15, 1895, pp. 4389-90.
28 Toronto *Globe*, October 9, 1877.
36 *Ibid.*
305 37 D. C. Harvey, 'Fielding's Call to Ottawa'.
307 15 Hansard, January 7, 1896.
34 Aberdeen Journal, p. 303.
308 8 *Ibid.*, p. 301.
23 *Ibid.*, p. 304.
310 6 *Ibid.*, p. 307.
38 *Ibid.*, p. 309.
311 34 Hansard, January 15, 1896.
312 6 *Ibid.*
313 18 Skelton, vol. I, pp. 470-1.
23 Aberdeen Journal, Introduction, p. lix.
314 37 Hansard, March 3, 1896.
316 17 *Ibid.*
318 1 *Ibid.*, April 15, 1896.
19 Dafoe, *Laurier*, p. 43.
319 10 Willison, *Reminiscences*, p. 161.
27 'Laurier, citoyen d'Arthabaska'.
320 20 Aberdeen Journal, p. 351.

Chapter Fifteen

pg. *ln.*
322 2 Aberdeen Journal, p. 361.
325 23 PAC: Laurier, 4384.
326 13 *Ibid.*, 6990-1.
331 31 Skelton, vol. II, pp. 15-16.
332 13 PAC: Laurier, 8635-7.
333 2 Skelton, vol. II, p. 20.
334 28 PAC: Pacaud Papers, 569-71.
33 Skelton, vol. II, p. 24.
335 3 *Ibid.*, vol. II, p. 31.
14 Proulx Papers, Séminaire Ste-Thérèse, copy of letter Laurier to David, March 28, 1896.
32 PAC: Laurier, 9624.

Chapter Sixteen

pg. *ln.*
336 14 John Dafoe, *Clifford Sifton in Relation to His Times*, pp. 105-6.
339 22 PAC: Laurier, 11019-20.
340 14 Fred Landon, 'A Canadian Cabinet Episode of 1897', p. 49.

342 37 Proulx Papers, Séminaire Ste-Thérèse, copy of letter Laurier to Proulx, March 22, 1897.
344 5 Hansard, April 23, 1897.
11 *Ibid.*, April 22, 1897.
31 *Ibid.*, April 26, 1897.
345 1 *Ibid.*, May 28, 1897.
12 Skelton, vol. II, pp. 57-8.
36 *Ibid.*, vol. II, p. 40.
348 8 PAC: Laurier, 13049, 13051, 13053.
353 18 Consulted for Jubilee description: Skelton, vol II, pp. 59-84; Richard Harding Davis in *Harper's* Magazine, December 1897; *London Illustrated News*, June 1897; *The Times*, June 1897.
355 18 Skelton, vol. II, p. 22.
21 John Buchan, *Lord Minto*, p. 127.
357 29 Skelton, vol. II, p. 77.
37 *Ibid.*, pp. 70-1.
360 1 David, *Laurier, sa vie, ses oeuvres*, p. 113.

Chapter Seventeen

pg. ln.
361 3 Skelton, vol. II, p. 67.
19 Story told writer by Professor Frank H. Underhill.
363 24 Skelton, vol. II, p. 126.
364 7 *Ibid.*, vol. II, p. 175.
366 19 PAC: Laurier, 18300-13.
367 17 Hansard, May 11, 1898.
369 15 PAC: Laurier, 31219, 31231, 31232.
370 12 *Ibid.*, 21661.
373 27 Aberdeen Journal, p. 484.
36 PAC: Laurier, 31219, 31231, 31232.
374 2 *Ibid.*, March 10, 1899.
375 9 Jean Bruchési, 'Sir Wilfrid Laurier et Monseigneur Bruchési'.
18 Langelier, *Souvenirs politiques*, vol. I, p. 19.
32 Bruchési, 'Sir Wilfrid Laurier et Monseigneur Bruchési'.

Chapter Eighteen

pg. ln.
378 15 PAC: Laurier, 24352.
35 *Ibid.*, 35582.
379 31 Hansard, July 31, 1899.
380 29 Robert Rumilly, *Histoire de la province de Québec*, vol. IX, p. 117.
36 Toronto *Globe*, October 4, 1899.
381 37 Buchan, *Lord Minto*, p. 139.
383 5 Willison, *Laurier*, vol. II, p. 322.
384 37 Rumilly, *Histoire de la province de Québec*, vol. IX, pp. 121-2.
386 35 *Ibid.*, vol. IX, pp. 152-3.
388 14 Hansard, March 13, 1900.
391 21 *Ibid.*
28 *Ibid.*
392 20 PAC: Laurier, 44240-2.
32 Hansard, June 7, 1900.
393 31 PAC: Laurier, 45657-8.
394 20 *Ibid.*, 46797-8.
36 *Ibid.*, 48789.

395 22 *Ibid.*, 48788-91.
38 *Ibid.*, 49586.
397 7 Willison, *Laurier*, vol. II, p. 341.

Chapter Nineteen

pg. ln.
398 21 Hansard, March 12, 1901, p. 1325.
399 12 PAC: Laurier, 57893.
401 37 Henri Bourassa, *Great Britain and Canada.*
404 25 Rumilly, *Histoire*, vol. X, p. 73.
405 33 Léon Trépanier in *La Patrie*, Montreal, March 31, 1957.
406 18 PAC: Pacaud Papers, 731.
21 Gabriel Nadeau, 'Le plus illustre de nos poitrinaires'.
30 PAC: Willison Papers, 17970-1.
407 3 Henry Borden, ed., *Robert Laird Borden, His Memoirs*, p. 92.
20 Bourassa, *Great Britain and Canada*, Preface to English edition.
31 Hansard, May 12, 1902, p. 4726.
33 Rumilly, *Histoire*, vol. X, p. 106.
408 3 PAC: Proceedings of Colonial Conference, 1902, p. 3.
409 6 Skelton, vol. II, p. 295.
7 Rumilly, *Histoire*, vol. X, p. 112.
410 8 Buchan, *Lord Minto*, p. 205.
11 Rudyard Kipling, *Something of Myself*, p. 196.
411 9 PAC: Laurier, 65654.
13 *Ibid.*
29 Rumilly, *Histoire*, vol. X. p. 151.
412 9 Skelton, vol. II, p. 178.
23 PAC: Laurier, 67501-3.
26 Rumilly, *Histoire*, vol. X, p. 162.

Chapter Twenty

pg. ln.
413 12 Walter Vaughan, *The Life and Work of Sir William Van Horne*, p. 201.
414 28 *Borden Memoirs*, vol. I, p. 148n.
38 PAC: Laurier, 68062.
415 6 *Ibid.*, 68065.
16 Nadeau, 'Le plus illustre de nos poitrinaires'.
28 Rumilly, *Histoire*, vol. X, p. 167.
34 PAC: Laurier, 69190-1.
421 8 Skelton, vol. II, pp. 143-4.
18 PAC: Laurier, 69632-3.
30 *Ibid.*, 70239.
34 Skelton, vol. II, p. 145.
423 4 PAC: Laurier, 69086.
424 24 Hansard, March 13, 1903, p. 39.
425 3 PAC: Laurier, 74973.
24 Hansard, July 30, 1903, p. 7676.
426 30 PAC: Laurier, 74969.
427 21 Hansard, July 30, 1903, pp. 7659-60.
30 *Ibid.*, September 29, 1903, p. 12656.
428 6 Toronto *Globe*, October 15, 1904

Chapter Twenty-One

pg. ln.
430 38 Skelton, vol. II, pp. 146-7.

431 9 PAC: Laurier, 77602.
32 *Ibid.*
432 17 Hansard, October 23, 1903, pp. 14814-18.
24 Dafoe, *Sifton*, p. 238.
434 10 Pacaud, *Letters*, pp. 127-8.
435 12 PAC: Laurier, 82781-2.
28 *Ibid.*, 79958.
34 *Ibid.*, 82032.
436 15 Letter of Senator Powers to Miss Norah Story, September 12, 1961.
437 29 *Borden Memoirs*, vol. I, p. 117.
34 Hansard, June 10, 1904, p. 4582.
438 6 Lieutenant-General the Earl of Dundonald, *My Army Life*, p. 191.
18 Hansard, June 10, 1904, p. 4606.
28 *Ibid.*, p. 4619.
439 5 *Ibid.*, June 24, 1904, pp. 5549-50.
440 8 Rumilly, *Histoire*, vol. XI, p. 162.
12 PAC: Laurier, 84108.
441 14 PAC: Willison Papers, 18044-6.
20 Rumilly, *Histoire*, vol. XI, p. 178.
27 Toronto *Globe*, October 15, 1904.
38 *Daily Telegraph*, Saint John, October 19, 1904.
442 23 Skelton, vol. II, p. 215.
32 *Ibid.*, vol. II, p. 211.
444 28 PAC: Laurier, 93729.
447 6 Hansard, February 17, 1890.
448 20 PAC: Laurier, 93969-73.
23 *Ibid.*, 93974-6.
26 *Ibid.*, 94915.
29 *Ibid.*, 94931.
35 *Ibid.*, 94932.
449 1 Hansard, May 3, 1905, p. 5339.
450 18 *Ibid.*, February 21, 1905, p. 1458.
451 35 PAC: Laurier, 95478-80.
452 13 *Ibid.*, 209161-6.
28 Rumilly, *Histoire*, vol. XI, p. 158.
453 31 Hansard, March 28, 1905, p. 3284.
454 10 Skelton, vol. II, p. 247.
28 PAC: Choquette Papers, 77-80.

Chapter Twenty-Two

pg. ln.
456 38 *Canadian Annual Review*, 1906, p. 542.
459 22 PAC: Laurier, 108890-3, 108921-4.
460 3 *Ibid.*, 108493-4.
461 10 Rumilly, *Histoire*, vol. XII, p. 135.
19 David, *Laurier, sa vie, ses oeuvres*, p. 223.
24 Skelton, vol. II, p. 312.
462 5 Bruchési, 'Sir Wilfrid Laurier et Monseigneur Bruchési'.
463 9 Hansard, February 19, 1907, p. 3316-17.
16 *Ibid.*, March 26, 1907, p. 5433.
27 *Ibid.*, p. 5463.
464 4 *Ibid.*, April 3, 1907.
29 Skelton, vol. II, p. 306.
465 16 *Canadian Annual Review*, 1907, pp. 331 ff.

24 PAC Microfilm, Report of Proceedings, Colonial Conference, 1907.
31 *Ibid.*
466 4 *Ibid.*
16 David, *Laurier, sa vie, ses oeuvres*, p. 114.
24 *Ibid.*
30 Montreal *Gazette*, July 20, 1907.
469 2 Rumilly, *Histoire*, vol. XIII, p. 105.
9 *Ibid.*, p. 138.
16 PAC: Grey Papers, 604.
470 17 *Ibid.*, 2114-15.
35 PAC: Laurier, 137993-8000.
471 27 *Canadian Annual Review*, 1908.
472 3 *Ibid.*
25 Skelton, vol. II, p. 347.
33 Rumilly, *Histoire*, vol. XIII, p. 143.
473 2 *Ibid.*, p. 144.
20 *Ibid.*, pp. 139-41.
25 *Ibid.*, p. 144.
475 5 Skelton, vol. II, p. 252.
12 Dafoe, *Sifton*, p. 342.
15 David, *Laurier, sa vie, ses oeuvres*, p. 115.
476 4 Skelton, vol. II, p. 281.
20 *Ibid.*, vol. II, p. 282.
23 Willison, *Laurier*, vol. II, p. 469.
37 PAC: Grey Papers, 986-7.
477 11 *Ibid.*, 990.
479 18 From a memorandum by A. Kirk Cameron, Montreal.

Chapter Twenty-Three

pg. ln.
480 12 Hansard, March 29, 1909, p. 3484.
481 17 Toronto, *Globe*, March 23, 1909.
482 6 Hansard, March 29, 1909, p. 3512.
13 *Ibid.*, p. 3512.
23 *Ibid.*
36 *Ibid.*, April 2, 1909, pp. 3843-9.
483 9 *Canadian Annual Review*, 1909, p. 216.
21 PAC: Grey Papers, 2442.
484 37 Hansard, March 4, 1909.
485 18 PAC: Laurier, 186770-3.
35 PAC: Grey Papers, 703-4.
487 8 *Ibid.*, 1442-3.
22 Rumilly, *Histoire*, vol. XIV, p. 39.
34 *Ibid.*, vol. XIV, p. 91.
488 11 *Ibid.*, vol. XIV, p. 80.
20 PAC: Laurier, 175693.
489 5 *Borden Memoirs*, p. 253.
20 PAC: Laurier, 159860.
31 Skelton, vol. II, p. 324.
490 11 *Borden Memoirs*, p. 249.
20 PAC: Laurier, 162089.
24 *Edmonton Bulletin*, November 22, 1909.
491 14 Rumilly, *Histoire*, vol. XIV, pp. 92-3.
23 PAC: Laurier, 175679.

492 3 *Ibid.*, 175688-91.
13 *Ibid.*, 175681-7.
32 PAC: Dandurand Papers, December 28, 1909.
493 7 PAC: Laurier, 162090-1.
32 *Le Devoir*, January 10, 1910.
494 5 Wade, *The French Canadians*, pp. 565-6.
496 3 Hansard, February 3, 1910.
10 *Ibid.*
22 *Ibid.*
497 7 *Ibid.*, January 12, 1910.
23 Rumilly, *Histoire*, vol. XIV, p. 135.
498 3 Henri Bourassa, *Le projet de la loi navale*, pp. 16, 37.
22 Told to writer by A. Kirk Cameron.

Chapter Twenty-Four

pg. ln.
500 5 *Canadian Annual Review*, 1907, pp. 377-8.
29 Skelton, vol. II, pp. 363-4.
501 27 PAC: Grey Papers, 2603.
502 2 Hansard, November 21, 1910; extract read to House by Laurier, p. 49.
35 *Canadian Annual Review*, 1910, pp. 27-8.
503 3 Rumilly, *Histoire*, vol. XIV, pp. 124-5.
28 *Canadian Annual Review*, 1910, p. 264.
504 11 Told by John Diefenbaker at speech in St-Eustache-sur-le-Lac, Quebec, during 1963 election campaign.
505 14 Rumilly, *Histoire*, vol. XV, p. 74.
22 PAC: Laurier, 173234.
506 5 *Ibid.*, 173817.
12 *Ibid.*, 173552.
507 5 *Ibid.*, 173817.
14 *Canadian Annual Review*, 1910, p. 282.
508 19 Rumilly, *Histoire*, vol. XV, p. 109n.
509 17 *Ibid.*, p. 116.
510 33 Skelton, vol. II, p. 337.
511 20 *Ibid.*, 336-7.
33 PAC: Laurier, 175698.
512 4 *Ibid.*, 175658.
11 *Ibid.*, 175656.
513 6 *Ibid.*, 175661.
14 *Ibid.*
514 16 Rumilly, *Histoire*, vol. XV, p. 157.
21 PAC: Laurier, 175910-14.
32 *Canadian Annual Review*, 1910, pp. 193-4.
515 3 Skelton, vol. II, p. 339.
13 *Canadian Annual Review*, 1910, p. 199.
21 Rumilly, *Histoire*, vol. XV, p. 159.
26 *Canadian Annual Review*, 1910, p. 199.
36 *Ibid.*, p. 200.
516 5 *Ibid.*, p. 207.
17 PAC: Laurier, 176379.
23 *Ibid.*, 176533-4.
32 *Ibid.*, 176410.
34 Willison, *Reminiscences*, p. 388.
517 3 Rumilly, *Histoire*, vol. XV, p. 162.

5 *Ibid.*, p.161.
11 *Ibid.*, pp. 164-5.
17 PAC: Laurier, 176585.
518 19 Dafoe, *Sifton*, p. 362.
519 1 Skelton, vol. II, p. 367.
520 6 PAC: Laurier, 180320-2.
7 *Ibid.*, 180323.
18 *Ibid.*, 180320-2.
26 *Borden Memoirs*, p. 303.
521 4 Bourassa, *The Reciprocity Agreement*, p. 2.
522 1 PAC: Laurier, 180919-21.
11 *Ibid.*, 180932.
18 Skelton, vol. II, p. 372.
523 3 Hansard, February 9, 1911.
16 Vaughan, *Van Horne*, p. 347.
22 PAC: Laurier, 180939.
28 *Borden Memoirs*, p. 307.
524 27 Hansard, February 28, 1911, pp. 4385-409.
31 PAC: Grey Papers, 1500.
525 26 Hansard, March 7, 1911, p. 4771.
38 PAC: Laurier, 184603.
526 13 *Borden Memoirs*, p. 315.
16 *Ibid.*, p. 317.
22 Hansard, April 28, 1911, p. 8038.
527 19 PAC microfilm, *Eye Opener*.
25 PAC: Laurier, 186210.
528 1 Skelton, vol. II, p. 340.
8 *Ibid.*, p. 343.
529 7 *Ibid.*, p. 290.
19 W. Stewart Wallace, ed., *The Memoirs of the Rt. Hon. Sir George Foster*, p. 153.
530 8 PAC: Laurier, 188041.
13 Skelton, vol. II, p. 375.
18 *Ibid.*
31 PAC: Laurier, 188374-5.
33 *Ibid.*, 188734-5.
531 13 Skelton, vol. II, p. 380.
22 Alfred D. DeCelles, *Discours de Sir Wilfrid Laurier*, vol. II, p. 7.
26 Skelton, vol. II, p. 379.
37 Rumilly, *Histoire*, vol. XVI, p. 75.
532 5 Bourassa, *La conférence impériale*, p. 5.
12 Skelton, vol. II, p. 379.
14 *Ibid.*
34 Rumilly, *Histoire*, vol. XVI, p. 86.
534 17 Ottawa *Free Press*, September 25, 1911.
536 3 R. MacGregor Dawson, *William Lyon Mackenzie King*, p. 221.
27 Ottawa *Free Press*, September 25, 1911.
537 2 *Borden Memoirs*, p. 336.
5 Pacaud, *Letters*, p. 143.
13 Skelton, vol. II, p. 382.
23 Rumilly, *Laurier*, p. 152.
538 6 PAC: Laurier, 190118-20.
20 *Canadian Annual Review*, 1912, p. 254.
24 *Ibid.*

25 *Ibid.*, p. 258.
539 32 Bourassa, *Pour la justice*, pp. 30-3.
540 6 Rumilly, *Histoire*, vol. XVII, p. 123.
14 *Canadian Annual Review*, 1912, p. 425.
29 PAC: Laurier, 191971.
541 9 Skelton, vol. II, pp. 469-70.
25 Bourassa, *The Spectre of Annexation*, p. 23.
34 *La Patrie*, Montreal, March 31, 1957.
542 22 *Canadian Annual Review*, 1912, p. 255.
543 4 *Ibid.*, p. 257.
17 *Ibid.*
544 1 *Ibid.*, p. 258.
8 *Ibid.*, p. 40.
22 Hansard, December 12, 1912, p. 1031.
36 *Ibid.*, December 5, 1912, p. 684.
545 18 *Ibid.*, p. 5336. *Canadian Annual Review*, 1913, p. 160.
546 6 Hansard, December 12, 1912, p. 1036.
13 *Ibid.*, p. 1037.
20 Skelton, vol. II, p. 406.
23 *Ibid.*
32 PAC: Laurier, 190462.
547 8 *Ibid.*, 190474-5.
22 *Ibid.*
548 15 Hansard, April 9, 1913, pp. 7412 ff.
33 Senate Debates, May 27, 1913.
550 21 *Canadian Annual Review*, 1913, pp. 277-8.
551 3 PAC: Laurier, 190566.
26 *Canadian Annual Review*, 1913, p. 279.
552 16 *Ibid.*
27 Hansard, January 19, 1914, p. 17.
554 36 *Canadian Annual Review*, 1913, p. 191.

Chapter Twenty-Six

pg. ln.
556 7 Hansard, August 19, 1914, p. 10.
9 *Ibid.*, p. 9.
15 *Ibid.*, p. 8.
20 *Ibid.*
557 4 *Ibid.*
12 *Ibid.*, August 22, 1914, p. 98.
18 Rumilly, *Histoire*, vol. XIX, p. 33.
21 *Ibid.*, p. 45.
24 Bourassa, *The Duty of Canada at the Present Hour*, p. 1.
36 Olivar Asselin, *L'Action Catholique – les évêques et la guerre*, p. 5.
559 3 G. W. L. Nicholson, *The Canadian Expeditionary Force* (Ottawa: Queen's Printer, 1962).
11 PAC: Laurier, 190806.
21 *Ibid.*, 190806-10.
28 Skelton, vol. II, p. 440.
560 4 *Ibid.*
18 Rumilly, *Histoire*, vol. XIX, p. 81.
561 8 *Ibid.*, p. 21.
11 Skelton, vol. II, p. 471.
563 3 *Ibid.*, p. 446.

24 *Ibid.*, p. 447.
27 *Ibid.*, p. 448.
564 3 *Borden Memoirs*, pp. 508-10.
14 PAC: Laurier, 192852.
21 Rumilly, *Histoire*, vol. XX, p. 29.
24 Skelton, vol. II, p. 500.
565 18 PAC: Laurier, 191552.
28 *Ibid.*, 191551-2.
38 *Ibid.*, 191551-3.
566 30 Pacaud, *Letters*, p. 144.
35 *Ibid.*, pp. 144-5.
567 8 Hansard, February 8, 1916, p. 632.
13 *Canadian Annual Review*, 1916, p. 566.
21 *Ibid.*, p. 526.
568 7 PAC: Laurier, 191259.
15 *Canadian Annual Review*, 1916, p. 567.
17 *Ibid.*, p. 526.
569 12 PAC: Laurier, 190987.
27 *Ibid.*, 191317-18.
37 *Ibid.*, 191968.
570 1 Ramsay Cook, 'Dafoe, Laurier and the Formation of Union Government'.
10 Hansard, 1916, vol. VII, p. 3619. Skelton, vol. II, pp. 477 ff.
571 4 Hansard, 1916, vol. VII, pp. 3704-5.
8 Skelton, vol. II, p. 478.
13 Hansard, May 10, 1916, p. 3697.
36 *Ibid.*, p. 3703.
572 35 Skelton, vol. II, pp. 483-4.
573 8 Wade, *The French Canadians*, p. 699.
14 Skelton, vol. II, p. 489.

Chapter Twenty-Seven

pg. ln.
574 9 PAC: Laurier, 192170.
13 *Canadian Annual Review*, 1916, p. 571.
17 PAC: Laurier, 192336.
575 37 Wade, *The French Canadians*, p. 684.
576 19 *Canadian Annual Review*, 1916, p. 344. Rumilly, *Histoire*, vol. XXI, p. 24.
27 Rumilly, *Histoire*, vol. XXI, p. 20.
577 4 Montreal *Gazette*, July 28, 1916.
29 Wade, *The French Canadians*, pp. 713 ff.
578 1 PAC: Laurier, 192469.
7 *Ibid.*, 193372.
8 Skelton, vol. II, p. 462.
26 PAC: Laurier, 193098.
28 *Ibid.*, 193268.
579 7 *Ibid.*, 193269.
14 *Ibid.*, 193437.
580 7 Skelton, vol. II, p. 498.
15 *Borden Memoirs*, p. 616.
26 *Ibid.*, p. 617.
27 PAC: Laurier, 194342.
581 2 Hansard, January 19, 1914, p. 13.
6 *Borden Memoirs*, p. 699.
17 PAC: Laurier, 195527b.

582 15 *Ibid.*, 195793.
37 *Ibid.*, 193757-9.
583 8 Hansard, July 24, 1917, p. 3722.
14 PAC: Laurier, 196471.
584 6 *Ibid.*, 195793.
16 *Ibid.*, 195527d.
20 *Ibid.*, 195527c.
25 *Ibid.*, 194342.
585 30 *Ibid.*, 196361-2.
586 2 *Ibid.*,
11 *Ibid.*, 199495.
32 *Ibid.*, 196555.
35 Skelton, vol. II, p. 526.
38 PAC: Laurier, 196600.
587 13 Told to writer by A. Kirk Cameron.
588 11 Bourassa, *Conscription*, p. 42.
15 Skelton, vol. II, p. 512.
589 19 *Canadian Annual Review*, 1917, p. 332.
27 *Ibid.*
590 5 PAC: Laurier, 197031.
13 *Ibid.*, 197137.
591 14 Skelton, vol. II, p. 530. F. A. McGregor, *The Fall and Rise of Mackenzie King*, pp. 298-302.
25 PAC: Laurier, 197497-8.
28 *Ibid.*, 197361.
32 *Ibid.*, 197669.
592 12 Rumilly, *Henri Bourassa*, pp. 586 ff.
19 PAC: Laurier, 194022-3.
593 15 Told to writer by A. Kirk Cameron.
30 PAC: Laurier, 197696.
594 8 *Ibid.*, 197683.
595 24 *Canadian Annual Review*, 1917, p. 621.
28 PAC: Laurier, 198276.
34 *Ibid.*, 198449.
38 *Ibid.*, 198413.
596 2 *Ibid.*, 198306.
5 *Ibid.*, 197108.
19 *Ibid.*, 198478.
35 *Ibid.*, 198501.
597 15 Bruchési, 'Sir Wilfrid Laurier et Monseigneur Bruchési'.
20 PAC: Laurier, 198554.
27 *Ibid.*, 198649.
36 *Ibid.*, 198785-6.
599 6 Skelton, vol. II, p. 537.
8 Toronto *News*, December 14, 1917.
10 *Canadian Annual Review*, 1917, p. 630.
14 *Manitoba Free Press*, December 7, 1917.
600 17 *Ibid.*, December 11, 1917.
35 PAC: Laurier, 198909.
601 24 Skelton, vol. II, p. 542.

Chapter Twenty-Eight

pg. ln.

602 5 PAC: Laurier, 198978.
8 *Ibid.*, 199037.
12 *Canadian Annual Review*, 1917, p. 642.
15 A. M. Williams, 'Conscription, 1917: A Brief for the Defence'.
22 Elizabeth H. Armstrong, *The Crisis of Quebec, 1914-18* (New York: Columbia University Press, 1937), p. 220n.
603 6 PAC: Laurier, 199112.
21 Skelton, vol. II, p. 544. PAC: Laurier, 198933.
604 3 PAC: Laurier, 198924.
23 *Ibid.*, 199787.
605 5 *Canadian Annual Review*, 1918, p. 463.
10 *Borden Memoirs*, pp. 787-8.
18 *Canadian Annual Review*, 1918, p. 640.
606 6 PAC: Laurier, 200228-34.
607 22 *Borden Memoirs*, pp. 795-6.
609 30 Hansard, May 23, 1918.
610 2 Pacaud, *Letters*, p. 147.
33 Skelton, vol. II, p. 274.
613 13 Told to writer by A. Kirk Cameron.
16 *Ibid.*
614 19 PAC: Laurier, 200836.
32 Rumilly, *Histoire*, vol. XXIII, p. 106.
615 14 PAC: Laurier, November 8, 1918.
616 8 *Ibid.*, 201241.
19 McGregor, *Mackenzie King*, p. 317.
24 PAC: Laurier, 201336-9.
33 *Ibid.*, 201075.
38 McGregor, *Mackenzie King*, p. 319.
617 34 *Ibid.*, p. 317.
618 11 PAC: Laurier, 201716-18.
15 *Ibid.*, 200984.
19 *Ibid.*, 201733.
22 *Ibid.*, 201285-6.
34 *Ibid.*, 202379.
619 3 *Ibid.*, 202348.
4 *Ibid.*, 202489.
17 *Ibid.*, 202540.
24 *Ibid.*, 202541.
27 *Ibid.*, 202542.
34 *Ibid.*, 202623.
38 *Ibid.*, 202624.
621 26 David, *Laurier, sa vie, ses oeuvres*, pp. 160 ff.
29 *Ibid.*
38 Skelton, vol. II, p. 555. Ottawa *Journal Press*, February 18, 1919.
622 9 Charles Murphy to a Press Gallery correspondent. See Arthur R. Ford, *As The World Wags On* (Toronto: Ryerson Press, 1950).

THE LAURIER MINISTRY

July 11th, 1896, to October 6th, 1911

PRIME MINISTER

The Right Honourable Sir Wilfrid Laurier

THE MINISTRY

President of the Privy Council	
Rt. Hon. Sir Wilfrid Laurier	July 11, 1896 – Oct. 6, 1911
Minister of Trade and Commerce	
Rt. Hon. Sir Richard John Cartwright (Senator)	July 13, 1896 – Oct. 6, 1911
Secretary of State of Canada	
Hon. Richard William Scott (Senator)	July 13, 1896 – Oct. 9, 1908
Hon. Charles Murphy	Oct. 10, 1908 – Oct. 6, 1911
Minister of Justice and Attorney General	
Hon. Sir Oliver Mowat (Senator)	July 13, 1896 – Nov. 17, 1897
Hon. David Mills (Senator)	Nov. 18, 1897 – Feb. 7, 1902
Vacant	Feb. 8, 1902 – Feb. 10, 1902
Hon. Charles Fitzpatrick	Feb. 11, 1902 – June 3, 1906
Hon. Sir Allen Bristol Aylesworth	June 4, 1906 – Oct. 6, 1911
Minister of Marine and Fisheries	
Hon. Sir Louis Henry Davies	July 13, 1896 – Sept. 24, 1901
Vacant	Sept. 25, 1901 – Jan. 14, 1902
Hon. James Sutherland	Jan. 15, 1902 – Nov. 10, 1902
Hon. Joseph Raymond Fournier Préfontaine	Nov. 11, 1902 – Dec. 25, 1905
Vacant	Dec. 26, 1905 – Jan. 5, 1906
Rt. Hon. Sir Wilfrid Laurier (Acting Minister)	Jan. 6, 1906 – Feb. 5, 1906
Hon. Louis-Philippe Brodeur	Feb. 6, 1906 – Aug. 10, 1911
Hon. Rodolphe Lemieux	Aug. 11, 1911 – Oct. 6, 1911

Minister of Militia and Defence

Hon. Sir Frederick William Borden	July 13, 1896 – Oct. 6, 1911

Postmaster General

Hon. Sir William Mulock	July 13, 1896 – Oct. 15, 1905
Hon. Allen Bristol Aylesworth	Oct. 16, 1905 – June 3, 1906
Hon. Rodolphe Lemieux	June 4, 1906 – Aug. 10, 1911
Hon. Henri Sévérin Béland	Aug. 11, 1911 – Oct. 6, 1911

Minister of Agriculture

Hon. Sydney Arthur Fisher	July 13, 1896 – Oct. 6, 1911

Minister of Public Works

Hon. Joseph Israel Tarte	July 13, 1896 – Oct. 21, 1902
Vacant	Oct. 22, 1902 – Nov. 10, 1902
Hon. James Sutherland	Nov. 11, 1902 – May 3, 1905
Vacant	May 4, 1905 – May 21, 1905
Hon. Charles Smith Hyman	May 22, 1905 – Aug. 29, 1907
Hon. William Pugsley	Aug. 30, 1907 – Oct. 6, 1911

Minister of Finance and Receiver General

Hon. William Stevens Fielding	July 13, 1896 – Oct. 6, 1911

Minister of Railways and Canals

Hon. Andrew George Blair	July 13, 1896 – July 20, 1903
Hon. William Stevens Fielding (Acting Minister)	July 21, 1903 – Jan. 14, 1904
Hon. Henry Robert Emmerson	Jan. 15, 1904 – Apr. 2, 1907
Vacant	Apr. 3, 1907 – Apr. 8, 1907
Hon. William Stevens Fielding (Acting Minister)	Apr. 9, 1907 – Aug. 29, 1907
Hon. George Perry Graham	Aug. 30, 1907 – Oct. 6, 1911

Minister of the Interior and Superintendent General of Indian Affairs

Vacant	July 13, 1896 – Nov. 16, 1896
Hon. Clifford Sifton	Nov. 17, 1896 – Feb. 28, 1905
Vacant	Feb. 29, 1905 – Mar. 12, 1905
Rt. Hon. Sir Wilfrid Laurier (Acting Minister)	Mar. 13, 1905 – Apr. 7, 1905
Hon. Frank Oliver	Apr. 8, 1905 – Oct. 6, 1911

Minister of Customs

Hon. William Paterson	June 30, 1897 – Oct. 6, 1911

Minister of Inland Revenue

Hon. Sir Henri Gustave Joly de Lotbinière	June 30, 1897 – June 21, 1900
Hon. Michel Esdras Bernier	June 22, 1900 – Jan. 18, 1904
Hon. Louis-Philippe Brodeur	Jan. 19, 1904 – Feb. 5, 1906
Hon. William Templeman	Feb. 6, 1906 – Oct. 6, 1911

Minister of Labour

Hon. Sir William Mulock	July 19, 1900 – Oct. 15, 1905
Vacant	Oct. 16, 1905 – Nov. 2, 1905
Hon. Allen Bristol Aylesworth	Nov. 3, 1905 – June 3, 1906
Hon. Rodolphe Lemieux	June 4, 1906 – June 1, 1909
Hon. William Lyon Mackenzie King	June 2, 1909 – Oct. 6, 1911

Minister of Mines

Hon. William Templeman	May 3, 1907 – Oct. 6, 1911

Secretary of State for External Affairs

Hon. Charles Murphy	June 1, 1909 – Oct. 6, 1911

Minister of the Naval Service

Hon. Louis-Philippe Brodeur	May 4, 1910 – Aug. 10, 1911
Hon. Rodolphe Lemieux	Aug. 11, 1911 – Oct. 6, 1911

Minister without Portfolio

Hon. Richard Reid Dobell	July 13, 1896 – Jan. 11, 1902
Hon. Christophe Alphonse Geoffrion	July 13, 1896 – July 18, 1899
Hon. James Sutherland	Sept. 30, 1899 – Jan. 14, 1902
Hon. William Templeman (Senator)	Feb. 25, 1902 – Feb. 5, 1906
Hon. Charles Smith Hyman	Feb. 5, 1904 – May 21, 1905

NOT OF THE CABINET

Solicitor General

Hon. Charles Fitzpatrick	July 13, 1896 – Feb. 9, 1902
Hon. Henry George Carroll	Feb. 10, 1902 – Jan. 28, 1904
Hon. Rodolphe Lemieux	Jan. 29, 1904 – June 3, 1906
Vacant	June 4, 1906 – Feb. 13, 1907
Hon. Jacques Bureau	Feb. 14, 1907 – Oct. 6, 1911

Controller of Customs

Hon. William Paterson	July 13, 1896 – June 29, 1897

Controller of Inland Revenue

Hon. Sir Henri Gustave Joly de Lotbinière	July 13, 1896 – June 29, 1897

Index

Abbott, J. J. C., 257, 266
Aberdeen, John Campbell Hamilton Gordon, 7th Earl, 292, 293, 294-6, 298, 302, 303, 306, 318, 319-20, 322, 333, 371, 373; refuses Bowell's resignation, 308-9; mediates in cabinet quarrel, 310-11
Aberdeen, Ishbel, Lady, 294-6, 302, 307-11 *passim*, 312, 317, 318, 319-20, 321-2, 371, 373
Achigan River, 9
Admiralty, British, 378, 483, 489, 494, 549
Affari Vos (papal encyclical on Manitoba schools), 366-7
Alaska boundary question, 326, 362, 413, 415; Joint High Commission, 363, 370-2, 381; treaty and board of arbitration, 399, 420-1, 429-32, 433
Alberta, creation of province, 440, 454; schools issue, 444-53 *passim*, 577
Allison, J. Wesley, 559
All-Red Route, 457, 465-6, 467
Alverstone, Richard Everard Webster, 1st Baron, 429, 431, 433, 470
Amherst, General Jeffery (and Jesuit Estates), 218
Angers, Auguste Réal, 302, 303, 307, 309, 335
Anglin, Frank A., 299, 305
Archambault, Oscar, 25, 85
Arthabaska (St-Christophe d'Arthabaskaville), 52-4, 58; Lauriers at home in, 71-6, 80-7, 89, 91-2, 160-3, 208-9, 229-31, 319, 371, 402, 553-5, 609-10
Asquith, Herbert Henry, 464, 494, 502, 527, 546
Asselin, Olivar, 557, 575
Assembly, Lower Canada, 3, 4
Atholstan, Lord, *see* Graham, Hugh
Atkinson, Joseph, 618
Autonomy Acts, Alberta and Saskatchewan, 444-53
Avenir, L', 33
Aylesworth, A. B., 429, 431, 460, 468, 469, 588, 591, 593, 618

Baldwin, Robert, 14
Barthe, Emilie, *see* Lavergne, Emilie
Bégin, Louis-Nazaire, Archbishop of Quebec, 319
Béland, Henri, 542, 616
Bellechasse, constituency, 468-9
Benedict XV, pope, 579
Bennett, R. B., 578, 580
Bering Sea, sealing dispute, 326, 479
Berthiaume, Treffle, 443-4
Bickerdike, Robert, 536
Bien Public, Le, 108
Blaine, James G., 248, 250
Blair, Andrew George, 323, 338-9, 340, 414, 419, 420, 423, 424, 426, 434, 437, 441-4
Blake, Edward, 92, 98, 103, 137, 139-42, 149, 152, 154-5, 174, 178, 181, 183, 185, 186, 187, 188, 201, 207, 211, 231, 235-8 *passim*, 256, 258-60, 333, 342, 343, 429, 445, 469, 551; on the C.P.R., 144-5, 157; on Riel and the Northwest, 98, 175, 179-80; resignation, 190-9; and reciprocity, 203-5 *passim*, 210, 213-16, 220-1, 223-5 *passim*, 246-7, 249-50, 252-3, 261-5; leaves to enter British Commons, 264-5
Bleu, Parti, 15, 33, 35, 57, 157; effect of Catholic Program, 90; move for coalition with *Rouges*, 147-9 *passim*
Boer War, *see* South African war
Bois-Francs country, 51-2
Bonaventure, constituency, 108-13
Borden, Frederick, 458, 459, 483
Borden, Robert, 397, 399, 407, 424, 426-7, 431, 434, 438-9, 444, 468, 471, 484, 510, 514, 516, 520, 522-3, 524, 526, 531, 534,

535, 536, 550, 570, 579-80, 605, 607, 615, 618; on Grand Trunk, 436-7; and the navy, 482, 483, 486, 489-90, 496-7, 498, 542, 544-9; wartime measures, extension of the life of parliament, 562-7, 575, 578; National Registration and conscription, 578-91 *passim*, 604
Boundary dispute, Alaska, *see* Alaska
Boundary dispute, Ontario, Quebec, and Manitoba, 151
Boundary waters treaty, 479, 500
Bourassa, Henri, 324-5, 330, 370, 371, 394-5, 397, 434, 439, 467, 468-9, 513-15, 516-17, 531-3, 536, 545, 592, 598, 613-14; on South African war, 380, 383-93 *passim*, 394, 398-9; on Canada and the Empire, 391, 400-2, 407, 415, 431, 453, 511, 539-40, 541; on schools issue, 331, 447-8, 452, 554, 560-1, 565; his following in Quebec, 397, 435-6, 454, 458, 469, 472-3, 487, 490-1, 513-15, 531-2; and the Church, 331, 502, 503, 506-10 *passim*; on Lord's Day Act, 460; on immigration, 461, 505; on navy, 496, 497-8, 515, 544, 545; on World War, 557, 560, 576; on conscription, 595, 596, 605; see also *Le Devoir*
Bourassa, Napoléon, 77
Bourbeau, Désiré-Olivier, 123
Bourget, Ignace, Archbishop of Montreal, 29, 55, 77; Guibord Case, 78, 104-5; Catholic Program, 81-2, 89-90; on duty of Catholics, 106; on political liberalism, 108, 113-14, 169
Bourne, Francis, Archbishop of Westminster, 508, 509
Bowell, Mackenzie, 99, 292-8 *passim*, 302-11 *passim*, 313, 318, 343, 369, 599
British Columbia, 103, 202, 289, 322, 326, 393, 418, 456, 490, 530
British Empire League, 378
British North America Act, 58, 273, 401, 440, 441, 445-6
Brodeur, Louis-Philippe, 465, 469, 483, 487, 514
Brown, George, 14, 31, 32, 35, 36, 44, 45, 58, 92, 105, 126, 342
Bruchési, Louis-Joseph Paul Napoléon, Archbishop of Montreal, 364, 365, 368, 375, 460, 462, 483, 506-8 *passim*, 557, 597, 613
Bryce, James, 469-70, 485, 500
Buies, Arthur, 85
Bulletin, Edmonton, 490, 610
Bureau, Jacques, 608, 609
Burpee, Isaac, 140, 195

Cabinet of 1896, 321, 323-4, 336-41, 646-8
Calder, James A., 590-1, 608
Cameron, A. Kirk, 478-9, 498, 587, 613, 615
Cameron, John, Bishop of Antigonish, 313
Canadian Expeditionary Force (1914), 558-9, 575-7; *see also* Conscription
Canadian Military Gazette, 380
Canadian Northern Railway, 416, 417, 419, 422, 423, 425, 522, 547, 550, 552, 553, 564, 584, 589
Canadian Pacific Railway, 144-6, 152, 153, 156-7, 168, 170-2, 174, 188, 203, 252, 274, 285-6, 326, 338-9, 413, 416, 417, 419, 433, 442, 456; land grants, 146, 337
Canadien, Le, 242, 244, 248
Cape Breton, constituency, 312
Caron, Joseph Philippe René Adolphe, 154, 167, 171, 177, 179, 242, 243, 266, 302, 303, 310
Cartier, George Etienne, 14, 31, 32-3, 35, 36, 44, 45, 58, 82, 88, 90, 98, 612
Cartwright, Richard, 93, 103, 135, 137, 140-1, 154, 174, 183, 191, 192, 195-8 *passim*, 215, 221, 222, 229, 231, 232, 235, 236, 246, 247, 249, 252, 256, 257, 266, 300, 311, 315, 318, 324, 338, 343, 344, 370, 371, 412, 414, 420, 439, 468, 535, 551; on reciprocity, 204-5, 210-14 *passim*, 224, 261, 263
Carvell, Frank, 590, 591, 611, 615
Casgrain, J. P. B., 516, 597, 601
Castors, 153, 167, 323, 364, 510
Catholic Association of French Canadian Youth, 452, 508
Catholic Church, *see* Roman Catholic Church
Catholic Program, 81-2, 89-90; Laurier's opposition, 84-5
Catholic schools, *see* Manitoba schools, Autonomy Acts
Cauchon, Joseph, 88, 105-9 *passim*, 114, 122
Chamberlain, Joseph, 212-13, 338, 346-8, 355-7, 363, 371, 373-4, 376-95 *passim*, 407-10, 421, 429, 432, 433, 464
Chapleau, Joseph Adolphe, 88-9, 142-3,

156, 157, 167, 177, 179, 185-6, 238, 240, 242, 243, 272, 307, 312, 363-4, 370, 374; relations with Mercier, 147-53 *passim*
Charlevoix, constituency, 103-4, 105, 113, 123, 209
Charlton, John, 226, 261, 370, 371
Choquette, P. A., 285
Chronicle, Halifax, 593
Churchill, Winston, 464, 465, 544-6 *passim*
Civil Service, 471-2
Clarke, Champ, 530
Closure (1913), 547-8
Club National, Montreal, 245, 334
Club Saint-Jean Baptiste, 48
Coalition government (1917), *see* Union Government
Colonial Conferences: (1897), 338, 355-7; (1902), 407-10; (1907), 457, 464-6; *see also* Imperial Conferences
Colonial Council, proposed, 356, 392
Commercial Union, 204, 211, 213-14, 253, 259, 261, 262, 269, 324; *see also* Reciprocity
Confederation, 30, 35-6, 43-6, 57-8, 64, 137, 159, 228, 275-6; the work of Laurier, 611-13
Connaught and Strathearn, H.R.H. Arthur William Patrick Albert, 1st Duke, 536
Conroy, Bishop, of Ardagh, 113-16 *passim*, 122
Conscription, 227; and Naval Act, 494, 497, 511, 514-15, 531; in World War, 563, 578-91 *passim*, 593, 595, 603, 604-7
Conventions: National Liberal (Ottawa, 1893), 268-70; Western Liberal (Winnipeg, 1917), 585-6
Cottineau, François (Champlaurier), 8
Coutu, François-Xavier, 43, 49, 65, 69
Coutu, Yvonne, 403-4, 405, 527
Crépeau, Eugène, 62, 66, 72, 75
Crerar, Thomas, 603, 611, 618
Crowsnest Pass, railway, 326, 338-9
Cuba, 363, 371
Cummings, Mrs. Emily Ann McCausland, 307-8

Dafoe, John, 299, 313, 518, 569, 573, 586, 599, 600, 602, 618
Daily Mail, London, 357
Dandurand, Raoul, 572
Dansereau, Arthur, 22, 123, 143, 323, 374-5, 386, 407, 443, 462, 563
David, Laurent-Olivier, 30, 41, 49, 50, 71, 108, 268, 333, 335, 406, 434, 466, 613, 614
Davies, Louis Henry, 197, 339, 370, 371, 414
Dawson, William, 4-5
Débats, Les, Quebec, 397
Défricheur, Le, 34, 50, 51, 54, 56, 59, 61
Democratic party, United States, 217, 363
Desaulniers, Henri Lesieur, 25
'Devil's Dozen', 226
Devoir, Le, Montreal, 493-4, 495, 497, 502, 506, 515, 529, 531, 540, 544
Devonshire, Victor Christian William Cavendish, 9th Duke, 578, 587
Dewart, Hartley, 593-4, 597, 601
Diamond Jubilee (1897), 346-55
Diefenbaker, John G., 504
Digby, constituency, 206
Doherty, Charles, 569-588
Dorion, Antoine-Aimé, 30, 31, 34-5, 41, 44-6, 49, 50, 58, 88, 93, 100, 283
Dorion, Eric, 30, 33-4, 41, 44-6, 49, 54, 56-7
Double mandate, 88, 89
Dougall, J. R., 451
Drolet, Gustave Adolphe, Chevalier, 330
Drummond, George, 298
Drummond-Arthabaska, constituency, 34, 64, 80, 85, 90, 92, 123-6, 132, 134, 208, 436, 512-17, 557
Dundonald, Major-General D. M. B. Hamilton, 12th Earl, 437-9
Duquet, Dr. Francis, 16
Durham, John George Lambton, 1st Earl, 13, 15

Eastern Townships, 33
Edgar, J. D., 191, 196, 197, 199, 210, 213-14, 221, 229, 231, 324, 342, 348
Edwards, Bob, 527
Electeur, L', Quebec, 143-4, 148-9, 171, 209, 235, 237, 244, 319, 333
Elections, general: (1867), 64; (1872), 90; (1878), 135; (1882), 152; (1887), 187-8; (1891), 250-3; (1896), 318-20; (1900), 395-7; (1904), 439-44; (1908), 475-7; (1911), 530-3; (1917), 593-601
Elgin, James Bruce, 8th Earl, 14
Elgin, Victor Alexander Bruce, 9th Earl, 464

Emmerson, Henry R., 458-60, 463-4, 545
Equal Rights Association, 227, 229, 267
Eucharistic Congress (Montreal, 1910), 506-9
Evénement, L', Quebec, 602
External Affairs, department formed (1909), 484-5
Eye Opener, Calgary, 527

Fallon, Michael Francis, Bishop of London (Ont.), 502-3, 506, 540, 561, 599
Farrer, Edward, 248, 250-1, 443
Ferguson, Howard, 562, 569
Fielding, William Stevens, 188, 202, 242, 269, 299, 305-6, 318, 320, 393, 410, 413, 414, 420, 451, 453, 459, 461, 467, 471, 477, 478-9, 495, 499, 533, 535, 546, 547, 550, 567, 590-1, 593, 607, 608, 611, 616, 617, 618, 620; Minister of Finance, 323, 338, 343-4, 412, 501, 517, 519-20, 525, 530
Fisher, Sydney, 190, 339, 412, 437-8, 459, 468, 471, 535, 615, 617
Fisheries disputes with U.S., 326, 479, 500
Fitzpatrick, Charles, 333, 341, 345, 370, 414, 448, 451, 452, 460, 462, 608
Flavelle, Joseph Wesley, 416, 579
'Forty Thieves' article and libel trial, 148-51
Foster, George Eulas, 262, 291, 292, 303, 306, 307, 317, 344, 379, 387, 392, 460, 462-3, 480-3, 490, 496, 520, 536, 557, 587, 606, 607-9 *passim*, 615
Franco-Prussian War, 76
Franchise: federal, 170, 172-4; women's, 173-4, 606
Fréchette, Louis, 94, 125-6
Free Press, Manitoba, 299, 518, 586, 599-601 *passim*
Free Press, Ottawa, 126, 128, 130
Frog Lake massacre (1885), 172

Gascoigne, Major-General W. J., 377
Gauthier, Emma, 38-43 *passim*, 65-70 *passim*, 403
Gauthier, Hannah, 38-43 *passim*, 63-70 *passim*, 405, 537, 541
Gauthier, Louis, 42
Gauthier, Phoebe, 38-43 *passim*, 63-70 *passim*, 155
Gauthier, Dr. Séraphin, 37-42 *passim*, 63-70 *passim*
Gazette, Montreal, 6, 8, 196, 205, 466, 596
Geoffrion, C. A., 149, 150
Globe, Toronto, 94-5, 127, 197, 198, 199, 229, 232, 246, 249, 251, 259, 308, 380, 416, 481, 596, 599, 610, 618; on bilingualism, 567-8, 569
Gosselin River, 52
Gouin, Lomer, 468, 473, 487, 491, 561, 587
Graham, George Perry, 468, 535, 537, 538, 542, 543, 555, 572, 594, 595, 611, 615, 616, 617
Graham, Hugh, 379, 442, 444, 486, 521, 587
Grain Growers Association, 507, 603
Grand Trunk Railway, 31, 34, 36, 44, 52, 417, 419, 421-8; Grand Trunk Pacific Railway, 424-8, 432-3, 435, 436-7, 441-3, 457, 483, 495, 505-6, 550, 553, 564, 584
Greenshields, J. N., 443
Greenway, Thomas, 232, 301, 302, 304, 317, 345, 386
Grey, Albert Henry George, 4th Earl, 463, 470, 476, 477-9 *passim*, 483, 487, 495, 500, 501, 518, 524, 536
Guibord Case, 78, 84, 104-5

Haggart, John Graham, 306
Hays, Charles, 422, 424, 505-6
Hazen, John, 547-8, 568
Herald, Montreal, 100, 299
Herschell, Farrer Herschell, 1st Baron, 370, 371
High Commission, boundary waters, 500
Holton, Luther, 107
Homesteads, western, 337
Howe, Joseph, 48
Hughes, Samuel, 378, 380, 381, 385, 415, 438, 462, 536, 539, 552, 558-9, 563, 564, 575, 576, 578, 606, 607, 608
Huntington, Lucius Seth, 106, 107
Hutton, Major-General Edward, 377-8, 380, 385
Hutton, Maurice, 552
Hyman, Charles, 299-301 *passim*, 458, 459, 463, 470, 594

Immigration, 286, 337, 397, 411, 416, 455-6, 461, 505, 547
Imperial Conferences: (1907), 464; (1911), 526, 527-9; *see also* Colonial Conferences

Imperial Council, proposed, 356, 409, 465
Imperial Council of State, proposed (1911), 527-8
Imperial defence, 356-7, 409, 465, 481, 483, 488, 511
Imperial Federation, 270, 271, 280, 338, 346-7, 355-7, 552, 608-9
Imperial Federation League, 211, 213, 216, 217, 227, 236, 267
Imperial preference, 216, 338, 341, 344-5, 357, 433, 501, 519; *zollverein*, 338, 341, 347, 357, 408, 409, 433
Imperial press conference, 483
Imperial South African Association, 378
Imperialism, 212-13, 227, 376-97 *passim*, 407-8, 409-10, 527-8; Blake on, 263-4; Bourassa on, 400; Laurier on, 432, 511; Round Table Group, 524-5; *see also* Imperial Council, Imperial defence, Imperial Federation, Imperial Federation League, Imperial preference
Industrial Disputes Investigation Act (1907), 486
Institut Canadien, 28-9, 40, 46, 55; *see also* Guibord Case
Institut des Lois, 40
Intercolonial Railway, 45, 78, 338, 343, 417, 419, 423, 437, 442
Irvine, George, 149-50
Irish Catholics *versus* French Catholics, 485

Jackson, Henry, 177
Jesuit Estates Question, 218-19, 225-7, 229, 231-5
Jetté, Louis-Amable, 429, 431, 491
Joint High Commission, Canada and United States (1898-9), 363, 370-2, 381
Journal d'Arthabaska, Le, 89, 108, 123, 124, 133, 135
Journal des Trois Rivières, Le, 57, 59, 122

Keewatin territory and schools issue, 538-9
King, William Lyon Mackenzie, 459, 485-6, 505-6, 535, 537, 538, 542, 543, 550, 555, 594-5, 611, 613, 616, 617-20 *passim*
Kirk family, New Glasgow, 19, 20
Klondike, 362, 367, 369
Knowles, W. E., 570, 597

Labelle, constituency, 324, 386
Labelle, François Xavier Antoine, 225
Lacombe, Father Albert, 313, 315
Laflamme, Rodolphe, 26-7, 28, 30, 37, 50, 72, 184; Guibord Case, 78, 104-5; election and appointment to cabinet, 108-9
Laflèche, Louis-François, Bishop of Three Rivers, 55, 59, 61, 77, 113, 161, 167, 302, 305, 312, 328, 375; Catholic Program, 81-2, 89-90
Lafontaine, Louis-Hippolyte, 14-15, 31-2, 511
Lafontaine, Napoléon-Godefroi, 39, 69
Lafontaine, Zoë, *see* Laurier, Zoë
Lafontaine, Mme Zoë, 39, 42, 43
Lanctôt, Médéric, 30, 41, 49, 50, 71, 184
Landerkin, George, 160, 268, 319
Langelier, Charles, 259
Langelier, François, 197, 511
Langevin, Hector, 88, 103-4, 123, 142, 153, 167, 173, 177, 179, 209, 238, 240, 242-4, 248, 255, 257, 266
Langevin, J. P. F. Laforce, Archbishop of St. Boniface, 302, 305, 312, 328, 331-2, 368-9, 498, 506, 508, 540
Lapointe, Ernest, 447, 531, 569-70, 595, 602
Larivière, Zélia, 72
Larkin, Peter, 610-11, 618, 621
Larkin, Connolly and Company, 242-3
Lash, Zebulon, 522, 523
L'Assomption, College of, 21-3, 614-15
Laurier, family: A. Charlemagne (half-brother), 395; Adeline Ethier (stepmother), 16-17, 37, 366, 434; Carolus (father), 9, 16, 17, 19, 37, 42, 185; Charles (grandfather), 17-19, 37; Henri (half-brother), 372, 461; Malvina (sister), 16, 17; Marcelle Martineau (mother), 16, 39, 94; Romuald (half-brother), 461; Ubald (half-brother), 372; Wilfrid (nephew), 395
Laurier, Wilfrid: ancestry and early family history, 8-9; immediate family, 16-19; education, 19-24; Montreal (1864-6), 25-9, 37-50 *passim*; L'Avenir, (1866), 50-2; Arthabaska (1867-8), 52-65; marriage, 66-70; Arthabaska (1868-71), 71-80; Quebec legislature (1871-4), 87-9; election to federal House (1874), 92; enters cabinet (1877), 122; elected in Quebec East, 127-30; leader of Liberal party (1887), 197-9; Prime Minis-

ter (1896), 320; knighthood (1897), 347-8; Liberal defeat (1911), 533; death, 621
and English institutions, 79, 100, 109-10, 119, 163-5, 359-60, 366-7, 375, 510; on political liberalism, 115-22; on autonomy, 335; and the Church, 55, 77, 84, 115-22, 133, 276, 328-35; and Riel, 96-102, 175-83 *passim*; and the schools issues, 241, 273-6 *passim*, 296-8, 301-6, 313-18, 328-35 *passim*, 341-2, 345, 366-7, 368-9, 375, 445-50, 561-2, 565-73 *passim*; on Canada and the Empire, 233, 237, 280, 344-5, 355, 409, 431-2, 472, 481-2, 500; and the French-Canadian position in the nation, 164-5, 181, 186-7, 228, 233, 238-41, 282-3, 335, 461, 569-73, 611-13, 616
Laurier, Zoë (*née* Lafontaine), 39-43 *passim*, 49-50, 62, 63, 65, 67-70, 71-6 *passim*, 82-3, 91-2, 110, 111, 128, 133, 160-3 *passim*, 196, 209, 221, 223, 230, 284, 295, 321-2, 346-8 *passim*, 350, 371, 373, 403-6, 413, 414, 459, 464, 527, 533, 537, 541, 542, 554, 617, 621, 622
Laurier, Archambault and Desaulniers, 25, 46
Laurier-Greenway settlement, 331-2, 343, 366-7
Laval University, 117, 218, 397
L'Avenir, 33-4, 50, 51, 54
Lavergne, Armand, 162, 277-80, 397, 404-5, 447, 454, 467, 488, 491-2, 502, 511-13, 517, 605; political activities, 435-6, 452, 461, 462, 473, 487-8, 490-1, 502, 513-14, 531, 532, 536, 539; on schools and the war, 561, 565, 567, 569, 576
Lavergne, Georgette (Mme Armand, *née* Roy), 488, 511-12
Lavergne, Joseph, 91, 110, 136, 160, 162, 208, 276, 284, 361-2, 404, 491, 512, 554
Lavergne, Emilie (Mme Joseph, *née* Barthe), 110-11, 161-3, 194, 208-9, 223, 258-9, 276-80, 284, 335, 361-2, 404, 491, 554, 566
Lavergne, Louis, 162, 436, 512, 515, 516, 554
Lemieux, Rodolphe, 447, 468, 485, 487, 503, 507, 521, 531, 569, 595, 608, 609, 616-17
Leo XIII, pope, 219, 341, 359
Liberal Information Office, Ottawa, 538
Liberalism, Catholic, 27, 122
Liberalism, political; Bishop Laflèche on, 56, 81; Laurier on, 115-22
Ligue Nationaliste, 452
Liquor traffic, bill for federal regulation, 158
Lloyd George, David, 464, 466
Lodge, Henry Cabot, 421
London, *see* Diamond Jubilee; Colonial Conferences; Imperial Conferences
Lord's Day Act (1906), 460-1, 462, 467
Lower Canada, 2-6, 57
Lynn Canal, 362, 372
Lyons, Lewis, 38

McBride, Richard, 490
McCarthy, D'Alton, 213, 216, 217, 226-7, 246, 267-8, 271, 273, 296, 315, 332, 334, 364-5, 370, 445, 449, 453
McCarthy, Leighton, 530
Macdonald, Hugh John, 386, 397
Macdonald, John A., 14, 31, 36, 44, 45, 58, 90-1, 95, 98, 102, 133-8 *passim*, 146, 151, 154, 157, 168, 170-5 *passim*, 180, 183, 188, 203, 216, 217, 226, 237-8, 242-4, 246, 250-2, 254-5, 272, 290, 325, 402, 417, 522, 532, 608, 611; and Riel, 169, 177-8; Laurier on, 158-9, 206-7, 228, 256
McGill, James, 2-4 *passim*
McGill University, 1-5 *passim*, 23-4
McGreevy, Robert, 153, 242-8 *passim*
McGreevy, Thomas, 153, 242-8 *passim*, 255, 257, 259
McInnes, Thomas, 393
Mackenzie, Alexander, 91, 92, 98, 102-6, 108-9, 114, 116, 122, 126-7, 131, 134, 135, 136, 140-1, 183, 212, 342
Mackenzie, William, and Mann, Donald A., 326, 416, 419, 420, 422-5 *passim*, 442-4, 457, 522, 552-3, 584
McKinley, William, 246, 363, 381, 399
McMaster, Andrew, 577, 582
Mail, Toronto, 178-9, 227
Manchester Guardian, 432
Manitoba schools, 232, 237-41, 259, 267, 271-6, 286-8, 294, 296-9 *passim*, 322, 328-35 *passim*, 343, 368-9, 375; debate on Remedial Bill, 301-7, 313-18; Laurier-Greenway settlement, 331-3; *Affari Vos*, papal encyclical, 366-7
Manitoba, 79, 96-101 *passim*, 103, 188, 274, 322, 386, 416, 568
Mann, Donald A., *see* Mackenzie, William

Maritime Provinces, 35, 322, 419-26 *passim*, 456
Martin, Joseph, 271-2, 284, 287, 288, 323-4, 336, 393
Meighen, Arthur, 496, 581, 589, 608
Mercier, Honoré, 143, 147-51 *passim*, 153, 156, 166-7, 178-9, 181, 184-6, 197, 202, 206, 209, 212, 217-19, 225-8 *passim*, 232-3, 244-7, 251, 254, 257-8, 259, 261, 262, 266, 281, 289, 388, 497
Merry del Val, Cardinal, 341-2, 345, 359, 364, 365, 366, 375, 503, 521
Métis, 55, 79, 97-8, 168, 169, 171, 175-6, 182-3
Military Service Act (1917), 581
Military Voters Bill (1917), 588-9
Militia, 378, 437-8
Mills, David, 195-8 *passim*, 261-3 *passim*, 305, 364, 365, 370, 414
Minerve, La, 123, 199
Minto, Gilbert John Elliot, 4th Earl, 373, 377-9 *passim*, 381, 385, 438, 463
Mitchell, Walter, 597, 601
Monk, F. D., 480, 489, 490, 496, 510-14 *passim*, 521, 529, 531, 536, 538-9, 543-4
Monk, S. C., 150
Montague, Walter Humphries, 310
Mont Christo, 52-3, 110
Montmagny, constituency, 435, 462
Montmorency, constituency, 251, 254, 272
Montreal, 1-2, 31, 36, 64, 131, 338; Eucharistic Congress (1910), 506-9 *passim*; conscription riots (August 1917), 589
Montreal East, constituency, 90
Mousseau, Joseph-Alfred, 99, 153, 156, 157, 167
Mowat, Oliver, 151, 158, 190, 194-8 *passim*, 210-11, 229, 231-4 *passim*, 249, 259, 318-19, 323, 329, 334, 364, 365, 434, 540-1
Mulock, William, 210, 213-14, 229, 236, 261, 323, 325, 339, 374, 395, 412, 414, 420, 458
Murphy, Charles, 484-5, 506, 508, 542-3 *passim*, 559, 569, 611, 618, 622
Murray, John, 19-20

National Policy, 112, 134, 136-8, 147, 152, 188, 203, 207, 222, 242, 246, 267, 274, 284, 519
National Service Board, 578
National Transcontinental Railway, 424-6, 437, 456, 457, 475, 547
Nationalism, French-Canadian: Papineau's influence, 10-11; Riel and reaction, 177-9; Laurier on, 282; South African war and reaction, 376-97; *see also* Bourassa, Henri
Natural Resources, committee on, 484, 518
Navy, 480-3, 486, 488-98, 538, 542-9
New Brunswick, 46, 79, 242, 297
New York Times, 345
News, Toronto, 175, 416, 440, 509, 571, 599
Niobe, H.M.C.S., 517, 549
'Noble Thirteen', 226, 237, 378
'No precedent' clause (1899), 382-3, 388, 390
Norris, Tobias C., 568, 589
North Shore Railway, 142, 148-53 *passim*, 156, 157; McGreevy-Mercier scandal, 244-5
North Simcoe, constituency, 530
North Victoria, constituency, 378
North York, constituency, 550, 595
Northrup, W. B., 548
Northwest Territories, attack on use of French, 237-41, 445-7

O'Brien, Colonel William Edward, 225-6
Oliver, Frank, 458, 469, 471, 490, 559, 585-6, 593, 597, 600, 610
Ontario, French language in schools, *see* Regulation 17
Orange Order, 99, 159, 229, 303, 306, 315, 332, 449, 450, 476, 496, 502, 536, 564, 569, 577-8, 599
Orders in Council: on Manitoba schools (March 1895), 297; on troops for South African war, 382-3, 388, 390
Ottawa, 93, 567
Ouimet, Joseph Alderic, 302, 303

Pacaud, Charles, 59-60, 80
Pacaud, Edouard, 59, 80, 81-3, 85
Pacaud, Ernest, 80, 89, 108, 123, 125, 126-7, 130, 135, 144, 148, 149, 156, 158, 171, 200, 202, 209, 224-5, 234-7 *passim*, 241, 251, 279-80, 284, 298-9, 305, 323, 334, 406, 415, 434; involvement with Mercier and McGreevy, 244-6, 254, 255, 257, 259, 266-7, 281

Pacaud, Georges-Jérémie, 80-1, 110
Pacaud, Marie-Louise (Mme Ernest), 130, 537, 566, 610
Pacific Scandal, 90-1
Papal infallibility, dogma, 77
Papal Zouaves, 28, 77
Papineau, Louis-Joseph, 4, 9-16, 18, 26, 28-9, 32, 461, 511
Papineau, Talbot, 562, 576-7, 582-3
Paquet, Abbé Benjamin, 117
Pardee, Frederick, 543, 590, 594, 611
Parti National, 90, 177, 179, 181
Paterson, William, 519, 520
Patrie, La, 163, 386
Patrons of Industry, 268
Pays, Le, 51, 56, 89
Pelletier, C. A., 140
Perrault, J. E., 513, 516
Pius IX, pope, 77
Poisson, Dr. Edouard Modeste, 54-5, 62, 66, 71
Pope, the, *see* Benedict XV, Leo XIII, Pius IX
Pope, Joseph, 161, 199, 256, 370, 444
Pope, Minette (Mrs. Joseph, *née* Taschereau), 161, 199
Prairies, 286, 337-8, 397, 413, 416-17, 455
Préfontaine, J. R. F., 413-14, 458, 469
Presse, La, 177, 386, 407, 443-4, 462
Princess Patricias, battalion, 562
Privy Council, 159, 272, 273, 290, 293, 296, 330, 333, 579
Prohibition referendum, 340, 373, 606
Protestant Defence Association, 106
Protestant Protective Association, 267, 281
Proulx, Abbé Jean-Baptiste, 330, 342, 366
Provencher, constituency, 96, 98, 100
Provincial Premiers Conference, Quebec, 202, 217-18
Pugsley, William, 442, 468, 469, 611, 621

Quebec City, 228, 359; tercentenary, 472; conscription riots, 604-5
Quebec Conference (1864), 30, 35
Quebec East, constituency, 127-31, 135
Quebec provincial legislature, 80, 87-9, 602-3

Railway Commission (established 1903), 420, 424, 434, 441
Railway reserves, 146, 337
Railways: *see* Canadian Northern, Canadian Pacific, National Transcontinental, Grand Trunk
Rainbow, H.M.C.S., 517, 549
Rebellion, Lower Canada (1837), 4, 9-13
Reciprocity, 31, 203, 204, 242, 249, 250-3, 286, 501-2, 518-26 *passim*, 529, 530, 532-3, 538; Unrestricted Reciprocity and Commercial Union, 203-5, 207-8, 210-17, 213-14, 219-21, 222, 224, 225, 234, 235, 236-7, 249-53, 259, 261-5, 269
Recruiting (1914-18), 559, 563, 564, 567, 574-7 *passim*, 581
Redistribution of constituencies, 151
Referenda: prohibition, 340, 373; navy, proposed, 489, 496, 498; conscription, proposed by Laurier, 582, 591, 593
Reform Club, Ottawa, 269
Reform Club, Toronto, 234
Regulation 17, 540-1, 554, 560-2, 565-73 *passim*
Remedial Bill, Manitoba, 314, 318; *see also* Manitoba schools
Renfrew, constituency, 209
Representation by population, 30, 35
Republican party, United States, 217, 224, 235, 363, 371, 469, 499, 500-1, 519
Richard, Edouard, 66, 71, 75, 76, 91
Riel, Louis, 79, 90, 92, 96-8, 98-102 *passim*, 168, 169, 171, 174-84 *passim*, 196, 199
Rogers, Robert, 536, 538, 559, 562, 568, 574-5, 578-81 *passim*, 586, 589
Roman Catholic Church, 3, 4, 11, 27, 44, 77, 113-14, 122, 328-9, 330
Roosevelt, Theodore, 399, 415, 421, 430, 431, 433, 499
Root, Elihu, 421, 469, 470, 479, 500, 501
Rouge, Parti, 15-16, 26-9, 31-3, 44-7, 58, 90, 106, 108, 119, 147-51 *passim*, 157, 281, 323
Round Table Group, 524-5, 527, 552, 567, 579, 586
Rowell, Newton W., 566, 567, 606, 608
Russell, Charles, 333, 341, 365-6, 604
Russell, David, 442-3

St-Eustache, 12, 13
St-Lin, 9, 12
St. Sauveur, constituency, 491
Saskatchewan: rebellion (1885), 169, 171-2; creation of province, 440, 454;

schools issue, 444-53 *passim*, 577
Sbaretti, Monsignor, 448, 452
Schools, denominational: *see* Manitoba schools; Autonomy Acts; Keewatin territory
Scott, Thomas, 79, 98, 100, 175, 177
Secret balloting, 104
Selkirk, constituency, 271
Senate, 343, 369, 373-4, 548
Sénécal, Louis-Adélard, 60-1, 64, 90, 125, 134, 142, 148-50 *passim*, 152, 153, 242, 244
Shaughnessy, Thomas Shaughnessy, 1st Baron, 326, 508, 587
Sifton, Arthur, 585, 615
Sifton, Clifford, 269, 271-2, 274, 275, 301, 302, 305, 323, 329, 332, 343, 370, 393-4, 397, 411, 414, 420, 423, 429, 431, 435, 437, 465, 466-7, 468, 475, 477, 484, 487, 531, 536, 550-1, 581, 584-7 *passim*, 616, 617, 618; Minister of the Interior, 336-8, 340-1, 362, 367, 369, 386, 458, 471; on schools issue and resignation, 446, 448, 450-3 *passim*; on reciprocity, 518, 522, 523-4, 529, 530
Sinclair, Captain John, 310
Skelton, O. D., 595
Smith, Alexander ('Silent'), 269, 518, 525, 537-8, 550, 569, 611, 616
Smith, Donald A., 133, 298, 385
Smith, Frank, 292
Smith, Goldwin, 203
Soleil, Le, Quebec, 333
Sorel, Quebec, 439, 475
South African war, 347, 376-97; in retrospect, 407-8, 409
South African League Congress, 378
Spanish American War, 370, 371
Sproule, Dr. Thomas, 439, 449, 450, 536
Star, Montreal, 180, 379, 381, 442, 521, 536, 560, 563
Star, Toronto, 618
Stephen, George, 144, 170
Strachan, John, Rector of York, 2, 3, 4
Strathcona, Lord, *see* Smith, Donald A.
Sutherland, James, 284, 413-14
Suzor, Father Philippe-Hippolyte, 55, 59, 61, 73, 81-5 *passim*, 86-7, 122, 161, 319

Taché, Alexandre A., Archbishop of St. Boniface, 272
Taché, Etienne-Pascal, 43
Taft, William, 479; reciprocity, 499-501 *passim*, 518-19
Tariff, 107, 112, 203, 340-1, 343-5, 499-502 *passim*; *see also* Reciprocity; Imperial preference; Sifton on reciprocity
Tarte, Joseph Israel, 22, 124, 127, 133, 166, 281, 305, 312, 313, 318, 340, 343, 363-4, 370, 374, 392, 394, 397, 414, 428, 434, 469; Langevin-McGreevy scandal and move to Liberals, 242-5, 247-8, 251, 254-5, 267; on Manitoba schools issue, 272, 273, 297, 329-33; Minister of Public Works, 323, 339; on South African war, 379-90 *passim*; attempt for the leadership, 410-12; on transcontinental railway, 428, 434
Taschereau, Elzéar Alexandre, Archbishop of Quebec (later Cardinal), 82, 117, 167, 319, 375, 510
Telegraph, Saint John, N.B., 441, 442
Territorial Ordinances (1901), 446
Thibeault, Charles, 124-5, 128
Thibodeau, Isidore, 127
Thompson, John, 238, 257, 266, 267, 268, 273, 276, 284, 290-1, 294
Thompson, Lady, 290, 292-3, 295
Tilley, Samuel Leonard, 49, 136, 167
Titles, debate on, 551, 607
Tupper, Charles, 46, 49, 133, 138-9, 144, 156-7, 167-8, 188, 191, 210, 216, 235, 250, 252, 256-7, 291-5 *passim*, 306-20 *passim*, 322, 329, 343, 344, 357, 368, 369, 387, 392, 397, 492, 551, 565
Tupper, Charles Hibbert, 257, 291-3 *passim*, 296-8, 303, 309, 311, 319, 369
Turner, George, 421

Ultramontanes, 147, 152-3, 281, 282, 503
Ultramontanism, 27, 77, 103-9, 113, 142, 328
'Undue influence' clause, and charges under, 104-5, 108, 113
Union des Cantons de l'Est, L', 57, 59, 61, 82-5 *passim*, 108
Union of Upper and Lower Canada (1841), 4, 13-16, 30-1
Union Government (1917), 585-93 *passim*, 599, 600, 610, 618
Union Nationale, L', 30, 48
United States: trade and tariffs, 137, 203, 286, 411-12, 417, 465, 469-70, 479, 499-502, 518-20 (*see also* Reciprocity); problems with, 326-7, 408, 417, 479,

495, 500; sentiments towards, 35, 45, 57, 58, 137, 270, 400-1, 407, 409, 523-4, 530; *see also* Alaska boundary question
University of Toronto, 517, 551
Unrestricted Reciprocity, *see* Reciprocity

Valois, Pierre, 43, 49, 63, 65, 68, 69
Van Horne, William, 144, 170-2 *passim*, 418, 420, 426, 456, 523
Victoria Museum, Ottawa, 569, 607, 622
Victoria, Queen, 348, 352-4, 398

Wallace, Clarke, 303, 306, 313, 315
War Times Election Act (1917), 589, 590, 603
Weekly Colonist, Victoria, B.C., 199
West Durham, constituency: Blake's letter to electors, 253, 258
Wheat, 286, 288, 327, 413, 416, 425, 428, 455
Willison, John, 127, 197-8, 221, 222, 229-31, 232, 234, 235, 249, 268, 271, 299, 380, 406, 415, 416, 440, 441, 451-2, 476, 486, 509, 524, 525, 567, 596
Wilson, Sir Charles Rivers, 422-4 *passim*
Wiman, Erastus, 203
Witness, Montreal, 451, 508
Woman suffrage, 173-4, 606
World, Toronto, 199, 571, 599
World Court, the Hague, 479, 500
Wyndham, George, 378

Young, James, 94, 100-1, 106, 109-10, 212
Young Men's Liberal Association, Quebec, 115
Young Men's Liberal Club, Toronto, 186, 229
Yukon territory, 326, 327, 336, 362, 367, 369, 373; *see also* Alaska boundary dispute